Laura Morrissey   3BCL

CASES ON IRISH COMPANY LAW

Cases on Irish Company Law

Michael Forde
B.A. (Mod.) and LL.B. (Dublin),
LL.M. (Brussels),
Ph.D (Cantab.),
of King's Inns,
Barrister-at-law,
Lecturer in Law,
University College Dublin

THE MERCIER PRESS
CORK and DUBLIN
1986

The Mercier Press Limited
4 Bridge Street, Cork
24 Lower Abbey Street, Dublin 1

© Michael Forde, 1986

British Library Cataloguing in Publication Data
Forde, Michael,
  Cases on Irish company law.
  1. Commercial law—Ireland—Cases
  I. Title
  344.1706'7'0264   KDK502

ISBN 0-85342-796-8

For Sue

-

Contents

Foreword

Those involved in commercial affairs today, be it as managers of businesses or as professional advisors, need to have a knowledge of Company Law.

It is a complex subject and until recently there were no books dealing with Irish Company Law.

Within the last two years, however, several excellent books on the subject have been published, including Dr Forde's *Company Law in Ireland* (1985, The Mercier Press), for which I had the pleasure of writing the Foreword.

Dr Forde has not rested on his laurels but has applied his wealth of knowledge and industry to writing this book, *Cases on Irish Company Law*, which should prove an invaluable complement to his earlier book.

Exhaustive as are the Companies Acts, there are many important areas of company law which are governed primarily by case law, either because there are no statutory provisions relating thereto or because the relevant statute gives the Courts a wide discretion.

As this book *Cases on Irish Company Law* so ably demonstrates, there is a wealth of cases on Company Law and this case book illustrates the major contribution made by the Irish Judiciary to the development of Company Law in this country.

Dr Forde's case book is a very welcome addition to Irish legal literature, providing as it does, in one volume, all the relevant cases.

He and his publishers, The Mercier Press, are to be congratulated for their combined efforts, which have resulted in this excellent production.

Liam Hamilton

President of the High Court

October 1986

Acknowledgements

I wish to thank the following for generously allowing me to reproduce copyright material: The Stationery Office for *The Statutes;* The Incorporated Council of Law Reporting for Ireland for *The Irish Reports;* The Round Hall Press for the *Irish Law Reports Monthly;* the Incorporated Council of Law Reporting for England and Wales for the *Law Reports;* Butterworth & Co. Ltd. for the *All England Law Reports* and the *British Company Law Cases;* the Scottish Council of Law Reporting and Messrs T. & T. Clark for the *Session Cases;* Butterworth & Co. (N.Z.) Ltd. for the *New Zealand Law Reports.* I would also like to thank the following judges for permission to reproduce their unreported judgments: Barron J., Carroll J., Costello J., Gannon J., Hamilton P., Keane J., Lardner J. and McWilliam J.

Preface

This book is simply a collection of the major cases on Irish Company Law, which it is hoped will prove useful to the student of the subject and to commercial law practitioners. The law regarding registered companies is governed principally by the Companies Act, 1963, and by the Amendment Acts of 1977, 1982, 1983 and 1986; and further statutory amendments are expected in the near future. Nevertheless, much of the law is contained in the cases. Indeed, on many of the most important aspects of the subject there are no directly relevant legislative provisions but there is an abundance of cases. Thus, mastering the cases is essential in order to understand Company Law.

Since Company Law in this country was originally United Kingdom Law, and because the Companies Acts, 1963-1986, are identical in numerous respects to U.K. law, the U.K. cases are highly relevant to the law here. Of the 114 cases reproduced in this book, 52 are decisions of Irish courts, and 6 are decisions of U.K. courts where the dispute either originated in Ireland or was closely connected with Ireland. The remainder are decisions of the English and Scots courts, and also of the New Zealand courts.

This book can perhaps be best used in conjunction with my *Company Law in Ireland* (Mercier Press, 1985). The cases are set out in accordance with the sequence in that book; and the reader should consult that book to see if the law as stated in some of the cases has been changed by legislation or in the light of other cases.

I wish to thank Catherine, Patrick and Peter for their patience while I assembled this book, and also Bernie Power, Mary Feehan and John Spillane of The Mercier Press for their persistence and assistance in getting it completed. Finally and once again I wish to thank Mr Justice Liam Hamilton for his most gracious foreword.

1. Introductory

Act for Establishing the Bank of Ireland
21 & 22 Geo. III, c.16, 1781-82

WHEREAS it will tend to the advancement of publick credit in this kingdom, and to the extension of its trade and commerce if a bank with publick security, shall be established therein; be it enacted by the King's most excellent Majesty by and with the advice and consent of the lords spiritual and temporal and commons in this present Parliament assembled, and by the authority of the same, That it shall and may be lawful to and for your Majesty, your heirs and successors, by commission under the great seal of Ireland, to authorize and appoint any number of persons, at any time after the first day of August next, to take and receive all such voluntary subscriptions as shall be made on or before the first day of January which shall be in the year of our Lord one thousand seven hundred and eighty four by any person or persons, natives or foreigners, bodies politick or corporate, for and towards the raising and paying into the receipt of your Majesty's treasury in this kingdom the sum of six hundred thousand pounds sterling, to be paid in money or by debentures which have been or shall be issued from your Majesty's treasury, by virtue of any act or acts of Parliament heretofore, and in this present session made in this kingdom, bearing an interest at the rate of four pounds per centum per annum, which debentures shall be taken at par from such subscriber or subscribers, and be considered as money by the persons to whom the same shall be paid; for which sums so to be subscribed, a sum, by way of annuity, equal in amount to the interest upon said debentures, at the rate of four pounds per centum per annum, shall be paid at your Majesty's treasury in manner herein after mentioned.

II. And be it enacted by the authority aforesaid, That if from competition for a preference amongst the persons desiring to subscribe, they shall be willing to pay or advance any sum or sums, by way of premium for obtaining such preference or permission to subscribe; in that case the amount of such sum so advanced and paid, over and above the said sum of six hundred thousand pounds to the said commissioners impowered to receive such subscriptions and premiums for such preference or permission, shall be applied towards any purposes for the beginning or better carrying on the

2   CASES ON IRISH COMPANY LAW

business of the said bank, and also towards the erecting a proper building
and convenient accommodation for the same, pursuant to such plan as
shall be furnished by said commissioners; which plan and situation for
such building, shall be subject to the approbation of the lord lieutenant,
or other chief governor or governors of this kingdom for the time being.

III. And be it further enacted by the authority aforesaid, That it shall
and may be lawful to and for your Majesty, your heirs and successors, by
letters patent under the great seal of Ireland, to limit, direct, and appoint,
how and in what manner and proportions, and under what rules and directions the said sum of six hundred thousand pounds sterling, and every or
any part or proportion thereof, may be assignable or transferable, assigned
or transferred to such person or persons only as shall freely and voluntarily
accept of the same, and not otherwise, and to incorporate all and every
such subscribers and contributors, their executors, administrators, successors, or assigns, to be one body politick and corporate, by the name of
the Governor and Company of the Bank of Ireland; and by the same name
of the Governor and Company of the Bank of Ireland, to have perpetual
succession, and a common seal; and that they and their successors, by the
name aforesaid, shall be able and capable in law, to have, purchase, receive,
possess, enjoy, and retain to them, and their successors, lands, rents, tene-
ments and hereditaments of what kind, nature or quality soever, and also
to sell, grant, alien, demise, or dispose of the same; and by the same name
to sue and implead, and be sued and impleaded, answer and be answered
in courts of record, or any other places whatsoever, and to do and execute
all and singular other matters and things by the name aforesaid, that to
them shall or may appertain to do, subject nevertheless, to the proviso or
condition of redemption herein after mentioned. Etc. Etc.
[This Act has twenty-five sections in all]

The Bank's Acts

Acts of the Parliament of Ireland

Session and Chapter	Title or Short Title
21 & 22 Geo III. c. 16.	An Act for establishing a Bank by the name of the Governor and Company of the Bank of Ireland.
31 Geo. III. c. 22.	An Act to extend the provisions of an Act passed in the 21st and 22nd years of His Majesty's reign entitled An Act for establishing a Bank by the Name of the Governor and Company of the Bank of Ireland.
37 Geo. III. c. 50.	An Act for further extending the provisions of an Act passed in the 21st and 22nd years

of His Majesty's reign entitled An Act for establishing a Bank by the name of the Governor and Company of the Bank of Ireland.

Acts of the United Kingdom Parliament

48 Geo. III. c. 103.	The Bank of Ireland Act, 1808.
1 & 2 Geo. IV. c. 72.	The Bank of Ireland Act, 1821.
1 Will. IV. c. 32.	An Act to explain two Acts of His present Majesty for establishing an agreement with the Governor and Company of the Bank of Ireland, for advancing the sum of £500,000 Irish currency and for the better regulation of co-partnerships of certain bankers in Ireland.
8 & 9 Vic. c. 37.	The Bankers (Ireland) Act, 1845.
23 & 24 Vic. c. 31.	The Bank of Ireland Act, 1860.
27 & 28 Vic. c. 78.	The Bank Notes (Ireland) Act, 1864.
35 & 36 Vic. c. 5.	The Bank of Ireland Charter Amendment Act, 1872.

Acts of the Oireachtas

Year and Number	
1929 no. 4 (Private)	The Bank of Ireland Act, 1929 (infra).
1935 no. 1 (Private)	The Bank of Ireland Act, 1935 (infra).

Bank of Ireland Act, 1929

(1) Notwithstanding anything to the contrary contained in the Charter or in the Bank's Acts.

(a) no banking company registered outside Saorstát Eireann or banking corporation trust or other company carrying on its principal business outside Saorstát Eireann shall be qualified to vote or capable of voting at any general court or otherwise through a trustee nominee or other person or otherwise in any matter relating to the affairs or government of the Bank, and

(b) the members of the Bank duly assembled in a general court may from time to time by resolution reduce or increase as they think fit the number of the Directors (exclusive of the Governor and the Deputy Governor) of the Bank and fix the amount of capital stock of the Bank which must be held as their qualifications by the Governor Deputy Governor and Directors respectively and may from time to time fix the quorum of Directors necessary for the transaction of business, and

(c) the Governor and Deputy Governor and at least three fourths of the other directors shall be domiciled and resident in Saorstát Eireann, and

(d) all members of the Bank holding the amount of the capital stock of the Bank necessary to qualify them to vote shall have the same rights of voting at general courts whether the capital stock of the Bank of which they are the registered holders or any part thereof is held by them in their own right or in trust for any other person or persons or for any company or corporation not disqualified to vote by paragraph (a) of this sub-section: Provided that where capital stock in the Bank is held in trust for the same company corporation person or persons by different members of the Bank not more than one of such members of the Bank shall be entitled to vote at any general court, and

(e) where capital stock of the bank is registered in the names of two or more persons as joint holders thereof any one of such persons shall have the same right to vote at any general court as if he were solely entitled thereto and if more than one of such joint holders be present at any general court that one of the said persons so present whose name stands first on the register in respect of such capital stock shall alone be entitled to vote, and

(f) any company or corporation holding the amount of the capital stock of the Bank necessary to entitle members to vote for the period prescribed by the Charter and not being disqualified to vote by paragraph (a) of this sub-section may by resolution of its directors or governing body appoint any person to vote at any general court and the person so appointed shall have the same right of voting at such general court on behalf of the company or corporation by which he shall have been appointed as if he were a member of the Bank: Provided that a duly authenticated copy of such resolution shall in every case be sent or delivered to the Secretary of the Bank at least seven days before the holding of the general court or courts at which such person is to be entitled to vote on behalf of such company or corporation, and

(g) at any general court a poll of the members of the Bank qualified to vote at general courts may be demanded by the Chairman presiding at such general court or by at least nine other persons qualified to vote and personally present and if a poll is duly demanded it shall be taken in such manner and at such time and place as the Chairman shall direct and the result of the poll shall be deemed to be the resolution of the general court at which the poll was demanded, and

(h) any member of the the Bank holding the amount of the capital stock of the Bank necessary to qualify members to vote may be required by the Directors to declare by statutory declaration whether he is entitled to the capital stock of which he is the registered holder in his own right or otherwise and if the whole or any part of such capital stock is held by him otherwise than in his own right to disclose and specify every company corporation person or persons in trust for whom or on whose behalf he holds the same and where any member has been required to make such declaration as aforesaid the making by him of such declaration shall be a condition precedent to the right of such member to vote at any general court, and

(i) the Bank shall not absorb any other bank without the consent in writing of the Minister for Finance previously obtained, and

(j) the Bank shall not be absorbed by any other bank corporation trust or other company whatsoever, and

(k) notwithstanding any notice of any trust the Bank so far as not restrained by Order or Rules of Court shall pay the dividends on the capital stock of the Bank for the time being to the members of the Bank appearing from the Register to be the owners thereof and shall allow such members to sell and transfer such capital stock, and

(l) the members of the Bank may by bye-laws duly made under the Charter determine the number of general courts to be held in every year and may for that purpose reduce or increase as they think fit the number of such general courts as fixed by the Charter or by such bye-laws, but so that no less than one general court shall be held in every year, and

(m) the members of the Bank may by bye-laws duly made under the Charter appoint the days on which general courts shall be held, and

(n) whenever the number of general courts is fixed or the dates for holding general courts are appointed by such bye-laws, general courts shall be summoned in accordance with such bye-laws and not otherwise.

(2) Nothing in this section shall prejudice or affect the summoning at any time in accordance with the Charter of a general court on the demand of nine or more members of the Bank qualified as mentioned in the Charter.

Bank of Ireland Act, 1935, §2

Notwithstanding anything contained in the Act of the Irish Parliament passed in the 21st and 22nd years of the reign of His late Majesty King George the Third and entitled 'An Act for establishing a bank by the name of the Governors and Company of the Bank of Ireland' or contained in the Charter or Letters Patent under the Great Seal of Ireland [on] the 10th day of May, 1783 and granted by His said late Majesty in pursuance of the said Act by which a Bank was established and a Company was incorporated by the name of the Governor and Company of the Bank of

Ireland hereinafter called the Bank or contained in the Acts amending the same or any of them, no past or present member of the Bank shall, in the event of a winding up, be liable to contribute towards the debts or liabilities of the Bank to an amount exceeding the amount, if any, unpaid on the stock of the Bank held by him at the date of the commencement of the winding up or within the period of twelve months prior to that date. . . .

The Dublin General Cemetery Company's Act, 1933, (preamble)

WHEREAS by an Act passed in the Session of Parliament held in the 4th and 5th years of King William the Fourth, Chapter 65, intituled 'An Act for Establishing a General Cemetery in the Neighbourhood of the City of Dublin' (which Act is hereinafter referred to as 'the Act of 1834') certain persons were united into a Company under the the name of 'The General Cemetery Company of Dublin' (hereinafter called 'the Company') and were authorised to raise a sum of £12,000 by means of shares and to borrow on mortgage £9,000 and to purchase and hold lands not exceeding twenty-five acres for the purpose of the said undertaking to be vested in trustees to be nominated by the directors of the Company:

AND WHEREAS by an Act passed in the Session of Parliament held in the 37th and 38th years of Queen Victoria, Chapter 28, intituled 'An Act to enable The General Cemetery Company of Dublin to enlarge their Cemetery to raise a further sum of money and for other purposes' (which Act is hereinafter referred to as 'the Act of 1874') the Company were authorised to hold a small piece of land containing about five acres and described in the First Schedule thereto in addition to the lands authorised to be purchased by the Act of 1834 and by the same Act sections 36 to 39 inclusive of the Act of 1834 relating to money to be borrowed by the Company upon mortgage were repealed and power was given to the Company to raise additional capital not exceeding £8,000 by means of shares or stock and to borrow on mortgage £5,000 and to purchase and hold additional lands not exceeding twenty-one acres one rood twenty perches:

AND WHEREAS the Company in pursuance of the said powers have constructed and enlarged near Harold's Cross, in the County Borough of Dublin, a cemetery which occupies a space of about forty-seven acres, and also hold the small piece of land containing about five acres described in the First Schedule to the Act of 1874:

AND WHEREAS by reason of the increase in the population of the County Borough of Dublin it has become necessary that additional space should be provided for the interment of the dead and it is expedient that the said cemetery should be further extended and enlarged and that the Company should be authorised to purchase for that purpose certain lands and property adjoining the said cemetery and described in the Schedule to this Act:

AND WHEREAS owing to the difficulty of finding twelve suitable directors as prescribed by section 70 of the Act of 1834 it is expedient that the Company should be permitted to reduce the number of directors but so that the minimum number shall not be less than six:

AND WHEREAS it is expedient that the provisions of sections 77 and 81 of the Act of 1834 in so far as they relate to any person being concerned or interested in any contract under the Company being chosen or continuing a director and to directors taking or being concerned or interested in any contract under the Company should be amended but not so as to permit any such director voting in respect of any such contract:

AND WHEREAS the payment by the Company of fees upon interment to incumbents of parishes is no longer necessary and it is expedient that the Company should be relieved from the payment of same and from other duties in connection therewith as prescribed by sections 90 to 96 inclusive of the Act of 1834:

AND WHEREAS the Company out of the authorised capital of £20,000 have raised the sum of £17,000 in shares and do not owe any money upon mortgage, it is expedient that the powers of the Company to borrow money on mortgage up to but not exceeding the sum of £5,000 should be extended so as to enable the Company to borrow on mortgage a sum not exceeding in the whole £10,000:

AND WHEREAS a plan showing the lands required or which may be taken for the purpose or under the powers of this Act and a book of reference containing the names of the owners or lessees or reputed owners or lessees and of the occupiers of such lands were duly deposited with the Principal Clerk of the Private Bill Office and are hereinafter referred to as the deposited plan and the deposited book of reference respectively:

AND WHEREAS it is expedient that the other powers in this Act mentioned should be conferred on the Company:

AND WHEREAS the purpose aforesaid cannot be effected without the authority of the Oireachtas:

BE IT THEREFORE ENACTED BY THE OIREACHTAS OF SAORSTÁT EIREANN AS FOLLOWS: . . .

II. Company Formation

A most convenient way of setting up business as a registered company is to buy an already-formed company from one of those firms of solicitors or accountants that specialise in selling companies 'off-the-shelf'. The purchasers would then make whatever alterations to that company they deem necessary, such as changing its name, the address of its registered office, directors, capital structure, articles of association, and the like. Alternatively, they may decide to form a new company themselves, which in any event is not a particularly onerous or complex task. Essentially all that is needed is two founders and a signed memorandum and articles of association; these documents must be accompanied by a statutory declaration and a cheque for capital tax, and be registered with the registrar of companies. A number of additional formalities must be complied with before some companies can commence doing business.

Irish Permanent Building Soc. v. Cauldwell
[1981] I.L.R.M. 242 (H.Ct.)

(From headnote) The Irish Life Building Society (the second named defendant) was registered as a building society by the registrar of Building Societies (the first named defendant), in 1979. The initial capital was provided by the Irish Life Assurance Co. (the third named defendant) which continued to retain an absolute controlling interest in the society's share capital. The major shareholder in Irish Life Building Society was the Minister for Finance, who directed the Assurance Co. to provide funds by way of mortgages for house purchase. The board of directors of the Assurance Co. (the fourth named defendant) agreed to do so and founded the Irish Life Building Society. The executives of the Irish Life Assurance Co. were invited to become founding members of the building society and each individual member acknowledged that he held his share on trust for the Assurance Co. and undertook to use his shares to vote as the Assurance Co. would direct. The plaintiffs sought a number of declarations against the defendants. The issue revolved around whether a building society having such close connections with a major financial institution, such as the Irish Life Assurance Co., was registrable under the Building Societies Act, 1976. The plaintiffs submitted that the society was not registrable because it was not an autonomous co-operative society but the subsidiary

of another body, the Irish Life Assurance Co.

BARRINGTON J.: . . . [259] I accept that the society is, in all respects, the creature of the Irish Assurance Company Limited. That company decided to set it up; provided its deposit at the Central Bank; assigned employees to be the founding members and the Board of Directors of the society; provided the founding members with their share capital on their undertaking to hold these shares in trust for the company and to use them to vote as directed by it; arranged the share capital so that its nominees could control the constitution of the society and outvote any opposition for the foreseeable future and generally provided the finance to set the society in business.

[261] The real issue in the present case is whether the law permits the kind of relationship which exists between the Irish Life Assurance Company and the [262] Irish Life Building Society. If such a relationship is permissible in law it is permissible and this abstract issue cannot be determined by whether a particular relationship does or does not give rise to possibilities of abuse. If abuses exist they are to be dealt with by the agencies set up to control the activities of Building Societies and Insurance Companies.

The defendants submit that the plaintiffs have failed to grasp the significance of the fact that a building society, under the 1976 Act, is an incorporated body and that certain incidents attach to the fact of incorporation. They submit that it is quite unreal for a great financial institution like the Irish Permanent Building Society to compare itself with the small unincorporated building societies contemplated by the 1836 Act. When, they say, s.9 of the Building Societies Act, 1874 provided for the incorporation of building societies it opened the way to the formation of a society such as the Irish Life Building Society.

The defendants submit that the plaintiffs have missed the significance of the concept of incorporation, and to illustrate their point, they refer to the judgment of the Court of Appeal in *Salomons Case* (1895) 2 Ch.D. 323.

In that case Salomon caused a limited liability company to be incorporated and the seven subscribers of the memorandum of association consisted of Mr Salomon, his wife, his daughter and his four sons. Twenty thousand shares were issued to Mr Salomon and one share only to each of the other six subscribers to the memorandum of association. Mr Salomon transferred his business to the company, took a floating charge over the company, became managing director and carried on his business as before. The other members of the company were merely his nominees.

Lopes LJ (at page 340 of the report) commented on this situation and his comments are interesting as they almost exactly reproduce the submissions made on behalf of the plaintiffs in the present case. He said:

The incorporation of the company was perfect – the machinery by which it was framed was in every respect perfect, every detail had been observed; but notwithstanding, the business was, in truth and in fact the business of Aron Salomon; he had the beneficial interest in it; the company was a mere nominis umbra, under cover of which he carried on his business as before, securing himself against loss by a limited liability of £1 per share, all of which shares he practically possessed, and obtaining a priority over unsecured creditors of the company by the debentures of which he had constituted himself the holder. It would be lamentable if a scheme like this could not be defeated. If we were to permit it to succeed, we would be authorising a perversion of the Joint Stock Companies Act. We would be giving vitality to that which is a myth and a fiction. The transaction is a device to apply the machinery of the Joint Stock Companies Act to a state of things never contemplated by that Act – an ingenious device to obtain the protection of that Act in a way and for objects not authorised by that Act, and in my judgment in a way inconsistent with and opposed to its policy and provisions. It never was intended that the company to be constituted should consist of one substantial person and six mere dummies, the nominees of that person, without any real interest in the company. The Act contemplated the incorporation of seven independent bona fide members, who had a mind and a will of their own, and were not the mere puppets of an individual who, adopting the machinery of the Act, carried on his old business in the same way as before, when he was a sole trader. To legalise such a transaction would be a scandal.

[263] The significance of these comments for the purposes of the present case is that they were totally rejected by the House of Lords (see post pp. 53-58) as revealing a failure to understand what was involved in the incorporation of a limited liability company under the Companies Act.

In his speech in the House of Lords Lord Herschell said (at page 45):

It was said that in the present case the six shareholders other than the appellant were mere dummies, his nominees, and held their shares in trust for him. I will assume that this was so. In my opinion it makes no difference. The statute forbids the entry in the register of any trust; and it certainly contains no enactment that each of the seven persons subscribing the memorandum must be beneficially entitled to the share or shares for which he subscribes. The persons who subscribe the memorandum, or who have agreed to become members of the company and whose names are on the register are alone regarded as, and in fact are the shareholders. They are subject to all the liability which attaches to the holding of the share. They can be compelled to make any payment which the ownership of the share involves. Whether they are beneficial owners or trustees is a matter with which neither the company nor creditors have anything to do: it concerns only them and their cestuis que trust if they have any. If, then, in the present case all the requirements of the Statute were complied with, and the company was effectually constituted and this is the hypothesis of the judgment appealed from, what warrant is there for saying that what was done was contrary to the true intent and meaning of the Companies Act?

The defendants submit that the Oireachtas, in the 1976 Act, by providing that a building society must have at least ten founding members and that it must make a deposit of not less than £20,000 with the Central Bank, has accepted that building societies have changed greatly from the small associations of working men contemplated by the 1836 Act. Likewise, they say the Minister by providing, in effect, by S.I. No. 119 of 1977 that the share qualification of directors must be £10,000 each has recognised the financial importance of building societies and has sought to protect the public by having them run by men of substance. Moreover the defendants say that shortly before the enactment of the 1976 Act the Norwich Union Insurance Group caused to be formed the Norwich Irish Building Society and the legislature could have been expected to intervene had it considered such a close relationship between an insurance company and a building society to be undesirable.

It therefore appears to me that I should approach this case on the basis that the incidents of incorporation attach to building societies as they do to limited liability companies except in so far as they are affected by the differing provisions of the Companies Act and the Building Societies Act.

The plaintiffs submit that there are relevant distinctions between the Companies Act of 1963 and the Building Societies Act 1976 concerning the formation of a company or building society. Section 5 of the 1963 Act provides that any seven or more persons, or in the case of a private company, any two or more persons 'associated for any lawful purpose' may by 'subscribing their names' to a memorandum of association form an incorporated company. Section 8 of the 1976 Act on the other hand provides that any ten or more persons not disqualified by law may form a building society by 'agreeing on rules'.

[264] The plaintiffs submit that an 'agreement' of ten persons contemplates ten individual wills converging on a particular course but, they submit, there can be no agreement if all of the ten persons are nominees of the same person and each is expressing not his own will but the will of the person who nominated him. For the same reason they submit that there can be no delivery of 'agreed' rules under s. 11 of the Building Societies Act as there had in fact been no agreement.

This submission appears to me to be answered in part by the extract from the speech of Lord Herschell in *Salomon*'s case. As a matter of fact I am satisfied that each of the ten founder members of the building society was pleased to act in the formation of the building society and that each of them accepted the rules. In these circumstances I reject the plaintiffs' submission on this score as being based on too fine and metaphysical a distinction to be useful in dealing with practical affairs.

Rex v. Registrar of Companies, ex p. Moore
[1931] 2 K.B. 197

It was sought to register in England a company, the principal object of which was to sell Irish Hospital Sweepstake tickets there.

SLESSER L. J.: [201] It is clear that a company cannot be formed whose proposed constitution necessarily involves an offence against the general law. That was assumed in *Rex v. Registrar of Companies. Ex parte Bowen* [1914] 3 K.B. 1161 and in [202] *Bowman v. Secular Society* [1917] A. C. 406. Mr Beyfus seeks to obtain a rule for a writ of mandamus requiring the Registrar of Companies to register a company, the object of which the Registrar has said is to carry out something which is contrary to law, because of s. 41 of the Lotteries Act, 1823. That section repeats the language of earlier Acts, making it illegal for a person to sell any ticket 'in any lottery or lotteries except such as are or shall be authorised by this or some other Act of Parliament.' It is not suggested that the lottery which is now being promoted in the Irish Free State is authorised by the Act of 1823, and therefore Mr Beyfus has to find some other Act of Parliament which authorises lottery tickets to be sold in England. He says that it is now lawful to sell these tickets in England, because since the passing of the Irish Free State Constitution Act, 1922, the Irish Free State has power to legislate in that State: see art. 2 of Sch. I. A constitution has been set up for the Irish Free State, and its Parliament in 1930 passed an Act which enables the Minister to sanction schemes for lotteries in Ireland notwithstanding anything to the contrary in any other Act. It still, however, remains for Mr Beyfus to satisfy the Court that the prohibition in s. 41 of the Lotteries Act, 1823, which forbids the selling of lottery tickets in England, has been in any way affected. I cannot accept the contention that the Irish Act is itself an Act of Parliament within the meaning of the exception in s. 41 of the Lotteries Act, 1823. The distinction is made clear throughout the history of the legislation. Thus, it appears that by a statute of George I (6 Geo. 1, c. 5) it was enacted by the British Parliament that 'the said kingdom of Ireland hath been, is, and of right ought to be subordinate unto and dependent upon the Imperial Crown of Great Britain, as being inseparably united and annexed thereunto; and that the King's

Majesty, by and with the advice and consent of the Lords spiritual and temporal, and Commons of Great Britain in Parliament assembled, had, hath, and of right ought to have full power and authority to [203] make laws and statutes of sufficient force and validity, to bind the Kingdom and people of Ireland.' The position thus stated was altered by 23 Geo. 3, c. 28, which provided (inter alia): 'that the said right claimed by the people of Ireland to be bound only by laws enacted by His Majesty and the Parliament of that Kingdom, in all cases whatever, . . . shall be, and it is hereby declared to be established and ascertained for ever, and shall, at no time hereafter, be questioned or questionable.' So after that date the Irish Parliament had power to pass Acts of Parliament, but only for Ireland. In 1800, by the Act of Union (39 & 40 Geo. 3, c. 67), the two Parliaments were united, and thereafter the words 'some Act of Parliament' mean an Act of Parliament of the United Kingdom. Now looking at the Lotteries Act, 1823, it is clear to me that the words 'some Act of Parliament', mean some Act of the Imperial Parliament. Although it is true that in 1922 an Act of the United Kingdom set up a Legislature for Ireland, that has not altered the meaning of the expression, 'Act of Parliament' in the Act of 1823, and it is impossible to say that an Act passed by the Irish legislature is an 'Act of Parliament' within the meaning of s. 41. The Irish Free State Constitution Act, 1922 (Session 2), by Article 2 of the First Schedule provided that 'all authority legislative. . . shall be exercised in the Irish Free State. . . through the organisations established by or under, and in accord with,' the Constitution. It follows that there has been no Act of Parliament within the meaning to be attributed to that expression in s. 41, which authorises the sale of lottery tickets in England. Permission to sell those tickets in Ireland is limited to Ireland, and therefore the sale in England of tickets in connection with the Irish lottery is as illegal now as it was before the Act of 1922.

III. Corporate Personality

The principal attraction that the registered company offers over other legal forms of business organisation is that the company has a separate legal personality from that of its owners. When it is said that an individual or thing possesses legal personality what is meant is that he, she or it enjoys rights and is subject to duties under a given legal system. That is to say, within that legal system he, she or it has a distinctive identity and autonomy in that they or it can acquire rights and incur liabilities in respect of themselves or itself, and not merely vicariously on behalf of others. Thus in Ireland neither trees nor dogs possess legal personality, although the law lays down certain rights and obligations that individuals possess and are subject to regarding trees and dogs. In many slave-owning societies, slaves are regarded as not possessing legal personality. Prior to the Married Women's Property Act, 1957, married women did not have quite the same legal capacity to act as their spouses. And it has been a matter of considerable political as well as legal controversy whether the human foetus is a legal person, and if it is, to what extent and with what effect. Adult citizens of sound mind, by contrast, possess as complete a legal personality as can exist in Irish law. Some of the general principles that are dealt with in this chapter, such as *ultra vires*, piercing the corporate veil and limited liability, recur in particular contexts throughout this book.

SCOPE OF LEGAL CAPACITY

Wedick v. Osmond & Son (Dublin) Ltd.
[1935] I.R. 820 (H.Ct.)

SULLIVAN P.: [833] James Wedick, the complainant in this case, is an Inspector of the Pharmaceutical Society of Ireland. The defendants are a Limited Company. . . . By the summonses the complainant charged the defendants with [several] offences. . . . [834] On the facts. . . found the District Justice convicted the defendants of the offences charged in the said summonses and on the application of the defendants stated a case for the opinion of this Court whether, having regard to the facts so found by him, he was right in law in so convicting.

[838] The third summons charges an offence under sect. 17 of the Pharmacy Act (Ireland), 1875, Amendment Act, 1890. That section provides:

> Any person or persons lawfully keeping open shop for selling, retailing, or mixing poisons shall personally manage and conduct such shop and the retailing and mixing of poisons therein, or shall employ for the purposes aforesaid, as an assistant or manager in such shop, a duly registered chemist and druggist, or registered druggist, or pharmaceutical chemist or licentiate apothecary, and such person or persons lawfully keeping open shop as aforesaid shall, for the purposes of this Act and of the principal Act, be held to be the retailer and compounder of poisons aforesaid therein;... and any person or persons acting in contravention of this enactment shall for every such offence be liable to pay a penalty not exceeding five pounds.

It was argued by counsel for the defendants that the conviction on this third summons was wrong, on the ground that the words 'person or persons' in that section do not include a Limited Company. In support of that argument counsel relied on the decisions in *Pharmaceutical Society* v. *London and Provincial Supply Association* (5 A.C. 857) and *Pharmaceutical Society of Ireland* v. *Boyd & Co.* [1896] 2 I.R. 344.

In *Pharmaceutical Society* v. *London and Provincial Supply Association* the question to be determined was whether the word 'person' in the first and fifteenth sections of the Pharmacy Act, 1868 (31 & 32 Vict. c. 121), applied to an incorporated company. The first section of that Act enacts that it shall be unlawful for any person to sell, or keep open shop for retailing, dispensing, or compounding poisons, or to assume, or use the title 'Chemist and Druggist', or Chemist or Druggist, or Pharmacist, or Dispensing Chemist or Druggist, unless such person shall be a Pharmaceutical Chemist or a Chemist and Druggist within the meaning of the Act and be registered under the Act and conform to such regulations as to the keeping, dispensing, and selling of such poisons as may from time [839] to time be prescribed. The fifteenth section enacts that any person who shall sell, or keep an open shop, for the retailing, dispensing, or compounding poisons, or who shall take, use or exhibit the name or title of Chemist and Druggist, or Chemist or Druggist, not being a duly registered Pharmaceutical Chemist or Chemist and Druggist, or who shall take, use, or exhibit the name or title Pharmaceutical Chemist, Parmaceutist, or Pharmacist, not being a Pharmaceutical Chemist, or shall fail to conform with any regulation as to the keeping or selling of poisons made in pursuance of the Act, or who shall compound any medicine of the British Pharmacopeia except according to the formularies of the said Pharmacopeia, shall for every such offence be liable to pay a penalty or sum of £5. It was held by the Court of Appeal and by the House of Lords, that the word 'person' in these sections did not include a corporation. In the House of Lords, Lord Selborne L.C. stated (p. 861):– 'There can be no question that the word "person" may, and I should be disposed myself to say *prima facie* does, in a public statute, include a person in law: that is a corporation, as well as a natural person,' but he accepted the principle that 'if a statute provided that no person shall do a particular act except on a particular condition, it is, *prima facie*, natural and reasonable (unless there be something in the context or in the manifest object of the statute, or in the nature of the subject-matter, to exclude that construction) to understand the Legislature as intending such persons, as, by the use of proper means, may be able to fulfil the condition; and not those who, though called "persons" in law, have no capacity to do so at any time, by any means, or under any circumstances, whatsoever.' He held that *prima facie* the first section contemplates persons such as may, or may not, be pharmaceutical chemists or chemists and druggists within the meaning of the Act and be registered under the Act, and that as it was clear that a corporation could not be a Pharmaceutical Chemist or a Chemist and Druggist, and be registered under the Act, the word 'person' did not include a corporation, in the absence of anything in the context or object of the Act to require that it should. Lords Blackburn and Watson were of the same opinion. In the *Pharmaceutical Society of Ireland* v. *Boyd & Co.* the same question arose on the construction of sect. 30 of the Pharmacy (Ireland) Act, 1875 (37 & 38 Vict. c. 57) which is practically identical in its terms with sects. 1 and 15 of the Pharmacy Act, [840] 1868. The Court of Queen's Bench in Ireland (O'Brien, Johnson and Holmes JJ.) following the decision in the *Pharmaceutical Society* v. *London and Provincial Supply Association* upon the construction of corresponding sections of the Pharmacy Act, 1868, held that the word 'person' in sect. 30 of the Pharmacy (Ireland) Act, 1875 did not include a body corporate. The principles stated by the House of Lords in the *Pharmaceutical Society* v. *London and Provincial Supply Association* were also accepted and applied in this country in *O'Duffy* v. *Jaffe* [1904] 2 I.R. 27 and *R. (King)* v. *Antrim JJ* [1906] 2 I.R. 298. In the latter case Palles C.B. at p. 327, having quoted from the opinion of Lord Blackburn the following passage: 'I am quite clear about this, that whenever you can see that the object of the Act requires that the word "person" shall have the more extended or the less extended sense, then, whichever sense it requires, you should apply the word in that sense and construe the Act accordingly,' proceeds:– 'Of course this principle is applicable only when the words are capable of being used in the extended sense. Therefore, if the special description in the statute of the person within it is one which cannot be answered by a body corporate, or if the Act, contemplated or prohibited, be one which a body corporate is incapable of committing, then the limited construction must prevail. *The Pharmaceutical Company's Case* and that of *O'Duffy* v. *Jaffe* are instances of the first class of limitation. Offences in which either intent or *mens rea* is an essential ingredient are illustrations of the other.' In that case the Court had to consider the question whether the word 'person' in sect. 80 of the Fisheries (Ireland) Act, 1842 (5 & 6 Vict. c. 106), included a corporation. The Court held that it did. Palles C.B. in the course of his judgment (p. 326), having referred to the Interpretation Act, 1889, sect. 2, sub-sect.1, which provides that, in the construction of every enactment relating to an offence punishable on summary conviction, 'person' shall, unless the contrary intention appears, include a body corporate, said: 'In determining this question, although the Act, as a whole, cannot be disregarded, the ultimate decision must be on the particular section itself. Of the various sections of the Act, there are many in which a contrary intention does appear, such as those which constitute offences of which intent is a material part. I, therefore, restrict my consideration to sect. 80 alone.'

[841] These words of the Chief Baron are singularly applicable to the present case. Mr Fitzgerald pointed out that in several sections of the Pharmacy Act (Ireland), 1875, Amendment Act, 1890, the word 'person' or the word 'persons' obviously means a natural person or persons and does not include a corporation; see sects. 5, 8, 10, 12, 13, 15. But when we consider the terms of sect. 17, upon which the third summons in this case was based, I think the word 'person' or 'persons' must receive a different interpretation. There is an obvious and very material difference between that section and sects. 1 and 15 of the Pharmacy Act, 1868, which were under consideration in the *Pharmaceutical Society* v. *London and Provincial Supply Association* and *The Pharmaceutical Society of Ireland* v. *Boyd & Co.* It was admitted by the defendants' counsel that a corporation can lawfully keep open shop for the sale of poisons, and it is obvious that a corporation can comply with the conditions imposed by sect. 17 on persons lawfully keeping open shop for selling, retailing, or mixing poisons, for though it cannot 'personally manage and conduct such shop' it can 'employ for the purpose aforesaid as an Assistant or Manager in such shop a duly registered chemist and druggist, or registered druggist, or pharmaceutical chemist, or licentiate apothecary.' There is, therefore, nothing in the special description in the section of the persons within it that cannot be answered by a corporation, and I can see nothing in the apparent object of the section to require that the word 'persons' should be so construed as to exclude corporations. I am, therefore, of the opinion that a corporation is a 'person' within the meaning of sect. 17 of 53 & 54 Vict. c. 48.

Dean v. John Menzies (Holdings) Ltd.
(1981) S.C. 23

(From headnote) The defendant company was charged in the Sheriff Court of North Strathclyde at Dumbarton on a complaint at the instance of Ian Dean, Procurator-fiscal, which set forth that 'On 30th January 1979 at the premises occupied by you at 50 High Street, Dumbarton, you did conduct yourself in a shamelessly indecent manner in respect that you did sell, expose for sale and have for sale 64 indecent and obscene magazines as specified in the Schedule annexed hereto, which magazines were likely to deprave and corrupt the morals of the lieges and to create in their minds inordinate and lustful desires.' The accused company stated pleas to both the competency and the relevancy of the libel and the Sheriff (Jardine), sustaining the plea to competency, dismissed the complaint.

At the request of the Procurator-fiscal, the Sheriff stated a case for the opinion of the High Court of Justiciary.

LORD CAMERON (dissenting): . . . [24] The issue of competency as presented in argument is short, substantial but not simple: it is whether by the law of Scotland a fictional person can be guilty of the common law offence libelled. It is of course a matter of necessary concession and of everyday practice, that such persons can be guilty of statutory offences even of those offences where proof of knowledge or even intention on the part of the accused is an essential element in proof of guilt.

Before I come to deal with the arguments which were presented by counsel I think it is desirable to set out in the simplest form what it is that the respondents are alleged to have done – it is the sale or exposure for sale as a transaction of commerce, presumably in shop premises occupied by them for the purpose of their business, of certain specified magazines. It is the alleged quality of these particular magazines and their consequent effects or potential effects on the minds of the purchaser and reader which constitute the criminal character of what would otherwise be a very ordinary everyday commercial transaction. Such prosecutions in the case of individual shopkeepers are not uncommon and the recent case of *Robertson* v. *Smith* 1980 J.C.1 makes it clear that sale to the public or exposure for sale of such literature constitutes a criminal offence in the common law of Scotland.

One obvious consequence of the Sheriff's decision would be that if an individual shopkeeper were to transfer the control of such a business as was conducted by the appellant in *Robertson* v. *Smith* from himself as an individual to a limited company controlled by him he could escape the penal consequences of his action. I make this observation because, while the present appeal is concerned with the affairs of a large company, with, as is well known, many trading outlets, the issue is equally applicable to a 'one-man company' operating in a back street in Glasgow.

[25] The submissions for the appellant were presented by the Advocate-Depute in a careful and able argument in which his broad submission was that those directing and controlling the activities of a limited company, being its responsible officers, are persons capable of supplying the 'will' of the company sufficient for the company to be able to possess the *mens rea* required for a common law offence and in particular the offence with which this company is charged in this complaint.

In elaboration of this submission the Advocate-Depute drew attention to the nature of the offence here charged as that has been identified in *Watt* v. *Annan* 1978 J.C. 84 and *Robertson* v. *Smith* 1980 J.C.1. The general question of the capacity of a corporate entity or fictional person to exercise a will and to form and carry into effect an intent had for long been settled in Scotland as in England. In *Gordon* v. *British & Foreign Metaline Co.* (1886) 14 R. 75 the capacity of such a 'person' to act with malice was affirmed, and the classic authority of *Lennard's Carrying Co. Ltd.* v. *Asiatic Petroleum Co. Ltd.* [1915] A.C. 705 left no room for doubt as to how the law would approach the question of a company's capacity to commit a common law offence and therefore to form the necessary wicked intent. A company's capacity to be guilty of malicious defamation was also recognised in English law: cf. *Triplex Safety Glass* v. *Lancegaye Safety Glass (1934) Ltd.* [1939] 2 K.B. 395, *per* du Parcq L.J. at p. 408, while the case of *D.P.P.* v. *Kent and Sussex Contractors* [1944] K.B. 146 showed that in England a company could be convicted of making statements which they knew to be false 'with intent to deceive'. This was a case of breach of regulation but that did not affect the principle.

There was ample authority in Scotland for the proposition for which he contended. . . .

[26] The broad proposition which Mr Kerrigan advanced was that as there was no reported case which decided that a limited company could be liable to a charge of criminal conduct at common law; the corollary of that proposition was that so to charge a limited company was by clear inference incompetent. The remedy lay not with the Court but with the legislature. For this Court to decide that a common law charge would lie against a limited company would be to make new law and in effect to create a whole catalogue of new offences; this was beyond the competence of the Court.

If what the Crown is seeking in this case to do were, as Mr Kerrigan argued, to induce the Court to create a new offence or offences which were previously unknown to the law then I would think there was great force in his argument, but the absence of direct authority affirming the Crown's submissions as to the competency of this charge is not by itself authority for the contrary; in any event the offence here libelled is not new: it is well known and has been the subject of more than one prosecution.

The question therefore is not one of the creation of new offences but the application of the existing law to a corporate body as that law applies to an individual. The width of Mr Kerrigan's argument is such that logically applied it would, in Scotland, apply equally to a partnership as to a limited company. But Mr Kerrigan's argument went much further. He drew a distinction between those *mala prohibita* the commission of which admittedly may involve the formation of a deliberate intent, but only in those areas or fields identified by Parliament, and *mala in se*; fictional persons as such could not be guilty of acts of moral turpitude, and it is that quality which is involved in the concept of the *malum in se*, and it is because of the nature of a company that the limits of its criminal liability require to be drawn by its creator i.e. Parliament. The nature of the offence here requires proof of dole, which while in substance the same as *mens rea* (cf. Hume on Crimes, Vol. 1, 25) differs in that dole infers a degree of moral obliquity. A company could not be [27] charged with culpable homicide, though it might be guilty of libel or even of criminal libel in England. In any event this was an offence in a 'subjective area' and there was no precedent for such a charge being brought against a company where the essence of the charge was of moral delinquency. Further, it was impossible to fasten the label of 'shameless conduct' to a limited company. The capacity for a sensation of shame was not within the necessary category of those senses which could be credited to a company. Therefore it could not (in the absence of expressed parliamentary enactment to the contrary) be guilty of shameless conduct, it being incapable of any sense of shame. This was a matter which should be left to the consideration and decision of Parliament. . . .

In considering the arguments addressed to the competency of the charge in this case it is necessary to have its precise terms in mind; it is a charge of an offence against public decency as specified in the complaint and is a charge at common law. The arguments presented against the competency of the proceedings were not directed to the nature of the charge as being one unknown to the common law if committed by an individual, but solely to the competency of charging a limited company, being a fictional person, with a common law offence. The argument proceeded in three steps (1) that a fictional person could not be charged with a common law offence, that being a matter for Parliament; (2) that in any case the particular offence charged, being one involving subjective considerations, could not be competently charged, and (3) that, as it was impossible for a company to have or feel a sense of shame, this offence in which subjective shamelessness was an essential ingredient could not be competently libelled against the respondents.

While the arguments were presented in general terms on both sides of the bar, I think it is necessary to isolate the precise issue which arises on the competency of the present complaint. It is whether a limited company, acting within its statutory powers and in pursuit of its objects as prescribed by its articles, can be competently charged with an offence at common law. The case is not concerned directly with any wider question, but solely with whether a limited company acting in course of its ordinary and legitimate business can be prosecuted for a common law offence, where its action in its specific facts would in the case of an individual render him liable to prosecution for a contravention of the common law. I think it is particularly important to limit the field of decision in this case to such action as falls within the powers of the corporation. This complaint and the issues arising upon it [28] are not concerned with actions which are *ultra vires* or in excess of the powers conferred on the corporation by its incorporating statutes or instruments or articles of association. The assumption here is that the sale or exposure was in course of the respondents' business.

The criminal law has long recognised that a corporate body may be guilty of breaches of statute and incur a penalty, and therefore be susceptible to prosecution as a person recognised in the eyes of the law. Further, the law has also recognised that an incorporation may be guilty of statutory offences the commission of which is the result of intended or deliberate action or inaction. It was not Parliament which specifically provided that corporate bodies such as limited companies should be subject to prosecution: the various statutes assumed that no distinction in capacity to offend should exist between natural and other persons recognised by law as legal entities with capacity to discharge certain functions and perform certain actions. The responsibility of both for breaches of statute is the same, and the individuals and the company alike can be cited and charged in their own names. . . .

[T]his is not a case of creating or declaring a new crime or offence which never existed before, nor of extending the boundaries of criminal responsibility to a group of legal persons on whose shoulders criminal responsibility had not been rested before. If therefore a limited company has the capacity to form an intention, to decide on a course of action, to act in accordance with that deliberate intent within the scope and limits of its articles, it is difficult to see on what general principle it should not be susceptible to [29] prosecution where that action offends against the common law. It must no doubt be conceded that this principle could not be applied to a crime where the law prescribes only one and that a custodial penalty; but the fact that *lex non cogit ad impossibilia* in a particular instance does not imply that as a consequence it follows that *lex non cogit ad possibilia* in other instances where penalties for breaches of the common law can be effectively imposed. It has long been settled in our civil law that a company can be guilty of malice: malice implies a harmful intention deliberately directed against another person or persons. The parallel between malice in the field of defamation and the essense of this *mens rea* which is essential to criminal liability at common law appears to me close. What then is criminal intent? While it is of course true that the 'wicked intent' – (which is *mens rea*) is a matter of proof in which the burden of proof lies upon the Crown, 'the wicked intent is an inference to be drawn from the circumstances of the deed, as well as from any explanations by the man. Although a man considers his deed meritorious, the law may hold him to have acted wickedly and feloniously. Whenever a person does what is criminal, the presumption is that he does so wilfully': MacDonald 5th edition p. 1. Further it was put by Hume in writing on the nature of dole thus 'It is not material to the notion of guilt, that the offender have himself been fully conscious of the wickedness of what he did': Hume on Crimes, Vol. 1, 25. No distinction is drawn by Hume between the concept of 'dole' and that of *mens rea*: dole being defined as 'that corrupt and evil intention, which is essential. . . to the guilt of any crime' *op. cit.* Vol. 1, 21. These are general principles applicable to all common law crimes and offences and therefore it follows that the presumption of law is precisely the same in all cases – whatever the degree of moral obliquity involved in the com- mission of the offence. Therefore the bald submission that a company cannot in Scotland in any circumstances be guilty of a common law offence does not commend itself to me as sound in principle. It is without any authority and if it be argued that a company cannot possess the capacity to exhibit *mens rea* it can be sufficiently answered that *mens rea* is no more than that 'wicked intent' which is the presumed element in all acts which are criminal at common law. It is trite law also that a company is legally capable of many deliberate actions within the limits of its powers as set out in its Articles of Association, these powers being exercised by those who are the 'directing mind' or 'will' of the company. In the case of *Len- nards' Carrying Co. Ltd.* v. *Asiatic Petroleum Co. Ltd.* [1915] A.C. 705 at p. 713 Lord Chancellor Haldane, with whom his colleagues, including Lord Dunedin, concurred, at p. 713, in analysing the elements which taken together demonstrate the basis on which a company can be held responsible as an entity for deliberate acts or omissions where these acts or omissions are those at least in the field of civil liability, said 'A corporation is an abstraction. It has no mind of its own any more than it has a body of its own; its active and directing will must consequently be sought in the person of somebody who for some purposes may be called an agent, but who is really the directing mind and will of the corporation, the very ego and centre of the personality of the corporation. That person may be under the direction of the shareholders in general meeting; that person may be the board of directors itself, or it may be, and in some companies it is so, that that person has an authority co-ordinate [30] with the board of directors given to him under the articles of association, and is appointed by the general meeting of the company, and can only be removed by the general meeting of the company.' This may well indicate that difficulties of proof will arise when a charge of criminal conduct at common law is brought against a limited company, but does nothing to suggest that such a charge may not be competently brought, and that without the necessity in all cases of specifying in the complaint or indictment which particular officer or employee of the company was in fact responsible for the act or omission charged. The argument put forward by Mr Kerrigan, who cast aside any support which he might get from *Miles* v. *Finlay* and the passage in Green's Encyclopaedia founded on by the Sheriff, that there is no reported authority in Scotland supporting the Crown's contention on competency does not seem to me to carry the matter very far: stood on its head the argument on the absence of direct authority is equally potent – that the absence of authority indicates that the matter is beyond argument. But the authorities demonstrate that a company can be guilty of *mala prohibita* even where the offence involves knowledge, intentional action of permission. Further, in the field of civil liability a company can be held liable in reparation for defamation where malice has to be established, while in England there is authority for the proposition that a company may be guilty of criminal libel. If a company can by law – by legal fiction, if you will – be endowed with a mind and will exerciseable by natural persons acting within the confines of the company's legal competence, and be held responsible for actings in pursuance of the exercise of that mind and will, then if those actings are contrary to the common criminal law, I find it difficult to see upon what basis of principle it can be said that the company is free of criminal liability, however this may be enforced. The wicked intent in all common law crimes is the intent to perform the criminal act. The motive or moral depravity of the actor is alike irrelevant to the quality of that act in the eye of the law. Therefore if the act is intentional, the criminal intent is presumed whatever the motive which inspired the actor.

The rules of law as to a company's capacity to exercise a conscious mind and will enunciated in the case of *Lennard's Carrying Company* have been further illustrated in the recent and important case of *Tesco Ltd.* v. *Nattrass* [1972] A.C. 153 (post pp. 27-33). No doubt the decision is concerned with a statutory charge and with the defences open to a company charged with a contravention of that statute, but in my view its importance lies in the extent to which the House of Lords held that a company could be susceptible to criminal proceedings whether under statute or at common law. In that case Lord Reid at page 171, after citing the passage I have quoted from the speech of Lord Haldane, went on to refer to a passage from the judgment of Lord Denning in *H. L. Bolton (Enginnering) Co. Ltd.* v. *T. J. Graham & Sons Ltd.* [1957] Q.B. 159 where he said at page 172 'A company may in many ways be likened to a human body. It has a brain and nerve centre which controls what it does. It also has hands which hold tools and act in accordance with directions from the centre. Some of the people in the company are mere servants and agents who are nothing more than hands to do the work and cannot be said to represent the mind or will. Others are directors and managers who represent the directing mind and will of the company, and [31] control what it does. The state of mind of these managers is the state of mind of the company and is treated by the law as such.' Having quoted that passage Lord Reid went on to say 'In that case the directors of the company only met once a year: they left the management of the business to others, and it was the intention of those managers which was imputed to the company. I think that was right.' I draw particular attention to the word 'intention'. Later in his speech Lord Reid referred to the case of *D.P.P.* v. *Kent and Sussex Contractors* cited by the Advocate-Depute and also *R.* v. *I.C.R. Haulage Ltd.* [1944] K.B. 551 where it was held that a company can be guilty of common law conspiracy. Lord Reid added in relation to this latter case at page 173 'I think that the true view is that the judge must direct the jury that if they find certain facts proved then as a matter of law they must find that the criminal act of the officer, servant or agent including his state of mind, intention, knowledge or belief is the act of the company. I have already dealt with the considerations to be applied in deciding when such a person can and when he cannot be identified with the company. I do not see how the nature of the charge can make any difference.'

No doubt the decision in the case of *Tesco* is one concerned with English criminal law, but the statute under which the prosecution was brought is a United Kingdom statute effective in Scotland and the judgment and opinions in the case, if technically not binding in this country, are necessarily to be treated with the highest respect. One thing may be taken as clear, that in England a charge of common law crime may be competently laid against a company, and while I agree that there is no reason why the criminal jurisprudence of the two countries should necessarily fall into line, at the same time I see no reason in principle why a different rule of law should operate in Scotland, the same statute governing the structure, powers and functioning of limited companies in both countries. In both countries the rules and principles governing the civil liabilities of companies are the same: in both countries the rules and principles governing criminal liability in respect of statutory offences are the same and it is therefore not easy to see upon what principle of Scots criminal law a company created by statute should not be amenable to the common law in matters criminal – the only authority for the contrary view which appealed to the Sheriff was thrown overboard by Mr Kerrigan and in my opinion rightly – particularly as in both countries the capacity of a company to form an intent, to carry it into effect, to exercise a will and to make a conscious choice of courses of action or inaction is undoubted and is precisely the same. In my opinion the competency of the present charge is not open to successful challenge on the broad general principle that a company cannot in Scots law be guilty of a common law offence.

This however is not the end of the matter. It must necessarily be conceded that certain criminal conduct cannot be ascribed to a company. Thus, where the only penalty prescribed or permitted by law is custodial or personally physical, it may be presumed that no charge will lie, but no such objection could be levelled here and that is a question that does not arise in the present case. The narrower question is whether this charge can be brought against a limited company, and it is to this particular aspect of the matter that Mr [32] Kerrigan's subsidiary argument was directed. Whatever might be the general liability of a limited company, this charge, it was submitted, was not one which could be competently brought. Mr Kerrigan's argument in brief was that as this charge involved as a critical element an accusation of 'shamelessness' it went far beyond any acceptable limits. His argument could be put in very simple form. He said that 'shame' or a 'sense of shame' was something which could not be attributed to a fictional person. Therefore a fictional person could not possess the capacity to act 'shamelessly'. But the charge was one of 'shameless' conduct. The accused was a fictional person, therefore the charge lacked its essential content because no fictional person could have a sense of shame. The simplicity of the argument thus presented is attractive. But the 'shameless' quality of the conduct here libelled is essentially an objective and not a subjective quality. It is of the essence of this offence that the conduct be directed towards some person or persons with an intention or in the knowledge that it should corrupt, or be calculated or be liable to corrupt or deprave in the manner libelled, those towards whom the conduct is directed. It is this which determines the shameless quality of the act, with which the moral obliquity of the actor – if any – has nothing to do. In the present case the qualification of the conduct is that the exposure for sale or sale to persons, members of the public, was done with the knowledge or intention of the company – knowledge of the calculated consequences or those liable to follow or intention that such consequences should follow. Now the respondents here are primarily a commercial company concerned in the sale of *inter alia* magazines. It may be presumed that the selection of stock is not a matter of accident but at least dictated to some extent by commercial considerations and in the hope and expectation that the articles exposed will be attractive and saleable and that the selection is at the will and intention of the seller. The transactions under consideration therefore represent conduct which is directed and deliberately directed to members of the public to influence them to purchase articles for sale. In these circumstances I do not see why that conduct directed, as it admittedly would be, towards members of the public as potential purchasers, should not be capable of bearing the qualitative description which the Crown seeks to put upon it. In effect, the test of criminality is objective and not subjective and it is here that Mr Kerrigan's subsidiary or 'subjective' argument appears to me unsound , because it is ill-founded. The question is not whether a company is an entity which is endowed with a conscience to be appeased or a capacity for moral sensation or an absence of a sense of shame or even a capacity to overcome a sense of shame by the prospect of financial profit. It may well be that the offence libelled is one which falls within the category of offences against public morals, but in order to commit it the offender does not require to be possessed of capacity to feel a sense of personal shame or even to lack it. What however is of the essence of the offence is that the action itself of an indecent character should be directed towards a person or persons with certain intentions or knowledge of the consequences or likely consequences to that person or those persons – the intention or knowledge that it should corrupt or be calculated or liable to corrupt or deprave those towards whom the conduct is directed. If these matters can be established by relevant and sufficient evidence then the [33] qualification and therefore the criminal character of the actions themselves are also proved.

In my opinion therefore Mr Kerrigan's two main attacks on the competency of this charge as directed against the respondents fail. By libelling this offence against the respondents it cannot be said the prosecutor is seeking to create a new offence. The offence is one known to the common law, as Mr Kerrigan conceded. Further I do not think that he succeeded in demonstrating that a company cannot possess a capacity in law to intend its actions and therefore be incapable of forming the wilful intent essential to the commission of a common law offence, and as I have already indicated, I think his argument on 'shamelessness' of conduct was misconceived. I do not intend to imply however that a limited company is in law to be regarded as capable of the commission of any and every common law offence, other than those for which the only penalty is custodial, or of offences – such as rape – which are obviously and necessarily physical acts of a natural person. In my opinion, and as at present advised, so to hold would go much further than is necessary for a decision as to the competency of libelling this offence against a limited company. Having considered the arguments presented in this case I am of opinion that a company may competently be charged with an offence at common law, where that offence consists of action purposely taken by the company within its statutory powers and in pursuance of its objects as defined and set out in its articles, and where such action if taken by a natural person would constitute a common law offence.

Tesco Supermarkets Ltd. v. Nattrass
[1972] A.C. 153 (H.L.)

The defendant (Tesco Ltd.) owned a large chain of supermarkets, and from time to time it sold products at prices considerably lower than their normal price. On one occasion there was advertised in a Tesco store a washing power as selling for 2s. 11d., when the normal selling price was 3s. 11d. A customer, relying on the advertisement, sought washing powder in the store at the advertised price, but could only find it at 3s. 11d. Tesco Ltd. were prosecuted for contravening §11(2) of the Trade Descriptions Act, 1968. According to §11(2):

> If any person offering to supply any goods, by whatever means, any indication likely to be taken as an indication that the goods are offered at a price less than that at which they are in fact being offered he shall, subject to the provisions of this Act, be guilty of an offence.

It was not disputed that that section applied to this case. Tesco Ltd. relied on section 24(1) which provides:

> In any proceedings for an offence under this Act it shall, subject to subsection (2) of this section, be a defence for the person charged to prove – (a) that the commission of the offence was due to a mistake or to reliance on information supplied to him or to the act or default of another person, an accident or some other cause beyond his control; and (b) that he took all reasonable precautions and exercised all due diligence to avoid the commission of such an offence by himself or any person under his control.

LORD REID: . . . [168] The relevant facts as found by the magistrates were that on the previous evening a shop assistant, Miss Rogers, whose duty it was to put out fresh stock found that there were no more of the specially marked packs in stock. There were a number of packs marked with the ordinary price so she put them out. She ought to have told the shop manager, Mr Clement, about this, but she failed to do so. Mr Clement was responsible for seeing that the proper packs were on sale, but he failed to see to this although he marked his daily return 'all special offers O.K.' The magistrates found that if he had known about this he would either have removed the poster advertising the reduced price or given instructions that only 2s. 11d. was to be charged for the packs marked 3s. 11d.

Section 24(2) requires notice to be given to the prosecutor if the accused is blaming another person and such notice was duly given naming Mr Clement.

In order to avoid conviction the appellants had to prove facts sufficient to satisfy both parts of section 24(1) of the Act of 1968. The magistrates held that they had exercised all due diligence in devising a proper system for the operation of the said store and by securing so far as was reasonably practicable that it was fully implemented and thus had fulfilled the requirements of section 24(1)(b).

But they convicted the appellants because in their view the requirements of sections 24(1)(a) had not been fulfilled: they held that Clement was not 'another person' within the meaning of that provision.

[169] The Divisional Court held that the magistrates were wrong in holding that Clement was not 'another person'. The respondent did not challenge this finding of the Divisional Court so I need say no more about it than that I think that on this matter the Divisional Court was plainly right. But that court sustained the conviction on the ground that the magistrates had applied the wrong test in deciding that the requirements of section 24(1)(b) had been fulfilled. In effect that court held that the words 'he took all reasonable precautions. . .' do not mean what they say: 'he' does not mean the accused, it means the accused and all his servants who were acting in a managerial or supervisory capacity. I think that earlier authorities virtually compelled the Divisional Court to reach this strange construction. So the real question in this appeal is whether these earlier authorities were rightly decided.

But before examining those earlier cases I think it necessary to make some general observations.

Over a century ago the courts invented the idea of an absolute offence. The accepted doctrines of the common law put them in a difficulty. There was a presumption that when Parliament makes the commission of certain acts an offence it intends that *mens rea* shall be a constituent of that offence whether or not there is any reference to the knowledge or state of mind of the accused. And it was and is held to be an invariable rule that where *mens rea* is a constituent of any offence the burden of proving *mens rea* is on the prosecution. Some day this House may have to re-examine that rule, but that is another matter. For the protection of purchasers or consumers Parliament in many cases made it an offence for a trader to do certain things. Normally those things were done on his behalf by his servants and cases arose where the doing of the forbidden thing was solely the fault of a servant, the master having done all he could to prevent it and being entirely ignorant of its having been done. The just course would have been to hold that, once the facts constituting the offence had been proved, *mens rea* would be presumed unless the accused proved that he was blameless. The courts could not, or thought they could not, take that course. But they could and did hold in many such cases on a construction of the statutory provision that Parliament must be deemed to have intended to depart from the general rule and to make the offence absolute in the sense that *mens rea* was not to be a constituent of the offence.

This has led to great difficulties. If the offence is not held to be absolute the requirement that the prosecutor must prove *mens rea* makes it impossible to enforce the enactment in very many cases. If the offence is held to be absolute that leads to the conviction of persons who are entirely blameless: an injustice which brings the law into disrepute. So Parliament has found it necessary to devise a method of avoiding this difficulty. But instead of passing a general enactment that it shall always be a defence for the accused to prove that he was no party to the offence and had done all he could to prevent it, Parliament has chosen to deal with the problem piecemeal, and has in an increasing number of cases enacted in various forms with regard to particular offences that it shall be a defence to prove various exculpatory circumstances.

In my judgment the main object of these provisions must have been to distinguish between those who are in some degree blameworthy and those [170] who are not, and to enable the latter to escape from conviction if they can show that they were in no way to blame. I find it almost impossible to suppose that Parliament or any reasonable body of men would as a matter of policy think it right to make employers criminally liable for the acts of some of their servants but not for those of others and I find it incredible that a draftsman, aware of that intention, would fail to insert any words to express it. But in several cases the courts, for reasons which it is not easy to discover, have given a restricted meaning to such provisions. It has been held that such provisions afford a defence if the master proves that the servant at fault was the person who himself did the prohibited act, but that they afford no defence if the servant at fault was one who failed in his duty of supervision to see that his subordinates did not commit the prohibited act. Why Parliament should be thought to have intended this distinction or how as a matter of construction these provisions can reasonably be held to have that meaning is not apparent.

In some of these cases the employer charged with the offence was a limited company. But in others the employer was an individual and still it was held that he, though personally entirely blameless, could not rely on these provisions if the fault which led to the commission of the offence was the fault of a servant in failing to carry out his duty to instruct or supervise his subordinates.

Where a limited company is the employer difficult questions do arise in a wide variety of circumstances in deciding which of its officers or servants is to be identified with the company so that his guilt is the guilt of the company.

I must start by considering the nature of the personality which by a fiction the law attributes to a corporation. A living person has a mind which can have knowledge or intention or be negligent and he has hands to carry out his intentions. A corporation has none of these: it must act through living persons, though not always one or the same person. Then the person who acts is not speaking or acting for the company. He is acting as the company and his mind which directs his acts is the mind of the company. There is no question of the company being vicariously liable. He is not acting as a servant, representative, agent or delegate. He is an embodiment of the company or, one could say, he hears and speaks through the persona of the company, within his appropriate sphere, and his mind is the mind of the company. If it is a guilty mind then that guilt is the guilt of the company. It must be a question of law whether, once the facts have been ascertained, a person in doing particular things is to be regarded as the company or merely as the company's servant or agent. In that case any liability of the company can only be a statutory or vicarious liability.

In *Lennard's Carrying Co. Ltd.* v. *Asiatic Petroleum Co. Ltd.* [1915] A.C. 705 the question was whether damage had occurred without the 'actual fault or privity' of the owner of a ship. The owners were a company. The fault was that of the registered managing owner who managed the ship on behalf of the owners and it was held that the company could not dissociate itself from him so as to say that there was no actual fault or privity on the part of the company. Viscount Haldane L.C. said, at pp. 713, 714:

> [171] For if Mr Lennard was the directing mind of the company, then his action must, unless a corporation is not to be liable at all, have been an action which was the action of the company itself within the meaning of section 502.... It must be upon the true construction of that section in such a case as the present one that the fault or privity is the fault or privity of somebody who is not merely a servant or agent for whom the company is liable upon the footing respondeat superior, but somebody for whom the company is liable because his action is the very action of the company itself.

Reference is frequently made to the judgment of Denning L.J. in *H. L. Bolton (Engineering) Co. Ltd.* v. *T. J. Graham & Sons Ltd.* [1957] 1 Q.B. 159. He said, at p. 172:

> A company may in many ways be likened to a human body. It has a brain and nerve centre which controls what it does. It also has hands which hold the tools and acts in accordance with directions from the centre. Some of the people in the company are mere servants and agents who are nothing more than hands to do the work and cannot be said to represent the mind or will. Others are directors and managers who represent the directing mind and will of the company, and control what it does. The state of mind of these managers is the state of mind of the company and is treated by the law as such.

In that case the directors of the company only met once a year: they left the management of the business to others, and it was the intention of those managers which was imputed to the company. I think that was right. There have been attempts to apply Lord Denning's words to all servants of a company whose work is brain work, or who exercise some managerial discretion under the direction of superior officers of the company. I do not think that Lord Denning intended to refer to them. He only referred to those who 'represent the directing mind and will of the company, and control what it does'.

I think that is right for this reason. Normally the board of directors, the managing director and perhaps other superior officers of a company carry out the functions of management and speak and act as the company. Their subordinates do not. They carry out orders from above and it can make no difference that they are given some measure of discretion. But the board of directors may delegate full discretion to act independently of instructions from them. I see no difficulty in holding that they have thereby put such a delegate in their place so that within the scope of the delegation he can act as the company. It may not always be easy to draw the line but there are cases in which the line must be drawn. *Lennard's* case [1915] A.C. 705 was one of them.

In some cases the phrase alter ego has been used. I think it is misleading. When dealing with a company the word alter is I think misleading. The person who speaks and acts as the company is not alter. He is identified with the company. And when dealing with an individual no other individual can be his alter ego. The other individual can be a servant, agent, delegate or representative but I know of neither principle [172] nor authority which warrants the confusion (in the literal or original sense) of two separate individuals. . .

[173] In the next two cases a company was accused and it was held liable for the fault of a superior officer. In *Director of Public Prosecutions* v. *Kent and Sussex Contractors Ltd.* [1944] K.B. 146 he was the transport manager. In *Rex* v. *I.C.R. Haulage Ltd.* [1944] K.B. 551 it was held that a company can be guilty of common law conspiracy. The act of the managing director was held to be the act of the company. I think that a passage in the judgment is too widely stated, at p. 559:

> Where in any particular case there is evidence to go to a jury that the criminal act of an agent, including his state of mind, intention, knowledge or belief is the act of the company, and, in cases where the presiding judge so rules, whether the jury are satisfied that it has been proved, must depend on the nature of the charge, the relative position of the officer or agent, and the other relevant facts and circumstances of the case.

This may have been influenced by the erroneous views expressed in the two *Hammett* cases. I think that the true view is that the judge must direct the jury that if they find certain facts proved then as a matter of law they must find that the criminal act of the officer, servant or agent including his state of mind, intention, knowledge or belief is the act of the company. I have already dealt with the considerations to be applied in deciding when such a person can and when he cannot be identified with the company. I do not see how the nature of the charge can make any difference. If the guilty man was in law identifiable with the company then whether his offence was serious or venial his act was the act of the company but if he was not so identifiable then no act of his, serious or otherwise, was the act of the company itself.

In *John Henshall (Quarries) Ltd.* v. *Harvey* [1965] 2 Q.B. 233 a company was held not criminally responsible for the negligence of a servant in charge of a weighbridge. In *Magna Plant* v. *Mitchell* (unreported) April 27, 1966, the fault was that of a depot engineer and again the company was held not criminally responsible. I think these decisions were right. In the *Magna Plant* case Lord Parker C.J. said:

> ... knowledge of a servant cannot be imputed to the company unless he is a servant for whose actions the company are criminally responsible, and as the cases show, that only arises in the case of a company where one is considering the acts of responsible officers forming the brain, or in the case of an individual, a person to whom delegation in the true sense of the delegation of management has been passed.

I agree with what he said with regard to a company. But delegation by an individual is another matter. It has been recognised in licensing cases but that is in my view anomalous (see *Vane* v. *Yiannopoullos* [1965] A.C. 486).

The latest important authority is *Series* v. *Poole* [1969] 1 Q.B. 676. That was an appeal against the dismissal of an information that the holder of a carrier's licence had failed to keep or cause to be kept records required by the Road Traffic Act, 1960 with regard to the driver of a vehicle. That was [174] an absolute offence but that was amended by the Road Traffic Act, 1962 which provided by section 20 that it should 'be a defence to prove that he used all due diligence to secure compliance with those provisions.' The respondent proved that he had given proper instructions to the driver, that he employed a secretary to check the driver's records and had to begin with supervised her work, but that thereafter she failed to make the proper checks. The justices held, possibly wrongly, that the accused had used all due diligence as required by the Act. The court accepted that finding but nevertheless sent the case back with a direction to convict.

Lord Parker C.J. dealt with the case on the basis that the accused had done everything that was reasonable. He said, at p. 684:

He may. . . acting perfectly reasonably appoint somebody else to perform his duty, his alter ego, and in that case it seems to me if the alter ego fails in his duty the employer is liable. Equally, if the employer seeks to rely on the defence under section 20, he must show that the alter ego has observed due diligence.

I have already said that the phrase alter ego is misleading. In my judgment this case was wrongly decided and should be overruled. When the second statute introduced a defence if the accused proved that 'he used all due diligence' I think that it meant what it said. As a matter of construction I can see no ground for reading in 'he and all persons to whom he had delegated responsibility.' And if I look to the purpose and apparent intention of Parliament in enacting this defence I think that it was plainly intended to make a just and reasonable distinction between the employer who is wholly blameless and ought to be acquitted and the employer who was in some way at fault, leaving it to the employer to prove that he was in no way to blame.

What good purpose could be served by making an employer criminally responsible for the misdeeds of some of his servants but not for those of others? It is sometimes argued – it was argued in the present case – that making an employer criminally responsible, even when he has done all that he could to prevent an offence, affords some additional protection to the public because this will induce him to do more. But if he has done all he can how can he do more? I think that what lies behind this argument is a suspicion that magistrates too readily accept evidence that an employer has done all he can to prevent offences. But if magistrates were to accept as sufficient a paper scheme and perfunctory efforts to enforce it they would not be doing their duty – that would not be 'due diligence' on the part of the employer.

Then it is said that this would involve discrimination in favour of a large employer like the appellants against a small shopkeeper. But that is not so. Mr Clement was the 'opposite number' of the small shopkeeper and he was liable to prosecution in this case. The purpose of this Act must have been to penalise those at fault, not those who were in no way to blame.

The Divisional Court decided this case on a theory of delegation. In that they were following some earlier authorities. But they gave far too wide a meaning to delegation. I have said that a board of directors can delegate part of their functions of management so as to make their delegate an [175] embodiment of the company within the sphere of the delegation. But here the board never delegated any part of their functions. They set up a chain of command through regional and district supervisors, but they remained in control. The shop managers had to obey their general directions and also take orders from their superiors. The acts or omissions of shop managers were not the acts of the company itself.

McMahon v. Murtagh Properties Ltd.
[1982] I.L.R.M. 342 (H. Ct.)

The defendant company was prosecuted for breach of the Licensing Acts in a public house that it owned. Among the questions raised in a case stated by way of appeal was the position of registered companies with regard to holding liquor licenses.

BARRINGTON J.: . . . [344] [This case] raises. . . issues of practical importance concerning the right of a limited liability company to hold an intoxicating liquor licence, and the practice of such companies holding their licences through nominees, and the complications which this practice may create in the prosecution of offenders against the licensing code and in the administration of Part 3 of the Intoxicating Liquor Act, 1927.

It was at one time thought that an incorporated company could not itself hold an intoxicating liquor licence, and that it required a nominee to hold the licence on its behalf. It is hard to find the logical basis for this theory.

On incorporation, a limited liability company becomes a body corporate capable of exercising all the functions of an incorporated company and having [345] a perpetual succession and a Common Seal. (See s. 18 of the Companies Act, 1963.) If the powers contained in the memorandum of association include power to carry on the business of selling intoxicating liquor by retail for consumption on or off the premises, the company has power to carry on that business on obtaining the appropriate licence and complying with other relevant legal requirements. One of these requirements is that the company should own an appropriate estate in premises in which to carry on the business, but it is well established that there is no property or goodwill in a licence itself apart from the ownership of the premises to which the licence is attached. (See *Kelly* v. *Montague*, 16 LRI 424). It would appear to follow logically from this, that the property and the licence should both be held by the same person.

However, notwithstanding this, the practice has grown up in Ireland of appointing nominees to hold licences for limited liability companies engaged in the intoxicating liquor trade. This practice has even secured Statutory recognition, and it is probably too late now to say that it is wrong.

The learned District Justice himself referred to s. 28 of the Intoxicating Liquor Act, 1960, which reads as follows:

> A licence held by a nominee of a body corporate in respect of premises in which the lowest estate or tenancy is held by the body corporate may, on the application by the body corporate to the court at any sitting thereof for the court area within which the premises are situate, be transferred, by indorsement made by the court on the licence or, if the licence is not available, on a copy thereof, to such other person as the body corporate may nominate.

It is quite clear, however, that such a nominee has himself, no beneficial interest whatsoever in the licence, and that he must comply with all lawful directions of the body corporate in relation to it. While the Statute acknowledges that he holds the licence, he holds it only for the body corporate which is the beneficial and, indeed, the real holder of the licence, just as it is the real holder of the premises in which the business is carried on.

The present practice of companies holding their licence through nominees probably goes back to a time when the implications of incorporation were not fully understood. It has, however, the authority of a passage in O'Connor's *The Licensing Laws of Ireland* which appears at page 86 of that book and which reads as follows: 'The provisions of the licensing code go to show that a licence cannot be granted to a limited company, but the application may be made in the name of the secretary or other servant or nominee.'

The cases cited for this proposition are:

R v. *Lyon* (1898), 14, TLR 357; 62 JP, 357 and
R v. *Jones* (1895) 59 JP 87.

In the first case, the Court of Appeal in England held that a notice of application for a licence, brought by the secretary of a company on behalf of a company was not necessarily bad on its face because brought in the name of the secretary as secretary of the company. The court accordingly issued an order of mandamus directing the justices to hear and determine the application. In the course of the argument in the case it was apparently conceded that the company itself could not hold the licence.

[346] In the second case (*R* v. *Jones*) the Queens Bench division for England and Wales refused to issue an order of mandamus to justices directing them to hear and determine an application by a branch manager of a company for an 'off' licence to sell spirits. Under the relevant statutory provision a licensed dealer in spirits might take an additional retail spirits licence for the sale of spirits not consumed on the premises. The branch manager was not such a dealer. The company was, but it held its 'on' licence in the name of three of its directors as nominees.

Neither case therefore appears to be strong authority for the proposition in support of which it is cited in O'Connor (supra).

However, two years after the publication of O'Connor's *Licensing Laws*, the matter was fully discussed in the case of *The King (Cottingham)* v. *Justices of County Cork* [1906] 2 IR 415.

In his judgment in that case, the Chief Baron Palles emphasised that a body corporate was a 'person' and that it could therefore have a 'character' or reputation and nailed the fallacy that a body corporate could not apply for a licence because it could not satisfy the justices that it had a 'good character'. At page 419 he goes so far as to say:

I am aware that much difference of practice, and as I believe, much irregularity, exists as to the names in which licences are taken out, even when the real trader is a natural person and not a company – still the questions will some day arise, IS A LICENCE RIGHTLY ISSUED TO THE MANAGER OF A COMPANY? CAN THE INCORPORATED COMPANY LAWFULLY SELL BEER UNDER SUCH A LICENCE? I am inclined to hold that each of these questions should be answered in the negative.

As I said earlier, it is probably too late now, to hold that the practice of companies holding licences through nominees is wrong. But Chief Baron Palles had no difficulty whatsoever in holding that a body corporate was a 'persons' capable of applying for and obtaining an intoxicating liquor licence and that it was capable of having a good character. He goes on to say:

I cannot see why a public company cannot have a character. No doubt it has no soul; but it can act by others, and through others do acts which in the case of a natural person would affect conscience, and be a foundation of that reputation which the law knows as 'character', be it good or bad. It can be guilty of fraud, or malice, and of various criminal offences, some of commission, others of omission; some punishable summarily, others by indictment. 'Character' as used in the section means 'reputation'. Reputation is acquired by conduct. The conduct of the authorised agents of a company is *its* conduct. Why should not that conduct give rise to a reputation as to this character, good, bad or indifferent. An unincorporated company of seven persons can acquire a reputation for fair dealing, for truth in their representations, for close supervision of their business, for carrying on their business in an orderly and peaceable manner. But this reputation is not that of an individual. It is, or may be, something different from the reputation of each. It may be a reputation acquired by the aggregation of the seven; as the reputation of an unincorporated bank for solvency. Why cannot those seven persons acquire a similar reputation by their action in aggregation, although that aggregation has assumed the more intimate form of incorporation? [347]

Johnson J agreed with the Chief Baron's reasoning. He said:

The second ground raises the question whether this company is a 'person' within the meaning of The Beerhouses (Ireland) Acts and the Licensing Act, 1874. The contention for the prosecutor is, as I understand it, that the whole scope of these Acts as ascertained from the language of the legislature in the Acts *ex visceribus actus* (C. Co. Litt, 381b), points to the individual and personal responsibility of the applicant for a licence or transfer of a licence, and that it is in this sense his character must be 'good'; and that in as much as 'Beamish & Crawford Ltd' is merely an impersonal incorporated legal entity, it cannot in the nature of things obtain from the justices a certificate of good character, and therefore cannot have a wholesale beerdealers' licence. But though this company is of such impersonal character, it is competent to employ and act, and practically must employ and act, by and through such individuals as by its constitution it is competent to engage, and engages, for its purposes, and by whose conduct within the scope of their employment, the 'company' is bound. A limited liability company is capable of suing, and liable to be sued, in almost every kind of action in the nature of tort or contract. It may be made criminally responsible for most offences which are not punishable solely by imprisonment or corporal punishment. It may be enjoined, and its property may be sequestrated for payment of its debts or fines imposed for offences. Good or bad character is a matter of local or public reputation and the widest discretion is given by Statute to justices in respect of their certificate. In *Leader* v. *Yell* (16.CB)(NS) 584, where this matter is discussed, Erle, CJ at 593, suggests how the words 'good character' came to be introduced into the Beer Acts.

I think if the house is conducted in a disorderly way, if convictions are had for breaches of the Licensing Acts, if improper characters were allowed to resort there for improper purposes, or public feeling is outraged by lewd or improper acts knowingly committed, this 'company' would, through their agent or manager, who they put in charge of, or whose omissions or acts they are liable for, have an evil reputation and a bad character; but if, on the contrary, the house is conducted in an orderly and decent manner, the provisions of the Licensing Acts observed, and perhaps I may venture to add, reasonably good and wholesome beer supplied, the local and public reputation of this company, through their agent or manager whom this company places in charge and for whom they are responsible, would be good, and this company would be, as the justices have certified them to be, of good character. (at 426)

The case of *The King (Cottingham)* v. *Justices of Cork* went to the Court of Appeal where the decision of the Divisional Court was upheld, but on a different point, and the *dicta* quoted are, therefore, in a certain sense *obiter*. Nevertheless they are of high authority and it is surprising that they appear to have had so little effect on practice.

The matter came up for discussion before the modern Supreme Court in the case of *The State (John Hennessy and Chariot Inns Ltd)* v. *Superintendent J. Commons*, [1976] IR 238. Again, the decision in the case turned upon a different point, but in his judgment, Kenny J went out of his way to cite with approval the judgments of Johnson J and the Chief Baron in *The*

King (Cottingham) v. *Justices of County Cork,* and referred to the 'myth' widely accepted by 'both branches of the legal profession' that a company incorporated under the Companies Acts cannot be granted a licence to sell intoxicating drink and that when it seeks to be licensed in respect of premises, or when it acquires licensed premises, the licence must be granted to its nominee.

From this discussion I drew three conclusions. First the present practice of [348] companies holding their licences through nominees has no basis in sound logic. Second the practice has however received statutory recognition so that it is now too late to say that it is wrong. Third the practice, not being based on sound logic, will necessarily give rise to difficulties in administering the licencing code so that one can sympathise with the position in which the learned District Justice found himself.

Nevertheless I drew the following practical conclusions. First, a limited liability company is entitled itself to hold its licence without resorting to the device of having a nominee.

Secondly, it is not incorrect to refer to the nominee as being the 'holder' of the licence as long as it is remembered that the company is the beneficial and as previously indicated, the real holder of the licence. The nominee must comply with all legal instructions of the company in relation to the licence, and he is, in effect, no more than a peg on which the company finds it convenient to hang its licence. This being so, if the company, through its agents, breaks the law in the running of the business, it is at all times liable as the holder of the licence. The nominee, provided he does no more than hold the licence, commits no offence, but if the nominee is also the manager of the business or if he assists in the commission of the offence then he may be liable for aiding and abetting the company as holder of the licence, notwithstanding that he is a nominal 'holder' himself.

Private Motorists Protection Soc. Ltd. v. Attorney General
[1983] I.R. 339

(From headnote) The first plaintiff was a body corporate which was registered as an industrial and provident society. The second plaintiff was a shareholder of the plaintiff society, which carried on a banking business. The loans made by the plaintiff society in the course of that business in the year 1970 amounted to £200,000 and such loans increased until they amounted to £11,700,000 in the year 1979. In 1971 the plaintiff society and others were expressly exempted from the provisions of legislation imposed on persons, other than licensed banks, who were carrying on banking businesses. The Act of 1978 was passed by the National Parliament on the 5th July, 1978. Section 5, sub-s. 2, of the Act of 1978 provided that, subject to a possible extension, the plaintiff society and others were not to accept or hold deposits after a period of five years commencing at the passing of that Act. The

plaintiffs claimed in the High Court a declaration that the Act of 1978 was invalid having regard to the provision of the Constitution of Ireland .

CARROLL J.: . . . [349] The first issue to be determined is whether the society, as such, can claim that its constitutional rights under Article 40, s. 3, and under Article 43 of the Constitution have been infringed. The property rights which are guaranteed by Article 40, s. 3, are those stated in Article 43: see p. 176 of the report of *The Attorney General* v. *Southern Industrial Trust Ltd.* (94 I.L.T.R. 161). In Article 43, s. 1, sub-s. 1, the State acknowledges that man, in virtue of his rational being, has the natural right, antecedent to positive law, to the private ownership of external goods. The remainder of Article 43 flows from that statement. In Article 43, s. 1, sub-s. 2, the word 'accordingly' shows a reference back to s. 1, sub-s. 1, of that Article. Article 43, s. 2, sub-s. 1, specifically refers to the rights mentioned in the foregoing provisions of the Article and s. 2, sub-s. 2, of the Article refers to 'the said rights'. In my opinion the provisions of Article 43, s. 1, sub-s. 1 cannot be construed as acknowledging or conferring a constitutional right on a corporate body – itself a creature of positive law. The right protected by Article 43 is the right of a human person.

Therefore, in so far as a claim is made by the Society that its constitutional rights under Article 40, s. 3 and Article 43 have been infringed by the Act, the claim is unsustainable as the Society does not have such rights. This view is in accord with the view expressed, in respect of s. 1 of Article 40, by the Supreme Court at p. 14 of the report of *Quinn's Supermarket* v. *The Attorney General* [1972] I.R. 1.

However, Mr Moore is a shareholder in the Society. He invested his money with other shareholders in a Society incorporated under the law which is entitled to carry on business *intra vires*. If the business of the Society is affected by the Act of 1978 in such a way that the property rights of Mr Moore as a shareholder are affected, then he is entitled, *prima facie*, to make a claim that his constitutional rights that are protected by Article 40, s. 3, and Article 43 have been infringed. Ownership of shares is one of the bundle of rights which constitute ownership of private property: *per* Mr Justice Kenny at p. 84 of the report of *Central Dublin Development Association* v. *The Attorney General* (109 I.L.T.R. 69).

SUPREME COURT: O'HIGGINS C.J.: . . . [358] The case for invalidity which the plaintiffs seek to establish rests on two allegations. In the first place it is contended that the impugned legislation (and, in particular, sub-s. 2 of s. 5 thereof) contravenes the provisions of Article 40, s. 3, of the Constitution in that it constitutes an unjust attack on property rights. In the second place it is contended that the legislation is an interference with the freedom of association which is guaranteed to citizens by Article 40, s. 6, sub-s. 1(iii), of the Constitution. This case has been put forward on behalf of both the Society and Mr Moore. The rights which are alleged to have been infringed are among the personal rights which the Constitution guarantees to citizens. The Society is a creature of statute law and it is argued that, as such, it does not enjoy that constitutional protection. However, Mr Moore, as a citizen, is entitled to complain if the impugned legislation interferes with any of his personal rights. This he does in the claim that both his property rights and his freedom of association have been violated. In the circumstances it is unnecessary to decide the question of the Society's rights. Therefore the Court does not express any opinion on this question.

Ashbury Railway Carriage & Iron Co. Ltd. v. Riche
(1875) L.R. 7 H.L. 653 (H.L.)

(From headnote) A company was registered under the *Joint Stock Companies Act,* 1862. Its objects, as stated in the Memorandum of Association, were these: 'to make, and sell, or lend on hire, railway carriages and waggons, and all kinds of railway plant, fittings, machinery, and rolling-stock; to carry on the business of mechanical engineers and *general contractors;* to purchase, lease, work, and sell mines, minerals, land, and buildings; to purchase and sell, as merchants, timber, coal, metals, or other materials, and to buy and sell any such materials on commission or as agents.' The directors agreed to purchase a concession for making a railway in a foreign country, and afterwards (on account of difficulties existing by the law of that country), agreed to assign the concession to a *Société Anonyme* formed in that country, which *société* was to supply the materials for the construction of the railway, and to receive periodical payments from the English company.

LORD CAIRNS L.C.: . . . [663] [T]he history and progress of the action out of which the present appeal arises is not, I must say, creditable to our legal proceedings. There was not in the case any fact in dispute; and the only questions which arose were questions of law, or questions, perhaps, as to the proper inference to be drawn from facts as to which there was no dispute. The action, however, was commenced so long ago as the month of May, 1868. The litigation appears to have been active and continuing, and yet seven years have been consumed, and the result of all, up to the present time, is this, that in the Court of Exchequer, two out of the three Judges were of opinion that the Plaintiff should have judgment; and when the case came before the Exchequer Chamber, it was heard before six Judges, three of whom were of opinion that the Plaintiff [664] was entitled to judgment, the other three thinking that the Defendant was entitled to judgment. The result, therefore, was that the judgment of the Court of Exchequer was affirmed.

My Lords, but for this difference of opinion among the learned Judges, I should have said that the only questions of law which arise in the case, the questions which appear to me to be sufficient altogether to dispose of the case, were of an extremely simple character. The action was brought by the Plaintiffs, who appear to be contractors in *Belgium*, and it was brought for damages for the breach of an agreement entered into between the Plaintiffs and the shareholders, constituting the *Ashbury Railway Carriage and Iron Company, Limited.*

These persons constituted a company established under the *Joint Stock Companies Act* of 1862. I think your Lordships will find it necessary to consider with some minuteness some of the leading provisions of that Act of Parliament. But, in the first place, you will find it convenient to ascertain the purposes for which this company was formed, and then the nature of the agreement, or contract, for the breach of which the present action was brought.

The purposes for which a company, established under the Act of 1862, is formed, are always to be looked for in the Memorandum of Association of the company. According to that Memorandum, the *Ashbury Railway Carriage and Iron Company, Limited,* is formed for these objects (see supra). Part of the argument at your Lordships' Bar was as to the meaning of two of the words used in this part of the memorandum – the words 'general contractors'. My Lords, as it appears to me, upon all ordinary principles of construction those words must be referred to the part of the sentence which immediately precedes them. The sentence which I have read is divided into four classes of works. First, 'to make and sell or lend on hire railway carriages [665] and waggons and all kinds of railway plant, fittings, machinery, and rolling stock.' That is an object *sui generis* and complete in the specification which I have read. The second is 'to carry on the business of mechanical engineers and general contractors.' That, again, is the specification of an object complete in itself; and, according to the principles of construction, the term 'general contractors' would be referred to that which goes immediately before, and would indicate the making generally of contracts connected with the business of mechanical engineers – such contracts as mechanical engineers are in the habit of making, and are in their business required, or find it convenient, to make for the purpose of carrying on their business. The third is, 'to purchase, lease, work, and sell, mines, minerals, land, and buildings.' That is an object pointing to the working and the acquiring of mineral property, and the generality of the last two words, 'land and buildings,' is limited by the purpose for which land and buildings are to be acquired, namely, the leasing, working, and selling, mines and minerals. The forth head is, 'to purchase and sell, as merchants, timber, coal, metals, or other materials, and to buy and sell any such materials on commission or as agents.' That requires no commentary.

My Lords, if the term 'general contractors' were not to be interpreted as I have suggested, the consequence would be that it would stand abso-

lutely without any limit of any kind. It would authorize the making, therefore, of contracts of any kind and every description, and the memorandum
in place of specifying a particular kind of business would virtually point to
the carrying on of business of any kind whatever, and would therefore be
altogether unmeaning.

My Lords, that being the object for which the company professes by
the memorandum of association to be incorporated, I now turn to examine
the contract upon which the present action is brought. I may relieve your
Lordships from any lengthened exposition of the nature of that contract
by referring you to the account given of it by Mr Baron *Bramwell* in the
Court of Exchequer. . . . 'The substance [666] of those contracts' – that is,
the contract upon which the action was brought, and two other contracts,
which are inseparably connected with it – 'The substance of those contracts
was this: *Gillon* and *Baertsoen* had obtained the right to make a railway in
Belgium. This right the Defendants' directors supposed to be valuable to
its owners; that is to say, the line could be constructed for a certain sum,
and a *société anonyme* could be constituted with shareholders to take its
shares to an amount which would give a large sum over the cost of construction. The benefit of this the directors desired to obtain for the Defendant
company, and to do so purchased the concession. This was their main
object. But the Plaintiffs held a contract with the concessionaries to con-
struct the line, and to accomplish the directors' object it was necessary or
desirable, or they thought it was, that they should agree with the Plaintiffs
that the Defendants should constitute a *société anonyme*, and, as the Plaintiffs
went on with the work, the Defendants should pay into the hands of the
société proportionate funds. The farther contract entered into in the Defendants' name, called *D.*, is of no importance in this case. The directors
accordingly entered into two contracts in the Defendants' name – one with
the concessionaries to purchase the concession; the other with the Plaintiffs
to furnish the *société anonyme* with funds, the latter contract being auxiliary
to the former. They paid the concessionaries £26,000, part of the price.
Now, whatever may be the meaning of 'carry on the business of mechanical
engineers and general contractors', to my mind it clearly does not include
the making of either of these contracts. It could only be held to do so by
holding that the words 'general contractors' authorized generally the making of any contracts; and this they certainly do not. . . . [667]

Those being the results of the documents to which I have referred, I
will ask your Lordships now to consider the effect of the Act of Parliament
– the *Joint Stock Companies Act* of 1862 – on this state of things. And here,
my Lords, I cannot but regret that by the two Judges in the Court of
Exchequer the accurate and precise bearing of that Act of Parliament upon
the present case appears to me to have been entirely overlooked or misap-
prehended; and that in the Court of Exchequer Chamber, speaking of the
opinion of those learned Judges who thought that the decision of the Court

of Exchequer should be maintained, the weight which was given to the provisions of this Act of Parliament appears to me to have entirely fallen short of that which ought to have been given to it. Your Lordships are well aware that this is the Act which put upon its present permanent footing the regulation of joint stock companies, and more especially of those joint stock companies which were to be authorized to trade with a limit to their liability.

The provisions under which that system of limiting liability was inaugurated, were provisions not merely, perhaps I might say not mainly, for the benefit of the shareholders for the time being in the company, but were enactments intended also to provide for the interests of two other very important bodies; in the first place, those who might become shareholders in succession to the persons who were shareholders for the time being; and secondly, the outside public, and more particularly those who might be creditors of companies of this kind. And I will ask your Lordships to observe, as I refer to some of the clauses, the marked and entire difference there is between the two documents which form the title deeds of companies of this description – I mean the Memorandum of Association on the one hand, and the Articles of Association on the other hand. With regard to the memorandum of association, your Lordships will find, as has often already been [668] pointed out, although it appears somewhat to have been over-looked in the present case, that that is, as it were, the charter, and defines the limitation of the powers of a company to be established under the Act. With regard to the articles of association, those articles play a part subsidiary to the memorandum of association. They accept the memorandum of association as the charter of incorporation of the company, and so accepting it, the articles proceed to define the duties, the rights and the powers of the governing body as between themselves and the company at large, and the mode and form in which the business of the company is to be carried on, and the mode and form in which changes in the internal regulations of the company may from time to time be made. With regard, therefore, to the memorandum of association, if you find anything which goes beyond that memorandum, or is not warranted by it, the question will arise whether that which is so done is *ultra vires*, not only of the directors of the company, but of the company itself. With regard to the articles of association, if you find anything which, still keeping within the memorandum of association, is a violation of the articles of association, or in excess of them, the question will arise whether that is anything more than an act *extra vires* the directors, but *intra vires* the company.

The clauses of the statute to which it is necessary to refer are four: in the first place, the sixth clause. That provides that 'Any seven or more persons associated for any lawful purpose may, by subscribing their names to a memorandum of association, and otherwise complying with the requisitions of this Act in respect of registration, form an incorporated company, with or without limited liability.' My Lords, this is the first section which speaks of the incorporation of the company; but your Lordships will observe that it does not speak of that incorporation as the creation of a corporation with inherent common law rights, such rights as are by common law possessed by every corporation, and without any other limit than would by common law be assigned to them, but it speaks of the company being incorporated with reference to a memorandum of association; and you are referred thereby to the provisions which subsequently are to be found upon the subject of that memorandum of association.

[669] The next clause which is material is the eighth: 'Where a company is formed on the principle of having the liability of its members limited to the amount unpaid on their shares, hereinafter referred to as a company limited by shares, the Memorandum of Association shall contain the following things' (I pass over the first and second, and I come to the third item which is to be specified): 'The objects for which the proposed company is to be established.' That is, therefore, the memorandum which the persons are to sign as a preliminary to the incorporation of the company. They are to state 'the objects for which the proposed company is to be established;' and the existence, the coming into existence, of the company is to be an existence and to be a coming into existence for those objects and for those objects alone.

Then, my Lords, the 11th section provides: 'The memorandum of association shall bear the same stamp as if it were a deed, and shall be signed by each subscriber in the presence of, and be attested by, one witness at the least, and that attestation shall be a sufficient attestation in *Scotland*, as well as in *England* and *Ireland*. It shall, when registered, bind the company and the members thereof to the same extent as if each member had suscribed his name and affixed his seal thereto, and there were in the memorandum contained, on the part of himself, his heirs, executors, and administrators, a covenant to observe all the conditions of such memorandum, subject to the provisions of this Act.' Your Lordships will observe, therefore, that it is to be a covenant in which every member of the company is to covenant that he will observe the conditions of the memorandum, one of which is that the objects for which the company is established are the objects mentioned in the memorandum, and that he not only will observe that, but will observe it subject to the provisions of this Act. Well, but the very next provision of the Act contained in the 12th section is this: 'Any company limited by shares may so far modify the conditions contained in its memorandum of association, if authorized to do so by its regulations as originally framed, or as altered by special resolution in manner hereinafter mentioned, as to increase its capital by the issue of new shares of such amount as it thinks expedient, or to consolidate and divide its capital into shares of larger amount than its existing shares, or to convert its [670] paid-up shares into stock, but, save as aforesaid, and save as is hereinafter provided in the case of a change of name, no alteration shall be made by any company in the conditions contained in its memorandum of association.' The covenant, therefore, is not merely that every member will observe the conditions upon which the company is established, but that no change shall be made in those conditions; and if there is a covenant that no change shall be made in the objects for which the company is established, I apprehend that that includes within it the engagement that no object shall be pursued by the company, or attempted to be attained by the company in practice, except an object which is mentioned in the memorandum of association.

Now, my Lords, if that is so – if that is the condition upon which the corporation is established – if that is the purpose for which the corporation is established – it is a mode of incorporation which contains in it both that which is affirmative and that which is negative. It states affirmatively the ambit and extent of vitality and power which by law are given to the corporation, and it states, if it is necessary so to state, negatively, that nothing shall be done beyond that ambit, and that no attempt shall be made to use the corporate life for any other purpose than that which is so specified.

Now, my Lords, with regard to the articles of association, observe how completely different the charter of the legislation is. The 14th section deals with those articles: 'The memorandum of association may, in the case of a company limited by shares, and shall, in the case of a company limited by guarantie, or unlimited, be accompanied, when registered, by articles of association, signed by the subscribers to the memorandum of association, and prescribing such regulations for the company as the subscribers to the memorandum of association deem expedient.' They are to be the masters of the regulations which (always keeping within the limit allowed by law) they may deem expedient for the internal regulation of the company. 'The articles shall be expressed in separare paragraphs, numbered arithmetically. They may adopt also any of the provisions contained in the table marked A. in the first schedule hereto.' I need not read the remainder of that section.

[671] But your Lordships must take, in connection with that, the 50th section of the Act. That provides that 'subject to the provisions of this Act, and to the conditions contained in the memorandum of association, any company formed under this Act may, in general meeting, from time to time, by passing a special resolution in manner hereinafter mentioned, alter all or any of the regulations of the company contained in the articles of association, or in the table marked A. in the first schedule, where such table is applicable to the company, or make new regulations to the exclusion of, or in addition to, all or any of the regulations of the company.' Of the internal regulations of the company the members of it are absolute masters, and, provided they pursue the course marked out in the Act, that is to say,

holding a general meeting and obtaining the consent of the shareholders, they may alter those regulations from time to time; but all must be done in the way of alteration subject to the conditions contained in the memorandum of association. That is to override and overrule any provisions of the articles which may be at variance with it. The memorandum of association is, as it were, the area beyond which the action of the company cannot go; inside that area the shareholders may make such regulations for their own government as they think fit.

My Lords, that reference to the Act will enable me to dispose of a provision in the articles of association in the present case which was hardly dwelt upon in argument, but which I refer to in order that it may not be supposed to have been overlooked. It appears that there has come into the articles of association of this company one which is in these words: 'An extension of the company's business beyond or for other than the objects or purposes expressed or implied in the memorandum of association shall take place only in pursuance of a special resolution.' In point of fact, no resolution for the extension of the business of the company was in this case come to; but even if it had been come to, it would have been entirely inept and inefficacious. There was, in this 4th article, an attempt to do the very thing which, by the Act of Parliament, was prohibited to be done – to claim and arrogate to the company a power under the guise of [672] internal regulation to go beyond the objects or purposes expressed or implied in the memorandum.

Now, my Lords, bearing in mind the difference which I have just taken the liberty of pointing out to your Lordships between the memorandum and the articles, we arrive at once at all which appears to me to be necessary for the purpose of deciding this case. I have used the expressions *extra vires* and *intra vires*. I prefer either expression very much to one which occasionally has been used in the judgments in the present case, and has also been used in other cases, the expression 'illegality'.

In a case such as that which your Lordships have now to deal with, it is not a question whether the contract sued upon involves that which is *malum prohibitum* or *malum in se*, or is a contract contrary to public policy, and illegal in itself. I assume the contract in itself to be perfectly legal, to have nothing in it obnoxious to the doctrine involved in the expressions which I have used. The question is not as to the legality of the contract; the question is as to the competency and power of the company to make the contract. Now, I am clearly of opinion that this contract was entirely, as I have said, beyond the objects in the memorandum of association. If so, it was thereby placed beyond the powers of the company to make the contract. If so, my Lords, it is not a question whether the contract ever was ratified or was not ratified. If it was a contract void at its beginning, it was void because the company could not make the contract. If every shareholder of the company had been in the room, and every shareholder of the company had said, 'That is a contract which we desire to make, which we authorize the directors to make, to which we sanction the placing the seal of the company,' the case would not have stood in any different position from that in which it stands now. The shareholders would thereby, by unanimous consent, have been attempting to do the very thing which, by the Act of Parliament, they were prohibited from doing.

But, my Lords, if the shareholders of this company could not *ab ante* have authorized a contract of this kind to be made, how could they subsequently sanction the contract after it had, in point of fact, been made. I endeavoured to follow as accurately as I could the very able argument of Mr *Benjamin* at the Lordships' [673] Bar on this point; but it appeared to me that this was a difficulty with which he was entirely unable to grapple. He endeavoured to contend that when the shareholders had found that something had been done by the directors which ought not to have been done, they might be authorized to make the best they could of a difficulty into which they had thus been thrown, and therefrom might be deemed to possess power to sanction the contract being proceeded with. My Lords, I am unable to adopt that suggestion. It appears to me that it would be perfectly fatal to the whole scheme of legislation to which I have referred, if you were to hold that, in the first place, directors might do that which even the whole company could not do, and that then, the shareholders finding out what had been done, could sanction, subsequently, what they could not antecedently have authorized.

My Lords, if this be the proper view of the Act of Parliament, it reconciles, as it appears to me, the opinion of all the Judges of the Court of Exchequer Chamber; because I find Mr Justice *Blackburn*, whose judgment was concurred in by two other Judges who took the same view, expressing himself thus (1): 'I do not entertain any doubt that if, on the true construction of a statute creating a corporation it appears to be the intention of the Legislature, expressed or implied, that the corporation shall not enter into a particular contract, every Court, whether of law or equity, is bound to treat a contract entered into contrary to the enactment as illegal, and therefore wholly void, and to hold that a contract wholly void cannot be ratified.' My Lords, that sums up and exhausts the whole case. In my opinion, beyond all doubt, on the true construction of the statute of 1862, creating this corporation, it appears that it was the intention of the Legislature, not implied, but actually expressed, that the corporation should not enter, having regard to its memorandum of association, into a contract of this description. If so, according to the words of Mr Justice *Blackburn*, every Court, whether of law or of equity, is bound to treat that contract, entered into contrary to the enactment, I will not say as illegal, but as *extra vires*, and wholly null and void, and to hold also that a contract wholly void cannot be ratified.

Northern Bank Finance Corp. Ltd.
v. Quinn and Achates Investment Co.
(Keane J., Nov. 8, 1979, H.Ct.)

The first defendant was indebted to the plaintiff bank, and his debts were secured by way of a guarantee given by the second defendant, the company. When the bank sought to enforce the guarantee the company contended that the guarantee was *ultra vires* and not binding on it.

KEANE J.: ... On the 15th November, 1973, the Plaintiffs (whom I shall call 'the Bank') wrote to the first-named Defendant (whom I shall call 'Mr Quinn') informing him that they would make loan facilities available to him on the terms and conditions set out in the letter.

The letter went on to state that the amount of the loan was £145,000.00 and that the rate of interest thereon would be 3% per annum over the average cost to the Bank of raising funds on the Inter Bank Market. It was also stated that the loan would [2] be repayable on demand, but that if no demand were made, it would be the Bank's understanding that, with effect from November 1st, 1974, monthly payments of £3,000.00 each would be made by Mr Quinn towards the payment of principal and interest.

The letter also stated that the loan was to be secured inter alia by the unconditional and continuing guarantee of the second-named Defendant (whom I shall call 'the Company') of the loan, interest and repayment arrangements, supported by a first legal mortgage on the title deeds and documents relating to 54 acres of land at Ratoath, County Meath and 56 aces at Jamestown, County Meath.

The Bank's Solicitor, Mr T. F. O'Connell, was asked by the Bank to attend to the legal formalities necessary to complete the transaction; and on November 29th, 1973, he sent to Mr Quinn's Solicitors a number of documents, including Requisitions on Title relating to the properties which were to be the subject of the mortgage, a draft Mortgage, a draft Guarantee by the Company and draft Resolution to be passed by the Directors of the Company empowering the Company to guarantee the sum of £145,00.00 and the [3] interest thereon. On the 30th November, 1973, the necessary Resolution was passed by the Directors of the Company; and on the same day a Guarantee was also executed by them, in respect of the sum of £145,000.00 and interest thereon. The Mortgage supporting the Guarantee was executed by the Company on the 13th December, 1973, the delay being due to the necessity to discharge a prior incumbrance on the land.

Mr O'Connell also received from Mr Quinn's Solicitors a copy of the Memorandum and Articles of Association of the Company. It will be necessary to refer to these documents in more detail at a later stage.

Mr Quinn having failed to pay certain of the instalments of £3,000.00 as they fell due, the Bank called in the balance of the loan and commenced these proceedings by way of Special Summons claiming as against Mr

Quinn payment of the sum of £50,829.38 as due and owing by him on foot of a covenant in the Mortgage; and as against the Company an Order declaring the same sum well charged upon the two properties already referred to together with the usual consequential relief.

[4] The liability in principle of Mr Quinn on foot of the covenant in the Mortgage was not disputed. Evidence was adduced on behalf of the Bank that the amount due in respect of principal and interest calculated in accordance with paragraph 1(1)(c) of the Mortgage at the date of the hearing was £56,524.60. Counsel for Mr Quinn submitted that the Bank had not properly proved the amount of interest properly payable having regard to the terms of paragraph 1(1)(c) and that accordingly the Summons should be dismissed against him. I rejected this submission and gave judgment against Mr Quinn for the sum of £56,524.60 and costs.

It was submitted on behalf of the Company that the execution of the guarantee was *ultra vires* the Memorandum and Articles of Association and that, accordingly, both the guarantee and the mortgage (insofar as it comprised the Company's property) were void. Counsel for the Bank submitted that the guarantee was *intra vires* the Memorandum and Articles of Association; but, that even if it were not, the Bank were protected by the modification of the *ultra vires* rule effected [5] by s. 8 of the Companies Act, 1963. He further submitted that, since the Memorandum had been subsequently altered by a Resolution of the 18th May, 1974, so as to put beyond doubt the power of the Company to execute guarantees, the Guarantee of 30th November, 1973, was retrospectively validated and he relied in this connection on s. 10 (1) of the Act. Counsel for the Bank finally submitted that, in any event, the Company were estopped from relying on the alleged lack of vires.

The Company is an unlimited company having a share capital. Its objects are set out in paragraph 2 of the Memorandum of Association. The first of them, in truncated form, reads as follows :

> To acquire and hold. . . shares and stocks of any class or description, debentures, debenture stock, bonds, bills, mortgages, obligations, investments and securities of all descriptions and of any kind issued or guaranteed by any company, corporation or undertaking. . . and investments, securities and property of all descriptions and of any kind. . . .

This, coupled with the fact that the Company is an unlimited company, would suggest, so far as it is relevant, that the Company was not intended to be a trading company in the [6] ordinary sense but rather an investment company.

Clause 2 (f) empowers the Company

> Incidentally to the objects aforesaid, but not as a primary object, to sell, exchange, mortgage (with or without power of sale), assign, turn to account or otherwise dispose of and generally deal with the whole or any part of the property, shares, stocks, securities, estates, rights or undertakings of the company. . . .

This clause was not relied on by Counsel for the Bank as empowering the transaction in question, but was relied on by Counsel for the Company as indicating that the Company was empowered to mortgage its property only where the execution of the mortgage was incidental to one of the objects of the Company set out in sub-paragraphs (a) to (e).

Sub-paragraph (k) empowers the Company

> to raise or borrow or secure the payment of money in such manner and on such terms as the directors may deem expedient and in particular by the issue of bonds, debentures or debenture stock, perpetual or redeemable, or by mortgage, charge, lien or pledge upon the whole or any part of [7] the undertaking, property, assets and rights of the Company, present or future, including its uncalled capital and generally in any other manner as the Directors shall from time to time determine and to guarantee the liabilities of the Company and any debentures, debenture stock or other securities may be issued at a discount, premium or otherwise, and with any special privileges as to redemption, surrender, transfer, drawings, allotments of shares, attending and voting at general meetings of the Company, appointment of Directors and otherwise.

This sub-paragraph – and in particular the words 'secure the payment of money' – was relied on by Counsel for the Bank as authorising the execution of the Guarantee. It was accepted that the words 'to guarantee the liabilities of the Company' in this clause were meaningless as they stood; but Counsel for the Bank submitted that the clear intention was to enable the Company to guarantee the liabilities of third parties and that these words in the sub-paragraph should be so read. Counsel for the Company submitted that, insofar as the words could be given any meaning, they should be read as empowering [8] the Company to procure the guaranteeing of its own liabilities by third parties.

Sub-paragraph (t) empowered the Company

> to do and carry out all such things as may be deemed by the Company to be incidental or conducive to the attainment of the above objects or any of them or calculated to enhance the value of or render profitable any of the Company's properties or rights.

It was submitted on behalf of the Bank that this sub-paragraph was sufficiently wide ranging in its terms to enable the Company to execute the Guarantee in question. It was submitted on behalf of the Company that the sub-paragraph merely authorised the doing of such things as were incidental to the attainment of any of the preceding objects and that since it could not be shown that the execution of a guarantee was incidental or conducive to the attainment of any of the objects referred to in the preceding sub-paragraphs, of itself it could not render the transaction in question *intra vires*.

It is clear that sub-paragraph (f) did not authorise the execution of the Guarantee in question and that, insofar as [9] it authorised the Company to execute a Mortgage, this could only be done incidentally to the objects set out in sub-paragraphs (a) to (e). Counsel for the Bank did not indeed advance any submission to the contrary. He did, however, as I have already indicated rely on sub-paragraph (k). I have set out that sub-paragraph in full, because I think the wording used plainly indicates that it was essentially intended to confer a power of borrowing on the Company. Viewed in this context, the words 'secure the payment of money' could not reasonably be read, in my opinion, as conferring a power to execute guarantees. The words 'secure the payment of' are used disjunctively in apposition to 'raise' and 'borrow', clearly indicating that it was intended to confer on the Company a power of obtaining money for its own purposes and not a power to guarantee advances made to other persons. Counsel also relied on the words 'to guarantee the liabilities of the Company' and submitted that, as this phrase literally construed was meaningless, it should be construed as though, in place of the [10] words 'the Company', there appear the words 'other persons' or similar words. While I accept that the words, literally construed, are meaningless, since a company cannot guarantee its own liabilities, I see no warrant in the wording of sub-paragraph (k) as a whole for giving the expression in question the meaning contended for by Mr O'Neill. To give it such a meaning would not merely be to do violence to the actual language used but would also be inappropriate in any event in the context of a sub-paragraph which, as I have said, is essentially concerned with enabling the Company, and not other persons, to borrow money. It seems more likely to me that it was intended by the use of this phrase to enable the Company to secure the guaranteeing by third parties of its own liabilities.

Sub-paragraph (t) was also relied on by Counsel for the Bank; but, in my view, the execution of a Guarantee could not reasonably be regarded as 'incidental or conducive to the attainment of' any of the objects set out in the preceding sub-paragraphs. The sole object of executing the Guarantee [11] was to facilitate the borrowing by Mr Quinn of the sum of £145,000.00 from the Bank. Only the Bank and Mr Quinn could possibly derive any benefit from this transaction; the Company could derive no benefit from the advancing of money to Mr Quinn. The securing by means of a Guarantee of a loan to Mr Quinn could not properly be regarded as being fairly incidental to the objects expressly authorised by the Memorandum within the meaning of the well known rule laid down in *Attorney General* v. *Great Eastern Railway,* (5 App. Cas. 473). The effecting of such a transaction was not 'incidental or conducive to the attainment of' any of the expressly authorised objects within the meaning of sub-paragraph (t); nor was it 'calculated to enhance the value of or render profitable any of the Company's properties or rights' within the meaning of that sub-paragraph.

It follows, in my view, that the Memorandum conferred neither expressly nor by implication any power on the Company to execute a Guarantee for the purpose of securing the payment of a Bank loan to Mr Quinn. In these circumstances, it is unnecessary to express any final opinion on a further [12] submission advanced by Mr McCracken that, even were the Memorandum to be read as conferring an express power on the Company to execute such a Guarantee, the transaction would nonetheless be *ultra vires* since no conceivable benefit could result to the Company from it. The celebrated observations of Bowen L. J., in *Hutton* v. *West Cork Railway,* (23 Ch. D. 654) that 'charity cannot sit at the boardroom table' and 'there are to be no cakes and ale except for the benefit of the company' may have been extended too far in *Re Lee, Behrens and Company* ([1932] 2 Ch. 46); and while this latter decision might appear to afford support for Mr McCracken's proposition, its authority as a persuasive precedent would require reconsideration to-day in the light of the decision in *Charterbridge Corporation Limited* v. *Lloyds Bank* [1970] Ch. 62. Having regard, however, to the conclusion I have arrived at, it is unnecessary that I should say anything more on this aspect of the case.

[On the effect of §8, see post p. 375.]

SEGREGATION FROM OWNERS

Salomon v. Salomon & Co. Ltd.
[1897] A.C. 22 (H.L.)

(From headnote) Mr Salomon (the vendor) sold a solvent business to a limited company with a nominal capital of 40,000 shares of £1 each, the company consisting only of the vendor, his wife, a daughter and four sons, who subscribed for one share each, all the terms of sale being known to and approved by the shareholders. In part payment of the purchase-money, debentures forming a floating security were issued to the vendor. Twenty thousand shares were also issued to him and were paid for out of the purchase-money. These shares gave the vendor the power of outvoting the six other shareholders. No shares other than these 20,007 were ever issued. All the requirements of the Companies Act, 1862 were complied

with. The vendor was appointed managing director, bad times came, the company was wound up, and after satisfying the debentures there was not enough to pay the ordinary creditors.

LORD HALSBURY L.C.: [29] [T]he important question in this case, I am not certain it is not the only question, is whether the respondent company was a company at all – whether in truth that artificial creation of the Legislature had been validly constituted in this instance; and in order to determine that question it is necessary to look at what the statute itself had determined in that respect. I have no right to add to the requirements of the statute, nor to take from the requirements thus enacted. The sole guide must be the statute itself.

Now, that there were seven actual living persons who held shares in the company has not been doubted. As to the proportionate amounts held by each I will deal presently; but it is important to observe that this first condition of the statute is satisfied, and it follows as a consequence that it would not [30] be competent to any one – and certainly not to these persons themselves – to deny that they were shareholders.

I must pause here to point out that the statute enacts nothing as to the extent or degree of interest which may be held by each of the seven, or as to the proportion of interest or influence possessed by one or the majority of the shareholders over the others. One share in enough. Still less is it possible to contend that the motive of becoming shareholders or of making them shareholders is a field of inquiry which the statute itself recognises as legitimate. If they are shareholders, they are shareholders for all purposes; and even if the statute was silent as to the recognition of trusts, I should be prepared to hold that if six of them were the cestuis que trust of the seventh, whatever might be their rights inter se, the statute would have made them shareholders to all intents and purposes with their respective rights and liabilities, and, dealing with them in their relation to the company, the only relations which I believe the law would sanction would be that they were corporators of the corporate body.

I am simply here dealing with the provisions of the statute, and it seems to me to be essential to the artificial creation that the law should recognise only that artificial existence – quite apart from the motives or conduct of individual corporators. In saying this, I do not at all mean to suggest that if it could be established that this provision of the statute to which I am adverting had not been complied with, you could not go behind the certificate of incorporation to shew that a fraud had been committed upon the officer entrusted with the duty of giving the certificate, and that by some proceeding in the nature of scire facias you could not prove the fact that the company had no real legal existence. But short of such proof it seems to me impossible to dispute that once the company is legally incorporated it must be treated like any other independent person with its rights and liabilities appropriate to itself, and that the motives of those who took part in the promotion of the company are absolutely irrelevant in discussing what those rights and liabilities are.

I will for the sake of argument assume the proposition that [31] the Court of Appeal lays down – that the formation of the company was a mere scheme to enable Aron Salomon to carry on business in the name of the company. I am wholly unable to follow the proposition that this was contrary to the true intent and meaning of the Companies Act. I can only find true intent and meaning of the Act from the Act itself; and the Act appears to me to give a company a legal existence with, as I have said, rights and liabilities of its own, whatever may have been the ideas or schemes of those who brought it into existence.

I observe that the learned judge (Vaughan Williams J.) held that the business was Mr Salomon's business, and no one else's, and that he chose to employ as agent a limited company; and he proceeded to argue that he was employing that limited company as agent, and that he was bound to indemnify that agent (the company). I confess it seems to me that that very learned judge becomes involved by this argument in a very singular contradiction. Either the limited company was a legal entity or it was not. If it was, the business belonged to it and not to Mr Salomon. If it was not, there was no person and no thing to be an agent at all; and it is impossible to say at the same time that there is a company and there is not.

Lindley L.J., on the other hand, affirms that there were seven members of the company; but he says it is manifest that six of them were members simply in order to enable the seventh himself to carry on business with limited liability. The object of the whole arrangement is to do the very thing which the Legislature intended not to be done.

It is obvious to inquire where is that intention of the Legislature manifested in the statute. Even if we were at liberty to insert words to manifest that intention, I should have great difficulty in ascertaining what the exact intention thus imputed to the Legislature is, or was. In this particular case it is the members of one family that represent all the shares; but if the supposed intention is not limited to so narrow a proposition as this, that the seven shareholders must not be members of one family, to what extent may influence or authority or intentional purchase of a majority among the shareholders be carried so as [32] to bring it within the supposed prohibition? It is, of course, easy to say that it was contrary to the intention of the Legislature – a proposition which, by reason of its generality, it is difficult to bring to the test; but when one seeks to put as an affirmative proposition what the thing is which the Legislature has prohibited, there is, as it appears to me, an insuperable difficulty in the way of those who seek to insert by construction such a prohibition into the statute.

As one mode of testing the proposition, it would be pertinent to ask whether two or three, or indeed all seven, may constitute the whole of the shareholders? Whether they must be all independent of each other in the sense of each having an independent beneficial interest? And this is a question that cannot be answered by the reply that it is a matter of degree. If the legislature intended to prohibit something, you ought to know what that something is. All it has said is that one share is sufficient to constitute a shareholder, though the shares may be 100,000 in number. Where am I to get from the statute itself a limitation of that provision that that shareholder must be an independent and beneficially interested person? . . .

[33] Vaughan Williams J. appears to me to have disposed of the argument that the company (which for this purpose he assumed to be a legal entity) was defrauded into the purchase of Aron Salomon's business because, assuming that the price paid for the business was an exorbitant one, as to which I am myself not satisfied, but assuming that it was, the learned judge most cogently observes that when all the shareholders are perfectly cognisant of the conditions under which the company is formed and the conditions of the purchase, it is impossible to contend that the company is being defrauded. . . .

My Lords, the truth is that the learned judges have never allowed in their own minds the proposition that the company [34] has a real existence. They have been struck by what they have considered the inexpediency of permitting one man to be in influence and authority (over) the whole company; and, assuming that such a thing could not have been intended by the Legislature, they have sought various grounds upon which they might insert into the Act some prohibition of such a result. Whether such a result be right or wrong, politic or impolitic, I say, with the utmost deference to the learned judges, that we have nothing to do with that question if this company has been duly constituted by law; and, whatever may be the motives of those who constitute it, I must decline to insert into that Act of Parliament limitations which are not to be found there.

LORD MACNAGHTEN: . . . [50] [The liquidator] disputed the validity of the debentures on the ground of fraud. On the same ground he claimed rescission of the agreement for the transfer of the business, cancellation of the debentures, and repayment by Mr Salomon of the balance of the purchase-money. In the alternative, he claimed payment of £20,000 on Mr Salomon's shares, alleging that nothing had been paid on them.

When the trial came on. . . it was not disputed that the 20,000 shares were fully paid up. The case presented by the liquidator broke down completely; but the learned judge suggested that the company had a right of indemnity against Mr Salomon. The signatories of the memorandum of association were, he said, mere nominees of Mr Salomon – mere dummies. The company was Mr Salomon in another form. He used the name of the company as an alias. He employed the company as his agent; so the company, he thought, was entitled to indemnity against its principal. The counter-claim was accordingly amended to raise this point; and on the amendment being made the learned judge pronounced an order in accordance with the view he had expressed.

The order of the learned judge appears to me to be founded on a misconception of the scope and effect of the Companies Act, 1862. In order to form a company limited by shares, the Act requires that a memorandum of association should be signed by seven persons, who are each to take one share at least. If those conditions are complied with, what can it matter whether the signatories are relations or strangers? There is nothing in the Act requiring that the subscribers to the memorandum should be independent or unconnected, or [51] that they or any one of them should take a substantial interest in the undertaking, or that they should have a mind and will of their own, as one of the learned Lord Justices seems to think, or that there should be anything like a balance of power in the constitution of the company. In almost every company that is formed the statutory number is eked out by clerks or friends, who sign their names at the request of the promoter or promoters without intending to take any further part or interest in the matter.

When the memorandum is duly signed and registered, though there be only seven shares taken, the subscribers are a body corporate 'capable forthwith,' to use the words of the enactment, 'of exercising all the functions of an incorporated company.' Those are strong words. The company attains maturity on its birth. There is no period of minority – no interval of incapacity. I cannot understand how a body corporate thus made 'capable' by statute can lose its individuality by issuing the bulk of its capital to one person, whether he be a subscriber to the memorandum or not. The company is at law a different person altogether from the subscribers to the memorandum; and, though it may be that after incorporation the business is precisely the same as it was before, and the same persons are managers, and the same hands receive the profits, the company is not in law the agent of the subscribers or trustee for them. Nor are the subscribers as members liable, in any shape or form, except to the extent and in the manner provided by the Act. That is, I think, the declared intention of the enactment. If the view of the learned judge were sound, it would follow that no common law partnership could register as a company limited by shares without remaining subject to unlimited liability. . . .

[52] Among the principal reasons which induce persons to form private companies, as is stated very clearly by Mr Palmer in his treatise on the subject, are the desire to avoid the risk of bankruptcy, and the increased facility afforded for borrowing money. By means of a private company, as Mr Palmer observes, a 'trade can be carried on with limited liability, and without exposing the persons interested in it in the event of failure to the harsh provisions of the bankruptcy law. A company, too, can raise money on debentures, which an ordinary trader cannot do. Any member of a company, acting in good faith is as much entitled to take and hold the

company's debentures as any outside creditor. Every creditor is entitled to get and to hold the best security the law allows him to take. . . .

[53] The unsecured creditors of A. Salomon and Company, Limited, may be entitled to sympathy, but they have only themselves to blame for their misfortunes. They trusted the company, I suppose, because they had long dealt with Mr Salomon, and he had always paid his way; but they had full notice that they were no longer dealing with an individual, and they must be taken to have been cognisant of the memorandum and of the articles of association. For such a catastrophe as has occurred in this case some would blame the law that allows the creation of a floating charge. But a floating charge is too convenient a form of security to be lightly abolished. I have long thought, and I believe some of your Lordships also think, that the ordinary trade creditors of a trading company ought to have a preferential claim on the assets in liquidation in respect of debts incurred within a certain limited time before the winding-up. But that is not the law at present. Everybody knows that when there is a winding-up debenture-holders generally step in and sweep off everything; and a great scandal it is.

It has become the fashion to call companies of this class 'one man companies'. That is a taking nickname, but it does not help one much in the way of argument. If it is intended to convey the meaning that a company which is under the absolute control of one person is not a company legally incorporated, although the requirements of the Act of 1862 may have been complied with, it is inaccurate and misleading: if it merely means that there is a predominant partner possessing an overwhelming influence and entitled practically to the whole of the profits, there is nothing in that that I can see contrary to the true intention of the Act of 1862, or against public policy, or detrimental to the interests of creditors. If the shares are fully paid up, it cannot matter whether they are in the hands of one or many. If the shares are not fully paid, it is as easy to gauge the solvency of an individual as to estimate the financial ability of a crowd.

Roundabout Ltd. v. Beirne
[1959] I.R. 423 (H.Ct.)

(From headnote) The owners of licensed premises, having closed the premises in circumstances giving rise to a trade dispute with the defendants, leased the premises with an option to purchase to the plaintiff company, the directors of which were the owners, their accountant, and three barmen. When the licensed premises were subsequently re-opened for business by the plaintiff company, the entire work of the premises was carried out by the directors themselves, no person being employed by them. The barmendirectors were paid a fixed yearly sum by way of directors' remuneration, which was paid at such irregular intervals and in such irregular proportions

as was found convenient. The defendants, who had been picketing the premises throughout the period that they were closed, continued to picket the premises subsequent to their re-opening. The plaintiff brough an action for, *inter alia*, an injunction to restrain the defendants from watching, besetting or picketing the plaintiffs' premises.

DIXON J.: . . . [426] There is no doubt that a trade dispute was raised and existed between the Trade Union and some of its members on the one hand and the Marian Park Inn Company on the other hand. [427]

That company has ceased to carry on business in these premises, and the only question in this case is whether the trade dispute survives as against the new company which has been formed and which has taken a lease of the premises from the Marian Park Inn Company. The trade dispute still exists with what I may call the old company, and the question is whether the Union can avail itself of that dispute for the purpose of picketing the premises which are now occupied, and in which business is now carried on, by the new company.

The new company is in law a distinct entity, as is the old company. Each company is what is known as a legal person. I have to regard the two companies as distinct in the same way as I would regard two distinct individuals. I must therefore proceed on the basis that a new and different person is now in occupation of the premises and carrying on business there.

It has been suggested – and there is some basis for the suggestion – that the new company was formed for the purpose of getting rid of the trade dispute and also of enabling the employment of Union staff to be dispensed with. There is considerable substance in that suggestion. I think that it is quite permissible to describe the formation of the new company as a subterfuge – a legal subterfuge – to put an end to the trade dispute and enable the business to be carried on without the inconvenience of being subject to the picket. To this description there are two qualifications: first, that even though the formation of the new company may be a subterfuge, the question I have to decide is not ruled by that; the question which I must determine is whether it is a successful subterfuge, capable of effectually achieving its purpose. The second qualification is that I do not think that the sole, or possibly even the primary, purpose of the formation of the new company was to get rid of the trade dispute. I think that there was a genuine idea of getting new blood into the business and a genuine idea of the business eventually being taken over in some way by which the Morans would cease to have a substantial interest, and might possibly cease to have any interest in the premises or business. At the moment, indeed, the Morans are in control, constituting the three permanent directors of the new company. The other directors of the new company are at their mercy in a sense – in the sense that if the permanent directors see fit to remove the other directors, they can require them to transfer their entire shares or interest in the company. The new directors, however, are satisfied with that position: they are satisfied to rely on the Morans, and to trust to the [428] Morans that the new directors will not, as it were, be thrown out, and that, to put it colloquially, there will eventually be something in it for them.

While this new arrangement contains a considerable element of subterfuge, as a scheme designed to get rid, if legally possible, of the existing trade dispute, that is not the whole end and object of the arrangement. I must regard the new company as what it is, a distinct legal entity, and approach the position from the same point of view as if some individual or company totally unconnected with the old company had taken a lease of these premises similar to the lease taken here. The question then is whether a picket can be placed on the premises of the new owner by reason of a trade dispute with the previous owner. In the only case decided in this country on that matter, *Ferguson* v. *O'Gorman and Others* [1937] I.R. 620, Meredith J. held that, in the circumstances of that case, the existing trade dispute did attach to the premises when purchased by the new company, but there are distinctions between the facts of that case and those of the present case, which, I think, render the decision in that case inapplicable to the present case. In that case a company was formed which purchased the premises and took over the business of a partnership as a going concern, so that a new owner of the premises was substituted for the old, and the legal effect was the same as if the partnership had converted itself into a company.

In the present case, that is not the legal position. The old company still has not merely an interest in, but the ownership of, the premises. The new company has taken a lease of the premises from the old company; it has not taken over the business as a going concern.

Another distinction between the two cases is that, in the present case, the new company are not 'employers' in the sense that would bring them within the terms of the Trade Disputes Act, 1906. To make picketing lawful within that Act it must be conducted 'in contemplation of furtherance of a trade dispute' and a 'trade dispute' is defined, in s. 5, sub-s. 3, of the Act as being (so far as material here) a 'dispute between employers and workmen. . .' There is no doubt that 'workmen,' within the definition thereof in the Trade Disputes Act, 1906, are involved in this dispute, but there must, on the other side, be employers. 'Workmen' are defined, in s. 5, sub-s. 3, of the Act as 'all persons employed in trade or industry, whether or not in the employment of the employer with whom a trade dispute arises.' The practical effect of that definition is that, if a [429] trade dispute arises between workmen and employers in one premises, it might, and in most cases would, be permissible for the workmen or for other members of their trade union to picket entirely different premises owned or occupied by a totally different employer. It is an everyday feature of trade disputes that the dispute does not exist with the particular employer who is being picketed; the object of that provision of the Trade Disputes Act is to legalise sympathetic or consequential picketing. Before such picketing can be legalised the person whose premises are being picketed must first be an employer, for the obvious reason that the object of the picketing must be to act by influence or persuasion on employees. The distinction is perhaps a fine one, but where there is no trade dispute with the individual owner or occupier of the premises which are being picketed, such picketing can be justified only if such owner or occupier is in fact an employer.

The new company here is not an employer. It is true that it is a potential employer in the sense that it may well in the future be compelled by circumstances to take on staff, but at present it is not, and never has been, an employer in the sense in which that term is used in the Trade Disputes Act, 1906. It is true that the directors of the company do work in the licensed premises, but a distinction must be observed between directors who do work for a company and workmen who are employed by the company. The former cannot be regarded as working in pursuance of any contract of employment, and, therefore, cannot be regarded as workmen of the company. The fact that the company may at some future time be an employer is not sufficient to entitle me to hold that it is at present an employer, so as to entitle the defendants to claim the protection of the Trades Disputes Act, 1906.

The onus of establishing the existence of a trade dispute lies on the persons alleging its existence; in my view no trade dispute has been shown to exist between the plaintiffs, Roundabout Ltd., and the defendants, and accordingly the plaintiffs are entitled to have the interim injunction continued in a more permanent form. I propose, however, to grant the perpetual injunction only against the four named defendants.

Macaura v. Northern Assurance Co.
[1925] A.C. 619 (H.L.)

LORD BUCKMASTER: . . . [623] [T]he appellant is the owner of the Killymoon estate in the county of Tyrone. The respondents are five insurance companies with whom at various dates in January and February of 1922, the appellant effected insurance against fire on timber and wood goods in the open situate on the Killymoon domain not within a hundred yards of any saw mill or any building [624] in which wood working by power other than wind or water was carried on. Neither the amounts not the exact language of the policies are material for the purposes of the present appeal, nor is the fact that the policies were really effected in the name of the appellant and the Governor and the Company of the Bank of Ireland, for the real questions that arise for determination are these:

1. Whether the appellant had any insurable interest in the goods the subject of the policies, and

2. Whether the respondents were, in the circumstances, at liberty to raise the contention that he had no such interest in the manner in which it was raised in the course of these proceedings.

The history of the matter can be stated in a few sentences. The appellant upon whose estate the timber in question was originally standing on December 30, 1919, assigned the whole of it to a company known as the Irish Canadian Saw Mills, Ltd., the amount to be paid for the timber felled and unfelled being £27,000, while a further £15,000 was to be paid for the cost incurred by the appellant in felling the timber that was then down. The total price paid was therefore £42,000, satisfied by the allotment to the appellant or his nominees of £42,000 fully paid £1 shares in the company; no further shares than these were ever issued. The company proceeded with the operations of cutting the timber, and by the end of August, 1921, it had all been felled and sawn up in the saw mills. In the course of these operations the appellant had become the creditor of the company for £19,000, and beyond this it is stated that the debts of the company were trifling in amount. The timber when cut remained lying on the appellant's land, and on February 22, 1922 the greater part of it was destroyed by fire. The appellant accordingly claimed against the companies upon the policies and, on May 30, 1922, in an answer sent on behalf of all the companies, it was stated that the companies must decline to accept liability for the loss of any timber within a hundred yards of the saw mill. The appellant and the Bank of Ireland accordingly instituted [625] proceedings by issuing writs against each of the respondent companies, and each of the statements of claim delivered contained the following allegation: '3. The plaintiffs were at the date of the effecting of the said policy of insurance and at the time of the loss and damage hereinafter mentioned interested in the said timber to the amount so insured thereon as aforesaid.' . . .

[626] Turning now to his position as shareholder, this must be independent of the extent of his share interest. If he were entitled to insure holding all the shares in the company, each shareholder would be equally entitled, if the shares were all in separate hands. Now, no shareholder has any right to any item of property owned by the company, for he has no legal or equitable interest therein. He is entitled to a share in the profits while the company continues to carry on business and a share in the distribution of the surplus [627] assets when the company is wound up. If he were at liberty to effect an insurance against loss by fire of any item of the company's property, the extent of his insurable interest could only be measured by determining the extent to which his share in the ultimate distribution would be diminished by the loss of the asset – a calculation almost impossible to make. There is no means by which such an interest can be definitely measured and no standard which can be fixed of the loss against which the contract of insurance could be regarded as an indemnity. This difficulty

was realized by counsel for the appellant, who really based his case upon the contention that such a claim was recognized by authority and depended upon the proper application of the definition of insurable interest given by Lawrence J. in *Lucena* v. *Craufurd* (2 Bos. & P.N.R. 269, 302). I agree with the comment of Andrews L.J. upon this case. I find equally with him a difficulty in understanding how a moral certainty can be so defined as to render it an essential part of a definite legal proposition. In the present case, though it might be regarded as a moral certainty that the appellant would suffer loss if the timber which constituted the sole asset of the company were destroyed by fire, this moral certainty becomes dissipated and lost if the asset be regarded as only one in an innumerable number of items in a company's assets and the shareholding interest be spread over a large number of individual shareholders. The authorities which have the closest relation to the present are those of *Peterson* v. *Harris* (I.B. & S. 336) and *Wilson* v. *Jones* (L.R. 1 Ex. 193; L.R. 2 Ex. 139). In the first of these cases a shareholder in a company that was established for the purpose of laying down a submarine cable between the United Kingdom and America, effected an insurance upon his interest in the cable. The shareholder's insurable interest in the cable does not appear to have been disputed and the real question, therefore, was never argued. In the case of *Wilson* v. *Jones,* where another policy was effected by a shareholder in the same company, it was distinctly held that the policy was not upon [628] the cable but upon the shareholder's interest in the adventure of the cable being successfully laid. It was attempted by the underwriters to limit the insurance to an interest in the cable itself, which would have lessened the risk, but it was held that this was not the true construction of the policy. It was not argued that, if it were, the shareholder had no interest to insure, but both Martin B. in the Court of Exchequer and Willes J. in the Exchequer Chamber, stated that the plaintiff had no direct interest in the cable as a shareholder in the company, and, so far as I can see, this consideration it was that assisted the Court in determining that the insurance was upon the adventure in which the shareholder had an interest, and not upon the cable in which he had none. There are no other cases that even approximately approach the present case, and, properly regarded, I think the case of *Wilson* v. *Jones* is against and not in favour of the appellant's contention. Upon the merits of this dispute, therefore, the appellant must fail. Neither a simple creditor nor a shareholder in a company has any insurable interest in a particular asset which the company holds.

Nor can his claim to insure be supported on the ground that he was a bailee of the timber, for in fact he owed no duty whatever to the company in respect of the safe custody of the goods; he had merely permitted their remaining upon his land.

Jones v. Lipman
[1962] 1 All E.R. 442 (Ch.D.)

(From headnote) The first defendant agreed to sell freehold land with registered title to the plaintiffs for £5,250. Pending completion he sold and transferred the land to the defendent company (having a capital of £100), which he acquired and of which he and a clerk of his solicitors were sole shareholders and directors, for £3,000, of which £1,564 was borrowed by the defendant company from a bank and the rest remained owing to the first defendant.

RUSSELL, J.: . . . [444] The affidavit evidence by the first defendant made it plain (i) that the defendant company was, and at all material times had been, under the complete control of the first defendant, and (ii) that the acquisition of the defendant company by the first defendant and the transfer to it of the real property comprised in the contract with the plaintiffs (for the chattels remained in the ownership of the first defendant) was carried through solely for the purpose of defeating the plaintiff's rights to specific performance and in order to leave them to claim such damages, if any, as they might establish. So much was, quite rightly, admitted by counsel for the defendants.

For the plaintiffs the argument was twofold. First: that specific performance would be ordered against a party to a contract who has it in his power to compel another person to convey the property in question; and that admittedly the first defendant had this power over the defendant company. Second: that specific performance would also, in circumstances such as the present, be ordered against the defendant company. For the first proposition reference was made to *Elliott v. Pierson.* [1948] Ch. 452. In that case resistance to specific performance at the suit of a vendor was grounded on the fact that the property was vested in a limited company and not in the vendor. The company, however, was wholly owned and controlled by the vendor, who could compel it to transfer the property, and on this ground the defence to the claim for specific performance failed. It seems to me, not only from dicta of the learned judge but also on principle, that it necessarily follows that specific performance cannot be resisted by a vendor who, by his absolute ownership and control of a limited company in which the property is vested, is in a position to cause the contract to be completed.

For the second proposition reference was made to *Gilford Motor Co., Ltd. v. Horne* [1933] Ch. 935. In that case the individual defendant had entered into covenants restricting his trading activities. It caused the defendant company in that case to be formed. This company was under his control and did things which, if they had been done by him, would have been a breach of the covenants. An injunction was granted not only against him but also against the company. In that case Lord Hanworth, M.R., after referring to *Smith* v. *Hancock* [1894] 2 Ch. 377 said:

> Lindley, L.J., indicated the rule which ought to be followed by the court. 'If the evidence admitted of the conclusion that what was being done was a mere cloak or sham, and that in truth the business was being carried on by the wife and Kerr for the defendant, or by the defendant through his wife for Kerr, I certainly should not hesitate to draw that conclusion, and to grant the plaintiff relief accordingly.' I do draw that conclusion. I do hold that the company was 'a mere cloak or sham'; I do hold that it was a mere device for enabling Mr. E. B. Horne to continue to commit breaches of [the covenant], and in those circumstances the injunction must go against both defendants. . . .

Lawrence, L.J., in his judgment, said:

> [385] . . . I agree with the finding by the learned judge that the defendant company was a mere channel used by the defendant Horne for the purpose of enabling him, for his own benefit, to obtain the advantage of the customers of the plaintiff company, and that therefore the defendant company ought to be restrained as well as the defendant Horne.

Similarly, Romer, L.J., said:

> In my opinion, Farwell, J., was perfectly right in the conclusion to which he came . . . that this defendant company was formed and was carrying on business merely as a cloak or sham for the purpose of enabling the defendant Horne to commit the breach of the covenant that he entered into deliberately with the plaintiffs on the occasion of and as consideration for his employment as managing director. For this reason, in addition to the reasons given by my Lords, I agree that the appeal must be allowed with the consequences which have been indicated by the Master of the Rolls.

Those comments on the relationship between the individual and the company apply even more forcibly to the present case. The defendant company is the creature of the first defendant, a device and a sham, a mask which he holds before his face in an attempt to avoid recognition by the eye of equity. The case cited illustrates that an equitable remedy is rightly to be granted directly against the creature in such circumstances. . . .

The proper order to make is an order on both the defendants specifically to perform the agreement between the plaintiffs and the first defendant, but excepting from the order against the defendant company that part of the agreement which involved the chattels. Accordingly, the court will declare that the contract dated February 27, 1961, mentioned in the writ of summons, ought to be specifically performed as to both the realty and personalty comprised therein by the first defendant and as to the realty comprised therein of the second defendant.

Power Supermarkets Ltd. v. Crumlin Investments Ltd.
(Costello J., June 22, 1981, H.Ct.)

The first defendant, a company that was later acquired by the Dunnes Stores group, leased a unit in a shopping centre to the plaintiff. In the lease the defendant covenanted not to allow any extra-large supermarket to be operated in the centre; specifically, not to 'grant a lease for or to sell or permit or suffer the sale of any of its tenants or. . . any sub or under tenants' of groceries in a unit greater than 3,000 square feet. Subsequently, the Dunnes group decided to open a 3,000 square feet-plus supermarket in the unit. To that end, it incorporated a new company, the second defendant, and the first defendant conveyed to it the fee simple in the unit. All the evidence showed that the Dunnes companies involved were merely vehicles for carrying out the wishes of the controlling family, and that their wishes prevailed in respect of each company in the group. The first defendant was the wholly-owned subsidiary of Cornellscourt Shopping Centre Ltd., which was a wholly-owned subsidiary of Dunnes Holding Co., which was an unlimited company whose shareholders were trustees of a discretionary trust for the Dunne family. Through another chain of subsidiaries, the second defendant's ownership could be traced back to Dunnes Holding Co. Since they were incorporated, there had been no meeting as such of either defendants' shareholders or board of directors. Instead, they were managed and controlled by members of the Dunne family meeting informally. Costello J. instanced the conveyance of the unit to highlight the reality of the relationship between the companies. The consideration was only £100, it contained none of the usual easements, and it was not registered.

COSTELLO, J.: . . . [7] The Plaintiffs submit that I should pierce the corporate veil and look to the realities in this case and hold, notwithstanding the fact that Crumlin Investments and Dunnes Stores (Crumlin) are two separate corporate entities, that the business in the unit is being carried on by a single entity. I was referred to *Smith Stone and Knight Ltd.* v. *Birmingham Corporation* [1939] 4 All E.R. 116, a case in which a parent company was held entitled to compensation in respect of a business carried on by its subsidiary on the basis that the subsidiary was in reality carrying it on on behalf of the parent company, and to *D.H.N. Ltd.* v. *Tower Hamlets London Borough Council* [1976] 1 W.L.R. 852 a case also dealing with the payment of compensation for the compulsory acquisition of property. The claimants in that case were a group of three companies associated in a wholesale grocery business. The Court of Appeal held that it should pierce the corporate veil, and that it should not regard the companies as separate legal entities but treat the group as a single economic entity for the purpose of awarding compensation. I need not refer to the facts of the case; however, the reasons which prompted [8] the court's approach are very material for the resolution of the issues in the present case. Lord Denning pointed out (at page 860) that the group of companies was virtually the same as a partnership in which all three were partners; that they should not be treated separately so as to defeat the claim to compensation on a technical point; that they should not be deprived of the compensation which should be justly payable for disturbance. So, he decided that the three companies should be treated as one. Lord Justice Shaw (at page 867) pointed out that if each member of the group of companies was to be regarded as a company in isolation that nobody at all could claim compensation 'in a case which plainly calls for it', and he said that the true relationship should not be ignored because to do so would amount to a denial of justice. He too considered that the group should be regarded as a single entity.

It seems to me to be well established from these as well as from other authorities (See *Harold Holdsworth & Co. Ltd.* v. *Caddies* [1955] 1 W.L.R. 353; *Scottish Co-operative Wholesale Society Ltd.* v. *Meyer* [1959] A.C. 324) that a Court may, if the justice of the case so requires, treat two or more related companies as a single entity so that the business notionally carried on by one will be regarded as the business of the group, or another member of the group, if this conforms to the economic and commercial realities of the situation. It would in my [9] view, be very hard to find a clearer case than the present one for the application of this principle. I appreciate that Crumlin Investments is a property-owning not a trading company but it is clear that the creation of the new company and the conveyance to it of the freehold interest in a unit in the shopping centre were means for carrying out the commercial plans of the Dunne family in the centre. The enterprise had a two-fold aspect (a) the creation of a new retail outlet for the Dunnes Stores Group in the shopping centre and (b) the enhancement of the rents in the centre as a whole which the creation of such an outlet would hopefully produce. To treat the two companies as a single economic entity seems to me to accord fully with the realities of the situation. Not to do so could involve considerable injustice to the Plaintiffs as their rights under the covenant might be defeated by the mere technical device of the creation of a company with a £2 issued capital which had no real independent life of its own. If it is established that the covenant is breached there should in my opinion be an injunction against both Defendants.

IV. Governance

By governance in the context of company law is meant the way in which companies are organisations and run by those who own and control them. It can be contrasted with management, which signifies how a company's ordinary business affairs are conducted, although the line between overall governance and day-to-day management is not watertight. Different companies possess different methods of governance, just as there is an enormous variety of management systems. The Companies Acts, however, lay down certain minimum ground rules for governance. Ultimate control over companies' destinies is consigned to their members or shareholders. Members' meetings must be convened at least once a year, and a significant minority of the membership may call such meetings at any time; and various matters concerning the company must be decided at such meetings. It is for companies themselves to determine how votes are to be allocated among their shareholders and what particular powers should be entrusted to the directors. Companies can change their own regulations provided sufficient members support such a change.

GENERAL MEETINGS

Re Moorgate Mercantile Holdings Ltd.
[1980] 1 All E.R. 40 (Ch.D.)

Notices were circulated of a proposed special resolution that the company's share premium account, standing at £1,356,900, be cancelled on the grounds that the entire amount was lost. Due to an oversight, the proposers did not make provisions for a premium of £321 that was obtained shortly before then. On discovering this amount, the chairman sought to amend the proposed resolution to a proposal to reduce the share premium account from £1,356,900 to £321.

SLADE J.: ... [44] Section 141(1) the Companies Act 1948 defines an extraordinary resolution as follows:

> A resolution shall be an extraordinary resolution when it has been passed by a majority of not less than three fourths of such members as, being entitled so to do, vote in person or, where proxies are allowed,

by proxy, at a general meeting of which notice specifying the intention to propose the resolution as an extraordinary resolution has been duly given.

Section 141(2) of that Act, omitting an immaterial proviso, defines a 'special resolution' as follows:

A resolution shall be a special resolution when it has been passed by such a majority as is required for the passing of an extraordinary resolution and at a general meeting of which not less than twenty-one days' notice, specifying the intention to propose the resolution as a special resolution has been duly given. . . .

Section 141(5) provides that for the purpose of the section –

. . . notice of a meeting shall be deemed to be duly given and the meeting to be duly held when the notice is given and the meeting held in manner provided by this Act or the articles.

[Compare s. 140 of the 1963 Act.]

The company's articles, so far as I am aware, contain no provisions which are relevant to the question which I have to decide. The doubts as to the validity of the special resolution of 26th April 1979 arise solely from the provisions of s. 141(2).

It will be seen that, under the terms of s. 141(2), one of the conditions precedent to the validity of any special resolution is that '. . . not less than 21 days' notice specifying the intention to propose the resolution as a special resolution, has been duly given'. As counsel as amicus curiae has submitted, the phrase 'the resolution' in this context in my judgment manifestly means 'the aforesaid resolution', that is to say, the resolution which has been actually passed. This is a point of crucial importance in the present case.

The problem which now arises may be briefly summarised as follows. The notices dated 2nd April 1979 specified the intention to propose as a special resolution the resolution that 'the share premium account of the Company amounting to £1,356,900.48p be cancelled'. However, the resolution which was actually passed at the meeting of 26th April 1979 was a resolution that 'the share premium account of the Company amounting to £1,356,900.48p be reduced to £321.17p'. In these circumstances, did the notices of 2nd April 1979 give notice within the meaning of s. 141(2), specifying the intention to propose the resolution which was in the event actually passed?

In the absence of authority, I would have thought that the answer to this short question of statutory construction was manifestly No. The notices of 2nd April 1979 specified the intention to propose one resolution; the resolution actually passed at the meeting of 26th April 1979 was another, different resolution. Furthermore, the difference was not one merely of form but also of substance, albeit of slight substance, inasmuch as one resolution provided for the entire cancellation of the company's share premium account, while the other provided merely for its reduction, albeit by almost the entirety thereof.

The terms of s. 141(2), at least if read in isolation and in the absence of authority, would seem to me to require that, if a special resolution passed at a meeting of members is to be valid, it must be the same resolution as that which the requisite notice has specified the intention to propose. As I have already indicated, the phrase 'the resolution' appearing in the later words of the subsection clearly refers back to and echoes the phrase 'a resolution' appearing at the beginning of the subsection. I can see strong arguments for contending that a resolution passed at a meeting of members may properly be regarded as *the* resolution (that is, the same resolution as that) referred to in the preceding notice, if the only differences between the two are merely clerical or grammatical; I will revert [45] to this point later. If, however, there is any difference whatsoever of substance between the two I would not, in the absence of authority, have regarded the later resolution, which was actually passed, as having been preceded by proper notice for the purpose of s. 141(2).

Do the authorities lead me to a different conclusion?... [53] I... find nothing in the authorities which precludes me from reaching the conclusion as to the construction of s. 141(2) of the 1948 Act which I would have reached [54] in the absence of authority and indeed I think this conclusion derives strong support from the *MacConnell* decision [1916] 2 Ch. 57. In the light of this analysis of the authorities and of the wording of s. 141(2), I shall now attempt to summarise what are in my judgment the relevant principles relating to notices of, and the subsequent amendment of, special resolutions:

(1) If a notice of the intention to propose a special resolution is to be a valid notice for the purpose of s. 141(2), it must identify the intended resolution by specifying either the text or the entire substance of the resolution which it is intended to propose. In the case of a notice of intention to propose a special resolution, nothing is achieved by the addition of such words as 'with such amendments and alterations as shall be determined on at such meeting'.

(2) If a special resolution is to be validly passed in accordance with s. 141(2), the resolution as passed must be the same resolution as that identified in the preceding notice; the phrase 'the resolution' in s. 141(2) means 'the aforesaid resolution'.

(3) A resolution as passed can properly be regarded as 'the resolution' identified in a preceding notice, even though (i) it departs in some respects from the text of a resolution set out in such notice (for example by correcting those grammatical or clerical errors which can be corrected as a matter of

construction, or by reducing the words to more formal language) or (ii) it is reduced into the form of a new text, which was not included in the notice, provided only that in either case there is no departure whatever from the substance.

(4) However, in deciding whether there is complete identity between the substance of a resolution as passed and the substance of an intended resolution as notified, there is no room for the court to apply the de minimis principle or a 'limit of tolerance'. The substance must be identical. Otherwise the condition precedent to the validity of a special resolution as passed, which is imposed by s. 141(2), namely that notice has been given 'specifying the intention to propose the resolution as a special resolution' is not satisfied.

(5) It necessarily follows from the above propositions that an amendment to the previously circulated text of a special resolution can properly be put to and voted on at a meeting if, but only if, the amendment involves no departure from the substance of the circulated text, in the sense indicated in propositions (3) and (4) above.

(6) References to notices in the above propositions are intended to include references to circulars accompanying notices. In those cases where notices are so accompanied, the notices and circulars can and should, in my judgment, ordinarily be treated as one document.

(7) All the above propositions may be subject to modification where all the members, or a class of members, of a company unanimously agree to waive their rights to notice under s. 141(2): see s. 143(4)(d) of the 1948 Act, *Re Pearce, Duff & Co Ltd* [1960] 3 All E.R. 222 and *Re Duomatic Ltd* [1969] 2 Ch. 365.

I would emphasise that these propositions are directed solely to special resolutions. Very different considerations may apply in the case of ordinary resolutions, in relation to which the criteria of permissible amendments suggested by counsel for the company could well be very relevant: see, for example, *Betts & Co Ltd* v. *Macnaghten* [1910] 1 Ch. 430. In relation to special resolutions, however, I think that my conclusions of principle accord not only with the wording of the 1948 Act and with the authorities, but also with the following considerations of public policy. The 1948 Act requires a special resolution only in about ten circumstances. Thus, for example, such a resolution is required by s. 5 for the alteration of a company's memorandum, by s. 10 for the alteration of its articles, by [55] s. 18(1) for the change of its name, by s. 66 for the reduction of its capital, by s. 222(a) for a resolution that the company may be wound up by the court, and is also required for a resolution for voluntary winding-up passed under s. 278(1)(b). It may, I think, fairly be said that all the situations in which special resolutions are required are special situations, where the resolutions in question are by their nature likely either to affect the company's constitution or to have an important effect on its future. Since the passing of the 1929 legislation, the shareholders of a company, when faced with the intention to propose a special resolution, no longer have the protection of a locus poenitentiae in the shape of a second confirmatory meeting, at which they can accept or reject a special resolution passed at the first meeting. It is therefore all the more important that each shareholder should now have clear and precise advance notice of the substance of any special resolution which it is intended to propose, so that he may decide whether he should attend the meeting or is content to absent himself and leave the decision to those who do; the provisions imposed by s. 141(2) of the 1948 Act must be intended as much for the protection of the members who in the event decide to absent themselves as for those who decide to attend: see for example *Tiessen* v *Henderson* [1899] 1 Ch. 861 per Kekewich J. If it were open to the members who did attend to propose and vote on a special resolution differing in substance (albeit slightly) from the resolution of which notice had been given, there would be a risk of unfair prejudice to those members who, after due consideration, had deliberately absented themselves. I do not think that their interests would be sufficiently protected by the safeguard suggested by counsel for the company, namely that an amendment could properly be put to and voted on by the meeting only if a member, who had formed a view or intention with regard to a resolution as circulated, could not reasonably adopt a different view on the amended version. Nor do I think that the alternative 'whittling down' criterion suggested by him would offer them adequate protection. In many circumstances, albeit not on the facts of the particular case, either test when applied in practice could involve serious uncertainties and difficult questions of degree. Furthermore, in many cases it would present substantial embarrassment both to the chairman of the meeting who had to apply it and to any persons holding 'two-way' proxies on behalf of absent members. The absent members would be correspondingly faced with unpredictable risks.

These considerations strengthen my conclusion that the strict interpretation which I have placed on s. 141(2) is likely to represent the true intention of the legislature, as well as the grammatical meaning of the words used. There must be absolute identity, at least in substance, between the intended resolution referred to in the notice and the resolution actually passed.

I now turn to apply the seven propositions set out above to the facts of the present case. The qualifications referred to in the last of them are not relevant here, since not all members of the company entitled to vote thereat were present at the meeting of 26th April 1979. While I have no reason to doubt that the amendment to the resolution was put to the meeting in good faith and on legal advice, it was in my judgment improperly put and voted on. Counsel as amicus curiae accepted, and I accept, the correctness of the advice given to Mr Silman, on the facts, that no shareholder who had made up his mind how to vote on the resolution in its original form could reasonably have adopted a different view in regard to the amended form. For this reason I have a measure of sympathy with this petition. This point, however, in my judgment is irrelevant in law. In my judgment, the crucial point is that the resolution which the meeting of 26th April 1979 approved was not the same resolution, either in form or in substance, as that of which the text had been circulated to shareholders in the notices of 2nd April 1979. There is no room for the application of any 'de minimis' principle; a resolution to reduce the share premium account of a company to £321 could not even be deemed to be the same as a resolution to reduce it to £320.

[56] In the circumstances the resolution was not in my judgment validly passed in accordance with s. 141(2) of the 1948 Act. The court, therefore, has no jurisdiction to confirm the reduction of the share premium account as asked for by this petition.

Cane v. Jones
[1981] 1 All E.R. 533 (Ch.D.)

All the members of a family company, the shares in which were split evenly between two factions, at one stage agreed in writing that the chairman should not possess a casting vote at directors' meetings. The plaintiff contended that this agreement had the effect of a special resolution altering the company's articles of association.

WHEELER Q.C.: . . . [537] Counsel for the plaintiff contends that it operated as an alteration of the articles on what was conveniently called in argument 'the *Duomatic* principle' based on *Re Duomatic Ltd* [1969] 2 Ch 365, and the principle is, I think, conveniently summarised in a short passage in the judgment of Buckley J in that case where he says:

> . . . I proceed on the basis that where it can be shown that all sharehol-
> ders who have a right to attend and vote at a general meeting of the
> company assent to some matter which a general meeting of the com-
> pany could carry into effect, that assent is as binding as a resolution
> in general meeting would be.

Applying that principle to the present case, counsel for the plaintiff says that the agreement of all the shareholders embodied in the 1967 agreement had the effect, so far as requisite, of overriding the articles. In other words, it operated to deprive the chairman for the time being of the right to use his casting vote except, perhaps, in so far as an independent chairman contemplated by cl.1 might need to do. I should add here that it is quite clear that Percy, who was actually chairman of the company at the time, was well aware of the terms of the 1967 agreement.

For the first and third defendants, counsel has two answers to counsel's argument for the plaintiff: first, that on its true interpretation in relation to a special or extraordinary resolution the *Duomatic* principle only applies if there has been (i) a resolution and (ii) a meeting; and that here he says, with some truth, there was neither a resolution nor a meeting of the four shareholders; second, he stresses that the agreement does not in terms purport to alter the articles at all: it rests, he says, solely in contract and Gillian, not being a party, cannot take either the benefit or the burden of the agreement.

On the first of these two arguments, counsel for the first and third defendants helpfully reminded me of the line of cases in which the effect of the unanimous consent of the corporators had been considered, starting with *Baroness Wenlock* v. *River Dee Co* [1883] 36 Ch.D. 675. I do not propose to refer to all these cases in detail but, for the record, I will list them. The other cases are *Re George Newman & Co* [1895] 1 Ch 674. [538] Then there is *Re Express Engineering Works Ltd* [1920] 1 Ch 466, *Re Oxted Motor Co Ltd* [1921] 3 KB 32, *Parker and Cooper Ltd* v *Reading* [1926] Ch 975, *Re Pearce Duff & Co Ltd* [1960] 3 All ER 222, *Re Duomatic*, to which I have already referred and finally a decision of Slade J in *Re Moorgate Mercantile Holdings Ltd* [1980] 1 All ER 40 (ante p. 67)

Counsel for the first and third defendants pointed out, correctly, that of these cases only three were concerned with special or extraordinary resolutions, namely *Re Pearce Duff & Co Ltd*, and *Re Moorgate Mercantile Holdings Ltd* (both of which were concerned with special resolutions) and *Re Oxted Motor Co. Ltd.* (which is concerned with an extraordinary resolution). All the rest were concerned with matters which, if capable of ratification at all, could have been validated by ordinary resolutions.

The starting point of counsel for the first and third defendants is s. 10 of the Companies Act 1948 which provides for the alteration of articles by special resolution; and from that he goes on to s. 141, mentioning sub-ss. (1) and (2) and including the particular proviso, laying down how special and extraordinary resolutions are to be passed. First of all s. 10:

> (1) Subject to the provisions of this Act and to the conditions contained in its memorandum, a company may by special resolution alter or add to its articles.
>
> (2) Any alteration or addition so made in the articles shall, subject to the provisions of this Act, be as valid as if originally contained therein, and be subject in like manner to alteration by special resolution.

Then s. 141:

> (1) A resolution shall be an extraordinary resolution when it has been passed by a majority of not less than three fourths of such members as, being entitled so to do, vote in person or, where proxies are

allowed, by proxy, at a general meeting of which notice specifying the intention to propose the resolution as an extraordinary resolution has been duly given.

(2) A resolution shall be a special resolution when it has been passed by such a majority as is required for the passing of an extraordinary resolution and at a general meeting of which not less than twenty-one days' notice, specifying the intention to propose the resolution as a special resolution, has been duly given. Provided that, if it is so agreed by a majority in number of the members having the right to attend and vote at any such meeting, being a majority together holding not less than ninety-five per cent. in nominal value of the shares giving that right, or in the case of a company not having a share capital, together representing not less than ninety-five per cent. of the total voting rights at that meeting of all the members, a resolution may be proposed and passed as a special resolution at a meeting of which less than twenty-one days' notice has been given. . .

Thus, says counsel for the first and third defendants, you can only alter the articles by special resolution. That is his first argument. Secondly, a special resolution must be passed at a meeting; thirdly, here there was neither a resolution nor a meeting. . . .

[539] The first of counsel's two arguments for the first and third defendants (namely that there must be a 'resolution' and a 'meeting') does not appear to have been raised in any of the three reported cases which were concerned with special or extraordinary resolutions. But it is not an argument to which I would readily accede because in my judgment it would create a wholly artificial and unnecessary distinction between those powers which can, and those which cannot, be validly exercised by all the corporators acting together.

For my part I venture to differ from counsel for the first and third defendants on the first limb of his argument, namely that articles can *only* be altered by special resolution. In my judgment, s. 10 of the Act is merely laying down a procedure whereby *some only* of the shareholders can validly alter the articles; and, if, as I believe to be the case, it is a basic principle of company law that all the corporators, acting together, can do anything which is intra vires the company, then I see nothing in s. 10 to undermine this principle. I accept that the principle requires all the corporators to 'act together'; but with regard to this I respectfully adopt what Astbury J said in *Parker and Cooper Ltd* v. *Reading*.

Now the view I take of both these decisions [those were in *Re Express Engineering Works Ltd* and *Re George Newman & Co*] is that where the transaction is intra vires and honest, and especially if it is for the benefit of the company, it cannot be upset if the assent of all the corporators is given to it. I do not think it matters in the least whether that assent is given at different times or simultaneously.

See also per Younger LJ in *Re Express Engineering Works Ltd* at 471 and [540] the passage from the judgment of Buckley J in *Re Duomatic Ltd* which I have read earlier in this judgment.

I should add that the evidence in the case before me is that the 1967 agreement was signed by 'the two sides' (if I may call them that) separately and that they did not meet together, however informally, for the purpose of signing the document. But it is clear beyond doubt that the agreement did represent a meeting of minds which is, after all, the essence of a meeting and the passing of a resolution.

Some light is also, I think, thrown on the problem by s. 143(4) of the 1948 Act. Section 143 deals with the forwarding to the Registrar of Companies of copies of every resolution or agreement to which the section applies (see 1963 Act s. 143), and sub-s. (4) reads as follows:

> This section shall apply to – *(a)* special resolutions; *(b)* extraordinary resolutions; *(c)* resolutions which have been agreed to by all members of a company, but which, if not so agreed to, would not have been effective for their purpose unless, as the case may be, they had been passed as special resolutions or as extraordinary resolutions; *(d)* resolutions or agreements which have been agreed to by all the members of some class of shareholders but which, if not so agreed to, would not have been effective for their purpose unless they had been passed by some particular majority or otherwise in some particular manner, and all resolutions or agreements which effectively bind all the members of any class of shareholders though not agreed to by all those members. . . .

Paragraph *(c)* thus appears to recognise that you can have a resolution, at least, which has been agreed to by all the members and is as effective as a special or extraordinary resolution would have been, but, as counsel for the first and third defendants was quick to point out, para *(c)* says nothing about 'agreements' in contrast to para *(d)* which refers to resolutions or agreements which have been agreed to by all members of some class of shareholders. I should say in passing that I think the reference in para *(d)* to 'resolutions or agreements' stems directly from Reg 4 of Part 1 of the 1948 Table A, which, dealing with class meetings, provides briefly as follows:

> If at any time the share capital is divided into different classes of shares, the rights attached to any class (unless otherwise provided by the terms of issue of the shares of that class) may, whether or not the company is being wound up, be varied with the consent in writing of

the holders of three-fourths of the issued shares of that class, or with the sanction of an extraordinary resolution passed at a separate general meeting of the holders of the shares of the class,

so that you have either a consent which might be termed an agreement or a resolution.

I cannot regard this difference in drafting between paras *(c)* and *(d)* of s. 143(4) as fatal to the basic argument. It may be, as counsel for the plaintiff suggested, that a document which is framed as an agreement can be treated as a 'resolution' for the purposes of para *(c)*. (I should add in passing that a copy of the 1967 agreement was never, as far as I am aware, sent to the Registrar of Companies for registration.) It may be that there is a gap in the registration requirements of s. 143. But be that as it may, the fact that the 1967 agreement was drafted as an agreement and not as a resolution, and that the four signatories did not sign in each other's presence does not in my view prevent that agreement overriding pro tanto, and so far as necessary, the articles of the company; in my judgment counsel for the first and third defendants' first argument fails and unless he can show that the 1967 agreement has been superseded, the chairman of the company has no casting vote at board or general meetings.

THE CORPORATE FRANCHISE

Bushell v. Faith
[1970] A.C. 1099 (H.L.)

The articles of association of a private company provided that, in the event of a resolution being proposed at a general meeting of the company for the removal of a director, any shares held by that director should carry three votes per share. The company had an issued capital of £300 in £1 shares, which were distributed equally between the plaintiff, the defendant (her brother) and B., their sister. The plaintiff and defendant were the only directors of the company. The two sisters, requisitioned a general meeting of the company for the purpose of passing a resolution removing him from office as a director. On a poll at the meeting they both voted for the resolution, and he voted against it. A dispute having arisen as to whether the resolution had been passed or defeated, the plaintiff contended that it had been passed by 200 votes, being those of herself and her sister, to 100, those of the defendant. The defendant contended that in accordance with article 9 his 100 shares carried 300 votes to 200. The plaintiff claimed a declaration that the resolution had been validly passed and an injunction restraining the defendant from acting as a director.

LORD UPJOHN: . . . [1107] [T]he whole question is whether special article 9 is valid and applicable, in which case the resolution was rejected by 300 votes to 200, or whether that article must be treated as overridden by section 184 and therefore void, in which case the resolution was passed by 200 votes to 100. So to test this matter the appellant began an action for a declaration that the respondent was removed from office as a director by the resolution of November 22, 1968, and moved the court for an interlocutory injunction restraining him from acting as a director. This motion comes by way of appeal before your Lordships.

The appellant argues that special article 9 is directed to frustrating the whole object and purpose of section 184 (s. 182 of the 1963 Act) so that it can never operate where there is such a special article and the director in fact becomes irremovable. So she argues that, having regard to the clear words 'notwithstanding anything in its articles' in section 184, special article 9 must be rejected and treated as void. The learned judge, Ungoed-Thomas J., so held. He said: 'It would make a mockery of the law if the courts [1108] were to hold that in such a case a director was to be irremovable.' And later he concluded his judgment by saying: 'A resolution under article 9 is therefore not in my view an ordinary resolution within section 184. The plaintiff succeeds in the application.'

The brother appealed, and the Court of Appeal (Harman, Russell and Karminski L.JJ.) allowed the appeal. Harman L.J. did so on the simple ground that the Act of 1948 did not prevent certain shares or classes of shares having special voting rights attached to them and on certain occasions. He could find nothing in the Act of 1948 which prohibited the giving of special voting rights to the shares of a director who finds his position attacked. Russell L.J. in his judgment gave substantially the same reasons for allowing the appeal and he supported his judgment by reference to a number of recent precedents particularly those to be found in *Palmer's Company Precedents*, 17th ed. (1956), but, with all respect to the learned Lord Justice, I do not think these precedents which, so far as relevant, are comparatively new can be said to have the settled assent and approbation of the profession, so as to render them any real guide for the purposes of a judgment; especially when I note the much more cautious approach by the learned editors of the *Encyclopaedia of Forms and Precedents*, 4th ed. (1966), Vol. 5, p. 428, where in reference to a form somewhat similar to special article 9 they say in a footnote:

> The validity of such a provision as this in relation to a resolution to remove a director from office remains to be tested in the courts.

My Lords, when construing an Act of Parliament it is a canon of construction that its provisions must be construed in the light of the mischief which the Act was designed to meet. In this case the mischief was well known; it was a common practice, especially in the case of private companies, to provide in the articles that a director should be irremovable or only removable by an extraordinary resolution; in the former case the articles would have to be altered by special resolution before the director could be removed and of course in either case a three-quarters majority would be required. In many cases this would be impossible, so the Act provided that notwithstanding anything in the articles an ordinary resolution would suffice to remove a director. That was the mischief which the section set out to remedy; to make a director removable by virtue of an ordinary resolution instead of an extraordinary resolution or making it necessary to alter the articles.

An ordinary resolution is not defined nor used in the body of the Act of 1948 though the phrase occurs in some of the articles of Table A in the First Schedule to the Act. But its meaning is, in my opinion, clear. An ordinary resolution is in the first place passed by a bare majority on a show of hands by the members entitled to vote who are present personally or by proxy and on such a vote each member has one vote regardless of his shareholding. If a poll is demanded then for an ordinary resolution still only a bare majority of votes is required. But whether a share or class of shares has any vote upon the matter and, if so, what is its voting power upon the resolution in question depends [1109] entirely upon the voting rights attached to that share or class of shares by the articles of association.

I venture to think that Ungoed-Thomas J. overlooked the importance of article 2 of Table A which gives to the company a completely unfettered right to attach to any share or class of shares special voting rights upon a poll or to restrict those rights as the company may think fit. Thus, it is commonplace that a company may and frequently does preclude preference shareholders from voting unless their dividends are in arrear or their class rights are directly affected. It is equally commonplace that particular shares may be issued with specially loaded voting rights which ensure that in all resolutions put before the shareholders in general meeting the holder of those particular shares can always be sure of carrying the day, aye or no, as the holder pleases.

Mr Dillon, for the appellant, felt, quite rightly, constrained to admit that if an article provided that Mr Faith's shares should, on every occasion when a resolution was for consideration by a general meeting of the company, carry three votes such a provision would be valid on all such occasions including any occasion when the general meeting was considering a resolution for his removal under section 184.

My Lords, I cannot see any difference between that case and the present case where special voting rights are conferred only when there is a resolution for the removal of a director under section 184. Each case is an exercise of the unfettered right of the company under article 2 whereby

any share in the company may be issued with such. . . special
rights. . . in regard to. . . voting. . . as the company may from time to
time by ordinary resolution determine.

Parliament has never sought to fetter the right of the company to issue a
share with such rights or restrictions as it may think fit. There is no fetter
which compels the company to make the voting rights or restrictions of
general application and it seems to me clear that such rights or restrictions
can be attached to special circumstances and to particular types of resolution. This makes no mockery of section 184; all that Parliament was
seeking to do thereby was to make an ordinary resolution sufficient to
remove a director. Had Parliament desired to go further and enact that
every share entitled to vote should be deprived of its special rights under
the articles it should have said so in plain terms by making the vote on a
poll one vote one share. Then, what about shares which had no voting
rights under the articles? Should not Parliament give them a vote when
considering this completely artificial form of ordinary resolution? Suppose
there had here been some preference shares in the name of Mr Faith's
wife, which under the articles had in the circumstances no vote; why in
justice should her voice be excluded from consideration in this artificial
vote?

I only raise this purely hypothetical case to show the great difficulty of
trying to do justice by legislation in a matter which has always been left to
the corporators themselves to decide.

Kinsella v. Alliance & Dublin Consumers Gas Co.
(Barron J., Oct. 5, 1982, H.Ct.)

Under the Companies Clauses Consolidation Act, 1845, every member
possessed one vote per share held, but no one shareholder could possess
more than a limited number of votes regardless of how many shares he
owned. In an attempt to wrest control of the company from its board of
directors, the plaintiff and his supporters bought substantial blocks of
shares in the company. Because many of the share transfers were not
registered, their anti-directors resolutions were defeated. They sought to
have the rejection of their resolutions set aside.

BARRON J.: This action challenges the validity of the proceedings at an
extraordinary general meeting of the company held on the 10th September,
1982. At that meeting, voting was permitted only by stockholders whose
names had been entered in the register of shareholders and only such
stockholders were permitted to attend the meeting. Persons to whom stock
had been transferred and in respect of which transfers had been received
by the secretary of the company, but whose names had not been entered
in the register of shareholders were not permitted to attend the meeting.

Before dealing with the legal issues raised I feel it necessary to refer to the facts to show how such a situation arose. The extraordinary general meeting was called upon the requisition of the plaintiffs and those who support them. The resolutions for consideration at the meeting were essentially to remove the existing Board and to replace its members with nominees of the plaintiffs. In the ordinary way, this trial of strength would have been decided by the respective shareholdings of the members supporting each side. However, [2] in the case of the Gas Company the voting rights of its members are governed by the Company Clauses Consolidation Act, 1845. Under this Act, which in the main, comprises the constitution of the company, each member has one vote for each share held by him up to ten, one additional vote for every five shares beyond the first ten shares up to one hundred, and an additional vote for every ten shares held by him beyond the first hundred shares. The original shares were of a nominal value of £10 each and for many years had been converted into stock. Reference to a vote per share or number of shares is accordingly a reference to multiples of stock of £10 denomination.

It was seen by each side in the coming trial of strength that it was to their advantage to subdivide larger holdings in order to increase the voting power attributable to the stock comprising such holdings. Because of the need to build up voting strength not only by purchasing stock in the market place but also by subdivision of exisiting holdings, a very large number of transfers were required and these were delivered to the Secretary in the days preceding the date fixed for the meeting. While less than ten such transfers a week was the norm, three hundred and eighty eight transfers were lodged in the last week of August, three hundred and forty one transfers on the 2nd and 3rd September, ten hundred and fifty two transfers on the 6th September, four hundred and forty nine transfers on the 7th September, three hundred and eighty six [3] transfers on the 8th September and seventy six transfers on the 9th September.

It was the secretary's duty to register these transfers. As might be expected, the facilities available to the secretary to process such a large number of transfers were inadequate and it became necessary for him to call in registration staff from Craig Gardner & Company the company's auditors to assist him in this job. The secretary's task was further complicated by the need to process some four thousand proxies delivered to him in respect of the meeting. Here again he was obliged to rely upon the assistance of the registration staff of Craig Gardner & Company.

I do not propose to deal in detail with the work done by this registration staff. At first two members of the staff of Craig Gardner's were called in. Later they were joined by two more, and ultimately by a further six. They worked long hours – up to 9 p.m. on some nights, to midnight on others, and the night before the meeting to 4 a.m. They were able to process all transfers received by the secretary of the company up to 4.15 p.m. on

Monday the 6th September, but none received after that time of which there were approximately eleven hundred. In addition, they checked all the proxies and were able to provide for the chairman of the meeting the number of votes attributable to such proxies. It is in relation to these approximately eleven hundred stockholders whose transfers were not registered that the dispute in [4] this action arises.

It became obvious to Mr Jackson, one of the two solicitors acting for the plaintiffs, that the weight of paper being delivered by him to the company both in the form of stock transfers and proxies was such that there was a serious doubt whether or not all the transfers could be registered in time for the meeting. He telephoned Mr Hogan his colleague acting for the company on Wednesday the 8th September and asked him whether or not unregistered stockholders would be allowed to vote. Mr Hogan said that he would consider the matter. Mr Jackson rang Mr Hogan again that evening and was told by Mr Hogan that he had no answer for him yet but that he was getting counsel's opinion the following morning. On the following day Thursday the 9th September Mr Jackson wrote to Mr Hogan as follows:

> Dear Mr Hogan,
>
> Further to my telephone conversation of the 8th instant, I wish to confirm my telephone conversation with you on the 8th in connection with the Alliance and Dublin Consumers Gas Company. My client, Donal Kinsella, shall be claiming a right to vote on foot of proxies lodged in respect of transfers which have been duly delivered to the Secretary and accepted by him prior to 11 o'clock on Wednesday the [5] 8th September, 1982.
>
> I particularly confirm that I referred you to Sections 61, 62 and 64, as well as Sections 14 to 20 inclusive of the Companies Clauses Consolidation Act 1845. In addition, I referred you to Halsburys Statutes of England, third edition, volume 5 page 49 and thereabouts as well as the case of *Nanney* v. *Morgan* (1887) 37 Ch.D. 346.
>
> My client's supporters through their proxy of my client will be claiming entitlement to vote on foot of those proxies lodged concerning any stocks that may remain unregistered (but having been duly delivered) at the time of the meeting.
>
> I would also point out that there appears to be no regulation whereby the register of transfers can be closed and it would be my client's contention that registration in any event can be completed by the time of the meeting of those transfers as yet unregistered in view of the number that were registered on Monday, the 6th September, 1982.
>
> I felt it best to put the basics of our conversation and my client's contentions in writing at this stage even though I realise that at the

time of writing you are urgently considering the contents of my telephone call.

Yours sincerely. [6]

On the same day Mr Hogan's secretary rang Mr Jackson to say that he had as yet no answer for him. He got no answer that day nor was he able to contact Mr Hogan the following morning prior to the meeting. He attended the meeting and learned from the opening remarks of the chairman of the meeting that the attendance of unregistered stockholders was not being permitted.

The plaintiffs complain that the failure to register all the transfers submitted was as a result of a conscious decision to deprive the transferees affected of their rights as stockholders and that the failure of Mr Hogan to answer the question put to him was part of that conscious decision and deprived them of the opportunity to apply to the Court for an injunction to restrain the holding of the meeting.

The evidence adduced shows that no more work could have been done by the registration staff prior to the meeting. It was the decision of Mr Mooney, the senior member actually carrying out the work, made on the afternoon of Tuesday the 7th September that he would be unable to register any more transfers than those upon which he and his staff were then engaged. On the following afternoon, the registration staff were instructed by the secretary of the company acting on the advice of Mr Fitzgerald, another member of the firm of solicitors acting for the defendants, that their priority was to have the proxies processed and that if this meant leaving transfers unregistered [7] this would have to result. I have no evidence that there was any conscious decision by the board of the company or any one acting on its behalf to leave these transfers unregistered. The evidence is all to the contrary as I have indicated. Mr Fitzgerald indicated that they would rely upon the expertise of Craig Gardner and Company. It was through no lack of expertise on their part that the total work could not be completed. In my view, they did much more than could have been expected of them and are to be commended for their efforts. They were beaten by the sheer volume of paper and the shortness of the time available to them.

No reasonable explanation was given for the failure by Mr Hogan to reply to the question raised by Mr Jackson. Although it was not known on the Wednesday evening whether the instruction given to the registration staff would result in any transfers being left unregistered, it was reasonable at that stage to expect that this would apply to a large number of transfers. However, what was known, if not on Wednesday, then on the Thursday, was that stockholders who were not registered in the register of shareholders at the time of the meeting would not be allowed to vote. Mr Fitzgerald in evidence said that the failure to answer Mr Jackson's question was that both he and Mr Hogan had a lot of things to do and that there was no obligation to answer it. This answer and [8] the manner in which it was given was unfortunate since it tended to support an allegation for which there was no evidence. I think that an answer should have been given.

The basic question raised in these proceedings is the stage at which a transferee of shares in the company becomes entitled to exercise his or her voting rights in respect of such shares. The plaintiffs say it is when the transfer of such shares is acknowledged by the secretary of the company to have been received by him. The defendants say it is when the stockholder is actually registered as a stockholder in the register of shareholders.

In support of his submission counsel for the plaintiffs relies on the wording of Section 15 of the 1845 Act and on a passage in the judgment of Cotton L.J. in *Nanney* v. *Morgan*, 37 Ch.D. 346. Section 15 of the 1845 Act in so far as it is material is as follows:

> The said deed of transfer (when duly executed) shall be delivered to the secretary, and be kept by him; and the secretary shall enter a memorial thereof in a book to be called the 'Register of Transfers', and shall endorse such entry on the deed of transfer, and shall, on demand, deliver a new certificate to the purchaser, . . . and on the request of the purchaser of any share an endorsement of such transfer shall be made on the certificate of such share, [9] instead of a new certificate being granted; and such endorsement being signed by the secretary, shall be considered in every respect the same as a new certificate, and until such transfer has been so delivered to the secretary as aforesaid the vendor of the share shall continue liable to the company for any calls that may be made upon such share, and the purchaser of the share shall not be entitled to receive any share of the profits of the undertaking, or to vote in respect of such share.

In *Nanney* v. *Morgan*, Cotton L.J. at page 353 cites Section 15 from the words 'and until such transfer has been so delivered' until the end of the section and continues:

> that as regards the company provides that the deeds shall not have any effect, so as to put the transferees into the position of the transferor until it has been left with the Secretary, and it must be not only left, but accepted by him as properly left, because if the secretary finds that it does not comply with the provisions of the Act it is his duty to refuse to receive it.

Further on in the same paragraph the Judge says:

> I do not place any reliance on the transferee being entered on the register, because when a deed of transfer duly executed is left with

the [10] secretary, it becomes the duty of the company to register the transferee as entitled to the shares, and the mere neglect of the company to do that, will not in my opinion affect the right of the transferee to be treated as the legal owner of the shares.

This was the view of the majority of the Court, although one member, Lopes L.J. regarded it as unnecessary to express an opinion on the point.

The defendants' reply to this submission is that it is well settled law that only shareholders are entitled to vote and that, for the purpose of ascertaining who are shareholders, the company, whether incorporated under the Companies Acts or a statutory corporation as in the present case, need look only to its register of shareholders. Counsel for the defendants relied so far as companies governed by the 1845 Act are concerned, upon a passage in the judgment of Linley L.J. in *Powell* v. *London and Provincial Bank* [1893] 2 Ch. 555. At page 560 Linley L.J. said:

> . . . in order to acquire the legal title to stock or shares in companies governed by the Companies Clauses Consolidation Act you must have a deed, executed by the transferor, and you must have that transfer registered. Until you have got both you have not got the legal title in the transferee.

Counsel for the defendants also referred to several sections in the 1845 [11] Act in support of his argument. He relied particularly upon Sections 3, 8, 9 and 75. These sections are as follows:

> 3. The following words and expressions both in this and the special Act shall have the several meanings hereby assigned to them, unless there be something in the subject or the context repugnant to such construction:
> the word 'shareholder' shall mean a shareholder, proprietor, or member of the company; and in referring to any such shareholder, expressions properly applicable to a person shall be held to apply to a Corporation.
> 8. Every person who shall have subscribed the prescribed sum or upwards to the capital of the company, or shall otherwise have become entitled to a share in the company, and those whose name shall have been entered on the register of shareholders herinafter mentioned, shall be deemed a shareholder of the company.
> 9. The company shall keep a book, to be called the 'register of shareholders'; and in such book shall be fairly and distinctly entered, from time to time, the names of the several corporators, and the names and additions of the several persons entitled to shares in the company, together with the number of shares to which such [12] shareholders shall be respectively entitled. . . .

75. At the general meetings of the company every shareholder shall be entitled to vote according to the prescribed scale of voting, and where no scale shall be prescribed every shareholder shall have one vote for every share up to ten, and he shall have an additional vote for every five shares beyond the first ten shares held by him up to one hundred, and an additional vote for every ten shares held by him beyond the first one hundred shares. . . .

Counsel further submitted that similar sections in the Companies Act 1862 and later Acts had been construed as he suggested, and relied amongst other decisions upon *Pender* v. *Lushington* (1877) 6 Ch. D. 471.

The provisions of the 1845 Act like any other document must be construed as a whole. I am of the view that they are quite clear. Persons entitled to stock must be registered in the register of shareholders. Until they are, they are not entitled to vote. This is a well established principle and I would be wrong not to follow it.

I do not regard either Section 15 of the 1845 Act or the decision in *Nanney* v. *Morgan* as being contrary to this view. *Nanney* v. *Morgan* was a case in which the issue for the Court was whether a settlor of stock in a railway company held such stock under a legal or an equitable title at the date of the [13] settlement. If he had held under a legal title, a settlement would have been invalid, whereas if he had held under an equitable title it would have been good. The Court took the view that if a valid transfer had been accepted by the secretary at the date of the settlement, the settlor would have had the legal estate, but that the failure of the company to do what it had to do, i.e. register the transferee in the register of shareholders, could not have affected the transferees rights. Presumably, the Court was acting on the equitable maxim that it regards as having been done that which ought to have been done and was not prepared to permit failure by a company to determine whether the settlement was effective or ineffective.

There is nothing either in section 15 which provides that the right to vote acquired by the transferee shall be exercisable before registration of the name of the transferee in the Register of Shareholders. Having regard to the view expressed in *Nanney* v. *Morgan* and the express words of Section 15 of the Act, it may be that the true interpretation of that section is that the legal interest when completed by registration relates back to the date of receipt of a valid transfer.

Jackson v. Munster Bank Ltd.
(1884) 13 L.R.Ir. 118

The bank's articles of association provided inter alia that the directors' remuneration should be determined by the company in general meeting; and that the company should not make any advance or allow any credit to a director, or to any firm of which a director should be partner, on his or their personal guarantee or security only, or otherwise than on adequate security. Complaints were made by certain shareholders that these provisions of the articles had not been adhered to; and a report of the company's auditor as to directors' overdrafts stated that, in some instances, these were inadequately secured. A meeting of shareholders was held, at which they expressed their dissatisfaction; and on the 10th of January, 1884, a sub-committee was appointed at one of these meetings to require the directors to give full information as to advances to directors, and the securities held for same, and the directors declined. A circular was issued convening an extraordinary general meeting of the Company at which resolutions were to be proposed altering the articles of association by authorising advances to directors on their personal security, subject to certain restrictions, and by increasing the remuneration of directors, and leaving to the discretion of the directors the future remuneration of the chairman and vice-chairman, as well as the remuneration of the former for past services. Proxy forms, drawn in favour of two of the directors, accompanied the circulars.

CHATTERTON V.C.: . . . [134] I am of opinion that a misleading circular has been published convening the meeting, by which the great body of the shareholders may have been misled, and that statements are contained in it which are calculated to have the effect of obtaining proxies from the shareholders without having the information which would enable them to form a just judgment as to who are the proper persons to whom their votes should be entrusted. It is an unfortunate thing that this circular should have been issued under the hand of the person who, above all others, should not have been the party to have proposed or advocated either one or other of the two Resolutions which are the main objects of contention before me now: for beyond all doubt – and this was not disputed on the part of the Defendants – there was considerable objection made by a number of shareholders, to which the Directors in part acceded, as to the permission to the Chairman, Mr Shaw, to overdraw his account without having, as is alleged, supplied adequate security. It is, therefore, unfortunate that Mr Shaw should be the person to propose to the shareholders at large that the proxies should be signed in the name of his three nominees. But this is not the only point, though it is a material one, upon which I base my decision. Another point is this, that in reference to the special Resolution E, which it was proposed either to rescind altogether or to alter by substituting for it clause C1, there has been, in my opinion, a statement which did not call the attention of the shareholders to the real operation that would be effected by such a change. It is alleged that the opinion of Mr Benjamin had been obtained about a year ago, he having been consulted on the question of the liability of the Directors for having been parties to, or [135] privy to, or for not complaining of, breaches of trust on the part of their co-Directors in reference to advances of loans to Directors of the Bank. That might be a reason for suggesting some alteration in the special Resolution of 1866; but this falls very short of the clause which is now proposed to be substituted for that special Resolution. One alternative put forward was that this special Resolution E should be altogether rescinded. If the facts now known upon this motion could have been communicated to them, I do not think that the majority of the shareholders would have been disposed to authorise by their proxies or their votes the alteration proposed which is so manifestly contrary to their interests. That special Resolution was passed, I suppose, because the occasion for it arose so far back as 1866, and it has been in force – whether acted upon or not I do not know or inquire – from that year to the present time. The first thing proposed to be done at this Extraordinary Meeting is to do away with that special Resolution, which provides a wholesome and a very moderate check upon the Directors in reference to granting loans to one another – namely, that they should not be allowed to lend money to each other upon 'personal guarantee or security alone, or otherwise than on adequate security.' Can anyone contend that it would be for the benefit of the shareholders of the Company, or for the benefit of anyone but the Directors themselves, that that provision should be rescinded? And yet this is one of the matters contemplated by the circular of the Chairman. But when I come to consider what is to be substituted for that Resolution, I doubt whether it does not make matters worse than if the Resolution were simply rescinded. It is as follows: 'The Company shall not make any advance or allow any credit to a Director, or to any firm of which a Director is a partner, on his or their personal guarantee or security only, or otherwise, unless the Board, without a division, by an entry in their minutes, sanction such advance or credit: that the applicant for such advance or credit shall not be present upon any motion respecting the loan or advance of money, or otherwise giving credit to himself or his partner or partners.' This in point of fact would authorise the lending of money belonging to the Bank on the personal guarantee or security only of the Director seeking to [136] borrow, provided his brother Directors in his absence should come to the conclusion that he ought to have the advance. Can anyone say that this would be for the benefit of the Company, or that it would be a *bona fide* exercise of their powers by the Directors for the benefit of the shareholders? It is not for the purpose of guarding shareholders against *bona fide* acts of Directors that restraining clauses are inserted in Articles of Association; it is for the purpose of guarding them against *mala fides* on the part of the Directors, amongst whom A.B. might to-day vote a sum of money to C.D., and C.D. might next day vote a similar sum to A.B. I do not go into the question whether the passing of these Resolutions will absolve the Directors from liability for acts already done by them. The Defendants may be right in arguing that it cannot do so; but this is not the point. The question I have to consider is whether the shareholders have been fully and fairly informed and instructed upon what is to be done, and for the doing of which their proxies have now been probably obtained.

Then I come to another of the proposed Resolutions, D1, 'That the ordinary Directors shall for their services receive in future and be paid such sum as may amount to but not exceed £250 per annum for each Director, to be divided between them in such manner as they may determine: and the Directors shall and are hereby authorised to make such arrangement for the remuneration of the Chairman for his past services as they shall deem right, and pay to him such sum as shall be agreed upon,' &c. How can it be for the benefit of the Company that the Directors should be invested with unlimited authority to pay an increased and uncovenanted remuneration to the Chairman for his services rendered in the past? His past services he has rendered to the Company as its Chairman, for the remuneration he has received. But the circular in this respect is also misleading, because a clause exists – the 86th – in the Articles of Association, which is not adverted to, and in the very teeth of which this new Resolution is brought forward; that clause providing that the remuneration of Directors must be fixed by the shareholders. Without their attention, then, being called to the 86th Article, the shareholders are asked by this circular to forego this right, and to entrust it to [137] the last persons who ought to be entrusted with it. I think that the effect of the proposed Resolution has not been fairly communicated to the shareholders; and I must add that, when a Chairman of a Company thinks proper to do an unnecessary act, namely, to make a commentary on the Resolutions which the Directors are about to bring forward – as Mr Shaw has done in this circular – it should be a fair and candid commentary; and in my opinion this circular is neither fair nor candid. Under these circumstances, and for these reasons, without disputing the proposition of law, which is well established, that no dissentient minority of shareholders has a right to come into Court for the purpose of interfering with the decision of the majority in reference to matters of internal management, in the absence of fraud or proceedings *ultra vires*, a rule of law which, in my opinion, does not affect this motion, I give my decision entirely upon what I consider to be the probable effect of this circular upon the general body of the shareholders. Bearing in mind the rule as to convenience affecting interlocutory injunctions, and not offering any opinion upon any facts that hereafter may be discussed, but simply being of opinion that this circular has a misleading tendency (whether intentional or unintentional it is unnecessary to consider), and that proxies have been obtained by the nominees of the Chairman by means of it, I think that greater inconvenience would be caused if the meeting were to come to a decision under such circumstances, than if such decision were postponed – more particularly when the Directors can call another meeting at any time to consider any Resolutions they may think necessary. I do not say that these Resolutions, when fully understood and fairly considered, may not hereafter be adopted and conclusively ratified, a matter as to which I offer no opinion. I think that under the circumstances which I have stated, they ought not to be brought forward at to-morrow's meeting, as the general body of the shareholders might thereby be seriously affected.

DIVISION OF POWERS BETWEEN THE MEMBERS AND THE DIRECTORS

Automatic Self-Cleansing Filter Syndicate Co. Ltd. v. Cuninghame
[1906] 2 Ch. 34 (C.A.)

(From headnote) A company had power under its memorandum of association to sell its undertaking to another company having similar objects, and by its articles of association the general management and control of the company were vested in the directors, subject to such regulations as might from time to time be made by extraordinary resolution, and, in particular, the directors were empowered to sell or otherwise deal with any property of the company on such terms as they might think fit. At a general meeting of the company a resolution was passed by a simple majority of the shareholders for the sale of the company's assets on certain terms to a new company formed for the purpose of acquiring them, and directing the directors to carry the sale into effect. The directors, being of opinion that a sale on those terms was not for the benefit of the company, declined to carry the sale into effect.

COLLINS M.R.: [41] At a meeting of the company a resolution was passed by a majority – I was going to say a bare majority, but it was a majority – in favour of a sale to a purchaser, and the directors, honestly believing, as Warrington J. thought, that it was most undesirable in the interests of the company that the agreement should be carried into effect, refused to affix the seal of the company to it, or to assist in carrying out a resolution which they disapproved of; and the question is whether under the memorandum and articles of association here the directors are bound to accept, in substitution of their own view, the views contained in the resolution of the company. Warrington J. held that the majority could not impose that obligation upon the directors, and that on the true construction of the articles the directors were the persons [42] authorized by the articles to effect this sale, and that unless the other powers given by the memorandum were invoked by a special resolution, it was impossible for a mere majority at a meeting to override the views of the directors. That depends, as Warrington J. put it, upon the construction of the articles. First of all there is no doubt that the company under its memorandum has the power in clause 3 *(k)* to sell the undertaking of the company or any part thereof. In this case there is some small exception, I believe, to that which is to be sold, but I do not think that that becomes material. We now come to clause 81 of the articles, which I think it is important to refer to in this connection. [His Lordship read the clause.] Then come the two clauses which are most material, 96 and 97, whereby the powers of the directors are defined. [His Lordship read clause 96 and clause 97 (1).] Therefore in the matters referred to in article 97 (1) the view of the directors as to the fitness of the matter is made the standard; and furthermore, by article 96 they are given in express terms the full powers which the company has, except so far as they 'are not hereby or by statute expressly directed or required to be exercised or done by the company,' so that the directors have absolute power to do all things other than those that are expressly required to be done by the company; and then comes the limitation on their general authority – 'subject to such regulations as may from time to time be made by extraordinary resolution.' Therefore, if it is desired to alter the powers of the directors that must be done, not by a resolution carried by a majority at an ordinary meeting of the company, but by an extraordinary resolution. In these circumstances it seems to me that it is not competent for the majority of the shareholders at an ordinary meeting to affect or alter the mandate originally given to the directors, by the articles of association. It has been suggested that this is a mere question of principal and agent, and that it would be an absurd thing if a principal in appointing an agent should in effect appoint a dictator who is to manage him instead of managing the agent. I think that that analogy does not strictly apply to this case. No doubt for some purposes directors are agents. For whom are they agents? You have, no doubt, in theory and law [43] one entity, the company, which might be a principal, but you have to go behind that when you look to the particular position of directors. It is by the consensus of all the individuals in the company that these directors become agents and hold their rights as agents. It is not fair to say that a majority at a meeting is for the purposes of this case the principal so as to alter the mandate of the agent. The minority also must be taken into account. There are provisions by which the minority may be over-borne, but that can only be done by special machinery in the shape of special resolutions. Short of that the mandate which must be obeyed is not that of the majority – it is that of the whole entity made up of all the shareholders. If the mandate of the directors is to be altered, it can only be under the machinery of the memorandum and articles themselves. I do not think I need say more.

One argument used by Warrington J. strongly supports that view. He says in effect: 'There is to be found in these articles a provision that a director can only be removed by special resolution. What is the use of that provision if the views of the directors can be overridden by a mere majority at an ordinary meeting? Practically you do not want any special power to remove directors if you can do without them and differ from their opinion and compel something other than their view to be carried into effect.' That argument appears to me to confirm the view taken by the learned judge.

COZENS-HARDY L.J.: . . . [44] [I]t seems to me that the shareholders by their express contract mutually stipulated that their common affairs should be managed by certain directors to be appointed by the shareholders in the manner described by other articles, such directors being liable to be removed only by special resolution. If you once get a stipulation of that kind in a contract made between the parties, what right is there to interfere with the contract, apart, of course, from any misconduct on the part of the directors? There is no such misconduct in the present case. Is there any analogy which supports the case of the plaintiffs? I think not. It seems to me the analogy is all the other way. Take the case of an ordinary partnership. If in an ordinary partnership there is a stipulation in the partnership deed that the partnership business shall be managed by one of the partners, it would be plain that in the absence of misconduct, or in the absence of circumstances involving the total dissolution of the partnership, the majority of the partners would have no right to apply to the Court to restrain him or to interfere with the management of the partnership business. I would refer to what is said in *Lindley on Partnership*, 7th ed. p. 574: 'Where, however, the partner complained of has by agreement been constituted the active managing partner, the Court will not interfere with him unless a strong case be made out against him' – that is to say, unless there is some case of fraud or misconduct to justify the interference of the Court. Nor is this doctrine limited to [45] a case of co-partners. It is not a peculiar incident of co-partnership: it applies equally to cases of co-ownership. I think in some of the earlier cases before Lord Eldon with reference to the co-owners of one of the theatres, he laid down the principle that when the co-owners had appointed a particular member as manager the Court would not, except in the case of misconduct, interfere with him. And why? Because it is a fallacy to say that the relation is that of simple principal and agent. The person who is managing is managing for himself as well as for the others. It is not in the least a case where you have a master on the one side and a mere servant on the other. You are dealing here, as in the case of a partnership, with parties having individual rights as to which there are mutual stipulations for their common benefit, and when you once get that, it seems to me that there is no ground for saying that the mere majority can put an end to the express stipulations contained in the bargain which they have made. Still less can that be so when you find in the contract itself provisions which shew an intention that the powers conferred upon the directors can only be varied by extraordinary resolution, that is to say, by a three-fourths majority at one meeting, and that the directors themselves when appointed shall only be removed by special resolution, that is to say, by three-fourths majority at one meeting and a simple majority at a confirmatory meeting. That being so, if you once get clear of the view that the directors are mere agents of the company, I cannot see anything in principle to justify the contention that the directors are bound to comply with the votes or the resolutions of a simple majority at an ordinary meeting of the shareholders. I do not think it true to say that the directors are agents. I think it is more nearly true to say that they are in the position of managing partners appointed to fill that post by a mutual arrangement between all the shareholders. So much for principle. On principle I agree entirely with what the Master of the Rolls has said, agreeing as he does with the conclusions of Warrington J.

Barron v. Potter
[1914] 1 Ch. 895 (Ch.D.)

Potter stated that Canon Barron arrived at the office of the company with the object of attending the extraordinary general meeting called by him. Mr Potter thereupon proposed to Canon Barron that Mrs Clara Rose Potter, Miss Florence Millicent Hewitt, and Mr Frank Burnett should be appointed additional directors of the company, proposing each name separately. Canon Barron disregarded the proposals and refused to vote thereon, whereupon Mr Potter voted in favour of them and declared the persons named to be duly elected directors.

According to Canon Barron's evidence, he attended at the registered office of the company at 3 o'clock p.m. to attend the extraordinary general meeting, and as he entered the inner room where the meeting was to be held Mr Potter came after him and said, 'I propose Mrs Clara Rose Potter and (mentioning another name) as directors. Have you any amendments?' Canon Barron answered laughingly, 'Yes, I have plenty of amendments which we shall discuss.' Here Mr Potter interrupted him and said, 'Then I give my casting vote; they are elected.'

WARRINGTON J.: . . . [902] The question then arises, Was the resolution passed at the general meeting of the company a valid appointment? The argument against the validity of the appointment is that the articles of association of the company gave to the board of directors the power of appointing additional directors, that the company has accordingly surrendered the power, and that the directors alone can exercise it. It is true that the general point was so decided by Eve J. in *Blair Open Hearth Furnace Co.* v. *Reigart* (108 L.T. 665), and I am not concerned to say that in ordinary cases where there is a board ready and willing to act it would be competent for the company to override the power conferred on the directors by the articles except by way of special resolution for the purpose of altering the articles. But the case which I have to deal with is a different one. For practical purposes there is no board of directors at all. The only directors are two persons, one of whom refuses to act with the other, and the question is, What is to be done under these circumstances? On this point I think that I can usefully refer to the judgment of the Court of Appeal in *Isle of Wight Ry. Co.* v. *Tahourdin* (25 Ch. D. 320), not for the sake of the decision, which depended on the fact that it was a case under the Companies Clauses Consolidation Act, 1845, but for the sake of the observations of Cotton and Fry L.JJ. upon the effect of a deadlock such as arose in the present case. Cotton L.J. says: 'Then it is said that there is no power in the meeting of shareholders to elect new directors, for that under the 89th section the power would be in the remaining directors. The remaining directors would no doubt have that power if there was a quorum left. But suppose the meeting were to remove so many directors that a quorum was not left, what then follows? It has been argued that in that case, there being no board which could act, there would be no power of filling up the board so as to enable it to work. In my opinion that is utterly wrong. A power is given by the 89th section to the remaining directors 'if they think proper so to do' to elect persons to fill up the vacancies. I do not see how it is possible for a non-existent body to think proper [903] to fill up vacancies. In such a case a general meeting duly summoned for the purpose must have power to elect a new board so as not to let the business of the company be at a dead-lock.' Fry L.J. says this: 'Then with regard to the objection that a general meeting cannot elect directors to fill up vacancies, it appears to me that a general meeting would at any rate have that power in the event of all the directors being removed. In my judgment it is quite impossible to read the 89th section as the only section relating to the filling up of vacancies in the office of directors. That applies only where there are remaining directors, and those remaining directors think proper to exercise their power. That does not, in my judgment, deprive the general meeting of the power to elect directors, where there are no directors, or where the directors do not think fit to exercise their powers.' Those observations express a principle which seems to me to be as applicable to the case of a limited company incorporated under the Companies (Consolidation) Act, 1908, as to a case falling under the Companies Clauses Consolidation Act, 1845, and moreover to be a principle founded on plain common sense. If directors having certain powers are unable or unwilling to exercise them – are in fact a non-existent body for the purpose – there must be some power in the company to do itself that which under other circumstances would be otherwise done. The directors in the present case being unwilling to appoint additional directors under the power conferred on them by the articles, in my opinion, the company in general meeting has power to make the appointment. The company has passed a resolution for that purpose, and though a poll has been demanded no date or place has yet been fixed for taking it. The result therefore is that I must grant an injunction on the motion in Canon Barron's action and refuse the motion in Mr Potter's action.

CONSTITUTIONAL CHANGES: ALTERING THE MEMORANDUM AND ARTICLES OF ASSOCIATION

Allen v. Gold Reefs of West Africa Ltd.
[1900] 1 Ch. 656 (C.A.)

The company passed a special resolution to the effect that its articles of association shall be amended by giving the company a lien over the shares in the company held by any member who was indebted to the company. A Mr Z. was then indebted to the company, and became bankrupt; and it was anticipated that the company would reimburse itself through the lien that the altered articles of association would give it over Z's shares.

LINDLEY M.R.: [669] This is an appeal [which] raises several questions of great general interest relating to the power of limited companies to alter their articles, and especially to their power to alter their articles so as to affect shares standing in the names of deceased shareholders, and to the effect of an alteration duly made on vendors' fully paid-up shares issued before the alteration is made. . . . [670]

The facts above stated raise the following very important questions, namely, (1.) Whether a limited company, registered [671] with articles conferring no lien on its fully paid-up shares, can by special resolution alter those articles by imposing a lien on such shares? (2.) Whether, if it can, the lien so imposed can be made to apply to debts owing by fully paid-up shareholders to the company at the time of the alteration of the articles? (3.) Whether, if it can, fully paid-up shares allotted to vendors of property to the company are in any different position from other fully paid-up shares issued by the company? (4.) Whether, assuming the altered articles to be valid and to be binding on the general body of the holders of fully paid-up shares in the company, there are any special circumstances in this particular case to exclude the fully paid-up shares held by Zuccani from the operation of the altered articles?

The articles of a company prescribe the regulations binding on its members: Companies Act, 1862, s. 14. They have the effect of a contract (see s. 16); but the exact nature of this contract is even now very difficult to define. Be its nature what it may, the company is empowered by the statute to alter the regulations contained in its articles from time to time by special resolutions (ss. 50 and 51); and any regulation or article purporting to deprive the company of this power is invalid on the ground that it is contrary to the statute: *Walker* v. *London Tramways Co.* [1893] 2 Ch. 311.

The power thus conferred on companies to alter the regulations contained in their articles is limited only by the provisions contained in the statute and the conditions contained in the company's memorandum of association. Wide, however, as the language of s. 50 is, the power conferred by it must, like all other powers, be exercised subject to those general principles of law and equity which are applicable to all powers conferred on majorities and enabling them to bind minorities. It must be exercised, not only in the manner required by law, but also bona fide for the benefit of the company as a whole, and it must not be exceeded. These conditions are always implied, and are seldom, if ever, expressed. But if they are complied with I can discover no ground for judically putting any other restrictions on the power conferred by the section than those [672] contained in it. How shares shall be transferred, and whether the company shall have any lien on them, are clearly matters of regulation properly prescribed by a company's articles of association. This is shewn by Table A in the schedule to the Companies Act, 1862, clauses 8, 9, 10. Speaking, therefore, generally, and without reference to any particular case, the section clearly authorizes a limited company, formed with articles which confer no lien on fully paid-up shares, and which allow them to be transferred without any fetter, to alter those articles by special resolution, and to impose a lien and restrictions on the registry of transfers of those shares by members indebted to the company.

But then comes the question whether this can be done so as to impose a lien or restriction in respect of a debt contracted before and existing at the time when the articles are altered. Again, speaking generally, I am of opinion that the articles can be so altered, and that, if they are altered bona fide for the benefit of the company, they will be valid and binding as altered on the existing holders of paid-up shares, whether such holders are indebted or not indebted to the company when the alteration is made. [673]

It was urged that a company's articles could not be altered retrospectively, and reliance was placed on Rigby L.J.'s observations in *James* v. *Buena Ventura Nitrate Grounds Syndicate* [1896] 1 Ch. 466. The word 'retrospective' is, however, somewhat ambiguous, and the concurrence of Rigby L.J. in *Andrews* v. *Gas Meter Co.* [1897] 1 Ch. 361 shews that his observations in *James* v. *Buena Ventura Nitrate Grounds Syndicate* are no authority for saying that existing rights, founded and dependent on alterable articles, cannot be affected by their alteration. Such rights are in truth limited as to their duration by the duration of the articles which confer them.

V. Management and the Directors

By law, every company must have directors and a secretary, and various duties regarding the company's affairs are imposed on these officers. In a typical company, there will be a board of directors comprising a managing director, some salaried executive directors who work full time for the company, and some non-executive directors who have significant business interests elsewhere as well. Especially in large companies, various managerial functions will be assigned to management committees. Occasionally, companies delegate the running of their business to outsiders through what are known as management contracts. Ordinarily, it is the shareholders who select the directors; and directors can be removed by a simple majority vote of the shareholders. Directors must not be negligent in exercising their functions, and they owe their company extensive fiduciary duties. The Companies Acts have established an elaborate set of rules governing directors' remuneration and the disclosure of information about directors' affairs to the shareholders and to the general public.

THE SYSTEM OF MANAGEMENT

Barron v. Potter
[1914] 1 Ch. 895 (Ch.D.)

Mr Potter's evidence was that owing to the refusal of Barron to attend any board meeting the position of the affairs of the company was becoming so serious that he was advised in the interests of the company to meet Barron wherever he could be found and to use his casting vote as chairman in case Barron should refuse to agree to the appointment of additional directors. Accordingly on February 23 he met the train at Paddington by which he expected Barron to arrive, and seeing him alight from it walked by his side along the platform and said to him, 'I want to see you, please.' Barron replied, 'I have nothing to say to you.' Mr Potter then said, 'I formally propose that we add the Reverend Charles Herbert, Mr William George Walter Barnard, and Mr John Tolehurst Musgrave as additional directors to the board of the British Seagumite Company, Limited. Do you agree or object?' Barron replied, 'I object and I object to say anything to you at all.' Mr Potter then said, 'In my capacity as chairman I give my casting vote in their favour and declare them duly elected.' He continued to walk with Barron a few steps and then said, 'That is all I want to say; thank you. Good day.'

WARRINGTON J.: ... [900] The question is whether certain additional directors appointed at a general meeting of the company were validly appointed or whether certain additional directors were validy appointed at a directors' meeting, in which case the resolution of the company in general meeting would be invalid. ... [901] What then took place is said to have been a directors' meeting at which a valid appointment was made of the three additional directors proposed by Mr Potter. The answer, in my opinion, is that there was no directors' meeting at all for the reason that Canon Barron to the knowledge of Mr Potter insisted all along that he would not attend any directors' meeting with Mr Potter or discuss the affairs of the company with him, and it is not enough that one of two directors should say 'This is a directors' meeting' while the other says it is not. Of course if directors are willing to hold a meeting they may do so under any circumstances, but one of them cannot be made to attend the board or to convert a casual meeting into a board meeting, and in the present case I do not see how the meeting in question can be treated as a board meeting. In my opinion therefore the true conclusion is that there was no board meeting, but that Canon Barron came with the deliberate intention of not attending a board meeting. If he had received the notice sent to him by Mr Potter summoning him to a board meeting different considerations might have arisen, but he had not received it and came with the fixed intention of not attending any such meeting. There was therefore no board meeting at which Canon Barron was present. Mr Potter was alone present, so that there was no quorum, and I must hold that the three additional directors named by him were not validly appointed.

Clark v. Workman
[1920] 1 I.R. 107

This dispute concerned the take-over of a company (see post p. 359). At a general meeting of the company held in March 1881, the following resolution was passed: 'That Mr John Workman and Mr Charles Workman be re-elected directors for the ensuing year, and Mr Frank Workman be elected chairman.' From that time on, Mr Frank Workman acted as chairman without objection on the part of the other directors.

ROSS J.: ... [114] The first question that arises is whether Mr Frank Workman [is] lawfully chairman of. . . the directors. . . . The articles dealing with this matter are 91, 92, and 93. Article 91 provides that questions arising at any meeting of directors shall be decided by a majority of votes of those present, and in case of an equality of votes the chairman of the

meeting shall have a casting vote. Article 92 provides that the directors
may appoint a chairman and vice-chairman of their meetings, and determine the period for which he or they shall hold office. There you have
the precise contract with the shareholders, and it is [115] essential that
the chairman should be elected by the machinery provided by that contract,
and in no other way. The power of electing a chairman having a casting
vote is of vital importance. The power having been delegated by the company to the directors, cannot be controlled or affected by the company,
unless the contract is altered by a special resolution, but no such special
resolution was passed. Article 93 provides that all meetings shall be pres-
ided over by the chairman of the directors (if any) if present. This article
contemplates the possibility of the elected chairman's death or the expiration of his period of office as fixed by Article 92. In that case the directors
are to choose one of their number to preside.

The defendant, Mr Frank Workman, was never appointed by the
directors as chairman of their meetings. The defendants say that the resolution passed at the general meeting of shareholders held on the 21st March,
1881, was sufficient. . . . This is claimed to have the effect of conferring
on Mr Frank Workman the chairmanship, not for the ensuing year only,
but for life or until removal.

But the election of a chairman of directors is not the function of a general
meeting. It can elect directors, but not the chairman of the directors. The
minute does not state who attended. It is thirty-eight years ago since the
meeting was held. But even assuming that nobody attended, it is not a
meeting of directors. It is a general meeting, and all attended as shareholders, and in no other capacity.

Morris v. Kanssen
[1946] A.C. 459 (H.L.)

(From headnote) On February 1, 1940, C. and K. were the only directors
and the only shareholders in a company, holding one share each. C. and
one S. falsely claimed that at a meeting held on that date S. was duly
appointed a director and a minute was concocted to record the alleged
appointment. On April 9, C. and S. requested K. to resign his office and
on April 12, they purported to hold a meeting of directors and to issue
one share to S. and seven more shares to C. On April 26, 1940, an extraordinary general meeting of the company was held at which C., K. and S.
were present; C. moved and S. purported to second a resolution to confirm
the appointment of S. as a director. C. voted in favour of the resolution
and K. against it and S. having purported to vote in favour of it, it was
treated as carried, so that S. thereafter purported to act as a director. In
March, 1942, C. and S. purported to hold a meeting of directors and
thereat to appoint one M. a director; all three then purported to allot

thirty-four shares to M.; thirty-two more shares to S., and twenty-four more shares to C. Subsequently S. transferred seventeen of his shares to M.

LORD SIMMONDS: . . . [470] Section 143 of the Companies Act, 1929, which is in the same terms as corresponding sections in previous Acts, provides that: 'The acts of a director or manager shall be valid notwithstanding any defect that may afterwards be discovered in his appointment or qualification.' (see s. 178 of the 1963 Act). Article 88 of Table A (Article 108 of 1963 Act's Table A), which does not materially differ from similar articles in earlier Tables, provides that 'All acts done by any meeting of the directors or of a committee of directors, or by any person acting as a director, shall notwithstanding that it be afterwards discovered that there was some defect in the appoinment of any such director or person acting as aforesaid, or that they or any of them were disqualified, be as valid as if every such person had been duly appointed and was qualified to be a director.' The section can be invoked only where there is a defect afterwards discovered in the appointment or qualification of a director; in the article the condition is that it is afterwards discovered that there was some defect in the appointment of a director or person acting as a director or that he was disqualified to act as a director. Though the language of the section differs in some respects from that of the article, it does not appear that the difference is material for the purpose of the present case.

The facts relevant to the question now under consideration have already been stated. I will very briefly tabulate them:(1.) On February 1, 1940, Cromie and Kanssen were the only directors and the only shareholders holding one share each. (2.) On or about that date the fraudulent assumption of office by Strelitz and a minute concocted to record an appointment which did not take place. (3.) On April 9, 1940, an ineffective attempt to expel Kanssen from his office. (4.) On April 12, [471] 1940, the ineffective allotment of one share to Strelitz and seven shares to Cromie at a purported meeting of directors. (5.) On April 26, 1940, an extraordinary general meeting of the company at which as I have pointed out nothing was effectively done. (6.) At the end of 1941 the determination of the term of office of Cromie and Kanssen and of Strelitz, if he was a director, and from that date no directors of the company.

It is in these circumstances that the question arises whether the section or article can be called in aid by Morris in order to validate the transactions of March 30, 1942, namely, the allotment to him of shares or the appointment of him as a director. Do the facts that I have stated establish a defect in the appointment or qualification of Cromie or Strelitz? There is, as it appears to me, a vital distinction between *(a.)* an appointment in which there is a defect or, in other words, a defective appointment, and *(b.)* no appointment at all. In the first case it is implied that some act is done which purports to be an appointment but is by reason of some defect inadequate for the purpose; in the second case there is not a defect, there is no act at all. The section does not say that the acts of a person acting as director shall be valid notwithstanding that it is afterwards discovered that he was not appointed a director. Even if it did, it might well be contended that at least a purported appointment was postulated. But it does not do so, and it would, I think, be doing violence to plain language to construe the section as covering a case in which there has been no genuine attempt to appoint at all. These observations apply equally where the term of office of a director has expired, but he nevertheless continues to act as a director, and where the office has been from the outset usurped without the colour of authority. Cromie's acts after the end of 1941 were not validated by the section: Strelitz's acts were at no time validated. I have so far dealt with defect in 'appointment' and what I have said in regard to the section covers the article also where the same words are repeated. Some argument was founded by counsel for the appellant upon the words in the section 'or qualification' and in the article 'disqualified'. This argument is not easy to follow. So far as both Cromie and Strelitz were concerned, there was no defect in their qualification after the end of 1941. They were not disqualified. They were, so far as I know, qualified to act, but they had not been appointed. [472] I do not suggest that qualification refers only to the holding of qualification shares. But whatever extended meaning may be given to 'qualification' or 'disqualified' I find it impossible to say that it covers the case of Cromie or of Strelitz. The point may be summed up by saying that the section and the article, being designed as machinery to avoid questions being raised as to the validity of transactions where there has been a slip in the appointment of a director, cannot be utilized for the purpose of ignoring or overriding the substantive provisions relating to such appointment.

DIRECTORS' STATUS AND RIGHTS

Re Dairy Lee Ltd., Stakelum v. Canning
[1976] I.R. 314 (H.Ct.)

Dairy Lee Ltd. was unable to pay its debts and passed a resolution for voluntary winding-up. The applicant was the liquidator and brought proceedings for a decision by the Court as to whether the respondent's claim for accrued holiday remuneration should be treated as a debt ranking in priority under s. 285 of the Companies Act, 1963.

The respondent, who held 3,000 shares of £1 each in the company which had an issued capital of £6,452, was a director of the company. He worked full time for it and was responsible for the day-to-day running of the business though he was not the managing director. He was paid £225 a month by the company but there are no entries in the minute book to show whether these payments were salary or director's fees. The respondent, who did not have any service agreement with the company, regarded the payments as salary. His employment was terminated by the applicant, and he claimed accrued holiday remuneration.

KENNY J.: . . . [316] A director holds his office under the articles of association of the company and so, as a director, is not an employee or a clerk or servant of the company. Article 85 of the articles in Table 'A', which applies to this company, permits him to hold any other office or place of profit under the company in conjunction with his office of director for such period and on such terms as to remuneration and otherwise as the directors may determine. The result is that a director may be employed by the company not as a director but as a salaried employee.

When a person who is a director claims priority under s. 285 of the Act of 1963, the relevant questions are whether he was a director only or a director and a salaried employee. When deciding this, it is relevant to consider whether the moneys received by him were paid as director's fees or as salary. If he was a director and a salaried employee, he is entitled to priority under s. 285 for salary and accrued holiday remuneration. When a person who is a director but is not a managing director is working whole-time with the company, the inference that he was a director and a salaried employee seems to me to be justified unless there is evidence that he was a whole-time director only and was paid as such.

It is impossible to reconcile all the decided cases but the view which I have expressed is supported by the modern authorities. Some of the confusion arises from the fact that in the 19th century the concept of an executive or whole-time director (other than a managing director) was almost unknown, and the earlier cases were dealing with the question whether a part-time director was a clerk or a servant. In *Hutton* v. *West Cork Railway Co.* (1883) 23 Ch.D. 654, Bowen L.J. said that a director is not a servant of the company but a person who is doing business for the company but not on ordinary terms. In *Re Newspaper Proprietary Syndicate Ltd.* [1900] 2 Ch. 349, Cozens-Hardy J. held that a managing director was not a clerk or servant of the company although he had entered into an agreement with it by which he was appointed managing director for three years at a salary. The judge said that a managing director is only *(sic)* an ordinary director entrusted with some special powers, and that it was not relevant that he was entitled to remuneration by virtue of a special bargain or that his remuneration was [317] described as salary. This reasoning cannot be reconciled with that in the later, and more authoritative, decision of the Inner House of the Court of Session and the case should now be regarded as having been wrongly decided. In *Normandy* v. *Ind. Coope and Co. Ltd.* [1908] 1 Ch. 84, Kekewich J. said that a managing or other director is not a person in the employment of the company.

In *Re Beeton & Co. Ltd.* [1913] 2 Ch. 279, the articles of association of a company provided that no director should be disqualified by his office from contracting with, or being employed by, the company, and that a director might hold any other office or place of profit under the company in conjunction with his office as director. The minutes of the board of directors showed that one of the directors was to do other work for the company. Mr Justice Neville said that there was a special contract outside the office of director under which the claimant had to perform duties and that, although *qua* director she had no valid claim to preferential payment, yet in her other capacity as a servant of the company she was entitled to it. This decision seems to me to have been correct and to recognise the difference between moneys due to a person as director and sums due to an employee who is a director. In *Re Lee, Behrens & Co. Ltd.* [1932] 2 Ch. 46, Eve J. said that a director is not a servant of the company, but this decision was subsequently dissented from by Lord Normand.

In *Anderson* v. *James Sutherland (Peterhead) Ltd.* (1941) S.C. 203, the articles of association provided that, whenever any member of the company who was employed by the company in any capacity was dismissed for misconduct, the directors might resolve that such person should cease to be a member of the company and should be deemed to have served the other members with an offer of his shares. The managing director, who held shares in the capital of the company, was removed from his post as managing director and, when the directors decided to acquire his shares, he resisted the claim because, he said, he was not employed by the company. The members of the Inner House rejected this argument. The Lord President (Lord Normand) said that while he accepted the view that a director as such is not the servant or employee of the company, he might occupy an employment subordinate to that of director and in that capacity have different functions from a director. He added that a managing director has two functions and two capacities. *Qua* managing director, he is a party to a contract with the company which is a contract of employment and of service. There is nothing anomalous in this because, as Lord Normand said: 'it is a [318] common place of our law that the same individual may have two or more capacities each including special rights and duties in relation to the same thing or matter or in relation to the same persons.'

A striking illustration of this distinction is given by the advice of the Privy Council in *Lee* v. *Lee Air Farming Ltd.* [1961] A.C. 12. Mr Lee, who was a pilot, was governing director of the company. As governing director he gave an instruction to himself to act as pilot. He was killed while flying and his widow claimed that he was a worker and was employed by the company. The Privy Council held that a person who is a governing director of a company may have a contract of service with it, not as governing director, but as an employee.

In this case the only reasonable inference is that the respondent was a director and a salaried employee, and that the money he received was salary and not director's fees. He was therefore an employee and servant of the company and I will declare that he is entitled to priority under s. 285, sub-s. 2(d), of the Companies Act, 1963, in respect of his claim in the winding up for accrued holiday remuneration.

<h3 style="text-align:center">Bushell v. Faith
[1970] A.C. 1099 (H.L.)</h3>

See ante p. 76.

<h3 style="text-align:center">Carvill v. Irish Industrial Bank Ltd.
[1968] I.R. 325 (S.Ct.)</h3>

(From headnote) The plaintiff had been a director of the defendant company. The articles of association of the company provided that the company could remove a director before the expiration of his term of office, that the directors of the company could appoint a director to be the managing director for a fixed term or indefinitely, that the provisions of the articles relating to the removal of directors should apply to a managing director 'subject to the provision of any contract between him and the company', and that a managing director would cease to hold that office upon ceasing to hold the office of director. The plaintiff was not appointed to be managing director of the company, but he had acted as such and he had been remunerated and treated by the company as its managing director.

While acting as managing director, the plaintiff bought a new carpet for his own house and at the same time he instructed the suppliers to take an old carpet from the house, to alter the old carpet and to re-lay it in the company's premises. The total cost of these transactions was £129 15s, of which £90 15s was apportioned by the plaintiff as a debt due by the company to the suppliers. The company paid that sum to the suppliers without having been informed of the plaintiff's interest in the matter. Later the company duly resolved that the plaintiff be removed from the office of director, without being aware of any misconduct by the plaintiff and without giving the plaintiff any notice of his removal.

The plaintiff sued the defendant company in the High Court and claimed damages, amounting to 12 months salary, for wrongful dismissal. At the hearing of the action in the High Court the plaintiff conceded that the defendant company could justify the dismissal by proof of sufficient misconduct by the plaintiff prior to the dismissal, while the defendant company conceded that (if any notice were required) twelve months notice of dismissal was reasonable, and the company justified the dismissal on the ground of the plaintiff's conduct in the carpet transaction.

Held by Kenny J., in dismissing the plaintiff's claim, that the defendant

company had been entitled to terminate the plaintiff's contract of employment as a salaried employee, who was called the managing director, without
giving the plaintiff 12 months notice of such termination, which otherwise
would have been necessary. The plaintiff appealed.

O'KEEFFE J.: . . . [339] [T]he plaintiff alleged that he was managing director
of the company, and this was not denied by the defendants. Mr. Justice
Kenny held that the plaintiff was not the managing director of the company,
but that he was a director and also a salaried employee of the company.
At the trial the defendants had applied for leave to amend their defence
by inserting, at the beginning of para 5 of the defence, the following plea:
'The defendant admits that the plaintiff was employed as managing director
but denies that he was so employed from year to year or for any fixed or
definite term and further denies that such employment was at the salary
and emoluments mentioned in the statement of claim. The defendant
further denies that the plaintiff was employed under any contract, express
or implied. If (which is denied) the plaintiff was employed under any
contract, it was not an implied term or condition of the said contract or
employment that the said employment of the plaintiff should be determinable by the defendant company only by reasonable notice to the plaintiff
or that the plaintiff [340] should be entitled to continue in such employment
until the expiration of such notice.' Leave to make this amendment was
refused, and from this refusal the defendants have appealed in their cross-
appeal. It appears to me that this amendment was necessary to enable the
real dispute between the parties to be decided, and that it should have
been allowed although, for the reasons which I set out hereafter, the
amendment may not materially affect the result of the proceedings.

The finding of Mr Justice Kenny, that the plaintiff was not managing
director of the company, appears to me to be neither in accord with the
pleadings nor in accord with the facts as adduced in evidence. The reasons
for this view are as follows.

Article 106 of the articles of association of the company provided that
the directors may from time to time appoint one or more of their body to
be managing director or managing directors, or to discharge any technical,
advisory or other special duties (such persons to be called 'Special
Directors'), and either for a fixed term or without any limitation as to the
period for which he or they is or are to hold any such office and may from
time to time remove or dismiss him or them from office and appoint another
or others in his or their place or places. Article 107 provides as follows :
'A Special Director shall not, while he continues to hold that office, be
subject to retirement by rotation and he shall not be taken into account in
determining the rotation by retirement of directors, but he shall (subject
to the provisions of any contract between him and the company) be subject
to the same provisions as to resignation and removal as the other directors

of the company, and if he cease to hold the office of director from any cause he shall *ipso facto,* and immediately, cease to be a Special Director.'

There is no evidence of a formal appointment of the plaintiff as managing director by resolution of the board, but there was evidence that he had acted as such and had described himself and had been described by the defendants as such, and had received remuneration from the defendants appropriate to the position of managing director. The resolutions put in evidence fixing the remuneration of the plaintiff did not in terms describe him as managing director, but a resolution of the board passed on 6th July, 1961, purported to remove him from office as managing director and to appoint a new managing director in his stead. I take the view that, if there is compelling evidence of a consensus of opinion among the directors, a formal resolution need not be proved in order to justify a finding in accordance with that consensus of opinion. In the present case, I consider that it is clearly established by the evidence that the plaintiff was regarded by his co-directors as appointed to the office of managing [341] director, and that he should be held to be validly appointed to that office, even though no formal resolution appointing him appears among the minutes of the meetings of the board of directors. Not only is this in accordance with the facts, but it is, I think, the case which both the plaintiff and the defendants wished to make on their respective pleadings.

The real dispute between the plaintiff and the defendants is not as to whether the plaintiff was a managing director, but as to the terms upon which he held that office. The plaintiff alleges that one of the terms of his appointment as such was that he should not be removed from office save on notice of not less than twelve months duration, while the defendants allege that the plaintiff could be removed from office at any time. Each party in turn relies upon Article 107 of the articles of association. The plaintiff says that the provisions in that Article were expressed to be subject to his contract with the company, and that that contract required notice of not less than twelve months to determine it. The defendants say that there was no contract or, alternatively, that there was no contract which required any notice; and they say that, on his ceasing to be a director, the plaintiff automatically ceased to hold his position as managing director.

Reference was made to a number of authorities. On the one hand reliance was placed on such cases as *Nelson* v. *James Nelson and Sons Ltd.* [1914] 2 K.B. 770, *Southern Foundries (1926) Ltd.* v. *Shirlaw* [1940] A.C. 701, and *Shindler* v. *Northern Raincoat Co. Ltd.* [1960] 1 W.L.R. 1038, (post p. 117) where it was held that a company which had appointed a managing director for a fixed term could not, without being liable for damages for breach of contract, put an end to his employment as managing director during that term, even by altering its articles of association. On the other hand reference was made to *Read* v. *Astoria Garage (Streatham) Ltd.* [1952] Ch. 637 in which the plaintiff had been appointed managing director at a salary of £7 per week, which salary was later increased. He continued in office for many years, but finally it was resolved by the directors that his employment be terminated, and he was given a month's notice. His salary was paid for approximately four months. He brought an action for wrongful dismissal on the ground that he had not been given reasonable notice. Article 68 of Table 'A' to the Companies Act, 1929, applied to the company. That Article provided: 'The directors may from time to time appoint one or more of their body to the office of managing director or manager for such term and at such remuneration [342] (whether by way of salary, or commission, or participation in profits, or partly in one way and partly in another) as they may think fit, and a director so appointed shall not, while holding that office, be subject to retirement by rotation, or taken into account in determining the rotation or retirement of directors; but his appointment shall be subject to determination *ipso facto* if he ceases from any cause to be a director, or if the company in general meeting resolve that his tenure of the office of managing director or manager be determined.' Harman J. held that, on an article of association in that form, it was not open to the directors to appoint a managing director on terms which would deprive the company of its power to revoke the appointment *ipso facto* by removing the director from his office. This decision was upheld by the Court of Appeal, which distinguished the *Southern Foundries Case* on two grounds, first, that in that case there was a contract of service between the company and the managing director *dehors* the articles of association and, secondly, the contract was sought to be determined by a power which was not present in the articles of association of the company as they stood at the date of the contract, but which had been inserted in the articles by subsequent alteration.

In *Shindler's Case*, Diplock J. (as he then was) regarded himself bound by the decision in the *Southern Foundries Case* and considered that Harman J. had arrived at a decision which could not be reconciled with that earlier decision. In the present case it is not necessary to decide whether Diplock J., was correct in this. The articles which was construed in *Read* v. *Astoria Garage (Streatham) Ltd.* did not contain the important phrase 'subject to the provisions of any contract between him and the company' which appear in Article 107 of the articles of association of the defendant company, and these words make an important difference. Once these words appear, it is open to the directors to enter into a contract with the managing director the effect of which may be to deprive the company in general meeting of the power to remove him from office without being liable to pay damages. The question is whether there is such a contract in the present case.

It appears to me that a person who is a director, and who is appointed by the board of directors to the office of managing director, must be deemed to hold that office under some contract, either express or implied. The contract may be for a fixed term, in which case it cannot properly be terminated before the expiration of that term without a liability [343] to pay damages. It may be for no fixed term and, indeed, may be for so long only as the person holds office as director, in which case, if the person concerned ceases to be a director, his office as managing director also comes to an end. An express contract might well provide that the office could be held without limitation as to term, but with a provision for notice to determine it, and in that case there would be implied a term that, until the proper notice had been given, the person concerned would not be removed from the position of director so as to bring his appointment as managing director to an end.

What were the terms of the plaintiff's contract in the present case? He must be considered to have been appointed shortly after the formation of the company. The first record we have of his remuneration being fixed is in the minutes of the meeting of directors held on the 27th April, 1955, when it was resolved that the plaintiff's salary be fixed at £1,750 p.a. for the period of one year from the 1st October, 1954, such amount to be payable monthly. On the 18th May, 1956, the board approved the plaintiff's salary at £2,000 for the year ensuing as from the 1st October, 1955. The last resolution recorded in the minutes and relating to his salary was passed on the 21st March, 1957, and is as follows: 'That the salary of Mr Michael Carvill be fixed as £2,000 per annum payable monthly for the year ensuing as from 1st November, 1956, plus a commission of 2% on the net profits of the Company as shown in the audited Accounts before any provision is made for Income Tax or Company Tax but after charging the said salary and commission.' There is no record of any decision to continue the plaintiff's salary at this rate after the end of the year to which this entry refers, viz. from the 1st November, 1957, but the plaintiff continued to receive a salary of £2,000 p.a. and no attempt has been made to suggest he was not entitled to this. I think it fair to regard the salary as continued by consensus of the board of directors without any formal resolution to that effect. The plaintiff says that towards the end of 1959 he had a conversation in Nottingham with Mr Stanley Keywood, another director, when the plaintiff was told that he should receive a further £500 p.a. (though not apparently in addition to 2% of the profits), and he says that as from that time he was paid his salary of £2,000 p.a. monthly and that he drew against the additional £500 from time to time. I do not regard this increase as shown to have been arrived at by any consensus of the directors, and I think that this salary must, on the evidence as it stands, be regarded as remaining at £2,000 p.a., with a percentage of profits.

[344] I then find a situation in which the plaintiff is appointed managing director and his salary if fixed on a yearly basis and, while the figure is altered by increasing it first to £2,000 and then to £2,000 with a percentage of profits, it remains fixed on a yearly basis. I think that the plaintiff must be regarded as employed under a contract from year to year as managing

director, and that it must be implied also that such contract could not be determined without such notice as is appropriate to an engagement of the kind mentioned. The trial judge considered that a year's notice (or salary in lieu of notice) was appropriate, and the defendants have not submitted that such length of notice was excessive, although they have contended that no notice at all was required. In the circumstances I see no reason for disturbing the finding of the trial judge that the appropriate period of notice was a year, although I might not myself have fixed so long a period. I think, however, that the salary payable during the period of notice would be £2,000 p.a., not £2,500 p.a. If the plaintiff is entitled to damages this is the figure which I would award.

The plaintiff was dismissed summarily, and no reason was assigned at the time. The defendants subsequently sought to justify the dismissal on the ground that the plaintiff misconducted himself in his employment before his removal and that he was discharged because of this. Particulars of the misconduct were sought, and they were furnished by letters dated the 28th October, 1963, and the 21st January, 1964. The particulars of misconduct were given as follows: '4. The defendants maintain that the plaintiff's management of the affairs of the Company was incompetent and in particular the following matters appeared to the Board to be extremely unsatisfactory. . . .' There followed particulars of twelve matters which the defendants wished to question. These matters were dealt with at the trial and the trial judge found, in respect of all except one, that they would not justify the plaintiff's summary dismissal. He found against the plaintiff on that one, and because of this he held that the plaintiff was lawfully dismissed summarily, and did not award him any damages for wrongful dismissal.

The plaintiff has appealed against the finding of the trial judge on the last-mentioned item, and the defendants cross-appealed against the findings of the trial judge in relation to the other eleven items. At the hearing of the appeal the defendants confined their submissions to five of the twelve items.

As I have already said, no reason for the plaintiff's summary dismissal was assigned at the time, but the defendants sought to justify the dismissal on the grounds of 'misconduct' and gave particulars of this alleged misconduct, [345] and gave evidence in support of their plea. There was no evidence that at the time of the dismissal any of the matters complained of subsequently were within the knowledge of the defendants, but the defendants relied upon the statement of the law contained in text books to the effect that it is not necessary that a master, dismissing a servant for good cause, should state the ground for such dismissal; and that provided good ground existed in fact, it is immaterial whether or not it was known to the employer at the time of the dismissal. Counsel for the plaintiff submitted that this statement of the law was erroneous, and this point was fully argued by both sides. The plaintiff's counsel submitted that, while a master need not assign any ground for the summary dismissal of a servant, he could not later justify the dismissal on a ground which was not within his knowledge at the time of the dismissal. Support for this view is to be found in the judgment of Parke B. in *Cussons v. Skinner* (11 M. & W. 161) at p. 172 of the report where he says: '. . . it would be necessary for the defendants, who justify the discharge, to shew that at the time the discharge took place in January, 1841, they knew at least of this act of misconduct.' Support for the proposition relied upon by the defendants, and stated in the text books, is to be found in a number of cases but particularly in the judgment of Cotton L.J. in *Boston Deep Sea Fishing & Ice Co.* v. *Ansell* 39 Ch.D. 339. The Court was referred to the statement of the law in Smith on Master and Servant and it appears that, in the first and second editions, the author considered that a master could not rely on an act of misconduct to justify a dismissal unless he at least knew of the act at the time of dismissal; but that in the third edition (published in 1870) and in later editions of the work the author considered that a master might rely on an act of misconduct to justify a dismissal even if he did not know of it at the time of the dismissal.

In principle it is difficult to understand how an act can be relied upon to justify a dismissal unless it is known at the time of the dismissal. It must be conceded that there can be some breaches of contract so fundamental as to show that the contract is entirely repudiated by the party committing them, and that such an act might be relied upon in an action for wrongful dismissal, not as justifying the dismissal, but as supporting a plea that the dismissed servant had himself put an end to the contract. Where the act is not of so fundamental a character but would warrant the dismissal of the servant at the option of the employer, it appears to me to be quite illogical to say that an employer may be heard to [346] say that he dismissed his servant on a ground unknown to him at the actual time of dismissal. This is the reasoning of Lord Abinger C.B. in *Cussons v. Skinner* at page 168 of the report where he says: 'This plea alleges disobedience to be the cause of the plaintiff's discharge. What act of disobedience is shewn in this case, excepting the act alleged, which is said to be proved by the plaintiff's own letter? But it is admitted by the counsel on both sides, that the defendants never discovered that act till after they discharged him. How, then, can they urge that that was the cause of his discharge? It is agreed that the plea could only be sustained by evidence that that was the cause of his discharge. If the defendants knew it before, and passed it over, and allowed the plaintiff to remain to the 1st of August, he would still be entitled to all his wages up to that time. If the defendants did not know it, it clearly was not the cause of his discharge.' I should mention that in *Boland* v. *Dublin Corporation* [1946] I.R. 88, where the question of wrongful dismissal was discussed incidentally in the Supreme Court, the case of *Cussons* v. *Skinner* appears not to have been mentioned in the course of the argument.

In my opinion, therefore, an employer cannot, as a defence to an action for wrongful dismissal, rely on an act of misconduct on the part of his servant, which was unknown to him at the time of the dismissal, unless the act is of so fundamental a character as to show a repudiation of the contract of employment by the servant. This does not mean that the employer is without rights in respect of the misconduct. He can, in my view, rely on it as a ground for reduction of damages, and in a proper case the result may be to reduce the damages to the point of extinction.

[His Lordship referred to four of the five allegations of misconduct upon which the defendants relied in support of their cross-appeal and, having expressed his agreement with the findings of Kenny J. with regard to those four allegations, continued as follows:]

I now come to the carpet transaction. I have to examine this transaction in some detail, though I need not repeat all the facts. Counsel for the plaintiff have relied strongly on the fact that fraud or dishonesty on the part of the plaintiff was not pleaded and in my opinion this is so, if one is to have regard to the nature of the fraud or dishonesty which the evidence was tendered to establish. When particulars in relation to this matter were furnished they were as follows: 'In April, 1961, a carpet was supplied to the plaintiff's house by Messrs. Strahan & Co. together with an [347] underfelt and an old carpet from the plaintiff's house was fitted in the defendant's premises at a total cost of £129 15s. 0d. Part of this sum (£90) was charged to the defendants. This was done without the knowledge or consent of the board of the defendant company.' The complaint made is apparently that the plaintiff did not disclose his financial interest in the transaction. No complaint is made in the particulars that what the defendants obtained was worth less than the £90 paid for it. The failure to disclose his interest to his co-directors was a rather trivial matter, and would not warrant his dismissal, but at the trial the defendants put forward a case in excess of that covered by the particulars, and alleged in effect that the company had been defrauded by charging it with an amount greatly in excess of the value of the second-hand carpet. I do not think that this should have been permitted. If fraud is to be relied on, it must always be clearly pleaded and clearly established. Here it was not, in my view, pleaded at all. Furthermore, the evidence to establish it was unsatisfactory. The carpet was fitted early in 1961. Mr Gillespie, of Strahan & Co., had looked at it for the purpose of the case sometime between the 28th and the 31st January, 1964. When he was asked what its highest value was in April, 1961, he said: 'Well, it would be difficult to say in so far as I did not pay particular attention to it then. I would imagine possibly £30 to £35.'

This is obviously not the considered opinion of an expert to be relied upon as bringing home to the plaintiff the fraud which the defendants sought to impute to him, but an opinion casually given to a question for which the witness was, apparently quite unprepared. Even if fraud were properly pleaded, I would be reluctant to convict the plaintiff on such evidence. In the result I find myself at variance with the trial judge in respect of this transaction, and I would not regard the defendants as having established in respect of it a ground for dismissing the plaintiff.

It follows that even had all these matters been within the knowledge of the defendants at the time of dismissal, they have failed to make out a sufficient case to warrant the summary dismissal of the plaintiff and accordingly the plaintiff is, in my view, entitled to damages for wrongful dismissal. I have already indicated that the amount should be £2,000 and not £2,500.

Glover v. B.L.N. Ltd.
[1973] I.R. 388 (S.Ct.)

(From headnote) By an agreement dated the 10th January, 1964, a holding company and its three subsidiaries appointed the plaintiff to be technical director of the four companies for a period of five years at an agreed salary, subject to termination in accordance with clause 12 (c) thereof. That clause provided that the plaintiff's appointment might be terminated, without giving rise to compensation, if he should be guilty of any serious misconduct or serious neglect in the performance of his duties which, in the unanimous opinion of the board of directors of the holding company, affected injuriously the business or property of the holding company or of any of the subsidiaries. On the 5th July, 1966, having considered several serious complaints made against the plaintiff, the board of the holding company found unanimously that the plaintiff had been guilty of serious misconduct and neglect affecting the business of one of the subsidiaries, and terminated the plaintiff's appointment as technical director. On the 13th July, 1966, each of the subsidiaries terminated the said appointment. The plaintiff was not given any prior notice of the complaints made against him. In an action brought by the plaintiff in the High Court in which he claimed damages from the four companies for wrongful dismissal and breach of contract, it was

Held by Kenny J., in deciding the issue of liability for damages,

1. That the decision of the board of the holding company was amenable to review by the court.

2. That, in making their decision, the board of the holding company could only take into account the matters known on the 5th July, 1966.

3. That the evidence of the matters known to the board of the holding company on that date established that the plaintiff had been guilty of serious misconduct and neglect affecting injuriously the business of one of the subsidiaries.

4. That the plaintiff's position as the holder of an office, as distinct from being only an employee, required the application of the rules of natural justice to the termination of his appointment as technical director.

5. That since, in breach of such rules, the plaintiff had not been given prior notice of the charges made against him, his dismissal was invalid and he was entitled to damages.

The defendants appealed.

WALSH J.: . . . [423] For the purpose of this limited appeal only, it is unnecessary to go into details of the particular complaints. I proceed on the assumption that the learned trial judge's assessment of the facts and his conclusion that the plaintiff was guilty of serious neglect of duty and of serious misconduct were correct, and that the nature of the neglect and misconduct was such that the directors could reasonably have considered them to have injuriously affected the business, property and management of the operating company.

At the time the plaintiff was given his notice of dismissal he knew nothing of these charges because he was not given notice of them nor was he given any opportunity to answer them. In fact, he did not find out what the charges were until April, 1967. On the 27th July, 1966, the plaintiff issued proceedings for damages for wrongful dismissal. His statement of claim was delivered on the 15th December, 1966. The defendants delivered their defence on the 9th March, 1967, and alleged that the plaintiff was guilty of misconduct and neglect and that the defendants acted in lawful exercise of their rights under the agreement. On the 13th March the plaintiff's solicitor asked for particulars of the alleged misconduct and neglect and, in a long and detailed reply of the 12th April from the defendants' solicitors, the plaintiff learned for the first time the charges upon which the defendants sought to justify his dismissal. The plaintiff in his reply, which was delivered on the 24th May, denied that he was guilty of the alleged or any misconduct, or neglect and claimed that the boards were acting in excess of the authority vested in them under the service agreement to dismiss the plaintiff. The reply also claimed that the opinion formed by the board was not a *bona fide* one based upon any fair or proper inquiry or investigation into the circumstances of the case or upon any reasonable or justifiable grounds, and that it was formed without [424] reasonable or probable cause. It also claimed that the several boards of directors, in passing the resolutions, acted contrary to the principles of natural justice.

Mr Justice Kenny held that, as the plaintiff did not get notice of the charges against him and as the directors of the holding company did not give him an opportunity to make his defence, the termination of the plaintiff's contract by the resolution of the 5th July and the letter of the 8th July, 1966, was invalid; the judge held that the plaintiff was entitled to damages against the defendants. Mr. Justice Kenny reviewed the various cases he mentioned in his judgment, in particular the decision of the House of Lords in *Ridge* v. *Baldwin* [1964] A.C. 40; the speech of Lord Reid in that decision led him to the conclusion that the plaintiff's position should

MANAGEMENT AND THE DIRECTORS

be equated to that of the holder of an office, and not that of an employee only, and that the principles of natural justice applied to a termination under clause 12 (c) of the plaintiff's agreement.

In my opinion, this case hinges entirely upon clause 12 (c) of the service agreement. The defendants have relied upon this particular clause to justify their summary dismissal of the plaintiff. I agree with Mr Justice Kenny when he states that, because of the express provisions of this clause, no implied term is to be read into the contract that the plaintiff might be summarily dismissed for misconduct. On the contrary, the clause expressly provides that the plaintiff could not be validly dismissed for misconduct unless it was serious misconduct and was of a kind which, in the unanimous opinion of the board of directors of the holding company present and voting at the meeting, injuriously affected the reputation, business or property of either that company or of the subsidiary companies. The question of whether or not such a contract could be terminated summarily for breach of fundamental condition on the part of the plaintiff was not raised in this case and was not relied upon by the defendants so I do not feel any need to offer any view upon that point. It appears to me quite clear that the operation of clause 12(c) would necessarily involve (a) the ascertainment of the facts alleged to constitute serious misconduct, (b) the determination [425] that they did in fact constitute serious misconduct, and (c) that the members of the board present and voting should be unanimously of opinion that the serious misconduct injuriously affected the reputation, business or property of the holding company or of the subsidiary companies. The parties by their conduct explicitly set up the machinery for dismissal specified in clause 12(c); that machinery designated the board of directors as the tribunal, and required unanimity of opinion upon the effect of such serious misconduct if it should be proved.

In my view, it was necessarily an implied term of the contract that this inquiry and determination should be fairly conducted. The arguments and submissions in this Court ranged over a very wide field particularly in the field of constitutional justice: see the judgments of this Court in *McDonald* v. *Bord na gCon* [1965] I.R. 265 and *East Donegal Co-operative* v. *The Attorney General* [1970] I.R. 317. The Constitution was relied upon; in particular Article 40, s. 3, of the Constitution. This Court in *In re Haughey* [1971] I.R. 217 held that that provision of the Constitution was a guarantee of fair procedures. It is not, in my opinion, necessary to discuss the full effect of this Article in the realm of private law or indeed of public law. It is sufficient to say that public policy and the dictates of constitutional justice require that statutes, regulations or agreements setting up machinery for taking decisions which may affect rights or impose liabilities should be construed as providing for fair procedures. It is unnecessary to decide to what extent the contrary can be provided for by agreement between the parties. In the present case the provisions of clause 12(c) do not seek expressly or by implication to exclude the right of any of the parties to a fair procedure.

The plaintiff was neither told of the charges against him nor was he given any opportunity of dealing with them before the board of directors arrived at its decision to dismiss him. In my view this procedure was a breach of the implied term of the contract that the procedure should be fair, as it cannot be disputed, in the light of so much authority on the point, that failure to allow a person to meet the charges against him and to afford him an adequate [426] opportunity of answering them is a violation of an obligation to proceed fairly.

Having regard to the evidence which was given at the trial, one could not say with any degree of certainty that the members of the board of directors would have come to the same conclusion on the facts as Mr Justice Kenny did, or that they would have arrived at a unanimity of opinion on the effects of such misconduct as they might have found proved, particularly when one has regard to the close personal relationships which existed between some members of the board and the plaintiff and their knowledge of his activities in the firm since he joined it. But even if one could say with certainty that, if he had been given a fair hearing, the result would still have been the same, in my view that does not offer any ground for validating retroactively a procedure which was clearly invalid. It is to be noted that the board acted with great haste in dismissing the plaintiff, and on a report which did not contain complaints or allegations of misconduct set out with the particularity with which they were set out subsequently in the reply to the plaintiff's notice for particulars. Furthermore, as was settled by this Court in *Carvill* v. *Irish Industrial Bank Ltd.* [1968] I.R. 325 (ante p. 103), an employer, in defending an action by an employee for wrongful summary dismissal, cannot rely upon misconduct which was not known by the employer at the time of the dismissal. I would add that the misconduct, if known but not in fact used as a ground for dismissal at the time, cannot be relied upon afterwards in an effort to justify the dismissal.

For the reasons I have already stated, I am of opinion that the plaintiff was wrongfully dismissed in that the dismissal was a violation of the provisions of clase 12(c) of the service agreement because of the failure to inform him of the charges against him and the failure to give him an adequate opportunity of answering them.

I am conscious of the fact that Mr Justice Kenny's conclusion that the defendants had acted in breach of the contract is based on somewhat different grounds and, therefore, I should deal with Mr Justice Kenny's reasons. He places great reliance upon the speech of Lord Reid in *Ridge* v. *Baldwin* and quoted with apparent approval the [427] passage at p. 65 of the report in which Lord Reid said: 'The law regarding master and servant is not in doubt. There cannot be specific performance of a contract of service, and the master can terminate the contract with his servant at any time and for any reason or for none. But if he does so in a manner not warranted by the contract he must pay damages for breach of contract.' This particular point does not arise for decision in this case but I wish to expressly reserve my opinion on the correctness of this statement if it is intended to convey that a court cannot make a declaration which would have the effect of reinstating a person wrongfully dismissed. I do not think that the decision in *Ridge* v. *Baldwin* is directly applicable to the present case. In that case the appellant was a Chief Constable and by a statutory provision the watch committee had power to suspend or dismiss him when they thought him negligent in the discharge of his duty or otherwise unfit for the same. The Chief Constable was not the servant of the watch committee, or of any one else, and he was the holder of an office from which he could be only dismissed in accordance with statutory provisions. It was held that the power of dismissal of this officer, contained in the Municipal Corporations Act, 1882, could not have been exercised until the watch committee had informed the officer of the grounds on which they proposed to proceed and had given him a proper opportunity to present his case in defence. It was a prerequisite that the question of neglect of duty should be considered in a judicial spirit and that could not be done without giving the officer in question the opportunity to defend himself against such a charge, and he would therefore have to be told what was alleged neglect of duty. As that had not been done the decision was a nullity.

Unlike the present case, *Ridge* v. *Baldwin* was not governed by the terms of a contract. In my view, once the matter is governed by the terms of a contract between the parties, it is immaterial whether the employee concerned is deemed to be a servant or an officer in so far as the distinction may be of relevance depending on whether the contract is a contract for services or a contract of service. In the present case it is immaterial whether the [428] plaintiff is an officer or a servant of his employers and, in my view, the case does not fall to be decided upon that distinction but rather upon the actual terms of the contract for the reasons I have already given.

Mr Justice Kenny attached importance to the fact that the plaintiff's position with any of the four companies involved could be terminated by the directors of one of them (namely, the holding company) and that this was a characteristic which equated his position to that of an officer. This particular position was the result of a contract between the parties, including the plaintiff, and clause 12(c) of the service agreement gave the directors of the holding company the final decision in whether or not he should be dismissed. I agree with Mr Justice Kenny in so far as he says that this situation strengthened the plaintiff's position in his claim to have a fair hearing, but it leads me to the conclusion that this right was an implied term of the contract by reason of the particular machinery set up by clause 12(c) and, therefore, it is not necessary to examine what might have been the plaintiff's position if such a machinery had not been provided.

The relationship between the plaintiff and the defendants was a contractual one in so far as this particular matter is concerned.

Even if there had not been a pre-existing contractual relationship and the plaintiff had been invited to attend such an inquiry it is probably correct to say, as Harman J. held in *Byrne* v. *Kinematograph Renters Society* [1958] 1 W.L.R. 762, that a contract between the plaintiff and the defendants that the inquiry would be fairly conducted could be implied. It never appears to have been doubted in cases decided in England that, if the basis of the jurisdiction to conduct such an inquiry was based on statute or on the agreement of the parties, public policy prevents the exclusion of the rules of what in England is called natural justice where they ought to be observed. It is unnecessary in this case to enter into an examination of the other aspects of this problem which have engaged English courts, namely, whether the obligation to observe the rules of natural justice can be relied upon in a case where the relationship [429] between the parties is not founded either on statute or on contract.

Lastly, I come to deal with the defendant's contention that, if a hearing had been given to the plaintiff, there was nothing he could usefully have said and the result would have been the same. I think this proposition only has to be stated to be rejected. The obligation to give a fair hearing to the guilty is just as great as the obligation to give a fair hearing to the innocent. Furthermore, in this case, by reason of the provisions of clause 12(c), it would not be simply a case of established guilt or innocence, because the most important and effective power of the board of the holding company was one which was mainly a discretionary power, namely, to form the opinion or not that the plaintiff's misconduct injured any of the four companies.

For the reasons I have already given, I am of opinion that the defendants' appeal on all the matters set out in para. (1) of the said notice of appeal should be dismissed. This appeal, which took the form of an appeal confined in the first instance to the issues set out in the said paragraph of the notice of appeal, was heard pursuant to the order of this Court of the 13th March, 1970, which gave liberty to the parties to have the appeal on these issues heard in the first instance. Summarised briefly, the issues set out in para. (1) of the notice of appeal were whether the plaintiff was entitled to receive notice of the charges against him and to be given an opportunity to reply to the same, by virtue of clause 12(c) of the service agreement, before he could be dismissed; and whether he was entitled to damages for wrongful dismissal when he did not receive such notice before his dismissal. I am expressing no view on what damages the plaintiff should receive, or on what basis they should be calculated, as that aspect of the appeal has not yet been heard.

Shindler v. Northern Raincoat Co. Ltd.
[1960] 2 All E.R. 239 (Assizes)

The plaintiff was appointed managing director of the defendant company for a 10 year period. Following a subsequent take over of the company and disagreements between the plaintiff and the new controllers, resolutions were passed removing him from his office as a director and terminating his service agreement in so far as that may still be subsisting. The company's articles of association included clauses along the lines of articles 110 and 99 of Table A.

DIPLOCK J.: . . . [240] The argument for the defendant company on this matter derives some support from the cases referred to and from another case, *Nelson* v. *James Nelson & Sons, Ltd.* [1914] 2 K.B. 770. The argument is put thus – where a company's articles of association include art. 68, the directors have no power to appoint a managing director on terms which purport to exclude the company's right to terminate his appointment ipso facto on either his ceasing to be a director or if the company shall by resolution in general meeting resolve that his tenure of office as managing director be determined. That argument can be put in alternative ways, either that the agreement for a fixed term which does not incorporate the right of the company set out in art. 68 is ultra vires, or else that the agreement for a fixed period of employment must be subject to the implied term that it is determinable in either of the circumstances set out at the end of art. 68.

It seems to me that this point is concluded against the defendant company by the decision of the House of Lords in *Southern Foundries (1926), Ltd.* v. *Shirlaw* [1940] A.C. 701. That case was somewhat complicated and gave rise to a division of opinion in the House of Lords. Two of their Lordships (Viscount Maugham and Lord Romer) who were most familiar with the Chancery side came to one conclusion and three of their Lordships (Lord Atkin, Lord Wright and Lord Porter) who were perhaps more familiar with the common law side, came to another. There are some references in subsequent cases in the Chancery Division which suggest that it is difficult to ascertain what *Southern Foundries (1926), Ltd.* v. *Shirlaw* determined. It does, however, seem to me that all five of their Lordships in the *Southern Foundries* case were agreed on one principle of law which is vital to the defendant company's contention in the present case. That principle of law is that laid down in *Stirling* v. *Maitland* (5 B. & S. 840), where Cockburn, C.J., said:

> . . . if a party enters into an arrangement which can only take effect by the continuance of a certain existing state of circumstances, there is an implied engagement on his part that he shall do nothing of his own motion to put an end to that state of circumstances, under which alone the arrangement can be operative.

Applying that respectable principle to the present case, there is an implied engagement on the part of the defendant company that it will do nothing of its own motion to put an end to the state of circumstances which enables the plaintiff to continue as managing director. That is to say, there is an implied undertaking that it will not revoke his appointment as a director, and will not resolve that his tenure of office be determined.

Coubrough v. James Panton & Co. Ltd.
[1965] I.R. 272 (H.Ct.)

(From headnote) The plaintiff was a director of, and a large shareholder in, the defendant company. An extraordinary resolution was required by the Articles of Association of the company for the removal of the plaintiff from the office of director before the expiration of his period of office, but such resolution could not be carried without the concurrence of the plaintiff. On the 9th June, 1961, despite the objection of the plaintiff, an ordinary resolution that the existing directors should retire and offer themselves for re-election was proposed and passed. Thereafter the four individual defendants were elected as directors of the company and the plaintiff was excluded from meetings of the board of directors. The plaintiff sought in his summons a declaration that the resolution purporting to remove the directors from office was invalid; a declaration that he was still a director of the defendant company and an order restraining the defendants from excluding him from meetings of the board of directors of the defendant company. At the trial of the action the defendants conceded that the plaintiff was still a director of the company but, nevertheless, they contended that, in view of the opposition to the plaintiff acting as director of the company, the Court should not restrain them by injunction from excluding him from meetings of the board of directors.

BUDD J.: . . . [274] The plaintiff and the individual defendants own between them all the shares in the defendant Company. It is convenient here to refer to Article 104 of the Company's Articles as it is important in relation to what follows. The relevant part reads: '104. The Company may by extraordinary resolution remove any Director before the expiration of his period of office, and appoint another qualified person in his stead.' The position is that the Company could not carry such a resolution against the plaintiff as the remaining shareholders had not a sufficient holding of votes to achieve the required majority. So the resolution of the 9th June, 1961, in so far as it purported to remove the plaintiff was invalid. Now the contention of the defendants is that, notwithstanding that the resolution may be invalid, if all the shareholders other than the plaintiff approve the resolution which plainly shows that they do not wish him to take part in the affairs of the Company as a director, then I should not grant him an injunction restraining them from excluding him from their meetings. They make the further point that, notwithstanding that the resolution may be invalid, yet if in reality and *de facto* they have expressed a wish to exclude him, then that is sufficient to exclude him under the Articles for the reason that he is a trustee of the shareholders and owes a duty to them and he should not act contrary to their wishes by participating in the Company's affairs.

The position therefore is that the plaintiff is now accepted as a director. That being so, may the other directors exclude him from meetings? . . . .

On the question as to whether directors of a company may exclude one of their fellow directors several cases were cited and a question of some difficulty arises. The first case cited was *Pulbrook* v. *Richmond Consolidated Mining Company* (1878) 9 Ch.D. 610. The relevant portion of the head-note reads: 'A director of a company can, if qualified, sustain an action in his own name against the other directors, on the ground of an individual injury to himself, for an injunction to restrain them from wrongfully excluding him from acting as a director.' The matter came before Jessel M.R. who at the beginning of his judgment stated the issue in the following words: 'The first question is, whether a director who is improperly and without cause excluded by his brother directors from the board from which they claim the right to exclude him, is entitled to an order restraining his brother directors from so excluding him.' He then continued: 'In this case a man is necessarily a shareholder in order to be [276] a director, and as a director he is entitled to fees and remuneration for his services, and it might be a question whether he would be entitled to the fees if he did not attend meetings of the board. He has been excluded. Now, it appears to me that this is an individual wrong, a wrong that has been done to an individual. It is a deprivation of his legal rights for which the directors are personally and individually liable. He has a right by the constitution of the company to take a part in its management, to be present, and to vote at the meetings of the board of directors. He has a perfect right to know what is going on at these meetings. It may affect his individual interest as a shareholder as well as his liability as a director, because it has been sometimes held that even a director who does not attend board meetings is bound to know what is done in his absence. Besides that, he is in the position of a shareholder, of a managing partner in the affairs of the company, and he has a right to remain managing partner, and to receive remuneration for his services. It appears to me that for the injury or wrong done to him by preventing him from attending board meetings by force, he has a right to sue. He has what is commonly called a right of action. . .'. And finally at page 616 he said: 'It appears to me that Mr Pulbrook is a director, lawfully elected, and that he has not vacated his office. Therefore I think he is entitled to an injunction to restrain the directors as asked.' The facts in that case are similar to the present in as much as the plaintiff was a shareholder and entitled to remuneration and by the action of the other directors was excluded from meetings which he had a right to attend under the constitution of the Company.

The second report that I wish to refer to is *Hayes* v. *Bristol Plant Hire Ltd.* [1957] 1 All E.R. 685. The head-note sets out the facts. By resolution of the board of the defendant company, passed by certain defendant directors in the absence of the plaintiff, who was also a director, the exclusion of the plaintiff from the board for his absence from board meetings, was confirmed. The consequences of the resolution, if it were valid, was that the plaintiff's office as a director of the company would be vacated. The articles of association did not require a director to hold a share qualification and did not confer on directors the right to any specified remuneration, but provided that, subject to the terms of any agreement between a director and the company, the directors should be paid, by way of remuneration for their services, such sums as the company in general meeting might prescribe. The plaintiff had no service agreement with the company. He was a shareholder in the [277] company. In an action for a declaration, among other declarations, that the resolution confirming the exclusion of the plaintiff was invalid, and for consequential relief by injunction, the defendants objected, as a preliminary point, that the plaintiff had no such proprietary interest as entitled him to equitable relief by declaration and injunction. It was held that the action would not be stopped on the preliminary objection because, although the articles of association of the company did not require a director to hold a share qualification and although they did not confer on directors a right to specified remuneration, yet the plaintiff had a sufficient proprietary interest to enable him to pursue an action for relief by way of declaration and injunction against his exclusion from the board.

That decision follows *Pulbrook's Case* and it was decided as recently as 1957. It will be helpful to read a few of the observations of Wynn-Parry J. which are relevant to the facts of this case. He first deals with the facts stating that it was the fact that the articles of association did not require a director to be a shareholder, nor did they provide any direct right to a stipulated amount for remuneration, they merely provided for the payment of such amount as the company in general meeting might prescribe. I digress for a moment to say that under the Articles of the defendant Company a director is entitled to such sum as the Company in general meeting shall from time to time prescribe. Then (at the bottom of page 686) he says: 'On those facts counsel for the defendants contends that there is no, or no sufficient, proprietary interest vested in the plaintiff as director. He cited to me a number of cases the principles underlying which I wholly accept. It is perfectly clear that in the case of any relationship which involves a personal relationship this court will not intervene by way of injunction to enforce on a person or on a limited company in the position of an employer a person whom the employer or the company, expressing its view through the shareholders, does not want; and it is perfectly true also to say that the cases establish that the basis of the court's interference is the existence of some right of property in the person seeking relief.' Then he goes on to deal with *Pulbrook's Case* and points out that the Master of the Rolls did not base his decision on the fact that in that case a director was necessarily a shareholder, but that his reasoning applied equally where the articles did not require a director to be a shareholder. He also took the view that the reasoning of the Masters of the Rolls in *Pulbrook's Case* applied equally well to cases where the [278] articles of association of a company did not give an express right to specified remuneration but merely provides for a director being paid such remuneration as the company may prescribe. He therefore held the plaintiff entitled to proceed. It is right to add that the learned judge made it clear that he was not dealing with the case on the basis that the majority of the company did not wish the plaintiff to continue as a director. The case was really decided on the basis of a sufficient proprietary interest to maintain an action. Reading the two cases together they go this far in my view – that the plaintiff in the present proceedings has a sufficient proprietary right to maintain this action. However, the question still remains whether the Court should grant the relief claimed in the circumstances existing.

The next case I wish to refer to is *Bainbridge* v. *Smith* 41 Ch.D. 462. I do not intend to brush it lightly aside, but it does not in my view deal with the same facts as are in issue here. The *ratio decidendi* is to be found on page 474, where Cotton L.J. says: 'But I think it right to say that in my opinion, and I believe that my learned Brother agrees with me, if the company says that even if the plaintiff has the qualification they do not desire him to act as one of their managing directors, we should not grant an injunction, because it would be contrary to the principles on which this Court acts to grant specific performance of this contract by compelling this company to take this gentleman as managing director, although he was qualified so to act, when they do not desire him to act as such.' It is clear that the plaintiff's rights in that case were rights under a contract and not rights arising out of the articles of association, or rights of directors or shareholders *inter se.* That case does not therefore advance matters very much.

But the next case, *Harben* v. *Phillips* (1883) 23 Ch.D. 14, does require careful consideration. The facts are complicated but may be stated briefly as follows: at the annual general meeting of the company concerned, two opposing groups arose relating to the number of directors, the persons to be elected as directors, the amount of dividend to be declared and the port of operation of the company's ships. Votes were taken and polls were demanded on them. The chairman ruled proxies valid which did not comply with the Articles. Had the proxies not been admitted, the plaintiffs' opponents would have been defeated and the five plaintiffs would have been

elected to the board. The plaintiffs brought proceedings seeking declarations that their motions had been carried, that they had been elected
directors and claiming *inter alia* an injunction to restrain the [279] other
directors from excluding them from board meetings. On the hearing of
an interlocutory motion before Chitty J. and the Court of Appeal it was
held that the proxies ruled valid by the chairman were invalid. Chitty J.
granted the injunction above-mentioned and other relief. His order was
discharged by the Court of Appeal and a series of orders made and undertakings exacted designed to preserve the *status quo* until a meeting of the
shareholders, convened with the concurrence of all parties, had been held
to deal with the matters in dispute. The extraordinary general meeting
was held and a motion carried rescinding the appointment of the plaintiffs
as directors. On the matter coming on again before the Court of Appeal,
it was agreed that the shareholders' resolution was ineffectual for removing
the plaintiffs from office, and the plaintiffs renewed their claim for an
injunction to restrain the other directors from excluding them. It was held
that the injunction should not be granted, for reasons which will later
appear.

The facts therefore are somewhat similar to those of the present case,
particularly in that there was an ineffective resolution of the shareholders
to remove a director. Mr McWilliam relies on part of the judgment of
Cotton L.J. as showing that he is entitled to succeed and that I should not
in any event grant an injunction. The relevant portion of the judgment of
Cotton L.J. is at page 39 of the report, where he says:

'If there is no power given by the articles of association to remove a
director, all the shareholders cannot say effectually that he is to be removed,
for it has been decided that there is no power to remove a director unless
it is given by the articles of association; but no one can doubt that the wish
of a corporation that certain persons should not be directors may effectually
be expressed by any meeting of the shareholders duly called for such
purpose, although such wish may not be effectual to remove the persons
appointed to the office of directors. Then it comes to this, that we have
in the resolution of the meeting an expression by the majority of the
shareholders of the company of a desire that the plaintiffs should not be
directors, and that the policy advocated by the plaintiffs should not be that
which should be adopted by the company, and what this Court is asked
to do is, as against the wish to the majority of the shareholders, to interfere
by injunction to compel in fact the company and the other members of
the board to allow the plaintiffs to act as directors.' Mr McWilliam asks
me to interpret that passage as a statement of the law that the Court should
not force a director on the board of a company where the shareholders
have made it [280] clear that they do not want him. Mr Parke's answer to
that is this: Cotton, L.J. was not in fact laying down the law as Mr McWilliam claims; the Lord Justice was posing the problem which had arisen on

an interlocutory application and there is no way of knowing what action the Court might have taken on a full trial of the action. The only clear view of what might have been done appears in the judgment of Bowen L.J., at page 42, where he says: 'I am not satisfied if it had now to be decided, that, assuming the plaintiffs to make out their case in other respects, this is a matter in which perpetual injunction is the relief to which they are entitled, but I wish to leave that entirely open, and to decide this case on the grounds simply that although there is a great inconvenience whichever way we decide, I am by no means satisfied that the balance of convenience is in favour of granting an injunction. One cannot help seeing that this company has got into a very unfortunate position for the transaction of even its most ordinary business, and it is difficult to say what can be done to relieve it so long as both parties insist on prosecuting their own views of their legal rights, but on the whole the best thing to do is, I think, to leave the matter to stand as it is and refuse the application of the plaintiffs, Mr Macnaghten giving the undertaking that the two directors whom he represents, and whose election is open to doubt, should not act until the hearing.' In short, the matter was left open.

Now in support of the view that Cotton L.J. was merely posing a question as to what might happen if shareholders did express a wish, Mr Parke points out that the Lord Justice proceeded as follows, at page 40 of the report: 'Now, in determining whether the Court should so interfere, we must not only consider the expression of the wish of the majority of the shareholders as shewn at that last meeting, but in my opinion we must also consider how it was that the plaintiffs came to be appointed to be directors.' So Cotton L.J. in Mr Parke's submission, did not decide as a matter of law that the shareholders' wish ends the matter, for that would have been the end of the case. It was only one matter to be considered. And the Lord Justice went on to say: 'I assume that they were effectually appointed directors of this company, although of course at the hearing we can listen to any argument which the defendants may think fit to advance to shew that they were not properly elected. But then assuming they were rightly elected, the election was only an accident arising from many of the shareholders who desired that some one else should be appointed, sending their proxies in such a way that the votes expressed by them could not be legally [281] used. Taking that, as I do, into consideration, this Court ought not, in my opinion, to interfere on this motion by compelling the company to put the management of its affairs into the hands of the plaintiffs, or by requiring the other directors to receive the plaintiffs as co-directors. Cases were referred to, to shew there was authority for the Court to so interfere; but there was no case which touched the point on which I decide this.'

Now I think it is clear from that passage that Mr McWilliam is not correct in suggesting that Cotton L.J. had decided as a matter of law that if the shareholders are opposed to a director the Court will not assist him to enforce his rights. It was a matter concerning the control of the company and he pointed out that the plaintiffs were directors only by the accident of the invalid proxies. That does not apply in this case. And in this case a director can only be removed by a three-fourths majority of the Company on an extraordinary resolution. I am then of opinion that *Harben* v. *Phillips* is not an authority for the proposition that if the shareholders are opposed to a director the Court will not act to aid that director. To take an extreme illustration, suppose a company had five directors and as a result of pro-longed differences of opinion a resolution was passed by the shareholders in general meeting that they did not want any of the directors to act. Then there would be nobody to carry on the affairs of the company. But directors have a duty to conduct their company's affairs. And further, if Mr McWil-liam were right, it would make nonsense of Article 194 which provides that directors can only be removed by extraordinary resolutions. It would mean that while a director could not be legally removed, nevertheless the same result could be achieved by barring him from attending meetings by a bare majority. Articles 114 and 115 provide that the management and control of the Company shall be vested in the directors. So that to accede to Mr McWilliam's argument and not grant the relief claimed would be to exclude the plaintiff from his right to act as a director; and one must remember that he would, as a director, be responsible for decisions of the board at a time when he was not allowed to attend and to give his advice and vote.

In my view, being a large shareholder and a director, the plaintiff is in fairness entitled to know what is happening and to vote at meetings. There is the further consideration that resolutions of the board may possibly be ineffectual and invalid if a person entitled to be present is excluded from meetings at which the resolutions are passed. So I have come [282] to the conclusion, on the basis of the cases of *Pulbrook* v. *Richmond Consolidated Mining Company* and *Hayes* v. *Bristol Plant Hire Ltd.* that in proper circum-stances a director has a right to attend board meetings which may be enforced against the other directors. What was said in *Harben* v. *Phillips*, an interlocutory application, is not sufficient to prevent me granting relief. I think it is clearly distinguishable on the facts from the present case.

So the plaintiff is in the position of being a director, not validly excluded from meetings. And he is also a large shareholder. He is in consequence deprived of information on the affairs of the Company, and important decisions are made in his absence. In all the circumstances I feel I should exercise my discretion in favour of the plaintiff and grant him the relief claimed relevant to that part of the action that I am dealing with.

Healy v. Healy Homes Ltd.
[1973] I.R. 309 (H.Ct.)

The plaintiff claimed an injunction to restrain the defendants from preventing the plaintiff and his accountant from examining and inspecting the statutory books and accounts of the defendant company and its share register, register of members and minute books.

KENNY J.: [310] The plaintiff and the second defendant are directors of the defendant company. The plaintiff, who complains that he has been excluded from the management of the company, sought an inspection of the register of members, the minute book and the books of account of the company, and wished to have an accountant with him when he was doing this. The defendants refused to allow anyone except the plaintiff to see the books of account. The right of the plaintiff and his accountant to inspect the register of members and the minute book of general meetings was not disputed, and the debate was limited to the question whether the right of inspection of the books of account is personal to a director or whether he may be accompanied by an accountant when exercising it. The parties have wisely agreed that this point should be decided under Order 25 of the Rules of the Superior Courts. . . .

[311] The purpose of the section [s. 147 of the Companies Act, 1963] is to compel companies to keep proper books of account: one of the ways in which this important object is achieved is by imposing an obligation on each director to make sure that this is being done. But a director who has not had a training in accountancy cannot decide whether proper books of account are being kept unless an accountant is allowed to inspect them; the phrase 'proper books of account' means books which give a true and fair view of the state of the company's affairs and which explain its transactions. It follows that a director's right to inspect the books of account necessarily involves that an accountant nominated by him may do this. The accountant may do this when he is accompanied by the director or when the accountant has been given a written authority to do so, and he may be required to give a written undertaking that the knowledge which he gets will not be used for any purpose except that of giving confidential advice to his employer in relation to the matter in connection with which he has been retained.

The purpose of the section shows that this is the correct interpretation of it. This view gets support from the judgment of Collins L.J. in the Court of Appeal in England in *Bevan* v. *Webb* [1901] 2 Ch. 59, where, at p. 68 of the report, he said that a permission to a man to do something which he cannot do effectually without an agent to help him carries with it the right to employ an agent. The right of a director to inspect the books of a company, when he has an obligation imposed on him the breach of which may involve him in criminal liability, necessarily implies that he has the right to employ a qualified agent to advise him. The question whether proper books are being kept is one on which an accountant is the only person qualified to advise as most directors would not be able to form a correct judgment on [312] the matter. The director and his accountant are also entitled to make copies of the books of account or any part of them.

Bevan v. *Webb* was a decision that the right of a partner to inspect the books of account of the partnership may be exercised by his agent also. It was decided on s. 24, sub-s. 9, of the Partnership Act, 1890, which provided that the partnership books were to be kept at the place of business of the partnership and that every partner might, when he thought fit, have access to and inspect and copy any of them. The court held that the right to inspect was not confined to the partners personally but that any of them could appoint an agent who was entitled to make the inspection if he was prepared to give the undertaking which I have already mentioned.

In this case the plaintiff is prepared to have his accountant with him when he is making the inspection. *Bevan* v. *Webb* decided that the accountant is entitled to make the inspection though he is not accompanied by his employer if he has the necessary authority from him.

Battle v. Irish Art Promotion Centre Ltd.
[1968] I.R. 242 (S.Ct.)

In the course of proceedings being brought against the defendant company, its managing director, who was also its principal shareholder, applied for liberty to conduct the company's defence at the hearing.

Ó DÁLAIGH C.J.: [243] The appellant says the company has not now sufficient assets to permit of solicitor and counsel being engaged to present the company's defence; he also says that the company has a good defence to the action and that if, in the absence of solicitor and counsel to conduct the defence, the company were to be decreed, it would be a reflection on the appellant's reputation and standing as a business man. It would appear that the appellant is now managing director of another company of which he is also the major shareholder. The appellant was unable to refer the Court to any authorities touching on his application; and in these circumstances the Court allowed the application to stand over in order that it might have an opportunity of examining the law.

I have not found any reported Irish case which bears on the Court's problem; but there are at least three English decisions. The first, *Scriven* v. *Jescott Leeds Ltd.* (53 Sol. Jo. 101) is reported as a note. The managing director sought a right of audience to represent the company. Bray J. is reported as having held that a company can only be represented by attorney and that it is not in the same position as a litigant in person. In *London County Council and London Tramways Company* (13 T.L.R. 254) the objection was taken but not ruled. The point arose again in *Frinton and Walton*

U.D.C. v. *Walton and District Sand and Mineral Co. Ltd.*[1938] 1 All E.R. 649 and it was again ruled in the same sense by Morton J. who said: 'the points to which my attention has been drawn are sufficient to satisfy me that a company cannot appear in person.' Lastly, the matter was the subject of a ruling in *Tritonia Ltd.* v. *Equity and Law Life Assurance Society* [1943] A.C. 584. Viscount Simon L.C. in his speech (with which all his brethren concurred) said at p. 586 of the report: 'In the case of a corporation, inasmuch as the artificial entity cannot attend and argue personally the right of audience is necessarily limited to counsel instructed on the corporation's behalf.' Having referred to an apparent exception in the case of the Appeal Committee (whose practice it was to hear agents in incidental petitions and other matters dealt with by the committee, but not in argument on the substantial appeal), he said that this 'cannot be held to constitute a real exception to the long established rule that an appeal cannot be argued on behalf of a party by any one except the party himself (if not a corporation) or by counsel.'

[244] I should also avert the case of *Charles P. Kinnell & Co.* v. *Harding, Wace & Co.* [1918] 1 K.B. 405, where it was held that in the English County Court a limited company may lawfully employ an agent who is not a solicitor to institute proceedings and file the necessary *praecipe* on its behalf and, with the leave of the judge, represent it in Court. The proceedings were to set aside a judgment which had been entered on default of appearance at the hearing by the defendant. The plaintiff company had, for the purpose of filing the necessary *praecipe* and affidavit, employed one of their own clerks instead of a solicitor. This was relied upon by the defendants as an irregularity such as to entitle them to have the judgment set aside. The Court of Appeal, hearing an appeal from a divisional court which refused the motion, examined the wider question on the right of a limited company to appear in the county court by its officer or agent, and the judges found warrant for their view that it could in the express provision of s. 72 of the County Courts Act, 1888.

This survey of the cases indicates clearly that the law is, as we apprehended it to be when this application was first made to us, *viz.* that, in the absence of statutory exception, a limited company cannot be represented in court proceedings by its managing director or other officer or servant. This is an infirmity of the company which derives from its own very nature. The creation of the company is the act of its subscribers; the subscribers, in discarding their own *personae* for the *persona* of the company, doubtless did so for the advantages which incorporation offers to traders. In seeking incorporation they thereby lose the right of audience which they would have as individuals; but the choice has been their own. One sympathises with the purpose which the appellant has in mind, to wit, to safeguard his business reputation; but, as the law stands, he cannot as major shareholder and managing director now substitute his *persona* for that of the company. The only practical course open to him would, it appears, be for him personally to put the company in funds for the purpose of presenting its defence. The Court in my judgment should refuse this application.

DIRECTORS' DUTIES

Re City Equitable Insurance Co. Ltd.
[1925] 1 Ch. 407 (C.A.)

(From headnote) In the winding up by the Court of the company an investigation of its affairs disclosed a shortage in the funds, of which the company should have been possessed, of over £1,200,000, due in part to depreciation of investments, but mainly to the instrumentality of the managing director and largely to his deliberate fraud, for which he had been convicted and sentenced.

Art. 150 of the company's articles of association provided (inter alia) that none of the directors, auditors, secretary or other officers for the time being of the company should be answerable for the acts, receipts, neglects or defaults of the others or other of them, or for any bankers or other persons with whom any moneys or effects belonging to the company should or might be lodged or deposited for safe custody, or for insufficiency or deficiency of any security upon which any moneys of or belonging to the company should be placed out or invested, or for any other loss, misfortune, or damage which might happen in the execution of their respective offices or trusts, or in relation thereto, unless the same should happen by or through their own wilful neglect or default respectively.

On a misfeasance summons under s. 215 of the Companies (Consolidation) Act, 1908 (s. 298 of the 1963 Act) the Official Receiver as liquidator sought to make the respondent directors, all of whom (except the managing director) had admittedly acted throughout, liable for negligence in respect of losses occasioned by investments and loans, and of payment of dividends out of capital.

In determining the questions of the liability of the respondent directors raised by the summons, Romer J. enunciated and adopted the following principles relative to the duties of directors and to the meaning to be attached to the words 'wilful neglect or default' in art. 150.

Duties of Directors.– The manner in which the work of a company is to be distributed between the board of directors and the staff is a business matter to be decided on business lines. The larger the business carried on by the company the more numerous and the more important the matters that must of necessity be left to the managers, the accountants, and the rest of the staff.

In ascertaining the duties of a company director, it is necessary to consider the nature of the company's business and the manner in which the work of the company is, reasonably in the circumstances and consistently with the articles of association, distributed between the directors and the other officials of the company.

In discharging those duties, a director *(a)* must act honestly, and *(b)* must exercise such degree of skill and diligence as would amount to the reasonable care which an ordinary man might be expected to take, in the circumstances, on his own behalf. But, *(c)* he need not exhibit in the performance of his duties a greater degree of skill than may reasonably be expected from a person of his knowledge and experience; in other words, he is not liable for mere errors of judgment; *(d)* he is not bound to give continuous attention to the affairs of his company; his duties are of an intermittent nature to be performed at periodical board meetings, and at meetings of any committee to which he is appointed, and though not bound to attend all such meetings he ought to attend them when reasonably able to do so; and *(e)* in respect of all duties which, having regard to the exigencies of business and the articles of association, may properly be left to some other official, he is, in the absence of grounds for suspicion, justified in trusting that official to perform such duties honestly.

A director who signs a cheque that appears to be drawn for a legitimate purpose is not responsible for seeing that the money is in fact required for that purpose, or that it is subsequently applied for that purpose, assuming, of course, that the cheque comes before him for signature in the regular way, having regard to the usual practice of the company. A director must of necessity trust to the officials of the company to perform properly and honestly the duties allocated to them.

Before any director signs a cheque, or parts with a cheque signed by him, he should satisfy himself that a resolution has been passed by the board, or committee of the board (as the case may be), authorizing the signature of the cheque; and where a cheque has to be signed between meetings, he should obtain the confirmation of the board subsequently to his signature.

The authority given by the board or committee should not be for the signing of numerous cheques to an aggregate amount, but a proper list of the individual cheques, mentioning the payee and the amount of each, should be read out at the board or committee meeting and subsequently transcribed into the minutes of the meeting.

It is the duty of each director to see that the company's moneys are from time to time in a proper state of investment, except so far as the articles of association may justify him in delegating that duty to others.

Before presenting their annual report and balance sheet to their shareholders, and before recommending a dividend, directors should have a complete and detailed list of the company's assets and investments prepared for their own use and information, and ought not to be satisfied as to the value of their company's assets merely by the assurance of their chairman, however apparently distinguished and honourable, nor with the expression of the belief of their auditors, however competent and trustworthy.

It is not the duty of a director of a big insurance company to supervise personally the safe custody of the securities of the company. It would be impracticable, on every purchase of securities, for actual delivery thereof to be made to the directors, or, on every sale, for the delivery to the brokers of the securities sold to await a meeting of the board or of a committee of directors. The duty of seeing that the securities are in safe custody must of necessity be left to some official of the company in daily attendance at the office of the company, such as the manager, accountant, or secretary.

A director is not responsible for declaring a dividend unwisely. He is liable if he pays it out of capital, but the onus of proving that he has done so lies upon the liquidator who alleges it.

Wilful Neglect or Default. – An act, or an omission to do an act, is wilful where the person who acts, or omits to act, knows what he is doing and intends to do what he is doing, but if that act or omission amounts to a breach of that person's duty, and therefore to negligence, he is not guilty of wilful neglect or default unless he knows that he is committing, and intends to commit, a breach of his duty, or is recklessly careless in the sense of not caring whether his act or omission is or is not a breach of his duty.

That the immunity afforded by art. 150 was one of the terms upon which the directors held office in the company, and availed them as much on a misfeasance summons by the Official Receiver under s. 215, as it would have done in an action by the company against them for negligence; and

Upon the evidence and in accordance with the principles enunciated above, that none of the respondent directors (other than the managing director) was liable for the losses covered by the points of claim, and that in those instances in which all or some of the directors had been guilty of negligence, such negligence was not wilful and art. 150 applied to exonerate them from liability.

Land Credit Co. of Ireland v. Lord Fermoy
(1870) L.R. 5 Ch. App. 763

The company's directors set up an executive sub-committee of the board. That committee, with the intention of raising the price of its shares in the market and keeping up fictitious appearance of credit, determined to employ the money of the company in the purchase of shares, and brokers were directed to purchase shares in the company, at a premium; and in order to conceal the irregularity of the transaction, the executive committee determined to use other persons' names, and untruly to represent the payments in respect of such transaction in the company's books as loans. The shares were paid for with cheques drawn on the company's bank account. At a board meeting, the secretary reported to the directors that various cheques had been paid, including the above-mentioned cheques.

LORD HATHERLEY L.C.: [770] I am exceedingly reluctant in any way to exonerate directors from performing their duty, and I quite agree that it is their duty to be awake, and that their being asleep would not exempt [771] them from the consequences of not attending to the business of the company. But we must look at the nature of the business of this company.

It appears that under the trust-deed they had the power of making loans, and the power of appointing a committee, to whom they might delegate all the powers they thought proper; and that, in fact, a committee was appointed, called the executive committee, and that the functions of the directors were transferred to this committee, so far as regarded proposals for business, and for loans and other matters. The committee from time to time reported to the directors, and the directors had a right to ask proper questions, and to decide thereon according to their discretion; and the directors must be tried as any other trustees accused of neglecting their duty. Now, setting aside all that was concealed by the executive committee, there was laid before the board a statement that the cheques for £2000 and £1733 11s 3d had been signed by the executive committee, and then, before the chairman, a paper, on which was written, amongst the agenda for the day, 'Loans to Mr. *Costelloe* and Mr *Oliphant.*' This we must take to have been read out, and it must have been stated that these loans had received the sanction of the executive committee, and that the sanction of the directors was sought. Now, suppose that Mr *Munster* is bound by everything which appears upon the books to have been discussed by the directors? He must be taken to have known of these loans; and the question is, how far he ought to have pursued his investigation? If there had been anything unreasonable or extravagant in the matter, or the loans had been of an unusual amount, one would expect further questions to be asked, but the loans amounted to £3733 only, and it would have been useless to ask the executive committee, who had already recommended the loans, whether the security was good. But the charge is, that the directors did not see to the application of these loans. The money was actually placed to the credit of these persons, and, in form, all was done that was recommended by the executive committee. The real transaction was, that the executive committee had adopted the very improper course of purchasing shares in their own company, and now wanted to pay for them by means of these apparent loans to *Oliphant* and *Costelloe.*

[772] But it would be carrying the doctrine of liability too far to say that the directors are liable for negligence, not because they did not ask whether

Costelloe and *Oliphant* were solvent and respectable, but because they did not inquire what they were going to do with the money. To do this would be carrying the doctrine of the responsibility of directors far beyond anything laid down in this Court. Whatever may be the case with a trustee, a director cannot be held liable for being defrauded; to do so would make his position intolerable.

The question, then, is, whether this was concealed. *Oliphant* says it was not; but this is denied by the evidence of others, and I think that it was in fact concealed: it was very unlikely that the executive committee would disclose their scheme to the other directors. Mr *Munster* has denied that the matter was ever brought before him, or that he had any knowledge of the transactions; and I give full belief to his denial.

The Plaintiff's have failed to establish against Mr *Munster* the thing which it was essential for them to establish; and the bill, as against him, must be dismissed with costs.

Jackson v. Munster Bank Ltd.
(1885) 15 L.R.Ir. 356

This action was brought by certain shareholders of the bank for a declaration that the making of advances out of the funds of the company to the directors, or to past directors while holding office, or to firms of which, while holding office, they were partners, constituted a breach of trust on the part of the board of directors, and that the defendants, other than the company, or such of them as might appear to the Court to be liable thereto, should be ordered to repay and make good to the company the amount of such advances not adequately secured. No advances had been made by the bank to Mr Dease or to any firm of which he was a partner; but very substantial advances had been made to all the other directors, with the exception of one. Some of these advances were made on dates after Mr Dease was appointed a director; but such advances were not made by his direct permission or authority. The question whether, he being a director, such advances were made by his permission or authority was at the desire of the plaintiffs, and the defendant Mr Dease reserved for the consideration of the Court on the further consideration of the action.

CHATTERTON V.C.: [360] The only question I have now to decide is whether the Defendant Edmund G. Dease is liable for the advance made, without security, to the Directors of the Munster Bank at any time since he was appointed Director. It appears that Mr Dease was nominated to be a Director of the Bank in the month of February, 1881, and that his appointment was confirmed at the half-yearly meeting held in Cork in the subsequent July. There can be no doubt that it was intended at the time that his services were to be made use of principally, at any rate, in Dublin, and I have now to decide how far he is responsible for the very great misfeasance and breaches of trust which were committed by his co-Directors in Cork since the date of his appointment. . . .

It is not a universal rule that a trustee is bound to make himself acquainted with all the circumstances relating to the trust fund, and the authorities cited [361] by Mr Robertson undoubtedly show that the Directors of Companies are not, in all respects, under the same liabilities as other trustees. In this case, however, the only doubt present to my mind is where the point of liability commences. There is much to be said in excuse for Mr Dease's inaction with reference to the transactions that occurred previously to the 11th January, 1883. It was expected of him that he would remain in Dublin, and there certainly was plenty of business to occupy him there. That enables a reasonable excuse to be urged for his not having taken a more active part in the business at Cork. I agree with the contention of the Plaintiffs that he was bound to perform the duties of his post, no matter how arduous; but the fact of his having been actively engaged in the business of the Company in Dublin may be an excuse for his non-intervention in the business at Cork, where no other would avail him. There can, however, be no reason for exempting him from liability from an early period in the year 1883.

On the 11th January, 1883, the following letter was written by Mr Thomas Fitzgerald, one of the Plaintiffs, to Mr La Touche, and this letter was shown to Mr Dease. [His Lordship here read the letter.] Here was a statement which, if Mr Dease had been hitherto ignorant of the affairs of the Company, should have startled him very much. It is strange that he should have been ignorant of them before; but, at any rate, after the receipt of that letter, he was bound at once to set about investigating all this misfeasance. If he had then gone down to Cork and done his duty and examined the accounts, he would have found that there had been a systematic fraudulent misappropriation of the property of the Bank, and the money of the customers of the Bank, extending over a period of years, conducted principally by the Chairman of the Bank, with the assistance of one who had been a manager, and was afterwards appointed a Director of it, and with the concurrence of several other Directors who formed the local Board in Cork. A firm man going down in the exercise of his duty, mastering the facts, and remonstrating with his brother Directors, could have put a stop to this nefarious system, and the Bank would, from that time out, have been protected against the fraudulent misconduct of its Directors. Mr Dease did not do so. He [362] attended at the general meeting, and was silent. He sat by and heard as false a statement as ever was made by a person in the same situation which he knew to be false, and for his own benefit put forward. That was the statement made by the Chairman of the Company to the meeting, that all these statements about overdrafts to the Directors were utterly without foundation, the account of that gentleman being actually overdrawn nearly £100,000 at the time the statement was made. Subsequently to this meeting Mr Dease was appointed to make an examination of the accounts of the Directors with the Company, but he did not go down to Cork for this purpose for some months afterwards. It was his bounden duty to have gone at once into an investigation of these transactions, and to have put a stop to them, and I can listen to no excuse for his not having done so. If no better course was open to him, he was, in my opinion, bound to institute a suit in Chancery to put a stop to these proceedings. He did nothing of the kind. Mr Dease is liable from February, 1883.

Nash v. Lancegaye Safety Glass (Ireland) Ltd.
92 I.L.T.R. 11 (1958) (H.Ct.)

The second defendant James Ryan and his supporters held about 49 per cent of the voting shares in the company and dominated the board. The plaintiff, with his own shares and the proxies he had obtained, controlled about 51 per cent of the voting shares. Major differences of policy arose between them, which led to the plaintiff requisitioning an extraordinary general meeting at which it was to be proposed to appoint new directors. In the meantime, the board decided to issue and allot 16,000 unissued voting shares; 5,000 of these were to be allotted to James Ryan, and the remainder were to be allotted to all the existing shareholders on a pro rata basis.

DIXON J.: . . . [19] According to Mr McNicholl, the Secretary of the Company, this minute was a conscientious record of what took place. His practice was to take notes at the meetings and prepare the minutes from the notes. His notes are not available. The minutes, as drafted, were read and signed at the meeting of 4th June, 1955 at which the directors who had taken part in the prior meeting, and also Dr Michael Ryan, were present. The only criticisms of the minutes were offered by Mr Nash and his proposed amendment of them was defeated, the Chairman stating (according to the minute of this meeting) 'that the Board was adamant that the minutes as recorded were correct'.

The Chairman's view has apparently not since altered, as, in evidence, he maintained that the minutes were correct. Mr Doyle, on the other hand, in cross-examination, expressed the view that the minutes did not give a true picture but said that it did not occur to him when he heard them read at the next meeting, or indeed until the matter arose in this action, that they might give a false picture. There is little doubt as to the picture the minutes give and it is one that is inconsistent with the account given by Dr Ryan and Mr Doyle. Mr Breen professed to have no clear recollection of what preceded the passing of the resolution. The plain meaning of the minute is that, as an alternative to rewarding Mr Ryan for his past services by paying him £1,000, he should be allowed to take up £5,000 worth of shares at par and in priority to the existing shareholders. The version given by Dr Ryan and Mr Doyle amounted to asserting that the matter of a recompense to Mr Ryan had been, as it were, interpolated in a general discussion of the capital position and had been turned down on the ground that nothing was due to Mr Ryan: that the discussion of the capital position had then been resumed and that the offer of £5,000 by Mr Ryan was merely mentioned as a means of raising capital and dealt with without any idea of conferring a benefit or advantage on Mr Ryan. Mr Doyle, in his evidence, said that, when the question of capital expenditure was being discussed, he thought it an opportune moment to mention the claim of Mr Ryan but not, he said, for the purpose of having any provision made for it, but simply to have the matter ruled on so that he would have an answer to Mr Ryan's importunities on the subject. I find this – as indeed, much of the evidence of Dr Thomas Ryan and Mr Doyle – unconvincing and unacceptable. I believe Mr Doyle did raise the matter as an item of capital expenditure for which some provision [20] would have to be made. I do not accept that the Chairman, as he and Mr Doyle stated in evidence, ruled out the claim as having no legal or moral basis, and that, therefore, the matter was at an end and had no bearing on the allocation of the shares. Such a view would be inconsistent, apart altogether from the minutes, with the admitted statement by the Chairman that there might be some appreciation in the shares which would meet Mr Doyle's point. Such an important view or ruling would, I feel, have been recorded in the minutes. Mr McNicholl, in his account of the meeting in evidence, made no reference to any such view being expressed and gave a short summary which was not inconsistent with a distinct relationship between the £1,000 and the proposed issue of shares. Finally, the account of Mr Nash, which I accept, fully bears out the apparent meaning and implications of the minutes. I accept that he was the only person at the meeting who queried the validity of the claim and the legality or propriety of making any payment, that Mr Doyle referred to the power under the Articles of giving gratuities to past employees, that the Chairman said the Board could do it if they wished but that he would suggest an alternative method, the alternative method being to allow his father to take the shares at par.

There was certainly no legal validity in the claim of Mr Ryan. Whether it had any moral force is a matter of opinion. It apparently related to the circumstances that, in July of 1952, he had agreed to his remuneration as managing director being reduced from £1,000 per annum to £500 per annum as from 1st January, 1952. That voluntary reduction was related to the increase of Mr Doyle's salary as general manager, which then was increased by £150 per annum as from 1st January, 1952. As Mr Ryan ceased to be managing director in November, 1953, his claim would appear to be that he had foregone nearly £1,000 over the two years 1952 and 1953. An alternative basis would be that he was not paid his salary of £500 as managing director as from 1st January, 1953; but this was because, on Mr Ryan's representation and request, Dr Michael Ryan, although only appointed managing director in November of 1953, was paid the salary as from 1st January, 1953. Neither claim would, therefore, appear to be well founded. Whatever the basis of it, the matter seems to have become an obsession with Mr Ryan. It was a topic that he mentioned at the Annual General Meeting of 3rd November, 1954, his view being that, instead of the critical and ungrateful attitude of the shareholders at that meeting towards his conduct of the affairs of the company, he should have been complimented and, in view of the good prospects for the next year, promised that the amount would then be voted to him. It was a grievance which, it was clear during the course of Mr Ryan's evidence, still rankled. It was also a consideration which, even according to himself, was in his mind, in March of 1955, when he discussed the question of investing £5,000 in Lancegaye with Dr Thomas Ryan. Both he and Dr Ryan gave evidence as to this discussion. Dr Ryan rather gave the impression that his father had volunteered to invest £5,000 and that the matter had been discussed from the point of view of the soundness of the investment. Mr Ryan's evidence gave more the impression that he had been asked by Dr Ryan to help the company financially and was induced to do so but he also stated, significantly, that he had lost £1,000 which he wanted to get back, that he debated whether he could get it back if he took shares, and that he calculated that an appreciation or profit of 1s per share on £5,000 worth at par would give him back the £1,000. His affidavit for the purposes of the interlocutory application put the matter simply as that he agreed to subscribe for the shares solely to encourage other shareholders to subscribe for shares also and so assist the company to secure the additional finances it needed. If this were his attitude, he could have been equally helpful by underwriting an issue of shares to that extent. It was in this affidavit that he swore categorically that the document drawn up prior to his co-option to the Board – which could only have been the minute of the agreement between himself, Mr Nash and Mr Breen – was one which did not concern him and to which he was not a party. In view of this, it is hard to receive any of his evidence without reserve.

Other, not insignificant, matters are that the balance sheets for 1954, which were then in draft and would show a substantial improvement in the position of Lancegaye, including a trading profit of over twice the amount in the previous year, were discussed between father and son in March, 1955; and that, at the meeting of 17th May, 1955, transfers were before the Board showing dealings with shares at over 6s a share, which fact was commented upon by the Chairman as showing that there was some public confidence in the Company.

I find it impossible to escape the conclusion that, in voting to allow James Ryan to take up £5,000 worth of shares at par, the directors Dr

Thomas J. Ryan, Daniel Breen [21] and Brendan Doyle, were largely influenced by the desire and intention of conferring a benefit or privilege of appreciable monetary value on James Ryan in reward for past services or to meet some supposed claim on moral grounds to compensation. This was, of course, a distinct prejudice to the position and interests of the existing shareholders. Of the £16,000 unissued capital there would only be available for issue to these shareholders £11,000, £5,000 having been allotted in priority to one relatively small shareholder. Apart from depriving the shareholders of the opportunity of taking up nearly one-third of the unissued capital, the issue of this one-third to one holder in priority was liable to depreciate the value of their existing holdings.

This transaction could not be justified under the power – referred to at the Meeting by Mr Doyle – under Article 124 (14) of the Articles of Association of giving retiring gratuities, pensions or annuities to ex-employees of the Company. The only provision it could be justified under is Article 6 which so far as material reads: 'Subject as aforesaid the shares shall be under the control of the directors who may allot or otherwise dispose of the same to such persons on such terms and conditions, and at such times, as the directors think fit.' In contrast, Article 48 which deals with the issue of new shares on an increase of capital, provides that 'subject to any direction to the contrary that may be given by the meeting that sanctions the increase of capital, all new shares shall be offered to the members in proportion to the existing shares held by them, and each offer shall be made by notice specifying the number of shares to which the member is entitled, and limiting a time within which the offer, if not accepted, will be deemed to be declined, and after the expiration of such time, or on the receipt of any intimation from the member to whom such notice is given, that he declines to accept the shares offered, the directors may dispose of the same in such manner as they think most beneficial to the Company.' This Article laid down a fair and reasonable method of issuing new capital. It was eighteen years since the formation of the Company and the original issue of the capital in 1937 and the method of Article 48 might, in the circumstances, have seemed more appropriate to the issue of the unissued portion of that capital in 1955. The plaintiff, however, does not dispute the power of the directors to deal with the unissued capital under Article 6 so long as the power is properly exercised. He relies on the well-established principle that the directors are trustees of the powers entrusted to them, including that of allotting shares and that the Court will intervene in the case of an improper use or the abuse of any of their powers: see e.g. *Punt* v. *Symons & Co.* [1903], 2 Ch. 506, *Piercy* v. *Mills & Co.* [1920], 1 Ch. 77; *York and North Midland Railway* v. *Hudson* 16 Beav. 485.

In addition to this matter of a reward to Mr Ryan, there is also the question of the alteration of the voting strength of the Ryan family and their supporters, including therein Rybar. The effect of this issue of shares to James Ryan would have been to confer on him 15,000 votes in respect of that number of preference shares. Unless, which was clearly not contemplated, the balance of the unissued shares were issued and allotted before the next general meeting of the Company, the total of votes would have been increased from the existing 96,000 to 111,000 of which about 13½% would have been freshly issued to one small shareholder. As will be seen, and can be assumed for the moment, this would almost certainly have assured an effective majority of the voting strength to the Ryan interests.

The Plaintiff contends that this was not only the effect of the allotment but was also its object. A clash of interests and outlook had clearly developed at the slightly stormy general meeting in November 1954 at which Mr Ryan clearly felt he had been treated with base ingratitude on the part of the shareholders and with open disloyalty on the part of a fellow-director, the Plaintiff. So far as it is material, I think the major part of the trouble, such as it was, at that meeting was occasioned by the autocratic and offensive attitude of Mr Ryan himself, as Chairman of the meeting, and his highly misleading statement as to his not having drawn money from the Company for two years. But, wherever the justice of the matter lay, it would have been obvious to persons far less intelligent than Mr Ryan and the directors who supported him that a struggle for control of the Company was developing and that the next general meeting might see a serious attempt to curb their power and influence if not to oust them altogether. This intention clearly appeared from the requisition of 10th June, 1955, by a number of the shareholders, including the plaintiff, for an extraordinary general meeting, at which it was proposed, among other things, to increase the number of directors to twelve and to appoint new directors. This, however, was of course, subsequent to the resolution of 17th May, but it, and the knowledge of the rather formidable number of proxies which had been [22] entrusted to the plaintiff, preceded the resolution of 16th June, effecting the actual allotment.

The defendant directors take up the position that the sole object of the resolution of 17th May, 1955, was to avail of an offer of fresh capital made at a time when fresh capital was not only needed but needed urgently. There can be a legitimate difference of opinion as to whether fresh capital was necessary. The plaintiff took the view, which he expressed at the meeting, that an issue of shares was quite unnecessary; and the expert witnesses differed in their views as to whether it was necessary or not. It is hard, however, to see how the issue could reasonably be regarded as an urgent necessity. Mr Breen both in evidence and when he learnt of the offer from Dr Thomas Ryan before the meeting, expressed the view that it was 'Manna from Heaven' and that it should be accepted at once lest Mr Ryan should change his mind. In that connection, it is one of the curiosities of this case that no formal application for shares was ever made by or required from Mr Ryan and that, according to himself, he did not subsequently regard himself as having offered to take shares and was reluctant to do so only that he felt the family honour was involved. The professed attitude of Mr Breen and the other defendant directors was, naturally, that the position and prospects of the company were so poor that any offer of help should be gratefully and unhesitatingly accepted. This was a curious appraisal of the fortunes of a company which, between 1948 and 1954, had been able to increase its fixed assets by over £40,000, while also increasing its excess of assets over liabilities to the position that this excess in 1954 was twice the issued capital, which had been able to write off £14,000 worth of stock which had paid a dividend of 6% or more for every year except 1953 (in which year a dividend *could* have been paid), while putting back over £26,000 in undistributed profits into the business, and which was about to declare a trading profit of more than twice that of the previous year. A more just appreciation of the position, but one inconsistent with this professed attitude of theirs, was shown by these directors in their appeal for proxies of 16th June, 1955 in which they stated, probably correctly, that the company 'has never been in a sounder position nor run on more efficient lines'. The suggestion of urgency was sought to be related to necessary capital expenditure, out of the items discussed at the meeting of 17th May, only a few amounting to a comparatively small figure which could easily be met out of undistributed profits, were agreed on. The two matters, alleged to have been the occasion of Mr Ryan's offer in the discussion in March, 1955, between him and his son, and on which so much stress was placed in evidence as matters of urgent and large expenditure were, in fact, not decided on at the meeting but postponed on a rather indefinite basis. One of these, the question of the replacement of a furnace, was left over to await the result of an examination of the furnace to take place in August. The other, and heavier item of expense, was the installation of a Vinyl plant, but it was decided that it was imperative that the company should obtain a long term agreement with Messrs Fords (who were the only customers who wished to have Vinyl glass) before undertaking further expense in the matter. This item is again referred to in the minutes of the subsequent meeting of 16th June, according to which 'the Chairman outlined a letter received from Messrs Fords concerning the use of Vinyl'. There is no record of any decision as to the installation of the plant or anything to suggest the matter had become more urgent or indeed that the plant would ever need to be installed. Of the items actually agreed on at the meeting, one, an engineering lathe at £800, represented about half the total amount, and was admitted by Dr Thomas Ryan in evidence not to be strictly necessary although he thought it would be an excellent addition to the factory and could be a source of considerable profit. Finally, although the overdraft of the company with its bankers would appear high if considered without relation to the general financial position of the company, there was no suggestion that the bankers were in any way pressing in the matter or had expressed any dissatisfaction nor does it appear that there was any definite intention or idea of paying off the overdraft.

I find the suggestion of urgency wholly unconvincing and quite inadequate to explain the somewhat indecent haste with which the matter was put through. No agenda or notice of any resolution was sent out beforehand, and in the agenda circulated at the meeting the only heading the matter could be related to was 'capital position', which was an item appearing in the agenda and discussed at nearly every meeting. Mr Nash's plea for adjournment and an opportunity of further consideration was rejected rather summarily. The board meeting was being held at a time when the draft accounts for the year 1954 had been prepared – they were, in fact, discussed at the meeting – and the annual general meeting of the company was due to be held within a month or so. Was [23] there any good or compelling reason why the matter should not have been held over and the whole position put before the company as a whole at that meeting? The defendant directors took and take the position that if money were required (and they say it was), past history had shown the futility of appealing to the shareholders. In his somewhat exaggerated way, Dr Thomas Ryan said they had 'tried and tried' unsuccessfully with the shareholders over all the years. In fact, only one appeal had been made to the shareholders to take up an issue of shares, that of October, 1953, made by Mr Ryan on his own initiative and in a form settled by him. His object was, allegedly, to test the pulse of the shareholders but, if that were genuinely the object of the appeal, it was very inept for its purpose. It is unnecessary to go into the detailed criticism that had been made of it. It is enough to quote a sentence from the advice of one of the two stockbrokers whom Mr Ryan and Mr Breen were, unknown to the other directors, consulting about the same time. He said 17th November, 1953: 'I do not, however, consider that this circular from the company could attract possible new subscribers of capital.' It is not unreasonable to suppose that, if the matter were put properly and fairly before the shareholders and in the light of the progress and prospects of the company as of May or June of 1955, the response would have been very different. The defendant directors did not choose to take that course but, if the matter were merely one of a legitimate difference of opinion or even of an error of judgment, their action could not be impugned. The net question in this case, however, is whether their action was taken in good faith in what they believed to be in the interests of the company. On the evidence, and in all the circumstances, I am of opinion that it was not so taken. I believe their action was primarily inspired by the dual desire to confer a privilege or benefit on James Ryan and to increase the voting strength of the Ryan interests.

Against this view two practical considerations were urged. One was that control, if desired, could have been obtained at any time previously in a manner that could not have been questioned. The only such manner, however, that could be suggested was the issue of a debenture giving, as it legitimately could, a controlling interest. It is useful to recall in this connection, that the issue of such a debenture to Rybar was actually mooted by Mr Ryan, at the meeting of 3rd May, 1952, as an alternative to the proposal of Mr Nash to seek accommodation from Lancegaye's bankers, or if such accommodation were refused. The suggestion of Mr Ryan, according to Mr Nash, was that Rybar, if it took a debenture, should get a controlling interest in Lancegaye or on the board. This was denied by Dr Ryan while Mr Ryan stated in evidence that he was never anxious that Rybar should take a debenture. I accept Mr Nash's evidence on the point. I also accept his evidence, although it does not appear in the minute, that it was he who was to approach the Bank. It is highly significant that, notwithstanding this, Mr Ryan wrote to the Bank two days later a letter couched in terms which courted a refusal and which, but for the intervention of Mr Nash resulting in the bank manager not putting the actual letter before his board, would almost certainly have evoked a refusal of accommodation. In the event of such refusal, I feel little doubt in that Rybar would have taken a debenture with a controlling interest. In the actual event, nothing further was heard from Rybar although Dr Thomas Ryan had stated at the meeting of 3rd May that he would investigate the matter on his return to England and inform Lancegaye. In his evidence, Dr Thomas Ryan said he did discuss the matter later with his father but they decided it would be foolish to make a large investment in Lancegaye, notwithstanding that, as he says he then told his father, Rybar had ample funds available – a fact which his father would have known better than himself. I believe this episode was a deliberate and well planned attempt to gain control of Lancegaye which failed only by reason of Mr Nash's insistence on first approaching the bank and by reason of the bank granting the accommodation which Mr Ryan did his best to ensure it would not grant. At any later stage, the difficulty in taking a debenture that a large sum would first have to be paid to discharge the bank overdraft, might have been a real obstacle. At the time in question, it was only an apparent one, because the overdraft was limited, prior to May, 1952 to £10,000 and securities were held amounting to approximately the same sum. Dr Thomas Ryan mentioned a sum of £60,000 as then necessary but this is arrived at by the device of relating figures of later years to that time. Lancegaye did not then require £30,000 nor was the bank overdraft, as has been seen, anywhere near another £30,000. I cannot, therefore, accept the reason he now gives as having operated then against taking a debenture. I believe the resolution of May 1955, was a belated attempt to secure the same [24] result as the abortive effort three years earlier.

The other practical consideration urged was that, in fact, the amount of shares agreed to be issued was insufficient to secure an absolute majority of the total voting strength of Lancegaye. This is so, but the amount was sufficient to ensure a strong likelihood of an effective or working majority. At the annual general meeting in November of 1954, the resolution supported by Mr Nash had been defeated on a poll by about 5,000 votes, and it might have seemed that a further 15,000 votes would ensure an ample majority. Again, the subsequent success of Mr Nash in mustering such a large measure of support was, possibly, not to be anticipated.

I have endeavoured to approach the question under consideration without paying regard to matters which mainly arose subsequent to the meeting of 17th May and, therefore, would not necessarily have a bearing on the motives inducing the resolution of that date. Those matters do, however, indicate an intention to put the transaction through and to regain control of Lancegaye at all costs, and, to that extent, they are at least consistent with the existence of such an attitude of 17th May. One of these matters was the determination to hold the annual general meeting before the extraordinary general meeting which had been requisitioned. This was for the ostensible purpose of putting the whole position of the directors before the shareholders so that their actions could be approved or disapproved. It is not very clear why this could not be done as satisfactorily at the extraordinary meeting, but the course adopted ensured that there would not be time for the shareholders to nominate directors. Again, the earlier date fixed for the annual meeting – in breach of, if not an undertaking, at least a very plausible representation to the Plaintiff – was sought to be justified by a supposed obligation to hold the extraordinary meeting within twenty-one days of the requisition. In the event, it was not fixed for a date within the twenty-one days nor did the articles require that it should be. Neither is it likely that anyone would have made any point, even if there had been any substance in it, as to a date being fixed outside the twenty-one days. The rapidity with which the printing for the annual meeting was accomplished – the possibility of which must always have been known to Mr Doyle – confirms the impression that the date of the annual meeting was deliberately fixed to frustrate so far as possible the wishes and intentions of the shareholders and to ensure the confirmation or re-election of the existing directors. The place of the meeting was fixed for Dublin, instead of, as normally, at Templemore, and Mr Breen made no secret of the fact that this was for the purpose of making it as difficult as possible for the local shareholders to attend.

Another matter of some relevance in this connection is the attempt, at the meeting of 25th June, 1955 to secure the position of Mr Doyle by granting him a ten-year contract as general manager, which would bind the company. This was on the eve of a meeting of the company which might well have been so dissatisfied with his services as not to have wished to retain him at all.

One other matter which extended over the period both before the meeting of 17th May, 1955, and after it, was the curious circumstances of Mr Breen's application for a revision of his agreement with the company and the withdrawal, amounting to suppression, of the application and the correspondence. The only thing that can be said about it is that the general air of obscurity and concealment about the whole matter is in keeping with other actions of the defendant directors. The evidence as a whole tends to the conclusion, that, in many of their actions, these directors and Mr Ryan were lacking in a sense of responsibility as to their fiduciary position and as to their duties to the shareholders and to the company and were concerned only with their own interests.

This attitude appears also from the lack of any consideration of the possible detrimental effect on the shares and shareholders of the company, in respect of Stock Exchange quotation or income tax relief, of the issue of shares in the manner adopted. In his letter of 17th June, 1955, the Secretary of the Stock Exchange said: 'the allotment of shares in a public company to an individual in this way is most unusual and is a procedure which is not favoured by my committee unless the consent of shareholders is first obtained and the reason for such allotment clearly explained to them.'

This was an unequivocal disapproval which might have led to serious consequences. Again, the preferred shares originally issued enjoyed an income tax remission under Section 7 of the Finance Act, 1932, and Section 7 of the Finance Act, 1935, and the deferred shares were subject to the requirements of a nationality declaration for the purposes of the Control of Manufacturers Acts. Both of these matters were ignored and serious prejudice could have resulted to the shareholders and to the Company.

[25] Another element of irresponsibility emerges in connection with the addendum to the resolution of 17th May, viz. 'subject to the action in so allocating shares be regular' (sic). Mr Nash, in opposing the resolution, had expressed his opinion that it was irregular and improper, that the existing shareholders were being deprived of the valuable right of first preference in taking up a large portion of the unissued capital, and that the only regular and fair method was to offer this capital to the existing shareholders in proportion to their holdings in the first instance. The board were not willing to accept this advice of the plaintiff, who was also their solicitor, but, presumably, the addendum meant that they were going to get competent advice on the matter. No legal advice was obtained by the board but, at the next meeting, it was stated that Mr Breen had obtained such advice but the advice, other than the effect of it, was not disclosed. In the meantime, the chairman, Dr Ryan, had discussed the matter with Mr Klingner, the company's auditor, who had previously advised him that the action would be within the powers of the board. Mr Nash had also

obtained legal opinion, to the contrary effect, as he mentioned at the same meeting. In these circumstances, it could hardly be said that the advice contemplated by the addendum had been obtained but, nevertheless, the board went ahead with the matter.

The resolution of 17th May, was defective, not only as to its being conditional in the sense just mentioned, but also because it did not specify the number and type of shares to be issued to Mr Ryan. The share capital of Lancegaye as already noted was divided in the Memorandum of Association between preferred and deferred shares in the proportion of three to one, and the original issue had been made on this basis; but it did not necessarily follow, nor could it be implied, that an issue or portion of the unissued capital must be made on that basis. The new shares were, in fact, issued on this basis and James Ryan was entered in the share register of Lancegaye on 2nd June, 1955, as the holder of 15,000 preferred shares and 5,000 deferred shares. For the two reasons mentioned, the resolution of 17th May, was not valid to justify this issue or registration and there was no other justification or authority.

An attempt was made at the meeting of 16th June, 1955, to remedy this matter by passing a resolution, particularising the shares. It was in the following terms: 'that the following shares, 15,000 6% Preferred Ordinary Shares numbered 96,001 to 111,000 inclusive and 5,000 6% Deferred Ordinary Shares numbered 32,001 to 37,000 inclusive be and are hereby allocated at par to Mr James Ryan, these above numbered shares to rank for dividend as from 1st July, 1955.' At the time of this meeting, one of the present actions had already been commenced and the summons served on some of the defendants. The resolution of 16th June, was clearly subsidiary and ancillary to that of May 17th, and tainted with the same lack of good faith and the same lack of due consideration of the matters relevant to be considered by directors in exercising their discretionary and fiduciary powers, and it must stand or fall with the resolution of 17th May.

For the defendants reliance was placed on *Foss* v. *Harbottle* (2 Hare 461) but I do not think the principle of that case applies to the present proceedings. It, and the cases which have followed and applied it, were concerned with wrongs alleged to be done to the company as a whole and in respect of which it was, therefore, for the company, as such to complain or not. See *Edwards* v. *Halliwell* [1950] 2 All E.R. 1064. In the present case, particular wrong has been done to individual shareholders, including the plaintiff, by the lack of good faith on the part of the directors in the purported exercise of their discretionary powers. In *Clark* v. *Workman* [1920] 1 I.R. 107, (post p. 359) Ross J. held, notwithstanding *Foss* v. *Harbottle* having been cited, that the transfer of a controlling interest in a company is not a matter of mere internal management, it may involve a complete transformation of the company, and consequently such a transfer may in a proper case be restrained. Again, the decision of Peterson, J., in *Piercy*

v. *S. Mills & Co. Ltd.* [1920] 1 Ch. 77, is very much in point here. He there held that directors are not entitled to use their power of issuing shares merely for the purpose of maintaining their control, or the control of themselves and their friends, over the affairs of the company, or merely for the purpose of defeating the wishes of the existing majority of shareholders.

Part of the principle of *Foss* v. *Harbottle*, if not the main feature of it, is that, in the case of a matter capable of being legalised or regularised by a majority of the shareholders, the person complaining of some action by the directors of the company, should await and abide by the outcome of a general meeting of the company; and, for this reason, it was contended that the present action was premature and unsustainable. I think, in the circumstances of the present case, this argument overlooks the fundamental point [26] that it was precisely the question whether the 15,000 votes of James Ryan could be used at the general meeting that was in issue. By the time of the commencement of the action, in June 1955, the forces of each side had been mustered and it was agreed, at the hearing, that the respective figures were approximately 51,000 votes for the plaintiff and his supporters, and nearly 53,000 for the Ryan family and their supporters. This 53,000 would include the 15,000 from the allotment to James Ryan. If he were entitled to use these votes, the Ryan family and supporters would not thereby have an absolute majority of the issued capital but there is little doubt that they would have had an actual majority at the meetings. Without the 15,000 votes ranking, the plaintiff would have had an absolute majority (51,000 out of a total voting strength of 96,000), but the general meeting would not have had power to undo or reverse what had been done by the directors in the exercise of the power and discretion delegated to them. On the other hand a majority at the meeting could have approved, if so minded of what had been done but this would leave the question undetermined and still outstanding whether the directors had acted in bad faith to the prejudice of individual shareholders. This position is, I think, recognised on the following portion of the passage from Buckley on the Companies Acts, dealing with the principle of *Foss* v. *Harbottle* and cited by Danckwerts, J., in *Palvides* v. *Jensen* [1956] 2 All E.R. 518, at p. 521 –'. . . it is idle to say that a meeting ought to be called in which the alleged wrongdoers should not vote, for that would be trying the question of fraud as a preliminary step for ascertaining the term of the action in which it is to be tried.' Again, if I am right in my view that the entry of James Ryan in the register of shareholders on 2nd June, 1955, was invalid, the plaintiff was entitled to bring the first action when he did without waiting for a general meeting to consider the matter. For these reasons, I think the proceedings were not premature or unsuitable. A somewhat similar position arose in *Punt* v. *Symons & Co. Ltd.* [1903] 2 Ch. 506 and Byrne J. there held that, where shares had been issued by directors, not for the general

benefit of the company but for the purpose of controlling the holders of
the greatest number of shares by obtaining a majority of voting power, the
directors ought to be restrained from holding the meeting at which the
votes of the new shareholders were to have been used. He considered and
distinguished *Foss* v. *Harbottle*. It makes no difference to my view, in this
respect, that in fact the number of shares issued would not have been
sufficient to ensure an absolute majority. I am concerned with motive and
it is irrelevant to that consideration whether the object would have been
fully achieved.

Having the two-fold object, as I hold, of conferring a privilege or advantage on James Ryan and also increasing the voting strength of the Ryan
family, is it of any avail to the defendant directors that they may also have
had the object, other things being equal, of benefiting the company. This
was certainly not, in my view, their sole object and I cannot say that it, in
fact, contributed to their decision. Even if it did, it was conceded in argument that would not suffice to validate the resolutions if the motives were
partly improper. If this matter were not conceded, the case of *Portland* v.
Tompson 11 H.L.C. 32, particularly at p. 54 would have been in point.

I have arrived at the conclusion that the resolutions of 17th May, and
16th June, 1955, were not an honest exercise of the directors powers in
the interests of either the shareholders or the company, and cannot be
allowed to take effect; and the entry of James Ryan in the share register
was invalid and must be set aside. . . .

[27] In the result, therefore, for the reasons given, I hold that the plaintiff
is entitled to an Order:

(1) Declaring that neither of the resolutions of 17th May, 1955 and 16th
June, 1955, was a *bona fide* exercise of their powers by the directors or
constituted a valid or effective allotment of shares to the defendant James
Ryan.

(2) Declaring the entry in the share register of the defendant James Ryan
on 2nd June, 1955, to be irregular and invalid;

(3) Directing the rectification of such register by the deletion of such entry;

(4) Directing the cancellation of the share certificates, if any, issued to
the defendant James Ryan pursuant to such resolution;

(5) An injunction restraining the defendants, other than James Ryan, from
proceeding further with or taking any steps under either of the said resolutions and restraining the defendant James Ryan from exercising any voting
or other rights in respect of the shares issued to him pursuant to such
resolutions.

Howard Smith Ltd. v. Ampol Ltd.
[1974] A.C. 821 (P.C.)

A company ('Millers Ltd.') that was somewhat short of funds was the subject of a take-over bid from an associate of its principal shareholder (Ampol Ltd.), which controlled 55 per cent of its shares. Another company (Howard Smith Ltd.) then made a take-over bid for Millers Ltd. In order to block the Ampol Ltd. bid, and to raise funds for the company, Millers Ltd.'s directors decided to make a substantial allotment of shares in the company to Howard Smith Ltd., and the effect of the allotment was to convert Ampol Ltd. and its associates into minority shareholders. Proceedings were brought to set aside the allotment.

LORD WILBERFORCE: . . . [831] The central findings of the judge, directed as they are to a determination of the purpose of the Millers' board of directors in making the disputed issue, and based as they are upon his estimate of the individual directors as seen in the witness box, are such as an appellate tribunal would necessarily respect. Their Lordships in fact are of opinion that upon the evidence given at the trial these findings are not only supportable, but inevitable. They will first endeavour to summarise them and will then consider to what conclusion they should lead in law.
Findings of fact

1. The judge found, as their Lordships think it right to make clear at once, that the Millers' directors were not motivated by any purpose of personal gain or advantage, or by any desire to retain their position on the board. The judge said:

> I discard the suggestion that the directors of Millers allotted these shares to Howard Smith in order to gain some private advantage for themselves by way of retention of their seats on the board or by obtaining a higher price for their personal shareholding. Personal considerations of this nature were not to the forefront so far as any of these directors was concerned, and in this respect their integrity emerges unscathed from this contest.

2. He then proceeded to consider the main issue which he formulated in accordance with the principle stated in the High Court of Australia by Dixon J. in *Mills* v. *Mills* (1938) 60 C.L.R. 150, 185-186. This was to ascertain the substantial object the accomplishment of which formed the real ground of the board's action. The issue before him he considered to be whether the primary purpose of the majority of directors was to satisfy Millers' need for capital or whether their primary purpose was to destroy the majority holding of Ampol and [its associate].

[832] In order to assist him in deciding upon the alternative motivations contended for, the judge considered first, at some length, the objective question whether Millers was in fact in need of capital. This approach was

criticised before their Lordships: it was argued that what mattered was not the actual financial condition of Millers, but what the majority directors bona fide considered that condition to be. Their Lordships accept that such a matter as the raising of finance is one of management, within the responsibility of the directors: they accept that it would be wrong for the court to substitute its opinion for that of the management, or indeed to question the correctness of the management's decision, on such a question, if bona fide arrived at. There is no appeal on merits from management decisions to courts of law: nor will courts of law assume to act as a kind of supervisory board over decisions within the powers of management honestly arrived at.

But accepting all of this, when a dispute arises whether directors of a company made a particular decision for one purpose or for another, or whether, there being more than one purpose, one or another purpose was the substantial or primary purpose, the court, in the Lordships' opinion, is entitled to look at the situation objectively in order to estimate how critical or pressing, or substantial, or, per contra, insubstantial an alleged requirement may have been. If it finds that a particular requirement, though real, was not urgent, or critical, at the relevant time, it may have reason to doubt, or discount, the assertions of individuals that they acted solely in order to deal with it, particularly when the action they took was unusual or even extreme. . . .

[833] [The Judge] found that the primary purpose so far as the management team was concerned (this is *not* the directors. . .) was to issue shares to Howard Smith so as to enable the Howard Smith takeover to proceed. As to the Millers' majority directors he said:

> They had found themselves enmeshed in a takeover struggle. The greater part, if not the whole, of their thinking in the critical days up to and including July 6 was directed to this takeover situation. It is unreal and unconvincing to hear them assert in the witness box that their dominant purpose was to obtain capital rather than to promote the Howard Smith's takeover offer, and I do not believe these assertions.
>
> The conclusion that I have reached is that the primary purpose of the four directors in voting in favour of this allotment was to reduce the proportionate combined shareholding of Ampol and [its associates] in order to induce Howard Smiths to proceed with its takeover offer. There was a majority bloc in the share register. Their intention was to destroy its character as a majority. The directors were, and had for some weeks been, concerned at the position of strength occupied by Ampol and Bulkships together. They were aware that in the light of the attitude of these two shareholders Howard Smiths could not be expected to proceed with its takeover offer that these directors

regarded as attractive. They issued the shares so as to reduce the interest of these two shareholders to something significantly less than that of a majority. This was the immediate purpose. The ultimate purpose was to procure the continuation by Howard Smith's of the takeover offer made by that company.

Their Lordships accept these findings.

[834] *The law*

The directors, in deciding to issue shares, forming part of Millers' unissued capital, to Howard Smith, acted under clause 8 of the company's articles of association. This provides, subject to certain qualifications which have not been invoked, that the shares shall be under the control of the directors, who may allot or otherwise dispose of the same to such persons on such terms as the directors think fit. Thus, and this is not disputed, the issue was clearly intra vires the directors. But, intra vires though the issue may have been, the directors' power under this article is a fiduciary power: and it remains the case that an exercise of such a power though formally valid, may be attacked on the ground that it was not exercised for the purpose for which it was granted. It is at this point that the contentions of the parties diverge. The extreme argument on one side is that, for validity, what is required is bona fide exercise of the power in the interests of the company: that once it is found that the directors were not motivated by self-interest – i.e. by a desire to retain their control of the company or their positions on the board – the matter is concluded in their favour and that the court will not inquire into the validity of their reasons for making the issue. All decided cases, it was submitted, where an exercise of such a power as this has been found invalid, are cases where directors are found to have acted through self-interest of this kind.

On the other side, the main argument is that the purpose for which the power is conferred is to enable capital to be raised for the company, and that once it is found that the issue was not made for that purpose, invalidity follows.

It is fair to say that under the pressure of argument intermediate positions were taken by both sides, but in the main the arguments followed the polarisation which has been stated.

In their Lordships' opinion neither of the extreme positions can be maintained. It can be accepted, as one would only expect, that the majority of cases in which issues of shares are challenged in the courts are cases in which the vitiating element is the self-interest of the directors, or at least the purpose of the directors to preserve their own control of the management; see *Fraser* v. *Whalley* (1864) 2 Hem. & M. 10; *Punt* v. *Symons & Co. Ltd.* [1903] 2 Ch. 506; *Piercy* v. *S. Mills & Co. Ltd.* [1920] 1 Ch. 77; *Ngurli Ltd.* v. *McCann* (1953) 90 C.L.R. 425 and *Hogg* v. *Cramphorn Ltd.* [1967] Ch. 254, 267.

Further it is correct to say that where the self-interest of the directors is involved, they will not be permitted to assert that their action was bona fide thought to be, or was, in the interest of the company; pleas to this effect have invariably been rejected (e.g. *Fraser* v. *Whalley*, 2 Hem. & M. 10 and *Hogg* v. *Cramphorn Ltd.* [1967] Ch. 254) – just as trustees who buy trust property are not permitted to assert that they paid a good price.

But it does not follow from this, as the appellants assert, that the absence of any element of self-interest is enough to make an issue valid. Self-interest is only one, though no doubt the commonest, instance of improper motive: and, before one can say that a fiduciary power has been exercised for the purpose for which it was conferred, a wider investigation may have to be made. This is recognised in several well-known statements [835] of the law. Their Lordships quote the clearest which has so often been cited:

> Where the question is one of abuse of powers, the state of mind of those who acted, and the motive on which they acted, are all important, and you may go into the question of what their intention was, collecting from the surrounding circumstances all the materials which genuinely throw light upon that question of the state of mind of the directors so as to show whether they were honestly acting in discharge of their powers in the interests of the company or were acting from some bye-motive, possibly of personal advantage, or for any other reason. *(Hindle* v. *John Cotton Ltd.* (1919) 56 Sc.L.R. 625, 630-631, *per* Viscount Finlay).

On the other hand, taking the respondents' contention, it is, in their Lordships' opinion, too narrow an approach to say that the only valid purpose for which shares may be issued is to raise capital for the company. The discretion is not in terms limited in this way: the law should not impose such a limitation on directors' powers. To define in advance exact limits beyond which directors must not pass is, in their Lordships' view, impossible. This clearly cannot be done by enumeration, since the variety of situations facing directors of different types of company in different situations cannot be anticipated. No more, in their Lordships' view, can this be done by the use of a phrase – such as 'bona fide in the interest of the company as a whole,' or 'for some corporate purpose.' Such phrases, if they do anything more than restate the general principle applicable to fiduciary powers, at best serve, negatively, to exclude from the area of validity cases where the directors are acting sectionally, or partially: i.e. improperly favouring one section of the shareholders against another. Of such cases it has been said:

> The question which arises is sometimes not a question of the interest of the company at all, but a question of what is fair as between different classes of shareholders. Where such a case arises some other test than

that of the 'interests of the company' must be applied... *(Mills* v. *Mills,* 164, *per* Latham C.J.).

In their Lordships' opinion it is necessary to start with a consideration of the power whose exercise is in question, in this case a power to issue shares. Having ascertained, on a fair view, the nature of this power, and having defined as can best be done in the light of modern conditions the, or some, limits within which it may be exercised, it is then necessary for the court, if a particular exercise of it is challenged, to examine the substantial purpose for which it was exercised, and to reach a conclusion whether that purpose was proper or not. In doing so it will necessarily give credit to the bona fide opinion of the directors, if such is found to exist, and will respect their judgment as to matters of management; having done this, the ultimate conclusion has to be as to the side of a fairly broad line on which the case falls.

> The application of the general equitable principle to the acts of directors managing the affairs of a company cannot be as nice as it is [836] in the case of a trustee exercising a special power of appointment. *(Mills* v. *Mills,* 185-186, *per* Dixon J.).

The main stream of authority, in their Lordships' opinion, supports this approach. In *Punt* v. *Symons & Co. Ltd.* Byrne J. expressly accepts that there may be reasons other than to raise capital for which shares may be issued. In the High Court case of *Harlowe's Nominees Pty. Ltd.* v. *Woodside (Lakes Entrance) Oil Co. N.L.* (1968) 121 C.L.R. 483, an issue of shares was made to a large oil company in order, as was found, to secure the financial stability of the company. This was upheld as being within the power although it had the effect of defeating the attempt of the plaintiff to secure control by buying up the company's shares. The joint judgment of Barwick C.J., McTiernan J. and Kitto J. contains this passage, at p. 493:

> The principle is that although primarily the power is given to enable capital to be raised when required for the purposes of the company, there may be occasions when the directors may fairly and properly issue shares for other reasons, so long as those reasons relate to a purpose of benefiting the company as a whole, as distinguished from a purpose, for example, of maintaining control of the company in the hands of the directors themselves or their friends. An inquiry as to whether additional capital was presently required is often most relevant to the ultimate question upon which the validity or invalidity of the issue depends; but that ultimate question must always be whether in truth the issue was made honestly in the interests of the company. Directors in whom are vested the right and the duty of deciding where the company's interests lie and how they are to be served may be

concerned with a wide range of practical considerations, and their judgment, if exercised in good faith and not for irrelevant purposes, is not open to review in the courts. Thus in the present case it is not a matter for judicial concern, if it be the fact, that the allotment to Burmah would frustrate the ambitions of someone who was buying up shares as opportunity offered with a view to obtaining increased influence on the control of the company, or even that the directors realised that the allotment would have that result and found it agreeable to the personal wishes. . . .

Their Lordships were referred to the recent judgment of Berger J. in the Supreme Court of British Columbia, in *Teck Corporation Ltd.* v. *Millar* (1972) 33 D.L.R. (3d) 288.This was concerned with the affairs of Afton Mines Ltd. in which Teck Corporation Ltd., a resource conglomerate, had acquired a majority shareholding. Teck was indicating an intention to replace the board of directors of Afton with its own nominees with a view to causing Afton to enter into an agreement (called an 'ultimate deal') with itself for the exploitation by Teck of valuable mineral rights owned by Afton. Before this could be done, and in order to prevent it, the directors of Afton concluded an exploitation agreement with another company 'Canex'. One of its provisions, as is apparently common in this type of agreement in Canada, provided for the issue to Canex of a large number of shares in Afton, thus displacing Teck's majority. Berger J. found, at p. 328:

> [837] their [*sc.* the directors'] purpose was to obtain the best agreement they could while. . . still in control. Their purpose was in that sense to defeat Teck. But, not to defeat Teck's attempt to obtain control, rather it was to foreclose Teck's opportunity of obtaining for itself the ultimate deal. That was. . . no improper purpose.

His decision upholding the agreement with Canex on this basis appears to be in line with the English and Australian authorities to which reference has been made.

In relation to a different but analogous power, to refuse registration of a transfer, the wide range of considerations open to directors, and to the court upon challenge to an exercise of the power, is set out in the judgment of the High Court of Australia in *Australian Metropolitan Life Assurance Co. Ltd.* v. *Ure* (1923) 33 C.L.R. 199.

By contrast to the cases of *Harlowe* and *Teck,* the present case, on the evidence does not, on the findings of the trial judge, involve any consider-ations of management, within the proper sphere of the directors. The purpose found by the judge is simply and solely to dilute the majority voting power held by Ampol and Bulkships so as to enable a then minority of shareholders to sell their shares more advantageously. So far as authority goes, an issue of shares purely for the purpose of creating voting power has repeatedly been condemned: *Fraser* v. *Whalley*; *Punt* v. *Symons & Co. Ltd.*; *Piercy* v. *S. Mills & Co. Ltd.* ('merely for the purpose of defeating the wishes of the existing majority of shareholders') and *Hogg* v. *Cramphorn Ltd.* In the leading Australian case of *Mills* v. *Mills*, it was accepted in the High Court that if the purpose of issuing shares was solely to alter the voting power the issue would be invalid. And, though the reported decisions, naturally enough, are expressed in terms of their own facts, there are clear considerations of principle which support the trend they establish. The constitution of a limited company normally provides for directors, with powers of management, and shareholders with defined voting powers having power to appoint the directors, and to take, in general meeting, by majority vote, decisions on matters not reserved for management. Just as it is established that directors, within their management powers, may take decisions against the wishes of the majority of shareholders, and indeed that the majority of shareholders cannot control them in the exercise of these powers while they remain in office (*Automatic Self-Cleansing Filter Syndicate Co. Ltd.* v. *Cuninghame* [1906] 2 Ch. 34), so it must be unconstitutional for directors to use their fiduciary powers over the shares in the company purely for the purpose of destroying an existing majority, or creating a new majority which did not previously exist. To do so is to interfere with that element of the company's constitution which is separate from and set against their powers. If there is added, moreover, to this immediate purpose, an ulterior purpose to enable an offer for shares to proceed which the existing majority was in a position to block, the departure from the legitimate use of the fiduciary power becomes not less, but all the greater. The right to dispose of shares at a given price is essentially an individual right to be exercised on individual decision and on which a majority, in the absence [838] of oppression or similar impropriety, is entitled to prevail. Directors are of course entitled to offer advice, and bound to supply information, relevant to the making of such a decision, but to use their fiduciary power solely for the purpose of shifting the power to decide to whom and at what price shares are to be sold cannot be related to any purpose for which the power over the share capital was conferred upon them. That this is the position in law was in effect recognised by the majority directors themselves when they attempted to justify the issue as made primarily in order to obtain much needed capital for the company. And once this primary purpose was rejected, as it was by Street J., there is nothing legitimate left as a basis for their action, except honest behaviour. That is not, in itself, enough.

Their Lordships therefore agree entirely with the conclusion of Street J. that the power to issue and allot shares was improperly exercised by the issue of shares to Howard Smith. It was not disputed that an action to set aside the allotment and for rectification of the register was properly brought by Ampol as plaintiff.

Cook v. Deeks
[1916] A.C. 554 (P.C.)

The Toronto Construction Co. Ltd. (the company) had prospered from contracts it had executed for the Canadian Pacific Railway Co. and its related enterprises. When a major new contract was being negotiated, three of the company's directors (who between them had a majority of the company's shares) succeeded in having the contract eventually being awarded to themselves rather than to the company. They never gave the company even an opportunity of having the contract for itself, and they concealed from the plaintiff (the remaining director and shareholder) all circumstances regarding the negotiation.

LORD BUCKMASTER L.C.: . . . [560] The negotiations for this contract were opened by a telephone message sent through to Mr Hinds at the Toronto Construction Company's office. Upon receipt of that message certain units of price were prepared in the company's office, and, the prices being ultimately fixed, the defendant Hinds was informed by Mr Leonard that, although the prices had been agreed to, the contract would not be then immediately let, as it was necessary that there should be an appropriation of the necessary cash made to authorize the contract by the Canadian Pacific Railway Company.

During the whole of this discussion, up till the time when these prices were fixed, it does not appear that at any moment the representatives of the Canadian Pacific Railway Company were told that this contract was in any way different from the others that had been negotiated in the same manner on behalf of the Toronto Construction Company, although it was plain that Mr Leonard had been told by Mr Deeks, when he was engaged on the Georgian Bay and Seaboard line, that when it was finished Messrs. Deeks and Hinds intended to go on their own account and leave Mr Cook. But after all the necessary preliminaries of the contract had been concluded Mr Hinds made to Mr Leonard this statement: 'Remember, if we get this contract it is to be Deeks and I, and not the Toronto Construction Company.'

On March 12, 1912, the Canadian Pacific Railway Company made the necessary appropriation for the contract, and this was communicated to Mr Deeks by Mr Ramsay, that company's engineer of construction, who said that they might proceed with the contract at once. As from this moment, although the formal contract was not signed until April 1, 1912, the defendants became certain of their position, and knew that they had obtained the contract for themselves. They then for the first time informed the plaintiff of what had happened. He protested without result, and the defendant the Dominion Construction Company was formed by the three defendants G. S. Deeks, G. M. Deeks, and T. R. Hinds, to carry out the work. The contract was accordingly taken over by this company, by whom the work was carried out and the profits made. . . .

[562] In other words, they intentionally concealed all circumstances relating to their negotiations until a point had been reached when the whole arrangement had been concluded in their own favour and there was no longer any real chance that there could be any interference with their plans. This means that while entrusted with the conduct of the affairs of the company they deliberately designed to exclude, and used their influence and position to exclude, the company whose interest it was their first duty to protect. . . .

[563] It is quite right to point out the importance of avoiding the establishment of rules as to directors' duties which would impose upon them burdens so heavy and responsibilities so great that men of good position would hesitate to accept the office. But, on the other hand, men who assume the complete control of a company's business must remember that they are not at liberty to sacrifice the interests which they are bound to protect, and, while ostensibly acting for the company, divert in their own favour business which should properly belong to the company they represent.

Their Lordships think that, in the circumstances, the defendants T. R. Hinds and G. S. and G. M. Deeks were guilty of a distinct breach of duty in the course they took to secure the contract, and that they cannot retain the benefit of such contract for themselves, but must be regarded as holding it on behalf of the company.

Regal (Hastings) Ltd. v. Gulliver
[1967] 2 A.C. 134n. (H.L.)

In order to enhance the plaintiff company's asset value (its business being running cinemas) with a view to selling the entire enterprise, the directors decided to take a lease on other cinemas. Because the company did not have sufficient funds to provide the lessor with security, its then directors and solicitor came to its assistance by putting some of their own money into the company's subsidiary, which then acquired the lease. Subsequently, the company and the subsidiary were taken over, and the directors and solicitor made substantial profits on their brief investment. The company then sued them to recover those profits.

VISCOUNT SANKEY: . . . [137] The appellants say they are entitled to succeed: (i) because the respondents secured for themselves the profits upon the acquisition and sale of the shares in Amalgamated by using the knowledge acquired as directors and solicitors respectively of Regal and by using their said respective positions and without the knowledge or consent of Regal; (ii) because the doctrine laid down with regard to trustees is equally applicable to directors and solicitors. Although both in the court of first instance and the Court of Appeal the question of fraud was the prominent feature, the appellants' counsel in this House at once stated that it was no part of his case and quite irrelevant to his arguments. His contention was that the respondents were in a fiduciary capacity in relation to the appellants and, as such, accountable in the circumstances for the profit which they made on the sale of the shares.

As to the duties and liabilities of those occupying such a fiduciary position, a number of cases were cited to us which were not brought to the attention of the trial judge. In my view, the respondents were in a fiduciary position and their liability to account does not depend upon proof of mala fides. The general rule of equity is that no one who has duties of a fiduciary nature to perform is allowed to enter into engagements in which he has or can have a personal interest conflicting with the interests of those whom he is bound to protect. If he holds any property so acquired as trustee, he is bound to account for it to his cestui que trust. The earlier cases are concerned with [138] trusts of specific property: *Keech* v. *Sandford* (1726) Sel. Cas. Ch. 261 *per* Lord King L.C. The rule, however, applies to agents, as, for example, solicitors and directors, when acting in a fiduciary capacity. . . .

[139] It is not, however, necessary to discuss all the cases cited, because the respondents admitted the generality of the rule as contended for by the appellants, but were concerned rather to confess and avoid it. Their contention was that, in this case, upon a true perspective of the facts, they were under no equity to account for the profits which they made. I will deal first with the respondents, other than Gulliver and Garton. We were referred to *Imperial Hydropathic Hotel Co., Blackpool* v. *Hampson* (1882) 23 Ch.D.1 where Bowen L.J., drew attention to the difference between directors and trustees, but the case is not an authority for contending that a director cannot come within the general rule. No doubt there may be exceptions to the general rule as for example, where a purchase is entered into after the trustee had divested himself of his trust sufficiently long before the purchase to avoid the possibility of his making use of special information acquired by him as trustee (see the remarks of Lord Eldon in *Ex parte James* (1803) 8 Ves.337) or where he purchases with full knowledge and consent of his cestui que trust. *Imperial Hydropathic Hotel Co., Blackpool* v. *Hampson* makes no exception to the general rule that a solicitor or director, if acting in a fiduciary capacity, is liable to account for the profits made by him from knowledge acquired when so acting.

It was then argued that it would have been a breach of trust for the respondents, as directors of Regal, to have invested more than £2,000 of Regal's money in Amalgamated, and that the transaction would never have been carried through if they had not themselves put up the other £3,000. Be it so, but it is impossible to maintain that, because it would have been a breach of trust to advance more than £2,000 from Regal and that the only way to finance the matter was for the directors to advance the balance themselves, a situation arose which brought the respondents outside the general rule and permitted them to retain the profits which accrued to them from the action they took. At all material times they were directors and in a fiduciary position, and they used and acted upon their exclusive knowledge acquired as such directors. They framed resolutions by which they made a profit for themselves. They sought no authority from the company to do so, and, by reason of their position and actions, they made large profits for which, in my view, they are liable to account to the company.

LORD RUSSELL OF KILLOWEN: . . . [144] The rule of equity which insists on those, who by use of a fiduciary position make a profit, being liable to account for that profit, in no way depends on fraud, or absence of bona fides; or upon such questions or considerations as whether the profit would or should otherwise have gone to the plaintiff, or whether the profiteer was under a duty to obtain the source of the profit for the plaintiff, or whether he took a risk or acted as he did for the benefit of the plaintiff, or whether the plaintiff has in fact been damaged or benefited by his action. [145] The liability arises from the mere fact of a profit having, in the stated circumstances, been made. The profiteer, however honest and well-intentioned, cannot escape the risk of being called upon to account.

The leading case of *Keech* v. *Sandford* is an illustration of the strictness of this rule of equity in this regard, and of how far the rule is independent of these outside considerations. A lease of the profits of a market had been devised to a trustee for the benefit of an infant. A renewal on behalf of the infant was refused. It was absolutely unobtainable. The trustee, finding that it was impossible to get a renewal for the benefit of the infant, took a lease for his own benefit. Though his duty to obtain it for the infant was incapable of performance, nevertheless he was ordered to assign the lease to the infant, upon the bare ground that, if a trustee on the refusal to renew might have a lease for himself, few renewals would be made for the benefit of cestuis que trust. Lord King L.C. said

> This may seem hard, that the trustee is the only person of all mankind who might not have the lease: but it is very proper that the rule should be strictly pursued, and not in the least relaxed. . . . [147]

My Lords, I have no hesitation in coming to the conclusion, upon the facts of this case, that these shares, when acquired by the directors, were acquired by reason, and only by reason of the fact that they were directors of Regal, and in the course of their execution of that office.

It now remains to consider whether in acting as directors of Regal they stood in a fiduciary relationship to that company. Directors of a limited company are the creatures of statute and occupy a position peculiar to themselves. In some respects they resemble trustees, in others they do not. In some respects they resemble agents, in others they do not. In some

respects they resemble managing partners, in others they do not. In *In re
Forest of Dean Coal Mining Co.* (1878) 10 Ch.D. 450 a director was held
not liable for omitting to recover promotion money which had been improperly paid on the formation of the company. He knew of the improper
payment, but he was not appointed a director until a later date. It was held
that, although a trustee of settled property which included a debt would
be liable for neglecting to sue for it, a director of a company was not a
trustee of debts due to the company and was not liable. I cite two passages
from the judgment of Sir George Jessel M.R.

> Directors have sometimes been called trustees, or commercial trus-
> tees, and sometimes they have been called managing partners, it does
> not matter what you call them so long as you understand what their
> true position is, which is that they are really commercial men managing
> a trading concern for the benefit of themselves and all other sharehol-
> ders in it.

Later, after pointing out that traders have a discretion whether they shall
sue for a debt, which discretion is not vested in trustees of a debt under
a settlement, he said:

> Again directors are called trustees. They are no doubt trustees of
> assets which have come to their hands, or which are under their control,
> but they are not trustees of a debt due to the company. . . . A director
> is the managing partner of the concern, and although a debt is due
> to the concern I do not think it right to call him a trustee of that debt
> which remains unpaid, though his liability in respect of it may in
> certain cases and in some respects be analogous to the liability of a
> trustee. . . . [149]

In the result, I am of opinion that the directors standing in a fiduciary
relationship to Regal in regard to the exercise of their powers as directors,
and having obtained these shares by reason and only by reason of the fact
that they were directors of Regal and in the course of the execution of that
office, are accountable for the profits which they have made out of them.
The equitable rule laid down in *Keech* v. *Sandford* and *Ex parte James* and
similar authorities applies to them in full force. It was contended that these
cases were distinguishable by reason of the fact that it was impossible for
Regal to get the shares owing to lack of funds, and that the directors in
taking the shares were really acting as members of the public. I cannot
accept this argument. It was impossible for the cestui que trust in *Keech*
v. *Sandford* to obtain the lease, nevertheless the trustee was [150] accountable. The suggestion that the directors were applying simply as members
of the public is a travesty of the facts. They could, had they wished, have
protected themselves by a resolution (either antecedent or subsequent) of

the Regal shareholders in general meeting. In default of such approval, the liability to account must remain. . . . [152]

There remains to consider the case of Garton. He stands on a different footing from the other respondents, but, in my opinion, he has a short but effective answer to the plaintiffs' claim. He was requested by the Regal directors to apply for 500 shares. They arranged that they themselves should each be responsible for £500 of the Amalgamated capital, and they appealed, by their chairman, to Garton to subscribe the balance of £500 which was required to make up the £3,000. In law his action, which has resulted in a profit, was taken at the request of Regal, and I know of no principle or authority which would justify a decision that a solicitor must account for profit resulting from a transaction which he has entered into on his own behalf, not merely with the consent, but at the request of his client.

Industrial Development Consultants Ltd. v. Cooley
[1972] 2 All E.R. 162 (Assizes)

The defendant, who was a managing director of an engineering company, was approached privately and offered a lucrative engineering contract for himself. He was told that in no circumstances would that contract ever be offered to his company. On the pretext of being ill, he resigned, and he took up the contract himself.

ROSKILL J.: . . . [166] There can be no doubt that the defendant got this Eastern Gas Board contract for himself and got it as a result of work which he did whilst still the plaintiffs' managing director. It is, of course, right to say that the contract for that work was not concluded until after he had left the plaintiffs. That work, as I have already said, was work which the plaintiffs would very much have liked to have had and, indeed, was in substance the same work as they had unsuccessfully tried to get in 1968. . . .

[167] At that time the defendant was still their managing director. He was still their managing director not only at the time when he met Mr Smettom on 13th June but when he prepared the documents over the ensuing weekend, sending them off on 17th June so as to get this work for himself. There was a point to make that on 13th June he went down to Watford in the plaintiffs' time and in the plaintiffs' car. That is, if I may use the phrase, and without wishing to condone such conduct, fiddling. It would be wrong to hold that sort of thing against the defendant, although perhaps it is not in accord with the strictest ethics, and I do not do so. However, at the meeting of 13th June Mr Smettom had made it absolutely plain to the defendant that no commitment was being made with the project, the time-table was likely to be urgent, it was necessary before there was any possibility of commitment being made, for the defendant to satisy Mr Smettom that he (the defendant) was free of all obligations to the plaintiffs

and it was up to the defendant to do whatever was necessary to obtain that freedom.

It is plain that at the meeting of 13th June the defendant became possessed of knowledge and information which was not possessed by his employers, the plaintiffs, knowledge which the plaintiffs would have wished to possess. . . .

Counsel for the defendant has forcefully described the cause of action for an account which is relied on in this case as misconceived. His admirable argument ran thus. True some directors are in a fiduciary relationship with their companies but when the defendant saw Mr Smettom on 13th June Mr Smettom made it plain that he was consulting the defendant not as managing director of the plaintiffs, but in a private capacity. Therefore, what the defendant did on 13th June and thereafter was not done qua managing director of the plaintiffs. The information he received was not received qua managing director of the plaintiffs. On the contrary the information was given and received in a purely private capacity. There was thus no breach of any duty, even the barest contractual duty, in failing to pass that information on to the plaintiffs. Still less was there any breach of any fiduciary duty because, [168] having regard to the fact this information was received by the defendant in his private capacity, there could be no fiduciary obligation to pass on this information to Mr Hicks or to his employers generally. The argument continued that, that being the position, the defendant did not and could not have got this valuable Eastern Gas Board work by virtue of his position as managing director of the plaintiffs. Indeed, the converse of that was true because the defendant could never have got that work so long as he was their managing director. . . .

Counsel for the defendant summarised his argument in this way. Any duty which might otherwise have been owed to the plaintiffs by the defendant was eliminated by the nature of Mr Smettom's approach which was from the outset a private approach. He pointed out that the contracts in this connection fell into two different classes, first, contracts with a company in which the director is interested – in relation to those counsel for the defendant said there was what he described as an inherent and inevitable conflict of interest and, therefore, there was a duty to disclose and a consequential liability in the event of a failure to disclose – and, secondly, contracts with a third party with which alone he submitted the court was concerned in this case. The relevant contract was not, as he put it, a contract with the plaintiffs at all. It was a contract with a third party and being a third party there was no inherent conflict between interest and duty unless it could be said that this contract was equally available to the plaintiffs as his employers. As it was a contract which was not available to the plaintiffs and with a third party there could be no duty to account. . . .

The first matter that has to be considered is whether or not the defendant was in a fiduciary relationship with his principals, the plaintiffs. Counsel for the defendant argued that he was not because he received this information which was communicated to him privately. With respect, I think that argument is wrong. The defendant had one capacity and one capacity only in which he was carrying on business at that time. That capacity was as managing director of the plaintiffs. Information which came to him while he was managing director and which was of concern to the plaintiffs and was relative for the plaintiffs to know, was information which it was his duty to pass on to the plaintiffs because between himself and the plaintiffs a [174] fiduciary relationship existed. . . .

It seems to me plain that throughout the whole of May, June and July 1969 the defendant was in a fiduciary relationship with the plaintiffs. From the time he embarked on his course of dealing with the Eastern Gas Board, irrespective of anything which he did or he said to Mr Hicks, he embarked on a deliberate policy and course of conduct which put his personal interest as a potential contracting party with the Eastern Gas Board in direct conflict with his pre-existing and continuing duty as managing director of the plaintiffs. That is something which for over 200 years the courts have forbidden. The principle goes back far beyond the cases cited to me from the last century. The well-known case of *Keech* v. *Sandford* is perhaps one of the most striking illustrations of this rule. . . .

[175] Therefore, I feel impelled to the conclusion that when the defendant embarked on this course of conduct of getting information on 13th June, using that information and preparing those documents over the weekend of 14th/15th June and sending them off on 17th June, he was guilty of putting himself into the position in which his duty to his employers, the plaintiffs, and his own private interests conflicted and conflicted grievously. There being the fiduciary relationship I have described it seems to me plain that it was his duty once he got this information to pass it to his employers and not to guard it for his own personal purposes and profit. He put himself into the position when his duty and his interests conflicted. As Lord Upjohn himself put it: 'It is only at this stage that any question of accountability arises.'

Does accountability arise? It is said: 'Well, even if there were that conflict of duty and interest, nonetheless, this was a contract with a third party in which the plaintiffs never could have had any interest because they would have never got it.' That argument has been forcefully put before me by counsel for the defendant.

The remarkable position then arises that if one applies the equitable doctrine on which the plaintiffs rely to oblige the defendant to account, they will receive a benefit which on Mr Smettom's evidence at least it is unlikely they would have got for themselves had the defendant complied with his duty to them. On the other hand, if the defendant is not required to account he will have made a large profit as a result of having deliberately put himself into a position on which his duty to the plaintiffs who were employing him and his personal interests conflicted. I leave out of account the fact that he dishonestly tricked Mr Hicks into releasing him on 16th June although counsel for the plaintiffs urged that that was another reason why equity must compel him to disgorge his profit. It is said that the plaintiffs' only remedy is to sue for damages either for breach of contract or maybe for fraudulent misrepresentation. Counsel for the plaintiffs has been at pains to disclaim any intention to claim damages for breach of contract save on one basis only and he has disclaimed specifically any claim for damages for fraudulent misrepresentation. Therefore, if the plaintiffs succeed they will get a profit which they probably would not have got for themselves had the defendent fulfilled his duty. If the defendant is allowed to keep that profit he will have got something which he was able to get solely by reason of his breach of fiduciary duty to the plaintiffs.

When one looks at the way the cases have gone over the centuries it is plain that the question whether or not the benefit would have been obtained but for the breach of trust has always been treated as irrelevant. I mentioned *Keech* v. *Sandford* a few moments ago and this fact will also be found emphasised if one looks at some of the speeches in *Regal (Hastings) Ltd.* v. *Gulliver* [1967] A.C. 134, (ante p. 155) although it is true, as was pointed out to [176] me, that if one looks at some of the language used in the speeches in *Regal* such phrases as 'he must account for any benefit which he obtains in the course of and owing to his directorship' will be found.

In one sense the benefit in this case did not arise because of the defendant's directorship; indeed, the defendant would not have got this work had he remained a director. However, one must, as Lord Upjohn pointed out, look at the passages in the speeches in *Regal* having regard to the facts of that case to which those passages and those statements were directed. I think counsel for the plaintiffs was right when he said that it is the basic principle which matters. It is an overriding principle of equity that a man must not be allowed to put himself in a position in which his fiduciary duty and his interests conflict. The variety of cases where that can happen is infinite. The fact there has not previously been a case precisely of this nature with precisely similar facts before the courts is of no import. The facts of this case are, I think, exceptional and I hope unusual. They seem to me plainly to come within this principle.

I think, although perhaps the expression is not entirely precise, counsel for the plaintiffs put the point well when he said that what the defendant did in May, June and July was to substitute himself as an individual for the company of which he was managing director and to which he owed a fiduciary duty. It is on the ground which I have stated that I rest my conclusion in this case. Perhaps it is permissible to say that I have less reluctance in reaching that conclusion on the application of this basic principle of equity since I know that what happened was enabled to happen because a release was obtained by the defendant from a binding contractual

MANAGEMENT AND THE DIRECTORS

obligation by the dishonest and unture misrepresentations which were made to Mr Hicks on 16th June. In my judgment, therefore, an order for an account will be issued because the defendant made and will make his profit as a result of having allowed his interests and his duty to conflict.

Percival v. Wright
[1902] 1 Ch. 421 (Ch.D.)

The company was a private company, and shares in it could not be transferred without the board's consent. Some shareholders offered to sell their shares to the directors at a stipulated price. The directors agreed to buy those shares, but at the time the directors were engaged in negotiations to have the company taken over at a much higher price per share. On discovering this, the plaintiffs sought to have the agreements to sell their shares set aside.

SWIFTEN EADY J.: [425] The position of directors of a company has often been considered and explained by many eminent equity judges. In *Great Eastern Ry. Co. v. Turner* (1872) L.R. 8 Ch.149, 152, Lord Selborne L.C. points out the twofold position which directors fill. He says: 'The directors are the mere trustees or agents of the company – trustees of the company's money and property – agents in the transactions which they enter into on behalf of the company.' In *In re Forest of Dean Coal Mining Co.* (1878) 10 Ch.D. 450, 453, Jessel M.R. says: 'Again, directors are called trustees. They are no doubt trustees of assets which have come into their hands, or which are under their control, but they are not trustees of a debt due to the company. The company is the creditor, and, as I said before, they are only the managing partners.' Again, in *In re Lands Allotment Co.* [1894] 1 Ch.616, 631, Lindley L.J. says: 'Although directors are not properly speaking trustees, yet they have always been considered and treated as trustees of money which comes to their hands or which is actually under their control; and ever since joint stock companies were invented directors had been held liable to make good moneys which they have misapplied upon the same footing as if they were trustees, and it has always been held that they are not entitled to the benefit of the old Statute of Limitations because they have committed breaches of trust, and are in respect of such moneys to be treated as trustees.'

It was from this point of view that *York and North Midland Ry. Co, v. Hudson* 16 Beav. 485, 491, 496, and *Parker v. McKenna* (1874) L.R. 10 Ch. 96, were decided. Directors must dispose of their company's shares on the best terms obtainable, and must not allot them to themselves or their friends at a lower price in order to obtain a personal benefit. They must act bona fide for the interests of the company.

The plaintiffs' contention in the present case goes far beyond this. It is urged that the directors hold a fiduciary position as trustees for the individual shareholders, and that, where negotiations for sale of the undertaking are on foot, they are [426] in the position of trustees for sale. The plaintiffs admitted that this fiduciary position did not stand in the way of any dealing between a director and a shareholder before the question of sale of the undertaking had arisen, but contended that as soon as that question arose the position was altered. No authority was cited for that proposition, and I am unable to adopt the view that any line should be drawn at that point. It is contended that a shareholder knows that the directors are managing the business of the company in the ordinary course of management, and impliedly releases them from any obligation to disclose any information so acquired. That is to say, a director purchasing shares need not disclose a large casual profit, the discovery of a new vein, or the prospect of a good dividend in the immediate future, and similarly a director selling shares need not disclose losses, these being merely incidents in the ordinary course of management. But it is urged that, as soon as negotiations for the sale of the undertaking are on foot, the position is altered. Why? The true rule is that a shareholder is fixed with knowledge of all the directors' powers, and has no more reason to assume that they are not negotiating a sale of the undertaking than to assume that they are not exercising any other power. It was strenuously urged that, though incorporation affected the relations of the shareholders to the external world, the company thereby becoming a distinct entity, the position of the shareholders inter se was not affected, and was the same as that of partners or shareholders in an unincorporated company. I am unable to adopt that view. I am therefore of opinion that the purchasing directors were under no obligation to disclose to their vendor shareholders the negotiations, which ultimately proved abortive. The contrary view would place directors in a most invidious position, as they could not buy or sell shares without disclosing negotiations, a premature disclosure of which might well be against the best interests of the company. I am of opinion that directors are not in that position.

There is no question of unfair dealing in this case. The directors did not approach the shareholders with the view of obtaining their shares. The shareholders approached the directors, and named the price at which they were desirous of selling. The plaintiffs' case wholly fails, and must be dismissed with costs.

DIRECTORS' REMUNERATION

Re Halt Garage (1964) Ltd.
[1982] 3 All E.R. 1016 (Ch.D.)

Mr and Mrs C. were the company's only directors and shareholders. Early on in the company's existence, both worked in the business and drew directors' remuneration. Then Mrs C. became ill and ceased working, but she remained a director and continued drawing remuneration. In the following year the company started to incur losses, and three years later it was wound up as insolvent. The liquidator contended that Mrs C. should not have been remunerated when she was not actively engaged in the business, and that Mr C.'s remuneration was excessive.

OLIVER J.: . . . [1023] [T]he claim originally made under s. 332 of the Companies Act 1948 (s. 297 of the 1963 Act) has not been proceeded with and the present claim is restricted to a claim for misfeasance and breach of trust under s. 333 (s. 298 of the 1963 Act). So it has to be shown that in making these payments the directors were in breach of some fiduciary duty which they owed to their beneficiary, which either was not or could not be sanctioned by that beneficiary. In relation to this claim, although it is alleged that the respondents (and that means, effectively, Mr Charlesworth) knew that the company was making losses and was unable to pay its debts without at least a further injection of funds or a measure of forbearance on the part of its major creditors, there is no allegation of fraud. . . .

The company's articles in the present case incorporate reg 76 of Table A, Part 1 (see Sch 1 to the 1948 Act), which provides that the remuneration of the directors shall from time to time be determined by the company in general meeting and shall be deemed to accrue from day to day. The directors, qua directors, are not, therefore, entitled as of right to any remuneration for their services, and in so far as remuneration has been drawn without the proper authority, they are bound to account to the company for it or to pay damages.

Obviously in the case of a lady who is as ill as Mrs Charlesworth is and whose illness, so far as the evidence goes, appears to have been contributed to by the long hours of work and irregularity of meals which she underwent whilst working up the business, the claim is not a very attractive one, but a liquidator has no discretion about the performance of his duties and if the claim is good in law it must succeed. If charity has, to use the words of Bowen L.J. in *Hutton* v. *West Cork Rly Co.* (1883) 23 Ch.D. 654 at 673, no business to sit at the board of directors, equally sympathy has no voice at the Bar of the court.

Counsel for the respondents takes his stand on the fact that the company has, by its constitution, an express power to determine and pay directors' remuneration, a power, moreover, which is recognised expressly in the case of every limited company by the Companies Act, 1948 (see, for instance, ss. 189 and 196). While it is true that a director, under an article in this form, has no entitlement to remuneration, nevertheless his agreement with the company when he accepts office is, impliedly, to serve the company as a director and to take the responsibilities which that office entails at whatever remuneration the company in general meeting may choose to vote to him, be it mean or generous, liberal or illiberal. It may vote nothing. But, if it votes him something, he is entitled to have it and it cannot be recovered from him in misfeasance proceedings, even if it is very greatly in excess of any possible value attributable to his services.

In the absence of fraud on the creditors or on minority shareholders, the quantum of such remuneration is a matter for the company. There is no implication or requirement that it must come out of profits only and indeed, any requirement that it must be so restricted would, in many cases, bring business to a halt and prevent a business which had fallen on hard times from being brought round.

There is, counsel for the respondents submits, no principle of law which establishes [1024] that the payment of a scale of remuneration which the court may consider overgenerous, having regard to the services performed by a particular director, is ultra vires the company, either in toto or pro tanto, and indeed it is not for the courts to decide how far remuneration is reasonable, absent some plea that its payment is a fraud on the creditors or on minority shareholders. As long as it is acting within its express powers, a company may be unwise, at least so long as it is honest, and, as I have said, there is now no suggestion of mala fides here. . . .

[1029] I cannot help thinking, if I may respectfully say so, that there has been a certain confusion between the requirements for a valid exercise of the fiduciary powers of directors (which have nothing to do with the capacity of the company but everything to do with the propriety of acts done within that capacity), the extent to which powers can be implied or limits be placed, as a matter of construction, on express powers, and the matters which the court will take into consideration at the suit of a minority shareholder in determining the extent to which his interests can be overridden by a majority vote. These three matters, as it seems to me, raise questions which are logically quite distinct [1030] but which have sometimes been treated as if they demanded a single, universal answer leading to the conclusion that, because a power must not be abused, therefore, beyond the limits of propriety it does not exist.

Nevertheless, it cannot, I think, be doubted that, whether it be logically defensible or not and whether it be labelled an application of the ultra vires doctrine of the protection of minorities, the courts have over the past hundred years evolved a series of principles which have been stated to be of general application to gratuitous dispositions of the property of trading companies. . . .

[1033] It is a commonplace in private family companies, where there are substantial profits available for distribution by way of dividend, for the shareholder directors to distribute those profits by way of directors' remuneration rather than by way of dividend, because the latter course has certain fiscal advantages. But such a distribution may, and frequently does, bear very little relation to the true market value of the services rendered by the directors and if one is to look at it from the point of view of the benefit of the company as a corporate entity, then it is wholly unjustifiable, because it deprives the company of funds which might otherwise be used for expansion or investment or contingency reserves.

Yet unless it is to be said that the *Lee, Behrens & Co.* [1932] 2 Ch. 46 test is to be applied also even to a unanimous exercise of the power of the company in general meeting to distribute profits by way of dividend (which I should hardly have thought was arguable) it is very difficult to see why the payment of directors' remuneration, on whatever scale the company in general meeting chooses, out of funds which could perfectly well be distributed by way of dividend, should be open to attack merely because the shareholders, in their own interests, choose to attach to it the label of directors' remuneration. After all, the close company provisions of the Income Tax Acts are specifically designed to compel distributions and deem them to have taken place if they fall short of the standard required. Is it then to be said that subsequently, perhaps years later, the company, by its liquidator or possibly at the instance of a purchaser of the shares, can come along and demand back profits paid out as remuneration with the active assent and concurrence of all the shareholders at the time because their payment was ultra vires? . . .

[1034] If it is truly beyond a company's capacity to make any gratuitous payment out of its funds that is not, viewed objectively, for the benefit of the company and to promote its business, then such a payment cannot logically be sanctioned or ratified even by all the shareholders acting in unison and it cannot logically matter how the company came by the funds. Company funds are company funds whether they are in the form of cash and representing profits earned by trading or in the form of credit from suppliers of moneys drawn on loan from the company's bankers. They do not belong to the shareholders unless and until they are paid to them by way of a properly declared dividend.

I do not find it altogether easy to reconcile the cases or to extract the principle from them, and it is not in this case of merely academic interest to seek to do so, because the payments under attack here were expressly sanctioned by all the shareholders and the liquidator's claim relates in part to a period when there were divisible profits from which the payments could be made and in part to a period when there were not. . . .

[1036] It does not appear to me that the group of cases culminating in
Parke v. *Daily News* [1962] Ch. 927 really has much bearing on a case
where what has been done is something expressly authorised by the company's constitution and has been expressly sanctioned by the unanimous
vote of all the shareholders in general meeting. Counsel for the liquidator,
however, submits that the liquidator is, in effect, in the position of a minority
shareholder. Suppose, he suggests, that the directors of a company vote
themselves a present and then use their majority votes as shareholders to
override a dissentient minority. Suppose that before the minority can act
to challenge this the company is wound up. Can it be said, he asks, that
the liquidator cannot pursue a claim on their behalf? That may be perfectly
right, but it does not seem to me that it really is of any help in the context
of a case where there is not and never has been any minority shareholder. . . .

[1037] No doubt the effectiveness even of a resolution in general meeting
will depend on its bona fides. Fraud opens all doors and the court will not
uphold or permit the fraudulent exercise of a power. *Re George Newman
& Co.* [1895] 1 Ch. 674 was a clear case of dishonesty, and it is not
surprising to find in the judgment of the court the doubt expressed whether
what was done there could have been sanctioned even by all the shareholders, although the point was not actually decided. But there is no suggestion
of bad faith in this case and, as is shown by *Re British Seamless Paper Box
Co.* (1881) 17 Ch.D. 467, which is referred to in the judgment of Lindley
L.J. in the *George Newman* case, the position is quite different where the
transaction is honest and is sanctioned by all members of the company at
the time. . .

[E]ven given a bona fide unanimous resolution in general meeting, it
still must be a resolution to do something which the company can lawfully
do. It cannot, for instance, lawfully return money to its shareholders out
of capital. . . . In the context of the instant case, however, counsel for the
liquidator submits that since (at any rate during most of the material time)
there were no profits available in the company for distribution and since
directors' emoluments are always gratuities, except where payable under
contract, and since the directors were shareholders as well, every payment
to them constituted an illegal reduction of capital except to the extent to
which it can be justified by the test of benefit to the company. One difficulty
about that, even accepting the submission for the moment, is that if 'the
benefit of the company' means, as Plowman J suggested in *Parke* v. *Daily
News*, 'the benefit of the shareholders as a whole', it leads him nowhere.

I accept entirely the submission of counsel for the liquidator that a
gratuitous payment out of the company's capital to a member, qua member,
is unlawful and cannot stand, even if authorised by all the shareholders.
What I find difficulty in accepting is that, assuming a sum to be genuinely

paid to a director-shareholder as remuneration under an express power, it becomes an illegal return of capital to him, qua member, if it does not satisfy some further test of being paid for the benefit of the company as a corporate entity. If he genuinely receives the money as a reward for his directorship, the question whether the payment is beneficial to the company or not cannot, as I see it, alter the capacity in which he receives it: see, for instance, *Cyclists' Touring Club* v. *Hopkinson* [1910] 1 Ch. 179. . . .

[1039] [A]ssuming that the sum is bona fide voted to be paid as remuneration, it seems to me that the amount, whether it be mean or generous, must be a matter of management for the company to determine in accordance with its constitution which expressly authorises payment for directors' services. Shareholders are required to be honest, but as counsel for the respondents suggests, there is no requirement that they must be wise and it is not for the court to manage the company.

Counsel for the liquidator submits, however, that if this is right it leads to the bizarre result that a meeting of stupid or deranged but perfectly honest shareholders can, like Bowen L.J.'s lunatic director, vote to themselves, qua directors, some perfectly outlandish sum by way of remuneration and that in a subsequent winding up the liquidator can do nothing to recover it. It seems to me that the answer to this lies in the objective test which the court necessarily applies. It assumes human beings to be rational and to apply ordinary standards. In the postulated circumstances of a wholly unreasonable payment, that might, no doubt, be prima facie evidence of fraud, but it might also be evidence that what purported to be remuneration was not remuneration at all but a dressed-up gift to a shareholder out of capital, like the 'interest' payment in the *Ridge Securities* case which bore no relation to the principal sums advanced.

This, as it seems to me, is the real question in a case such as the present. I do not think that in circumstances such as those in the instant case the authorities compel the application to the express power of a test of benefit to the company which, certainly construed as Plowman J held that it should be construed, would be largely meaningless. The real test must, I think, be whether the transaction in question was a genuine exercise of the power. The motive is more important than the label. Those who deal with a limited company do so on the basis that its affairs will be conducted in accordance with its constitution, one of the express incidents of which is that the directors may be paid remuneration. Subject to that, they are entitled to have the capital kept intact. They have to accept the shareholders' assessment of the scale of that remuneration, but they are entitled to assume that, whether liberal or illiberal, what is paid is genuinely remuneration and that the power is not used as a cloak for making payments out of capital to the shareholders as such.

[1040] Turning now to the facts of the instant case, it seems to me that the question which I have to determine is whether, on the evidence before me, I can say that the payments made to Mr Charlesworth and to Mrs Charlesworth were genuinely exercises of the company's power to pay remuneration, and counsel for the liquidator very properly concedes that he is in some difficulties as regards the case of Mr Charlesworth. Despite some rather confusing statements made by Mr Charlesworth to the Official Receiver which indicate the contrary (at any rate as regards part of the relevant time), I am satisfied on the evidence that, except for the period from December 1967 to March 1968 when Mr Gore was in charge and the period from September 1970 to March 1971 when he was away (save for two weeks or so in December), he was working more or less full-time in the business. . . .

[1041] I do not think that, in the absence of evidence that the payments made were patently excessive or unreasonable, the court can or should engage on a minute examination of whether it would have been more appropriate or beneficial to the company to fix the remuneration at £X rather than £Y, so long as it is satisfied that it was indeed drawn as remuneration. That is a matter left by the company's constitution to its members. In my judgment, a general meeting was competent to sanction the payments which he in fact drew and the claim in misfeasance against Mr Charlesworth under this head must fail.

I have felt considerably greater difficulty over the payments to Mrs Charlesworth. . . . It was known from, at the latest, December 1967 onwards, that Mrs Charlesworth could never return to render any services in the actual conduct of the company's business, and she was never thereafter called on, nor was she ever expected, to fulfil any function save that of being a director and carrying out such minimal formal acts as the holding of that office entailed. Mr Charlesworth in his evidence admitted that the company derived no benefit at all from the payments made to her, save such as may be thought to flow from the fact that she held office. She was incurably ill and living at a distance of several hundred miles from the company's place of business. Yet in each of the years 1968-69 and 1969-70 she received a sum of some £1,500 and in the year 1970-71 something over £500. It is true that Mr Charlesworth said in his evidence that it had always been the company's practice to continue the payment of full wages to employees who were off sick, and indeed the company's memorandum of association contains a wide express power in these terms:

> To pay gratuities or pensions or allowances on retirement to any directors who have held any other salaried office or place of profit with the company or to their widows or dependants and to make contributions to any fund and to pay premiums [1043] for the purchase or provision of any such gratuity, pension or allowance and to promote or assist, financially, whether by way of contributions, donations, the payment of premiums or otherwise, any fund or scheme for the benefit,

wholly or in part, of directors, ex-directors, or employees, or ex-employees, of the company, or their dependants or relatives, or for charitable purposes generally.

But it cannot be contended, I think, that Mrs Charlesworth came within that clause. She had never held any office other than that of director and that she retained. Moreover, Mr Charlesworth was not prepared to say that this practice of the company to which he referred had, or was thought to have, any effect on the loyalty of his staff.

The fact is that, however valuable and exacting may have been the services which Mrs Charlesworth had rendered in the past, her continued directorship contributed nothing to the company's future, beyond the fact that she was and remained responsible as a director and was able to make up the necessary quorum for directors' meetings (of which remarkably few took place if the minutes are any accurate guide).

On the other hand, it is said that the Companies Act 1948 imposes on every company incorporated under its provisions an obligation to have a director and it contemplates that those who assume the responsibilities of office, whether they carry them out well or ill, may be paid for that service in such way and in such measure as the company's regulations prescribe or permit. Here the company's constitution conferred on it in express terms a power to award to a director as reward or remuneration for the bare fact of holding office, and that power the company purported to exercise. If it be legitimate for the company to award some remuneration, however nominal, to Mrs Charlesworth for acting as a director and taking on herself, for good or ill, the responsibilities which that office entails, at what point, counsel for the respondents asks, does it become beyond the company's power to do that which its constitution permits it to do and how can the court take on itself the discretion as to quantum which is vested in the shareholders, there being, ex concessis, no mala fides? I have not found the point an easy one, but on the view that I take of the law the argument of counsel for the respondents is very difficult to meet *if* the payments made really were within the express power conferred by the company's constitution.

But of course what the company's articles authorise is the fixing of 'remuneration', which I take to mean a reward for services rendered or to be rendered; and, whatever the terms of the resolutions passed and however described in the accounts of the company's books, the real question seems to me to be whether the payments really were 'directors' remuneration' or whether they were gratuitous distributions to a shareholder out of capital dressed up as remuneration.

I do not think that it can be said that a director of a company cannot be rewarded as such merely because he is not active in the company's business. The mere holding of office involves responsibility even in the absence of any substantial activity, and it is indeed in part to the mere holding of office that Mrs Charlesworth owes her position as a respondent in these proceedings. I can see nothing as a matter of construction of the article to disentitle the company, if the shareholders so resolve, from paying a reward attributable to the mere holding of the office of director, for being, as it were, a name on the notepaper and attending such meetings or signing such documents as are from time to time required. The director assumes the responsibility on the footing that he will receive whatever recompense the company in general meeting may think appropriate. In this case, however, counsel for the liquidator is entitled to submit that the sums paid to Mrs Charlesworth were so out of proportion to any possible value attributable to her holding of office that the court is entitled to treat them as not being genuine payments of remuneration at all but as dressed-up dividends out of capital. . . .

Taupo Totara Timber Co. Ltd. v. Rowe
[1978] A.C. 537 (P.C.)

The plaintiff was hired as the defendant company's managing director for a five year period. It was provided in the service contract that, in the event of the company ever being taken over during the contract period, the plaintiff could resign, and would thereupon become entitled to a sum equivalent to five times his annual salary. The company was taken over, and he resigned and claimed that sum.

LORD WILBERFORCE: . . . [545] [T]he company's contention [is] that payment of the sum claimed by the respondent would be unlawful by virtue of section 191 of the Companies Act 1955 (cf. s. 186 of the 1963 Act). This is as follows:

> *Approval of the company requisite for payment by it to director for loss of office, etc.* – It shall not be lawful for a company to make to any director of the company any payment by way of compensation for loss of office, or as consideration for or in connection with his retirement from office, without particulars with respect to the proposed payment (including the amount thereof) being disclosed to members of the company and the proposal being approved by the company in general meeting.

This section is identical with section 191 of the Companies Act 1948 (U.K.) and, with one qualification, with section 129 of the Companies Act 1961 (Victoria). That qualification is that the Victorian section adds, after 'compensation for loss of office,' the words 'as director', and refers to 'retirement from *such* office'. These changes may be either clarificatory or restrictive. Since there is no obvious reason why Australian legislatures should wish to narrow the scope of the section, the former alternative seems more likely. The belief of the draftsman as to what the section was intended to mean is of course not decisive.

The New Zealand section raises two questions. First, whether it extends to payments made to persons who are directors in connection, not simply with the office of director, but also with some employment held by the director. Secondly, whether it applies to payments which the company is obliged, under contract, to make, or is limited to payment which the company, not being obliged to make, proposes to make. Although the section deals first with 'compensation for loss of office,' which is a well enough known type of transaction popularly described as a golden handshake, it is said that in continuing with a reference to payments as consideration for, or in connection with, retirement from office, the section is casting a wider net, capable of including contractual payments.

There is only one reported case, to their Lordships' knowledge, in which these points have been considered: the Victorian case of *Lincoln Mills (Aust.) Ltd.* v. *Gough* [1964] V.R. 193, a case like the present concerned with a managing director. Hudson J. gave a careful judgment, the relevant part (at p. 199) of which was fully quoted by Richmond P., in which he decided, on both the points above mentioned, that the payment was not illegal.

Their Lordships agree with the judgment of Hudson J., and, although [546] unassisted by the additional words appearing in the Victorian statute, would apply it to the present case. The respondent, as well as being a director, was an employee, and, as other employees with this company, had the benefit of a service agreement; he was described as 'employee' in it. In certain events, which might not happen, he could become contractually entitled to a sum of money, on resignation or dismissal, the amount of which was not fixed by the agreement and could only be ascertained if and when the event happened. The directors had full power under article 116 to appoint him as managing director on such terms as they thought fit. There was no obligation on them to seek approval of this agreement by the company in general meeting; to do so indeed would be both unusual and possibly undesirable. Then, if the agreement was, as (subject to any point as to vires; see below) it undoubtedly was, valid in itself, does section 191 require the directors to seek approval of a general meeting for carrying it out? Presumably this approval would be sought at a time when the obligation to make the payment had arisen and when its amount was known, but meanwhile the position of the employee would be uncertain and difficult. In their Lordships' view the section imposes no such requirement. The section as a whole read with sections 192 and 193 which are in similar form and the words 'proposed payment' and 'proposal' point to a prohibition of uncovenanted payments as contrasted with payments which the company is legally obliged to make. Their Lordships note that this contrast is drawn by the authoritative Report of the Jenkins Committee (1962)

(Cmnd. 1749), para. 93; there is also textbook support for it. Their Lordships on this point also agree with the Court of Appeal.

There remains an argument based upon vires. It was suggested that the agreement was ultra vires the company or ultra vires the directors of the company. Their Lordships cannot accept either of these contentions. There can be no doubt as to the general power of the company to engage servants and to enter into service agreements with them. There is no question as to the bona fides of the directors in entering into this particular agreement. It was shown that similar agreements had been entered into with other employees and that to do so had been the company's policy for several years. The view that inclusion of a provision giving protection in the event of a take-over was in the interests of the company, was clearly one that reasonable and honest directors might take. In its absence, the staff might be likely to go elsewhere. In the case of the respondent, as had been noted, an agreement in substantially similar form had been entered into in 1969 and there could be nothing suspicious, or open to criticism, in replacing that agreement in 1972 when he became managing director. As has been pointed out, there is explicit power in the articles to appoint a managing director on such terms as the directors – acting of course bona fide – think fit.

VI. Accounts and Audit

Re City Equitable Fire Insurance Co.
[1925] Ch. 407 (C.A.)

(From headnote) On the same misfeasance summons the Official Receiver sought to make the respondent auditors liable for negligence and breach of duty with respect to the audit by them of the balance sheets for the three years immediately previous to the winding up.

In determining the question of liability of the respondent auditors raised by the summons, Romer J. applied the principles enunciated by Lindley L.J. in *In re London and General Bank (No. 2)* [1895] 2 Ch. 673 and also the following further principles relative to the duties of auditors.

An auditor is not ever justified in omitting to make personal inspection of securities that are in the custody of a person or company with whom it is not proper that they should be left, whenever such personal inspection is practicable.

A company's stockbrokers, however respectable and responsible they may be, are not proper persons to have the custody of its securities except on such occasions when, for short periods, securities must of necessity be left with them; but immediately such necessity ceases the secutities should be lodged in the company's strongroom or with its bank, or placed in other proper and usual safe keeping.

Whenever an auditor discovers that securities of the company are not in proper custody, it is his duty to require that the matter be put right at once, or, if his requirement is not complied with, to report the fact to the shareholders, and this whether he can or cannot make a personal inspection:

Held, on the evidence and in accordance with the principles enunciated above: (1.) that the auditors were not guilty of any breach of duty as auditors –

> (a) In describing, after a full investigation in which they were misled and deceived, and their reports to the board suppressed, by the chairman of the company, large sums of money left in the hands of the company's stockbrokers and lent to the general manager of the company as 'Loans at call or short notice,' 'Loans' or 'Cash at hand and in bank': or

(b) In failing to discover that the company's stockbrokers, in order to reduce their indebtedness to the company for the purposes of the audit, made purchases, on behalf of the company, immediately before the close of the company's financial year, of Treasury Bills which in fact never came into the possession of the company and were sold immediately the new financial year had opened.

(2.) That the auditors committed a breach of duty in not personally inspecting the securities of the company in the hands of the stockbrokers of the company, and in accepting from time to time the certificate of the brokers that they had large blocks of such securities, and in not either insisting upon those securities being put in proper custody or in reporting the matter to the shareholders; but that inasmuch as throughout the audit the auditors honestly and carefully discharged what they conceived to be the whole of their duty to the company, such negligence was not wilful, and art. 150 applied to exonerate them from liability.

On the appeal of the Official Receiver from the above decision so far only as it affected the respondent auditors,

The Court (Pollock M.R., Warrington and Sargant L.JJ.), in affirming as a whole the decision of Romer J.:–

Held, (1.) That s. 215 was a procedure section only and created no new or additional liability.

(2.) That the measure of the auditor's responsibility depends upon the terms of his engagement. There may be a special contract defining the duties and liabilities of the auditors. If there is, then that contract governs the question. The articles will, however, be looked at if there is no special agreement, because the auditors will presumably have taken their duties upon the terms (among others) set out in the articles. That is not to say that auditors can set aside a statutory obligation. No agreement or article of association can remove an imperative or statutory duty.

(3.) Sect. 113 does not lay down a rigid code. The duty imposed on the auditors by it is not absolute, but depends upon the information given and explanations furnished to them, so that there is abundant scope for discretion. Art. 150 is not in conflict with the section. The onus lies upon the auditors, who would not be excused for total omission to comply with any of the requirements of the section, or for any consequences of deliberate or reckless indifferent failure to ask for information on matters which call for further explanation.

(4.) Auditors should not be content with a certificate that securities are in the possession of a particular company, firm, or person unless the company, etc., is trustworthy, or, as it is sometimes put, respectable, and further is one that in the ordinary course of business keeps securities for its customers. In all these cases the auditor must use his judgment.

The definition of 'wilful misconduct' by Lord Alverstone C.J. in *Forder*

v. *Great Western Ry. Co.* [1905] 2 K. B. 532, 536, adopted by Pollock M.R.

Quaere, whether in the particular circumstances of the case, apart from art. 150, there was negligence on the part of the auditors (as held by Romer J.) in not personally inspecting the securities which were in the possession of the company's stockbrokers and in accepting their certificate instead.

Kelly & ors v. Haughey Boland & Co.
(Lardner J., July 1985, H.Ct.)

The facts of this case are somewhat complicated, and would take far too long to recount in full. In brief, the plaintiffs purchased the assets and business of Royal Tara China Ltd. (Tara) in November 1977 for £380,000. The defendants were Tara's auditors, who had conducted the negotiations for the sale of the business. There was a considerable conflict in the evidence about what occurred during the negotiations. According to the plaintiffs, they relied on accounts that the defendants had prepared and in which the figure for stock was inaccurate, and that on taking over the business they found that their projected production from the factory and sales were not being achieved. In November 1977 the plaintiffs commenced proceedings against the vendors claiming damages for breach of a warranty contained in the sales agreement; but the action was stayed pending submission of the dispute to arbitration. In May 1983 proceedings were instituted claiming damages against the defendants for negligent misrepresentation and negligence in negotiations.

LARDNER J.: . . . [22] The first issue that arises on the pleadings is whether the Defendants owed a duty of care to the Plaintiffs in the auditing of the company's accounts and if so in respect of which years?

During the course of the trial Counsel for the Defendants conceded that such a duty of care was owed in respect of the accounts for the year ending 31st of December 1976. As I understand it, this concession was made on the basis that these accounts were being audited by Mr Stan McHugh of the Defendants in the months of April and May 1977 and were certified by the auditors in June of 1977, and in evidence he freely admitted that at that time, after Mr O'Sullivan's (owner of Tara) death, he was aware that Mrs O'Sullivan and her family were actively considering and canvassing the sale of the business. But it was not admitted that in regard to the [23] accounts for the years ended the 31st of December 1975 or the 31st of December 1974 or the 31st December 1973 any duty of care was owed by the Defendants to the Plaintiffs because it was said that no sale was in contemplation or reasonably should have been foreseen by Mr McHugh at the time of auditing the accounts in those years.

In his submissions relating to the duty of care, Counsel for the Plaintiffs substantially relied on the test adumbrated by Lord Wilberforce in *Anns v. Merton London Borough Council* [1978] A.C. at pp. 751 to 752 where he said:

Through the trilogy of cases in this House – *Donoghue* v. *Stevenson* [1932] A.C. 562, *Hedley Byrne & Co. Ltd.* v. *Heller & Partners Ltd.* [1964] A.C. 465, and *Dorset Yacht Co. Ltd.* v. *Home Office* [1970] A.C. 1004, the position has now been reached that in order to establish that a duty of care arises in a particular situation, it is not necessary to bring the facts of that situation within those of previous situations in which a duty of care has been held to exist. Rather the question has to be approached in two stages. First one has to ask whether, as between the alleged wrongdoer and the person who has suffered damage there is a sufficient relationship of proximity or neighbourhood such that, in the reasonable contemplation of the former, carelessness on his part may be likely to cause damage to the latter – in which case a prima facie duty of care arises. Secondly, if the first question is answered affirmatively, it is necessary to consider whether there are any considerations which ought to negative, or to reduce or limit the scope of the duty [24] or the class of person to whom it is owed or the damages to which a breach of it may give rise.

Counsel for the Defendants submitted that in cases of negligent statement or misrepresentation the issue fell to be considered within the formulation of principle expressed in *Hedley Byrne and Company Limited* v. *Heller and Partners* [1964] A.C. at p. 502. Lord Morris said:

> I consider that it follows and that it should now be regarded as settled that if someone possessed of a special skill undertakes, quite irrespective of contract, to apply that skill for the assistance of another person who relies upon such skill, a duty of care will arise. The fact that the service is to be given by means of or by the instrumentality of words can make no difference. Furthermore, if in a sphere in which a person is so placed that others could reasonably rely upon his judgment or his skill or upon his ability to make careful inquiry, a person takes it upon himself to give information or advice, or allows his information or advice to be passed on to, another person who, as he knows or should know, will place reliance upon it, then a duty of care will arise.

This latter test if applied would require reliance by the Plaintiffs on the skill and care of the auditor of the accounts as part of the test of liability as well as part of the chain of causation. Both Counsel referred me to and relied upon a recent English decision of *J.E.B. Fastners* v. *Marks, Bloom and Co.* [1981] 3 All E.R. 299, a case in which issues very similar to those in this case arose and which contains [25] a helpful review of the English decisions and a certain New Zealand decision. At p. 296 Wolfe J. said:

> Without laying down any principle which is intended to be of general application, on the basis of the authorities which I have cited, the

appropriate test for establishing whether a duty of care exists appears in this case to be whether the Defendants knew or reasonably should have foreseen at the time the accounts were audited that a person might rely on those accounts for the purpose of deciding whether or not to take over the company and therefore could suffer loss if the accounts were inaccurate. Such an approach does place a limitation on those entitled to contend that there has been a breach of duty owed to them. First of all, they must have relied on the accounts, and, second, they must have done so in circumstances where the auditors either knew that they would or ought to have known that they might. If the situation is one where it would not be reasonable for the accounts to be relied on, then, in the absence of express knowledge, the auditor would be under no duty. This places a limit on the circumstances in which the audited accounts can be relied on and the period for which they can be relied on. The longer the period which elapses prior to the accounts being relied on, from the date on which the auditor gave his certificate, the more difficult it will be to establish that the auditor ought to have foreseen that his certificate would, in those circumstances, be relied on.

[26]I respectfully adopt that as a statement of the appropriate test of liability to apply in this case.

Applying this test to the accounts for the year ended the 31st of December, 1976, I have no doubt that the Defendants did owe such a duty of care and indeed Counsel for the Defendants as I have said conceded as much during the course of the trial. The audit for that year appears to have occurred during the months of April and May 1977, and the accounts were certified in the month of June 1977. The first approach by Mr Murphy and Mr Murray to the O'Sullivans occurred at the end of March and the O'Sullivans were actively considering a sale of the business from April 1977. Mr Stan McHugh was made aware of this at the time the audit was being done and subsequently became aware that there were a number of potential purchasers of whom the Plaintiffs were one prior to certification of the accounts.

In regard to the accounts for the year ended 31st of December, 1975 the Defendants do not admit that they owe any duty of care to the Plaintiffs. The auditors' certificate on these accounts is dated the 28th October 1976 and the audit was presumably conducted in the preceding months. During 1976 Mr Kerry O'Sullivan was in declining health and this was affecting the management and performance of the business. Mr McHugh says, and I accept his evidence, that in this year he was not aware that a sale was being considered by the O'Sullivans and there has been no evidence that it was, but that it was a possibility at this time. There is, however, the further factor relied on by the Plaintiffs in regard to the 1975 accounts, namely that the figures in the balance sheet and the profit and loss account for that year appeared by way of [27] comparison in the 1976 accounts which were certified and put forward by the Defendants in the course of the negotiations for sale in 1977 to the Plaintiffs and to other interested parties. In my view the auditors in auditing the 1975 accounts should reasonably have foreseen and considered that there might be a sale of the business and the persons interested in purchasing it might rely on the 1975 accounts. As to the accounts for the year ending 31st of December, 1974 and the 31st of December 1973 there has been no evidence that these acccounts were put forward by the Defendants as auditors in the course of 1977, for the purposes of negotiations with an intending purchaser. The evidence has been so far as the present Plaintiffs are concerned that these accounts were delivered to them by Mrs O'Sullivan without the intervention of any of the Defendants. At the times they were prepared, I am not satisfied from any evidence which I have heard, that any sale of the business was in contemplation by the O'Sullivan family or might reasonably have been foreseen by the Defendants as auditors. And in the circumstances of this case I do not think it has been established that any duty of care lay upon the Defendants in the preparation of the accounts for these years, in regard to the Plaintiffs as intending purchasers or in regard to intending purchasers in general.

It will be convenient at this point if I refer generally to the professional duty of an auditor in regard to accounts. Evidence, which I accept and which was not really contested, was given for the Plaintiffs by Mr Alan Maloney, an independent chartered accountant, who qualified and has been in practice since 1963, and has worked for Messrs. Craig Gardner since 1965 [28] and has for some years lectured in accountancy in University College Dublin.

He described the essential features of an audit as 'making an independent report for the shareholders on accounts prepared by the directors'. In order to do this an auditor would begin by trying to obtain a general idea of the existing business by examining the accounts of two or three previous years. He would then ascertain what arrangements the company had made that would result in reliable accounts being prepared and he would make whatever examination and tests of those arrangements he considered appropriate to determine their reliability; he would then compare the actual draft accounts prepared by the directors with the arrangements leading to them, that is the company's accounting records. And finally, having established (a) that the company has made adequate arrangements leading to proper accounts, (b) that the system is reliable by testing and (c) having compared the accounts with the output of that system, he would make an overall review of the draft accounts to see whether they give a true and fair view in relation to the profit and loss account and the balance sheet.

It is clear that an auditor cannot conduct an examination of all the company's transactions during the particular accounting period. Rather he is concerned to see that there is an adequate and proper system for recording transactions, that such transactions are properly authorised and that the assets of the company are properly looked after and safeguarded.

Passing from these general considerations to the particular matter of stocktaking, Mr Maloney said that stocktaking was a [29] best way of checking the adequacy of the stocktaking. But the auditor as a professional person might make up his own mind what he would do in the circumstances of the particular case.

Having decided that a duty of care existed in regard to the accounts for the years ended 1975 and 1976, the next question I have to consider is whether Mr McHugh as auditor of the company was guilty of negligence in auditing the company's accounts for these years.

The substantial thrust of the Plaintiff's case was that owing to the negligence of the Defendants and in particular of Mr McHugh the company's audited accounts for the years ended 31st December, 1973 to 31st December, 1976 inclusive were incorrect; they incorrectly stated, that is understated, the stock in trade of the company for these years which in turn resulted in a misleading overstatement of the trading profit or reduction of the trading loss for these years. This case was formulated in two ways. Firstly, it was alleged that in breach of the duty of care Mr McHugh owed, no serious audit of the stocks was carried out in any year. And secondly, in order to establish that the figures for stock in the audited accounts for each of these years were erroneous, an exercise was undertaken by the Plaintiff's accountant whereby he attempted to estimate or calculate what the true figures for stocks in each year should have been. I will consider each of these matters in turn.

The main evidence in relation to them was given by Mr Kenneth McQuillan, a chartered accountant in practice for over thirty years. His evidence was that an examination on the auditors' working papers for each year did not show that any physical stock observation took place or that any serious audit of the stocks was carried out for any year other than [30] 1977. There were no working papers showing pricing policy, the basis of valuation of the stock or how such valuation was established. There was no comment in regard to the stock or whether it was in good condition. There was no qualification of the audit report in any year which would inform a person reading the accounts that the stocks might not have been adequately examined or properly valued. The Institute of Chartered Accountants had issued statements and recommendations on stock and work in progress which set out the professional standards required. These were:

K.1.U.9 on auditing, dealing with attendance at stocktaking issued in 1968

K.1.U.11 statement dealing inter alia with stock and work in progress issued in 1969 and G9 – Statement of Standard Accounting practice – stocks and work in progress applicable from 1st January 1976.

In Mr McQuillan's opinion, which I understand was based upon an examination of the audit working papers from 1973 to 1977, the recommendations and professional standards set out in these statements had not been followed or adhered to in any year up to and including the accounts for 1976.

The Defendant's defence in relation to these allegations of failure to carry out a proper audit of the company's accounts and of inaccuracy and negligence in relation to the audited accounts necessarily depends greatly upon the evidence of Mr Stan McHugh, the fourth Defendant, who was the auditor of Royal Tara China Limited during all the years in question and was responsible for the audit of the accounts which have been impugned. I turn now to consider his evidence. . . .

[35]Having considered his demeanour as a witness and his testimony, I find him to be a truthful and reasonably careful witness, not given, so far as I could judge, to exaggeration or distortion. In a number of instances he candidly admitted matters which were adverse to his case and did not try to conceal them though he gave reasons or explanations in justification of his conduct. He is a witness whose evidence generally I accept as truthful and reliable.

I now come to consider whether the Plaintiffs have established that Mr McHugh failed to show the care and skill which a reasonably careful and skilful accountant should show [36] firstly in relation to the stocktaking for the years 1975 and 1976 and secondly that he failed to carry out any proper investigation or verification of the information in which the accounts for these years were based.

There was really no dispute between the parties about the duties of an accountant in relation to stocktaking. Both accepted the statements of professional standards of the Institute of Chartered Accountants. These require that the auditor should ascertain what arrangements a company has made for accurate stocktaking and that he should test them. One way in which the auditor might fulfil this duty and which was recommended was to attend at the stocktaking and to observe the procedures being followed. Mr Alan Moloney said there was no professional standard or practice which required that an auditor must attend. He had an option to attend or not to attend. It was considered in the profession and recommended that attendance at stocktaking was the best way of testing or checking the adequacy of the procedures of the company's servants. But the auditor, as a professional man, might make up his own mind what he would do in the circumstances of each particular case. At the end of the stocktaking the auditor's duty was to judge whether he could reasonably rely on the company's stocktaking or not and whether the stock appeared to be of an amount which was material in relation to the balance sheet and the turnover of the company.

In the present case at the stocktaking and audit for the 1975 and 1976 accounts, Mr McHugh had been auditing the company's accounts for over twenty years. He knew Mr Kerry O'Sullivan well and had discussed the accounts and matters such as stocktaking on many occasions with him. He [37] was familiar with Mr O'Sullivan's way of managing the business and knew that he personally took stock. He had long experience of the company's accounting arrangements and of the books of account which were kept. He had a good opinion of them and of Mr Keane, the company's secretary. He said in his judgment he thought he could rely on Mr O'Sullivan's stocktaking and on Mr Keane's books of account. But he admitted that neither in 1975 nor in 1976 or any previous year back to 1954 had he ever attended at stocktaking and observed the procedure followed by Mr O'Sullivan.

In regard to the accounts for the year 1976 he said he did not know whether or not Mr O'Sullivan had taken stock or who had done it. Mr O'Sullivan was not able at this time and might not have taken stock. When he went to do the audit he was given stocksheets which had figures with the word 'estimated' written opposite them. But he said this referred to the values and that he was satisfied stock had been taken. He made checks in the books of account of purchases and sales for the following weeks and he was satisfied that the figures in the stocksheets were consistent and that the figures for stock in the audited accounts were correct. Considering all the evidence on this aspect, did Mr McHugh fail to exercise reasonable care in regard to the stocktaking – in particular by failing to attend the stocktaking in either 1975 or 1976?

If these two years were exceptional and if in some previous years he had attended, observed and been satisfied, I should have been slow for reason only of non attendance in these two years to conclude that there was any want of care. But 1975 and 1976 followed on twenty earlier years in which he never attended at stocktaking. I am aware from the evidence that [38] over the past forty or fifty years the standards in the profession have tended to become more exacting. In 1975 and 1976 Mr McHugh was drawing close to the end of his professional career and to retirement and it may be that his conduct in regard to stocktaking would in earlier years have been regarded as acceptable. But I have come to the conclusion that having regard to the professional standards which were recognised in 1975 and 1976 there was a failure by Mr McHugh, in not attending at and observing the stocktaking, to exercise reasonable care.

The further allegation is made by the Plaintiffs that Mr McHugh failed to carry out any proper investigation or verification of the information on which the accounts for these years were based. I consider this as a distinct and more extensive allegation than that of failing to attend at the stocktaking and it is linked by the Plaintiffs to the allegation that the auditors working papers for 1975 and 1976 and for earlier years which were forthcoming were sketchy and incomplete and that others which one would have expected to be available were simply not there. There was only an audit programme produced for one year between 1973 and 1976 and the narrative record of audit work done in most of these years was deficient and incomplete or missing altogether. And in effect it is alleged that the fact that such papers are defective or incomplete or missing is evidence that the requisite audit work was not done at all.

Mr McHugh's answer in evidence to these allegations was firstly that when an auditor was personally conducting the audit without the assistance of staff and was the principal of the firm who would sign the audit certificate and report [39] there was not the same need for working papers to comprise a narrative record of work done.

Secondly, he positively asserted that for each year that he audited the company's accounts and in particular for 1975 and 1976 there were stocksheets containing lists of all stock in the factory which had been counted and that he checked the figures for stock against the account book of purchases, the annual ledger and the records of subsequent sales in the sales ledger.

Perhaps it should also be remembered that the accounts for 1975 and 1976 were audited over eight years ago and six or seven years prior to the Plenary Summons in this action and there is certainly the possibility that papers may have been mislaid. It was accepted by the parties that there is no professional standard requiring the retention of working papers for any period.

In regard to all these matters Mr McHugh was subjected to a searching cross-examination. Having considered all the material evidence, in my judgment the allegation of failure to investigate or verify the information on which the accounts for 1975 and 1976 were based has not been made out. I accept Mr McHugh's evidence and I am not at all convinced that the incompleteness of the audit working papers establishes that the appropriate audit work was not done. . . .

[41]Having found that in one respect, viz his failure to attend at and observe the stocktaking in either the year 1975 or 1976, Mr McHugh was guilty of negligence and failure to conform to the standard of care recommended by and adhered to in the profession I now turn to consider whether the Plaintiffs have made out their claim that stock figures in the audited accounts for 1975 and 1976, the only years I am concerned with, were as a result false and misleading, leading to incorrect profit or loss figures. . . .

[48][Having considered the evidence] I find that the Plaintiffs have failed

to discharge the onus of proof which rests upon them to prove their case on the balance of probabilities.

In these circumstances it is not necessary for me to consider whether in entering into the agreement of 4th November [49] 1977 with the vendors the Plaintiff relied upon the figures in the audited accounts for 1975 and 1976 which have been challenged. Nor do I need to consider any question of damages.

The Plaintiffs' claim fails and will be dismissed.

VII. Finance and Raising Capital

There are various ways in which companies finance their operations, such as through shareholders' funds, funds borrowed either from shareholders or from outside lenders, retained earnings ploughed back into the business, and different kinds of state grants and aids. The Companies Acts contain elaborate provisions about companies issuing their shares and debentures, and especially where securities are offered to the general investing public. Among the principal concerns of these rules is to ensure that existing shareholders control allotments of unissued shares being made by the directors, and to insure that investors are not deceived or misled into acquiring shares.

ISSUING SECURITIES

Hilder v. Dexter
[1902] A.C. 474 (H.L.)

Immediately after its incorporation, the company issued £1 shares to raise working capital. Under the terms of issue, the shares were allotted at par, and the allottees would have the option at some later stage to subscribe for additional shares at par. Some time later when the shares were worth over £2, the defendant sought to exercise his option.

LORD DAVEY: . . . [478] [T]here is nothing whatever in the case to throw doubt upon the good faith of the directors in selecting this mode of issuing the shares of the company, in preference to offering them for public subscription in the ordinary way, or to impeach their exercise of the discretion vested in them by the articles. It appears from the affidavits that the scheme was to raise the necessary working capital by the issue of one-half of the share capital for cash, the other half being used for the purpose of payment in shares credited as fully paid up for the concessions to be purchased by the company. But it was said that this mode of raising the sum required for working capital is prohibited by s. 8, sub-s.2, of the recent Act of 1900, and is therefore beyond the power of the company. This is the only question which has been argued at the bar.

Now, before construing the words of the section which is relied on, your Lordships are entitled to consider the state of the law before the section was passed, with a view to ascertaining the mischief to which the enactment is directed. It was decided by this House in *Ooregum* v. *Roper* [1892] A.C.125 that a stipulation or agreement that a less cash sum than the nominal amount of the share shall be accepted as payment for the share is repugnant and void. On the other hand, there was authority for saying that the payment of a commission to brokers or others who undertook to procure subscriptions, or in default to subscribe for a certain number of shares, was legitimate. . . .

[480] The argument seems to be that the company, by engaging to allot shares at par to the shareholder at a future date, is applying or using its shares in such a manner as to give him a possible benefit at the expense of the company in this sense, that it foregoes the chance of issuing them at a premium. With regard to the latter point, it may or may not be at the expense of the company. I am not aware of any law which obliges a company to issue its shares above par because they are saleable at a premium in the market. It depends on the circumstances of each case whether it will be prudent or even possible to do so, and it is a question for the directors to decide. But the point which, in my opinion, is alone material for the present purpose is that the benefit to the shareholder from being able to sell his shares at a premium is not obtained by him at the expense of the company's capital. The prohibited application of the shares may be direct by allotting them as fully or partly paid up to the person underwriting the shares, or by allotting them in some other way with the intention that they shall ultimately find their way to such person or be applied in payment of his commission.

[481] My Lords, it may be that in some particular case a contract such as that which your Lordships have before you would be open to impeachment as improvident, or an abuse, or in excess of the powers of management committed to the directors. In this case the question is as to the powers of the company itself, and not as to the the due exercise of the directors' powers. I have come to the conclusion from a consideration of the language of s.8, sub-s.2, that the prohibition therein contained extends only to the application, direct or indirect, of the company's capital in payment of a commission by the company, and the transaction impeached in this case is not within it.

Mutual Life Insurance Co. of New York v. Rank Organisation Ltd.
[1985] B.C.L.C.11 (Ch.D.)

The defendant company proposed to issue additional shares but without giving all of its shareholders a first option on them. Principally in order not to be obliged to comply with U.S. securities regulations, it proposed to offer the new shares pro rata to all its members except for the U.S. shareholders. A New York based shareholder challenged the proposal.

GOULDING J.: . . . [18] The main support of counsel for the plaintiff's argument was an anthology of judicial pronouncements regarding the equality of a company's individual shareholders in point of rights save as otherwise clearly provided by its constitution. On the basis of such authority, he submitted that shareholders of one and the same class are to be given equal treatment, having in that respect an individual right which any shareholder can enforce against the company, a right, moreover, that is broken if the company by its directors or even by resolution of a general meeting, gives some shareholders an advantage not given to others of the same class, whether or not those others suffer any disadvantage beyond such mere denial of the advantage. So, counsel for the plaintiffs contends, shareholders not connected with North America received here in their capacity as shareholders an advantage not allowed to Guaranty, and Guaranty has a right of action against Rank accordingly. . . .

[21] I do not, of course, disagree with any of the judicial statements that I have recited. I think they were all clearly right in the respective contexts in which they were uttered, but they and other authorities that have been used in argument do not in my opinion justify the inference of an overriding term in the membership contract of the sort which the plaintiffs assert. To my mind the wide powers and provisions contained in art. 7, being themselves an express term of the membership contract which the members have accepted, ought not to be whittled down by any implication beyond what is required in the circumstances of the membership contract by the ordinary principles of the law of contract. That law in such circumstances, and so far as relevant to this action, requires in my judgment but two implied terms. First, the time honoured rule that the directors' powers are to be exercised in good faith in the interests of the company, and secondly that they must be exercised fairly as between different shareholders. I doubt whether it is possible to formulate either of the stipulations more precisely because of the infinity of circumstances in which they may fall to be applied. . . .

[23] The making of the offer was clearly actuated by a genuine belief that Rank needed more equity capital and less indebtedness to banks.

Then as to its terms, did the directors exercise their discretionary power under art. 7 in good faith in the interests of the company? In my opinion it is abundantly clear that they did so. The motive for refusing applications from North American members of the public appears in great detail from the documentary evidence, and it is in my judgment perfectly plain that they were excluded only to avoid legal requirements that the directors reasonably considered it would be disadvantageous for Rank to comply with. . . .

[24] I turn to the remaining test which I have proposed, namely, that of fairness between different shareholders. It must be borne in mind that in my view the equality of individual shareholders in point of right, does not

always require an identity of treatment. Compare the first of the passages that I cited from Lord Macnaghten's speech in the *British and American Trustee* case [1894] A.C. 399. After reflection on all that counsel for the plaintiffs said in argument I remain of opinion that the North American shareholders were fairly treated on the occasion of the offer for sale, notwithstanding their exclusion from participation along with their compatriots who were not already shareholders. Such exclusion did not in any way affect the existence of a shareholder's shares nor the rights attached to them. I do not know whether the transaction had any effect upon their market price. None has been alleged by the plaintiffs, and counsel for the plaintiffs disclaimed any suggestion that the terms of the offer for sale were improvident, heavily oversubscribed though it was. In any case, no shareholder in Rank, while its articles of association retain their present form, has any right to expect that his fractional interest in the company will remain forever constant. Moreover, the reason why North American shareholders were excluded was because of a difficulty resulting only from their own personal situation. It was not the fault of Rank that they were nationals or residents of countries whose laws impose onerous obligations.

Finally, it is not in my judgment unfair to the North American shareholders that Rank should raise capital in the way which it was advised, and its directors believed, was most advantageous for the purposes of maintaining its investment programme, since the successful fulfilment of the programme would give a prospect of continuing benefit to all members whatever their personal situation.

INVESTOR PROTECTION

Gluckstein v. Barnes
[1900] A.C. 240 (H.L.)

The defendant was a member of a syndicate that bought the Olympia exhibition hall for £140,000, then formed a company, and sold it the hall for £180,000, disclosing a profit of £40,000. But no disclosure was made of a profit of £20,000 he made by previously having bought up various charges on the property.

LORD MACNAGHTEN: . . . [248] These gentlemen set about forming a company to pay them a handsome sum for taking off their hands a property which they had contracted to buy with that end in view. They bring the company into existence by means of the usual machinery. They appoint themselves sole guardians and protectors of this creature of theirs, half-fledged and just struggling into life, bound hand and foot while yet unborn by contracts tending to their private advantage, and so fashioned by its makers that it could only act by their hands and only see through their eyes. They issue a prospectus representing that they had agreed to purchase the property for a sum largely in excess of the amount which they had, in fact, to pay. On the faith of this prospectus they collect subscriptions from a confiding and credulous public. And then comes the last act. Secretly, and therefore dishonestly, they put into their own pockets the difference between the real and the pretended price. After a brief career the company is ordered to be wound up. In the course of the liquidation the trick is discovered. Mr Gluckstein is called upon to make good a portion of the sum which he and his associates had misappropriated. Why Mr Gluckstein alone was selected for attack I do not know any more than I know why he was only asked to pay back a fraction of the money improperly withdrawn from the coffers of the company.

However that may be, Mr Gluckstein defends his conduct, or, rather I should say, resists the demand, on four grounds, [249] which have been gravely argued at the bar. In the first place, he says that he was not in a fiduciary position towards Olympia Limited, before the company was formed. Well, for some purposes he was not. For others he was. A good deal might be said on the point. But to my mind the point is immaterial, for it is not necessary to go back beyond the formation of the company.

In the second place, he says, that if he was in a fiduciary position he did in fact make a proper disclosure. With all deference to the learned counsel for the appellant, that seems to me to be absurd. 'Disclosure' is not the most appropriate word to use when a person who plays many parts announces to himself in one character what he has done and is doing in another. To talk of disclosure to the thing called the company, when as yet there were no shareholders, is a mere farce. To the intended shareholders there was no disclosure at all. On them was practised an elaborate system of deception.

The third ground of defence was that the only remedy was rescission. That defence, in the circumstances of the present case, seems to me to be as contrary to common sense as it is to authority. . . .

The last defence of all was that, however much the shareholders may have been wronged, they have bound themselves by a special bargain, sacred under the provisions of the Companies Act, 1862 , to bear their wrongs in silence. In other words, Mr Gluckstein boldly asserts that he is entitled to use the provisions of an Act of Parliament, which are directed to a very different purpose, as a shield and shelter against the just consequences of his fraud.

LORD ROBERTSON: . . . [256] To my thinking, the central fact in the history is, that while the object of the syndicate was to make profit out of the resale of Olympia, it was an essential part of the enterprise, as originally designed and as actually carried out, that the same individuals who sold as syndicate should buy as directors.

[W]here speculators have formed, exclusively of themselves, the directorate of a company, to be immediately floated for the purpose of buying the property which those same individuals are associated to acquire and resell, they have brought themselves directly within Lord Cairns's statement of the law in *Erlanger's Case* (1878) 2 App. Cas. 1218. They have taken a decisive step in shaping and limiting the company. It may well be asked, if this be not an act of promotion what is? The hypothesis of all the law which we are considering is that the company is not yet formed; and unless these gentlemen had registered the company (and thus passed out of this stage altogether) it is difficult to see what more overt acts of promoting and forming the company they could have done.

[257] And now I pass to the next stage of the case. Assuming the members of the syndicate to have been promotors at the date of the purchase of the mortgages, did they properly disclose it? In the skilful argument for the appellant the duty of disclosure on this hypothesis was conceded. But his concession must not disarm the criticism which, in considering the adequacy of the disclosure, first ascertains the relevancy of the transaction to the question what sum ought to be paid by the directors for the mortgaged property.

The theory of the appellant is that the purchase of the mortgages was a collateral and independent transaction. It seems to me, on the contrary, to be an essential and inseparable part of one and the same transaction, and for this plain reason that the syndicate's gain on the mortgages had to be paid by the company. The relevancy of the mortgage transaction to the [258] question solved by the syndicate sitting as directors is this – a company, or any one else, considering what price shall be paid draws inferences as to the true value from the price paid by the seller and the proposed advance on that price. In short, what the possible buyer wants to know is the profit to be made by his seller.... I consider that the transaction in mortgages was so relevant to the question what price should the company pay for the property that it was necessary that it should be disclosed to the company completely and in detail, and the question is whether this was done. There are several overwhelming reasons for a negative answer.

In the normal case, where the directors are truly and not merely in name the executive of the company, it may be assumed that they will be vigilant and critical of the particulars of a bargain of such paramount importance as the purchase of the property to be traded with, and that, dealing at arm's length, they will examine into anything bearing on that matter that does not tell its own story in its face. But, in the present case, the company was paralyzed so far as vigilance and criticism were concerned; for the board-room was occupied by the enemy. [259] Now, the question whether adequate disclosure had been made to a company by a vendor bound to do so must necessarily depend upon the intelligence brought to bear on the information. And if, by his own act, the promoter has weakened, or, as here, has annulled the directorate, his case on disclosure becomes extremely arduous – for he has to make out such disclosure to shareholders as makes directors unnecessary. How this could be done we have no occasion to consider, for the appellant is not within sight of doing it. Indeed, the case is so clear that I do not think it is a case of inadequate disclosure, but of direct misrepresentation.

Prospectus of the Components Tube Co. Ltd., which was considered in *Components Tube Co. Ltd.* v. *Naylor* [1900] 2 I.R. 1 (infra, p. 201).

The List of Applications will OPEN on MONDAY, the 1st FEBRUARY, and CLOSE on or before WEDNESDAY, the 3rd of FEBRUARY, 1897, for London, and on or before the following day for Country.

THE COMPONENTS TUBE COMPANY, LIMITED
INCORPORATED UNDER THE COMPANIES ACTS, 1862 to 1893.

CAPITAL: £150,000, in Ordinary Shares of £1 each, payable: 2s.6d. on Application; 7s.6d. on Allotment; Balance, 10s., on 1st March.

Directors: *Harvey Du Cros, Junr., Metchley House, Edgbaston, Birmingham, (Managing Director, Cycle Components Manufacturing Company, Limited).

*Frederick Faber MacCabe, M.B., Belleville, Donnybrook, Dublin (Director, Singer Cycle Company, Limited).

Richard James Mecredy, Gortmore, Dundrum, Co. Dublin (ex-Director, Pneumatic Tyre Company, Limited),

Charles Sangster, Bristol Road, Edgbaston, Birmingham (Director, Cycle Components Manufacturing Company, Limited).

Alexis M. DeBeck, St. Joseph's, Edgbaston, Birmingham (Managing Director, Singer Cycle Company (Russia), Limited).

Benjamin B. Tuke, Coventry (Director Austral Cycle Agency, Limited).

Bankers: Lloyds Bank, Limited, 222 Strand, London; and all other Branches.

National Bank, Limited, College Green, Dublin, and all Country Branches.

Solicitor: John B. Purchase, 11 Queen Victoria-street, London, E.C.

Brokers: London - Basil Montgomery & Co., 19, Throgmorton Avenue, E.C., and Stock Exchange. *Birmingham* – W. & F. Cuthbert, 103, Colmore-row, and Stock Exchange. *Dublin* –Daniel D. Bulger, 16 College-green, and Stock Exchange. *Limerick* – Thomas McSwiney, George's-street, Limerick.

Auditors: Felton & Walker, Chartered Accountants, 5, Waterloo-street, Birmingham.

Secretary (pro. tem.): Charles Freake.

Offices (pro.tem.): 5, Waterloo-street, Birmingham.

Registered Offices: The Works, Bournbrook, Birmingham.

PROSPECTUS

This Company has been formed to acquire, carry on, and develop the well known profitable and extending Tube manufacturing business carried on by The Cycle Components Manufacturing Company, Limited, at Bournbrook, Birmingham. This business was established by Mr James Hudson in 1882, and carried on by him till 1892, when it was converted into a Company under the title of Hudson & Company, Limited, and successfully carried on by that Company till taken over by The Cycle Components Manufacturing Company, Limited in 1894.

In dealing with the acquisition of Hudson & Co., Limited, the Prospectus of The Cycle Components Manufacturing Company, Limited, said: 'It would be difficult to exaggerate the importance of this purchase in view of the improvements contemplated and the exceptional facilities of which the amalgamation has obtained control. This Company has hitherto depended almost exclusively upon the demands of the cycle trade for tubing; but it is now intended to develop other branches of the tube trade, such as boiler tubes, tubes for gas conveyance, tubular shafting and a multitude of other articles which are made from weldless steel tube.'

The manufacture of weldless tubing has become such an important feature of businesses, other than the cycle industry, that it is desirable that a separate Company should be formed to work and extend this important and long established business, which, under the style of Hudson & Co., Limited, and later as a branch of The Cycle Components Manufacturing Co., Limited, has maintained a great reputation for tubing of the highest grade.

Since the date of sale of this branch of the business by The Cycle Components Manufacturing Company, Limited, contracts for the alteration and extension of the machinery and plant are being entered into at a cost of £20,000, which when complete will be capable of increasing the output from the present figure of 35,000 to about 100,000 feet per week.

This sum has been guaranteed by the Vendor out of the purchase moneys.

An additional £20,000 will be reserved for working capital, and will be provided out of the first subscriptions to the capital of the Company.

The Company will thus be strengthened by the addition of £40,000 of fresh capital, and the Directors claim that this sum will place the Company in the forefront of the tube trade and enable it to compete most successfully with any other concern.

Orders for tubing at remunerative prices have been received from the following Companies:

Singer Cycle Co., Ltd.	Riley Cycle Co., Ltd.
Swift Cycle Co., Ltd.	Allday & Onions Engineering Co., Ltd.
Birmingham Small Arms, Ltd.	Raglan Cycle and Anti-Friction Ball
Triumph Cycle Co.,Ltd.	Co., Ltd.
Bayliss Thomas, Ltd.	Fulwell Cycle Co., Ltd.
Thomas Smyth & Sons, Ltd.	Tyne Cycle Mfg. Syndicate, Ltd.
New Buckingham & Adams Cycle Co.	B.F. Williams, Wolverhampton.

In addition to these Orders the Cycle Components Manufacturing Company, Limited, has undertaken to take the whole of the balance of the output for the current season, after all orders received by the Company have been satisfied.

The Cycle Components Manufacturing Company, Limited, one of the largest consumers of Weldless Steel Tube, has also undertaken to purchase, at remunerative prices to this Company, its full requirements for the subsequent two years.

It will thus be seen that the Company starts under most favourable and exceptional circumstances. In addition to its already large *clientèle*, new and important markets are being exploited.

It is also contemplated to lay down plant for the drawing of aluminium tubes, for which there is an increasing demand. The Directors anticipate that the next development in cycle and other light vehicle construction will be in this direction.

The works are situated alongside the works of the Cycle Components Manufacturing Company, Limited, at Bournbrook, within easy reach of the centre of the city of Birmingham. Important railway and canal communication adjoins the premises. The property comprises an area of about 9040 square yards, and is held under lease for 21 years from the Cycle Components Manufacturing Company, Limited, at an annual rental of £400, with the option of renewal or puchase on very favourable terms.

The business will be taken over as a going concern as from the 1st September, 1896, and all profits accruing from that date will belong to the Company.

The purchase price has been fixed by the Vendor at £130,000, out of which he provides the £20,000 above-mentioned for alteration and extension of the plant and machinery. The Vendor undertakes to accept payment of the purchase-money in cash or shares at the option of the Directors, but he stipulates that he may subscribe for and require the Directors to allot to him at least a third of the capital.

The Company has been fortunate in securing the valuable services of Mr Harvey Du Cros, junior, who has undertaken to give every assistance in his power, and to at all times place the benefit of his experience at the disposal of the Directorate. The Vendor fully recognising the great importance of Mr Du Cros' experience, has, at his own expense, entered into a contract with Mr Du Cros, securing his services, as above, to the Company.

Mr Charles Sangster, who has been so prominently connected with the economic and energetic management of the Cycle Components Manufacturing Company as Works Manager, is taking a seat on the Board. This ensures a continuance of the same energetic supervision.

Mr Harvey Du Cros, junior, having made an agreement with the Vendor, will receive no payment beyond the ordinary fees to each Director. Mr Chas. Sangster, whose services might easily be valued at a higher figure, is also content to take only the ordinary Director's fees. The Company is therefore saved very heavy salaries which would otherwise have been incurred.

The following contracts have been entered into, viz.:

(1) Dated the 1st day of October, 1896, between the Cycle Components Manufacturing Company, Limited, of the one part, and Ernest Terah Hooley, of the other part.

(2) Dated the 27th day of January, 1897, between Ernest Terah Hooley, of the one part and William Henry Weekes of the other part.

(3) Dated the 28th day of January, 1897, between William Henry Weekes, of the one part, and Ernest Piercy, as Trustee for and on behalf of the Company, of the other part.

(4) Dated the 27th day of January, 1897, between William Henry Weekes, of the one part, and Harvey Du Cros, junior, of the other part.

(5) Dated the 27th day of January, 1897, between the Cycle Components Manufacturing Company, Limited, of the one part, and the said Ernest Piercy, of the other part.

The Vendor will pay all expenses up to and including the final allotment of shares.

There may be also other contracts, including certain trade contracts, particulars of which, for obvious reasons, the Directors deem it inadvisable to specify, relating to the formation of the Company, and subscriptions to the capital and otherwise, which may technically fall within Section 38 of the Companies Acts, 1867. Subscribers will be held to have had notice of all these contracts, and to have waived all right to be supplied with particulars of such contracts, and to have agreed with the Company as Trustee for the Directors and other persons liable not to make any claim whatsoever, or to take any proceedings under the said section in respect of any non-compliance therewith.

Application for a special settlement and quotation will be made in due course.

Applications for shares should be made on the forms enclosed, and forwarded to the bankers of the Company, with the amount of the deposit.

If no allotment is made the deposit will be returned in full, and where the number of shares allotted is less than the number applied for, the balance will be applied towards payment due on allotment, and any excess will be returned to the applicant.

Copies of the Prospectus, with Forms of Application for Shares, can be obtained at the offices of the Company, or from their bankers, brokers, or solicitors.

The Memorandum and Articles of Association, and contracts specified above, can be seen at the offices of the solicitor to the Company.

30th January, 1897.

Jury v. Stoker
(1882) 9 L.R.Ir. 385

When the Cork Milling Co. Ltd.'s shares were offered for sale to the public, a prominent member of the company's board had become a director in consequence of an agreement that he would get 150 shares in the company for joining its board. This fact was not disclosed either in the prospectus or to the registrar of companies.

SIR EDWARD SULLIVAN M.R.: . . . [400] A serious question is raised whether this prospectus is not expressly fraudulent within the thirty-eighth section of the Companies Act, 1867. It is a question of very great importance as between those who launch Companies before the public and those who take shares in them. The section was passed for the protection of honest shareholders. All the Judges agree with that view of it. The section is a very short one, and it is a curious illustration of the difficulty there is in framing a set of words on which there could be no difference of opinion. Here are the words of the section: 'Every prospectus of a Company, and every notice inviting persons to subscribe for shares in any Joint Stock Company shall specify the dates and the names of the parties to any contract entered into by the Company, or the promoters, directors, or trustees thereof, before the issue of such prospectus or notice, whether subject to adoption by the directors of the Company, or otherwise; and any prospectus or notice not specifying the same shall be deemed fraudulent on the part of the promoters, directors, and officers of the Company knowingly issuing the same, as regards any person taking shares in the Company on the faith of such prospectus, unless he shall have notice of such contract.' The object of that section was to compel promotors, directors, or trustees, of a Company to tell the public what their contracts were when they issued the prospectus. It is a most important provision. When a man sees in a prospectus the names of men like Stoker and Sikes, men of credit and position in the city of Cork, he would naturally say, 'this is a perfectly safe concern; can I imagine that this is not a good concern when I see the names of two such men in it?' Apart from the statute, the contracts with Stoker and Sikes would be most vital and most material for any person thinking of taking shares in this Company to know. It was material to know that Stoker's and Sikes' names were bought by Jackson; that Jackson, who was the getter up of the Company, made Stoker trustee for the Company for the purpose of making a contract with himself – Jackson being the whole Company, with Stoker's name as director in his pocket, and Stoker being the only person on the other side of the business acting for the intended Company. Such a state of facts never arose before: Jackson was about to start a Company, he was about to sell the mills to the Company, but before the sale he makes sure of Stoker [401] as a director; he makes an arrangement to give him one hundred and fifty fully paid-up shares in hand for allowing his name to be used as director, and then Jackson agrees with Stoker as trustee for the Company to sell his interest in the mills for two thousand five hundred shares. Was it not material for a man before he became a shareholder to know all this? I would say nothing could be more material for the public to know; and my impression is that, if any man in Cork had an idea of taking shares in the Company, the moment he heard that Stoker's name had been bought by Jackson he would not have taken shares, or have had anything to do with a Company based on a contract between men so circumstanced.

However, the material question is, is this contract within the section? What is the nature of a contract which brings it within the 38th section? On that question the Judges in England have differed. Some of them held that it must be a contract affecting the Company or its assets or property. Others put a wider interpretation on the words of the section, and held that a contract affecting the position of the promoters, directors, or trustees of the property, which it is material for intended shareholders and the public to know, are within the mischief and express provisions of the section. I am of opinion that the strong weight of authority is in favour of the extended construction. There is high authority on both sides, but my opinion is strongly with the Judges who put the extended construction on the statute. As to contracts with the Company, the question is closed by authority. The case which, in my opinion, rules the present is *Sullivan* v. *Metcalfe*, decided by the Court of Appeal in England, and reported 5 C.P.Div. 455. In that case there was, no doubt, a difference of opinion. The case was this, as it appears by the headnote. B and C, being possessed of a patent, agreed to sell it to the Company for £56,000, but by a series of contracts it was arranged that only £2,000 out of that sum should be retained by them for their own use, and that £54,000 should be divided between the promotors of the Company. The prospectus issued on behalf of the Company did not mention the contracts relating to the disposal of the purchase-money of the patent. The defendants were promoters and directors of the Company. The plaintiff [402] subcribed for shares, but he afterwards sued the defendants to recover the price of the shares subscribed for by him. It was held, upon demurrer, by Baggallay and Thesiger, L.JJ. (Bramwell, L.J., dissenting), that the contracts as to the disposal of the purchase-money of the patent ought to have been specified in the prospectus, pursuant to the Companies Act, 1867, s.38, and that the defendants were liable to the plaintiff for the price of his shares. The judgments of the majority of the Court of Appeal are given at length in the report, as well as the judgment of the dissentient Lord Justice, which is of less moment, for – as in the House of Lords, where there is a division of opinion – it is the opinion of the majority we must look to as the decision in the case; and, although the judgment of Lord Justice Bramwell in the case contains most elaborate and able arguments, I am bound to say that the construction of the section adopted by Thesiger and Baggallay, L.JJ., appears to me the right one; and if I was free myself to lay down what contracts are within the 38th section, I would adopt the language of Lord Justice Baggallay, at p.465 of the report: 'Upon the construction, then, of the language of the section, I am prepared to hold that every contract which, upon a reasonable construction of its purport and effect, would assist a person in determining whether he would become a shareholder in the Company is a contract within the meaning of the 38th section of the Act of 1867; and having arrived at this conclusion from the considerations which I have mentioned, I abstain from saying more in support of it, as it is in accordance with the conclusions which have been arrived at by other Judges, whose opinions on the subject are to be found in the published reports.'

Lord Justice Thesiger, after reviewing the opinions of the Judges in *Twycross* v. *Grant* (1877) 2 C.P.D. 469 lays down a rule for himself thus (pp. 460, 461): ' I am therefore content to put the condition, which would otherwise attach only to the remedy for non-disclosure of a contract as a further limitation or restriction upon the generality of the description of the contract itself, and to adopt the view that every contract relating to the formation of a Company, or its promoters or vendors, of the directors, or other (403) officers of the Company, and which is material to be made known to persons invited to take shares, in order to enable them to form a judgment as to the policy of so doing, is a contract within the meaning of s. 38 of the Companies Act, 1867, and as such must be disclosed under the circumstances and to the extent which the section points out; provided that one of the parties to it is, at its date, or subsequently becomes, a promoter, director, or trustee of the Company.' The contract here was made between Stoker, who assumed the character of a trustee for the Company, and Jackson, who was the real promoter of the Company. I entertain no doubt that, if he had known that Stoker had got £750 for allowing himself to be named as a director of the Company, he would have hesitated before he advanced his money in a concern which could bring nothing but danger and loss to him. But that is not the point. The question is, was this contract a thing which a man who was about to subscribe his money to the concern ought to have known? I am clearly of opinion that it was, and that this was a contract within the 38th section of the Companies Act, 1867.

Aaron's Reefs Ltd. v. Twiss
[1896] A.C. 273 (H.L.)

A prospectus was issued by a company in Februay 1890 offering 200,000 £1 shares for sale. The company had acquired a gold mine of doubtful value in Venezuela. The prospectus promised in so many words that handsome dividends would be paid once the mine got under way, and the defendant subscribed for one hundred shares. When a year later a call of four shillings per share was made, he refused to pay it; and when the company then sued him in respect of the unpaid calls, his defence was that the prospectus was untrue in material respects, and he claimed rescission.

LORD HALSBURY L.C.: . . . [280] Was there evidence for the jury that this contract was obtained by fraud of the plaintiff company? And was there evidence for the jury of the falsehood of the statements which are contained in the prospectus? My Lords, I cannot entertain the smallest doubt upon either of those questions. With reference to the first, whether the contract was obtained by fraud of the company, assuming there to be a fraud (a matter with which I will deal in a moment) I cannot entertain the least doubt that this was a very fascinating prospectus: there were statements in it which I will deal with more particularly hereafter, but they were statements calculated to shew that it was a very good thing – that it was a commercial adventure which was likely to produce very large profits, perhaps not 100 per cent., but at all events large profits. But I must protest against it being supposed that in order to prove a case of this character of fraud, and that a certain course of conduct was induced by it, a person is bound to be able to explain with exact precision what was the mental process by which he was induced to act. It is a question for the jury. If a man said he was induced by such and such an inducement held out in the prospectus, I should not think that conclusive. It must be for the jury to say what they believed upon the evidence. Looking at the evidence in this case, I should say if I were a juryman that this was a very fascinating prospectus, and was [281] calculated to induce any one who believed the statements in it to invest his money in the concern.

Then, inasmuch as the jury have found that, I think, upon very good evidence in the prospectus itself, it remains only to consider the final question, namely, whether or not there was evidence for the jury which would justify them in finding that this was a fraudulent prospectus – that these statements were fraudulent and false. Now, in dealing with that question, again I say I protest against being called on only to look at some specific allegation in it; I think one is entitled to look at the whole document and see what it means taken together. Now, if you look at the whole document taken together, knowing what we now know and what the jury had before them, I suppose nobody can doubt that this was a fraudulent conspiracy. I observe that one or two of the learned judges below used very plain language upon it, and remarked upon the fact that Mr Gilbert, who seems to have been the head and front of it, was not subjected to an inquiry in a criminal court. But, be that as it may, the question before your Lordships now is whether the jury were justified in finding with these facts before them what they did find.

It is said there is no specific allegation of fact which is proved to be false. Again I protest, as I have said, against that being the true test. I should say, taking the whole thing together, was there false representation? I do not care by what means it is conveyed – by what trick or device or ambiguous language: all those are expedients by which fraudulent people seem to think they can escape from the real substance of the transaction. If by a number of statements you intentionally give a false impression and induce a person to act upon it, it is not the less false although if one takes each statement by itself there may be a difficulty in shewing that any specific statement is untrue.

But I do not shrink from the question whether any of these statements are untrue. I think some of them are absolutely untrue. I will take one or two for example, although I think that the whole thing exhibits falsehood. I observed in the prospectus there is a statement to the effect that reports of the [282] most favourable character had been made upon this mine. That is not true. I only mention it in passing – I do not propose to rely upon it. The reports were made in respect of another company, and made some of them eight or nine years before. That is untrue, and, of course, even assuming what I shall deal with in a moment and what the words 'proved to be rich' may imply – assuming that there had been an inquiry into the state of the mine, a prospecting, as it is called, eight or nine years before – to treat that as something which had happened at the formation of this company is of itself a gross misrepresentation. Much may have happened in the eight or nine years intervening; and we now know as a fact that much did happen in those eight or nine years, shewing that, whatever opinion might reasonably have been entertained eight or nine years before, there was no ground for thinking that such a belief would have been entertained by skilled persons if they had just been inquiring into the state of this concession at the time when the company was formed. . . .

[283] But further than that, I wish to say for myself I do not think any particular form of words is necessary to convey a false impression. Supposing a person goes to a bank where the people are foolish enough to believe his words, and says, 'I want a mortgage upon my house, and my house is not completed, but in the course of next week I expect to have it fully completed.' Suppose there was not a house upon his land at all, and no possibility, therefore, that it could be fully completed next week, can anybody say that that was not an affirmative representation that there was a house which was so near to completion that it only required another week's work upon it to complete it? Could anybody defend himself if he was charged upon an indictment for obtaining money under false pretences, the allegation in the indictment being that he pretended that there was a house so near completion that it only required a week's work upon it, by saying that he never represented that there was a house there at all? So here, when I look at the language in which this prospectus is couched, and see that it speaks of a property which requires only the erection of machinery to be either at once or shortly in a condition to do work so as to obtain all this valuable metal from the mine, it seems to me that, although it is put in ambidextrous language, it means as plainly as can be that this [284] is now the condition of the mine, that such and such additions to it will enable it shortly to produce all those great results, and that that is a representation of an actually existing fact. I should quite agree with the proposition that the Lord Chancellor of Ireland and the Master of the Rolls put forward – if you are looking to the language as only the language of hope, expectation, and confident belief, that is one thing; but it does not seem to have been in the minds of the learned judges that you may use language in such a way as, although in the form of hope and expectation, it may become a representation as to existing facts; and if so, and if it is brought to your knowledge that these facts are false, it is a fraud.

My Lords, as to the rest of the case, if there was evidence for the jury no one can doubt that the jury were right in coming to the conclusion to which they came. The whole of this transaction seems to me to have been fraudulent to the last degree, and I entirely concur with those learned judges who, in very plain language, said that the persons engaged in this transaction were guilty of a fraudulent conspiracy, and might have been indicted for it.

Components Tube Co. Ltd. v. Naylor
[1900] 2 I.R. 1.

The company issued a prospectus (see supra p. 192) on the footing of which the defendant subscribed for and was allotted shares in the company. But the defendant refused to pay calls made in respect of those shares, claiming that the prospectus had been so misleading as to entitle him to rescission.

PALLES C.B.: . . . [37] After the incorporation of the company, the directors adopted the prospectus which had been previously prepared, issued it to the public, and upon the faith of it obtained a subscription from the defendant. Those directors were the agents of the company, and, in issuing the prospectus, they acted within the scope of their authority as such.

The defendant alleges: first, that the prospectus contains representations of fact which were untrue to the knowledge of the directors, or some of them, that is, fraudulent misrepresentations; secondly, that the directors concealed from, and omitted to state in the prospectus material facts which were within their knowledge, and which it is reasonable to hold would, if stated, have so operated upon the minds of those to whom the prospectus was addressed as to prevent them from applying for shares.

From the scope of the argument before us, I am driven to refer to principles absolutely elementary. What is the principle upon which a contract such as this, made by a company, is voidable, if induced by the fraud of its directors? It is not that the fraud of the directors is imputed to the company, but it is that even an innocent person is not permitted to retain a benefit obtained through the fraud of an agent, if the contract be repudiated within a reasonable time. Such a principal is not liable in an action for damages for the fraud of his agent, but, in relation to retaining a benefit obtained through the fraud, he cannot be in a better position than the fraudulent agent himself. The law is luminously stated by Lord Selborne in *Houldsworth* v. *City of Glasgow Bank* (1880) 5 App. Cas. 317. (post p. 210).

> In equity, one of the main heads of which has always been the redress of fraud, the constructive imputation of fraud to persons not really guilty of it has never been treated as a ground of relief, though the law of agency was administered according to the same rules in equity as at common law, and though in equity, as well as at law, an innocent principal might suffer for the [38] fraud of an agent. . . Vice-Chancellors Knight Bruce and Parker, and Lord Chancellor Campbell (all very eminent Judges), said (as Lord Cranworth and Lord Chelmsford also said in this House), that the law does not impute the fraud of directors to a company; and the same proposition would, I apprehend, be equally true, in the sense in which they intended it, if the principal

whose agent was guilty of fraud were not a corporation, but an individual. The real doctrine which Lord Cranworth, in *Addie's Case*,
meant (as I understand him) to affirm, was one of substance and not
of form: 'An attentive consideration' (he said) 'of the cases has convinced me that the true principle is that these corporate bodies, through
whose agents so large a portion of the business of the country is now
carried on, may be made responsible for the frauds of those agents,
to the extent to which the companies have profited by those frauds,
but that they cannot be sued as wrongdoers, by imputing to them the
misconduct of those whom they have employed.' . . . The words in
this passage, 'to the extent to which the companies have profited by
those frauds', may perhaps require some enlargement or explanation;
but, subject to that qualification, I am of opinion that this doctrine is
in principle right.

The same principle is thus stated by Lord Hatherley in the same case:

I think that the following points may be considered as concluded by
authority; at all events, I shall assume them so to be for the purposes
of the case before the House. First, that an agent, acting within the
scope of his authority, and making any representation whereby the
person with whom he deals on behalf of his principal is induced to
enter into a contract, binds his principal by such representation *to the
extent of rendering the contract voidable*, if the representation be false,
and the contracting party take proper steps for avoiding it whilst a
restitutio in integrum is possible. Secondly, that a corporation is bound
by the wrongful act of its agent, no less than an individual, and that,
such misrepresentation by the agent being a wrongful act, the result
of such misrepresentation must take effect in the same manner against
the corporation as it would against an individual.

The company being thus, *quoad* the rescission of the contract, responsible for the frauds of its directors, the next question is, Was there evidence
that the directors were guilty of fraud? To determine this question, it is
essential to consider what is the exact obligation of the company to those
whom it invited to apply for its shares? . . . [39]
    In giving judgment in *The Central Railway Co. of Venezuela* v. *Kisch* (L.R.2
H.C. 99) Lord Chelmsford, C., said:

But although, in its introduction to the public, some high colouring,
and even exaggeration, in the description of the advantages which are
likely to be enjoyed by the subscribers to an undertaking, may be
expected, yet no mis-statement or *concealment* of any material facts or
circumstances ought to be permitted. In my opinion, the public, who
are invited by a prospectus to join in any new adventure, *ought to have*

the same opportunity of judging of everything which has a material bearing on its true character *as the promoters themselves possess*. It cannot be too frequently or too strongly impressed upon those who, having projected any undertaking, are desirous of obtaining the co-operation of persons who have no other information on the subject than that which they choose to convey, that the utmost candour and honesty ought to characterize their published statements. As was said by Vice-Chancellor Kindersley, in the case of *The New Brunswick and Canada Railway Co.* v. *Muggeridge*, 'Those who issue a prospectus holding out to the public the great advantages which will accrue to persons who will take shares in a proposed undertaking, and inviting them to take shares on the faith of the representations therein contained, are bound to state everything with strict and scrupulous accuracy, and not only to abstain from stating as fact that which is not so, but to omit no one fact within their knowledge, the existence of which might in any degree affect the nature, or extent, or quality of the privileges and advantages which the prospectus holds out as inducements to take shares.' . . .

[56] *The New Sombrero Phosphate Company* v. *Erlanger* (5 Ch. D. 73) was a decision of Sir George Jessel, Lord Justice James, and Lord Justice Baggallay, which was affirmed in the House of Lords by Lord Cairns, C., Lord Penzance, Lord Hatherley, Lord O'Hagan, and Lord Blackburn; and in its circumstances has a strong similarity to the present. The question there was in reference to the purchase of an island in the West Indies, which on the 30th August, 1871, the liquidator of the company, then in the course of being wound up, contracted to sell for £60,000, subject to the sanction of the court of Chancery, to one Evans, who was the agent of Baron Erlanger, and who purchased for a syndicate of speculators. This contract was confirmed by the Judge in chambers on the 15th September following; and upon the 20th of the same month Evans agreed to sell the same property for £110,000 to one Francis Pavy, who purchased as a trustee for a then intended company. There were five directors named in the articles of association. Two were away from England when the company was formed, and took no part in the management till after the purchase was completed. Another [57] was Evans, the trustee who purchased on behalf of the syndicate. A fourth, by arrangement made before the registration of the company, obtained his share qualification by gift or loan from Baron Erlanger, the principal member of the syndicate, who in fact, directly or indirectly, selected all the directors. The fifth was independent of the syndicate. The three directors who were in England, at a Board meeting of the 29th September, adopted the contract for purchase. The bill was by the company, against the syndicate and directors, to set aside the purchase. Of course *Gover's Case* (1 Ch.D. 182) was cited. It was argued for the plaintiffs that the fact showed conclusively that Erlanger was the promoter of the company.

It will, perhaps, be suggested (said the plaintiff's counsel) that the law has been changed by *Gover's Case* and that it is necessary to show that when the first contract was entered into the company was actually in course of formation. But *Gover's Case* only decided that an application by contributories to be relieved from liability on shares could not be granted on the ground that the contract was made with a person who afterwards became a promoter of the company, though some of the *dicta* may lend colour to the argument sought to be founded on that case. Here the company was entirely the creation of Erlanger, and the inception of it must be carried back to the time of the purchase by the syndicate.

Lord Justice James says:

In this case the Vice-Chancellor appears to have proceeded, to a great extent, upon what was supposed to have been said in *Gover's Case*. Now, I adhere entirely to what I have said in *Gover's Case*, that is to say, it is quite open to a man to buy any property, at any price he likes, with a view or in the hope of selling that property to any company that he can get to buy it. . . but that has nothing whatever, as it appears to me, to do with the question in this case, which is, whether a man who has bought at a low price has obtained a higher price fairly and properly in accordance with the view which the Court of Equity takes of such transactions. . . A promoter is, according to my view of the case, in a fiduciary relation to the company which he promotes or causes to come into existence. If that promoter has a property which he desires to sell to the company, it is quite open for him to do so; but upon him, as upon any other person in a fiduciary position, it is incumbent to make full and fair disclosure of his interest and position with respect to the property. I can see no difference in this respect [58] between a promoter and a trustee, steward or agent. Such full and fair disclosure was not made in this case by the syndicate, which syndicate, it is admitted, were the promoters.

Later on he says:

Therefore it is not a technical rule at all which requires that a vendor who in any respect is in a fiduciary position should tell the exact truth, should say he is the vendor, or state the interest that he has.

The case was then brought to the House of Lords, where the judgment was affirmed. . . [59]

[N]one of the cases, either those mentioned by our own Master of the Rolls in *Aaron's Reefs* v. *Twiss* or those referred to in Lord Justice Lindley's book on Company Law, or *Gover's Case* as explained in *The New Sombrero Phosphate Co.* v. *Erlanger*, establish the proposition for which they are cited.

In my opinion, the result of all these cases is:

1. That where the circumstances are such that there can be rescission, and *restitutio in integrum*, the rule as to disclosure is that laid down in *The New Brunswick and Canada Railway Co.* v. *Muggeridge,* and *The Central Railway Co. of Venezuela* v. *Kisch;*

2. That, where the question is not the right of rescission, but is the right to damages for deceit, evidence must be given of active fraudulent misrepresentation, and that mere concealment, although fraudulent, is not sufficient; but –

3. That this second rule, as applicable to an action for deceit, is subject to this explanation, that omissions may, upon the construction of the entire document, render false a statement which would have been true had the omitted statement been contained in the document; and that, where the omission is of this character, the deceived party has a right not only to rescind the contract [60] which he would have been entitled to do even had the representation not been of this character, but in addition he can treat it as active misrepresentation, as distinguished from mere concealment, and therefore make it the ground of an action for damages for deceit – an action which mere concealment would not be sufficient to maintain.

My object in thus travelling through this long line of cases is not to establish a mere abstract proposition of law, but because the true principle, when once ascertained, is conclusive upon the case before us, and renders it unnecessary for us to critically examine small matters which are found upon the fringe of the gigantic fraud perpetrated here. It goes to the root of that which every commercial man, reading the prospectus, must know and recognise as the real fraud. It is not that a syndicate of promoters, having it in their power to acquire an undertaking for £50,000, by themselves and their creatures invite the public to become shareholders in a company formed by them to purchase the undertaking, at a profit to the promoters of £60,000. That might have been done, possibly, in such a way as to be consistent with honesty, morality, and law. But the real fraud is that their invitation to the public suppresses the two material facts: 1, that the real vendors are the promoters themselves; and 2, that their sale to the company is part of one entire transaction, by the other part of which they acquire the undertaking at £60,000 less than the price at which they offer it to the public. A contract obtained by such suppression we cannot uphold without violating the most elementary principles of common law and of justice. . . . [61]

Courts of Equity have always applied the rule of *caveat emptor,* in relation to the only subject-matters to which they held it applicable, viz. sales between parties who stood at arm's length from one another. In *Walters* v. *Morgan* (3 De G.F. & J. 718), Lord Campbell lays down:

There being no fiduciary relation between vendor and purchaser in the negotiation, the purchaser is not bound to disclose any fact exclusively within his knowledge which might reasonably be expected to influence the price of the subject to be sold. Simple reticence does not amount to legal fraud, however it may be viewed by moralists. But a single word, or (I may add) a nod or a wink, or a shake of the head, or a smile from the purchaser intended to induce the vendor to believe the existence of a non-existing fact, which might influence the price of the subject to be sold, would be sufficient ground for a Court of Equity to refuse a decree for a specific performance of the agreement. . . .

The fifth question left to the jury was: 'Was the prospectus as a whole substantially misleading and calculated to deceive?' It is found in the affirmative. . . . [68] There is no evidence of the fixing of terms, or of any agreement whatsoever. The terms in the prospectus were those of the promoters only. Upon the evidence, the other directors did little more than consent to become such, and agree to the prospectus; but these matters, taken together, will not amount to such a contract as a court of equity will hold to be binding upon a subsequently formed company. . . . [69]

Having now gone back behind these writings, and having ascertained the truth of the transaction, it is right to recall to mind the views which, before the Judicature Act, a Court of Equity, and since that Act any Division of the High Court, would be bound to take of such a matter, if, under the circumstances, the transaction really amounted to a contract.

The following are the words of Lord Cairns. L.C., in the case already referred to – *Erlanger* v. *New Sombrero Phosphate Co.*:

They (i.e. the promoters of a company) stand, in my opinion, undoubtedly in a fiduciary position. They have in their hands the creation and moulding of the company; they have the power of defining how and when, and in what shape, and under what supervision, it shall start into existence, and begin to act as a trading corporation. If they are doing all this in order that the company may, as soon as it starts into life, become, through its managing directors, the purchasers of the property themselves, it is, in my opinion, incumbent upon the promoters to take care that in forming the company they provide it with an executive, that is to say, with a board of directors, who shall both be aware that the property which they are asked to buy is the property of the promoters, and who shall be competent and impartial judges as to whether the purchase ought or ought not to be made. I do not say that the owner of property may not promote and form a joint stock company, and then sell his property to it, but I do say that if he does he is [70] bound to take care that he sells it to the company through the medium of a board of directors who can and do exercise an independent and intelligent judgment on the transaction.

Unquestionably, the proof of the affirmative of these propositions lies upon him who attempts to support the transaction; and so far from there being evidence that the directors here were 'competent and impartial judges as to whether the purchase ought or ought not to be made,' or that they 'could or did exercise an independent and intelligent judgment on the transaction,' the inferences to be drawn from the facts proved are entirely the other way. . . .

It may be said that the present case is distinguishable from *Erlanger* v. *New Sombrero Phosphate Co.*, because the present case is not one between the promoters and the company. No doubt this distinction exists, but in my opinion it is not material; and I arrive at that conclusion for the following reasons. By accepting the allotment of shares, the defendant here agreed that £130,000, upwards of four-fifths of the capital, should be applied in a payment under an alleged contract, which is called a purchase, but which in fact was an unreality and a fraud, which was not binding upon the company. When the case I have referred to was before the Court of Appeal both Sir George Jessel, M.R., and James, L.J., considered it as well in reference to the rights of individual shareholders, as of the company in its corporate capacity. It was necessary to do so, because it was urged in the argument that as there may have been many shareholders of the company who were parties to the fraud, the company itself was not the proper plaintiff, and that it was impossible to do equity between the defendants and the different shareholders, unless every shareholder filed his own bill or brought [71] his own action against the parties who misled him. Sir George Jessel shows how the representation to the shareholders could be relied upon there, although the action was one by the company. He says:

> How does the representation made by the prospectus to the shareholders become material? It is a question of substance. These gentlemen who were nominated as directors had a duty to perform, not to the then nominal shareholders, who are nobodies – there were really none, although there were persons who had agreed to take shares – but the future shareholders, who were to form the real company.

James, L.J. says:

> The ordinary remedy of a shareholder, in a case of this kind would be to say: 'You, the company, through and by your directors, led us into the thing, – we want to rescind the contract by which we became shareholders.' The remedy of the shareholder is to be relieved of his character of shareholder, and the company alone has the right to deal with the contract to which the company as a company is a party.

These passages seem to be express authorities that such a misrepresentation as that the alleged contract of purchase here was a *bona fide* contract, is a sufficient ground for rescission.

I am of the opinion that it was competent to the jury, upon the evidence, to find that there was a misrepresentation as to the motive for floating the company; and that, in relation to the contract to purchase, there were at least four distinct misrepresentations. They might have held –

1. That there was a misrepresentation, because, in truth and fact, there was no contract at all.

2. Because, if there were the *factum* of a contract, it was not an honest or binding one, or one which the directors, acting for the company, could honestly adopt.

3. Because, even if honest and binding, it was a contract not with Weekes, but the promoters.

4. Because it was not a contract for purchase at £130,000, but a contract in which the real purchase-money was fraudulently swollen, by an addition to it of £60,000, either as plunder or as commission. . . . [74]

Admitting, as I have in the commencement of my judgment, that the frauds of the promoters and directors cannot be imputed to the company, the company cannot retain benefits which were procured through the fraud of its authorised agents. Secondly, even assuming that, as MacCabe and Du Cros were not directors until after the allotment, they were not authorised agents of the company at the time of the issue of the prospectus and the payment by the defendant of his deposit, I hold that the company cannot retain benefits which have been obtained by the misrepresentation of persons purporting, although without authority, to act their part; and further that, as the directors, and MacCabe and Du Cros were acting together for a common purpose, the floating of the company, their acts are admissible to show the object and intention of the directors who were acting with them towards the common purpose.

Seddon v. North Eastern Salt Co. Ltd.
[1905] 1 Ch. 326 (Ch. D.)

JOYCE J.: . . . [331]The litigation in this case arises out of an arrangement for the acquisition by the plaintiff, Mr Seddon, of the property of the London Salt Company, by the purchase of the shares of that company from the persons who really owned those shares. . . . [I]t asks for a rescission of the arrangement and for restitution on the ground of misrepresentation. . . . [332]

[I]t appears to me, as it has done all through, that the plaintiff's way to succeeding in his claim is beset with difficulties. Now, in the first place, there is no allegation of fraud, and, in point of fact, the imputation of fraud upon the defendants has been expressly disclaimed, and properly so. Well, then, it is a claim to rescind or set aside for an innocent misrepresentation a contract for the sale of property, not executory, but executed, and under which nothing whatever still remains to be done. Lord Campbell states the rule on the question. In *Wilde* v. *Gibson* (1 H.L.C. 632), he says: 'My Lords, after the very attentive and anxious consideration which this case has received, I have come to the clear conclusion that the decree appealed against ought to be reversed; and I must say that in the Court below the distinction between a bill for carrying into execution an executory contract, and a bill to set aside a conveyance that has been executed, has not been very distinctly borne in mind.

With regard to the first: If there be, in any way whatever, misrepresentation or concealment, which is material to the purchaser, a Court of Equity will not compel him to complete the purchase; but where the conveyance has been executed, I apprehend, my Lords, that a Court of Equity will set aside the conveyance only on the ground of actual fraud.' Lord Selborne in *Brownlie* v. *Campbell* (5 App. Cas. 936), to which I have been referred, says, after explaining the circumstances of that particular case: 'The contract is ultimately entered into upon those terms. Passing from the stage of correspondence and negotiation to the stage of written agreement, the purchaser takes upon himself the risk of errors. I assumed them to be errors unconnected with fraud in the particulars, and when the [333] conveyance takes place it is not, as far as I know, in either country' – that means in Scotland or England – 'the principle of equity that relief should afterwards be given against that conveyance, unless there be a case of fraud.' Now I do not entertain the slightest doubt about that being a correct statement of the law. It has been acted upon by Cotton L.J. in *Soper* v. *Arnold* (37 Ch. D. 96). But the rule is not only a rule of equity, it is also a rule of law. In *Kennedy* v. *Panama, New Zealand and Australian Royal Mail Co.* (L.R. 2 Q.B. 580) Blackburn J. delivers the judgment of the court. He says: 'There is, however, a very important difference between cases where a contract may be rescinded on account of fraud, and those in which it may be rescinded on the ground that there is a difference in substance between the thing bargained for and that obtained. It is enough to shew that there was a fraudulent representation as to *any part* of that which induced the party to enter into the contract which he seeks to rescind; but where there has been an innocent misrepresentation or misapprehension, it does not authorise a rescission unless it is such as to shew that there is a complete difference in substance between what was supposed to be and what was taken, so as to constitute a failure of consideration. For example, where a horse is bought under a belief that it is sound, if the purchaser was induced to buy by a fraudulent representation as to the horse's soundness, the contract may be rescinded. If it was induced by an honest misrepresentation as to its soundness, though it may be clear that both vendor and purchaser thought that they were dealing about a sound horse and

were in error, yet the purchaser must pay the whole price, unless there
was a warranty; and even if there was a warranty, he cannot retain the
horse and claim back the whole price, unless there was a condition to that
effect in the contract.' And of course there can be no successful claim,
after completion, for damages for misrepresentation unless that misrepresentation was fraudulent.

It appeared to me from the first, upon this case, that this fact – the
absence of fraud and the absence of any allegation of fraud – was a fatal
objection to the action, and I should be [334] perfectly justified in disposing
of it on those grounds alone, and saying no more about the facts of the
case. But I will add just a few words about the facts as they have been
gone into so fully. If the plaintiff be right, the contract in question, of
course, is not void but voidable only, and it was the duty of the plaintiff,
bearing in mind the peculiar nature of the property, to repudiate the contract at the very earliest possible moment when he found out that any
misrepresentation had been made, if, in fact, any was made. In my opinion
the plaintiff did not do this, but, taking possession, he went on treating
the property as his own in many ways for many months, and continued to
do so long after the time when he had the information which would lead
him, and ought to have led him, at once to the conclusion that he had
been misinformed, if, in fact, he had been misinformed. It is quite plain
to my mind that the correspondence between the plaintiff and Mr Storr
does not amount to an arrangement that the plaintiff is to be entitled to
go on dealing with the property as his own without prejudice to the question
of whether he is to be entitled to rescind the contract and repudiate the
property or not. Really, as far as I understand it, there never was a suggestion about repudiating the property and rescinding the contract until the
commencement of the action. In the solicitor's letter which precedes the
commencement of the action there is not even a suggestion of repudiating
the property and rescinding; but all that he says is, 'I am going to commence
an action and claim against you compensation in damages.'

I think I ought to add also that upon the whole evidence I am not satisfied
that there was any misrepresentation that induced the plaintiff to enter
into the contract. I very much doubt whether there was any misrepresentation at all.

Houldsworth v. City of Glasgow Bank
(1880) 5 App. Cas. 317 (H.L.)

The plaintiff bought shares in the defendant bank, which was an unlimited
company. In the following year the bank failed, and was put into liquidation
with an enormous deficiency. The plaintiff, who was liable to the company
for calls on his shares, sued it for damages in fraud; he alleged that he
had been induced by the bank's own fraud to buy its shares.

EARL CAIRNS L.C.: . . . [324]A man buys from a banking company shares
or stock of such an amount as that he becomes, we will say, the proprietor
of one hundredth part of the capital of the company. A representation is
made to him on behalf of the company that the liabilities of the company
are £100,000, and no more. His contract, as between himself and those
with whom he becomes a partner, is that he will be entitled to one hundredth
part of all the property of the company, and that the assets of the company
shall be applied in meeting the liabilities of the company contracted up to
the time of his joining them, whatever their amount may be, and those to
be contracted afterwards, and that if those assets are deficient the deficiency
shall be made good by the shareholders rateably in proportion to their
shares in the capital of the company. This is [325] the contract, and the
only contract, made between him and his partners, and it is only through
this contract, and through the correlative contract of his partners with him,
that any liability of him or them can be enforced. . . .

[But H]e finds out, however, after he joins the company, that the
liabilities were not £100,000 but £500,000. He is entitled thereupon, as I
will assume, to rescind his contract, to leave the company, and to recover
any money he has paid or any damages he has sustained; but he prefers
to remain in the company and to affirm his contract, that is to say, the
contract by which he agreed that the assets of the company should be
applied in paying its antecedent debts and liabilities. He then brings an
action against the company to recover out of its assets the sum, say £4,000,
which will fall upon his share to provide for the liabilities, over and above
what his share would have had to provide had the liabilities been as they
were represented to him. If he succeeds in that action, this £4,000 will be
paid out of the assets and contributions of the company. But he has contracted, and his contract remains, that these assets and contributions shall
be applied in payment of the debts and liabilities of the company, among
which, as I have said, this £4,000 could not be reckoned. The result is,
he is making a claim which is inconsistent with the contract into which he
has entered, and by which he wishes to abide; in other words, he is in
substance, if not in form, taking the course which is described as approbat-
ing and reprobating, a course which is not allowed either in Scotch or
English law.

LORD SELBOURNE: . . . [329]This is not a case of parties at arm's length
with each other, one of whom has suffered a wrong of which damages are
the simple and proper measure, and which may be redressed by damages
without any unjust or inconsistent consequences. For many purposes a
corporator with whom his own corporation has dealings, or on whom it
may by its agents inflict some wrong, is in the same position towards it as
a stranger; except that he may have to contribute, rateably with others,
towards the payment of his own claim. But here it is impossible to separate

the matter of the Pursuer's claim from his status as a corporator, unless that status can be put an end to by rescinding the contract which brought him into it. His complaint is, that by means of the fraud alleged he was induced to take upon himself the liabilities of a shareholder. The loss from which he seeks to be indemnified by damages is really neither more nor less than the whole aliquot share due from him in contribution of the whole debts and liabilities of the company; and if his claim is right in principle I fail to see how the remedy founded on the principle can stop short of going to this length. But it is of the essence of the contract between the shareholders (as long as it remains unrescinded) that they should all contribute equally to the payment of all the company's debts and liabilities.

Such an action of damages as the present is really not against the corporation as an aggregate body, but is against all the members of it except one, viz., the Pursuer; it is to throw upon them the Pursuer's share of the corporate debts and liabilities. Many of those shareholders (as was observed by Lord Cranworth in *Addie's Case* (L.R. 1 H.L.Sc. 145), may have come and probably did come into the company after the Pursuer had acquired his shares. They are all as innocent of the fraud as the Pursuer himself; if it were imputable to them it must, on the same principle, be imputable to [330] Pursuer himself as long as he remains a shareholder; and they are no more liable for any consequences of fraudulent or other wrongful acts of the company's agent than he is. Rescission of the contract in such a case is the only remedy for which there is any precedent, and it is in my opinion the only way in which the company could justly be made answerable for a fraud of this kind. But for rescission the Appellant is confessedly too late.

Jury v. Stoker
(1882) 9 L.R.Ir. 385

The plaintiff acquired shares in the newly formed company on the footing of a prospectus which contained the following:

CORK MILLING COMPANY, LIMITED

The above Company have acquired the very valuable concern described below, with the vendor's trade business and good-will, on exceptionally favourable terms, viz.:

For the small sum of £8000, payable by the debentures of the Company, at 6 per cent. per annum, redeemable in three years, and one thousand fully paid-up shares; in addition to which the vendor will purchase fifteen hundred shares fully paid up, thus putting a cash capital of £7500 into the concern.

No promotion money has or will be paid.

The vendor never did agree to invest in the company. The company eventually went into liquidation, and the plaintiff lost his entire investment. He sued the defendant, who was responsible for issuing the prospectus, claiming damages for deceit

SIR EDWARD SULLIVAN M.R.: . . .[396] [W]hen one reads the prospectus, it represents that the cash capital of £7500 was not arising out of a sale by him, but to arise by a future transaction, whereby he was not to put in, but to purchase, one thousand five hundred shares. That is Jackson, after the Company was formed, was to apply for one thousand five hundred shares, and was at once, without call or instalment, to place on its table £7500 in cash. Now, Stoker's counsel of course have done all they could to gloss that passage in the prospectus, and to make it in conformity with the facts of the case; but they have failed to do so. It is manifest beyond a doubt that it was a deliberate misrepresentation, and entirely false; and I have as little doubt that it was deliberately [397] done with a view to make the company attractive in the eyes of the public, putting on the face of the prospectus an untrue allegation that the company was to start with £7500 down, which was to be paid by one person. That prospectus was for several weeks in preparation, and was the subject of deliberation, and it is essential to the Defendant's case to make it consistent with the original agreement of the 10th of July, 1877; but it is impossible to do so. It is impossible, in any view, to justify the insertion, in the passage of the prospectus which I have read, of the word 'cash' before 'capital'. In my opinion, it was a false representation. In my opinion, it was a fraudulent misrepresentation, and Jackson and Stoker are responsible for it. The Plaintiff Jury acted on that statement, and on the authorities I hold the Defendants answerable for the false representation.

My view of the law is that contained in the three propositions laid down in *Barry* v. *Croskey* (2 John & Hem. 1). Lord Hatherley says: First. Every man must be held responsible for the consequences of a false representation made by him to another, upon which the other acts, and, so acting, is injured or damnified. Secondly. Every man must be held responsible for the consequences of a false representation made by him to another, upon which a third person acts, and, so acting, is injured or damnified; provided it appear that such false representation was made with intent that it should be acted upon by such a third person in the manner that occasions the injury or loss. In *Langridge* v. *Levy* (2 M. & W. 519) the false representation was made to the father; the party who sustained the injury was the son; but the son brought the action, and recovered damages. The Court treated the representation as made by the defendant with the intent that it should be acted upon by the son in the manner that occasioned the injury. In warranting the gun 'to have been made by Nock, and to be a good, safe, and secure gun,' the defendant must have contemplated, as a natural consequence, that the father, confiding in that warranty, might place the gun in the hands of his son, or of any other third person; and, such third person using the gun, and sustaining injury by using it, the [398] defendant was liable for that injury as a consequence of his false warranty. Thirdly. But, to bring it within the principle, the injury, I apprehend, must be the immediate, and not the remote, consquence of the representation thus made. To render a man responsible for the con-sequences of a false representation made by him to another, upon which a third person acts, and, so acting, is injured or damnified, it must appear that such false representation was made with the direct intent, that it should be acted upon by such third person in the manner that occasions the injury or loss. In my opinion, the shareholders of this Company were entitled to have all the circumstances bearing on the affairs and formation of the company in the prospectus. There is no document in which it is of more consequence to state fully and fairly the real facts than the prospectus of a projected Company. Some men will speculate by taking shares in a Company, no mater how ridiculous it may be. But the law was not made for such persons. Thousands of persons of small property are striving to increase their income by investment in the shares of a Company, and in nine cases out of ten, persons who are not lawyers act on the prospectus, which ought to be a fair *resumé* of the affairs of the Company.

The law, as stated by Lord Hatherley, in *Barry* v. *Croskey* is not new law. That case was decided in 1861. In *Scott* v. *Dixon*, which was decided in 1855, and which is reported in a note to *Bedford* v. *Bagshaw* (29 L. J. (N. S.) Exch. 62), Lord Campbell and the other Judges of the Court of Queen's Bench in England held that, if there be a false and untrue rep-resentation in the report of the directors of a banking company, the persons issuing the report must answer for it. And in *Bedford* v. *Bagshaw* (4 H. & N. 538), decided in 1859, will be found the judgments of Chief Baron Pollock and Baron Bramwell to the same effect. Chief Baron Pollock says, p. 548, 'The defendant acted fraudulently, and made representations to the committee of the Stock Exchange with a view to induce persons to believe the existence of a particular state of things as to these shares. All persons buying [399] shares on the Stock Exchange must be considered as persons to whom it was contemplated that the representation would be made. I am not prepared to lay down as a general rule, that if a person makes a false representation, every one to whom it is repeated, and who acts upon it may sue him. But it is a different thing where a director of a Company procures an artifical and false value to be given to the shares in the Company which he professes to offer to the public. Generally, if a false and fraudulent statement is made with a view to deceive the party who is injured by it, that affords a ground of action. But I think that there must always be this evidence against the person to be charged, viz. that the plaintiff was one of the persons to whom he contemplated that the representation should be made, or a person whom the defendant ought to have been aware he was injuring or might injure. If a director of a Company, one of the persons who puts the shares forth into the world, deliberately adopts a scheme of falsehood and fraud, the effect of which is that parties buy the shares in consequence of the falsehood, I should feel no difficulty in saying that in such a case an action is maintainable.'

The law was laid down in the same manner in a series of subsequent cases; but so far back as 1855 the law on the subject was settled. In my opinion the prospectus was deliberately and fraudulently adopted to make the concern attractive. The Plaintiff Jury acted on the prospectus and took the shares. I have a very strong opinion that the representation was false and fraudulent, to induce men to take shares in this Company, and if loss has resulted from it, the person who made the false representation should be made to answer for the loss, even if the matter rested at common law, and outside any statute. The representation was false, fraudulent, and material, made to induce a man to take the shares, and loss has resulted to the Plaintiff. The Defendant who makes such a representation cannot be heard to say, 'Oh you might have found out that it was wrong if you had gone to the office and seen the instrument itself.' I am, therefore, clearly of the opinion, on the first part of the case, that Mr Stoker is answerable to the Plaintiff for the loss which he has sustained by the false statement in the prospectus as to the cash capital of £7500.

Securities Trust Ltd. v. Hugh Moore & Alexander Ltd.
[1964] I.R. 417 (H.Ct.)

(From headnote) K.A., who was a registered shareholder of the defendant company, applied for, and obtained from the company a copy of its memorandum and articles of association. K.A. held his shares in the company as trustee for the plaintiff company. His application for the memorandum and articles was in his own name and the defendant was unaware that he held his shares in trust. The copy articles supplied to him contained an error which suggested that on a winding up of the defendant both ordinary and preference shareholders would participate in a distribution of surplus assets. On the faith of this copy of the articles, the plaintiff made several purchases of preference shares in the defendant at prices in excess of their true value. Subsequent to these purchases, the said error was discovered by the defendant and it notified K.A. that the error existed in the copy articles supplied to him. On the winding up of the defendant, the plaintiff claimed to be entitled to participate in the distribution of surplus assets in respect of their holding of preference shares. The liquidator refused to allow their claim, and the plaintiff commenced proceedings for damages for negligent misrepresentation.

DAVITT P.: . . . [421]The law to be applied in this case is not in controversy. It would appear that the proposition that innocent (i.e. non-fraudulent) misrepresentation cannot give rise to an action for damages is somewhat too broadly stated, and is based upon a misconception of what was decided by the House of Lords, in *Derry* v. *Peek* (14 App. Cas. 337). Such action may be based on negligent misrepresentation which is not fraudulent. This was pointed out in *Nocton* v. *Lord Ashburton* [1914] A.C. 932, particularly in the speech of Haldane L.C. At page 948 he says:

> Although liability for negligence in word has in material respects been developed in our law differently from liability for negligence in act, it is none the less true that a man may come under a special duty to exercise care in giving information or advice. I should accordingly be sorry to be thought to lend countenance to the idea that recent decisions have been intended to stereotype the cases in which people can be held to have assumed such a special duty. Whether such a duty has been assumed must depend on the relationship of the parties, and it is at least certain that there are a good many cases in which that relationship may be properly treated as giving rise to a special duty of care in statement.

It was apparently considered in some quarters that such a special duty could arise only from a contractual or fiduciary relationship. In *Robinson* v. *National Bank of Ireland* (1916) S.C. (H.L.) 150, Haldane L.C. was at pains to dispel this idea. At page 157 he said:

> The whole of the doctrine as to fiduciary relationships, as to the duty of care arising from implied as well as express contracts, as to the duty of care arising from other special relationships which the Courts may find to exist in particular cases, still remains, and I should be very sorry if any word fell from me which would suggest that the Courts are in any way hampered in recognising that the duty of care may be established when such cases really occur.

The proposition that circumstances may create a relationship between two parties in which, if one seeks information from the other and is given it, that other is under a duty to take reasonable care to ensure that the information given is correct, has been accepted and applied in the case of *Hedley Byrne & Co. Ltd.* v. *Heller and Partners Ltd.* [1964] A.C. 465. Counsel for the defendant [422] Company did not seek to dispute the proposition. He submitted, however, that the circumstances of this case created no such special relationship.

Sect. 18, sub-s. 1, of the Companies (Consolidation) Act, 1908, provides:

> Every company shall send to every member, at his request, and on payment of one shilling or such less sum as the company may prescribe, a copy of the memorandum and of the articles (if any).

At the time that Mr Anderson made his request to the secretary of the defendant Company for a copy of their Memorandum and Articles of Association he was a shareholder. The plaintiff Company had not then been registered as owner of any shares. He was a member of the defendant Company; his Company was not. The position was that he was entitled to receive a copy of the Memorandum and Articles; his Company was not. He was entitled to receive it personally *qua* member; he was not entitled to receive it *qua* agent of the plaintiff Company. In these circumstances I must, I think, conclude that the copy was requested and supplied, in accordance with the provisions of s. 18, sub-s. 1 of the Act, by the defendant Company to Mr Anderson personally and not as agent for the plaintiff Company. It seems to me that there was no relationship between the parties in this case other than such as would exist between the defendant Company and any person (other than Mr Anderson) who might chance to read the copy supplied to him; or, indeed, between that Company and any member of the community at large, individual or corporate, who chanced to become aware of the last sentence in Article 155 of the defective reprint of the Memorandum and Articles. It can hardly be seriously contended that the defendant Company owed a duty to the world at large to take care to avoid mistakes and printer's errors in the reprint of their Articles. In my opinion, counsel is correct in his submission that in this case the defendant Company owed no duty to the plaintiff Company to take care to ensure that the copy of the Articles supplied to Mr Anderson was a correct copy. For these reasons there must, in my opinion, be judgment for the defendant Company.

VIII. Capital Integrity

One of the fundamental doctrines of company law is that of capital integrity, which has spawned a number of sub-principles and sub-rules. Many of these were discovered by judges between 1880 and 1900, the evidence for their existence being the underlying scheme of the Companies Acts. Their principal objective is to provide company creditors with a degree of security. As Jessel M.R. explained,

> [t]he creditor has no debtor but that impalpable thing the corporation, which has no property except the assets of the business. The creditor, therefore... gives credit to that capital, gives credit to the company on the faith of the representation that the capital shall be applied only for the purposes of the business. ...

That is to say, the law enables persons to do business under the aegis of registered companies which are legally segregated from their owners and almost invariably have limited liability. Accordingly, all that persons dealing with such companies can look to for satisfaction of obligations owing to them is the company's own assets. However, there is always a danger of the shareholders withdrawing funds from the company in the shape of dividends or otherwise, with resultant diminution of the amount creditors can claim against. It, therefore, is necessary to provide that the subscribed capital be protected against the depredations of shareholders and to the detriment of creditors, and indeed of the minority shareholders as well.

We have already come across one distinctive manifestation of the capital integrity principle in *Houldsworth* v. *City of Glasgow Bank* (ante p. 210) which was decided before most of the leading cases in this field. It was held there that persons who were wrongfully induced by a company to subscribe for shares in it have no remedy in damages against the company once the shares have been allotted to them. The reasons given by the Law Lords is somewhat obscure, but one justification for the rule, which flies in the face of the principle of separate legal personality (and *Houldsworth* was decided long before the *Salomon & Co.* case (ante p. 52)) is that awarding damages against the company depletes the fund to which outsiders can look for satisfaction of the company's obligations to them.

The rules regarding capital integrity have been extended significantly by the 1983 Act, which was adopted in response to the E.E.C. Second

Directive, it being based on some major features of French and German law. That Directive's central objective is summed up in its preamble:

> Whereas Community provisions should be adopted for maintaining the capital, which constitutes the creditors' security, in particular by prohibiting any reduction thereof by distribution to shareholders where the latter are not entitled to it and by imposing limits on the company's rights to acquire its own shares.

2nd Dir re

Some of this Directive's requirements were already incorporated in the 1963 Act, such as those regarding companies buying and financing the purchase of their own shares. But other parts of that Act had to be drastically amended, notably in respect of paying dividends from capital, and requiring that P.L.C.s have a minimum capital and that consideration paid for shares in P.L.C.s must be shown to be adequate.

MINIMUM AMOUNTS

Ooregum Gold Mining Co. of India Ltd. v. Roper
[1892] A.C. 125 (H.L.)

(From headnote) A company limited by shares, formed and registered under the Act of 1862, has no power to issue shares as fully paid up, for a money consideration less than their nominal value.

Issuing Sh at a discount

The memorandum of association of a company registered under the Act of 1862 stated that the capital of the company was £125,000 divided into 125,000 shares of £1 each, and that the shares of which the original or increased capital might consist might be divided into different classes and issued with such preference, privilege, or guarantee as the company might direct. The company being in want of money and the original shares being at a great discount, the directors in accordance with resolutions duly passed issued preference shares of £1 each with 15s. credited as paid, leaving a liability of only 5s. per share. A contract to this effect was registered under the Companies Act 1867 s. 25. The transaction was bona fide and for the benefit of the company. In an action by an ordinary shareholder to test the validity of the issue:

Held, affirming the decision of the Court of Appeal, that reading the Companies Acts of 1862 and 1867 together the issue was beyond the powers of the company, and that the preference shares so far as the same were held by original allottees were held subject to the liability of the holder to pay to the company in cash the full amount unpaid on the shares.

Now contained in S60(14) '63 Act

WATERING SHARES

Re Wragg Ltd.
[1897] 1 Ch. 796 (C.A.)

Wragg and another formed a company, and they sold it their livery-stable business, which the company paid for partly by allotting them its entire capital of 20,000 fully paid £1 shares. When the company failed, the liquidator sought to show that the real value of the business acquired was £18,000 less than what was paid for it, and that accordingly the issued shares must be treated as only partly paid.

LINDLEY L.J.: . . . [826] It has never been doubted, so far as I know, that the obligation of every shareholder in a limited company to pay to the company the nominal amount of his shares could be satisfied by a trans- action which amounted to accord and satisfaction or set-off as distinguished from payment in cash. In 1867 the Legislature rendered all such transac- tions invalid unless they were made pursuant to a duly registered contract; but if there is such a contract the law is now what it always was.

As regards the value of the property which a company can take from a shareholder in satisfaction of his liability to pay the [827] amount of his shares, there has been some difference of opinion. But it was ultimately decided by the Court of Appeal that, <u>unless the agreement pursuant to</u> <u>which shares were to be paid for in property or services could be impeached</u> <u>for fraud, the value of the property or services could not be inquired into.</u> In other words, <u>the value at which the company is content to accept the</u> <u>property must be treated as its value as between itself and the shareholders</u> <u>whose liability is discharged by its means.</u> . . .

[829]I understand the law to be as follows. The liability of a shareholder to pay the company the amount of his shares is a statutory liability, and is declared to be a specialty debt (Companies Act, 1862, s. 16), and a short form of action is given for its recovery (s. 70). But specialty debts, like other debts, can be discharged in more ways than one – e.g., by payment, set-off, accord and satisfaction, and release – and, subject to the qualifica- tions introduced by the doctrine of ultra vires, or, in other words, the limited capacity of statutory corporations, any mode of discharging a spe- cialty debt is as available to a shareholder as to any other specialty debtor. It is, however, obviously beyond the power of a limited company to release a shareholder from his obligation without payment in money or money's worth. It cannot give fully paid-up shares for nothing and preclude itself from requiring payment of them in money or money's worth: *In re Eddystone Marine Insurance Co.* [1893] 3 Ch. 9; nor can a company deprive itself of its right to future payment in cash by agreeing to accept future payments in some other way. It cannot substitute an action for the breach of a special

agreement for a statutory action for non-payment of calls.

[830]From this it follows that shares in limited companies cannot be issued at a discount. By our law the payment by a debtor to his creditor of a less sum than is due does not discharge the debt; and this technical doctrine has also been invoked in aid of the law which prevents the shares of a limited company from being issued at a discount. But this technical doctrine, though often sufficient to decide a particular case, will not suffice as a basis for the wider rule or principle that a company cannot effectually release a shareholder from his statutory obligation to pay in money or money's worth the amount of his shares. That shares cannot be issued at a discount was finally settled in the case of the *Ooregum Gold Mining Co. of India* v. *Roper* [1892] A.C. 125, the judgments in which are strongly relied upon by the appellant in this case. It has, however, never yet been decided that a limited company cannot buy property or pay for services at any price it thinks proper, and pay for them in fully paid-up shares. Provided a limited company does so honestly and not colourably, and provided that it has not been so imposed upon as to be entitled to be relieved from its bargain, it appears to be settled by *Pell's Case* and the others to which I have referred, of which *Anderson's Case* is the most striking, that agreements by limited companies to pay for property or services in paid-up shares are valid and binding on the companies and their creditors. The Legislature in 1867 appears to me to have distinctly recognised such to be the law, but to have required in order to make such agreements binding that they shall be registered before the shares are issued.

MAINTENANCE OF CAPITAL

Re Exchange Banking Co., Flitcroft's Case
(1882) 21 Ch.D. 519 (C.A.)

(From headnote) The directors of a limited company for several years presented to the general meetings of shareholders reports and balance-sheets in which various debts known by the directors to be bad were entered as assets, so that an apparent profit was shewn though in fact there was none. The shareholders, relying on these documents, passed resolutions declaring dividends, which the directors accordingly paid. An order having been made to wind up the company the liquidator applied, under Sect. 165 of the Companies Act, 1862, for an order on the directors to replace the amount of dividends thus paid out of capital:

Held, by *Bacon*, V.C., and by the Court of Appeal, that as regards each half-yearly dividend the persons who were directors when it was paid were liable for the whole amount paid for the dividends of that half-year.

The order of *Bacon*, V.C., declared them to be jointly liable, but this was varied on appeal by declaring them jointly and severally liable:

Held, that even if the shareholders had known the true facts, so that their ratification of the payment of dividends would have bound themselves individually, they could not bind the company, for that the payment of dividends out of *corpus* was *ultra vires* the company, and incapable of ratification by the shareholders:

Held, further, that the fact that the capital thus improperly applied was distributed *pro rata* among the whole body of shareholders did not protect the directors, for that the shareholders were not the corporation, and that payment to them would not prevent the corporation before winding-up, or the liquidator after winding-up, from compelling the directors to replace the money that it might be applied to proper purposes.

Re Halt Garage (1964) Ltd.
[1982] 3 All E.R. 1016 (Ch.D.)

See ante p. 165.

Trevor v. Whitworth
(1887) 12 App. Cas. 409 (H.L.)

(From headnote) A limited company was incorporated under the Joint Stock Companies Acts with the objects (as stated in its memorandum) of acquiring and carrying on a manufacturing business, and any other businesses and transactions which the company might consider to be in any way conducive or auxiliary thereto or in any way connected therewith. The articles authorised the company to purchase its own shares. The company having gone into liquidation a former shareholder made a claim against the company for the balance of the price of his shares sold by him to the company before the liquidation and not wholly paid for:

Held, reversing the decision of the Court of Appeal, that such a company has no power under the Companies Acts to purchase its own shares, that the purchase was therefore ultra vires, and that the claim must fail.

Belmont Finance Corp. v. Williams Furniture Ltd. (No. 2)
[1980] 1 All E.R. 393

The defendant company sold property, allegedly worth £60,000, to the plaintiff company for £500,000. That money was then used by the defendant company's subsidiary to buy all the shares in the plaintiff company. Damages were claimed against the defendant and its directors for conspiracy.

Immediately before the transaction out of which the claim arises Belmont was a wholly-owned subsidiary of the second defendant, City Industrial Finance Ltd ('City'). City was and is a wholly owned subsidiary of the first defendant, Williams Furniture Ltd ('Williams') formerly called Easterns Ltd. Williams was then owned or controlled by a Colonel Lipert. He was anxious to sell Belmont to Mr Grosscurth. . . .

Early in those negotiations in answer to an enquiry by Colonel Lipert as to how Mr Grosscurth proposed to finance the deal, Mr Grosscurth stated in a letter dated 5th June 1963 that his present intention was 'to arrange the consideration for the purchase of Belmont from Belmont's own resources. . . by selling to Belmont the whole of the issued share capital of Rentahome Limited'. Later, in a letter dated 2nd Spetember 1963 to Mr James, Mr Grosscurth said that for fiscal reasons he was unable to sell shares in Rentahome and suggested as an alternative that Belmont should purchase the whole of the share capital of Maximum for £500,000. . . .

The outcome of the agreement when completed was (1) that, whereas previously (a) Mr Grosscurth and his associates had owned all the capital of Maximum, of which a company which I shall call Cityfield was a wholly owned subsidiary, and (b) Mr James and his associates had owned a controlling interest in Williams, of which City was a wholly owned subsidiary and Belmont a wholly owned sub-subsidiary, after completion (i) Mr Grosscurth and his associates owned all the capital of Belmont, of which Maximum was a wholly-owned subsidiary and Cityfield a wholly-owned sub-subsidiary, and (ii) City had parted with Belmont, (2) that City received £489,000, out of which it subscribed at par for 230,000 £1 5% cumulative redeemable preference shares of Belmont retaining £259,000 in cash, and Mr Grosscurth and his associates received £11,000 in cash, (3) that the paid-up capital of Belmont was increased by an amount of £300,000 consisting of 230,000 preference shares subscribed by City, 20,000 like shares subscribed by Mr Grosscurth and 50,000 ordinary shares subscribed by Mr Grosscurth, (4) that Belmont had £200,000 on loan from Williams and City for 12 months, which altogether with the proceeds of the new share capital, restored to Belmont for the time being the £500,000 cash employed in buying Maximum, (5) that Belmont had the undertaking of Mr Grosscurth that the profits of Maximum and its subsidiaries for the period 22nd May 1962 to 31st May 1968, net of all expenses but subject to tax, should be not less than £500,000 (representing net profits after tax at the rates of tax then in force of £156,250), such undertaking being secured on the share capital of Rentahome, and (6) that the programme for the redemption of the preference shares was such that they would become due for redemption by prescribed instalments in each of the sixth to the twentieth years following allotment.

BUCKLEY L.J.: . . . [400] The first question for consideration is whether the agreement did contravene s. 54 of the 1948 Act (§60 of the 1963 Act). Only if the answer to that question is affirmative does the question whether the defendants or any of them are guilty of conspiracy arise, for it is the illegality of the agreement, if it be illegal, which constitutes the common intention of the parties to enter into the agreement a conspiracy at law.

There is little judicial authority on the section. . . .

[402]If A Ltd buys from B a chattel or a commodity, like a ship or merchandise, which A Ltd genuinely wants to acquire for its own purposes, and does so having no other purpose in view, the fact that B thereafter employs the proceeds of the sale in buying shares in A Ltd should not, I would suppose, be held to offend against the section; but the position may be different if A Ltd makes the purchase in order to put B in funds to buy shares in A Ltd. If A Ltd buys something from B without regard to its own commercial interests, the sole purpose of the transaction being to put B in funds to acquire shares in A Ltd, this would, in my opinion, clearly contravene the section, even if the price paid was a fair price for what is bought, and a fortiori that would be so if the sale to A Ltd was at an inflated price. The sole purpose would be to enable (i.e. to assist) B to pay for the shares. If A Ltd buys something from B at a fair price, which A Ltd could readily realise on a resale if it wished to do so, but the purpose, or one of the purposes, of the transaction is to put B in funds to acquire shares of A Ltd, the fact that the price was fair might not, I think, prevent the transaction from contravening the section, if it would otherwise do so, though A Ltd could very probably recover no damages in civil proceedings, for it would have suffered no damage. If the transaction is of a kind which A Ltd could on its own commercial interests legitimately enter into, and the transaction is genuinely entered into by A Ltd in its own commercial interests and not merely as a means of assisting B financially to buy shares of A Ltd, the circumstance that A Ltd enters into the transaction with B, partly with the object of putting B in funds to acquire its own shares or with the knowledge of B's intended use of the proceeds of sale, might, I think, involve no contravention of the section, but I do not wish to express a concluded opinion on that point. . . .

[403]In truth the purchase of the share capital of Maximum was not a commercial transaction in its own right so far as Mr James and his group of companies were concerned: it was part of the machinery by which City obtained £489,000 for the share capital of Belmont, £259,000 in cash and £230,000 by redemption of the redeemable preference shares subscribed in Belmont. It was not a transaction whereby Belmont acquired anything which Belmont genuinely needed or wanted for its own purposes: it was one which facilitated Mr Grosscurth's acquiring Belmont for his own purposes without effectively parting with Maximum. That the purpose of the sale of Maximum to Belmont was to enable Mr Grosscurth to pay £489,000 for Belmont was at all relevant times known to and recognised by Mr James and the members of his team as well as by Mr Copeland. There is no good reason disclosed by the evidence to suppose either that

Mr Grosscurth and his associates could have sold Maximum to anyone else for £500,000 or that Belmont could have disposed of Maximum for £500,000 to anyone else at any time. The purchase of the share capital of Maximum may have been intra vires of Belmont (a matter which we have not been invited to consider), but it was certainly not a transaction in the ordinary course of Belmont's business or for the purposes of that business as it subsisted at the date of the agreement. It was an exceptional and artificial transaction and not in any sense an ordinary commercial transaction entered into for its own sake in the commercial interests of Belmont. It was part of a comparatively complex scheme for enabling Mr Grosscurth and his associates to acquire Belmont at no cash cost to themselves, the purchase price being found not from their own funds or by the realisation of any asset of theirs (for Maximum continued to be part of their group of companies) but out of Belmont's own resources. In these circumstances, in my judgment, the agreement would have contravened s.54 of the 1948 Act even if £500,000 was a fair price for Maximum. . . .

It follows that in my judgment the agreement was unlawful, for it was a contract by Belmont to do an unlawful act, viz to provide financial assistance to Mr Grosscurth and his associates for the purpose of, or in connection with, the purchase of Belmont's own share capital.

SANCTIONS AND REMEDIES

Belmont Finance Corp. v Williams Furniture Ltd. (No. 2)
[1980] 1 All E.R. 393 (C.A.)

For background, see supra, p. 222.

BUCKLEY L.J.: . . . [404]The next question is whether in these circumstances the alleged conspiracy is established in respect of those defendants against whom the action is still on foot, i.e. the first three defendants. To obtain in civil proceedings a remedy for conspiracy, the plaintiff must establish (a) a combination of the defendants, (b) to effect an unlawful purpose, (c) resulting in damage to the plaintiff. . . .

The unlawful purpose in this case was the provision of financial assistance in contravention of s. 54 of the 1948 Act (s. 60 of the 1963 Act). That the purpose of the sale of Maximum to Belmont was to enable Mr Grosscurth to pay £489,000 to City for the share capital of Belmont was known to all concerned. For reasons which I gave in my judgment on the earlier appeal in this action, the alleged conspiracy sued on must, in my view, have preceded the signing of the agreement, but its object is made clear by the agreement, namely that Belmont should give the financial assistance to Mr Grosscurth which the carrying out of the agreement would afford him. Williams and City were parties to the agreement and so, in my opinion, are fixed with the character of parties to the conspiracy. Moreover, Mr James knew perfectly well what the objects of the agreement were. He was director of both Williams and City. Mr Harries and Mr Foley, who also knew the objects of the agreement, were a director and the secretary respectively of City. Mr Foley was also the secretary of Williams. Their knowledge must, in my opinion, be imputed to the companies of which they were directors and secretary, for an officer of a company must surely be under a duty, if he is aware that a transaction into which his company or a wholly-owned subsidiary is about to enter is illegal or tainted with illegality, to inform the board of that company of the fact. Where an officer is under a duty to make such a disclosure to his company, his knowledge is imputed to the company (*Re David Payne & Co Ltd* [1904] 2 Ch. 608, *Re Fenwick, Stobart & Co Ltd* [1902] 1 Ch. 507). In these circumstances, in my opinion, Williams and City must be regarded as having participated with Mr Grosscurth in a common intention to enter into the agreement and to procure that Belmont should enter into the agreement and that the agreement should be implemented. That Mr Grosscurth was a party to that common intention is, in my opinion, indisputable.

In my judgment, the alleged conspiracy is established in respect of these three defendants, and they are not exempt from liability on account of counsel's opinion or because they may have believed in good faith that the transaction did not transgress s. 54. If all the facts which make the transaction unlawful were known to the parties, as I think they were, ignorance of the law will not excuse them: see *Churchill* v. *Walton* [1967] 2 A.C. 224. That case was one of criminal conspiracy, but it seems to me that precisely similar principles must apply to a conspiracy for which a civil remedy is sought. Nor, in my opinion, can the fact that their ignorance of, or failure to appreciate, the unlawful nature of the transaction was due to the unfortunate fact that they were, as I think, erroneously advised excuse them (*Cooper* v. *Simmons* (1862) 7 H. & N. 707, and see *Shaw* v. *Director of Public Prosecutions* [1962] A.C. 220, where the appellant had taken professional legal advice).

If they had sincerely believed in a factual state of affairs which, if true, would have made their actions legal, this would have afforded a defence (*Kamara* v. *Director of Public Prosecutions* [1974] A.C. 104); but in my view of the effect of s. 54 in the present case, even if £500,000 had been a fair price for the share capital of Maximum and all other benefits under the agreement, this would not have made the agreement legal. So a belief in the fairness of the price could not excuse them.

I now come to the constructive trust point. If a stranger to a trust (a) receives and becomes chargeable with some part of the trust fund or (b) assists the trustees of a trust with knowledge of the facts in a dishonest design on the part of the trustees to misapply some part of a trust fund, he is liable as a constructive trustee (*Barnes* v. *Addy* (1874) 9 Ch. App. 1035 per Lord Selborne LC).

A limited company is of course not a trustee of its own funds: it is their beneficial owner; but in consequence of the fiduciary character of their duties the directors of a limited company are treated as if they were trustees of those funds of the company which are in their hands or under their control, and if they misapply them they commit a breach of trust (*Re Lands Allotment Co* [1894] 1 Ch. 616, per Lindley and Kay LJJ). So, if the directors of a company in breach of their fiduciary duties misapply the funds of their company so that they come into the hands of some stranger to the trust who receives them with knowledge (actual or constructive) of the breach, he cannot conscientiously retain those funds against the company unless he has some better equity. He becomes a constructive trustee for the company of the misapplied funds. This is stated very clearly by Jessel MR in *Russell* v. *Wakefield Waterworks Co*, where he said:

> In this Court the money of the company is a trust fund, because it is applicable only to the special purposes of the company in the hands of the agents of the company, and it is in that sense a trust fund applicable by them to those special purposes; and a person taking it from them with notice that it is being applied to other purposes cannot in this Court say that he is not a constructive trustee.

In the present case, the payment of the £500,000 by Belmont to Mr Grosscurth, being an unlawful contravention of s. 54, was a misapplication of Belmont's money and was in breach of the duties of the directors of Belmont. £489,000 of the £500,000 so misapplied found their way into the hands of City with City's knowledge of the whole circumstances of the transaction. It must follow, in my opinion, that City is accountable to Belmont as a constructive trustee of the £489,000 under the first of Lord Selborne LC's two heads.

Bank of Ireland v. Rockfield Ltd.
[1979] I.R. 21 (S.Ct.)

The bank had agreed to advance money to two individuals to enable them to buy a certain piece of land, and it was intended that the security would be an equitable mortgage of the certificate of title to the land. In the event, the money was advanced to the order of the defendant company; and since the land was in its name, it deposited the certificate of title with the bank. The individuals then used the money that was advanced to acquire control of the company. When the bank sought to enforce the equitable charge, the company claimed that the charge was ineffective because it was used to assist financing the purchase of the company's shares.

KENNY J.: . . . [34] McWilliam J. . . held that the agreement of the 30th July, 1973, had been ratified by the defendants, that the plaintiffs had not actual notice that the £150,000 was to be applied in purchasing the shares in the defendant company, that the doctrine of constructive notice did not apply, and that 'notice' in s. 60, sub-s. 14, of the [35] Act of 1963 means actual notice; he then went on to say: 'I fully accept the view expressed by Lindley L.J. but it seems to me that there must be some limit to the extent to which a person may fail to accept information available to him or fail to make the inquiries normal in his line of business so as to leave himself in the position that he has no notice of something anyone else in the same line of business would have appreciated.' Counsel for the plaintiffs has complained that this blurs the distinction between actual notice and constructive notice, and I confess that I find considerable difficulty in understanding what the judge meant by this passage. He went on to say that the limit he had mentioned was reached in this case 'and I hold that the plaintiff should have had notice of the purpose for which the money was being applied, namely, the purchase of the defendant's own shares.' This meant that the judge was applying the doctrine of constructive notice to s. 60, sub-s. 14, of the Act of 1963.

It was agreed by counsel that the appeal was confined to the questions of ratification and s. 60, sub-s. 14, of the Act of 1963.

The principles governing ratification by a principal of an act by an agent when the agent had no authority to act for the principal have been stated by Wright J. at p. 75 of the report of *Firth* v. *Staines* [1897] 2 Q.B. 70, in a passage which has been cited with approval in many subsequent cases: the passage reads:

I think the case must be decided upon the ordinary principles of the doctrine of ratification. To constitute a valid ratification three conditions must be satisfied: first, the agent whose act is sought to be ratified must have purported to act for the principal; secondly, at the time the act was done the agent must have had a competent principal; and, thirdly, at the time of the ratification the principal must be legally capable of doing the act himself.

At the meeting with the plaintiffs on the 5th September, 1973, Mr Costello and Mr Blakemore signed a promissory note which bore on its face over their signatures the words 'for and on behalf of Rockfield Limited'. They were not directors or members of the defendant company at the time when they signed this note but they had agreed to buy all the shares in that company. Mr Blakemore said that he knew that he was going to be a director of that company in a short time. I have no doubt whatever that Mr Blakemore and Mr Costello purported to act for the principal, the defendant company. The first condition in the passage from the judgment of Wright J. is satisfied.

[36]It was strenuously argued by counsel for the defendants that the transaction could not be ratified because it was illegal. The transaction was the borrowing of money; it was not the borrowing of money for the purchase of the shares in the defendant company, and indeed, only part of the money was applied for that purpose. The defendants had power to borrow money and so the agents had a competent principal that was legally capable of doing the act itself. The defendants' argument on this branch of the case confuses two things – the borrowing of the money and the borrowing of the money for the purpose of buying the shares in the defendant company. The defendants also ratified the transaction by accepting the two cheques of £15,300 and £5,100 which were part of the agreed total advance. The amounts of the loan represented by these two cheques were subsequently repaid and this is also an act of ratification – as was the authorised deposit of the land certificate in May, 1974. I fully agree with the trial judge's finding that Mr Costello and Mr Blakemore did not enter into the transaction on the 5th September, 1973, on behalf of the defendant company; they could not have done so because they had not been authorised but I have no doubt whatever that the judge's finding that the act of agreeing to borrow the money was subsequently validly ratified by the defendants.

I come now to deal with the much more difficult question which arises under the provisions of s. 60 of the Act of 1963. In 1963 this section was new to our company law; it was enacted to prevent a limited company from purchasing its own shares or giving assistance to anyone who wanted to buy shares in it. When a company buys its own shares, it is reducing its share capital without the sanction of the court and so damnifying the position of its creditors. The introduction of the section had been recommended in the report of the Company Law Reform Committee.

[The judge referred to the provisions of sub-ss. 1 and 14 of s. 60 of the Act of 1963 and continued] Sub-sections 2, 12 and 13 of s. 60 have no relevance to this case and, although sub-s. 1 of s. 60 appears in the (British) Companies Act, 1948, nothing corresponding to sub-s. 14 appears in that Act. This is the first case, as far as I know, in which the meaning of sub-s. 14 of s. 60 has been considered by any court in this country. The onus of proving that the money was advanced for the purchase of shares in the defendant company lies on the person who alleges this. The plaintiffs do not have to prove that they had no notice of facts which constituted a breach of section 60. What has to be established is that the plaintiffs had notice when lending the money that it was to be used for the purchase of shares in the defendant company. The fact [37] which constituted such breach in this case was the application of £150,000 to the purchase of the shares in the defendant company. As the purchase followed the loan, the defendants must establish that the plaintiffs knew at the time when they made the loan that it was to be applied for this purpose. If they got notice of this subsequently, that is irrelevant.

The notice referred to in sub-s. 14 of s. 60 is actual notice and not constructive notice. As there has been considerable confusion as to the meaning of the terms 'actual notice' and 'imputed notice' and 'constructive notice' – a confusion which has been pointed out by many judges and text-book writers – I wish to say that I use the term 'actual notice' as meaning in this case that the plaintiff bank, or any of its officals, had been informed, either verbally or in writing, that part of the advance was to be applied in the purchase of shares in the defendant company, or that they knew facts from which they *must* have inferred that part of the advance was to be applied for this purpose. This difficult branch of the law is well summarised at p. 50 of the 27th edition of Snell's Principles of Equity (of which the editors were The Hon. Sir Robert Megarry, now the Vice-Chancellor, and Professor Baker) where it is stated:

> From this it is clear that a purchaser is affected by notice of an equity in three cases:
> (1) Actual notice: where the equity is within his own knowledge;
> (2) Constructive notice: where the equity would have come to his own knowledge if proper inquiries had been made; and
> (3) Imputed notice: where his agent as such in the course of the transaction has actual or constructive notice of the equity.

See also s. 3 of the Conveyancing Act, 1882. I include in 'actual notice' cases where the agent gets actual notice of the equity.

There is strong authority that the doctrine of constructive notice is not to be extended to commercial transactions. In *Manchester Trust* v. *Furness* [1895] 2 Q.B. 539, Lindley J., a great authority upon company law, said at p. 545 of the report:

> . . . as regards the extension of the equitable doctrines of constructive notice to commercial transactions, the Courts have always set their faces resolutely against it. The equitable doctrines of constructive notice are common enough in dealing with land and estates, with which the Court is familiar; but there have been repeated protests against the introduction into commercial transactions of anything like an extension of those doctrines, and the protest is founded on perfect good sense. In dealing with estates in [38] land title is everything, and it can be leisurely investigated; in commercial transactions possession is everything, and there is no time to investigate title; and if we were to extend the doctrine of constructive notice to commercial transactions we should be doing infinite mischief and paralyzing the trade of the country.

That passage was approved by Lopes and Rigby JJ. It was cited with approval by Scrutton L.J. in the Court of Appeal in *Greer* v. *Downs Supply Co.* [1927] 2 Q.B. 28.

Section 60 of the Act of 1963 deals with financial assistance, not with mortgages. The word 'mortgage' does not appear in the section and sub-s. 14 applies to all commercial transactions. The fact that there was a mortgage involved in this transaction does not mean that the sub-section is to be read in one sense for financial assistance without security and in another sense when a mortgage is involved. That would be a ludicrous interpretation. Therefore 'notice of the facts which constitute such breach' means 'actual notice' in the sense in which I have defined those words.

In the puzzling passage in the trial judge's judgment, he refers to a person failing to accept information available to him or failing to make the inquiries normal in his line of business; but these are the criteria of constructive notice. What he seems to be saying is that constructive notice becomes actual notice at some undefined point. This is incorrect; it is blurring the distinction between actual notice and constructive notice. There is nothing in this case which indicates that the plaintiffs or any of their officials knew that any part of the advance was to be applied to the purchase of shares in the defendant company, and what they did know does not lead to a conclusion that they must have inferred that the money was to be applied for the purchase of shares in the defendant company.

The matters which were relied on as fixing the plaintiffs with constructive notice were, first, the failure to inspect or get a copy of the folio; secondly, the estimate of stamp duty in the estimate of the cost of the transaction which was submitted to them early on in the discussions; thirdly, the fact that planning permission was granted to the defendants in 1972 when application was made for it by them; and, fourthly counsel's opinion which is headed 'Rockfield Limited with Wicklow County Council.' The opinion is dated the 18th January, 1973. I think the failure to get a copy of or to inspect the folio would be held to be constructive notice for this was a matter that the plaintiffs ought to have investigated and, if the doctrine of constructive notice applied, that failure would certainly have fixed them with that type of notice; but, as it [39] is an omission to do something which they ought to have done, it is not actual notice. I confess that I find it incomprehensible why the plaintiffs did not ask for a copy of the folio, but then lawyers tend to think that everyone will take the same precautions as they do. I think that the plaintiffs ought to have inquired as to the estimate of stamp duty but, again, the fact that the stamp duty estimate was 1% of the purchase price was not notice that the money was to be applied for the purchase of the shares in the defendant company; it indicated that the purchase of another company was contemplated but not necessarily the defendant company. Knowledge that the defendants applied in 1973 for planning permission and that it was granted to them by Wicklow County Council was not either actual or constructive notice for, as I have already pointed out, until the 30th July, 1974, when this Court decided otherwise it was generally assumed in the legal, architectural and engineering professions that anybody could apply for planning permission without having any interest in the land. This transaction took place long before that date.

It follows that the plaintiffs are entitled to succeed in this action. Although they had constructive notice that the defendant company was the owner of the land, the plaintiffs had not actual notice and that is the knowledge which is referred to in s. 60, sub-s. 14, of the Act of 1963.

IX. Shareholder Status and Rights

The Companies Acts contain elaborate provisions concerning what may be called the personal property aspect of company law, viz. questions of title to shares, and their transfer and transmission. Shareholders generally owe their companies one principal obligation, which is to pay up any unpaid amount on their shares when called upon to do so. Subject to the company in question's own regulations, shareholders generally are entitled to transfer their shares, to vote in general meetings, to a dividend whenever one is declared, and where possible when the company is wound up to a return of their capital and a share in any surplus remaining. Companies with preference shares usually have special rules on these matters.

TITLE TO SHARES

Rearden v. Provincial Bank of Ireland
[1896] 1 I.R. 532

The assets of a trust included shares in the defendant bank, and the shares were registered in the trustee's [Mr Barry's] name. The bank was fully aware of the trust's existence and terms. When the trustee failed to pay his own debts to the bank, it claimed a lien over the shares registered in his name, contending that it was entitled to do so in the light of what today is s. 123 of the 1963 Act and article 7 of Table A.

PORTER M.R.: . . . [555] The bank say, here are certain shares in Barry's name. Whether he is the owner or not does not matter. By the effect of the Companies Act of 1862, section 30, and by virtue of our own articles of association, and neglecting the knowledge given to us that he is merely a trustee for another, we are entitled to hold the shares answerable for his debt. That is the way the question of law arises.

In the case of *The New London and Brazilian Bank* v. *Broclebank* (21 Ch.D. 302), the articles of association were substantially the same as here. But in that case, there was no notice even alleged by the company of the absence of benefical ownership on the part of the registered owners of the shares. The lien of the bank prevailed, and rightly; but the case has no authority or bearing on the point, when the clearest notice I have ever known (whatever the result of it may be) is proved. . . .

[562] Is it then the case that any notice 'if given to a Company would be absolutely inoperative to affect the Company with any trust'? In my opinion the case of *The Bradford Bank* v. *Briggs* (1889) 12 App. Cas. 29, shows that this is not so, and that for some purposes, at any rate, notice may bind the Company, not with specific trusts, but with knowledge that shares are held by one who has no interest in them which he can lawfully deal with for his own benefit.

That case came originally before Field, J. The articles of association of a Company provided that the Company should have a first and permanent lien and charge on every share of every person who was the holder for all debts due by him to the Company. A shareholder deposited the certificates of some shares belonging to him in the Company with his bankers as security for the balance due, or which should become due, on his current account, and the bank gave notice to the Company of the deposit, the certificates deposited stating that the shares were held subject to the articles of association of the Company. It was held in the House of Lords, reversing the decision of the Court of Appeal, which had in turn reversed the decision of Field, J., that the Company could not, in respect of moneys which became due from the shareholder to the Company after notice of the deposit with the bank, claim priority over advances by the bank made after such notice, but that the principle of *Hopkinson* v. *Rolt* (9 H.L. Cas. 514) applied.

[563] On this question of notice there are two important distinctions to be noted between the case of the Bradford Bank and the present. In that case there was no clause in the articles of association similar to clause 8 in the present. The question of notice there turned upon the effect of section 30 of the Act. Again, the equity affecting the shares there was that they had been deposited with a bank to secure advances, not as here, where they were held by a trustee.

Bearing these two points in mind, it is necessary to see exactly what was decided in *The Bradford Bank* v. *Briggs*. It is to be observed that there were three transactions – first, a lien by the Company; secondly, a mortgage by equitable deposit of the certificates of the shares by the shareholder for advances made by the bank; and, thirdly, further advances by them after notice to the Company; and the contest was as to whether the Company were enabled, notwithstanding notice of the intervening security, to draw up their subsequent advances and tack them to the previous advances. . . .

[566] [I]n *Bradford Bank* v. *Briggs* the transaction of which the bank had notice was this – the legal and equitable owner of shares had pledged them by depositing the share certificates with his bankers. He remained the legal owner after the deposit; but in equity the bank were the real owners subject to being redeemed at the option of the shareholder. The position of the bank was not disputed, that is, it was not denied that they were equitable mortgagees. The contest was between their equitable rights and

the claims of the defendant Company to a lien for advances to the shareholder after and with actual notice of the bank's equitable mortgage.

That such a transaction did for some purposes constitute the relation of trustee and *cestui que trust* between the bank and Easby could not I think be questioned. One person is legal owner. The other is the equitable owner (to the extent of his charge). If instead of a mortgage the transaction had been a sale, the certificates being deposited pending completion, it could not be doubted that the vendor would have held the legal title as a trustee for the purchaser so soon as the price was paid; and a mortgage is only a conditional sale.

But though undoubtedly for some purposes a trust, the condition or state of facts in *Bradford Banking Co.* v. *Briggs*, did not amount to a trust within the meaning of section 30, of the Act of 1862. Why is this?

The judgments in the House of Lords seem to say that the notice was not notice of a trust, in the sense of being notice of such a character as to attach to the Company the character of trustee. Section 30 deprives it of this character. It is not, therefore, the case of an attempt to affect the Company with a trust. It is merely notice that the person with whom the Company deals, that is the registered shareholder, is not really the owner of the shares. It does not enable the Company to 'charge what they knew was one man's property with another man's debt if only that property consisted of shares in the Company.'

[567] [T]he real object of the Legislature in enacting section 30, and that of similar provisions embodied in articles of association, may supply the key to the whole matter. It cannot be doubted that the intention was to spare the Company the responsibility of attending to any trusts or equities whatever attached to their shares, so that they might safely and securely deal with the person who is registered owner, and with him alone, recognising no other person and no different right; freeing them, in short, from all embarrassing inquiries into conflicting claims as to shares, transfers, calls, dividends, right to vote, and the like; and enabling them to treat the registered shareholder as owner of the shares for all purposes, without regard to contract as beween himself and third persons. But it could never have been the object of the Legislature to enable the Company, say a trading Company like the Provincial Bank, to ignore for their own purposes and interests the rights of other persons of which they have actual knowledge, so as, in the words of Lord Blackburn, 'to charge what they knew was one man's property with another man's debt.' There is no obligation upon a bank or other Company to lend money on its shares, and no reason why any special protection should be afforded them if they do: or why, if they choose to do so, they should be exempt from the rules of law and justice. . . . [568]

Sect. 30 provides 'No notice of any trust, expressed or implied or constructive, shall be entered on the register, or be receivable by the registrar, in case of Companies under this Act, and registered in England or Ireland,' and clause 8 of the articles of association provides, 'No person shall be recognised by the Company as holding any share upon any trust, and the Company shall not be *bound* by, or recognise, any equitable, future, or partial interest in any share... or any other right in respect of any share except an absolute right to the entirety thereof in the registered holder.' In both cases the language is, I think, intended for the protection of the Company; not to enable it to commit frauds, or knowingly take the benefit of them.

In the present case it is not sought (any more than in *Bradford Banking Co.* v. *Briggs*), to affect the bank with any particular trust, or with direct notice of any trust whatever. It is sought to show that no matter what trust or equity may have attached to the shares or to Barry, yet the bank had notice that Barry was not owner of the shares, and that they had this knowledge before they lent him the money in respect of which they claim to have a lien. I cannot see how in this point of view, the special facts of the present case render the reasoning in *Bradford Banking Co.* v. *Briggs* inapplicable.

But in the present case there is far more than mere notice to the Company of the rights of the plaintiff, or the absence of right and title in Barry. There is conduct on the part of the bank amounting to positive aquiescence in her position, or rather in the position that Barry had no property or right to the shares which he could use for his own benefit.

Casey v. Bentley
[1902] 1 I.R. 376

The plaintiff executed a transfer of shares to the defendant and was paid the purchase money. Under the company's regulations, the directors could refuse to register the defendant as a shareholder.

LORD ASHBOURNE C.: ... [384] This case raises a novel and interesting question on the duty of registering a transfer of shares purchased on the Stock Exchange, and the question is, What is the position of buyer and seller when the directors of the Company, acting within their powers, refuse to register the transfer though the purchaser has paid his money?

It appears that the plaintiff, Mrs Casey, was possessed of two shares in the Dublin and Glasgow Steam Packet Company, which is an unlimited Company, and being desirous of escaping from a Company with unlimited liability, she agreed on the 31st January, 1898, through her stockbroker, Mr Kelly, to sell her shares to the defendant. In pursuance of that agreement the transfer was signed by the plaintiff, and accepted, and the purchase money was paid. When the defendant sought to have his name placed on the list of shareholders, the directors of the Company refused to register the transfer, relying on their 15th Regulation, which prescribes: 'It shall be lawful for the directors to decline to register the transfer of shares to any person not approved of by the directors as transferee, and thereupon such a transfer shall be void, and the directors shall not be compellable to give any reason for such refusal.'

The defendant unquestionably acted with perfect good faith, and exhausted all the opportunities open to him of getting the transfer registered; on the other hand, it is not denied that the Company are within their rights in acting as they did in the matter. The dividends which have accrued since the sale of the shares have been regularly paid to Mrs Casey, and she has paid them over to the defendant, on his demand, but under protest.

Matters have stood thus for four years. The plaintiff desired to bring the question to an issue, and in order to elucidate her position she issued an equity civil bill in January, 1901, before the Recorder, [385] claiming specific performance of the agreement so far as the same remained unperformed, and asking that the defendant might be ordered to procure the shares to be registered in his own name or in that of some other person. When the matter came before the Recorder in February, 1901, it was found that that civil bill would not really present the case, and therefore an amendment was assumed to be necessary by all the parties. The civil bill was accordingly amended by the Court, a claim being added to the prayer for specific performance, asking for an indemnity and also for rescission of the contract. This amendment was made because the plaintiff, who was the vendor, finding that the original purchaser could not give her the relief she sought, thought that the best thing to do was to get rescission of the contract, and than seek for another purchaser, to whom the Company would not object. . . .

There is a clear distinction between the purchase of shares on the Stock Exchange and by private contract, and it is essential to keep this distinction clearly in view when reading the authorities, and when considering the comments in Fry on Specific Performance and Lindley on Companies.

There are many cases where purchasers have proceeded against vendors of shares on the Stock Exchange seeking for relief where the directors have refused to register the transfers, and thus complete their legal title. But I have been unable to find any case, like the present, where the vendor, having been paid the purchase money and executed the transfer, and the purchaser having *bona fide* failed to obtain registration owing to a legitimate refusal on the part of the directors acting within the scope of their legal powers, is perfectly willing to remain equitable owner of the shares and let matters rest, but is nevertheless, sued by the vendor praying for the rescission of the contract, in consequence of the purchaser not having succeeded in getting the shares registered in his name, which he admittedly could not have done.

The general position is stated by Fry, L.J., in his work on Specific

Performance, 1519: 'Where the constitution of the Company gives the directors a power to refuse to register transfers, the question arises whether the refusal on the part of the directors to register the purchaser relieves him from the obligation of performing the contract. This question must be answered [387] differently according to circumstances. Where the contract is not made on the Stock Exchange, but is made in the reference to the constitution of the Company or subject to its rules, and the constitution of the Company requires the vendor to do all that is essential to the transfer, the vendor is under an obligation to procure the assent of the directors, and if he fail so to do, the purchaser is relieved from the contract, and if he have already paid his purchase money in ignorance of this refusal he may recover it back. Where the contract is made on the Stock Exchange, and subject to its rules, it is clear that the refusal of the directors to register the transfer is immaterial, for, according to the construction put upon such a contract, it is performed on the vendor's part by the delivery of the transfer and certificates, and the vendee is entitled to the right which he thereby acquires to procure himself to be registered, if the directors so choose; he is not entitled to an absolute and unconditional right to registration. In a sale on the Stock Exchange it is no part of the vendor's duty, irrespective of express contract, to procure the registration of the transfer.'

The position of the purchaser I take to be sufficiently clear from the cases cited by the learned writer. . . .[391]

It is thus abundantly clear on the authorities that the purchaser cannot rescind the contract because he cannot obtain registration. The effort is now made for the first time to turn the tables and say that the vendor is entitled to rescind the contract because the directors have refused the most urgent requests of the purchaser to be registered. There is no authority for this to be found in any case of transfer of shares on the Stock Exchange. . . .

In his judgment in *Stray* v. *Russell* (I E. & E. 888), Crompton, J., said (at p. 913) – 'The fact of the payment being to be made on the handing over of the certificates and transfers, and the practice stated as to no prior consent being ever asked for, and as to no assent being ever refused, make it very probable that the vendee in such case bargains only for the delivery of the shares and transfers and takes the chance of getting himself or his nominee or subvendee accepted and registered. The plaintiff must be taken to have known of the clause in the deed as to the consent, and he may well have bought, taking the chance of procuring such acceptance or registration on himself. He seems to have bought the shares, certificates and transfers, on the agreement to pay for them on delivery of the documents. In *Wilkinson* v. *Lloyd*, (7 Q.B. 27) the Court assumed that the consent to the assignment was a part of the vendor's title, as in the case of sale of a lease; but whatever may have been the case of the purchase of the partnership shares in the mines (real [392] property to some extent), in that case on a sale between the parties not according to any course of business on the Stock Exchange, I can make no such assumption in the present case, where the sale was, according to the regulations of the Stock Exchange, which made the price payable on handing over the shares and transfers, and according to which it is at least probable that the vendee was to take upon himself the duty of getting the transfers completed and the shares registered, and where from the nature of the transaction, it seems to me very unlikely that the vendor should undertake for the acceptance of any particular name or person when he may have been entirely ignorant at the time of the contract of the name and responsibility of the intended transferee.'

It is said that it would be hard on the plaintiff to hold her bound to the shares she had sold and struggled to get rid of. But it was equally hard to hold the parties bound in the decided cases to which I have referred. If the plaintiff had been well advised she could have safeguarded her position and stipulated with her stockbroker that he was to stipulate for registration as a clear term in his Stock Exchange contract. In *Cruse* v. *Paine* (L.R. 6 Eq. 461) where the purchaser expressly guaranteed the registration of the shares, he was held liable to indemnify the seller. The sale note in that case had written across it the words 'registration guaranteed'. Lord Hatherley in his judgment expressly pointed out that the superadded provision of 'registration guaranteed' made the defendant liable to procure registration.

INCIDENTS OF MEMBERSHIP

Re Discoverers Finance Corp. Ltd., Lindlar's Case
[1910] 1 Ch. 312 (C.A.)

Fearing that the company was in difficulties and that he might be obliged to pay further calls on his shares, which were not fully paid up, the owner of 2,000 shares of £1 par sold them for £5 in all to a journeyman tanner. The consideration was never paid, or even sought.

BUCKLEY L.J.: . . . [316] The decisions upon the branch of the law with which we are here concerned are numerous. Care is necessary to avoid the danger which exists of allowing the attention to be distracted from the principles which underlie all those decisions, and to be drawn into an examination of the minute differences of fact and inferences of fact upon which judges have in different cases acted in forming their conclusions as to the facts to which they are about to apply those principles.

We propose first to state the principles as we understand them. By s. 22 of the Companies Act, 1862, which is reproduced as s. 22 of the Companies (Consolidation) Act, 1908, it is provided that the shares in a company under these Acts shall be capable of being transferred in manner provided by the regulations of the company. The regulations of the company may impose fetters upon the right of transfer. In the absence of restrictions in the articles the shareholder has by virtue of the statute the right to transfer his shares without the consent of anybody to any transferee, even though he be a man of straw, provided it is a bona fide transaction in the sense that it is an out and out disposal of the property without retaining any interest in the shares – that the transferor bona fide divests himself of all benefit. . . .[317] It was the policy of these Acts to give a free right of disposition, leaving it to the regulations of the company to impose such restrictions upon its exercise as might be desired. In the absence of restrictions it is competent to a transferor, notwithstanding that the company is in extremis, to compel registration of a transfer to a transferee notwithstanding that the latter is a person not competent to meet the unpaid liability upon the shares. Even if the transfer be executed for the express purpose of relieving the transferor from liability, the directors cannot upon that ground refuse to register it unless there is in the articles some provision so enabling them.

The cases which are generally regarded as the leading cases upon this branch of the law are cases decided before 1862. [Many of those] were cases in which the right to transfer rested not upon the statutory provision which has been mentioned, but upon such rights as arose upon the delivery of an instrument by whose delivery the shares were taken to pass. In the subsequent cases since 1862 (and they have been numerous) we do not remember that reference was made to the difference which arises by reason of the fact that the right to transfer is in cases under the Companies Acts a statutory right. It is a difference which in our judgment gives the transferor a greater right if that be necessary than existed in such a company as was the subject of the [Pre-1862] decision[s].

In that which follows the authorities are divided into three classes. . . .

[318] The first is the case where the articles contain no clause allowing the directors to reject a transferee. In such case the law is that a shareholder may up to the last moment before liquidation, and for the express purpose of escaping liability, transfer his partly-paid shares to a transferee, even though the latter be a pauper, and may compel the directors to register that transfer made avowedly for the purpose of avoiding liability, provided his transfer be an out and out transfer reserving to himself no beneficial right to the shares, direct or indirect. Whether the transfer is of that character is a question of fact. . . . [320] [Any] liability of the transferor in every case arises not from the fact that he has paid or become liable to pay something to the transferee, but upon the fact that he has reserved to himself a benefit in respect of the shares. If that be found not to be the case, then the transfer to a man of straw is effectual to protect the transferor.

The investigation whether the transfer is or is not an out and out transfer, is, of course, an investigation of the true relations subsisting between the transferor and the transferee. But if this inquiry is answered by finding that the transfer is out and out, there is in the absence of an approval clause in the articles, and in the absence of facts which bring the case within the third class presently mentioned, an end of the matter so far as any rights of the liquidator are concerned. Suppose the out and out transfer was procured by misrepresentation practised by the transferor towards the transferee. This will give the latter rights against the former, but with these the liquidator is not concerned. He has no right arising from this cause of action, assuming it to exist as between the other [321] parties. If the transferee initiates against the transferor successful proceedings, the liquidator no doubt can and ought to give his sanction under s. 131 of the Act of 1862, or s. 205 of the Act of 1908, if the result will be that he will obtain as contributory a solvent transferor in place of an insolvent transferee. But in such case the result is attained not by virtue of any right subsisting in the liquidator, but by the liquidator consenting to the successful assertion of a right subsisting in some one else. . . .

The second class of case is where the articles do contain a clause empowering the directors to reject a transferee whom they do not approve. In these cases the principle is that the transferor cannot escape liability if he has actively by falsehood or passively by concealment, induced the directors to pass and register a transfer (even though it be an out and out transfer) which, if he had not so deceived or concealed, they would have refused to register. Here again the question is one of fact. It is not sufficient to shew that the transferee's address was incorrect or that the description of his occupation was not accurate, or the like. The Court must arrive at the conclusion that therefrom resulted such a state of things as that if the directors had known the truth they would not have registered the transfer.

The third class of case is one which may arise in either one of the two classes of case above mentioned. It is the case in which the transferor has obtained the advantage of executing and registering his transfer to a man of straw upon an opportunity obtained by him fraudulently or in breach of some duty which he owed the corporation. As, for instance, if he (being in a position so to do) has procured the postponement of the commencement of the winding-up in order to get time to execute and tender such a transfer for registration, or if by collusion with the directors he has procured them in breach of their duty to pass a transfer which they ought not to have passed. The last is a ground which might have been material in the present case if it had been proved, which it has not.

Tangney v. Clarence Hotels Ltd.
[1933] I.R. 51

The company's articles of association empowered the directors to refuse to register any transfer of shares to someone who in their opinion 'is not a desirable person to admit to membership'. The plaintiff, who held some shares in the company bought more shares; but the directors refused to register those shares in his name.

JOHNSTON J.: ... [59] The first matter that was discussed by counsel for the Company, namely, the point that the plaintiff, being merely the transferee of the shares, has no *locus standi* as such and no right to take proceedings against the Company to compel the Company to register him as the owner of the shares, is wholly unsustainable. The transferee of shares is the proper person to take such a step, and were it not that the transferor has been given a statutory right, notwithstanding the fact that by the transfer the shares have passed from him outright, to apply to the Company to enter the transferee's name on the register, he would have no power whatsoever to do so. A transferee's right and privileges in regard to this matter are perfectly plain when the nature of a public company registered under the Companies Acts is considered and when the provisions of those Acts as to shares, stock and the proprietary interest that a 'member' of the company is entitled to, and the rights of transfer, and the method by which that proprietary interest may be transferred, are taken into account; and I would be prepared to hold, even without the assistance of sects. 28 and 32 of the Companies (Consolidation) Act, 1908, that a transferee's right was as I have stated it.

It is quite idle for this Company and the Directors to contend, as they both have done, that a person to whom a member of a company has transferred his stock or his share has no such privity with the company as would entitle him to go to the company with his deed of transfer and insist upon his being registered as the owner of the shares. Even were sects. 28 and 32 less clear than they are, the whole course of the existing statutory law would point to that conclusion. As a matter of fact, however, the matter has been set at rest by *Skinner's Case* (14 Q.B.D. 882) – a case to which I was not referred during the course of the argument. In that case a claim had been brought against [60] a company by a transferor of shares for damages for delay on the part of the company in registering the transfer. It was held by the Court of Appeal (Brett M.R. and Baggalley and Brown L.JJ.) that it was primarily the duty of the transferee to have procured the registration; and, as the consideration appearing on the face of the deed was merely a nominal sum, the plaintiff could, under the particular circumstances, recover only nominal damages from the company. Brett, M.R., at p. 887, says: 'So that when the transfer has been executed and handed over to the transferee, it is then for the latter to pay the consideration money and to get the transfer registered. Now is there any difference made in respect of this by sect. 26 of the Companies Act, 1867? I think not. It was not, I think, intended by the Legislature that that enactment should alter or have any effect on the duty of the transferee, and that it is still his duty, as it was before that enactment, to get himself registered as a member of the company in respect of the shares which have been transferred to him, and that this sect. 26 of the Companies Act, 1867, was only for the protection of the transferor in case the transferee failed to perform his duty.'

There must therefore be a declaration in favour of the plaintiff that this action is properly constituted and that the plaintiff as transferee of the shares referred to in the statement of claim is entitled to have brought the action to have the respective rights of the parties determined.

The second question that has been raised is that, on the true construction of Article 21 of the Articles of Association, it was, and is, a condition precedent that before any member of the Company can transfer his shares to any person he must serve a notice upon the Company of his intention to do so, giving the name and address of the proposed transferee, and that no valid transfer can take place unless and until that notice has been served. Article 21 is in the following terms:

'Any member proposing to transfer any share shall give notice in writing of this intention so to do to the Directors, giving the name and address of the proposed transferee; and if the Directors are of opinion that the proposed transferee is not a desirable person to admit to membership, they may decline to register the transfer of any such share, and it shall be lawful for them, within three months from the receipt of such notice, to transfer any such share to such person as the Directors shall nominate, at such price as the person giving notice and the nominee of the Directors may agree upon; and in default of agree[61]ment at such price as the Directors may determine, and the Directors may cause the name of their nominee to be entered in the Register in respect of the share transferred by them, and the receipt of the Company shall be a full discharge to the nominee of the Directors, and after his name has been entered in the Register the validity of the transaction shall not be questioned by any person. The proceeds of any share transferred by the Directors under this Article shall be applied in or towards satisfaction of the debts, liabilities, or engagements (if any) to the Company of the member whose share is transferred, and the residue (if any) paid to such member, his executors, administrators, or assigns.' . . . .

It seems to me that Article 21 must be construed reasonably and not oppressively, and I do not think that it was intended by the framers of the same that service of such a notice was to be a condition precedent to the execution by the holder of shares of an agreement to transfer or even to the execution of an actual tranfer deed. A transfer is not legally complete until the transferee has been registered in the books of the Company, and it was not incorrect for the Article to refer to a person to whom shares had been transferred by deed but who had not yet [62] been registered as 'the proposed transferee'. The Directors are given the power, not 'to decline to permit the execution by the proposed transferor of a deed of transfer' but merely to 'decline to register the transfer of any such share'. This point was made clear by Eve J., in *In re Copal Varnish Co. Ltd.* [1917] 2 Ch. 349, where the provision in question was this: 'No share shall be transferred to any person who is not already a member of the company without the consent of the directors.' Even that clause was held not to amount to a condition precedent. Eve J. said: 'So long as prior to the completion of the transaction an opportunity is given to the directors sitting as a board to determine whether the proposed transferee is a person whom they are prepared to admit as a member of the company, the conditions imposed by the Article are, in my opinion, complied with, and the contract into which the vendor on becoming a shareholder entered with his co-shareholders is sufficiently discharged.' In a somewhat analogous case – namely that of the pre-emption clause in sect. 1 of the Land Law (Ireland) Act 1881 – the Vice-Chancellor and Bewley J. arrived at a similar result in the cases of *Fisher* v. *Coan* [1894] 1 I.R. 179, and *Meath* v. *Megan* [1897] 2 I.R. 39 at p. 48. I am, therefore, prepared to give a declaration that on the construction of Article 21 service upon the Company of the notice referred to in that Article was not a condition precedent to the execution of a transfer of the shares by the Hibernian Bank to the plaintiff.

The third argument that has been addressed to me by the defendants, on the construction of this Article, is that the power given therein to the Directors is absolute and unrestricted, and is not confined to the case of a transfer of shares to persons who are not already shareholders and, as such, members of the Company. I am asked by the defendants to hold that the word 'membership' should be read as meaning 'membership in respect of the shares which are proposed to be transferred'. The plaintiff, on the other hand, says that the Article should be read as it stands, and that, read in that way, its meaning and intention are perfectly plain. Whenever a deed of transfer is submitted to the Directors they are empowered to decline to register the transfer; but their power to do so is not unlimited. It only arises whenever they are of the opinion that the proposed transferee is not a desirable person to admit to membership. It seems to me that that clause [63] was intended to meet the case of a stranger proposing to come into the family, as it were. In such a case the Directors were given the power to determine whether such person was 'a desirable person', and their power to decide that question seems to be absolute and cannot be questioned, except by showing affirmatively that they are exercising their powers capriciously or wantonly: *Ex parte Penney* (8 Ch. App. 446). As was pointed out by Eve J., in *In re Bede Shipping Co., Ltd.* [1917] 1 Ch. 123, the right of an owner of shares to get rid of them by transfer is absolute except in so far as it is restricted by contract *inter socios*, and 'it is to the Articles of Association that we must turn for the purpose of ascertaining the nature and the extent of the restrictions imposed'. The powers that have been conferred upon Directors in this respect vary widely in their extent and operation. One of the commonest forms of such restrictions, as Cozens Hardy M.R. pointed out in the same case (p. 132), was and is the power to restrict the transfer of shares except to persons who were already members of the company. That device has been adopted by company draftsmen in many different forms – that is, to place no restrictions upon the circulation of the shares amongst the members of the company, but to enable the heavy hand of the Directors to come down when a stranger seeks to enter into the charmed circle. This is the policy that is to be discerned in Articles 42 and 43 in the present case. Whenever the Directors with the sanction of the company decide to increase the capital of the Company by the issue of new shares, all such new shares must, subject to any direction of the Company that sanctions the increase of capital 'be offered to the members in proportion to the existing shares held by them'; and if new shares are issued in the future the plaintiff will be entitled to his proportion of them as a matter of course, and the Directors cannot refuse to let him have them on the ground that he is not 'a desirable person'.

The case of *In re Dublin North City Milling Co.* [1909] 1 I.R. 179, which is relied upon by the defendants, is of no assistance in this case. The article in question there provided that the Directors 'may decline to register any transfer of shares. . . unless the transferee is approved of by the board'; and it was held that the Directors could decline to register a transfer of shares to a person who was already a member of the company. This was not a decision upon [64] the construction of an Article of Association. It was an ordinary case where the Directors had an unrestricted power to decline to permit the registration of any transfer of shares. The transferee sought to get behind the power conferred by the Article by contending that because he was already a member of the company, the action of the board could not possibly be *bona fide*. The argument of the transferee's counsel opened in this way: 'The refusal of the directors to register the transfer is not *bona fide*'; and Meredith M.R. decided that he could not come to such a conclusion of fact upon the mere ground that the transferee was already a member of the company.

I cannot accede to the argument of the defendants that a shareholder is a member of the Company in regard to the particular shares he holds. That is too narrow a view of the principles of the law as to the nature and constitution of a public company. The Act of 1862, under which this Company was constituted, provides (sect. 18) that upon the registration of the company, 'the subscribers of the Memorandum of Association, together with such other persons as may from time to time become members of the company, shall thereupon be a body corporate by the name contained in the Memorandum of Association, capable forthwith of exercising all the functions of an incorporated company'. Sect. 23 provides further that the subscribers 'and every other person who has agreed to become a member of a company under this Act, and whose name is entered on the register of members, shall be deemed to be a member of the company'. These provisons are continued with small verbal differences, by sect. 16, sub-sect. 2, and sect. 24 of the Act of 1908. It seems to me, therefore, that the word 'membership' in Article 21 can only mean membership of the corporate body of which the members in the aggregate consist.

I shall therefore declare that on the true construction of Article 21 the Directors had no power to refuse to register the transfer of shares by the Hibernian Bank to the plaintiff, he being at the time a shareholder and a member of the Company.

In re Hafner
[1943] I.R. 426

The company was a small family company, and one of its articles of association was very similar to clause 3 of part II of Table A. The plaintiff inherited some shares in the company; but without assigning any reasons, the directors refused to register him as a member. Among the facts that came out in evidence was that one director drew £7,000 per annum in remuneration; and another director had a service contract providing for £3,000 per annum salary, the duration was 20 years, but if the company was wound up before that term expired, the director would become entitled to the equivalent of £1,500 per annum for the residue of the term.

BLACK J.: . . . [438] [W]hen discovery was obtained, it came to light that the company, or in reality, the three directors, who are the defendants in this action, had voted or agreed to pay various salaries and emoluments to one another, which, the plaintiff says, would swallow up the net profits, and thereby reduce the value of the 500 shares bequeathed to him to a cipher. He says that this procedure would amount to a fraudulent abuse of their fiduciary position by the defendants, and that the directors' refusal to register him in respect of these 500 shares was decided upon with the intention and for the purpose of facilitating them in making this fraudulent procedure more easily effective. That being his view, he seeks to have the refusal of registration overridden by order of the Court. Having made the discovery and formed the conclusion in question, the plaintiff sought leave of this Court to amend his statement of claim so as to raise the contentions mentioned. This leave was granted by me and my decision in that regard was upheld by the Supreme Court. The statement of claim has accordingly been amended, and a new ground is now put forward for requiring the defendants, as directors of the company, to register the transfer of the 500 shares to the plaintiff, namely, that in refusing such registration the directors, instead of exercising a *bona fide* discretion, acted with a view to compel the plaintiff to sell the said shares at an undervalue, and also with a view to preventing the plaintiff from questioning the payment of the impugned emoluments.

In dealing with this question, two Articles of Association are in question. These are as follows:

Article 6. 'The directors may, in their absolute and uncontrolled discretion and without assigning any reason, refuse to register any transfer of shares, and clause 20 of Table 'A' shall be modified accordingly.'

Article 7. 'No member may transfer or dispose of his shares or any of them without first offering them to the directors of the company, who shall have the first option of purchasing same at a fair market price to be fixed, in [439] the event of dispute, by the auditors of the company at the expense of the vendor. On payment of the price so fixed, the registered owner shall forthwith transfer the shares in manner directed by the directors.'

Now it seems to me that unless the plaintiff was entitled as a matter of law to demand to be registered, he cannot compel the company to register him however fraudulent the directors' object in refusing registration might be. The statement of claim does not expressly allege that the plaintiff was entitled to be registered. But if I might paraphrase it freely, it alleges certain facts from which the plaintiff considers that his right *prima facie* to be registered must follow. Of course it is the pleader's business to plead facts and not law. What, then, are these facts? Freely paraphrased they are as follows:

(a) The late Frederick A. Hafner was the registered holder of the 500 shares in question.

(b) By his last will he bequeathed them to the plaintiff absolutely.

(c) The executors by a proper form of transfer transferred the said shares to the plaintiff.

(d) The plaintiff duly transmitted this transfer to the company for registration.

The plaintiff then alleges in substance that the directors' refusal to register him was fraudulent, and claims that he is therefore entitled to be registered. He plainly assumes that the defendants have refused to register him purporting to exercise the discretion given them by Art. 6. But the defendants have taken care not to admit either by their pleadings or by their evidence that they purported to act under Art. 6. They have not disclosed which of the Articles they purported to act under, and this information has not been elicited from them either by pleading or by cross-examination. The mystery had been well guarded. But their counsel have claimed for them that they were entitled to refuse registration because the requirement in Art. 7 was not, as they say, complied with.

I am thus obliged to deal with both Articles.

First, Article 6. It is well settled that under such an Article as this the directors may refuse to register a transfer. It is equally settled that the directors' power in this regard is a fiduciary one and must be exercised in the interest of the company as a whole. They must not exercise it arbitrarily, capriciously, or corruptly. They are not bound to assign their reasons, and the Court is not entitled to infer merely from their omission to do so that their reasons were not legitimate.

[440] Hedged round with the privilege of remaining mute and the *prima facie* presumption of rectitude, the astutely silent director who wishes to exercise this power illegitimately may well consider himself all but invulnerable. No need to speak and no unfavourable inference from reticence – that is the settled rule. Yet, like many another settled rule, I am persuaded that it is not proof against possible exceptions. The case of *Bell Brothers* (7 T.L.R. 689), was one illustration of this, and I have to consider whether the present case provides another.

In *Bell's Case*, certain directors exercised an unrestricted power to refuse a transfer and also stood upon their privilege of declining to give any reasons. But it so happened that one of the directors, like Mr McGrath in this case, was executor of the will of the deceased owner of the shares in question. The shares were directed to be sold to raise money to provide for the widow's annuity. A Mr Hodgson purchased, and took out a summons for confirmation of the contract. The executor-director opposed; but the contract was confirmed and he was reluctantly obliged to execute the transfer as executor – just as Mr McGrath as executor executed the transfer of 500 shares to the plaintiff here, although it does not appear that he did it reluctantly. The director in *Bell's Case*, then, as director, proceeded to join with his co-directors in refusing registration of the transfer he had himself executed as executor, precisely as Mr McGrath joined in refusing as director to register the very transfer he had himself executed as executor. So far the likeness of the two cases is remarkable. But it turned out in *Bell's Case* that the director in question, when opposing the sale to Hodgson, had admitted that he wanted to have the shares sold to his father and co-director for the purpose of keeping all the company shares in the Bell family. Upon these facts Mr Justice Chitty put two and two together. He concluded that the admitted motive for opposing the sale to Hodgson was also likely to be a motive for refusing registration to Hodgson, and he held that a refusal actuated by such a motive would not be a legitimate exercise of the directors' discretion. If the learned Judge had stopped there, it seems to me that the directors might still have defied interference by the Court; for proof that they had a motive which was illegitimate, would not negative the possibility that they might also have had another and sufficient motive which was not illegitimate, and I apprehend that if directors had a good [441] and adequate reason for refusing a transfer upon which they would have acted in any case, the fact that they had at the same time an ulterior and perhaps still stronger motive of an illegitimate character would not invalidate the exercise of their discretion. I think that in order to interfere the Court must not only find that the directors had an invalid motive, but it must also find that they had no valid motive that might be itself sufficient. That is precisely what Mr Justice Chitty did. Yet this finding would have been impossible if the rule continued to apply that directors who do not state any reason for refusing a transfer must be presumed to have had valid reasons and that no unfavourable inference can be drawn from their silence. Once a reason which was invalid was proved to the satisfaction of the Court, the rule ceased to hold good, and the Court felt itself free to examine the possibility of other reasons that would not be invalid and even to comment upon and draw inferences from the directors' failure to state their reasons, although in *Bell's Case* their solicitor presumed to suggest possible reasons for them which the Court rejected. They themselves gave no reasons.

Now in the present case it is very clearly alleged in the statement of claim that the defendant directors had an illegitimate purpose in refusing to register the plaintiff in respect of his 500 shares, and this alleged purpose is plainly specified. It is alleged that the object was to compel the plaintiff to sell the 500 shares at an under value and also to prevent him from questioning the acts of the defendants in voting themselves large emoluments, which, it is said, would have the effect of reducing, if not of extinguishing altogether, the dividends which otherwise the plaintiff would be entitled beneficially to receive, whether registered as a member or not. When the statement of claim refers to 'compelling' the plaintiff to sell, of course it means putting pressure upon him to do so by rendering it unprofitable for him to refuse to sell, such pressure as an average business man would think amounted to virtual compulsion. Similarly, when mention is made of 'preventing' the plaintiff from questioning the defendants' act, I interpret 'preventing' to mean 'making it more difficult' for the plaintiff to question those acts, and thereby tending to prevent him from doing so. I do not think the defendants could literally prevent him from questioning the emoluments concerned, but I do think that if he were deprived of the privilege of attending the [442] company's meetings, he would lose a valuable opportunity of questioning the acts of its directors; and, moreover, by not being a member of the company his remedy, while not in my opinion taken away, might well be rendered more difficult – a possibility made very obvious by the fact that Mr FitzGibbon and Mr Leonard seemed to take different views as to what that remedy would be.

In partial, but only partial, reply to all this it is said that, even if refusal of registration would virtually compel the plaintiff to sell the shares, it would not compel him to do so at an undervalue, since the price would be fixed by the auditor and would have to be the fair value on the assumption that the impugned emoluments, if excessive, were reduced to proper and legitimate amounts. I am disposed to agree with that view of the auditor's duty in fixing the fair value. But, even so, as I suggested during the arguments, the refusal to register the plaintiff might still virtually compel him to sell at an undervalue, because the directors might decline to exercise any right of pre-emption, and I think it is only when they exercise that right that they are bound to pay the price fixed by the auditor. If they waived that right and left the plaintiff free to sell his shares as best he could, I think the directors, like any outsider, would be free to buy at any price they could get the plaintiff to accept. Hence, if the directors declined to pre-empt as of right, refusal of registration would be calculated to put pressure upon the plaintiff to get rid of these shares, whether to the directors or to outside purchasers, at an unfair under-value, always assuming that the payment of the emoluments complained of would be illegitimate and would, therefore, illegitimately reduce the market value of the shares.

Were, then, the impugned emoluments justified as a reasonable commercial proposition? . . . [443]I feel no manner of doubt that the payment of these bloated emoluments would convert this flourishing company from a dividend-paying concern into a director-remunerating [444] enterprise, either paying no dividends at all or at best paying only such reduced dividends as would amount to a grave injustice to the plaintiff, who, after all, was the nephew of the men who made the business and had been left 500 shares in it. The payments of these sums would benefit Mr and Mrs Powderley to a substantial extent at the expense of the plaintiff, and for the reasons I have mentioned would be facilitated by the refusal to put the plaintiff on the register of members. I hold that it would be a natural, and I imagine an inevitable, consequence of that refusal that the payment of these indefensible emoluments would be facilitated, and that Mr and Mrs Powderley would be more easily enabled to reap unjustifiable benefits to a substantial extent at the expense of Mr Olhausen. Now, when parties take a decision calculated to bring them personal gain as its natural, if not inevitable, result, it is in accord with a well known legal principle to infer that they intended that decision to produce or facilitate that result, and that the facilitating of that result was at least a motive for taking the decision. This inference seems the more justifiable when one is not given, and cannot regard as apparent, any other reason that could justify such a decision on the part of the directors, who were bound to have regard only to the interests of the company as a whole. I am, therefore, forced to the conclusion that a desire to facilitate the payment of these emoluments was at least a motive actuating the decision of the defendants to refuse to register the plaintiff in respect of the 500 shares.

I consider such an exercise of their discretion so actuated would not be a *bona fide* discharge of their fiduciary duty, and that, if they acted under Art. 6, at least one illegitimate motive must be attributed to them. Once an illegitimate motive for such a decision is brought home to directors, I think the normal legal presumption that they acted legitimately must go by the board, and that I am set free to consider whether they should be given credit for having had other and better reasons, and, further, that I am free to comment – as Mr Justice Chitty did in *Bell's Case* – upon their omission to state what any of their reasons were. I feel no longer bound to ignore their silence, or to refuse to draw any inference from it. It was not ignored in *Bell's Case* and I cannot ignore it in this case. So far as I am aware, the judgment in *Bell's Case* has never been dissented from in any particular. It has stood the [445] test of a good many years. While no reasons have been volunteered by the defendants, who stood firmly on their privilege of reticence, certain innuendos loomed up in the evidence, based on unconfirmed and not very precise rumours and also on a query made by the plaintiff regarding one of the Hafner formulae at a time when he was being paid at the rate of £1,000 a year as a kind of general supervisor of the business. It seems he also ventured to offer some critical opinion about the methods of the firm's pig buyer. Without further elucidation I could only regard these complaints about the plaintiff as trumpery reasons for refusing to register him as a shareholder, if, indeed, they were meant to do more than hint that something graver lurked in the background. Without special information I can think of only one plausible reason for this refusal, namely, that he was an important member of a competing firm. But this reason was not even suggested by the defendants' counsel, or by their solicitor, Mr Beatty, who gave evidence, as a like reason was insinuated by the directors' solicitor in *Bell's Case*. In that case, Mr Justice Chitty remarked that if the directors themselves had sworn it was the true reason, he might have accepted it, but that as they did not do so, he inferred that was not the true reason. I adopt the same attitude here. Perhaps it would have seemed daring to suggest such a reason after Mrs Powderley had gone out of her way to bring the plaintiff into the firm and to give him a supervising job at £1,000 a year.

On account of the considerations I have detailed, I consider that I am entitled, as a matter of law, and coerced, as a matter of fact, to conclude that if, and so far as, the defendants' refusal to register the plaintiff was based upon the discretion given them by Art. 6, it cannot be justified at all. But, as I have said, the defendants have taken care to fit their bow with two strings, and although one of them is sundered, there remains another tougher texture. Art. 7 has still to be reckoned with.

The judgment was appealed to the Supreme Court.

SULLIVAN C.J.: ... [471] In seeking to establish that the action of the directors was not *bona fide* in exercise of the fiduciary power conferred upon them by Art. 6, the plaintiff was faced with the difficulty that under that Article the directors need not assign any reason for their refusal to register the transfer, and that the mere omission of the directors to state their reasons would not entitle the Court to infer that their reasons were not proper and legitimate.

And accordingly the plaintiff had to adduce evidence of relevant circumstances from which the Court could legitimately infer that the directors had acted improperly. From the evidence given at the hearing Black J. was satisfied that such an inference should be drawn, and he accordingly held as a fact that the refusal to register the transfer was not the result of a *bona fide* exercise by the directors of their discretion under Art. 6. The evidence was read to this Court and was discussed at length by counsel on both sides, and after full consideration we have come to the conclusion that the decision of the learned Judge on that matter was right. Any difficulty that we have had in arriving at that conclusion was mainly attributable to the fact that, in respect of some incidental but material matters, inconsistent and contradictory evidence was given by the same witness. In such circumstances it was for the learned Judge to decide which evidence he accepted, and, in the absence of any statement to the contrary by him, we think that we are entitled to assume, and should assume, that he accepted the evidence that would tend to support the conclusion at which he arrived on the main question, and we accordingly do so. . . . [474]

There can be little doubt that, if the transfer to the plaintiff had been registered, he would at the next meeting of shareholders have challenged the action of the directors in fixing such salaries, and there can be as little doubt that this was in the minds of the directors, when they decided to refuse the plaintiff's application. It may be, as Mr FitzGibbon contended, that the plaintiff, while not a member of the company, would be entitled to apply to the Court for a declaration that the resolutions authorising these salaries were void, and for an injunction to restrain the directors from paying them but even if that be so, the directors would realise that the plaintiff would be more likely to make such an application if he was a member.

We are satisfied that the learned Judge was entitled to come to the conclusion, as an inference of fact, that a desire that the payment of these salaries should not be questioned by the plaintiff was a motive actuating the directors' refusal to register the transfer to the plaintiff, and, in the absence of any evidence that would indicate a different motive – and there was no such evidence beyond a general statement by each director that it was in the interest of the company that registration of the transfer should be refused – we think that conclusion is unassailable. That a refusal actuated by such a motive could not be supported as a decision arrived at by the directors *bona fide* in exercise of their power conferred upon them by Art. 6 is not denied.

It was further contended on behalf of the plaintiff that in refusing to register the transfer the directors had in view a further object, namely, to compel the plaintiff to sell his shares to the directors, or to some of them at an undervalue. In support of that contention it was said that the directors contemplated that when, by reason of the salaries payable to them, the plaintiff had been deprived of any reasonable prospect of receiving a dividend on his shares, he would be willing to sell them at almost any price, and that the directors, who would under Art. 7 have the first option of purchasing them, would then purchase them at an undervalue.

In answer to that argument counsel for the defendants pointed out that Art. 7 provides that on a sale to the directors under that Article the fair market price of the shares must, if the plaintiff so requires, be fixed by the auditors of the company, and they contended that in fixing the price the [475] auditors would have regard to such remuneration only as it would be reasonable to pay, and not to the remuneration that was in fact paid, to the directors.

The expert evidence on that matter was given by three chartered accountants: Mr Brock, who was examined on behalf of the plaintiff, and Mr Purtill and Mr Shortall, who were witnesses for the defendants. The evidence of Mr Purtill and of Mr Shortall would support the contention of the defendants' counsel, as would the evidence of Mr Brock on his examination-in-chief, with which his evidence on re-examination does not seem to be quite consistent.

We think that the weight of evidence on this point is in favour of the view expressed by Mr Purtill and Mr Shortall, and Black J., who had the advantage of seeing and hearing these witnesses, says that he was disposed to agree with that view.

We are, therefore, not satisfied that by refusing to register the transfer the directors could compel the plaintiff to sell his shares to them at an undervalue if they purchased the shares by virtue of their right of pre-emption under Art. 7, and there is nothing in the evidence that would suggest – and it would not, we think, be reasonable to suppose – that they ever contemplated the possibility of purchasing the shares otherwise than in exercise of that right.

We are, therefore, of opinion that, while it would be quite a reasonable inference from the evidence that the object that the directors had in view in refusing to register the transfer was to compel the plaintiff to sell his shares to them, it would not be reasonable to infer that their object was to compel him to sell the shares to them at an undervalue.

But as we are satisfied that the directors were actuated by one improper motive, the fact that we are not satisfied that they had a second improper motive is not material, as it would not affect the plaintiff's right to a declaration that the refusal of the directors was not *bona fide* in exercise of their discretion under Art. 6.

The relief, however, which the plaintiff seeks is a declaration that he is entitled to be registered as the holder of the 500 shares, and an order directing the company to register the transfer of these shares to him.

Black J. refused to make such a declaration or order on the ground that Art. 7 of the Articles of Association, when read in conjunction with s. 29 of the Companies (Consolidation) Act, 1908, and with Art. 22 of Table A, applied to the transfer of these shares by the executors of the testator's will to the plaintiff, and that as, admittedly, these shares had not in the first instance been offered to the directors [476] as prescribed by Art. 7, the executors were not entitled to transfer the shares to the plaintiff, and the directors were therefore entitled to refuse to register the transfer.

Counsel for the plaintiff contend that in so holding the learned Judge misdirected himself in law, and, in the alternative, that the directors, by their action in entertaining under Art. 6 the plaintiff's application to register the transfer, waived the right to refuse registration on the ground that the provision of Art. 7 had not been complied with. Both questions have been fully and ably argued before us.

The conclusion at which we have arrived on the latter question renders it unnecessary to finally determine the former. But in deference to the learned Judge and to the arguments that were addressed to this Court, we think it right to say, that, as at present advised, we are of opinion that, for reasons which he states, he was right in holding that the provisions of Art. 7 applied to the transfer of the shares by the executors to the plaintiff.

In considering the question of waiver we must in any event assume the existence of the right, the waiver of which is in question, and accordingly we assume that these shares should in the first instance have been offered by the executors to the directors.

The law on the subject of waiver is reasonably clear and it is not in controversy in this case. It is sufficient to say that a person, who to his knowledge, is entitled to a right may waive it by conduct which is inconsistent with the continued existence of that right, and the fact that another person acts upon such waiver is sufficient consideration to make it effectual.

In the present case the directors could, in our opinion, waive their right to require that the shares should be first offered to them. They would, admittedly, do so if they registered the transfer to the plaintiff, and we think that they also do so if, instead of calling upon the plaintiff to offer the shares to them, they proceed to deal with and dispose of the application for registration under Art. 6 by refusing to register the transfer.

We are of opinion that the directors should consider and decide whether they will exercise their option to purchase the shares under Art. 7 before they proceed to consider the exercise of their discretionary power under Art. 6.

The Articles contemplate that when a member proposes to transfer his shares he will first offer them to the directors. On that being done two alternative courses are open to the directors: 1, they may decide to purchase the shares, and, if they do so, they are then bound to purchase them at [477] a price to be fixed in default of agreement by the auditors of the company, or 2, they may decline to purchase the shares. In either event the directors' rights under Art. 7 are at an end, but in the latter event their rights under Art. 6 would be exercisable when a transfer of the shares is submitted to them for registration.

Accordingly it seems to us that the fact that the directors have considered and disposed of an application to register a transfer under Art. 6, whether such application is granted or refused, indicates clearly that the directors have waived their rights under Art. 7, as those rights should have been exercised before the application was finally disposed of.

In the present case the directors, with the knowledge of their rights under Art. 7, considered and refused the plaintiff's application under Art. 6. They have by so doing waived their rights under Art. 7, and the plaintiff has acted upon that waiver by bringing this suit in which he challenges the validity of their action under Art. 6.

We are therefore of opinion that they are not entitled to rely on the fact that the shares were not offered to them in compliance with Art. 7 as a ground for their refusal to register the transfer of those shares to the plaintiff, and accordingly that the plaintiff is entitled to a declaration that he is entitled to be registered as the holder of the shares, and to an order directing the company to register the transfer to him.

Walsh v. Cassidy & Co. Ltd.
[1951] Ir. Jur. Rep. 47

(From headnote) The defendant was a private limited company whose articles of association dealing with the transfer of shares contained inter alia the following provisions:

'31 (a) No share shall. . . be transferred to a person who is not a member so long as any member or any person selected by the directors as one whom it is desirable in the interests of the company to admit to membership is willing to purchase the same at the fair value.

(b) In order to ascertain whether any member or person selected as aforesaid is willing to purchase any share, the person proposing to transfer the share (hereinafter called 'the proposing transferor') shall give notice in writing (hereinafter called the 'transfer notice') to the company at its registered office that he desires to transfer the same. Such transfer notice shall specify the sum he fixes as the fair value of the share and shall constitute the company his agent for the sale of the share. . . .

(j) The directors may, in all or any circumstances, and at all or any time or times refuse to register any transfer of any share or shares without assigning any reason therefor and whether the share or shares which it is proposed to transfer be fully paid up or not. . . .'

'32 Whenever any member of the company who is employed by the company in any capacity ceases to be so employed by the company the directors may at any time thereafter resolve that such member do retire and thereafter he shall be deemed to have served the company with a transfer notice pursuant to Art. 31 hereof and to have specified thereon the amount paid up on his shares as the fair value and subsequent proceedings may be taken on that footing and in accordance with the clauses of Art. 31 hereof. Notice of the passing of any such resolution shall be given to the member affected thereby.'

The plaintiff in the first action, while a director and member of the company, was dismissed from the office of director and thereupon served on the company a notice under Art. 31 (b) for the purpose of enabling him to transfer his shares at a fair value fixed by him. The remaining directors subsequently passed a resolution pursuant to Art. 32 deeming the plaintiff to have served on the company a notice under Art. 31 specifying the amount paid up on his shares as their fair value. The plaintiff in the second action, while a director and member of the company, served the company a similar notice under Art. 31 (b) and on the following day gave three months notice of his intention to leave the employment of the company. The remaining directors thereupon determined this plaintiff's employment, paying him three months salary in lieu of notice, and passed a resolution pursuant to Art. 32 similar in effect to that passed in relation to the first plaintiff. In each case the value which would attach to the shares by virtue of the resolutions was less than the value which would attach by virtue of the notice served by the member.

In separate actions brought by the plaintiffs claiming, inter alia, declarations that the notices served by them under Art. 31 (b) were valid and effective and that the resolutions passed pursuant to Art. 32 were ultra vires.

KINGSMILL MOORE J.: [51] The question in this case is one of construction of the articles of the defendant company, more particularly of articles 31 and 32, more particularly still of article 32. Fraud on the part of the directors is not pleaded and therefore cannot be suggested; and it was further conceded at a late stage that no issue as to lack of *bona fides* was before the Court. The facts common to the case of all parties are only of importance as raising in a net form the problem of construction. Certain further facts, alleged in affidavits filed on behalf of the defendants and not expressly contradicted by the plaintiffs would be vital if any question of *bona fides* were involved; but in the absence of this issue I am not at liberty to take them into account nor to make any assumption as to their truth or falsity. If true they would, certainly in the case of Mr Walsh, dispose of any suggestion that the defendant directors had acted in any way harshly. If untrue, but believed by the defendant directors to be true, they would justify a claim by them that they were acting in what they believed to be the best interests of the company. If false and known by the defendant directors to be false, but nevertheless put forward by the defendant directors as the reasons for their action, a case of fraud might be made out; but the plaintiffs have carefully refrained from putting forward any such case.

Article 31, with certain minor and chiefly verbal variations, and one important addition, follows the standard form for private companies to be found in successive editions of vol. 1 of *Palmer's Company Forms*. The important addition is to be found in the first sentence of paragraph (j) which give the directors an unqualified and uncontrolled power to refuse to register any transfer. It is not suggested that there is anything illegal in this power and counsel for the defendants assert that a power of this nature is, if not usual, yet certainly not exceptional in private companies formed to take over a family business and to preserve the family interest. It certainly indicated clearly the desire of the draftsmen and the adopters of the articles that the directors should have an ultimate and unfettered control over transfers. The second sentence of this paragraph is the usual *Palmer* form and it is suggested by Mr Lavery that there is such an inconsistency between the two sentences as to show that the articles were not framed as a logically connected whole but were the result of some casual work with scissors and paste. I am invited in the [52] light of this conclusion to hold that the whole of articles 31 and 32 are inconsistent with each other and so to refrain from approaching the construction of these articles with a desire so to interpret them as to give to them both the maximum effective validity.

It is quite true that the second sentence of article 31 (j) is unnecessary if the first sentence is to be given its full meaning. Mr Wilson suggests that the second sentence, though not necessary, is put in as a reminder of what would be the practice in normal circumstances in the same way as articles often repeat unnecessarily what are statutory provisions in the Companies Acts. This may be so, though it seems more likely that the draftsmen after adopting the standard form considered that the nature of the company demanded something more universal and added the first paragraph. Be this as it may I think the apparent surplusage is not by itself sufficient ground to make me approach the construction of articles 31 and 32 with a disposition to find an inconsistency between them or to assume that article 32 is not to be given its face value.

Article 32 also follows in its essentials an established *Palmer* form. The contention for the plaintiffs was that a service of the requisite notice under article 31 altered irrevocably the previous position and set in motion a machinery which must grind out to the end. Once such a notice was served, it was said, article 32 was displaced and the directors, even if they were entitled ultimately to refuse to register a transfer under article 31, yet could not call to their aid the provisions of article 32. On this view the serving of a notice under article 31 ensured that the shareholder must at least receive the fair price of his shares if his shares were disposed of at all. For the defendants it was argued that article 32 meant what it said, no more and no less. If the shareholder who served the notice under article 31 happened also to be a servant of the company and subsequently ceased to be so employed the directors might at any time thereafter resolve that he do retire (a phrase which it was agreed meant 'cease to be a member') and thereupon he was to be deemed to have served a transfer notice specifying the amount actually paid up on his shares. The result would be that he would only recover for his shares at most the paid-up value even though this might be but a fraction of the market value.

There would seem to be no half way house between these two interpretations of the articles; at least none was suggested. Either interpretation might in certain circumstances result in apparent hardship or absurdity. If the defendants are right a person who had bought the shares at their full market value and who subsequently took some minor employment under the company (e.g. as a visiting dentist under a welfare scheme) could never vacate such employment without the risk of having his shares forcibly transferred from him at their paid-up value. If the plaintiffs are right a trusted employee who had been allotted shares, perhaps free, perhaps at an undervalue, can betray his trust, damage the company, serve a notice ensuring that he gets the full value of his shares, retire from his position and use his realised money to set up a rival business. If an employee is dismissed his rights depend on whether he can serve a notice on the company under article 31 before the directors take action under article 32.

Mr Lavery for the plaintiffs was faced with this obvious argument that article 32 was clear and unambiguous and that in the absence of ambiguity effect must be given to the plain meaning of its words, even if its operation might sometimes work hardship; and with the second argument that the articles must be construed as a whole so as to give the fullest practical effect to both articles 31 and 32, whereas his contention, if successful, might have the effect of nullifying for all practical purposes the provisions of article 32. To displace these he called attention, by way of general observation, to the fact that the shareholders between them were the real owners of all the assets [53] of the company, and urged that a court should avoid, if in any way possible, a construction which would enable the directors to alienate compulsorily the property of a shareholder 'at a gross undervalue'. This argument perhaps goes too far, for in a case where no notice has been served under article 31 there is no doubt that article 32 enables directors to alienate, and indeed to acquire for themselves, shares of a member at less than their real value.

But the position of a shareholder cannot be so simply stated. He is not a mere owner in common, subject to certain restrictions in the articles. His position was carefully laid down by Kenny J. in the case of *Attorney-General* v. *Jameson* [1904] 2 I.R. 644.

The property of the shareholder is really a bundle of contractual rights and obligations and among those obligations is the disadvantage of having to submit to the operation of article 32 if the shareholder finds himself in the position of an employee whose employment has terminated. It has long been decided that there is nothing illegal in provisions whereby compulsory retirement is enforced *Sidebottom* v. *Kershaw Leese Co.* [1920] 1 Ch. 154; *Phillips* v. *Manufactures' Securities Ltd.* (1917) 116 L.T. 290 is an authority that an article is valid even if it provides for compulsory expropriation at a gross undervalue, and that it may be operated to secure this result with a deliberate intention of punishing the member whose retirement has been enforced. Any person acquiring a share in Cassidy and Company, Limited, must be deemed to have known that in certain circumstances he might become liable to be expropriated on the terms of article 32. If on a fair reading of those terms they involve harshness he cannot subsequently ask the Court to endeavour to give them a more lenient interpretation or to find in their harshness a reason why they should not be invoked.

[54] Mr Lavery, I think, fully appreciated such considerations, and his main argument was that article 32 contained in its own words a clear indication that it was not meant to apply to any case where a member had already taken steps which, unless deliberately nullified by the directors, would result in his ceasing to be a member. The main — indeed the only object — of article 32 was, he argued, to enforce the retirement of a member. If that retirement was already in train this article was displaced and could not be operated. The provisions which fixed the price to be paid to a retiring member were only ancillary and if a member was in the way of retiring it was not contemplated that a resolution should be passed under article 32 merely for the purpose of bringing those auxiliary provisions into operation. He cited the case of *Robert Batcheller & Sons Ltd.* v. *Batcheller* [1945] 1 Ch. 169, which at first seemed very greatly in his favour. In that case Romer J. refused to apply an article on the ground that it only operated where the known circumstanes of a particular case are such as sensibly and legitimately admit of its application. His view was that the circumstances in *Batcheller's Case* did not warrant such a conclusion and he said 'To deem, however, that a thing happened when not only is it known that it did not happen, but it is positively known that precisely the opposite of it happened, is a conception which to my mind, if applied to a subject matter such as that of article 93, amounts to a complete absurdity'.

Mr Lavery points out that if article 32 is to be applied in the present case it will be necessary to deem that a notice had been served naming the amount paid up on the shares (namely £1) as their fair value, when not only has such notice not been served but a completely different notice naming £5 as their value has actually been served. *Batcheller's Case* may be summarised as one in which – to borrow the terse phraseology of Mr Wilson – the Judge came to the conclusion that the article was only intended to come into operation on a hypothesis which on the particular facts had not come into existence. If I were of opinion that there was a lack of clarity in the wording of article 32 and that common sense led me irresistibly to the conclusion that it was never intended to apply where a notice had already been served under article 31, *Batcheller's Case* would be an authority. I have not been able to reach this conclusion, despite the resemblences between this case and *Batcheller's Case* which Mr Lavery pointed out. I would agree that the main object of article 32 as drafted and adopted was to provide a power of compulsory retirement. I do not agree that this was its sole object.

The practice of encouraging employees to take an interest in the business which employs them by allotting to them shares either free or at a value less than the market value is one which has increased very greatly in the last fifty years. It is natural that directors should desire to keep some control over such shares and not allow them to be retained as of right when employees leave the service. It is also natural that directors should desire to have some lever whereby employees may be prevented from misconducting themselves while in employment and then, when they are dismissed or anticipate dismissal by retirement, enjoying the full fruits of shares allotted to them. I have said that I am not in any way basing my judgment on the truth of the allegations in Mr Cassidy's affidavit, but I am of opinion that the possibility of such conduct as is alleged is a matter normally present to the minds of commercial men and that it is natural to suppose that they desire to arm themselves against its occurrence by providing means of penalising it. It will be noted that article 32 is optional. In any case the directors may or may not avail themselves of the power it gives to them. The existence of such a power, arbitrary if you like, punitive if you like, may be a powerful weapon to secure diligence and loyalty among the employees and so be in the best interests of the company and the shareholders as a whole.

[55] I would draw the conclusion that article 32 was deliberately framed, inserted and adopted to give the directors such a power. If it is exercised fraudulently it may be restrained. If exercised in the case of shares acquired at full value by a person who was not then an employee (as in the instance I suggested) it might perhaps be possible to argue, that this was a hypothesis not contemplated by the article and so to afford relief along the lines of *Batcheller's Case.* But in the present case I find myself forced to decide against the contention of the plaintiffs, first because I find that the article read in its ordinary and grammatical sense is free from ambiguity, and secondly because, even if I should admit ambiguity, I have reached the conclusion that it was intended to confer power to take such action as was taken in the present case even if a prior notice had been served under article 31.

PREFERENCE SHARES

In re Lafayette Ltd.
[1950] I.R. 100

(From headnote) An incorporated company provided, by its articles of association, that the capital of the company should be divided into specified
numbers of preference and ordinary shares. Article 10 provided: '10. The
holders of the Preference Shares shall be entitled to receive out of the
profits of the Company a cumulative preferential dividend for each year
of £6 per cent. per annum on the amount for the time being paid on the
Preference Shares held by them respectively, such dividend shall be
cumulative, and arrears thereof shall be the first charge on the subsequent
profits of the Company. The Preference Shares shall also have a preferential right in distribution of assets of the Company.' Article 142 provided:
'142. The Directors may, notwithstanding the provisions of Article 132,
but shall not be obliged before recommending or declaring any dividend
or bonus, or interest on capital, in respect of any class of shares, out of,
or in respect of the earnings or profits of the Company for any yearly or
other period, cause to be reserved, or retained and set aside out of such
profits, such sums as they may think proper to form a reserve fund, and
such reserve fund is to be regarded as allotted to meet contingencies, or
for equalising dividends, or for repairing, improving and maintaining any
of the property of the Company, or in payment or satisfaction of any moneys
for the time being owing by the Company on mortgage or otherwise, and
for such other purposes as the Directors, in their absolute discretion, may
think conducive to the interests of the Company.' Articles 11, 132, and
133 provided, respectively, *(a)* that surplus profits in each year, after payment of the dividend (and arrears) on the preference shares, should be
applied to payment of dividend on the ordinary shares; *(b)* that, subject to
the provisions of the articles, the net profits should be applied to payment
of a dividend on the capital paid up, or credited as paid up, on the shares;
(c) that an appropriate dividend might be declared in general meeting of
the Company but such dividend should not be larger than that recommended by the directors.

A reorganisation of the Company being contemplated, questions arose
as to 1, whether the preference shareholders were entitled on a winding
up of the Company, to have any credit balance shown on the profit and
loss account, together with all moneys placed in reserve funds, which
represented undistributed profits, applied to pay off arrears of dividend;
2, whether, if such funds and moneys were insufficient to discharge all
arrears, capital assets should be applied to discharge the outstanding
arrears; 3, whether capital subscribed by preference shareholders was pay-

able out of assets in priority to capital subscribed by the ordinary shareholders; 4, whether any surplus assets after such repayment of capital to both
classes of shareholders, should be divided equally between both classes.

KINGSMILL MOORE J.: . . . [109] It has been admitted that the articles are
not perfectly drafted or entirely consistent. The inconsistency may not be
as great as at first appears. There was power in the articles to create new
classes of shares (though such shares were not to affect 'the priority or
privileges' of the existing preference shareholders without their consent),
and the use of the words in arts. 132, 133 and 142, which are relied on
by Mr FitzGibbon as clearly referring to more than one class of shares,
and so, presumably, including the preference shares in their provisions,
may be explained as being designed to apply to any future class of shares
which might be created after the formation of the Company. Article 11,
if anything, seems to tell against Mr FitzGibbon's contention. It deals with
'surplus profts', a very different thing from the 'net profits' referred to in
art. 132. Surplus profits must mean 'surplus of net profits' after something
has already been taken from them. What that something is, would be
abundantly plain from the foregoing art. 10, even if it was not defined as
being 'the surplus profit after payment of the said dividend on the preference shares and all arrears thereof'. Article 11 appears to me to deal only
with such profits as would be applicable to pay dividends on the ordinary
shares after satisfying all claims of preference shareholders to current
dividend and arrears, and only such profits are to be subject to the powers
given to the directors (including the power to create a reserve). It is significant that in art. 11 the permissory phrase, 'shall be applicable', is used, in
contrast with the mandatory words, 'shall be entitled to receive', in art. 10.

The position of the words, 'subject to the powers hereafter given to the
directors', is not very happy. This phrase would come in more properly
either at the beginning of the clause or after the word, 'thereof', but it
does not appear to me that this malposition can alter the meaning I have
given to the article as a whole.

I have suggested a way in which the articles may be interpreted so as
to avoid manifest inconsistency, but, if there is inconsistency between the
articles, I hold that the general phraseology of arts. 132, 133, and 142
must yield to [110] the clear and specific wording of art. 10, and that the
rights given to preference shareholders by that article cannot be diminished
by the subsequent articles unless such articles make evident an intention
to do so. I do not find any such intention. If the articles are in fact entirely
inconsistent, not only must the general yield to the particular, but there is
authority to show that the earlier article must prevail over the latter; *Forbes
v. Git* [1922] 1 A.C. 256.

The interpretation which I have given does not, as has been suggested,
stultify the power conferred on the directors to create a reserve fund. If

in any year the preference dividends and any outstanding arrears have been paid, then the directors may set aside a sum to reserve, and this sum is not available to satisfy future preference dividends, for art. 10 expressly limits the rights of the preference shareholders to be paid their arrears out of 'subsequent profits of the Company'.

Mr FitzGibbon, if forced reluctantly to concede that my interpretations of the present articles, standing by themselves, was correct, or, at least, not plainly erroneous, would – and does – maintain that, nevertheless, the general principles of company law and the accepted manner of interpreting articles prevents me from giving effect to the claim of the preference shareholders to be paid arrears out of the reserve fund and any undistributed net business profits, and he has cited many authorities for his view. I shall examine them separately, with the general prefatory remark that they seem to me all to be decisions on the particular wording of particular, though, no doubt, commonly used, articles, and that general principles are referred to in such cases merely as an aid to the interpretation of the particular articles. The articles in Lafayette Ltd. are different in form, and contain at least one provision which I have found nowhere else, viz., the provision that arrears are to be a 'first charge' on subsequent profits. This is a strong expression. A charge is a hypothec, and the thing charged cannot be released for purposes other than those of satisfying the charge, until that charge has been satisfied. It seems to me a mere begging of the question to say that the use of the words, 'first charge,' is equivalent to the use of the word, 'cumulative'. That is exactly what it is not. A charge earmarks the property which is subject to it for one particular purpose in priority to all others, and, if that purpose is one legally possible of being attained, then attained it must be. None of the cases cited by Mr FitzGibbon go so far as to lay down that there is anything illegal in providing that any particular sum is to be applied [111] in a winding up for the discharge of arrears of dividends. They do lay down that certain forms of articles are not sufficient to attain this end. Again, none of the cases cited lay down that articles may not give to preference shareholders an absolute right to be paid their fixed dividend and arrears out of profits without any previous declaration of dividend by the directors or the company. They do lay down that certain forms of articles require a dividend to be declared before it is presently payable.

I turn to the authorities. The first is *Bishop* v. *Smyrna and Cassaba Railway Co.* [1895] 2 Ch. 265, in which Kekewich J. decided that the provisions in the memorandum overrode inconsistent provisions in the articles, and that a sum of money standing to reserve account at the date of the commencement of liquidation was properly applicable to payment of arrears of dividend due at that date to the preference shareholders. Somewhat astonishingly the terms of the memorandum are nowhere given in the report but may be found in the judgment of Byrne J. in *In re Odessa Water-*

works Co. (printed in a note to *In re Crichton's Oil Company* [1901] 2 Ch. 184). From this it appears that the memorandum in the *Smyrna Railway Case* provided that the preference shares should have a right 'to a dividend of 7 per cent. per annum upon the amount paid up by preference and priority over the ordinary shares' and 'It is, however, understood and agreed, that if in any year or years the dividend on the ordinary shares shall fall below 7 per cent., and that in subsequent years means shall exist of dividing larger profits than the above-mentioned first dividend of 7 per cent. per annum, the surplus profits shall be first of all applied to make up the deficiency borne by the ordinary shares in previous years. . . .' It will be seen that the rights of the preference shares were declared in terms less extensive than they are in the present case, but Kekewich J. found them sufficient to ensure payment of arrears on a winding up. He held that in a winding up, when the powers of the directors to recommend, and the company to declare, a dividend were at an end, the rights of the preference shareholders still remained and were enforceable. Their rights were conferred as a right independent of the declaration of a dividend. The judgment was, indeed, rested on the fact that the rights of the preference shareholders were conferred by the memorandum, and so not assailable by contradictory provisions in the articles. I think, however, that if, on a fair interpretation of the articles themselves, a conclusion is reached that they were intended to confer similar rights on the preference shareholders, the [112] same result must follow as if those rights were declared in the memorandum. The *Odessa Waterworks Co. Case* [1901] 2 Ch. 190 is of no assistance because the rights of the preference shareholders were considered by Byrne J., on the construction of the articles, to be absolutely dependent on the declaration of a dividend. There was no article, such as art. 10 in the present case, purporting to give particular rights to the preference shareholders.

In re Crichton's Oil Co. is, on the wording of the articles, nearer to the present case. Article 6 provided that the holders of the preference shares should be entitled to a cumulative preference dividend at the rate of £6 per cent. per annum. Article 103 gave the directors power to set aside a reserve fund out of profits. Article 108 provided that the profits available for dividends should be applicable first to the payment of a fixed cumulative preference dividend on the preference shares in the original capital. The company was wound up and, on the taking of the accounts, it was found that there had been a profit on the last year of trading sufficient to pay the last year's preference dividend and some of the arrears of previous years. Wright J. held that this sum was not available for dividend but must be applied to repayment of capital in the winding up. He was of opinion that the dividend was only payable out of profits made available for dividend and that, as the directors had not recommended a dividend and no dividend had been declared by the company, the claim of the preference shareholders must fail. The terms of art. 6 were somewhat similar to those of art. 10 of Lafayette Ltd., but they lack the essential provisions that arrears shall be the first charge on subsequent profits, words which, in my view, make any recommendation by directors or declaration by the Company unnecessary.

I respectfully accept the interpretation of the *Crichton's Oil Company Case* which was given by Bennett J. in *Re W. Foster & Son, Ltd.* [1942] 1 All E.R. 314 and adopted by Wynn-Parry J. in *Re Catalinas Warehouses and Mole Co., Ltd.* [1947] 1 All E.R. 51 namely, that when once a company has passed a resolution for liquidation the provisions in the articles for declaration of dividends come to an end, and so, when a winding up has commenced, *prima facie* a dividend is no longer payable; but it seems to me that in Lafayette Ltd. the articles give the preference shareholders a right to their dividend, irrespective of any declaration, and, again without any declaration automatically charge arrears of preference dividend on any [113] future profits.

Bond v. *Barrow Hœmatite Steel Co.* [1902] 1 Ch. 353 turned on a small point of construction. The articles contained provisions for declaration of a dividend by the directors, with the consent of the company; for payment of dividends out of business profits and creation of a reserve fund; and for power to increase capital by creation of new shares, which were, however, to be subject to the provisions of the original articles, save that they might be given priority over the old shares by the resolutions creating them. In pursuance of this power new preference 8 per cent. shares were created in the year 1872, and new 6 per cent. preference shares in the year, 1876. The resolutions creating the 6 per cent. shares contained the following words, 'in case in any year the net profits of the company shall not be sufficient for the payment in full of the dividends on such new preference shares, the net profits of any subsequent year shall. . . be applied in payment to the holders of the said new preference shares of the amount by which the dividends of any previous year or years may have fallen short of the fixed rate of £6 per cent.' It was argued that these words gave to the 6 per cent. preference shareholders an absolute right to their fixed dividends out of any year's profits before any sum was carried to reserve, applied to replace lost capital, or carried forward. Farwell J., with apparently some little doubt, rejected this contention, but only on the ground that, as the original articles had subjected any new shares to the provisions of such original articles, any preference dividend must be declared, and was subject to the powers given to the directors to create a reserve. It may be gathered from his Judgment that, but for the express provision in the original articles, he would have upheld the contention of the preference shareholders.

The case which seems to me most in point, and, indeed, decisive, is a recent decision of our own Courts, viz., *In re The Imperial Hotel (Cork) Ltd.*

[1950] I.R. 115. In a voluntary liquidation of the Company the liquidator, after discharging the claims of creditors who were not members and his own costs and repaying the capital of the preference shareholders, found himself with about £6,500 in hand. The ordinary shareholders claimed that this sum should be applied in repaying their capital. The preference shareholders argued that the arrears of the cumulative dividend – some £4,477 – should first be paid, and the President unhesitatingly accepted their argument.

Article 13 of the articles in the *Imperial Hotel Case* was almost identical with the first sentence of art. 10 in the [114] present case, save that, instead of the words, 'such dividend shall be cumulative, and arrears thereof shall be the first charge on the subsequent profits of the Company,' there appeared the words, 'such dividend to be computed from the date of allotment and such holders to have the right to resort to the profits of subsequent years to make up the deficiency, if any, in preceding years.' Of the two phrases, the former, creating an actual first charge, seems to me the more emphatic in favour of the preference shareholders. The other articles in the *Imperial Hotel Case* in regard to declaration of dividends, creation of a reserve fund, payment out of net profits, and application of surplus after paying preference dividends, are similar in effect to those in Lafayette Ltd., though their order and wording are not identical.

The learned President held that the profits of each financial year must first be applied to the payment of the cumulative preference dividend, including any outstanding arrears; that the right of the preference shareholders to receive their dividend was independent of any declaration of dividend by the Company in general meeting; and that the right of the directors to create a reserve fund out of profits was irreconcilable with, and must yield to, the right of the preference shareholders to receive their dividends and arrears thereof. With those findings and the reasoning on which they are based I respectfully agree, and, applying the reasoning of the President, I hold that the preference shareholders are entitled to be paid their arrears of dividend out of profits shown in the profit and loss account for subsequent years; that this right is one independent of any recommendation by the directors or declaration of dividend by the Company; that this right takes precedence over the power of the directors to set aside sums for a reserve fund, and that, if such reserve fund has been set aside, it is applicable to pay the arrears; that this right to be repaid arrears is a charge upon subsequent profits and on the reserve fund; and that, on a winding up, the reserve fund and any undistributed profits shown in the profit and loss account are applicable, after payment of creditors of the Company, to the discharge of such arrears.

In re Cork Electric Supply Co. Ltd.
[1932] I.R. 315 (S.Ct.)

A company that ran trams and supplied the city with electricity had its undertaking nationalised under the Electricity Supply Act, 1927, and the company received substantial compensation. One question that then arose was whether, in a liquidation, any surplus remaining must be divided between the ordinary shareholders and the preference shareholders. The articles did not expressly indicate what was to become of the surplus.

KENNEDY C.J.: . . . [327] We cannot approach the question with the advantage of statutory guidance to the answer. Sect. 186 of the Companies (Consolidation) Act, 1908, leaves the matter as follows, as regards voluntary winding-up: '(i). The property of the Company shall be applied in satisfaction of its liabilities *pari passu*, and, subject thereto, shall, unless the Articles otherwise provide, be distributed among the members according to their rights and interests in the Company.' Sect. 170 provides that, in the case of a winding-up by the Court: 'The Court shall adjust the rights of the contributories among themselves, and distribute any surplus among the persons entitled thereto.' Hence a problem appears in every case in so far as specific provision is not made in the Articles of Association. A rule was, however, established by the decision of the House of Lords in England in the case of *In re The Bridgewater Navigation Co., Ltd., Birch* v. *Cropper* (14 App. Cas. 328), that, on the voluntary winding-up, the assets remaining after discharging all debts and liabilities and repaying to the ordinary and preference shareholders the capital paid on their shares, ought to be divided among all the shareholders (both preference and ordinary), not in proportion to the amounts paid on the shares, but in proportion to the shares held. The decision is very important for the elementary principles it affirmed (of which there is a tendency to lose sight in argument). Preference shareholders are holders of shares in the capital of a company in the same way as ordinary shareholders are holders of shares in its capital. Both classes of shareholders are equally members of the Company. Their respective positions are differentiated only to the extent to which the rights and privileges attaching to their respective shares are qualified contractually by the Memorandum and Articles of Association of the Company.

I turn, therefore, to the Memorandum and Articles of Association of the plaintiff Company to ascertain whether the right of the preference shareholders to participate in surplus assets on a winding-up of the Company has been [328] abrogated, cut down, or qualified in any way. There is no such specific provision, and we have to look for a limitation by implication. No. 10 of the Articles of Association (already quoted) is the basis of the argument on behalf of the ordinary shareholders. That Article confers on the preference shareholders two special privileges, viz.:(1) the right to a fixed dividend at the rate of £5 per cent. per annum out of the profits of each half-year, 'but to no further dividend,' and (2) the right in a winding-up to priority in payment of capital over the ordinary shares. The effect of the two amendments of the Article (already quoted) was to make the preferential dividend cumulative and to delete the words 'but to no further dividend.' We have been asked to hold with Johnston J. that the Article (as amended) is an exhaustive statement of the rights of the preference shareholders which excludes any other right or privilege and deprives (by implication) these shareholders of their right to participate in a distribution of surplus assets on a winding-up. We were referred to a series of decisions of Judges of first instance in England on analogous questions, in which, though they were cases of constuction arising on a variety of forms of Articles, a certain conflict of opinion appeared among the Judges: *In re Espuela Land and Cattle Co.* [1909] 2 Ch. 187; *In re National Telephone Co.* [1914] 1 Ch. 755; *In re Fraser and Chalmers Ltd.* [1919] 2 Ch. 114; *Anglo French Music Co., Ltd.,* v. *Nicoll* [1921] 1 Ch. 386; *Collaroy Co., Ltd.* v. *Giffard* [1928] 1 Ch. 144. We have also been referred to *Will* v. *United Lankat Plantations Co., Ltd.* [1914] A.C. 11. Out of all these cases, after consideration, what we derive is only this, that the right to participate in a distribution of surplus assets on a winding-up will be taken from preference shareholders by a clause in the Articles of Association delimiting their rights exhaustively to the exclusion of any other rights, and that the question whether a particular clause does so delimit the rights attached to the preference shares exhaustively and exclusively is a question of the construction of the particular Articles of Association in each case, and that we cannot construe one set of Articles by the construction applied by some Court to another set of Articles of another Company (save, of course, as to any principle or rule of construction of general application authoritatively declared for the purpose of such construction).

[329] Upon the construction of the Articles of Association before us it is to be observed that, while as regards participation in profits, the words of exclusion 'but to no further dividend' were carefully inserted, no such limitation was added to the immediately following clause as to priority in payment of capital. Moreover, I can find no gound for cutting down the word 'shareholders' in Art. 114, or the words 'members of the Company for the time being' in Art. 115, to ordinary shareholders only, from which it follows that Art. 10 is not an exhaustive statement of the rights of the preference shareholders. In answer to another argument borrowed from a passage in the judgment of Astbury J. in *Collaroy Co., Ltd.* v. *Giffard,* I must say that there is not, so far as I know, any rule of law or construction requiring a Court of construction to find a logical consistency between the rights of preference shareholders while a company is a going concern and their rights on a winding-up. It is difficult to know what is meant precisely by 'logical consistency' in this connection, but, as I understand it, it is

quite foreign to the great diversity of bargain which may lawfully be made in these business contracts.

In my opinion, therefore, the question in paragraph 3 of the claim on the summons should be answered in the affirmative – 'rateably.' I am also of opinion that an affirmative answer – *'pro rata'* – should be given.

FITZGIBBON J.: [331] In construing a document such as that with which we have to deal, decided cases are of little assistance, except in so far as they lay down principles of general application, or place a judicial interpretation upon a clause identical with that which is under consideration. The slightest [332] variation in the language employed may alter the effect of the clause, as, for instance, in the present case, reliance was placed upon the substitution of 'the' for 'a' in the phrases 'the right to be paid out of the profits,' and 'the right in a winding-up,' as indicative of an intention to limit the right of the preference shareholders to that which was expressed, rather than to define the preferential advantages which they were to enjoy in addition to their ordinary rights as members of the Company.

The House of Lords in *Birch* v. *Cropper* [1889] 14 App. Cas. 525, laid down as a principle of general application, that where the right of preference shareholders in a winding-up is not negatived or restricted by the Memorandum or Articles of the Company the surplus remaining after the payment off of the preference shares and the capital paid up on the ordinary shares is distributable amongst the shareholders of both classes in proportion to the shares held by them respectively. Lord Herschell says : 'When the whole of the capital has been returned both classes of shareholders are on the same footing, equally members and holding equal shares in the Company, and it appears to me that they ought to be treated as equally entitled to its property. It may be that the principle which I recommend your Lordships to adopt will not secure absolutely equal or equitable treatment in all cases, but I think that it will in general attain that end more nearly than any other which has been proposed.' I do not find that either Lord Macnaghten or Lord FitzGerald dissented from or qualified in any way the principle which Lord Herschell recommended them to adopt, and it appears to have received universal acceptation thenceforth at the hands of text writers, and what is more important, company draughtsmen. Bearing that principle in mind, I have read the Memorandum and Articles of Association, the latter as originally adopted, and then as amended by the successive resolutions increasing the capital of the Company, with a view to ascertaining whether there was any provision in them which conveyed to my mind an intention on the part of the Company to negative or restrict the right of the holders of the preference shares, in the event of a winding-up, to share in any surplus which might remain after the whole of the capital had been returned to the shareholders. In my opinion the provision in Art. 10 that the preference shareholders were to be repaid the amount contributed by them in priority to the ordinary shareholders does not by implication negative or restrict their right to share in a surplus, if any. It is a definition [333] of the amount of preferential treatment which they are to receive, not a deprivation or restriction of any other right to which they are, *prima facie*, entitled.

Having arrived at this interpretation without reference to decisions upon other and different Articles, I read all the cases to which we were referred in argument, and several others, in order to see whether there was any rule of law, recognised canon of construction, or binding decision, which precluded me from giving effect to that which appeared to me to be the natural interpretation of the Articles, because I think that if a particular article, clause, or expression has received a judicial interpretation, and has been subsequently adopted as a precedent in the formation of other Companies, it is better, in a doubtful question of construction, to adhere to previous decisions rather than upon a nice balance of opinion to disaffirm a construction in reliance upon which large amounts of capital may have been invested. The old reluctance of Courts – to which Lord Westbury and Lord Cranworth referred in *Young* v. *Robertson*, (4 Macq. H.L. 314, 337) – to disturb decisions upon which titles of land depended, seems to me, when we are called upon to construe commercial documents, to be no less applicable to 'decisions which, not being manifestly erroneous and mischievous, have stood for some time unchallenged, and from their nature and the effect which they may reasonably be supposed to have produced upon the conduct of a large portion of the community. . . in matters affecting rights of property, may fairly be treated as having passed into the category of established and recognised law': *Pugh* v. *Golden Valley Railway Co.* (15 Ch.D. 330).

I have not discovered any decision, or even any dictum, which can be regarded as having placed a definite interpretation upon the Article with which we are concerned, and accordingly I feel quite free to adopt the construction which commends itself to me. I think that little assistance can be derived from an elaborate discussion of cases such as that to be found in the judgment of Astbury J. in *Collaroy Co.* v. *Gifford*, where the point, as he says, 'must necessarily depend upon the exact language and context of the contract in each case.' He has, however, stated in that case one 'proposition' as of general application, which I am not at present prepared to accept. 'There ought to be a logical consistency between the preference shareholders' rights while the Company is a going concern [334] and their rights in a winding-up.' I do not see any reason for this. In every case the promoters of a company will consider the terms which are best calculated to induce the public to subscribe the capital required, and the conditions which should be attached to shares allotted to a vendor as part of the purchase consideration. An examination of the precedents in the different editions of Palmer's works and of other text-writers will

show that there is an almost infinite variety of conditions attached to preference shares both as concerns dividends and capital, and that there is
no 'logical consistency' required or observed. It is not unworthy of observation that Mr Palmer, in discussing the question 'whether the preference
shares are to have any preference as regards return of capital in a winding-
up or in relation to a reduction of capital,' after referring to *Birch* v. *Cropper*
as deciding that in the absence of provisions negating or restricting their
rights they will be entitled to share in the surplus after paying off the
preference shares and the capital paid up on the ordinary shares, proceeds:
'But very commonly it is desired to negative the right of the preference
shareholders to participate in such a surplus, and accordingly words are
inserted to the effect that the holders shall *not* be entitled to participate
any further in the profits or assets,' and he gives a form containing such
negative words. In the present case the framers of the Articles appear to
have recognised the necessity for or advisability of such negative words,
as in the clause dealing with capital, which defines the preferential rights
of the preference shares there is an express limitation of the preferential
dividend 'to £5 per cent. per annum, *but to* no further dividend,' while no
such restriction or negation is attached to the condition for repayment of
the capital. The right of priority is conferred, but the right to participate
in any possible surplus is not negatived.

In my opinion question No. 3 upon the summons should be answered
in the affirmative.

Scottish Insurance Corp. Ltd. v. Wilsons & Clyde Coal Co. Ltd.
[1949] A.C. 462 (H.L.)

The company's undertaking, coal mines, were nationalised, and substantial
compensation was paid to the company. The company then proposed to
repay its preference shareholders under the powers given in the equivalent
of §72 et seq. of the 1963 Act. Preference shareholders claimed that they
should not be repaid because, firstly, they had a right to share in the
surplus on the winding up, and that repayment would deprive them of that
right. The articles of association did not indicate expressly who was to
participate in any surplus.

LORD SIMONDS: . . . [486] The first plea makes an assumption, viz., that
the articles give the preference stockholders the right in a winding up to
share in surplus assets, which I for the moment accept but will later
examine. Making that assumption, I yet see no validity in the plea. The
company has at a stroke been deprived of the enterprise and undertaking
which it has built up over many years: it is irrelevant for this purpose that
the stroke is delivered by an Act of Parliament which [487] at the same
time provides some compensation. Nor can it affect the rights of the parties
that the only reason why there is money available for repayment of capital

is that the company has no longer an undertaking to carry on. Year by year the 7 per cent. preference dividend has been paid; of the balance of the profits some part has been distributed to the ordinary stockholders, the rest has been conserved in the business. If I ask whether year by year the directors were content to recommend, the company in general meeting to vote, a dividend which has left a margin of resources, in order that the preference stockholders might in addition to repayment of their capital share also in surplus assets, I think that directors and company alike would give an emphatic negative. And they would, I think add that they have always had it in their power, and have it still, by making use of arts. 139 or 141, to see that what they had saved for themselves they do not share with others. I observe that the learned Lord President was of opinion that such a use of one or other of these articles would be an impropriety which would at least be open to challenge in a court of law, but learned counsel for the appellants candidly admitted that he could not support this view. Reading these articles as a whole with such familiarity with the topic as the years have brought, I would not hesitate to say, first, that the last thing a preference stockholder would expect to get (I do not speak here of the legal rights) would be a share of surplus assets, and that such a share would be a windfall beyond his reasonable expectations and, secondly, that he had at all times the knowledge, enforced in this case by the unusual reference in art. 139 to the payment off of the preference capital, that at least he ran the risk, if the company's circumstances admitted, of such a reduction as is now proposed being submitted for confirmation by the court. Whether a man lends money to a company at 7 per cent. or subscribes for its shares carrying a cumulative preferential dividend at that rate, I do not think that he can complain of unfairness if the company, being in a position lawfully to do so, proposes to pay him off. No doubt, if the company is content not to do so, he may get something that he can never have expected but so long as the company can lawfully repay him, whether it be months or years before a contemplated liquidation, I see no ground for the court refusing its confirmation. To combat the suggestion that, so far as any benefit to the preference stock-[488]holders is concerned, the position is substantially the same whether they are now repaid their capital or full use is made of arts. 139 and 141, it was urged that the incidence of income tax would be a sufficient deterrent of this alternative measure. I do not, however, consider that the court can properly have regard to such a consideration as this in determining what is fair between the parties. It might indeed be considered improper to do so if it drove the ordinary stockholders to a course less advantageous to themselves but no more advantageous to the preference stockholders.

It will be seen, my Lords, that, even making an assumption favourable to the appellants, I reject their first plea. But it is perhaps necessary, in case there should be a division of opinion which would make this a decisive issue, that I should shortly examine the assumption. It is clear from the authorities, and would be clear without them, that, subject to any relevant provision of the general law, the rights inter se of preference and ordinary shareholders must depend on the terms of the instrument which contains the bargain that they have made with the company and each other. This means, that there is a question of construction to be determined and undesirable though it may be that fine distinctions should be drawn in commercial documents such as articles of association of a company, your Lordships cannot decide that the articles here under review have a particular meaning, because to somewhat similar articles in such cases as *In re William Metcalfe & Sons Ltd.* [1933] Ch. 142, that meaning has been judicially attributed. Reading the relevant articles, as a whole, I come to the conclusion that arts. 159 and 160 are exhaustive of the rights of the preference stockholders in a winding up. The whole tenor of the articles, as I have already pointed out, is to leave the ordinary stockholders masters of the situation. If there are 'surplus assets' it is because the ordinary stockholders have contrived that it should be so, and, though this is not decisive, in determining what the parties meant by their bargain, it is of some weight that it should be in the power of one class so to act that there will or will not be surplus assets.

There is another somewhat general consideration which also, I think, deserves attention. If the contrary view of arts. 159 and 160 is the right one and the preference stockholders are entitled to a share in surplus assets, the question will still arise what those surplus assets are. For the profits [489] though undrawn, belong, subject to the payment of the preference dividend, to the ordinary stockholders and, in so far as surplus assets are attributable to undrawn profits, the preference stockholders have no right to them. This appears to follow from the decision of the Court of Appeal in *In re Bridgewater Navigation Company* [1891] 2 Ch. 317, in which judgment of the House of Lords in *Birch* v. *Cropper* (14 App. Cas. 525) is worked out. This again is not decisive of the construction of particular articles, but I am unwilling to suppose that the parties intended a bargain which would involve an investigation of an artificial and elaborate character into the nature and origin of surplus assets.

But, apart from those more general considerations, the words of the specifically relevant articles, 'rank before the other shares. . . on the property of the company to the extent of repayment of the amounts called up and paid thereon', appear to me apt to define exhaustively the rights of the preference stockholders in a winding up. Similar words, in *Will* v. *United Lankat Plantations Co. Ltd.* [1914] A.C. 11, 'rank both as regards capital and dividend, in priority to the other shares', were held to define exhaustively the rights of preference shareholders to dividend, and I do not find in the speeches of Viscount Haldane L.C. or Earl Loreburn in that case any suggestion that a different result would have followed if the dispute had been in regard to capital. I do not ignore that in the same case in the Court of Appeal [1912] 2 Ch. 571, the distinction between dividend and capital was expressly made by both Cozens-Hardy M.R. and Farwell L.J., and that in *In re William Metcalfe & Sons Ltd.*, Romer L.J. reasserted it. But I share the difficulty, which Lord Keith has expressed in this case, in reconciling the reasoning that lies behind the judgments in *Will's* case and *In re William Metcalfe & Sons Ltd.* respectively. In *Collaroy Co. Ltd.* v. *Giffard* [1928] Ch. 144, Astbury J., after reviewing the authorities, including his own earlier decision in *In re Fraser and Chalmers* [1919] 2 Ch. 114, said: 'But whether the considerations affecting them [sc. capital and dividend preference respectively] are "entirely different" is a question of some difficulty', and approved the proposition [490] there urged by the ordinary shareholders that a fixed return of capital to shareholders in a winding up is just as artificial as a provision for a fixed dividend and that, if the latter is regarded as exhaustive, there is no prima facie reason why the former should not be similarly regarded. So also that learned judge was influenced by the consideration which appears to me to have much weight, that, if such an article as our art. 159 is regarded as a complete definition of the rights of the preference stockholders in a winding up, then there is a logical consistency between their rights before and after the company is put into liquidation. In effect I prefer the reasoning of Astbury J. in the case last cited to that of Eve J. and the Court of Appeal in *In re William Metcalfe & Sons Ltd.* Counsel for the appellants in the present case sought to draw a distinction between the right to repayment of capital and the right to some further share in surplus assets and pointed to the fact that arts. 159 and 160 said nothing about surplus assets. But this distinction is not in my opinion in the present context a valid one. Articles 159 and 160 are the first two in a number of articles headed 'Distribution of assets in winding up' and there is nothing in them to suggest a distinction between 'surplus assets' and 'property of the company', the expression in fact used in arts. 159 and 160, required for repayment of capital or distributable as surplus assets. Nor, I think, is the latter expression used throughout the articles: it is perhaps an expression which is better avoided.

Finally on this part of the case I ought to deal with an observation made by Lord Macnaghten in *Birch* v. *Cropper* upon which counsel for the appellants relied. 'They,' he said '[sc. the preference shareholders] must be treated as having all the rights of shareholders, except so far as they renounced these rights on their admission to the company.' But, in my opinion, Lord Macnaghten can have meant nothing more than that the rights of the parties depended on the bargain that they had made and that the terms of the bargain must be ascertained by a consideration of the articles of association and any other relevant document, a task which I have endeavoured in this case to discharge. I cannot think that Lord Macnaghten intended to introduce some new principle of construction and to lay down that preference shareholders are entitled to share in surplus assets unless they expressly and specifically renounce that right.

X. Minority Shareholder Protection

Almost invariably, differences will arise between shareholders about their company's affairs. One of the fundamental principles of company law is majority rule: that it is for the majority of shareholders with voting rights to decide most matters concerning the company, and that certain fundamental matters should be resolved by super-majorities (usually either a special resolution or decision of three quarters in value of the shareholders). Consequently, the dissatisfied shareholder or shareholders who cannot persuade the majority to come around to their point of view will often have to choose between having their preferences ignored or selling out their shares. In companies whose shares are quoted on the Stock Exchange, the threat to dispose of a large block of shares may persuade the majority to make their peace with the minority. In private companies, on the other hand, restrictions in the articles of association on the transferability of shares may render a minority stake virtually unsaleable.

Judges have always been somewhat hesitant about adjudicating on inter-shareholder disputes. Many of the matters that give rise to conflict between shareholders concern essentially business judgments, such as hiring and firing employees, expanding or contracting particular lines of activity, paying dividends or placing profits in reserve. If such matters were readily reviewable by the courts, then the spectre of judges 'taking on the management of every playhouse and brewhouse' in the country would be realised. Lawyers do not possess any special competence in business matters, and legal procedures are far too expensive and cumbersome for resolving differences of policy between shareholders. There nevertheless are several grounds on which the courts will intervene on the minority shareholder's behalf. Many of the Companies Acts' provisions entitle individual members to bring suit in order to enforce the statutory requirements. A shareholder may bring suit alleging breach of the 'section 25 contract' that is contained in the memorandum and articles of association; or alleging unfair discrimination against a minority; or a derivative suit claiming that the majority defrauded the company; or a petition under §205 of the 1963 Act claiming 'oppression'; or the drastic step of petitioning to have the company wound up on 'just and equitable' grounds or on the grounds of 'oppression'. A channel of shareholder redress that has not so far been used in Ireland is an investigation by inspectors under §§165-173 of the 1963 Act. Before addressing the substantive law of minority shareholder protection and related procedural questions, the basis for the reluctance of judges to intervene in inter-shareholder disputes must be considered.

ANTI-INTERVENTIONISM

Moylan v. Irish Whiting Manufacturers Ltd.
(Hamilton J., Apr. 14, 1980, H.Ct.)

HAMILTON J.: In this case the plaintiff claims; inter alia:-1. A Declaration that he is a Director of Irish Whiting Manufacturers Limited, the first-named Defendant herein, and is entitled to attend all meetings of the Board of Directors of the said Company. 2. An Injunction restraining the second, third and fourth-named Defendants from excluding the Plaintiff from meetings of Directors of the said Company.

Prior to the incidents of which the Plaintiff complains and which led to the institution of the proceedings herein, the Plaintiff was the Chairman of the Board of Directors of Irish Whiting Manufacturers Limited, the first-named Defendant, . . . having been so appointed in the year 1972, after serving as a Director since 1964. Prior to the 6th day of February, 1975, the Board of Directors of Irish Whiting Manufacturers Limited (hereinafter called 'the Company') consisted of [3] the Plaintiff and the second, third and fourth-named Defendants, all of whom were shareholders in 'the Company'.

At the Annual General Meeting of 'the Company' held on that day, a resolution was proposed, seconded and approved that all the directors of 'the Company' should retire and seek re-election. This resolution was opposed by the Plaintiff and though proposed he was not elected to the Board of Directors of 'the Company'. . . .

[6] Prior to the 6th day of February 1975, the Plaintiff and the second, third and fourth-named Defendants constituted the Board of Directors of 'the Company' and at all relevant times, there were no permanent Directors of 'the Company'. It is quite clear from a consideration of the minutes of the Annual General Meetings of 'the Company' held between the 27-9-1965 and the 6-2-1975 inclusive that the requirements of Table A with regard to the retirement and election of Directors were never complied with.

At the Annual General Meetings [7] [held between 1965 and 1969] respectively resolutions that the Directors be re-appointed collectively and that the outgoing Directors be re-elected Directors of the Company were passed. Two separate resolutions were necessary at each Annual General Meeting because of the terms of Section 181 of the Companies Act, 1963. . . . Though, during this period, the Directors did not retire in accordance [8] with the rota established by Table A, all were treated as having retired and were re-elected, the resolutions necessitated by the provisions of Section 181 of the Companies Act 1963 having been passed.

At the Annual General Meeting of 'the Company' held on Monday November 9th 1970, however, it was proposed by Dr H. Counihan and seconded by Mr McMahon that the same Directors be appointed for another year. It does not appear from the minutes that the resolution necessitated by the provisions of Section 181 of the Companies Act 1963 was passed at the Annual General Meeting.

Due to the illness of the Secretary of the Company, Mrs McCormack, the minutes of the Annual General Meeting held in 1971 were never completed. During this year the Chairman of the Company died and the Plaintiff was appointed Acting Chairman.

At the Annual General Meeting held on the 15th day of March 1972, the Plaintiff was appointed Chairman of 'the Company' and it was proposed by Dr H. Counihan and seconded by Mr McMahon that the four existing Directors be re-appointed. There is no record in the minutes that this resolution was passed [9] but I presume it was as the then existing Directors continued to act in that capacity. The resolution required by the provisions of Section 181 of the Companies Act 1963 does not appear to have been passed at this meeting.

At the Annual General Meeting held on the 24th day of January 1974 under the Chairmanship of the Plaintiff, the fourth-named Defendant was elected a Director of 'the Company'.   There is no record in the minutes of the election of any other Directors or of the retirement of any Directors in accordance with the requirements of Table A but the Plaintiff and the second, third and forth-named Defendants continued to act as Directors of 'the Company' with the Plaintiff acting as Chairman. That was the last Annual General Meeting of 'the Company' prior to the Annual General Meeting at which occurred the events that have led to the proceedings herein. It is quite clear from the evidence that 'the Company' was experiencing certain trading difficulties, was involved in litigation, had to contend with local agitation which culminated in portion of the mine being blown up and that relations between the Directors were not exactly harmonious.

[10] In January 1975 proceedings between 'the Company' and a man called Clive, with whom 'the Company' was in dispute were settled on the second day of the hearing. Though the second and third named Defendants were present with the Plaintiff at the hearing and authorised the settlement, the second-named Defendant criticised the settlement as not being in the best interests of 'the Company' at the meeting of the Board of Directors held on the 31st day of January 1975. It appears that the third-named Defendant then supported the second-named Defendant. After some heated discussion, the second-named Defendant proposed and the fourth-

named Defendant seconded the proposal that the Plaintiff retire as Chairman of 'the Company'. The Plaintiff asked for time to consider the position and there is a conflict of evidence as to what then transpired. The Plaintiff states that the matter ended there: that the resolution was not voted on as he did not put the resolution to the meeting.

The Defendants, other than 'the Company', however allege that they refused to allow the Plaintiff time to consider his position, insisted that the resolution be voted on, that it was voted on and passed.

[11] On the balance of probabilities, I accept the Defendants' evidence on this point though I am satisfied that the Plaintiff is convinced that what he alleges is true. The evidence of the Defendants is confirmed by the minutes of this meeting. The notice convening the Annual General Meeting was signed by the fourth-named Defendant and states 'We wish to inform you that the Annual General Meeting for the year ending 31st December 1974 of Irish Whiting Manufacturers Ltd., will be held at these offices on the 6th February 1975 at 4.30 p.m.'

Having regard to the events which transpired at the said Annual General Meeting this notice is impugned on the grounds that it:

(a) did not contain any agenda for the said meeting

(b) did not give notice of any special business to be transacted at the said meeting.

At the meeting held on the 6th day of February 1975 the notice concerning the meeting was read by the second-named Defendant, who stated that his understanding was that there were no officials or Directors of the Company in being and that the correct procedure was to elect a Chairman.

[12] After a discussion during the course of which objection was taken to this course, a vote was taken and by a majority it was decided to elect a Chairman for the Annual General Meeting. The second-named Defendant defeated the Plaintiff in the vote to elect a Chairman. Subsequently during the course of the meeting the second, third and fourth-named Defendants were individually proposed, seconded and elected as Directors of 'the Company'. The Plaintiff was proposed and seconded but not elected as a Director of 'the Company'. It is submitted on behalf of the Plaintiff that this meeting was invalid for the reasons set out in detail in Paragraph 6 of the Statement of Claim. It is further submitted that a resolution was passed at the said meeting that all the Directors be retired and put up for re-election and that that resolution was invalid in that it constituted a removal of the Directors otherwise than in accordance with Section 182 of the Companies Act 1963 and in that it also constituted special business of which notice had not been given in the letter purported to summon the said Meeting.

I am satisfied that no such resolution was proposed or passed at this meeting. [13] What transpired was that the second-named Defendant stated his belief that there were no Directors or officers of 'the Company' in

existence and that the meeting should elect a Chairman. It is true that
subsequently the practice previously adopted of electing the Directors
collectively was abandoned and that the Directors were elected individually
but there is nothing unlawful or invalid in adopting this course, rather
does the law require it in the absence of a specific resolution.

While there may have been certain deficiencies in the Notice convening
the meeting, such as failure to comply with the requirements of Clause
49 of Table A and irregularities in the manner in which the meeting was
conducted, it is quite clear that the majority of the shareholders gave their
approval to the course adopted at the meeting and the decisions reached
at the said meeting; and the first question I have to consider is whether I
have any jurisdiction to interfere with the conduct by 'the Company' of its
internal affairs.

In the course of his judgment in *MacDougall* v. *Gardiner* [1875] 1 Ch.
13 James L.J. stated:

> I think that it is of the utmost importance in all these Companies that
> the Rule which is well known to this Court as the rule in *Mozley* v.
> *Alston* and *Lord* v. *Copper Miners Co.* and *Foss* v. [14] *Harbottle* should
> be always adhered to: that is to say that nothing connected with internal
> disputes between the shareholders is to be made the subject of a Bill
> by some one shareholder on behalf of himself and others unless there
> be something illegal, oppressive or fraudulent – unless there is some-
> thing ultra vires the Company qua Company or on the part of the
> majority of the Company so that they are not fit persons to determine
> it; but that every litigation must be in the name of the Company if the
> Company really desire it.

In the course of his judgment in *Burland* v. *Earle* [1902] A.C. 83, Lord
Davey stated that:

> It is an elementary principle of the law relating to joint stock companies
> that the Court will not interfere with the internal management of
> companies acting within their powers and in fact has no jurisdiction
> to do so. . . . The cases in which the minority can maintain such an
> action are, therefore, confined to those in which the actions com-
> plained of are of a fraudulent character or beyond the powers of the
> Company.

In *Russell* v. *Wakefield Waterworks Ltd.* (1875) L.R.20 Eq. 474, Sir George
Jessel M.R. stated:

> But this is not a universal rule, that is, it is a rule subject to [15]
> exceptions and the exceptions depend very much on the necessity of

the case, that is the necessity for the Court doing justice. . . . The rule is not an inflexible rule and it will be relaxed where necessary in the interests of justice.

In *Heything* v. *Dupont* [1964] W.L.R. 854, Lord Justice Harman stated:

There are cases which suggest that the rule is not a rigid one and that an exception will be made where the justice of the case demands it.

Having regard to the provisions of Bunreacht na hÉireann I am satisfied that an exception to the rule must be made when the justice of the case demands it.

Does the justice of this case require that I abandon what has been described as 'an elementary principle' of the law relating to joint stock companies that the Court will not interfere with the internal manangement of companies acting within their powers and in fact has no jurisdiction to do so?

While the Plaintiff may with a certain degree of justification feel that he has been unfairly treated by his former co-Directors, the second, third and fourth-named Defendants, that is not to say that there has been anything illegal oppressive or fraudulent in their actions and I so find.

[16] Was their action and the action of 'the Company' ultra vires the Company? Their action could, in my opinion, only be ultra vires the Company if on the 6th day of February 1975 he was a duly appointed Director of 'the Company' and not due to retire on rotation. It appears to me that all the resolutions appointing Directors of 'the Company' passed at the Annual General Meetings of the Company held on the 9-11-1970, 15-3-1972 and the 24-1-1974 whereby Directors were elected collectively were void having regard to the provisions of Section 181 of the Companies Act, 1963. Consequently I am not satisfied that the Plaintiff was at the date of the Annual General Meeting on the 6th day of February 1975 a duly appointed Director of 'the Company' not due to retire on rotation. It follows that I am not satisfied that the actions of the Defendants were in any way ultra vires the Company.

I do not consider that the circumstances of this case and the Plaintiff's complaints with regard to the procedures adopted by the Defendants before and at the Annual General Meeting are such as to justify the Court in interfering with matters which relate to the internal management of 'the Company'.

BREACH OF THE MEMORANDUM OR
ARTICLES OF ASSOCIATION

Cockburn v. Newbridge Sanitary Steam Laundry Co. Ltd.
[1915] 1 I.R. 237

The company had a contract to do certain work for the military authorities in the Curragh for £3,000, but payment was to be made to the defendant director, who handed over only £1,000 to the company.

O'BRIEN L.C.: [252] The principle of law applicable to cases of this kind are well settled and, indeed, as has been said, are elementary. The difficulty arises in applying well-settled principles to the particular facts of each case, and the only trouble in the present instance arises from the circumstance that the facts do not at once readily group themselves under any of the reported cases.

Thomas Llewellyn, one of the defendants, was a director of the Newbridge Sanitary Steam Laundry Co., Ltd., and acted, although not possibly legally qualified, as managing director. The business had been founded by the husband of Louisa Cockburn, the plaintiff, and on his death practically the entire management of the company was carried on by Llewellyn, and, as the Master of the Rolls accurately puts it, the plaintiff did not control the affairs of the company, never inquired into them, and was in fact a mere dummy; and I see no reason to form the conclusion, even if the question could affect the result, that she was in a way privy or party to the transaction which gives rise indirectly to the present claim.

Owing to the proximity of the large military establishments near Newbridge, the business carried on by the defendant company is large, and appears to have been very remunerative. In the years 1909, 1910 and 1911, contracts were entered into between the military authorities and the defendant Llewellyn in his own name, for washing to be done in connexion with the military hospital, and otherwise under circumstances which would make the War Office liable to pay large sums for laundry work.

It is not disputed that although Llewellyn's name only appeared in the contracts, he really entered into them on behalf of the company. The washing was done by the company, and the remuneration to be paid for the work done was earned by the company, and, prima facie, the whole of it should be payable to them. The amount admittedly received by Llewellyn from the War Department was £3268, and the amount which he paid into the coffers of the company was only £1038, leaving an extraordinarily large balance for which he refuses to account.

[253] The plaintiffs, who hold a large number of shares in the company, but not a preponderating amount, seek to make him account, or, more simply, to pay to the company the money which he has received, and which

he refuses to pay.

The Master of the Rolls came to the only conclusion that a court could come to, that, as between Llewellyn and the company, there could be no answer to the action if the company had been the plaintiffs, but he was pressed by, and yielded to, the argument that in substance this was merely an attempt to enforce by a member of a company a claim against a director which the company might lawfully and reasonably refuse to enforce; that accordingly the question was one merely relating to the 'internal management' of the company, and therefore that a shareholder could not invoke the aid of the Court against the will of the company, and compel Llewellyn to account to the company.

There is no doubt that if this was merely a matter of 'internal management' the decision of the Court below could not be disturbed, and the sole question that we have to determine is whether on the peculiar facts of this case this is a question of merely 'internal management'.

The rule of law and of good sense laid down in *Foss* v. *Harbottle* (2 Hare 461) is indisputable, but it is subject to the exception that where the acts complained of are of a fraudulent character, or beyond the powers of the company, the action may be maintained by a shareholder suing on behalf of himself and the other shareholders, the company being made a defendant in the action. *Dominion Cotton Mills Co., Ltd.* v. *Amyot* [1912] A.C. 546, and *Burland* v. *Earle* [1902] A.C. 83, are recent cases where the rule had been considered and expounded, and its limitations defined.

Let us now return to the evidence. The defendant Llewellyn refuses to disclose what he did with the money, because he says [254] that the disclosure might criminate him. Mr Beck, the secretary of the company, says that it would be unwise to investigate Llewellyn's dealings, presumably because the criminality of some kind lying at the root would be laid bare. On being pressed, Llewellyn said that to give an account might incriminate him, because it would show that the differences in the amounts paid to the company and received by him had been disbursed in secret commissions, which of course would be a criminal offence. It is very hard to understand, even on the wildest scheme of bribery, that £2230 out of £3268 were paid in secret commissions, but it makes the case no better for Llewellyn that he claims the right of secrecy on this ground alone.

It has been argued most ingeniously by counsel for the company that there was a contract with Llewellyn, which it is suggested would be perfectly lawful, that he was to give the company whatever he thought right out of what he received. There is no evidence of such a contract having been made, even if it could lawfully be made; and the only question is whether, on the facts as we have now got them, it would be within the powers of the company to take up the attitude, 'We will not inquire.' If this company had entered into a contract with Llewellyn, giving him authority to commit a crime on behalf of himself and the company, such a contract would, of course, be absolutely illegal, and it requires no argument to see that it would be equally illegal to adopt such a contract either affirmatively or indirectly.

Illegality and ultra vires are not interchangeable terms, but it is difficult, if not impossible, to conceive a case in which a company can do an illegal act, the illegality arising from public policy, and act within its powers.

Dealing with a case not of this class, but of ultra vires unaffacted by criminality, Lord Cairns, says, in *Ashbury Railway Carriage & Iron Co.* v. *Riche* (L.R. 7 H.L. 653, at p. 672): 'But, my Lords, if the shareholders of this company could not *ab ante* have authorized a contract of this kind to be made, how could they subsequently sanction the contract after it had, in point of fact, been made... [255] It appears to me that it would be perfectly fatal to the whole scheme of legislation to which I have referred, if you were to hold that, in the first place, directors might do that which even the whole company could not do, and that then the shareholders finding out what had been done, could sanction, subsequently, what they could not antecedently have authorized.'

How much stronger is the position when the whole matter is tainted with criminality. The real agreement which it is suggested the directors did make in this case would have been an agreement, if made, so tainted with crime and so subversive of public policy as to be illegal in itself. It would, accordingly, have been quite beyond the powers of the company to have entered into it, nor could any memorandum or articles have given it power; it would be equally wrong for the company to ratify it, and it would be idle to give them an opportunity to vote on such a question, because the carrying of the resolution would be, in my judgment, nugatory as being illegal, and consequently wholly outside the powers of a company. To do a thing which would have for its main object either the commission of a crime, or the aiding or abetting of a crime, or the hushing up of a crime, could not be in any way within the powers of a company, and a matter of 'internal management' in which the Court should not interfere.

In this view of the case I do not find myself constrained by the difficulties which affected the Master of the Rolls. I do not go into the question of the sufficiency or insufficiency of the demand which was made for the plaintiff on the directors to summon a meeting of their company. In the view that I take of the case it would not be within the power of the company either to make, ratify or adopt a proceeding of the scandalous character sought to be cloaked over in the present case by such a resolution.

The appearance of the company, and the arguments of the counsel, are sufficient in my judgment to justify the Court in holding that the plaintiffs are entitled to direct relief in the present case, and that an account should be directed against the defendant Llewellyn in respect of the moneys which the company earned by these contracts, and which he either received or ought to have received.

HOLMES L.J.: ... [258] The Master of the Rolls was satisfied that, on the facts before him, the company was entitled to enforce an account. When the director who manages the business of a company, like that of this steam laundry, admits that he has entered into many contracts on behalf of the company, that he has been paid the contract prices, and that he has not accounted therefor, he could have no answer to an action of account by the company; and O'Connor M.R. would have so held, if such an action had been brought by them; but the difficulty he feels is that the company not only refuse to assist the plaintiffs, but, being named as defendants, actively defended the suit on the well-known legal ground that the matter in controversy relates to the mode of managing the company's business. The company may have such a question settled by action; but, if it does not desire to do so, one or more shareholders cannot, by constituting themselves plaintiffs, do so. There is, however, one well-recognized exception to this rule. Where the question involves the investigation of misconduct or criminality on the part of the company and one or more of its officers, or something ultra vires the company itself, the arm of the law cannot be stayed by the rule of law to which I have referred.

O'Connor M.R. was of opinion that there was no evidence of this exception in the present case. . . On this point I have come to a different conclusion. The only evidence in favour of himself given by Mr Llewellyn is that he neither kept nor used any of the contract prices for himself. [But h]e declined to answer the simple question as to what he had done with the portion thereof which he had not paid over to or for the company. When asked the ground of his refusing to answer, he said that to do so would criminate himself. The case has been tried in the Rolls and argued in this Court, in the shadow of this answer. Surely, without some explanation, it is a matter of certainty that what became of this money involves some criminality or misconduct by the managing director. . .

Salmon v. Quin & Axtens Ltd.
[1909] 1 Ch. 311 (C.A.)

The company's articles of association gave each of two named managing directors, who as well were the company's principal shareholders, what in effect was a veto over major property transactions envisaged by the company. Against the objections of the plaintiff, who was one of them, the board and then the members in general meeting, resolved to enter into such a transaction. The plaintiff sought to enjoin the company from acting on that resolution.

FARWELL L.J.: . . .[318] The articles, by s. 16 of the Act of 1862, are made
equivalent to a deed of covenant signed by all the shareholders. The Act
does not say with whom that covenant is entered into, and there have no
doubt been varying statements by learned judges, some of them saying it
is with the company, and with the shareholders. Stirling J. in *Wood* v.
Odessa Waterworks Co. (1889) 42 Ch.D. 636 says: 'The articles of association constitute a contract not merely between the shareholders and the
company but between each individual shareholder and every other.' I think
that that is accurate subject to this observation, that it may well be that the
Court would not enforce the covenant as between individual shareholders
in most cases. Now the general power of the board to manage here is
qualified by the stipulation which follows, that it is to be subject to the
provisions of these articles. I therefore turn to article 80, and I find this
provision to which these general powers of management are made subject:
(His Lordship read the article.) In the present case Mr Salmon did so
dissent according to the terms of that article, and therefore the veto therein
provided came into operation. That was met by the company being called
together by a requisition of seven shareholders and by passing general
resolutions for the acquisition of this property and the letting of the vacant
premises. It is said that those resolutions are of no effect, and I am of
opinion that the contention is right. I base my opinion on the words of
article 75, 'subject, nevertheless, to the provisions of any Acts of Parliament
or of these articles,' which I read to be [320] 'subject, nevertheless, to
article 80' and to such regulations (being not inconsistent with any such
provisions of these articles) as may be prescribed by the company in general
meeting.' That is to say, 'subject also to such regulations not inconsistent
with article 80 as may be prescribed by the company in general meeting.'
But these resolutions are absolutely inconsistent with article 80; in truth
this is an attempt to alter the terms of the contract between the parties by
a simple resolution instead of by a special resolution. The articles forming
this contract, under which the business of the company shall be managed
by the board, contain a most usual and proper requirement, because a
business does require a head to look after it, and a head that shall not be
interfered with unnecessarily. Then in order to oust the directors a special
resolution would be required. The case is, in my view, entirely governed,
if not by the decision, at any rate by the reasoning of the Lords Justices
in *Automatic Self-Cleansing Filter Syndicate Co.* v. *Cuninghame* [1906] 2 Ch.
34 (ante p. 89) and *Gramophone and Typewriter, Ltd.* v. *Stanley* [1908] 2
K.B. 89. I will only refer to one passage in Buckley L.J's judgment in the
latter case. He says: 'This Court decided not long since, in *Automatic
Self-Cleansing Filter Syndicate Co.* v. *Cuninghame*, that even a resolution of
a numerical majority at a general meeting of the company cannot impose
its will upon the directors when the articles have confided to them the
control of the company's affairs. The directors are not servants to obey

directions given by the shareholders as individuals; they are not agents appointed by and bound to serve the shareholders as their principals. They are persons who may by the regulations be entrusted with the control of the business, and if so entrusted they can be dispossessed from that control only by the statutory majority which can alter the articles. Directors are not, I think, bound to comply with the directions even of all the corporators acting as individuals.' That appears to me to express the true view. Any other construction might, I think, be disastrous, because it might lead to an interference by a bare majority very inimical to the interests of the minority who had come into a company on the footing that the business should be managed by the board of directors.

Beattie v. E. & F. Beattie Ltd.
[1938] 1 Ch. 708 (C.A.)

One provision in the company's articles of association was that whenever 'any. . . . dispute shall arise between the members of the company, or between the company and any member or members,' it shall be referred to arbitration. The plaintiff shareholder sought to bring a derivative action against the company's chairman and managing director, who was also a shareholder, for breach of fiduciary duty. A central issue was whether the above clause obliged the plaintiff to have the matter resolved by arbitration.

SIR WLFRED GREENE M.R.: . . . [720] The appellant . . . seeks to find in the articles themselves a contract to which he is a party giving him the right to demand an arbitration in the present circumstances. . . . [His counsel] says – Here is a member, [and] here is an article which provides that a dispute between the company and a member shall be referred to arbitration. It covers, among other things, a dispute relating to an act or default of a director. And he says that what he is seeking in the present case to do is to enforce that right as a member under that article and not any right as a director; that he has a right, and all other members have a right, when they find the company disputing with a director, to insist on that dispute being referred to arbitration. [His counsel] says that the case must be treated as though the circumstance that the appellant happens to be a director is immaterial. He says that it is quite immaterial that the member who is demanding arbitration is himself the member attacked.

[721] In my judgment, that argument is based on an incorrect view both as to the effect of the article and as to the effect of s. 20 of the Companies Act. The question as to the precise effect of s. 20 has been the subject of considerable controversy in the past, and it may very well be that there will be considerable controversy about it in the future. But it appears to me that this much, at any rate, is good law: that the contractual force given to the articles of association by the section is limited to such provisions of the articles as apply to the relationship of the members in their capacity

as members.

I do not think, in saying that, that I am in any way departing from or extending (and it certainly is not my intention to depart from or extend) certain observations of Astbury J. in the well-known case of *Hickman* v. *Kent or Romney Marsh Sheep-Breeders' Association* [1915] 1 Ch. 881. In that case Astbury J. made a careful review of all the decisions, and he expressed his conclusions with regard to them in this way. He referred to *Eley* v. *Positive Life Assurance Co., Ltd.* (1876) 1 Ex.D. 21, and certain other cases, and pointed out that those decisions amounted to this: 'An outsider to whom rights purport to be given by the articles in his capacity as such outsider, whether he is or subsequently becomes a member, cannot sue on those articles treating them as contracts between himself and the company to enforce those rights. Those rights are not part of the general regulations of the company applicable alike to all shareholders and can only exist by virtue of some contract between such person and the company.' Then, again, he said: 'no right merely purporting to be given by an article to a person, whether a member or not, in a capacity other than that of a member, as, for instance, as solicitor, promoter, director, can be enforced against the company.'

With those two statements I respectfully agree. They are statements with regard to the true construction and operation of s. 20, and they have the result in the present case of preventing that section from giving contractual force to the article as between the company and its directors as such.

[722] It is to be observed that the real matter which is here being litigated is a dispute between the company and the appellant in his capacity as a director, and when the appellant, relying on this clause, seeks to have that dispute referred to arbitration, it is that dispute and none other which he is seeking to have referred, and by seeking to have it referred he is not, in my judgment, seeking to enforce a right which is common to himself and all other members. He is seeking to enforce a quite different right. I will explain what I mean. Let me assume that this article on its true construction entitles any member of the company to say to the company, when it is in dispute with a director: 'You, the company, are bound by your contract with me in the articles to refer this dispute to arbitration, and I call upon you so to do.' That is the right, and the only right in this respect, which is common to all the members, under this article. If that were the right which the appellant was seeking to exercise, there might be something to be said for that argument but, with all respect to the able argument of [his counsel] it appears to me that that is not at all the right which the appellant is seeking to enforce. He is not seeking to enforce a right to call on the company to arbitrate a dispute which is only accidentally a dispute with himself. He is asking, as a disputant, to have the dispute to which he is a party referred. That is sufficient to differentiate it from the right which is common to all the other members of the company under this article,

which I have tried to define. That right is one which a member might find very great difficulty in enforcing in the Courts, because it concerns a matter relating to the internal management of the company, with which the Courts will not, in general, interfere.

But quite apart from that consideration, the two rights are, in my judgment, perfectly distinct and quite different – the general right of a member as a member and the right which the appellant as a party to the dispute is seeking to enforce. Indeed, [counsel] agrees that his argument really amounted to saying that the present application is in essence the same as proceedings brought by Mr Ernest Beattie, as a shareholder, to restrain the company from litigating and [723] to obtain a mandatory order on the company to go to arbitration. But that is a very different thing from what he is now seeking since his claim, as I have said, is to insist on a reference of his own dispute.

FRAUD ON THE COMPANY

Cook v. Deeks
[1916] 1 A.C. 554 (P.C.)

See ante p. 154 for the background to this case. After several shareholders' meetings, resolutions were passed, with the aid of the defendants' votes, approving the sale of part of the plant of the company to the Dominion Construction Company, and a declaration was made that the company had no interest in the Shore Line contract, and that the directors were authorized to defend this action, which had in the meantime been instituted.

LORD BUCKMASTER L.C.: . . . [560] Two questions of law arise out of this long history of fact. The first is whether, apart altogether from the subsequent resolutions, the company would have been at liberty to claim from the three defendants the benefit of the contract which they had obtained from the Canadian Pacific Railway Company; and the second, which only arises if the first be answered in the affirmative, whether in such event the majority of the shareholders of the company constituted by the three defendants could ratify and approve of what was done and thereby release all claims against the directors. . . .

[563] There remains the more difficult consideration of whether this position can be made regular by resolutions of the company controlled by the votes of these three defendants. The Supreme Court of Canada have given this matter the most careful consideration, but their Lordships are unable to agree with the conclusion which they reached.

In their Lordships' opinion the Supreme Court has insufficiently recognized the distinction between two classes of case and has applied the principles applicable to the case of a director selling to his company property which was in equity as well as at law his own, and which he could dispose of as he thought fit, to the case of a director dealing with property which, though his own at law, in equity belonged to his company. The cases of *North-West Transportation Co.* v. *Beatty* (1887) 12 App. Cas. 589 and *Burland* v. *Earle* [1902] A.C. 83 both belonged to the former class. In each, directors had sold to the company property in which the company had no interest at law or in equity. If the company claimed any interest by reason of the [564] transaction, it could only be by affirming the sale, in which case such sale, though initially voidable, would be validated by subsequent ratification. If the company refused to affirm the sale the transaction would be set aside and the parties restored to their former position, the directors getting the property and the company receiving back the purchase price. There would be no middle course. The company could not insist on retaining the property while paying less than the price agreed. This would be for the Court to make a new contract between the parties. It would be quite another thing if the director had originally acquired the property which he sold to his company under circumstances which made it in equity the property of the company. The distinction to which their Lordships have drawn attention is expressly recognized by Lord Davey in *Burland* v. *Earle* and is the foundation of the judgment in *North-West Transportation Co.* v. *Beatty* and is clearly explained in the case of *Jacobus Marler Estates* v. *Marler*, (1913) 85 L.J.P.C. 167n, a case which has not hitherto appeared in any of the well-known reports.

If, as their Lordships find on the facts, the contract in question was entered into under such circumstances that the directors could not retain the benefit of it for themselves, then it belonged in equity to the company and ought to have been dealt with as an asset of the company. Even supposing it be not ultra vires of a company to make a present to its directors, it appears quite certain that directors holding a majority of votes would not be permitted to make a present to themselves. This would be to allow a majority to oppress the minority. To such circumstances the cases of *North-West Transportation Co.* v. *Beatty* and *Burland* v. *Earle* have no application. In the same way, if directors have acquired for themselves property or rights which they must be regarded as holding on behalf of the company, a resolution that the rights of the company should be disregarded in the matter would amount to forfeiting the interest and property of the minority of shareholders in favour of the majority, and that by the votes of those who are interested in securing the property for themselves. Such use of voting power has never been sanctioned by the Courts, and, [565] indeed, was expressly disapproved in the case of *Menier* v. *Hooper's Telegraph Works* (1874) L.R. 9 Ch. 359.

If their Lordships took the view that, in the circumstances of this case, the directors had exercised a discretion or decided on a matter of policy (the view which appears to have been entertained by the Supreme Court) different results would ensue, but this is not a conclusion which their Lordships are able to accept. It follows that the defendants must account to the Toronto Company for the profits which they have made out of the transaction.

Daniels v. Daniels
[1978] Ch. 406 (Ch.D.)

Minority shareholders sought to sue a director and controlling shareholder who had purchased property from the company for significantly less than its current value. The defendant applied to have the action struck out for not disclosing a reasonable cause of action.

TEMPLEMAN J.: . . . [408] The plaintiff's complaint appears from paragraphs 3 and 4 of the statement of claim. Paragraph 3 alleges that in October 1970 the company sold certain land in Warwickshire to the second defendant for £4,250 on the instructions and by the direction of the directors, who were the first and second defendants. Paragraph 4 alleges that the price of £4,250 paid to the company by the second defendant was less than the current value of the land at the time of the sale, as the first and second defendants well knew or ought to have known. The particulars of that allegation are first that the first and second defendants purported to adopt a probate value made on the death, which took place on 8 June 1969, of the father of the plaintiffs and the first defendant; secondly, that 'probate values being conservative in amount, are customarily less than the open market value obtainable as between a willing vendor and a willing purchaser'; thirdly, that in 1974 the land was sold by the second defendant for the sum of £120,000.

Putting it broadly, all the allegations will be denied by the defendants if the action proceeds. But it is common ground that for the purpose of this application I must proceed upon the basis that all the allegations in the statement of claim can be sustained.

Mr Richards, for the first two defendants who bring this application to strike out, says there is no cause of action shown because the statement of claim does not allege fraud, and in the absence of fraud, minority shareholders are unable to maintain a claim on behalf of the company against a majority. For that proposition he referred first of all to the principles set out in *Foss* v. *Harbottle* (1843) 2 Hare 461. That case established the general proposition that minority shareholders cannot maintain an action on behalf of the company, subject to certain exceptions. The exceptions are four in number, and only one of which is of possible application in the present case. The first exception is that a shareholder can sue in respect of some attack on his individual rights as a shareholder; secondly, he can sue if the company, for example, is purporting to do by ordinary resolution that which its own constitution requires to be done by special resolution; thirdly, if the company has done or proposes to do something which is ultra vires; and fourthly, if there is fraud and there is no other remedy. There must be a minority who are prevented from remedying the fraud or taking any proceedings because of the protection given to the fraudulent shareholders or directors by virtue of their majority.

[409] Mr Richards says, and it is conceded, that the statement of claim in its present form does not allege fraud. Mr Blackburne, for the plaintiffs, says of course he is not alleging fraud because the plaintiffs do not really know what happened: all they know is what is set out in the statement of claim. There has been a sale at an undervalue and the second defendant has made a substantial profit; therefore, fraud is not pleaded. But, says Mr Blackburne, when the authorities are considered, the rights of a minority are not limited to cases of fraud; they extend to any breach of duty. In the present case if the defendants sold at an undervalue then that was a breach of duty. As the plaintiffs cannot remedy the breach, save by a minority shareholders' action, they should be entitled to bring the action. *Foss* v. *Harbottle*, 2 Hare 461, was a case in which there was no oppression by a majority.

The next case in point of time, to which I was referred, was *Atwool* v. *Merryweather* (1867) L.R. 5 Eq. 464n. The exception of fraud in *Foss* v. *Harbottle* was emphasised, the reason being, according to Page Wood V.-C., at p.468:

> If I were to hold that no bill could be filed by shareholders to get rid of the transaction on the ground of the doctrine of *Foss* v. *Harbottle*, it would be simply impossible to set aside a fraud committed by a director under such circumstances, as the director obtaining so many shares by fraud would always be able to outvote everbody else. . . .

[410] In *Menier* v. *Hooper's Telegraph Works* (1874) L.R. 9 Ch.App. 350, a minority shareholders' action was allowed where the majority intended to divide the assets of the company more or less between themselves to the exclusion of the minority. Mellish L.J. said, at p.354:

> I am of the opinion that although it may be quite true that the shareholders of a company may vote as they please, and for the purpose of their own interests, yet that the majority of shareholders cannot sell the assets of the company and keep the consideration, but must allow the minority to have their share of any consideration which may come to them. . . .

[413] Then in 1956 there was a case on which Mr Richards very strongly relies and from which Mr Blackburne asked me to differ. In *Pavlides* v. *Jensen* [1956] Ch. 565, it was alleged that directors had been guilty of

gross negligence in selling a valuable asset of the company at a price greatly below its true market value, and it was alleged that the directors knew or well ought to have known that it was below market value. Danckwerts J. struck out the statement of claim as disclosing no cause of action because no fraud was pleaded. The headnote says, at p. 566:

> ... since the sale of the asset in question was not beyond the powers of the company, and since there was no allegation of fraud on the part of the directors or appropriation of the assets of the company by the majority shareholders in fraud of the minority, the action did not fall within the admitted exceptions to the rule in *Foss* v. *Harbottle*. ...

Danckwerts J. said, at p. 576:

> On the facts of the present case, the sale of the company's mine was not beyond the powers of the company, and it is not alleged to be ultra vires. There is no allegation of fraud on the part of the directors or appropriation of assets of the company by the majority shareholders in fraud of the minority. It was open to the company, on the resolution of the majority of the shareholders, to sell the mine at a price decided by the company in that manner, and it was open to the company by a vote of the majority to decide that, if the directors by their negligence or error of judgment had sold the company's mine at an undervalue, proceedings should not be taken by the company against the directors.

Mr Richards relies very stongly on this decision as showing that, whatever the exceptions to *Foss* v. *Harbottle* may be, mere gross negligence is not actionable, and he says all that is pleaded in the present case is gross negligence at the most. But in *Pavlides* v. *Jensen* no benefits accrued to the directors. Mr. Blackburne asks me to dissent from *Pavlides* v. *Jensen* but the decision seems to me at the moment to be in line with the authorities, in what is a restricted exception to the rule in *Foss* v. *Harbottle*.

In *Birch* v. *Sullivan* [1957] 1 W.L.R. 1247 the decision really went off on a point of pleading; moreover the judge was not satisfied that the dissenting shareholders could not put matters right by a meeting of the company. Finally I was referred to *Heyting* v. *Dupont* [1963] 1 W.L.R. 1192; [1964] 1 W.L.R. 843. But that was only an instance of the court refusing on its own initiative to hear an action begun by minority shareholders where the *Foss* v. *Harbottle* exceptions did not come into play.

The authorities which deal with simple fraud on the one hand and gross negligence on the other do not cover the situation which arises where, without fraud, the directors and majority shareholders are guilty [414] of a breach of duty which they owe to the company, and that breach of duty not only harms the company but benefits the directors. In that case it seems to me that different considerations apply. If minority shareholders can sue if there is fraud, I see no reason why they cannot sue where the action of the majority and the directors, though without fraud, confers some benefit on those directors and majority shareholders themselves. It would seem to me quite monstrous – particularly as fraud is so hard to plead and difficult to prove – if the confines of the exception to *Foss* v. *Harbottle*, were drawn so narrowly that directors could make a profit out of their negligence. Lord Hatherley L.C. in *Turquand* v. *Marshall*, L.R. 4 Ch.App.376, 386, opined that shareholders must put up with foolish or unwise directors. Danckwerts J. in *Pavlides* v. *Jensen* accepted that the forbearance of shareholders extends to directors who are 'an amiable set of lunatics.' Examples, ancient and modern, abound. To put up with foolish directors is one thing; to put up with directors who are so foolish that they make a profit of £115,000 odd at the expense of the company is something entirely different. The principle which may be gleaned from *Alexander* v. *Automatic Telephone Co.* [1900] 2 Ch. 56 (directors benefiting themselves), from *Cook* v. *Deeks* (ante p. 289) (directors diverting business in their own favour) and from dicta in *Pavlides* v. *Jensen* (directors appropriating assets of the company) is that a minority shareholder who has no other remedy may sue where directors use their powers, intentionally or unintentionally, fraudulently or negligently, in a manner which benefits themselves at the expense of the company. This principle is not contrary to *Turquand* v. *Marshall*, because in that case the powers of the directors were effectively wielded not by the director who benefited but by the majority of independent directors who were acting bona fide and did not benefit. I need not consider the wider proposition for which Mr Blackburne against some formidable opposition from the authorities contends that any breach of duty may be made the subject of a minority shareholder's action.

I am certainly not prepared to say at this stage of the game that the action brought by the plaintiffs in the present instance is bound to fail. What the result of the action will be I know not, but if the statement of claim is right, and the husband and wife who control 60 per cent. of the shares were responsible for a sale by the company to the wife at an undervalue, which they knew or ought to have known, then a remedy for the minority shareholders ought to lie.

BREACH OF FAITH AND UNFAIR DISCRIMINATION

Greenhalgh v. Arderne Cinemas Ltd.
[1951] 1 Ch. 286 (C.A.)

This case is part of a series of litigation between parties interested in the company in question. Under the company's articles of association, no shares could be transferred to outsiders until they were first offered to and refused by the existing shareholders; and the directors were empowered to refuse to register any transfer of shares. Principally to enable a controlling shareholder to sell his shares to an outsider, the company resolved to alter these provisions by adding to them a clause whereby, with the approval of an ordinary resolution in general meeting, any member could transfer his shares to any named outsider. The plaintiff claimed that this resolution was unlawful.

EVERSHED M.R.: [290] The burden of the case is that the resolution was not passed bona fide and [291] in the interests of the company as a whole, and there are, as Mr Jennings has urged, two distinct approaches.

The first line of attack is this, and it is one to which, he complains, Roxburgh, J., paid no regard: this is a special resolution, and, on authority, Mr Jennings says, the validity of a special resolution depends upon the fact that those who passed it did so in good faith and for the benefit of the company as a whole. The cases to which Mr Jennings referred are *Sidebottom* v. *Kershaw, Leese & Co. Ltd.* [1920] 1 Ch. 154, Peterson, J.'s decision in *Dafen Tinplate Co. Ltd.* v. *Llanelly Steel Co. (1907) Ltd.* [1920] 2 Ch. 24, and, finally, *Shuttleworth* v. *Cox Brothers & Co. (Maidenhead), Ltd.* [1927] 2 K.B. 9. Certain principles, I think, can be safely stated as emerging from those authorities. In the first place, I think it is now plain that 'bona fide for the benefit of the company as a whole' means not two things but one thing. It means that the shareholder must proceed upon what, in his honest opinion, is for the benefit of the company as a whole. The second thing is that the phrase, 'the company as a whole', does not (at any rate in such a case as the present) mean the company as a commercial entity, distinct from the corporators: it means the corporators as a general body. That is to say, the case may be taken of an individual hypothetical member and it may be asked whether what is proposed is, in the honest opinion of those who voted in its favour, for that person's benefit.

I think that the matter can, in practice, be more accurately and precisely stated by looking at the converse and by saying that a special resolution of this kind would be liable to be impeached if the effect of it were to discriminate between the majority shareholders and the minority shareholders, so as to give the former an advantage of which the latter were deprived. When the cases are examined in which the resolution has been successfully attacked, it is on that ground. It is therefore not necessary to require that persons voting for a special resolution should, so to speak, dissociate themselves altogether from their own prospects and consider whether what is thought to be for the benefit of the company as a going concern. If, as commonly happens, an outside person makes an offer to buy all the shares, prima facie, if the corporators think it a fair offer and vote in favour of the resolution, it is no ground for impeaching the resolution that they are considering their own position as individuals.

Accepting that, as I think he did, Mr Jennings said, in effect, that there are still grounds for impeaching this resolution: first, because it goes further than was necessary to give effect to the particular sale of the shares; and, secondly, because it prejudiced the plaintiff and minority shareholders in that it deprived them of the right which, under the subsisting articles, they would have of buying the shares of the majority if the latter desired to dispose of them.

What Mr Jennings objects to in the resolution is that if a resolution is passed altering the articles merely for the purpose of giving effect to a particular transaction, then it is quite sufficient (and it is usually done) to limit it to that transaction. But this resolution provides that anybody who wants at any time to sell his shares can now go direct to an outsider, provided that there is an ordinary resolution of the company approving the proposed transferee. Accordingly, if it is one of the majority who is selling, he will get the necessary resolution. This change in the articles, so to speak, franks the shares for holders of majority interests but makes it more difficult for a minority shareholder, because the majority will probably look with disfavour upon his choice. But, after all, this is merely a relaxation of the very stringent restrictions on transfer in the existing article, and it is to be borne in mind that the directors, as the articles stood, could always refuse to register a transfer. A minority shareholder, therefore, who produced an outsider was always liable to be met by the directors (who presumably act according to the majority view) saying, 'We are sorry, but we will not have this man in'.

Although I follow the point, and it might perhaps have been possible to do it the other way, I think that this case is very far removed from the type of case in which what is proposed, as in the *Dafen* case, is to give a majority the right to expropriate a minority shareholder, whether he wanted to sell or not, merely on the ground that the majority shareholders wanted the minority man's shares.

As to the second point, I felt at one time sympathy for the plaintiff's argument, because, after all, as the articles stood he could have said: 'Before you go selling to the purchaser you have to offer your shares to the existing shareholders, and that will enable me, if I feel so disposed, to buy, in effect, the whole of the shareholding of the Arderne company'. I think that the answer is that when a man comes into a company, he is not entitled to assume that the articles will always remain in a particular form; and that, so long as the proposed alteration does not unfairly discriminate in the way which I have indicated, it is not an objection, provided that the resolution is passed bona fide, that the right to tender for the majority holding of shares would be lost by the lifting of the restriction. I do not think that it can be said that that is such a discrimination as falls within the scope of the principle which I have stated.

[293] Mr Jennings further says that, if that is wrong, he falls back on

his other point that the defendant Mallard acted in bad faith. He concealed, it is said, various matters; he confessed to feelings of envy and hatred against the plaintiff; he desired to do something to spite him, even if he cut off his own nose in the process. Following the judge's line of reasoning, it is said that the defendant Mallard did control all these other submissive persons who supported him, so that they are equally tainted with the defendant Mallard's bad faith. I agree with Mr Jennings that, if an ordinary shareholder chooses to give what Mr Jennings called 'carte blanche' to the promotor of a scheme and that promoter is then found to have been acting in bad faith, the persons who gave him carte blanche cannot then say that they exercised any independent judgment, and they would likewise be tainted with the evil of their leader.

Mr Jennings had, early in his argument, formulated his grounds for bad faith against the defendant Mallard at greater length, and I need not, I think, go through the several heads.

[His lordship considered certain specific criticisms of the defendant Mallard's conduct, and continued:] Mr Jennings says that all these various matters cast such doubt upon the transaction that the defendant Mallard must be taken to have been acting in bad faith. I think that he acted with grave indiscretion in some respects; but the judge has said that he was in no way guilty of deliberate dishonesty; and I cannot see where and how it can be suggested that he was grinding some particular axe of his own. He was getting 6s. a share; but he was getting no more and no less than anyone else would get who wished to sell; and I am unable and unwilling to put upon the actions of the defendant Mallard, because of his unfortunate secrecy and other conduct, so bad a complexion as to impute bad faith in the true sense of the term, of which, indeed, Roxburgh, J., acquitted him.

In my opinion, in spite of all these complexities, this was, in substance, an offer by an outside man to buy the shares of this company at 6s. a share from anybody who was willing to sell them. As commonly happens, the defendant Mallard, as the managing director of the company, negotiated and had to proceed on the footing that he had with him sufficient support to make the negotiation a reality. That was the substance of what was suggested. It discriminated between no types of shareholder. Any who wanted to get out at that price could get out, and any who preferred to stay in could stay in.

Clemens v. Clemens Bros. Ltd.
[1976] 2 All E.R. 268 (Ch.D.)

The company here had only two shareholders, the plaintiff who held 45 per cent of the voting shares and the second defendant who held the other 55 per cent. Resolutions were passed in general meeting to issue additional shares in the company to the second defendant and her associates. The effect of implementing those resolutions would have been to dilute the plaintiff's stake in the company to just less than 25 per cent of the shares, and thereby deprive her of the power to block alterations of the company's articles of association. Among the relevant facts were that the plaintiff was not a director whereas the second defendant and her associates were on the board; for some years no dividends were paid; directors' generous emoluments exceeded the substantial profits that the company earned; shares could not be transferred to an outsider without them being first offered to the existing members; and the second defendant declined to give evidence.

FOSTER J.: . . . [280] For the plaintiff it was submitted that the proposed resolutions were oppressive, since they resulted in her losing her right to veto a special or extraordinary resolution and greatly watered down her existing right to purchase Miss Clemens' shares under art. 6. For the defendants it was submitted that if two shareholders both honestly hold differing opinions, the view of the majority must prevail and that shareholders in general meeting are entitled to consider their own interests and vote in any way they honestly believe proper in the interests of the company.

There are many cases which have discussed a director's position. A director must not only act within his powers but must also exercise them bona fide in what he believes to be the interests of the company. The directors have a fiduciary duty, but is there any, or any similar, restraint on shareholders exercising their powers as members at general meetings?

Menier v. *Hooper's Telegraph Works* (1874) L.R. 9 Ch.350, is a very clear case, since it involved the majority shareholders expropriating the company's assets to the exclusion of the minority. In *North-West Transportation Co. Ltd.* v. *Beatty* (1887) 12 App. Cas. 589, Sir Richard Baggallay said:

> The general principles applicable to cases of this kind are well established. Unless some provision to the contrary is to be found in the charter or other instrument by which the company is incorporated, the resolution of a majority of the shareholders, duly convened, upon any question with which the company is legally competent to deal, is binding upon the minority, and consequently upon the company, and every shareholder has a perfect right to vote upon any such question, although he may have personal interest, in the subject-matter opposed to, or different from, the general or particular interests of the company. On the other hand, a director of a company is precluded from dealing, on behalf [281] of the company, with himself, and from entering into engagements in which he has a personal interest conflicting, or which possibly may conflict, with the interests of those whom he is bound by fiduciary duty to protect; and this rule is as applicable to the case of one of several directors as to a managing or sole director. Any such

dealing or engagement may, however, be affirmed or adopted by the company, provided such affirmance or adoption is not brought about by unfair or improper means, and is not illegal or fraudulent or oppressive towards those shareholders who oppose it.

Here I find for the first time the word 'oppressive', but in that case the question in issue was whether a director could exercise his vote as a shareholder in general meeting to ratify a voidable contract to which he was party.

In *Allen* v. *Gold Reefs of West Africa Ltd.* (ante p. 94) Lindley MR said:

The power thus conferred on companies to alter the regulations contained in their articles is limited only by the provisions contained in the statute and the conditions contained in the company's memorandum of association. Wide, however, as the language of s. 50 is, the power conferred by it must, like all other powers, be exercised subject to those general principles of law and equity which are applicable to all powers conferred on majorities and enabling them to bind minorities. It must be exercised, not only in the manner required by law, but also bona fide for the benefit of the company as a whole, and it must not be exceeded. These conditions are always implied, and are seldom, if ever, expressed.

In *Greenhalgh* v. *Arderne Cinemas Ltd.* (ante p. 294) Evershed MR said:

Certain things, I think, can be safely stated as emerging from those authorities. In the first place, it is now plain that '*bona fide* for the benefit of the company as a whole' means not two things but one thing. It means that the shareholder must proceed on what, in his honest opinion, is for the benefit of the company as a whole. Secondly, the phrase, 'the company as a whole', does not (at any rate in such a case as the present) mean the company as a commercial entity as distinct from the corporators. It means the corporators as a general body. That is to say, you may take the case of an individual hypothetical member and ask whether what is proposed is, in the honest opinion of those who voted in its favour, for that person's benefit.

If that is right the question in the instant case which must be posed is this: did Miss Clemens, when voting for the resolutions, honestly believe that those resolutions, when passed, would be for the benefit of the plaintiff?

In *Re Scottish Co-operative Wholesale Society Ltd.* (post p. 301), which was a case under s. 210 of the Companies Act 1948 (s. 205 of the 1963 Act), the Lord President (Lord Cooper) said:

The section is not concerned with the results to the oppressor but with the results to those who complain of the oppression. When the section inquires whether the affairs of the company are being conducted in a manner oppressive to some part of the members including the complainer, that question can still be answered in the affirmative even if, *qua* member of the company, the oppressor has suffered the same or even greater prejudice.

[282] That case went to the House of Lords, where Viscount Simonds took the dictionary meaning of the word 'oppressive' as 'burdensome, harsh and wrongful.'

In *Ebrahimi* v. *Westbourne Galleries Ltd.* [1973] A.C. 360, the House of Lords was dealing with s. 222(*f*) and the 'just and equitable' ground for winding up a company. Lord Wilberforce said:

> The 'just and equitable' provision does not. . . entitle one party to disregard the obligation he assumes by entering a company, nor the court to dispense him from it. It does, as equity always does, enable the court to subject the exercise of legal rights to equitable considerations; considerations that is, of a personal character arising between one individual and another, which may make it unjust, or inequitable, to insist on legal rights, or to exercise them in a particular way.

I think that one thing which emerges from the cases to which I have referred is that in such a case as the present Miss Clemens is not entitled to exercise her majority vote in whatever way she pleases. The difficulty is in finding a principle, and obviously expressions such as 'bona fide for the benefit of the company as a whole,' 'fraud on a minority' and 'oppressive' do not assist in formulating a principle.

I have come to the conclusion that it would be unwise to try to produce a principle, since the circumstances of each case are infinitely varied. It would not, I think, assist to say more than that in my judgment Miss Clemens is not entitled as of right to exercise her votes as an ordinary shareholder in any way she pleases. To use the phrase of Lord Wilberforce, that right is 'subject. . . to equitable considerations. . . which may make it unjust. . . to exercise (it) in a particular way'. Are there then any such considerations in this case?

Conclusion

I do not doubt that Miss Clemens is in favour of the resolutions and knows and understands their purport and effect; nor do I doubt that she genuinely would like to see the other directors have shares in the company and to see a trust set up for long service employees. But I cannot escape the conclusion that the resolutions have been framed so as to put into the hands of Miss Clemens and her fellow directors complete control of the company and to deprive the plaintiff of her existing rights as a shareholder with more than 25 per cent of the votes and greatly reduce her rights under art. 6. They are specifically and carefully designed to ensure not only that the plaintiff can never get control of the company but to deprive her of what has been called her negative control. Whether I say that these proposals are oppressive to the plaintiff or that no one could honestly believe they are for her benefit matters not. A court of equity will in my judgment regard these considerations as sufficient to prevent the consequences arising from Miss Clemens using her legal right to vote in the way that she has and it would be right for a court of equity to prevent such consequences taking effect.

OPPRESSION, INJUSTICE AND INEQUITY

Scottish Co-Operative Wholesale Soc. v. Meyer
[1959] A.C. 324 (H.L.)

The petitioners and the Scottish Co-Op. agreed to establish a company that would be run as a joint enterprise. The company was a subsidiary of the Co-Op.'s, and was very dependant on the Co-Op. for its raw materials (yarn). Five years later the Co-Op.'s stake in the company was increased to 70 per cent. Shortly afterwards it sought to buy out the petitioners' £1 shares at par even though the shares were then worth about £6 each; but they refused to sell out. From then on the company was allowed to run down; supplies of raw materials to the company were effectively cut off, and the majority directors, who were the Co-Op.'s nominees, did nothing to halt the company's decline. The petitioners sought to have the company wound up under the U.K. Act's equivalent of §205 of the 1963 Act (s. 210 of the 1948 Act).

VISCOUNT SIMONDS: . . . [339] It is common ground that at the date of presentation of the petition on July 13, 1953, it was just and equitable that the company should be wound up. It could hardly be denied that to wind up the company would unfairly prejudice the repondents. The only question is whether its affairs were being conducted in a manner oppressive to the respondents and, if so, whether the court ordained the appropriate remedy. . . .

It is, however, necessary, if section 210 is to be successfully invoked, to show, not only that there has been oppression of the minority shareholders of a company but also that it has been the affairs of the company which have been conducted in an oppressive manner, and it was to this point that a large part of the appellants' argument was directed. I must therefore state in broad outline the course of events which led to the presentation of the petition.

The last event that I mentioned was the failure of the society to acquire at par shares that were worth a far greater sum. This was at a time of the company's great prosperity which, subject to the ups and downs of the textile trade, might be expected to continue. It was, however, followed by a recession in the rayon trade, of which the dates of beginning and ending were a matter of dispute. Such dates cannot be precisely determined and are of no consequence. It is, however, to be noted that it was in the course of it that rayon control came to an end, so that neither the society nor the company any longer depended on the personality [340] of the respondents to get supplies of yarn. It was also in the course of it that the respondent Meyer was anxious to visit Germany with a view to increasing the company's trade in that country but was prevented by his co-directors from doing so. This was undoubtedly the cause of much ill-feeling. . . .

An important consequence of the removal of cotton control was this. In or about June, 1951, a new department of the society had been formed called the merchant converting department. It was under the control of a Mr Wand, the manager of the drapery department, and its function was to convert loom state cloth by dyeing, printing and finishing into material for manufacture into garments. It therefore became possible upon the removal of cotton control and upon a revival of the rayon trade for the society to divert to their own converting department the product of their Falkland Mill. It was the fact, as they were well aware, that the company which had throughout been practically tied to them for the greater part of its supplies, would have great difficulty upon a revival of trade in getting them elsewhere. Deliberately they supplied the necessary material to the converting department but, in spite of Meyer's protests, declined to supply the company except at higher and non-competitive prices. An attempt to justify this discrimination was rightly regarded by their Lordships of the First Division as unsatisfactory. I have no doubt that at any rate by the end of 1952 it was the policy of the society by one means or another to destroy the company it had created, knowing that the minority shareholders alone would suffer in that process . . . . Robert Taylor, a director of the society and then chairman of the company, had an interview with [the petitioners] and told them frankly that the society was out to destroy the company, that they had no chance against such a powerful organisation, and that they should make their peace with the society by offering to sell their shares. . . .

At this time the three nominee directors of the company were aware (Taylor by his own confession) of the policy of the society. It is undeniable that persons so placed may find themselves in a difficulty. But in all the evidence I have not been able to find the least trace that they regarded themselves as owing any duty to the company of which they were directors. They were the nominees of the society and, if the society doomed the company to destruction, it was not for them to put out a saving hand. Rather, they were to join in that work, and, when a frank and prompt statement to their co-directors might have enabled them to retrieve its fortunes, they played their part by maintaining silence. That is how they conducted the affairs of the company, and it is impossible to suppose that that was not part of the deliberate policy of the society. As I have said, nominees of a parent company upon the board of a subsidiary company may be placed in a difficult and delicate position. It is, then, the more incumbent on the parent company to behave with scrupulous fairness to the minority shareholders and to avoid imposing upon their nominees the alternative of disregarding their instructions or betraying the interests of the minority. In the present case the society pursued a different course. It was ruthless and unscrupulous in design and it was effective in operation, and, as I have said, it was promoted by the action or inaction of the nominee directors. The company, which might have recovered [342] its former prosperity, had 'served its purpose.' It would conveniently be liquidated. I have omitted much which reflects no credit on the society and its officers, for I do not want to repeat what has already been said, or to anticipate what will fall from some of your Lordships. I will only mention the final fact that on August 24, 1953 (that is, after the presentation of the petition under section 210) Meyer and Lucas were given three months' notice of termination of their appointments as managing directors, and Mr Wand, the manager of the society's drapery department was appointed manager of the company.

My Lords, upon the facts, as I have outlined them and as they appear in greater detail in the judgments of their Lordships of the First Division, it appears to me incontrovertible that the society have behaved to the minority shareholders of the company in a manner which can justly be described as 'oppressive.' They had the majority power and they exercised their authority in a manner 'burdensome, harsh and wrongful' — I take the dictionary meaning of the word. But, it is said, let it be assumed that the society acted in an oppressive manner: yet they did not conduct the affairs of the company in an oppressive manner. My Lords, it may be that the acts of the society of which complaint is made could not be regarded as conduct of the affairs of the company if the society and the company were bodies wholly independent of each other, competitors in the rayon market, and using against each other such methods of trade warfare as custom permitted. But this is to pursue a false analogy. It is not possible to separate the transactions of the society from those of the company. Every step taken by the latter was determined by the policy of the former. I will give an example of this. I observed that, in the course of the argument before the House, it was suggested that the company had only itself to blame if, through its neglect to get a contract with the society, it failed in a crisis to obtain from the Falkland Mill the supply of cloth that it needed. The short answer is that it was the policy of the society that the affairs of the company should be so conducted and the minority shareholders were content that it shoud be so. They relied — how unwisely the event proved — upon the good faith of the society, and, in any case, they were impotent to impose their own views. It is just because the society could not only use the ordinary and legitimate weapons of commercial warfare but could also control from within the operations of the company that it is illegitimate to regard the conduct of the company's affairs as a matter for which they had no responsibility. After much [343] consideration of this question, I do not think that my own views could be stated better than in the late Lord President Cooper's words on the first hearing of this case. 'In my view,' he said, 'the section warrants the court in looking at the business realities of a situation and does not confine them to a narrow legalistic view. The truth is that, whenever a subsidiary is formed as in this case with an independent minority of shareholders, the parent company must, if it is engaged in the same class of business, accept as a result of having formed such a subsidiary an obligation so to conduct what are in a sense its own affairs as to deal fairly with its subsidiary.' At the opposite pole to this standard may be put the conduct of a parent company which says: 'Our subsidiary company has served its purpose, which is our purpose. Therefore let it die,' and, having thus pronounced sentence, is able to enforce it and does enforce it not only by attack from without but also by support from within. If this section is inept to cover such a case, it will be a dead letter indeed. I have expressed myself strongly in this case because, on the contrary, it appears to me to be a glaring example of precisely the evil which Parliament intended to remedy.

Some criticism was made of the relief given by the order of the court. It was said that only that relief could be given which had as its object and presumably its effect the 'bringing to an end of the matters complained of' and that an order upon the society to purchase the respondents' shares in the company did not satisfy that condition. This argument is without substance. The matter complained of was the oppression of the minority shareholders by the society. They will no longer be oppressed and will cease to complain if the society purchase their shares.

Finally, it was said that the court had not properly exercised its discretion in fixing a price of £3.15s.0d. per share. I see no ground for interfering with this decision. Necessarily a price cannot be scientifically assessed, but I heard no argument, nor had any evidence called to my attention, which suggested that their Lordships had acted on any wrong principle or adopted a measure too generous to the respondents.

In re Greenore Trading Co. Ltd.
(Keane J., March 28, 1980, H.Ct.)

The facts are stated in the judgment.

KEANE J.: These proceedings were commenced on the 15th June, 1979, by a petition presented on behalf of Adolph Parge, a shareholder in the company. The petition claimed *inter alia*:

    (a) declarations that certain transactions relating to the issue and transfer of shares in the company to Omer Vanlandeghem were invalid;

    (b) an order requiring Omer Vanlandeghem to purchase the shares of the Petitioner in the company;

    (c) in the alternative to (b), an order for the winding-up of the Company under the Companies Act, 1963.

On the 23rd July, 1979, on a motion for directions, it was ordered that a number of issues be set down for plenary hearing with the Petitioner as the plaintiff and the company and Omer Vanlandeghem as the defendants. The trial of the [2] issues took place before me last term when oral evidence was adduced by both sides.

The order of 23rd July, 1979, directs the trial of eighteen issues, but the principal matters in controversy between the parties can be reduced to three, viz:

    (1) whether an issue of 10,000 ordinary shares of £1 each at par to Mr Vanlandeghem on the 5th February, 1975, was invalid,

    (2) whether the transfer of 8,000 ordinary shares of £1 each in the company held by Sean Boyle to Mr Vanlandeghem in March, 1978, was invalid,

    (3) whether the affairs of the company were conducted or the directors' powers exercised in a manner which was oppressive to the Petitioner or in disregard of his interests as a member.

The facts of the case, so far as they are not in controversy, are as follows. The company was incorporated on the 5th May, 1963, under the name of International Estate Agents Limited. The name of the company was changed to Greenore Trading Company Limited on the 3rd August, 1965. [3] The first shareholders and directors of the company were the Petitioner, who resided in Germany, and Mr Sean Boyle, who is an auctioneer. The capital of the company was originally £10,000 divided into 10,000 ordinary shares of £1 each. It was subsequently increased to £20,000 and then to £24,000. The company appears to have commenced life as essentially a property development enterprise, but in 1965 it embarked on what was to prove its main business, namely, the provision of a service at the port of Greenore for exporters of cattle through that port. With this object in view, the company took a lease from the owners of the port, Greenore Ferry Services Limited of a site in the port area on which there were already cattle pens and on which they proposed to erect further cattle pens.

In August, 1965, i.e. very shortly after the company had commenced its new business, Mr Vanlandeghem became a customer of the company. He is a substantial livestock exporter and farmer and his becoming a customer of the company was and is acknowledged by all concerned to have been a significant asset to the company. Shortly after he [4] became a customer, the suggestion was broached that he might acquire a financial interest in the business itself and, as a result, in January 1966 he became a director and shareholder. At that stage the capital of the company was increased to £24,000 consisting of 24,000 ordinary shares of £1 each, which were owned equally by the Petitioner, Mr Boyle, and Mr Vanlandeghem. The Petitioner was the chairman of the company and both Mr Boyle and Mr Vanlandeghem were directors. Mr Boyle was the manager of the company and responsible for its day to day operations. On the 14th January, 1966, a resolution was passed at an extraordinary general meeting of the company which precluded any one shareholder from holding more than 8,000 ordinary shares in his name or in the name of his nominee. This resolution is important in the light of later events.

The company's operations proved relatively successful, at least until the year 1973. Mr Vanlandeghem took the view that, as the company's major customer, he should be given preferential treatment so far as rates for the shipment of his cattle were concerned. At a meeting of the directors [5] on the 1st December, 1966, it was resolved that he should be given such preferential treatment for a specific time; and a further resolution to the same effect was passed on the 28th May, 1972, but subsequently rescinded on the 21st September, 1972.

While the Petitioner visited Ireland at fairly regular intervals, he was obviously not as actively involved in the company as time went by as Mr Boyle and Mr Vanlandeghem. Differences between the two latter gentlemen began to occur with growing frequency and ultimately in the years 1973 and 1974 Mr Vanlandeghem withdrew his custom from the port entirely, although he remained, of course, a shareholder and director of the company. The company's fortunes had already begun to decline due to the fact that they were not in a position to comply with the regulations which became effective so far as the export of cattle were concerned upon Ireland's accession to the European Economic Community. Mr Vanlandeghem's withdrawal of his custom was a major additional blow and by the year 1975 the company was in serious financial difficulties. An extraordinary general meeting was held on [6] the 20th January, 1975, at which the Petitioner, Mr Boyle and Mr Vanlandeghem were all present. At that meeting the Petitioner and Mr Boyle both made it clear that they were unable to come to the rescue of the company financially. Mr Vanlandeghem enquired whether his co-directors would be willing to transfer their shares to him. The Petitioner said that he could not do so, since his shares were pledged to a bank in Germany. Mr Boyle said that he was unwilling to transfer his shares to Mr Vanlandeghem. Mr Vanlandeghem said that he was prepared to come to the assistance of the company, but on condition that he became a holder of the majority of the ordinary shares. As this was not possible, the suggestion was then made that Mr Vanlandeghem might take a debenture to secure the sum of £60,000 and undertake to discharge the present liabilities of the company. (The liabilities at that date were estimated to amount to £10,000 but it was anticipated that further monies might be required from time to time to keep the company in business). This appeared to be acceptable to all concerned. At this meeting the Petitioner resigned as a director and Mr [7] Vanlandeghem was appointed managing director. The meeting was then adjourned in order to enable the debenture to be prepared and executed. The meeting was resumed on the 5th February, 1975, but on this occasion the Petitioner was not present, Mr John Kieran, solicitor, attending the meeting on his behalf under a power of attorney which had been executed by the Petitioner in 1970. The company having been advised that their interests would be better protected if Mr Vanlandeghem's advance was secured by an allocation of shares to him rather than by the execution of a debenture, 10,000 ordinary shares of £1 each were purportedly allotted to him at the adjourned meeting, and Mr Vanlandeghem paid a cheque for £10,000 to the company.

In the years which followed, the company's trading position improved until the year 1978. In that year its fortunes went into decline again and it ceased trading entirely in August, 1978. A major factor which contributed to this decline in the company's fortunes was the existence of disagreements between the company and its lessors which, at one stage, led to litigation.

[8] In 1978, Mr Boyle indicated to Mr Vanlandeghem that he would be willing to leave the company and sell his shares to Mr Vanlandeghem provided he got an acceptable sum. An agreement was reached under which Mr Boyle transferred his shares to Mr Vanlandeghem and was paid a total sum of £22,500. This was paid by two cheques, one for £8,000 drawn on Mr Vanlandeghem's account and one for £14,500 drawn on the company's account. The explanation given for payment being made in this fashion was that the £14,500 did not form any part of the consideration for the shares, but was in the nature of a severance payment to Mr Boyle on his leaving the company. The Petitioner was not notified of this latter transaction and on learning of it instructed solicitors to protest to the company and Mr Vanlandeghem. Solicitors on his behalf wrote to the company and Mr Vanlandeghem complaining both about this transaction and the manner in which it was alleged the affairs of the company had been conducted by Mr Vanlandeghem in a manner oppressive to the Petitioner for a number of years. No reply having been received to these complaints, the present proceedings [9] were then instituted. As I have already noted, the company ceased trading in August, 1978, and Mr Vanlandeghem wished to use his shareholding in the company for the purpose

of putting it into voluntary liquidation. Following an application to the Court, however, Mr Vanlandeghem gave an undertaking that no step would be taken or resolution passed to put the company into liquidation pending the determination by the Court of these proceedings.

I shall consider first the general complaint that the affairs of the company have been conducted and his powers as a director exercised by Mr Vanlandeghem in a manner which is oppressive to the Petitioner and in disregard of his interests as a member of the company. (It was further submitted that the transaction involving the purchase of Mr Boyle's shares also constituted such conduct.) The general complaint is essentially based on two allegations: first, that Mr Vanlandeghem abused his position as a director and shareholder to obtain preferential treatment for himself as a customer of the company and, secondly, that he induced other customers of the company not to trade with it in order [10] to obtain for himself the exclusive benefit of the company's services. So far as the first allegation is concerned, it is common case that for a limited period at least, Mr Vanlandeghem was, in fact, afforded preferential treatment so far as the rates of payment were concerned in respect of cattle exported by him through the port, but that this was with the express approval of his fellow directors and shareholders. It is also not in dispute that Mr Vanlandeghem's custom was of very great importance to the company: it might not, indeed, be overstating the position to say that it was of paramount importance, to such an extent that, when he withdrew his custom in the years 1973 and 1974, the company did virtually no business.

It would not be surprising to find preferential treatment being accorded to such a customer; and I very much doubt whether Mr Vanlandeghem in seeking it could be said to be acting oppressively towards his fellow shareholders. It was claimed that in the post-1975 period, he was charged an all-in figure per head in respect of cattle shipped by him through the port, in contrast to his competitors who [11] had to pay extra sums in respect of weighing, lairage, etc. I do no think that the evidence went so far as to establish that the company to any significant extent afforded Mr Vanlandeghem preferential treatment because of pressure brought to bear on them by him. If he was afforded such preferential treatment – and it is not in dispute that at one stage it was given to him with the full accord of his fellow shareholders and directors – it was simply the consequence of his dominant position as a customer and as such did not, in any way, reflect oppressive treatment by him of the Petitioner or any disregard of his interests.

It was also alleged that Mr Vanlandeghem systematically discouraged other exporters of cattle from using the port of Greenore with a view to securing a virtual monopoly of the cattle trade out of the port. Doubtless if it could be established in evidence that Mr Vanlandeghem acted in a manner which was so patently detrimental to the company's interests, this would constitute the sort of conduct envisaged by s. 205. The evidence in support of this allegation was principally that of Mr Boyle; and it was strenuously disputed [12] by Mr Vanlandeghem. I think that the significant feature of this conflict of evidence was that no attempt was made on behalf of the Petitioner to call any of the persons who were alleged to have been actively discouraged by Mr Vanlandeghem from exporting their cattle through Greenore. In my opinion, the Petitioner failed to discharge the onus of proof resting on him so far as this allegation was concerned.

The two transactions concerning the share capital of the company which were challenged must next be considered. So far as the issue of 10,000 additional shares to Mr Vanlandeghem at the meeting of the 5th February, 1975, is concerned, it was submitted on behalf of the Petitioner that it was invalid for the following reasons:

(1) although the allotment involved an increase in the capital of the company, no notice was given of any intention to propose a special resolution to that effect, nor was any such resolution passed;

(2) the resolution of 14th January, 1966, to the effect that the shareholding of individual members should not [13] be increased beyond £8,000 was not rescinded;

(3) although the meeting of 5th February, 1975, was an extraordinary general meeting of the company and not a meeting of directors, it purported to allot the shares to Mr Vanlandeghem, whereas this should have been done at a meeting of directors alone.

I think that it is clear that each of these grounds of objection is well founded. It is also the case, however, that the issue of shares was made to Mr Vanlandeghem in order to give him some security in respect of the £10,000 which he was prepared to advance to the company in order to get it out of its serious financial problems. The money was made available by him when it became obvious that neither the Petitioner nor Mr Boyle could nor would come to the rescue of the company. The Petitioner was present at the commencement of the meeting on the 20th January, 1975, and was represented at the adjourned meeting on 5th February, 1975, by his solicitor, Mr John Kieran, acting under a power of attorney. It was not seriously disputed that had Mr Vanlandeghem not been willing to advance the sum of £10,000 [14] the company would have been in very serious financial trouble and might well have gone to the wall. The Petitioner and Mr Boyle were obviously perfectly happy that Mr Vanlandeghem should come to the company's assistance and were willing that he should be secured by the issue of the debenture. It was only when the company's solicitors advised that it would be more in the interests of the company for Mr Vanlandeghem to be allotted the 10,000 shares that this course was adopted. It was not questioned by the Petitioner until long afterwards. While the procedure adopted was technically not in conformity with the Companies Act 1963 and the terms of the earlier resolution, the Petitioner, although not present at the meeting when the shares were allotted by his conduct clearly indicated that he was satisfied that the additional shares should be allotted to Mr Vanlandeghem, provided he came to the aid of the company financially. This Mr Vanlandeghem did: but if the contention advanced on behalf of the Petitioner is well founded it means that, should the company go into liquidation, Mr Vanlandeghem will have to prove for his £10,000 as an ordinary creditor and will be without any [15] security whatsoever. This would be the result of his having foregone the debenture, which would have made him a secured creditor, and which was abandoned simply because the company's solicitor advised that it was against the company's interest. The company, and the Petitioner, will accordingly have had the benefit of Mr Vanlandeghem's £10,000 while he will be deprived of all security in relation to it, although he had acted in the reasonable belief, which his fellow shareholders did nothing to dispel, that the transaction was not merely fully acceptable to them, but the only means available of saving the company.

It would seem to me entirely contrary to justice and to be singularly unfair and unreasonable that, in these circumstances, the Petitioner could successfully assert that the issue of shares was invalid. I think, however, that in these circumstances the doctrine of estoppel in pais is applicable: because where a person has so conducted himself that another would, as a reasonable man, understand that a certain representation of fact is intended to be acted on, and the other has acted on the representation and thereby [16] altered his position to his prejudice, an estoppel arises against the party who made the representation, and he is not allowed to aver that the fact is otherwise than he represented it to be. This principle of law, which is to be found summarised in Halsbury's *Laws of England*, Fourth Edition, Volume 16, paragraph 1505, is fully applicable, in my view, to the resolution of January 14th 1966. The Petitioner, by his conduct, having led Mr Vanlandeghem to believe that he was treating that resolution as of no effect, and thereby induced him to alter his position to his prejudice, cannot now aver that the resolution is binding on the company. Similarly, he cannot now aver that the necessary notice was not given of an intention to pass a special resolution or that no such special resolution was passed; nor can he aver that the meeting was a meeting of shareholders only and not of directors. It is, of course, clear that a party cannot set up an estoppel in the face of a statute; but that principle does not seem to me to be directly applicable [17] to a case such as the present, where the transaction in issue was not prohibited by law and its recognition or enforcement by the court would violate no principle of public policy or social policy. (See *Re Stapleford Colliery Company, Barrow's Case*, 14 Ch. D. 432 at 441, *Bradshaw* v. *McMullan* [1920] 2 I.R.47, 412, 490, and *Kok Hoong* v. *Leong Cheong Kweng Mines Ltd.* [1964] A.C. 993). In this case the Petitioner is clearly estopped, in my opinion, from asserting the irregularity of a transaction which he tacitly approved of when it was being implemented, which does not offend against any principle of law and which was entirely for the benefit of the company and indeed its creditors.

Different considerations entirely apply to the transfer of Mr Boyle's shares to Mr Vanlandeghem. It is immaterial whether the real price paid for the shares was £22,500 or whether the sum of £14,500 represented compensation to Mr Boyle for his quitting the company, as the respondents claim. If it was compensation of this nature, then the transaction was clearly unlawful having regard to the provisions of section 186 of the Companies Act 1963, since the proposed [18] payment was not disclosed to the other member of the company (the Petitioner) nor was it approved by the company in general meeting. Indeed, the illegality of the transaction, if this was its nature, was compounded by the fact that the sum paid in respect of compensation was not specified in the company's accounts, as required by s. 191 of the Act. If, on the other hand, the sum of £14,500 did represent part of the consideration for the shares, the transaction was also unlawful, since it was in violation of s. 60 of the Act, which prohibits a company from giving financial assistance for the purchase of its shares. On any view, accordingly, this transaction was not merely irregular, but grossly irregular.

I am satisfied that this latter transaction constituted conduct of such a nature as to justify, and indeed require, the making of an order under s. 205 (3) of the Act. Prior to that transaction, Mr Vanlandeghem, as a result of the issue of 10,000 shares to him in 1975, was the holder of just over 50% of the issued share capital. Had the transfer of shares by Mr Boyle to him gone unchallenged, he would have become [19] the owner of more than 75% of the company share capital. 'Oppressive' conduct for the purposes of the corresponding s. 210 of the English Companies Act 1948 has been defined as meaning the exercise of the company's authority 'in a manner burdensome, harsh and wrongful.' (See *Scottish C.W.S. Ltd.* v. *Meyer* [1959] A.C. 324 at p. 342 (ante p. 301)). The patent misapplication of the company's monies for the purpose of giving Mr Vanlandeghem a dominant position in its affairs seems to me to be properly described as 'burdensome, harsh and wrongful' *quoad* the Petitioner. It cannot be equated to the allotment of shares in *Re Jermyn Street Turkish Baths Ltd.* [1971] 3 A.E.R. 184, which was treated by the Court of Appeal as being one entered into in good faith for the benefit of the company. Nor can the actual misapplication of the funds be properly treated as an isolated act of oppression (which would not normally be sufficient to justify relief under the section: see *Re Westbourne Galleries Ltd.* [1970] 3 A.E.R. 374 at p. 385). As I have already noted, not merely were the company's monies purportedly applied towards an unlawful purpose, i.e. the payment of compensation [20] to a director for loss of office without the sanction of a general meeting: the payment of that compensation was not separately dealt with in the company's accounts for the relevant year, as required by law.

It is true that the wording of the section envisages that the oppression complained of is operative at the time when the petition is launched. (See *Re Jermyn Street Turkish Baths Ltd.* at p. 198). In this case the transfer of shares took place in March, 1978. The accounts for the year were certified by the company's auditors on the 9th June, 1978. The petition was presented just over a year later on the 15th June, 1979, after protests had been made in correspondence on behalf of the Petitioner at the manner in which the company's affairs were being conducted. The company had not merely failed to take any steps to deal with these gross irregularities in its affairs prior to the issuing of the petition; it had also wholly ignored letters written on behalf of the Petitioner which clearly called for an answer. It seems to me that in these circumstances the oppressive conduct can properly be regarded as having [21] continued up to the date of the issuing of the petition.

It is obvious that the present circumstances would justify an order being made for the winding up of the company under s. 213 (f) and (g). It is agreed, however, that such an order, in the present circumstances, would not be in the interests of the members; and, accordingly, the remedy for the oppressive conduct must be the alternative remedy provided by s. 205. I think that the only effective method of bringing to an end the oppressive conduct of which the Petitioner complains is an order for the purchase of his shares by Mr Vanlandeghem.

The shares, accordingly, must be purchased by Mr Vanlandeghem at a fair price; and it remains to consider what that price should be, in all the circumstances of the case. Having regard to the findings I have made, it is clear that the Petitioner's shareholding must be valued on the assumption that the purported purchase of Mr Boyle's shares had not taken place. This would leave the Petitioner owning 8,000 shares, Mr Vanlandeghem 18,000 shares and Mr Boyle 8,000 shares. I doubt very much whether a shareholder [22] already in control of more than 50% of the share capital would, in the particular circumstances of this company, have paid more than their par value to acquire the shareholding of the Petitioner. I do not think that the fact that Mr Boyle may have got £22,500 for his shareholding is of much assistance in determining the value of the Petitioner's shareholding. In the first place, the purchaser was not willing to pay more than £8,000 for the shares from his own resources. In the second place, Mr Boyle was more conspicuously involved in the company's affairs – usually in contest with Mr Vanlandeghem – and, accordingly, had more of a nuisance value from the point of view of Mr Vanlandeghem than the Petitioner. In the third place, there remains the possibility that some, at least, of the consideration was genuinely, if illegally, related to compensation for the loss of office rather than the purchase price of the shares themselves. Having regard to the uncertain financial future of the company I doubt very much whether, from the point of view of the majority shareholder, it would have been worth paying more than £8,000 for the Petitioner's shareholding; [23] nor do I think that somebody buying an interest in the company, who had not already any interest in it, would have been willing to pay more than that sum.

That, however, does not conclude the matter, since it is clear that, in prescribing the basis on which the price is to be calculated, the Court can, in effect, provide compensation for whatever injury has been inflicted by the oppressors. (See *Scottish Co-operative Wholesale Society* v. *Meyer* (ante p. 301). The accounts in the present case show that the company had been pursuing a conservative policy in relation to the payment of dividends in the years immediately preceding the wrongful purchase of Mr Boyle's shares; and this policy may well have been justified by the company's uncertain trading future. There seems to me, however, no reason why the Petitioner should be deprived of the share to which he would have been entitled of the £14,500 wrongfully applied in the transaction regarding Mr Boyle's shares. It is immaterial whether that sum comes back to the company following these or other proceedings and is ultimately paid out by way of dividend or as a return on capital to the contributories, since the Petitioner will derive no [24] benefit from that once his shares have been purchased by Mr Vanlandeghem. It follows that he is entitled, in my view, to be paid a sum bearing the same proportion to that sum of £14,500 as his share-holding of £8,000 did to the total issued share capital of £34,000 prior to the unlawful transaction in relation to Mr Boyle's shares; and I will order that sum to be paid, in addition to the sum of £8,000 representing the par value of his shares.

In re Murph's Restaurants Ltd. (No.2)
(Gannon J., July 31, 1979, H.Ct.)

The facts are stated in the judgment.

GANNON J.: Murph's Restaurants Ltd. is a private company which was incorporated on the 17th January, 1972 with a share capaital of 3,000 ordinary shares of £1 each of which 2,400 are fully paid up. There are only three shareholders namely Brian Suiter, Kevin O'Driscoll and G. Murph O'Driscoll who are also directors of the company. The present value of the assets of the company is estimated by the company's accountant to be little short of £190,000. Brian Suiter has petitioned the Court pursuant to section 213 of the Companies Act, 1963 to order that the company be wound up on the grounds that the affairs of the company are being conducted and the powers of the directors being exercised in a manner which is oppressive to him and in disregard of his interests and also that it is just and equitable so to order. The company on the hearing of this petition is requested by the other two shareholders/directors Kevin and

Murph O'Driscoll, who on their part claim that the petitioner had been removed from the position of director for good reason and that it would be neither in the interests of [2] the company nor just nor equitable to wind up the company. Each of the three shareholders/directors, to whom I shall refer hereafter as Brian, Kevin and Murph, and the company's accountant gave evidence on the hearing of the petition which was amended by consent to include a claim by Brian, the petitioner, for alternative relief under section 205 of the 1963 Act.

Prior to the formation of the company Brian worked as a computer salesman in IBM Ltd. in which Kevin also was employed and they were close friends. They discussed the idea of setting up as a joint venture a snack bar business and engaging Kevin's brother Murph, who was then not in any employment, to manage the business. After three or four months discussion this company was incorporated following agreement that Brian and Kevin would advance £800 each as capital and that each would advance a further £400 on behalf of Murph so that all three would be equal partners. It was agreed that Murph would not be required to refund these two advances made on his behalf but would give equivalent value in his whole time attention to the business while Kevin and Brian remained in their salaried employments. Within three years Kevin also became whole-time engaged in the work of the company, but Brian retained his employment having moved from IBM Ltd. to Honeywell Ltd. [3] and then to Memory Ireland Ltd. with whom he was general manager at a salary of about £10,000 per annum from 1976 until he too became whole-time engaged in the company in June, 1977. Up to that time neither Kevin nor Murph was in receipt of an annual income as high as that which Brian was receiving in his employment.

The business of the company had commenced as a sandwich bar at 99 Lower Baggot Street, Dublin and next a delicatessen and cold foods shop was opened in Suffolk Street, Dublin. The company opened a hot food restaurant with wine licence at Bachelor's Walk, Dublin and later engaged in contract catering before opening a restaurant in Cork in October, 1977. In 1978 premises were acquired adjoining the Baggot Street premises and the range of catering there extended. Although the registered office of the company is at Lower Baggot Street the offices used by the directors as head office are at Bachelor's Walk. At each of the branches of the business the company employs either a manager or manageress and other necessary staff.

The business of the company of its nature involved long working hours, and in the earlier years, while expanding, the returns from the business provided Murph and later Kevin with a reasonable annual income [4] but little profit. In 1976 after the Bachelor's Walk branch of the business was established the company became profitable. By 1977 all aspects of the business were going well and the company became significantly profitable.

The company did not hold annual meetings nor have annual accounts prepared nor were there regular or formal board meeting of directors nor minutes nor other formal company records kept. Brian, Kevin and Murph met every Monday night for management meetings and had their meals in the company premises and met regularly over lunch and the affairs of the company were conducted and the decisions taken at the Monday night meetings and the informal meetings. No dividends were paid on shares nor fees paid to directors and salaries were paid by regular drawings against estimated annual amounts finally determined at the end of the year. In addition to these, however, each of the three of them could and did take from cash at the Baggot Street premises sums up to £200 per month in respect of which no record was kept. This was described in evidence by one of the witnesses as 'slush money'. Regular sums of money were taken out of cash of the business and paid into building society accounts in the names or variations of the names of one or other of the three in different branches of building societies but these did not appear in the company's accounts. [5] Special care was taken to ensure that the salaries, cash receipts and the value of perquisites including the use of cars were equated so as to ensure that at all times equality was maintained as between the three of them. The services of qualified accountants, Messrs. Kidney & Co., were first engaged in March, 1977 but the accountants were not aware of the cash drawings or building society deposits.

The decision to open a branch of the business in Cork was taken early in 1977. According to Murph his brother Kevin tried to persuade Brian to give up his employment and to come into the company business whole-time. This Brian agreed to do in June, 1977 on the basis that he would look after the Cork business and would have the same salary and drawings as each of the other two. Brian said his sole job 'was to ensure that Cork got off the ground properly' and the Cork branch opened on the 12th October, 1977. According to Murph the Cork business exceeded expectations, and within 18 months the business there was almost as good as at Bachelor's Walk which they considered the best of the branches. The accountant said it would be difficult to say which of the two, Cork or Bachelor's Walk, is the more profitable. In or about November, 1977 the three directors contemplated investing company money in property development and through Messrs. Lisneys made two bids which were not accepted for the purchase of a former hotel known as Strawberry Hill on [6] Vico Road, Dalkey. 1978 was a most significant year. In March of that year Kevin and Murph without telling Brian made a very much higher bid for Strawberry Hill than did the company the previous November and after negotiations in April and May purchased this property for themselves about the end of May. In connection with this property and its development by conversion and reconstruction into three separate dwellings they borrowed about £190,000. One of the dwellings is occupied by the parents of Kevin and Murph, another is occupied by Murph and his wife, and the third is intended for Kevin or for resale. In connection with this development both Kevin and Murph gave a lot of time which otherwise would have been devoted to the business of the company. During the summer of 1978 an expansion of the business at 99 Lower Baggot Street under the direction of an architect was undertaken by the company which by reason of restricted working area and hours rendered the work more difficult for the contractor and more expensive for the company than had been anticipated. In the autumn of that year Brian purchased a house in Cork and in connection with it devoted time which otherwise would have been given to the business of the company. When Kevin and Murph purchased Strawberry Hill and informed Brian of their purchase it was agreed that a record of time taken away from the company business on that [7] account should be recorded so that Brian should be allowed the equivalent time off at a future date if the occasion arose. It was later agreed that the purchase by Brian of a house in Cork gave rise to such an occasion. On the 6th August, 1978 Kevin drew and signed a cheque payable to himself for the sum of £15,681.02. This cheque was drawn on the company's bank account in Cork. On the 28th September Kevin signed another cheque drawn on the company's Cork bank account payable to himself for the sum of £9,318.98. These two sums together make up a sum of £25,000 which is an amount Kevin and Murph say Brian agreed could be borrowed by them from the company in the financing of the Strawberry Hill project. They did not tell Brian anything about the cheques at the times they were drawn nor did the cheques show for what purpose they were drawn and no explanation was given for the determination of the amount for which each or either cheque was drawn. Brian says he agreed they could borrow £10,000 from the company and pay to him the amount of interest thereon at the rate of one-third of the rate they would have had to pay to a finance company. Kevin and Murph say that Brian proposed this idea to them to reduce their liability for interest and agreed that the amount should be £25,000 at a rate of 15% for interest and Brian would be paid 5% on that. Kevin and Murph at Christmas 1978 took a three and half week holiday in [8] Florida which extended into January 1979

According to Murph's evidence he and Kevin had arrived at a decision on the 2nd February, 1979 that they did not want Brian working in the company, and on Saturday afternoon, 3rd February, 1979, they handed him notices to this effect. These comprised a letter on company notepaper signed by Murph as secretary in the following terms.

Mr. Brian E. Suiter,
East Wing,
Holyrood Castle,
Dublin 4.   3rd February, 1979.

Dear Sir,

I send you herewith a copy of a Notice which has been received by
Murph's Restaurants Limited of a resolution which, as appears from
the said Notice, is intended to be moved at the General Meeting of
the Company convened for the 12th day of March 1979.

Your attention is drawn to the provisions of Section 182 of the
Companies Act, 1963.

I also enclose Formal Notice of the calling of the meeting referred
to above.

Yours faithfully,

Secretary

[9] The enclosure referred to therein was also on company notepaper
signed by Murph as secretary and reads as follows:

The Secretary,
Murph's Restaurants Limited,
21 Bachelors Walk,
Dublin 1.

Dear Sir,

TAKE NOTICE that we, the undersigned, being shareholders in the
company, intend at the next General Meeting of Murph's Restaurants
Limited to move a resolution that Mr. Brian E. Suiter a director of
the said company be removed from his office of director.

Dated the 2nd day of February 1979.

G. Murph O'Driscoll
Kevin O'Driscoll

No meeting was held on the 12th March, 1979 nor had there been a
meeting of the board or of the directors/shareholders convened or held
on or prior to the 3rd February, 1979 at which a decision was taken either
to hold a meeting on the 12th March, 1979 or to propose a resolution as
stated. In the course of his evidence Murph said 'I am told I am the
secretary of the company. [10] This is a recent development. We did not
keep minutes'. He described this meeting of the 3rd February when the
notices were handed to Brian as being 'pretty much a non-meeting'. He
said 'we handed Brian the legal documents. He studied them and asked
why. We said we had been through all the specifics. The basic reason is
you are not performing your job satisfactorily. I can't remember what he

said. There were long periods of silence.' The same occasion was described
by Kevin in his evidence as follows: 'on Saturday afternoon we handed
Brian the legal documents giving notice of an extraordinary general meeting
and resolution for his removal. He asked what was it all about. We said
he should know. We are not going to go into detail. His questions were
why? what is it about? Our responses were you should know. You have
been told before. We are not going over it again. We offered to purchase
his shares at a valuation and to pay his salary for the next three months. I
don't remember if he said anything. We said we are relieving you of responsibility as a working director and want you to clear out your desk. He said
"I will do it on Monday." We have a policy never to let anybody work out
their notice. Effectively he was given notice and his coming in on Monday
caused chaos.' The evidence given by Brian was that he had got a phone
call to say they [11] wanted to have a meeting urgently on Saturday, the
3rd February 'and when we met I was handed these notices. There hadn't
been anything about this at any previous meeting. It came as a shock. I
got no explanation and was advised to see a solicitor.' He denied that there
was any mention of 'unsatisfactory performance'. He said that 'at the end
I said "do you want me to resign?" with a smile on my face as it hadn't
reached that stage.' In his evidence Murph referred to this and said it was
not at this February meeting but at a meeting the previous March, 1978
when Brian asked 'do you want me to resign' and it was said in seriousness
and that he and Kevin in reply said 'no we would rather see you improve
in the work you are doing'. Having regard to the course of the affairs
throughout 1978 involving many undertakings and continued dealings
between the three which necessarily involved mutual confidence and trust
I do not believe Murph is correct and I accept Brian's evidence in relation
to this meeting of 3rd February, 1979.

From seeing Kevin and Murph in the witness box and observing the
way in which they gave their evidence I have no confidence in the reliability
of their evidence. I have a strong feeling they were withholding or avoiding
evidence on material matters, but I make no attempt to take into account
or speculate upon what they omitted. The particular area in which this is
most [12] significant and most obvious is on all references to financial
matters including the earnings and expenses of the company and their
own incomes, expenses and financial arrangements.

I have no doubt that prior to the 3rd February, 1979 Kevin and Murph
had decided that they should, were entitled to, and would, dismiss Brian
from the employment of the company and that in respect of his salary and
term of notice he was in the position of an employee of the company whose
services could be dispensed with peremptorily but legally by giving him
three months salary in lieu of notice. I draw no inference from the forms
of the documents presented to Brian and the statements made to him as
he gave in evidence (which I believe) as to whether or not Kevin and

Murph had gone to the trouble of taking legal advice on this matter. It is clear from the evidence that from the 3rd February, 1979 the previous relationship essential to the continued association between Brian on the one part and Kevin and Murph on the other had effectively come to an end. Subsequent events have made this position irretrievable.

The cause for this is attributed by Brian to an agreement on the part of Kevin and Murph to takeover Brian's interests and to exclude him completely from the company at a time when the company and Kevin and Murph had achieved [13] considerable prosperity and great prospects for further success. The cause for this is attributed by Kevin and Murph to matters of complaint of which they gave the following evidence. Brian had been put in charge of the Cork branch which opened on the 12th October, 1977 and Kevin and Murph used to pay visits together to the Cork branch from time to time to get their own view of things there. By January, 1978 they began to realise that the sort of problems which arose, as expected after opening the new branch, were continuing and were not being resolved, such as, quality of food, purchasing of stock, hygiene, and financial control. The policy and standards achieved in the Dublin branches were not being observed. These different matters used to be mentioned at the regular meetings in Dublin after their periodic trips.

There were three meetings held at which Kevin and Murph raised with Brian matters of complaint. Apart from the latest of these held on the 3rd February, 1979 previous to which Kevin and Murph had agreed they wanted Brian out, as Murph put it, they held meetings in March, 1978 and November, 1978. They said they complained to Brian at the March meeting that the quality of food in Cork 'was disastrous; that he should not have left the purchase of food and cutlery to be done by the Manager; that there was no proper control of cash and the paper work from Cork was unsatisfactory.' They [14] say they told him he showed marked lack of responsibility or of co-operation and that he had deceived them. As to the former the only example given was that when they would phone the Cork branch from Dublin at lunch time Brian would not be there and he would not phone back until after 4 p.m. As to the alleged deception they gave two instances. One was that he gave a false explanation of being unable to get a flight to London as his reason for not coming over there for a meeting with them when called there by them. The other was that when asked to get an estimate for work to be done at the Cork branch he said he had had a meeting with a builder named Weldon and this was found to be untrue. In relation to the meeing in November, 1978 they said they were getting pretty fed-up with things in Cork where a third manager was then starting, the first having left voluntarily and the services of the second having been dispensed with. These managers were engaged by Kevin and Brian, and presumably the third was engaged at or shortly after the time the second was dismissed. Many of the matters of complaint deposed to in the affidavit of Kevin were not substantiated in oral evidence.

Brian's evidence about these matters was that at the various meetings it was normal and usual that they used to criticise each other roundly and matters of supposed complaint would be accepted and explained. He felt that [15] Kevin and Murph used to come down to the Cork branch together and go through it 'with a fine comb' and consequently faults were always to be found. He said he was always accessible when required and that the figures for the Cork branch showed that the performance was satisfactory.

On this last aspect it is significant that in relation to the purchase by Kevin and Murph of Stawberry Hill for which £25,000 was borrowed from the Cork branch Kevin said in his evidence that at that time 'the Cork account was running at a surplus to that extent' and 'these monies were available as profits and not required for running Cork'. Contrary to what Kevin swore in his affidavit both Kevin and Murph gave evidence that when they decided to buy Strawberry Hill for themselves and negotiated the purchase they did not tell Brian. This was in the period March/April, 1978, but they did tell him after they had made the contract. When they did so they discussed with him the arrangements about keeping records of their time away from the company and devoted to work at Strawberry Hill and the arrangements about making a borrowing from the company so as to save two-thirds of finance company rates of interest on loans.

It is quite clear from the evidence as a whole and from practically every aspect of evidence relating to the different events and the conduct of [16] affairs of the company that Brian, Kevin and Murph were equal partners in a joint venture, and that the company was no more than a vehicle to secure a limited liability for possible losses and to provide a means of earning and distributing profits to their best advantage with minimum disclosure. The company was never conducted in accordance with statutory requirements nor in accordance with normal regular business methods. The directors received no fees, the shareholders received no dividends, and all three directors/shareholders received by mutual agreement exactly the same income from the earnings of the company adjusted according to profitability in the form of drawings recorded as salary, drawings from cash unrecorded, credit deposits of cash in building societies' accounts, perquisites of meals and cars, and various expenses for purely personal purposes in respect of all of which strict equality was always maintained. This was achieved, and could be achieved, only by a relationship of mutual confidence and trust and active open participation in the management and conduct of the affairs of the company particularly in the irregularity or informality of its corporate quality of existence. The co-operation of the brothers, Kevin and Murph, in a close personally related venture such as this is understandable, particularly as Murph who had been unemployed was thereby provided with employment and a career for which he has proved himself eminently suited. But the participation [17] of Brian was achieved through his personal friendship with Kevin acquired while working in employment very different from this class of business and through the persuasion exercised by Kevin, Brian was persuaded to and did give up regular employment with what was then a very good annual salary and attendant security to take his chances in participation in a business for which he did not appear to have had any of the working skills associated with catering. So far as the company is concerned he appears to have no more than 800 shares of nominal value of £1 upon which no dividends are payable with no right to offer them to the public or to dispose of them save in accordance with the approval of one or both of the other two directors. It is said that he remains a director, but without fees, and is being and will be denied any active participation in the affairs of the company. He is being and has been treated by his two co-directors as if he was an employee of theirs liable to be and purported to have been dismissed by them peremptorily and not under any colour of regular exercise by directors of their powers under the articles of association of the company. The action of Kevin and Murph on the 3rd February, 1979 was entirely irregular, and no attempt has been made to make or confirm this action in regular manner on behalf of the company. The action of Kevin and Murph on the 3rd February was not and could not be accepted in law as an action of the company. The action of Kevin and Murph [18] on the 3rd February was a deliberate and calculated repudiation by both of them of that relationship of equality, mutuality, trust and confidence between the three of them which constituted the very essence of the existence of the company. The action of Kevin and Murph on the 3rd February, 1979 deprived Brian of a livelihood, and not simply of an investment, which he was induced by their representations to take and in so doing to abandon to his irretrievable loss a secure means of livelihood in a career for which, judging by his progress, he must have had some considerable aptitude. The justification offered by evidence for the action of Kevin and Murph on the 3rd February was their dissatisfaction with his performance of duties allotted to him by them which they described as of a working director. But the evidence shows that the matters of exemplification are all within the normal range of duties of a manager, and related to a branch of the business from which two successive managers were replaced during the period to which their complaints related. Their own evidence also shows that during the same period the business of that branch had shown profitability beyond their expectations, and sufficed in a period of less than 12 months to provide a surplus income large enough to afford them a significant amount of capital on loan for a private investment. Whatever cause of complaint or fault Kevin [19] and Murph may have found in Brian it did not relate to the talents or qualifications which he had shown, and must have been known to them to have had, at the time he was induced to join with them in a venture of strictly drawn equality.

In his petition Brian asks that the company be wound up under paragraphs (f) and (g) of section 213 of the Companies Act, 1963. In reply Kevin and Murph on behalf of the company submit that Brian has been deprived of his directorship for good reason and as a shareholder can be afforded sufficient relief under section 205 of the Act by allowing them to purchase his shares at a valuation. It is also submitted that it would not be in the best interests of the company to have it wound up because in the course of compulsorily winding up the assets of the company would not meet the liabilities and Brian could gain nothing from it, and because his interest as a shareholder has not been affected he is not entitled to an order under section 213. As to the matter of his removal from directorship I am satisfied from the evidence that the reasons advanced are neither good nor sufficient and are wholly inadequate to justify that action. But the evidence further discloses that the purported removal was irregular and ineffective in law. Furthermore it is clear from the evidence that in the conduct of the affairs of the company the directors did not exercise their [20] powers in a regular manner so far as the company is concerned, and the purported exclusion of Brian by Kevin and Murph in an irregular and arrogant manner is undoubtedly oppressive. As to the matter of what would be the best interests of the company and the consequences of an order for winding up evidence was given on behalf of the company by Mr. Kidney who is the accountant for the company. He was first engaged by the company about March, 1977. On instructions he prepared a draft balance sheet for the company as of the 3rd February, 1979 from information obtained from the books of the company and given to him by Kevin and Murph. He estimated the assets (including the presumed repayment of the £25,000 loan) to be £189,672 and the liabilities to be £185,829. He expressed the opinion that in a winding up of the company under Court order the apparent net balance could not be achieved because all assets would not realise the estimated values and consequently there would be no surplus or dividend for shareholders. He had not included monies in building societies' accounts and he was not aware of the 'siphoning off of funds'. From my observation and assessment of the evidence of Kevin and of Murph I believe they would not be as truthful and forthcoming when instructing the accountant as the Court would require them to be in order to be in a position to place reliance on the opinion of the accountant founded on [21] their information to him.

It is clear from the evidence that there is no form of order of the nature indicated in section 205(3) which could bring to an end the matters complained of by Brian in the proceedings or which could regulate the affairs of the company for the future. It appears to me that the circumstances in which by order under section 205 the Court may direct the purchase of the shares of a member by other members or by the company are circumstances in which the Court would do so 'with a view to bringing to an end the matters complained of by the person applying to the Court. It is my opinion that in this case with the fundamental relationship between Brian, Kevin and Murph sundered that proceedings under section 205 would not in any circumstances be appropriate.

In the course of argument and submissions I was referred to the judgment of the House of Lords in England in *Re Westbourne Galleries Ltd.*, [1973] A.C. 360 in support of the claim of the petitioner Brian to have the company wound up on the grounds that such order would be just and equitable. It was relied upon also in answer to the contentions of the company, per Kevin and Murph, that Brian is not entitled to such an order on the grounds that there was no disregard of his interests [22] as a member, he had nothing to gain as a contributory, there was no lack of probity or unfair dealing on their part, that their conduct was based on their concern for the welfare of the company and to ensure the business would prosper, and that it would not be in the best interests of the company, its staff, customers or creditors that it be wound up.

The claim before the House of Lords was by one of three directors/shareholders of a limited company for an order to have the company wound up pursuant to section 222(f) of the English Companies Act, 1948, the wording of which corresponds exactly with section 213(f) of the Companies Act, 1963. I find the opinions delivered in the course of this judgment in the House of Lords very helpful because of the statements of principle the application of which depends upon the facts under consideration. I have accordingly set out first the facts in the case before me from which it can be seen where they may be distinguishable from those in the case to which the House of Lords judgment relates. But that judgment reminds us that the principles of equity which are applicable in every Court of law are the same and should be given application in the like manner in cases affecting the commercial relations of companies, in which rules of law tend to be technical and rigid, as much as in cases of personal relations between private individuals.

[23] Having regard to the contentions advanced on behalf of Kevin and Murph I think it appropriate to quote the following passage from the report of the speech of Lord Wilberforce in *Re Westbourne Galleries Ltd.*:

> For some 50 years, following a pronouncement by Lord Cottenham L.C. in *Ex parte Spackman* (1849) 1 Mac. and G. 170, 174 in 1849, the words 'just and equitable' were interpreted so as only to include matters *ejusdem generis* as the preceding clauses of the section, but there is now ample authority for discarding this limitation. There are two other restrictive interpretations which I mention to reject. First, there has been a tendency to create categories or headings under which cases must be brought if the clause is to apply. This is wrong.

Illustrations may be used, but general words should remain general and not be reduced to the sum of particular instances. Secondly, it has been suggested, and urged upon us, that (assuming the petitioner is a shareholder and not a creditor) the words must be confined to such circumstances as affect him in his capacity as shareholder. I see no warrant for this either. No doubt, in order to present a petition, he must qualify as a shareholder, but I see no reason for preventing him from relying upon any [24] circumstances of justice or equity which affect him in his relations with the company, or, in a case such as the present, with the other shareholders.

One other signpost is significant. The same words 'just and equitable' appear in the Partnership Act, 1892 section 25 as a ground for dissolution of a partnership and no doubt the considerations which they reflect formed part of the common law of partnership before its codification. The importance of this is to provide a bridge between cases under section 222(f) of the Act of 1948 and the principles of equity developed in relation to partnerships.

Before proceeding further with consideration of the speech of Lord Wilberforce it would be helpful to refer at this stage to what was said by Lord Cross of Chelsea in his speech:

> In some of the reported cases in which winding up orders have been made those who opposed the petition have been held by the Court to have been guilty of a 'lack of probity' in their dealings with the petitioners.

He then cites two examples and then goes on the say 'but it is not a condition precedent to the making of an order under the subsection that the conduct of [25] those who oppose its making should have been unjust or inequitable. This was made clear as early as 1905 by Lord M'Laren in his judgment in *Symington* v. *Symington's Quarries Ltd.* (8 F. 121. 130). To the same effect is the judgment of Lord Cozens-Hardy M.R. in *Re Yenidje Tobacco Co. Ltd.* [1916] 2 Ch. 426, 431-432. It is sometimes said that the order in that case was made on the ground of deadlock. That is not so.' Having explained why he takes that view he goes on to say:

> People do not become partners unless they have confidence in one another and it is of the essence of the relationship that mutual confidence is maintained. If neither has any longer confidence in the other so that they cannot work together in the way originally contemplated then the relationship should be ended – unless, indeed, the party who wishes to end it has been solely responsible for the situation which has arisen. The relationship between Mr Rothman and Mr Weinberg (the names of parties in the case under his then consideration) was

not, of course, in form that of partners; they were equal shareholders in a limited company. But the Court considered that it would be unduly fettered by matters of form if it did not deal with the situation it would have dealt with it had the parties been partners in form as well as in substance.

[26] Turning again to the speech of Lord Wilberforce I draw attention to the nature of the submissions made to the Court in that case as summarised in the speech of Lord Wilberforce and the manner in which he expressed his opinion on these matters following examination of a number of cases dealing with the partnership features of companies. At page 379 he then says:

> My Lords, in my opinion these authorities represent a sound and rational development of the law which should be endorsed. The foundation of it all lies in the words 'just and equitable' and if there is any respect in which some of the cases may be open to criticism, it is that the Courts may sometimes have been too timorous in giving them full force. The words are a recognition of the fact that a limited company is more than a mere legal entity, with a personaility in law of its own; that there is room in company law for recognition of the fact that behind it, or amongst it, there are individuals, with rights, expectations and obligations inter se submerged in the company structure. That structure is defined by the Companies Act and by the articles of association by which shareholders agree to be bound. In most companies and in most contexts, this definition is sufficient and [27] exhaustive, equally so whether the company is large or small. The 'just and equitable' provision does not, as the respondents suggest, entitle one party to disregard the obligation he assumes by entering a company, nor the Court to dispense him from it. It does, as equity always does, enable the Court to subject the exercise of legal rights to equitable considerations; considerations, that is, of a personal character arising between one individual and another, which may make it unjust or inequitable, to insist on legal rights, or to exercise them in a particular way.

Lord Wilberforce then gives examples of circumstances in which relations of a special personal character may be essential to the members of a company with particular reference to mutual confidence. At page 380 he goes on to say:

> My Lords, this is an expulsion case, and I must briefly justify the application in such cases of the just and equitable clause. The question is, as always, whether it is equitable to allow one (or two) to make use of his legal rights to the prejudice of his associate(s). The law of

companies recognises the right, in many ways, to remove a director
from the board. Section 184 of the Companies Act, 1948 confers this
right upon the [28] company in general meeting whatever the articles
may say. Some articles may prescribe other methods; for example, a
governing director may have the power to remove (compare in *Re
Wondoflex Textiles Pty. Ltd.* [1951] V.L.R. 458). And quite apart from
removal powers, there are normally provisions for retirement of
directors by rotation so that their re-election can be opposed and
defeated by a majority, or even by a casting vote. In all these ways a
particular director/member may find himself no longer a director,
through removal, or non-reelection; this situation he must normally
accept, unless he undertakes the burden of proving fraud or mala
fides. The just and equitable provision nevertheless comes to his assistance if he can point to, and prove, some special underlying obligation
of his fellow member(s) in good faith, or confidence, that so long as
the business continues he shall be entitled to management participation, an obligation so basic that, if broken, the conclusion must be
that the association must be dissolved. And the principles on which
he may do so are those worked out by the Courts in partnership cases
where there has been exclusion from management (see *Const* v. *Harris*
(1824) Tur. and Rus. 496, 525) even where under the partnership
agreement there is a power of expulsion (see *Blisset* v. *Daniel* (1853)
10 Hare 493; Lindley on Partnership, 13th Ed.(1971) pp 331, 595).

[29] I make one final quotation from this speech which concludes as follows
at page 381:

> I must deal with one final point which was much relied on by the
> Court of Appeal. It was said that the removal was, according to the
> evidence of Mr Nazare, bona fide in the interests of the company;
> that Mr Ebrahimi had not shown the contrary; that he ought to do so
> or to demonstrate that no reasonable man could think that his removal
> was in the company's interest. This formula 'bona fide in the interests
> of the company' is one that is relevant in certain contexts of company
> law and I do not doubt that in many cases decisions have to be left to
> majorities or directors to take which the Courts must assume had this
> basis. It may on the other hand, become little more than an alibi for
> a refusal to consider the merits of the case, and in a situation such as
> this it seems to have little meaning other than 'in the interests of the
> majority'. Mr Nazar may well have persuaded himself, quite genuinely,
> that the company would be better off without Mr Ebrahimi, but if Mr
> Ebrahimi disputed this, or thought the same with reference to Mr
> Nazar what prevails is simply the majority view. To confine the appli-
> cation of the just and equitable clause to proved cases of mala fides

would be to [30] negative the generality of the words. It is because I do not accept this that I feel myself obliged to differ from the Court of Appeal.

I accept the statements of principles given in the Lords' speeches in that case as the correct guidance for my consideration of the questions before me on this petition.

Reverting now to the facts: there is only one answer to the question, was Brian lawfully removed from the office of director of this company? Was this not a business in which all three engaged on the basis that all should participate in its direction and management? Was it an abuse of wrongfully or mistakenly arrogated power and a breach of the good faith which these three partners owed to each other to exclude him from all participation in the business of the company? To these questions there can be only an affirmative answer. Even if the intended resolution for his removal had been proposed in a regular manner, and even if the resolution had been considered at a regularly convened meeting what justification could have been offered to support it? The only matters of complaint of their nature were such that they probably could have been resolved by a temporary spell of personal attention by one of the other directors more experienced in that area of work. But the facts belie the complaints. The business at the Cork branch was exceeding [31] expectations and seemed likely to outstrip the business of the best branch in Dublin and provided support for private investment for the partners making the complaints. The action of Kevin and Murph on the 3rd February, 1979 was wholly unjustified as well as being irregular. But by that action, and in their evidence relating to it, they made it clear that they did not regard Brian as a partner but simply as an employee. Their refusal to recognise any status of equality amounted to a repudiation of their relationship on which the existence of the company was founded. By ceasing to be a director Brian would lose not director's fees for there were none, nor dividends on his shares for there were none, but his very livelihood consisting of an equal share of all capital and profits and active participation in direction and management of the company.

I am satisfied that the petitioner has made out a case for a winding up order, and has shown that proceedings under section 205 would not be appropriate. A liquidator will be appointed and notice of the presentation of the petition and the making of the winding up order will be advertised. The petitioner will have his costs of the hearing to be borne by Kevin and Murph and the company will bear such of its own costs as are not related to these of Kevin and Murph.

PROCEDURAL MATTERS

In re Murph's Restaurants Ltd.
(McWilliam J., Apr. 5, 1979, H.Ct.)

The facts are stated in the judgment.

McWILLIAM J.: These proceedings have been initiated by the Petitioner to
wind up Murph's Restaurants Limited (hereinafter called the Company).
At the time of the filing of the petition, my copy of which does not bear
any date, the Petitioner appears to have been a director of the Company.
He had been served with a notice calling an extraordinary general meeting
of the Company on 12th March, 1979, for the purpose of considering a
resolution that the Petitioner be removed from office as a director of the
Company. There were three directors and the Petitioner has objected that
he was not given any notice of the meeting of the Board at which it was
decided to convene the extraordinary general meeting. It is unlikely that
this is very material, even if correct. It appears that the meeting called for
12th March did not take place and it may be assumed that the Petitioner
is still a director. It is admitted that the Petitioner has been refused any
participation in the [2] affairs of the Company as a director and he also
alleges that the other directors are attempting to purchase his shares at a
gross undervalue. The three directors are the only shareholders in the
Company and they have equal shareholdings. In correspondence prior to
the issue of the Petition it was stated on behalf of the Petitioner that the
petition for winding up was being filed pursuant to the provisions of section
213(g) of the Act.

The present motion is brought on behalf of the Company for an Order
restraining the Petitioner from advertising the petition. . . .

[4] It has been urged on behalf of the company that the advertisement
of the petition would greatly damage the Company, that the matters complained of by the Petitioner are such as could properly be dealt with under
the provisions of section 205, that the petition is not presented in good
faith, and that it is a case in which the Court would, under the provisions
of paragraph (g) of section 213, dismiss a petition to wind up on the grounds
that proceedings under section 205 would be more appropriate. I was
referred to the case entitled *Re A Company* [1894] 2 Ch. 394 as authority
for the proposition that I have jurisdiction to restrain the advertisement
of the petition if it is not presented in good faith but for the purpose of
putting pressure on the company.

For the Petitioner it is argued that his co-directors are trying to acquire
his shares on unfavourable terms and that, if any of the matters complained
of could be a ground for [5] winding up, this application should be refused.
I was referred to the case of *Bryanston Finance Ltd.* v. *de Vries* [1976] 1 All

E.R. 25. I was also referred to the case of *Mann* v. *Goldstein* [1968] All E.R. 769 in support of the proposition that pursuing a valid claim in a normal manner is not an abuse of the process of the court even though it is done with personal hostility and with some ulterior motive.

It occurs to me that some confusion may have been caused in the minds of both parties by the reference in the correspondence to paragraph (g) of section 213. This paragraph and section 205 apply only to members of a company as members. Apart from the allegations in paragraph 13 of the petition, which are not grounded on any facts, the petition is based on facts which prejudice the Petitioner in his capacity as director. Although there has been an offer to purchase the Petitioner's shares, this did not arise until the Petitioner had threatened to issue his petition to have the company wound up on the ground that he was being deprived of his rights as a director and there does not appear to have been a threat of any sort to the Petitioner's shareholding or [6] to his rights as a member.

On the other aspect of the case, it is perfectly clear that the directors are at loggerheads and that the Petitioner has been deprived of all his functions as director. This appears to be a case, similar to that of *Re Lundi Brothers Ltd.* [1965] 1 W.L.R. 1051, in which, in substance, a partnership exists between the three persons carrying on the business of the company together and that, prima facie, the Petitioner would have been entitled to a dissolution of the partnership if it were a partnership and not a company, and that, accordingly, he has a bona fide claim to have the Company wound up.

On the views I have taken that the petition is based on the Petitioner's office of director and as to the application of section 205 and paragraph (g) of section 213, it does not appear to me to be open to the Court to dismiss the petition on the grounds that proceedings under section 205 would be more appropriate.

Under these circumstances, I will refuse the application to restrain the Petitioner from advertising the petition, [7] although it may well be that the Petitioner should consider whether it is to his advantage to proceed with his petition or not.

I should add that I would be hesitant to restrain the advertisement of a petition if the circumstances were not such that I should also restrain any further proceedings on the petition, as was done in the Case of *Re A Company*.

Wallersteiner v. Moir (No. 2)
[1975] Q.B. 373 (C.A.)

This decision is just one of several that was made in a protracted and complicated case. A minority shareholder (Moir), in a derivative proceeding, contended that the appellant had been defrauding the company by various elaborate devices.

LORD DENNING M.R.: . . .

[390] 2. *The Derivative Action*

It is a fundamental principle of our law that a company is a legal person, with its own corporate identity, separate and distinct from the directors or shareholders, and with its own property rights and interests to which alone it is entitled. If it is defrauded by a wrongdoer, the company itself is the one person to sue for the damage. Such is the rule in *Foss* v. *Harbottle* (1843) 2 Hare 461. The rule is easy enough to apply when the company is defrauded by outsiders. The company itself is the only person who can sue. Likewise, when it is defrauded by insiders of a minor kind, once again the company is the only person who can sue. But suppose it is defrauded by insiders who control its affairs – by directors who hold a majority of the shares – who then can sue for damages? Those directors are themselves the wrongdoers. If a board meeting is held, they will not authorise the proceedings to be taken by the company against themselves. If a general meeting is called, they will vote down any suggestion that the company should sue them themselves. Yet the company is the one person who is damnified. It is the one person who should sue. In one way or another some means must be found for the company to sue. Otherwise the law would fail in its purpose. Injustice would be done without redress. In *Foss* v. *Harbottle*, Sir James Wigram V.-C. saw the problem and suggested a solution. He thought that the company could sue 'in the name of some one whom the law has appointed to be its representative.' A suit could be brought

> by individual corporators in their private characters, and asking in such character the protection of those rights to which in their corporate character they were entitled, . . .

This suggestion found its fulfilment in the *Merryweather* case which came before Sir William Page Wood V.-C. on two occasions: see (1864) 2 Hem. & M. 254 (sub nom. *East Pant Du United Lead Mining Co. Ltd.* v. *Merryweather*) and L.R. 5 Eq. 464n. It was accepted there that the minority shareholders might file a bill asking leave to use the name of the company. If they showed reasonable ground for charging the directors with fraud, the court would appoint the minority shareholders as representatives of the company to bring proceedings in the name of the company against the wrong-doing directors. By that means the company would sue in its own name for the wrong done to it. That would be, however, a circuitous course, as Lord Hatherley L.C. said himself, at any rate in cases where the fraud itself could be proved on the initial application.

To avoid the circuity, Lord Hatherley L.C. held that the minority shareholders themselves could bring an action in their own names (but in truth on behalf of the company) against the wrong-doing directors for the damage done by them to the company, provided always that it was impossible to get the company itself to sue them. He ordered the fraudulent directors in that case to repay the sums to the company, be it noted, with interest. His decision was emphatically approved by this court in *Menier* v. *Hooper's Telegraph* (1874) 9 Ch.App. 350 and *Mason* v. *Harris* (1879) 11 Ch.D. 97. The form of the action is always 'A.B. (a minority shareholder) on behalf of himself and all [391] other shareholders of the company' against the wrongdoing directors and the company. That form of action was said by Lord Davey to be a 'mere matter of procedure in order to give a remedy for a wrong which otherwise would escape redress': see *Burland* v. *Earle* [1902] A.C. 83, 93. Stripped of mere procedure, the principle is that, where the wrongdoers themselves control the company, an action can be brought on behalf of the company by the minority shareholders on the footing that they are its representatives to obtain redress on its behalf.

I am glad to find this principle well stated by Professor Gower in *Modern Company Law*, 3rd ed. (1969), p. 587, in words which I would gratefully adopt:

> Where such an action is allowed, the member is not really suing on his own behalf nor on behalf of the members generally, but on behalf of the company itself. Although. . . he will have to frame his action as a representative one on behalf of himself and all the members other than the wrongdoers, this gives a misleading impression of what really occurs. The plaintiff shareholder is not acting as a representative of the other shareholders, but as a representative of the company. . . . In the United States. . . this type of action has been given the distinctive name of a 'derivative action,' recognising that its true nature is that the individual member sues on behalf of the company to enforce rights derived from it.

As it happens in the present case the formula has been discarded. The counterclaim by Mr Moir was prepared by a careful, learned and skilful member of the bar, Mr William Stubbs. It is not headed 'on behalf of himself and all the other shareholders.' It is just headed 'M. J. G. Moir, plaintiff on counterclaim.' The two companies were made parties by being added to the counterclaim. The prayer is: 'Mr Moir counterclaims for' several declarations of wrongs done to the two companies and orders on Dr Wallersteiner to pay specified sums to the two companies, and that he do pay the costs of Mr Moir and the two companies. No objection has been taken to that form of proceeding. No suggestion has been made that it should be amended. Quite right. Let it stand as it is. It is in accord with principle. Mr Moir sues in his own name but in reality on behalf of the companies: just as an agent may contract in his own name but in reality on behalf of his principal.

3. *Indemnity*

Now that the principle is recognised, it has important consequences which have hitherto not been perceived. The first is that the minority shareholder, being an agent acting on behalf of the company, is entitled to be indemnified by the company against all costs and expenses reasonably incurred by him in the course of the agency. This indemnity does not arise out of a contract express or implied, but it arises on the plainest principles of equity. It is analogous to the indemnity to which a trustee is entitled from his cestui que trust who is sui juris: see *Hardoon* v. *Belilios* [1901] A.C.118 and *Re Richardson, Ex parte Governors of St Thomas's Hospital* [1911] 2 K.B. 705. Seeing that, if the action succeeds, the whole benefit will go to the company, it is only just that the minority [392] shareholder should be indemnified against the costs he incurs on its behalf. If the action succeeds, the wrongdoing director will be ordered to pay the costs: but if they are not recovered from him, they should be paid by the company. And all the additional costs (over and above party and party costs) should be taxed on a common fund basis and paid by the company: see *Simpson and Miller* v. *British Industries Trust Ltd.* (1923) 39 T.L.R. 286. The solicitor will have a charge on the money recovered through his instrumentality: see section 73 of the Solicitors Act 1974.

But what if the action fails? Assuming that the minority shareholder had reasonable grounds for bringing the action – that it was a reasonable and prudent course to take in the interests of the company – he should not himself be liable to pay the costs of the other side, but the company itself should be liable, because he was acting for it and not for himself. In addition, he should himself be indemnified by the company in respect of his own costs even if the action fails. It is a well known maxim of the law that he who would take the benefit of a venture if it succeeds ought also to bear the burden if it fails. *Qui sentit commodum sentire debet et onus.* This indemnity should extend to his own costs taxed on a common fund basis.

In order to be entitled to this indemnity, the minority shareholder soon after issuing his writ should apply for the sanction of the court in somewhat the same way as a trustee does: see *Re Beddoe, Downes* v. *Cottam* [1893] 1 Ch. 547, 557-558. In a derivative action, I would suggest this procedure: the minority shareholder should apply ex parte to the master for directions, supported by an opinion of counsel as to whether there is a reasonable case or not. The master may then, if he thinks fit, straightaway approve the continuance of the proceedings until close of pleadings, or until after discovery or until trial (rather as a legal aid committee does). The master need not, however, decide it ex parte. He can, if he thinks fit, require notice to be given to one or two of the other minority shareholders – as representatives of the rest – so as to see if there is any reasonable objection. (In this very case another minority shareholder took this very point in letters to us). But this preliminary application should be simple and inexpensive. It should not be allowed to escalate into a minor trial. The master should simply ask himself: is there a reasonable case for the minority shareholder to bring at the expense (eventually) of the company? If there is, let it go ahead. . . .

[393] 5. *Contingency fee*

English law has never sanctioned an agreement by which a lawyer is remunerated on the basis of a 'contingency fee', that is that he gets paid the fee if he wins, but not if he loses. Such an agreement was illegal on the ground that it was the offence of champerty. In its origin champerty was a division of the proceeds (campi partitio). An agreement by which a lawyer, if he won, was to receive a share of the proceeds was pure champerty. Even if he was not to receive an actual share, but payment of a commission on a sum proportioned to the amount recovered – only if he won – it was also regarded as champerty: see *Re Attorneys and Solicitors Act 1870* [1875] 1 Ch.D. 573, 575, *per* Sir George Jessel M.R. and *Re A Solicitor, Ex parte Law Society* [1912] 1 K.B. 302. Even if the sum was not a proportion of the amount recovered, but a specific sum or advantage which was to be received if he won but not if he lost, that too, was unlawful: see *Pittman* v. *Prudential Deposit Bank Ltd.* (1896) 13 T.L.R. 110, *per* Lord Esher M.R. It mattered not whether the sum to be received was to be his sole remuneration, or to be an added remuneration (above his normal fee), in any case it was unlawful if it was to be paid only if he won, and not if he lost.

Prudential Assurance Co. Ltd. v. Newman Industries Ltd. (No. 2) [1981] 1 Ch. 257 (Ch.D. and C.A.)

This decision also forms part of protracted and complex litigation. A minority shareholder (Prudential Ltd.) contended that the company's de facto controllers had effectively defrauded the shareholders and the company by arranging for the company to buy a business in which those controllers had a large financial interest.

VINELOTT J.: . . .[304] The real issue in this action is whether the derivative claim is barred by the rule commonly known as the rule in *Foss* v. *Harbottle* (1843) 2 Hare [305] 461. This rule was stated by Jenkins L.J. in *Edwards* v. *Halliwell* [1950] 2 All E.R. 1064, 1066-1067, in the following terms:

> The rule in *Foss* v. *Harbottle*, 2 Hare 461, as I understand it, comes to no more than this. First, the proper plaintiff in an action in respect of a wrong alleged to be done to a company or association of persons is prima facie the company or the association of persons itself. Secondly, where the alleged wrong is a transaction which might be made binding on the company or association and on all its members by a simple majority of the members, no individual member of the company

is allowed to maintain an action in respect of that matter for the simple reason that, if a mere majority of the members of the company or association is in favour of what has been done, then cadit quaestio. No wrong has been done to the company or association and there is nothing in respect of which anyone can sue. If, on the other hand, a simple majority of members of the company or association is against what has been done, then there is no valid reason why the company or association itself should not sue. In my judgment, it is implicit in the rule that the matter relied on as constituting the cause of action shall be a cause of action properly belonging to the general body of corporators or members of the company or association as opposed to a cause of action which some individual member can assert in his own right.

Jenkins L.J. went on to point out that the rule so formulated can have no application unless the members of the company can by ordinary resolution, passed in general meeting, validly resolve that no proceedings should be instituted to remedy the wrong to the company. Thus, the rule cannot apply (a) to cases where the minority seek to restrain the commission of an act which is ultra vires or illegal or to recover on behalf of the company property disposed of under an ultra vires or illegal transaction; (b) to cases where the minority seeks to have a resolution of the company in general meeting declared void upon the ground that the resolution was one which could only be passed by a special resolution; or (c) to cases where the wrong done to the company is also an infringement of the minority's own individual rights, whether as members or otherwise.

These three categories of cases are sometimes referred to as exceptions from the rule in *Foss* v. *Harbottle*. They are exceptions only in the sense that cases within these categories fall outside the ambit of the rule as formulated by Jenkins L.J. There is another exception which is an exception in a different sense, namely that it operates to exclude from the rule cases which would otherwise fall within its apparent scope. This exception, which I shall call simply 'the exception', is stated by Jenkins L.J. in these terms, at p. 1067:

It has been further pointed out that where what has been done amounts to what is generally called in these cases a fraud on the minority and the wrongdoers are themselves in control of the company, the rule is relaxed in favour of the aggrieved minority who are allowed to bring what is known as a minority shareholders' action on behalf of themselves and all others. The reason for this is that if they [306] were denied that right, their grievance could never reach the court because the wrongdoers themselves, being in control, would not allow the company to sue.

The exception is commonly stated in terms which require the plaintiff in a minority shareholders' action to establish two things. First, that the wrong to the company which it is sought to remedy was a wrong of a fraudulent character and, secondly, that the wrongdoers are in control of the company. I shall examine each of these two requirements in turn. . . .

[316] Th[e] authorities show that the exception applies not only where the allegation is that directors who control a company have improperly appropriated to themselves money, property or advantages which belong to the company or, in breach of their duty to the company, have diverted business to themselves which ought to have been given to the company, but more generally where it is alleged that directors though acting 'in the belief that they were doing nothing wrong' (*per* Lindley M.R. in *Alexander v. Automatic Telephone Co.* [1900] 2 Ch. 56, 65) are guilty of a breach of duty to the company, including their duty to exercise proper care, and as a result of that breach obtain some benefit. In the latter case it must be unnecessary to allege and prove that the directors in breaking their duty to the company acted with a view to benefiting themselves at the expense of the company; for such an allegation would be an allegation of misappropriation of the company's property. On the other hand, the exception does not apply if all that is alleged is that directors who control a company are liable to the company for damages for negligence it not being shown that the transaction was one in which they were interested or that they have in fact obtained any benefit from it. It is not easy to see precisely where the line between these cases is to be drawn. For instance, is an action to be allowed to proceed if the allegation is that the controlling director is liable to the company for damages for negligence and that as a result of his negligence a benefit has been obtained by his wife or a friend or by a company in which he has a substantial shareholding? In *Pavlides* v. *Jensen* [1956] Ch. 565 would it have been enough if, in addition to the allegation of negligence, it had been alleged that Portland Tunnel had a substantial shareholding in the Cyprus company and therefore benefited indirectly? It is also not easy to see what principle underlies the distinction. Whether the claim is for property improperly withheld or for damages for negligence or breach of fiduciary duty and, in the latter case, whether those controlling the company have or have not obtained some benefit the reason for the exception is the same, namely that the claim is brought against persons whose interests conflict with the interest of the company. It may be said, in a perfectly intelligible sense, to be a fraud on the minority that those against whom the claim would be brought are in a position to procure, and, if the derivative claim is not brought, will procure, that the company's claim, however strong it may appear to be, will not be enforced. Mr Scott, very frankly, admitted that he could not put forward any valid [317] ground of distinction between a case where the claim by the company is of a proprietory nature and one where it is for damages only, nor between a

claim for damages for negligence where the loss to the company is either not matched by any benefit to anybody or is not matched by a benefit to those in control. However, Mr Scott also conceded that the claim by Prudential is a claim founded on acts of a 'fraudulent character,' whatever meaning is attributed to those words. I have endeavoured to state the principle which underlies the first limb of the exception, because the second limb cannot be construed in isolation from it, but it is unnecessary for me to decide precisely where the boundary limiting the category of cases which permit of a minority shareholder's action is to be drawn and it would be wrong for me to attempt to do so.

The central issue in this case is whether a derivative action can be brought against defendants who do not have voting control of the company on whose behalf the derivative claim is brought and, if it can, in precisely what circumstances such claim will be allowed to proceed. . . .

[323] If the rule and the exception cannot be confined within the rigid formulation expressed in terms of voting control by the persons against whom relief is sought on behalf of the company, then the question whether a given case falls within the exception can only be answered by reference to the principle which underlies the rule and the exception to it. Mr Scott submitted, I think rightly, that the principle which underlies the rule is that it would be wrong to allow a minority shareholder to bring proceedings joining the company as defendant and claiming against other defendants relief on behalf of the company for a wrong alleged to have been done to it if the majority of the members of the company take the view that it is not in the interests of the company that the proceedings should be pursued. Indeed, it would be so plainly wrong that it might be said that, in a broad sense, the court would have no jurisdiction to allow the wishes of the minority to override the wishes of the majority in that way. The principle which underlies the exception to the rule is that in ascertaining the view of the majority whether it is in the interests of the company that the claim be pursued, the court will disregard votes cast or capable of being cast by shareholders who have an interest which directly conflicts with the interest of the company. Those are general principles of substantive law and are not mere rules of procedure. But in any derivative action the plaintiff must allow in his statement of claim some ground which, if established at the trial, would bring the case within the exception and justify an order that the company recover damages or property from the other defendants.

XI. Fundamental Structural Changes

The system laid down in the Companies Acts for the governance of companies can be divided into four distinct tiers. The board, which ordinarily runs the business, is subject to the *de facto* control of a simple majority of the shareholders, who have the power to remove directors by an ordinary resolution. Most provisions of a company's regulations can be altered by special majorities of the members in that the articles of association can be changed by special resolution. Thirdly, certain vital or fundamental changes in the nature of companies cannot be made unless they are approved of by super-majorities of the members and either are not vetoed by or are endorsed by the court: notably, altering the objects clause, reducing or repaying capital, varying class rights, and making an arrangement under §201 of the 1963 Act. In dealing with most of these matters, the Companies Acts override or modify any special voting rights and disabilities that may exist under the company's regulations, and wholly or partly enfranchise shareholders to the extent of their shares' nominal values. Thus, a §201 arrangement must be approved by a majority representing 75 per cent in value of those members of each class affected by it *who vote* on the proposal. Somewhat similarly, the holders of not less than 15 per cent in nominal value of the company's issued share capital, or of any class of shares or debentures, may apply to the court to veto a change in the company's objects; and the holders of not less than 10 per cent of the issued shares of the class in question can apply to the court to have an agreed variation of class rights blocked. The Acts also empower the court, when approving some of these changes, to order appraisal for dissenting shareholders, i.e. order that their shares be bought out at an objectively determined price. The fourth tier in the statutory system of governance is provided for in §§ 9 and 28 of the 1963 Act, which permit matters to be 'entrenched' in the memorandum of association so that they can be altered only in some special way, or indeed be unalterable.

CHANGING THE NATURE OF THE BUSINESS

In re Munster & Leinster Bank Ltd.
[1907] 1 I.R. 237

The bank proposed to alter its objects clause so as to give itself power to act as trustees. Some shareholders applied to the court to veto this proposal.

PORTER M.R.: [247] So far as the proposed change relates to the undertaking and execution of the duties of treasurer there is no objection to the prayer of the petition. The opposition is confined to the proposed extension of the business of the bank to the business of trustee or executor. I am impressed by the fact that the seven gentlemen represented here today (who are shareholders, holding in all 398 shares) had full knowledge of the proposed alteration in the memorandum of association, and had due notice of the meetings of the company at which the special resolution was passed and confirmed, yet did not raise any objection, or take any exception, to the proposed alteration until the hearing of this petition. It appears. . . that the special resolution was passed without dissent, and was confirmed without opposition. If these seven gentlemen had even now come forward and opposed this petition, as shareholders, I should, perhaps, have given more weight to their objections, and to the argument offered on their behalf; but the learned counsel who nominally appeared for them did not seek to deny, but rather prided himself on the fact, that he represented, not individual shareholders, but the Incorporated Law Society of Ireland and the Southern Law Society. I have read the resolutions passed by these eminent bodies, on which the present opposition is based, and in accordance with which the petition of the bank is resisted today, and it is apparent that they were framed not really in the interests of shareholders, but in apprehension of the injury which might result to the solicitor profession from the proposed extension of the objects of the bank. The apprehension is that the new business would prove so attractive that other banks in Ireland would follow the lead of the Munster and Leinster Bank, and that the general body of solicitors would, under the circumstances suggested, suffer no inconsiderable injury. Mr Ronan and Mr O'Connor urge that the resolutions demonstrate that the extension of the business of the bank would prove beneficial to the shareholders. Why should there be apprehension of sustained and severe competition unless the real truth is that the Munster and Leinster Bank have discovered [248] something new, something likely to be advantageous to their shareholders, and profitable in one way or another? . . . I have the fact that, after the fullest notice, the shareholders at two meetings voted in favour of the enlargement of the bank's powers, and I have the fact that Mr Lillis, the general manager, and a director of the bank, states to the Court on oath his opinion that the proposed extension of the objects of the company is required to carry on certain businesses and classes of business which may conveniently and advantageously be combined with the business of the company. Mr Lillis is a business man, and, as manager of the bank, he should be, and, I think, he would be, the last person in the world to propose any change except in the interest of the bank and of its shareholders.

In support of the petition, I have positive statements, while, on the other side, I have nothing but vague apprehensions, vague fears; not so much that the bank or its shareholders may suffer, but that the general body of solicitors may suffer. Far be it from me to say that the eminent bodies whose duty it is to safeguard the interests of their profession were wrong in viewing the proposed new departure in banking business with some dislike; but I think that they have taken an exaggerated view of the situation, and apprehend misfortune which is not likely to occur. That this bank, or any other bank, would be able to carry out on a large scale the duties of executors or trustees, without the assistance of the general body of solicitors, is, to my mind, absolutely impossible. I am rather inclined to think that the proposed alteration, if carried into effect, would probably result in benefit to the solicitors' profession, as it certainly would result in benefit to the public in many respects. All these considerations are, however, beside the question. I am bound, as Mr Wilson says, to concentrate my attention on the bank and the shareholders, and taking all the circumstances of the case into consideration it appears to me that material advantage may accrue to the bank, not so much from the few cases in which they may receive remuneration for their services, as from the attraction to customers [249] arising from knowledge of the fact that they can rely upon the bank to act as their trustee or executor, in full confidence that property entrusted to the bank will be in safe custody; not liable to be lost or made away with by ignorance, negligence, or default.

I see good grounds for supposing that this knowledge and confidence may retain and attract customers, and thus ultimately result in benefit to the shareholders. At all events, so the great majority of the shareholders appear to think, and I see no reason why I should set the apprehension of the solicitors in opposition to the views of the shareholders. I, therefore, exercise the discretion which I possess by confirming the resolution, with one alteration. I do not think it desirable that any question should be raised as to the power of the bank to accept trusts in cases where the trust estate or property is situate altogether outside the jurisdiction of this Court. Some words must be inserted limiting the extended powers to cases where at least some portion of the trust estate or some portion of the assets is within the jurisdiction of the High Court of Justice in Ireland. As regards change of name, I am of opinion that the cases cited by Mr Wilson are not such as to make it incumbent upon me to direct any alteration in the name of the bank.

VARIATION OF CLASS RIGHTS

White v. Bristol Aeroplane Co. Ltd.
[1953] 1 Ch. 65 (C.A.)

The company's capital was comprised of 600,000 £1 preference shares and 3,000,000 £1 ordinary shares. It was proposed to increase the capital by issuing 660,000 new £1 cumulative preference shares and 1,000,000 new £1 ordinary shares, and that the entirety of the new issue should be distributed among the present ordinary shareholders. The preference shareholders sought to block this proposal, claiming that it was an impermissible interference with their class rights. The company's articles of association contained the following class rights variation clause: 'Subject to the provisions of. . . the Companies Act. . . all or any of the rights and privileges attached to any class of shares forming part of the capital for the time being of the company may be affected, modified, varied, dealt with, or abrogated in any manner with the sanction of an extraordinary resolution passed at a separate meeting of the members of that class. To any such separate meeting all the provisions of these articles as to general meetings shall. . . apply.'

LORD EVERSHED M.R.: . . . [73] [W]ill the effect of this proposed distribution, if carried out, be to 'affect' the rights of the preference stockholders? . . .

[74] It is necessary, first, to note – although on this matter Mr Gray has not argued to the contrary – that what must be 'affected' are the rights of the preference stockholders. The question then is – and indeed, I have already posed it – are the rights which I have already summarised 'affected' by what is proposed? It is said in answer – and I think rightly said – No, they are not; they remain exactly as they were before; each one of the manifestations of the preference stockholders' privileges may be repeated without any change whatever after, as before, the proposed distribution. It is no doubt true that the enjoyment of, and the capacity to make effective, those rights is in a measure affected; for as I have already indicated, the existing preference stockholders will be in a less advantageous position on such occasions as entitle them to register their votes, whether at general meetings of the company or at separate meetings of their own class. But there is to my mind a distinction, and a sensible distinction, between an affecting of the rights and an affecting of the enjoyment of the rights, or of the stockholders' capacity to turn them to account. . . .

[80] I have no doubt, as I have already indicated, that upon a sufficient analysis what is here suggested will 'affect' the preference stockholders 'as a matter of business'; but we are concerned with the question whether the rights of the preference stockholders are 'affected', not as a matter of business, but according to the articles, that is, according to their meaning

construed under the rules of construction and as a matter of law. I further think that having regard to the fact that the word 'affected' was in the article in the *Mackenzie* case [1916] 2 Ch. 450, it would be wrong for this court now to say that its presence in this set of articles – and I dare say it has appeared in many others before and since that case – has so restrictive an effect upon the ordinary shareholders in the company that separate meetings of preference stockholders and shareholders would have to be held whenever it could be shown that as a matter of business, upon a close analysis, that which was proposed would, or might, affect in some degree the value of the preference shares, or the way in which the rights conferred upon them by the regulations of the company were to be enjoyed.

CAPITAL REDUCTION AND REPAYMENT

In re Holders Investment Trust Ltd.
[1971] 2 All E.R. 289 (Ch.D.)

The company's issued share capital comprised of ordinary shares and 5 per cent cumulative preference shares that were to be redeemed in 1971. In 1970 it was proposed that the 5 per cent preference shareholders should be repaid by being allotted 6 per cent unsecured loan stock 1985-1990 in the same nominal amounts. This proposal was approved by a special resolution of the company, and also by a special resolution of the preference shareholders meeting separately. Of the latter, however, approximately 3 per cent did not vote; 7 per cent opposed the proposal; and the remaining 90 per cent who supported the proposal were trustees who also held over half of the ordinary shares. From the evidence it was clear that, in voting for the proposed capital repaymemt, the trustees were influenced solely by the benefit to the trust as a whole and were not concerned with the advantages to themselves *qua* preference shareholders.

MEGARRY J.: . . . [290] Put briefly, counsel for the opposing trustees' opposition to the confirmation of the reduction is twofold. First, he contends that the extraordinary resolution of the [291] preference shareholders was not valid and effectual because the supporting trustees did not exercise their votes in the way that they ought to have done, namely, in the interests of the preference shareholders as a whole. Instead, being owners of much ordinary stock and many shares as well, they voted in such a way as to benefit the totality of the stocks and shares that they held. Secondly, he contends that even if the extraordinary resolution was valid, the terms on which the reduction of capital is to be effected are not fair, in particular in that the increase in the rate of interest from 5% to 6% is not an adequate recompense for having the right of repayment or redemption postponed from 31 July 1971, until at earliest 31 October 1985, and at latest some unspecified date in 1990. I may say at the outset that it is common ground that the proposed reduction is not in accordance with the class rights of the preference shareholders. . . .

Counsel for the company put before me four propositions based on the authorities. Discarding what does not apply in this case, and putting the matter shortly, I think that three relevant propositions emerge. First, a reduction of capital which is not in accordance with the class rights is nevertheless regular if it is effectually sanctioned in accordance with the regulations of the company. Second, there is an effectual sanction to the modification of class rights if those holding a sufficient majority of the shares of that class vote in favour of the modification in the bona fide belief that they are acting in the interests of the general body of members of that class. Third, the burden of proof depends on whether or not there is any such sanction. If there is, the court will confirm the reduction unless the opposition proves that it is unfair; if there is not, the court will confirm the reduction only if it is proved to be fair. These propositions were based on *Carruth* v. *Imperial Chemical Industries Ltd.* [1937] A.C. 707, when read in conjunction with *British America Nickel Corpn Ltd.* v. *M. J. O'Brien Ltd.* [1927] A.C. 369, and *Shuttleworth* v. *Cox Bros & Co. (Maidenhead) Ltd.* [1927] 2 K.B. 9. Whatever may be said about the formulation of the propositions, their substance was, I think, common ground between the parties. Accordingly, I must first consider the validity of the class resolution.

In the *British America* case, Viscount Haldane, in speaking for a strong Board of the Judicial Committee, referred to 'a general principle, which is applicable to all authorities conferred on majorities of classes enabling them to bind minorities; namely, that the power given must be exercised for the purpose of benefiting the class as a whole, and not merely individual members only. . . .' The matter may, I think, be put in the way in which Scrutton LJ put it in the *Shuttleworth* case, where the question was the benefit of the company rather than of a particular class of members. Adapting his language. . . I have to see whether the majority was honestly endeavouring to decide and act to the benefit of the class as a whole, rather than with a view to the interests of some of the class and against that of others. . . .

[292] I pause here to point the obvious. Without guidance from those skilled in these matters, many members of a class may fail to realise what they should bear in mind when deciding how to vote at a class meeting. The beneficial owner of shares may well concentrate on his own personal interests: even though he regards the proposal per se as one to be rejected, collateral matters affecting other interests of his may lead him to vote in favour of the resolution. Trustees, too, are under a fiduciary duty to do the best they properly can for their beneficiaries. A proposal which, in isolation, is contrary to the interests of those owning the shares affected may nevertheless be beneficial to the beneficiaries by reason of the

improved prospects that the proposal will confer on other shares in the company which the trustees hold on the same trusts: and that, in essence, is what is in issue here. . . .

[His Lordship referred to correspondence between the 'supporting trustees' and their professional advisers, and continued:] [294] That exchange of letters seems to me to make it perfectly clear that the advice sought, the advice given, and the advice acted upon, was all on the basis of what was for the benefit of the trusts as a whole, having regard to their large holdings of the equity capital. From the point of view of equity, and disregarding company law, this is a perfectly proper basis; but that is not the question before me. I have to determine whether the supporting trustees voted for the reduction in the bona fide belief that they were acting in the interests of the general body of members of that class. From first to last I can see no evidence that the trustees ever applied their minds to what under company law was the right question, or that they ever had the bona fide belief that is requisite for an effectual sanction of the reduction. Accordingly, in my judgment there has been no effectual sanction for the modification of class rights. It may be observed that I have said nothing as to the burden of proof on this issue whether the sanction to the modification of class rights has been validly given, and I propose to continue to say nothing. However that burden lies, in my judgment there was no effectual sanction. The result is therefore that on the issue of fairness the burden of proof devolves on those supporting the reduction to prove that it is fair. Unless this burden is discharged, confirmation of the reduction will be refused.

[His Lordship considered the evidence and ruled that the reduction had not been shown to be fair to the preference shareholders. Accordingly, he refused to confirm the reduction.]

SECTION 201 ARRANGEMENT AND RECONSTRUCTION

In re John Power & Son Ltd.
[1934] I.R. 412 (S.Ct.)

The company was established in 1921 with a capital of 400,000 £1 ordinary shares and 400,000 £1 preference shares carrying an 8 per cent per annum cumulative preferential dividend. After ten years of continuously falling profits, the directors concluded that there was no prospect of the company ever earning enough to meet the preference dividend every year and at the same time provide for depreciation. The directors, therefore, proposed to reduce the ordinary shares' nominal value to 50p per share, and that each preference share to be exchanged for a redeemable loan of £1 at 5 per cent per annum interest. This proposal was approved by a special resolution of the company, and by large majorities of the ordinary shareholders and the preference shareholders meeting separately.

FITZGIBBON J.: . . . [423] It seems to have been contended in the Court of first instance, and the appellants certainly adumbrated a similar contention here, that where a proposal for a reduction of capital under sect. 46, and a scheme of arrangement under sect. 120, have been approved by majorities considerably in excess of those prescribed by the Companies Act, the Court is practically bound, in the absence of bad faith, or unless there is some statement or omission likely to mislead the shareholders, to give its confirmation or sanction, as the case may be, to the proposed reduction or scheme. In my opinion the duty of the Court is not confined to these considerations. Until 1908 the power of the Court to bind a minority by the vote of a majority was limited to creditors and to cases of winding-up, but sect. 120 extended the power in the case of a compromise or scheme of arrangement, in the same words, to the 'members or any class of them', and the decisions under the earlier Acts have always been treated, and in my opinion necessarily so, as authorities to be followed in exercising the extended powers conferred by sect. 120 of [424] the Act of 1908, in cases where no winding-up was in progress.

The rule was stated by the Court of Appeal in England in *Re Alabama, New Orleans, Texas and Pacific Junction Railway Co.* [1891] 1 Ch. 213, by a Court consisting of Lindley, Bowen and Fry LL.JJ., and I take the following passage from the judgment of Lindley L.J.: 'What the Court has to do is to see, first of all, that the provisions of that statute [the Joint Stock Companies Arrangement Act, 1870, which corresponds, with the addition of the provisions as to 'members', with sect. 120 of the Companies Act, 1908] have been complied with; and, secondly, that the majority have been acting *bona fide*. The Court *also* has to see that the minority is not being overridden by a majority having interests of its own clashing with those of the minority whom they seek to coerce. *Further than that*, the Court has to look at the scheme, and see whether it is one as to which persons acting honestly, and viewing the scheme laid before them in the interests of those whom they represent, take a view which can be reasonably taken by business men, The Court must look at the scheme, and see whether the Act has been complied with, whether the majority are acting *bona fide*, and whether they are coercing the minority in order to promote interests adverse to those of the class they purport to represent; *and then* see whether the scheme is a reasonable one, *or* whether there is *any reasonable objection* to it, *or such an objection* to it as that *any reasonable man* might say that he could not approve of it.' That decision came up for consideration two years later in the very important case of *Re English, Scottish, and Australian Chartered Bank* [1893] 3 Ch. 385, when Sir Horace Davey *arguendo* in support of the scheme contended that the passage I have cited meant no more than that the Court should see 'whether the majority are acting *bona fide*'. Vaughan Williams J. – a great authority not only on Company Law but especially on the law and practice in bankruptcy, where similar principles in the case of creditors were of daily application – corrected him, and pointed out in a luminous judgment, in which they are set forth as clearly and concisely as in any judgment I have read, the principles and considerations which should govern a Court in dealing with such a scheme, and he put his interpretation upon the words of Lindley L.J. An appeal was taken from this decision, which was affirmed in the Court of Appeal, where Lindley L.J. expressly reaffirmed all that [425] he had said in the *Alabama Case* [1891] 1 Ch. 213, and Lopes and A. L. Smith LL.JJ. agreed that the law had been most clearly stated there. The House of Lords, in *British and Amercian Trustee and Finance Corp.* v. *Couper* [1894] A.C. 399, and in *Poole* v. *National Bank of China Ltd.* [1907] A.C. 229, affirmed the right of a majority to bind a minority both on the question whether there should be a reduction of capital, and on the mode by which that reduction should be carried out, provided always that it was fair and equitable as between the different classes of shareholders, and in the latter case Lord Macnaghten deprecated 'a growing tendency to narrow and restrict the power conferred by the Act of 1867 on companies limited by shares'.

Having dealt with the principles which I think should govern the Court, I now come to the objections which have been urged in this particular case against the proposals of the Company.

I confess that I find great difficulty in ascertaining the ground upon which the learned Judge based his rejection of the proposals.

He says that 'if a simple proposal, under sects. 46 and 120 of the Companies Act, 1908, had been brought forward for the conversion, to put it shortly, of the 400,000 preference shares into 400,000 £1 5 per cent. Debenture Stock' (I think his '£1' has been misplaced) 'and if all requisite formalities had been observed, and if the statutory majority had been obtained, I should have had no difficulty whatever in giving the required sanction. Under existing circumstances I consider that the £5 Debenture Stock may quite reasonably be regarded as a more attractive investment than the 8 per cent. Cumulative Preference.' He then points out that this 'simple proposal' is complicated by an additional proposal that half the ordinary capital should be cancelled by the reduction of the £1 shares to 10*s.* shares, and adds: 'It is obvious that this addition to the scheme cannot prejudice the preference shareholders.' No wonder he says 'That being so, it may well be asked "Is not that all the more reason for sanctioning the scheme?" The scheme has the unanimous approval of the ordinary shareholders, and opposition only comes from a comparatively small number of preference shareholders. If, then, the Court would readily have sanctioned the simple scheme for conversion, should it not all the more readily give its sanction when the scheme is only complicated by being indissolubly bound up with [426] a cancellation of half of the ordinary share capital which must make the scheme more attractive to the preference shareholders.' He then proceeds to point out what he calls 'the fallacy in this argument'. 'No doubt,' he says, 'if the preference shareholders had approved by the required majority of a simple scheme for the conversion of the preference shares into 5 per cent. Debenture Stock the Court would have sanctioned the scheme at once. Further, if the preference shareholders would have so approved they would, of course, also approve of the scheme with the addition of the provision for the cancellation of half the ordinary capital. But there is no use stressing the attractiveness of the simple scheme for conversion when the preference shareholders were not given an opportunity for voting on that, but were only presented with the complex scheme, as one integral whole, recommended to them mainly on the ground that a reduction of capital was necessary.' What does this mean but that a man, presumably reasonable, would approve of the substitution of 5 per cent. Debenture Stock for 8 per cent. Cumulative Preference Shares as, 'under existing circumstances a more attractive investment', and would 'of course, also approve of the scheme with the addition of the provision for the cancellation of a half of the ordinary capital', as 'it is obvious that this addition to the scheme cannot prejudice the preference shareholders,' while the same reasonable man would be justified in rejecting either or both of the proposals because they were propounded simultaneously? The learned Judge appears to think that there is something improper or unfair in propounding a composite scheme involving the reduction of capital under sect. 120, or in making the one conditional or dependent upon the other. The contrary was expressly decided in Re Hoare [1910] W. N. 87, not long after the passing of the Act. In that case it is true there was no opposition, but in Re Odham's Press, Ltd. [1925] W.N. 10, to which my brother Hanna referred during the argument, the question was argued, and Eve J. decided against the objection. The procedure has become so common that the precedent books contain examples of the necessary and usual forms. The learned Judge then appears to regard the statement in the Directors' circular that 'the earning capacity of the Company is not equal to the strain of providing the cumulative [427] preference dividend (requiring an annual sum of £32,000, less income tax) if proper provision for depreciation, reserves, etc., is to be made in the future' as 'a direct threat to the preference shareholders that if they do not accept the integral scheme, or, to adopt Mr Overend's simile, if they do no swallow the physic the doctor has prescribed in a prescription that cannot be changed or tampered with, the Directors must resort, at least as a matter of prudence, to the annual profits to make good as far as possible all the depreciation in the fixed assets.' I am unable to regard a simple statement of essential facts as 'a direct threat', and I confess, that if the Directors had not drawn the attention of the shareholders to the fact that for several years nothing had been set aside for depreciation, and had allowed the shareholders to cast their votes under the false impression that, as the respondents' circular stated, 'the Company is able not only to pay the preference dividends in full but to carry forward very large credit balances', they would have laid themselves open to a far stronger charge of misleading the shareholders than any that has been suggested. I do not know whence the proposition was derived that the preference shareholders must 'swallow the physic the doctor has prescribed in a prescription *that cannot be changed or tampered with*'. The resolution proposed 'a scheme to be framed in accordance with the terms following:' of which No. 4 was: 'The Company may assent to any modification or condition which the Court may think fit to approve or impose.' No condition or modification was suggested by the opponents of the scheme, either in the Court below, in response to the express invitation of the Judge (who stated that he had 'jurisdiction to intervene in an appropriate manner, either by refusing sanction *or by imposing appropriate conditions*'), or here; their demand was to stand upon their original rights, no matter how ruinous such a course might be to the Company and their fellow preference shareholders who had approved the scheme by a vast majority, and this is a matter upon which reliance was placed by Lord Loreburn C. (at p. 236) and Lord Macnaghten (at p. 239) when dismissing the appeal of the dissentient shareholders in *Poole* v. *National Bank of China.*

It might be supposed from some passages in the judgment of the learned Judge that he thought it possible that some shareholders had been misled by the Directors' circular. It is certain that the three shareholders who opposed the scheme were not misled, and the concluding paragraph of [428] the learned Judge's opinion seems to me to demonstrate that he did not believe that anyone not before the Court could have been under any misconception, because he says: 'Now that the position has been fully investigated, the "objectors" – (who had not been misled) – might consent to withdraw their objections and if *they* so consented, I would be satisfied that the circular would only leave matters where they stand, and accordingly would allow the scheme to go through.' He could not allow the scheme to go through, if he believed that shareholders not before the Court had been, or might have been, misled into supporting, or into refraining from opposing it, and the action of the three opponents, who *ex concessis* had not been misled, in withdrawing their opposition, based upon totally different grounds, ought not to be allowed to prejudice the ignorant absentees. This passage shows that the learned Judge had disregarded the suggestion, if it was ever made by counsel for the opponents, that the circular had inadvertently misled anyone. He says 'Personally I think it unlikely that any preference shareholder would desire to withdraw his approval of the scheme if he were sent a further circular,' an expression of opinion with which I entirely agree, and agreeing also, as I do, 'that the circular would only leave matters where they stand,' I 'accordingly would allow the scheme to go through.'

I can find nothing misleading in the circular, and the proposals seem to me quite intelligible to any person of ordinary intelligence. The only omission which has occurred to me is one which was not stressed, or even mentioned during the argument, of a statement as to the probable market value of the new Debenture Stock, but as any expression of opinion on this point would be purely speculative, and might be challenged as misleading, I am satisfied that it was properly omitted, and that it was not unfair to leave the shareholders to form their own estimates of the merits of the exchange which the learned Judge considered might 'reasonably be regarded as a more attractive investment'.

That the substitution of debentures for shares is not *per se* an objection to the sanctioning of a scheme was settled by the decisions in *Re Nixon's Navigation Co.* [1897] 1 Ch. 872, and *Re Thomas De la Rue & Co.* [1911] 2 Ch. 361, which dispose of the objection by the respondents that the scheme would alter their position from that of shareholders to that of [429] creditors.

The *bona fides* of the Directors is conceded; it has been stated without challenge or contradiction that the required majority of preference shareholders was obtained without reckoning the votes of any preference shareholders who were also holders of ordinary shares; there is, in my opinion, nothing by way of statement or omission in connection with the circular which could have the effect of misleading even a less then ordinarily intelligent shareholder; and there is nothing about the proposed scheme which appears to me intrinsically unfair or inequitable.

Finally, no suggestion of any modification of the proposal has been put forward by the three dissentients, and in these circumstances I am of opinion that the proposed reduction of capital should be confirmed, and that the scheme of arrangement should be sanctioned by the Court.

XII. Take-Overs and Mergers

By take-overs and mergers is meant where one company (or exceptionally an individual) acquires control of another company or where both companies amalgamate. There are no general definitions for these terms in the Companies Acts. Such transactions can be brought about in significantly different ways. For instance, one company may simply sell its entire undertaking to another – either for cash or for securities in that other company. Section 260 of the 1963 Act provides a convenient mechanism where it is sought to sell the undertaking for shares in the acquiring company and then distribute those securities to the seller's own shareholders. The procedure under § 201 of the 1963 Act for arrangements can be used in order to take over or merge with another company. But the most common method today is where one company simply acquires most or all of the shares in another company, so that the latter becomes a subsidiary of the former.

AUTHORITY

Automatic Self-Cleansing Filter Syndicate Co. Ltd. v. Cuninghame
[1906] 2 Ch. 34 (C.A.)

See ante p. 89.

FINANCING

Belmont Finance Corp. v. Williams Furniture Ltd. (No. 2)
[1980] 1 All E.R. 393 (C.A.)

See ante p. 222.

Bank of Ireland v. Rockfield Ltd.
[1979] I.R. 21 (S.Ct.)

See ante p. 227.

In re Wellington Publishing Co. Ltd.
[1973] 1 N.Z.L.R. 133

A company borrowed approximately $NZ 3 million in order to finance the take-over of another company. When the take-over was completed, the acquired company's assets were revalued and were shown to be worth far more than their stated value. In anticipation of the profit that would be made on those properties if ever realised, a dividend of approximately $NZ 3 million was paid, which the successful bidder then used to pay off the overdraft. It was contended that these transactions contravened the New Zealand near-equivalent of §60 of the 1963 Act.

QUILLIAM J.: . . . [136] Section 62 of the Companies Act 1955, so far as is material for the present purpose, is as follows:

> (1) Subject as provided in this section, it shall not be lawful for a company to give, whether directly or indirectly, and whether by means of a loan, guarantee, the provision of security or otherwise, any financial assistance for the purpose of or in connection with a purchase or subscription made or to be made by any person of or for any shares in the company.

This case resolves itself into the question of whether the declaration and payment of a dividend by Blundell Brothers Limited is the giving to the Wellington Company of 'financial assistance'.

There is no doubt that the words of s. 62 are intended to have a wide application. This does not mean that they are to have unlimited application. Nor does it mean that they are to be given any strained or unnatural interpretation. The purpose of the section would seem to be the protection of minority shareholders and creditors. If, therefore, a transaction in question is likely to detract from that protection then the words of the section may the more readily be regarded as extending to embrace that transaction.

I think the first approach should be to look at the words of the section and see whether, giving those words their normal and popular meanings, they appear to extend to the declaration and payment of a dividend. I find it very difficult to say that this is the case. It is necessary first to eliminate the words 'loan, guarantee, the provision of security'. By no process of reasoning can those words be regarded as including a dividend. There remain the words 'or otherwise' which undoubtedly have the widest application and will presumably include transactions of any kind. Any transaction which is being considered, however, must be of a kind which gives 'any financial assistance for the purpose of or in connection with a purchase' of shares. The expression 'financial assistance' is an indefinite one and it is beyond normal experience to regard that expression as applying to the payment of a dividend. The payment of a dividend is part of the normal functions of a company, and indeed, in the final analysis, is probably as much the reason for the company's existence as is the earning of profits the reason for an individual trader being in business. To be more precise, a dividend must be regarded as first and foremost a return on an investment. In the customary usage of words the payment by a company of a dividend to a shareholder is not to be regarded as giving financial assistance to that shareholder.

I think it is beyond doubt that the payment of a dividend is not something which will ordinarily be regarded as the giving of financial assistance. It is necessay therefore to inquire whether there is anything in the decided cases or the substance of the transaction itself which would [137] require the payment of a dividend to be treated as falling within a special category so as to bring it under s. 62. . . .

[140] It is, I think, clear that the Court may go beyond the form of a transaction in a case such as this and look at the substance of it. It was suggested by Mr Blank that once this is done the payment of the dividend must be regarded as giving financial assistance to the Wellington Company for the purchase of the shares. As I understand Mr Blank's argument it was that assistance would arise principally in two ways. First, it would enable the Wellington Company to purchase on a cheaper basis than if it had to adopt an alternative method. It is true that the evidence was that the use of dividend money to make the payment would save the Wellington Company from adoping more expensive methods of financing and would also free it from the limitations upon its activities which would result from the need to raise a substantial loan liability. It may be that a situation such as that could in appropriate circumstances amount to financial assistance as contemplated in *Dey's* case [1966] V.R. 464, but I do not think any such conclusion is to be reached here. All that the Wellington Company proposes is to use money to which it as a shareholder would be entitled. It does not amount to any disadvantage to Blundell Brothers Limited which would be applying revenue reserves which would properly be the subject of a dividend. The second matter raised by Mr Blank was that the dividend proposed would be non-taxable in the hands of the Wellington Company by virtue of the provisions of s. 86c(1) of the Land and Income Tax Act of 1954, whereas if the dividend had been paid to the former shareholders (at least as private individuals) it would have been taxable (s. 81(1)(f)). This meant that the Wellington Company by being relieved from a liability for tax, would be able to pay more for the shares than would otherwise be the case. Here again there may be circumstances in which this could be the case but I can see no basis upon which it could be a relevant situation in the present circumstances. The proposed method of payment forms no part of the offer made by the Wellington Company. Before the offer was made the Wellington Company was already aware that doubt had been expressed as to the validity of what it proposed and [141] in fact the present originating summons had been issued before the offer was sent to sharehol-

ders. I can, therefore, see no basis upon which it could be said that the declaration of a dividend could have had any bearing on the amount offered for the shares. There is certainly nothing in the evidence to suggest that the price offered has been influenced by the company's belief that it may be able to use the dividend payment.

Finally, I should say a word about the effect of the payment of the dividend on the financial structure of the two companies. It was common ground that the Wellington Company's proposed treatment of the dividend payment in its accounts was correct. That treatment involved deducting the amount of the dividend from the cost of acquisition of the shares so that the balance sheet would then record the net cost of acquisition. So far as Blundell Brothers Limited is concerned a notional balance sheet of its position after payment of the dividend shows that it would then have assets totalling $5,690,478 and term and current liabilities of $2,546,652. If the purpose of s. 62 is the protection of minority shareholders and creditors, there would appear to be no detriment involved. There are in this case no minority shareholders because all the shareholders have accepted the offer. Existing creditors are amply protected by the substantial excess of assets over liabilities. It was suggested by Mr Blank that future creditors should also be taken into account. On principle I think this is incorrect. It would be unrealistic to say that a company should never make a financial move which might involve an inability to meet the demands of creditors who may at some indefinite time appear and who of course may never appear at all, unless of course it were to do so at a time when it had no reasonable margin of assets over liabilities.

In summary, the position is that the proposal involves the declaration of a dividend by Blundell Brothers Limited out of money which is in every respect a proper subject for a dividend. What is intended is that the Wellington Company will apply the money to which it is entitled in this way towards the purchase of the shares. I consider this to be a normal application by it of funds to which it is entitled and I cannot regard this upon the facts of the present case as constituting 'financial assistance' within the meaning of s. 62.

Securities Trust Ltd. v. Associated Properties Ltd.
(McWilliam J., Nov. 19, 1980, H.Ct.)

McWILLIAM J.: The plaintiff has brought these proceedings for the cancellation under the provisions of section 60 of the Companies Act, 1963, of a special resolution passed on 15th August 1979, by the first-named defendant, hereinafter called Associated. At that time, the second-named defendant, hereinafter called Estates, was in process of acquiring all the shares in Associated under the powers conferred by Section 204 of the 1963 Act.

The special resolution was in the following terms: 'That the making of an interest-free loan of £1,800,000 by the Company to Estates Development Limited which shall be repayable on demand to assist the said Estates Development Limited to purchase ordinary, ordinary A and preference shares in the capital of the Company be and is hereby approved.'

[2] Associated and Estates are two companies which have carried on business in conjunction for a number of years. The directors and managers of the two companies are the same. At the time Estates commenced the operation for the acquisition of the shares in Associated the plaintiff owned shares of each denomination in Associated, and the Bank of Nova Scotia Trust Company Channel Islands Limited, which supports the plaintiff in these proceedings, owned a number of preference shares.

By letter dated 2nd July 1979, sent to all shareholders of Associated an offer was made and recommended by Allied Irish Investment Bank Limited, hereinafter called the Bank, on behalf of Estates for the purchase of the shares in Associated not already held by Estates, at the following prices, that is to say: £7.10 for each ordinary share of £1, £6.75 for each ordinary 'A' share of £1, and 65p for each cumulative preference share of £1. Appendix IV to the said letter, which was expressed to form part of the offer, furnished the following information. Under the heading 'Responsibility for Statements': (a) The information contained in this document in relation to Estates has been [3] supplied by the directors of Estates, who have taken all reasonable care to ensure that the facts stated and the opinions expressed herein in relation to Estates are fair and accurate and that no material facts or considerations have been omitted. All the directors of Estates jointly and severally accept responsibility accordingly. (b) The information contained in this document in relation to Associated has been supplied by the directors of Associated who have taken all reasonable care to ensure that the facts stated and the opinions expressed herein in relation to Associated are fair and accurate and that no material facts or considerations have been omitted. All the directors of Associated jointly and severally accept responsibility accordingly. These two paragraphs are probably some sort of 'common form' which does not take any account of the fact that the directors of both companies were and are identical. Under the heading 'General' are the following paragraphs: (a) No agreement, arrangement or understanding exists between Estates or any person acting in concert with it and any of the directors or recent directors, shareholders [4] or recent shareholders of Associated having any connection with or dependence on the offers. (c) No contracts material to the offers have been entered into by Estates or Associated within the last two years. (e) Allied Irish Investment Bank Limited is satisfied that adequate resources are available to Estates to satisfy full acceptance of the offers (which would entail cash payments by Estates totalling £2.294 million).

In the letter of offer full particulars were given with regard to the position of Associated. No particulars were given with regard to the position of

Estates, except that Estates financed the purchase of houses by tenants of Associated and that the directors and managers of both companies were the same. On 4th May, 1979, the Bank offered loan facilities to Estates in the sum of £2,300,000 for the purchase of the shares in Associated on the security of a letter of hypothecation over all the ordinary and preference shares in the capital of Associated. This offer was accepted by the board of Estates by resolution dated 8th May, 1979, by which time the necessary number of ordinary shareholders in each category had agreed to sell their holdings. By 15th May [5] 1979, Estates had borrowed £1,900,000 for the purchase of shares in Associated. Further sums were borrowed later to complete the purchases. On 8th August 1979 the directors acting in their capacity as the board of Associated resolved to call an extraordinary general meeting of Associated to consider a resolution that Associated should make an interest free loan to Estates for the purchase by Estates of shares in Associated. This extraordinary general meeting was held on 15th August 1979, and a representative of the plaintiff attended and objected to the proposed resolution on the ground that it was not within the power of Associated to make the loan by reason of the provisions of Article 5 of the articles of association of Associated. Nothwithstanding the objection, the resolution was passed and this is the resolution which is challenged in these proceedings. As a result of the objection which had been made on behalf of the plaintiff, a further extraordinary general meeting of Associated was called for 21st August 1979, and, at this meeting, Article 5 of the articles of association was amended, and the objects of Associated as set out in the memorandum of association were also amended.

[6] It appears that, on 15th August 1979, Associated had lodged £862,493.89 with the Bank in discharge of part of the loan Estates had obtained from the Bank for the purchase of shares in Associated and that, on 21st August 1979, after the extraordinary general meeting Estates repaid Associated the sum of £862,493.89 and that, thereupon, Associated lent a sum of £1,800,000 to Estates to repay to the Bank the money borrowed by Estates to purchase the shares.

In the summons herein the plaintiff claims that the special resolution of 15th August 1979 was unlawful as being in contravention of Section 60, subsection (1) of the Act of 1963 and in contravention of Article 5 of the articles of association of Associated. In argument it was also claimed that there had been a breach of faith in calling the general meeting of 21st August 1979 to pass the resolution altering the memorandum and articles after the loan had been made, and also in concealing in the offer document that the resources available to pay for the shares were the resources of Associated itself. . . .

[9] Article 5 of the articles of association of Associated provided as follows: 'None of the funds of the Company shall be empolyed in the purchase of, or lent on, shares of the Company.'

On the facts as they have been put before me, I have difficulty in accepting the accuracy of the statement at paragraph (a) under the heading 'General' in Appendix IV in the letter of offer. It may be assumed, in the absence of compelling evidence to the contrary, that, in a transaction involving the borrowing of a sum in the nature of two million pounds, the parties organising the transaction had worked out the method of completing it before embarking on the transaction. As the directors of the two companies were the same, nothing in the nature of a written agreement between the two boards was required.

I do not know what is the reason for the provisions of section 204 of the 1963 Act or why is should be thought desirable that minority shareholders may be compulsorily bought out, but I am of opinion that, on a compulsory [19] purchase of this nature, the people whose shares are being compulsorily purchased are entitled to be given full particulars of the transactions, its purpose, the method of carrying it out and its consequences. The purpose of the transaction and its consequences have not yet been disclosed and the method of carrying it out was not disclosed to the persons concerned.

I have not been addressed on the duty of directors towards their own members or their positions as agents or otherwise vis-à-vis the shareholders on such a transaction but, although a director is not a trustee of the shareholders, directors are to some extent in a fiduciary position and I am of opinion that, on a transaction such as this, the shareholders are entitled to be given reasonably full particulars by their directors about the matters I have just mentioned. Certainly, in the offer documents in this case there was no indication that the money for the purchase of the shares was to be provided by Associated itself.

As a result of the procedures adopted, the plaintiff's ordinary shares had been compulsorily acquired before the [11] meeting of 15th August 1979, at which, if the plaintiff had then held its ordinary shares, it would have been able, under the provisions of subsection (7) of section 60, to have prevented the transaction being carried out in the way in which it was carried out. In itself this is not a matter of great importance but it may help to explain the procedures adopted by the directors.

However this may be, I am of opinion that the special resolution of 15th August 1979 was one which came within the provisions of subsection (2) of section 60 of the 1963 Act so as to avoid the prohibition contained in subsection (1) and would have been effective to authorise the loan had such a resolution been within the power of the company under its memorandum and articles of association.

I am also of opinion, however, that Associated had no power under its memorandum and articles of association to advance money by way of loan or otherwise for the purchase of its own shares. Lending money was not one of the objects in the memorandum and Article 7 stated unequivocally that none of the funds of the company could be employed for [12] the purchase of shares in the company. Section 25 of the 1963 Act provided that the articles and memorandum bind the company and the members. Accordingly, at the time of the resolution of 15th August 1979, Associated had no power to pass the resolution making the interest free loan of £1,800,000 to Estates. This circumstance was brought to the attention of the company and its directors at the meeting but the resolution was passed notwithstanding.

The subsequent proceedings by Association to rectify the position were also unsatisfactory. The general meeting of 21st August to alter the memorandum and articles of association was effective for that purpose but, in my opinion, this would not retrospectively validate the resolution of 15th August. There should have been a new resolution after there was authority to pass it. Again, this is not in itself a matter of great importance but it is a matter which I should take into consideration with regard to the attitude of the directors in conducting the transaction.

I am not impressed by the procedures of repaying the [13] earlier loan and making new loans which are alleged to have taken place immediately after the resolutions of 21st August had been passed. I am sure that the necessary book entries were made but what was required at that stage was a new resolution authorising the loan.

One of the matters mentioned in the arguments on behalf of the plaintiff was that the Bank had been left in an invidious position by the statements of the directors. This may be so, but the Bank issued the letter of offer under its own name and recommended the offer and advanced the money for the purchase of the shares and was completely identified with the transaction, although I accept it acted in accordance with current practice in such matters.

On the matter being adjourned, the case was settled between the parties and no order of the Court is necessary.

PROFITEERING

Regal (Hastings) Ltd. v Gulliver
[1967] 2 A.C 134n. (H.L.)

See ante p. 155.

Percival v. Wright
[1902] 2 Ch. 421 (Ch.D.)

See ante p. 163.

Coleman v. Myers
[1977] 2 N.Z.L.R. 225

(From headnote) The first and second respondents, a son and his father, were managing director and chairman of an old established private company in which many of the shareholders, individually or through trusts, were relatives. They were also directors of a wine and spirit company in which the family company owned a half share, the book value of which was about $NZ5 million. It also owned properties, including the Strand-Coburg block, and had about $NZ1.8 million in cash. The first respondent, who had only a small shareholding in the family company, evolved a plan whereby he would acquire all the shares at a price of $4.80 each and would pay for them entirely out of the company's assets, by using the cash and selling Strand-Coburg and other properties, leaving him sole owner of the company with remaining interests (principally the share in the wine and spirit company) worth some millions. The major shareholders included certain family trusts of which the second respondent was a trustee. As a result of approaches by both respondents, the shares of these trusts were secured at $4.80; before the subsequent take-over offer they had consequently been transferred to the second respondent's trust. As opposition from a minority was feared, the first respondent formed a new company (the third respondent) of which he was sole owner. This enabled a take-over offer to be made to all the then shareholders in the name of an offeror which, not already holding any shares, could expect to obtain acceptance from holders of nine-tenths of the shares for which offers were made, so making available the compulsory acquisition provisions of the Companies Act 1955, s. 208 (cf. s. 204 of the 1963 Act). The new company made such an offer. In their statutory statement under the Companies Amendment Act 1963 the first and second respondents, as directors of the offeree company, recommended shareholders to accept.

The appellants, who were minority shareholders, reluctantly accepted when served with notice that the offeror had acquired nine-tenths. The first respondent successfully carried out his plan, selling Strand-Coburg at much above book value soon after the take-over and using the proceeds of $3.5 million and the $1.8 million cash to pay for the shares. He made these resources available to himself by temporary loans from the company, followed by capital dividends. When they learnt these facts the appellants brought action, claiming fraud, breach of fiduciary duty, negligence and breach of the Companies Act 1955, s. 62. They alleged that the first respondent's plan and the magnitude of his potential gain had not been disclosed to shareholders; and that he had represented that he intended to keep Strand-Coburg, whereas in fact he had engaged property consultants to sell it and had himself been negotiating for its sale and had advice as to its true value; and that he had also represented that the cash was committed to the wine and spirit company, whereas in fact it was available for capital dividends. They gave evidence of these representations; the documentary evidence included a letter in which the first respondent indicated that because of doubts as to legality he had been advised to keep the method of financing to himself. The appellants claimed rescission and alternatively damages. The respondents gave no evidence themselves but called expert witnesses. In the Supreme Court the action was dismissed. The plaintiffs appealed.

Held, allowing the appeal and awarding damages, 1. The respondent directors owed fiduciary duties to the shareholders, the circumstances from which their duties arose being the family character of the company; the position of father and son in the family and in the company; their high degree of inside knowledge; and the way in which they went about the take-over and the persuasion of shareholders. They were therefore obliged not to make to shareholders statements on matters material to the proposed dealing which were either deliberately or carelessly misleading, and to disclose material matters as to which they knew or had reason to believe that the shareholder whom they were trying to persuade to sell was inadequately informed. On the take-over bid, asset-backing was a material factor. On the facts breach of fiduciary duty and causation were established.

2. Per Woodhouse and Cooke JJ. The respondent directors, being admittedly under a duty of care in recommending shareholders to accept the take-over offer, were also in breach of that duty, in that the circumstances, including the knowledge of the directors as to asset-backing and the plan, the recommendation to sell at $4.80 was not made with reasonable care for the interests of shareholders.

3. Per Woodhouse and Casey JJ. As to fraud, which allegation was pursued on appeal against the first respondent only, although an appellate court will hesitate to differ from the trial judge on questions of fact upon the uncontradicted oral evidence of the appellants and the documentary evidence fraudulent misrepresentations by the first respondent had been established.

DEFENCES

Kinsella v. Alliance & Dublin Gas Consumers Co. Ltd.
(Barron J., Oct. 5, 1982, H.Ct.)

See ante p. 79.

Howard Smith Ltd. v. Ampol Petroleum Ltd.
[1974] A.C. 821

See ante p. 147.

Clark v. Workman
[1920] 1 I.R. 107

Consideration was being given to reconstructing a company owned by two families, the Workmans and the Clarks. Negotiations began with a U.K. consortium with a view to the company being taken over; and after protracted discussions, the consortium offered to buy the company's shares. By this stage, the directors and shareholders were deeply divided about the company's future. At a board meeting which was attended by all eight directors, resolutions dealing with the transfer of a controlling interest in the company were passed with the casting vote of the chairman, the defendant. The defendant had been elected to the chair in 1881, and since then he had acted as chairman without objection from any director.

ROSS J.: [111] Prior to [this] meeting there had been no less than five attempts to deal with the matter, either by reconstruction or by the sale of all or portion of the shares of the company. No unfriendly attempt had been made to prevent Sir George Clark from purchasing. Everybody was willing to accept his offer until he withdrew it, on discovering that it had been made in error. But all this could not get rid of the fiduciary obligations incumbent on every director when he attended that all-important meeting on 26th November. They were bound to consider the interests of all the shareholders, unfettered by any undertaking or promise to any intending purchaser. They were bound to consider all offers, by whomsoever made, and they were bound to weigh and consider the desirability of admitting the persons or companies who proposed to come into their concern. If they failed in any of these matters, they disabled themselves from performing their duty to the shareholders, and nothing that they did would in the eye of the law be held to have been done in good faith.

[His Lordship then read the minutes of the meeting of 26th November 1919.]

The notice of motion now before me is for an interlocutory injunction until the hearing of the action or until further order restraining the defendant directors in respect of three matters: First, from approving of or voting in favour of a resolution approving of any sale or sales or transfers of shares of the company, submitted under Article 139 of the Company's Articles of Association, to any person or persons or body corporate without complying with the provisions of the said Article 139(2).

[112] The second matter in respect of which an injunction is required I pass over, as it is not pressed for the present.

The third is that the defendant company and the named defendants be restrained from acting on the resolution of the directors passed at a meeting of the directors on 26th November, 1919, which resolution purports to have been carried by the casting vote of the defendant, Frank Workman.

I have granted an application of the plaintiffs that they be at liberty to amend the writ of summons by a statement that they are suing on behalf of themselves and other shareholders of the company associated with them.

There is no real controversy, as I have said, as to the facts, but there is much as to the proper inferences to be derived from these facts. There is no real controversy between the parties as to the legal principles, but there is much as to the application of these principles to the facts of the case.

We must first consider what is the position of a shareholder in this and similar companies. He does not hold his property simply at the mercy of the majority. His rights are carefully guarded, and his chief protection consists in the articles of association. Now, what do the articles of association amount to in point of law? They constitute a contract between every shareholder and all the others, and between the company itself and all the shareholders. It is a contract of the most sacred character, and it is on the faith of it that each shareholder advances his money (sect. 14 Companies Act, 1908): *Wood* v. *Odessa Waterworks* (42 Ch.D. 636); see judgment of Farwell L.J. in *Salmon* v. *Quin* [1910] 1 Ch. 311 (ante p. 285). Can this contract be altered or varied?

It can only be varied by a special resolution. A special resolution is defined by sect. 69 of the Act of 1908. It must first be passed as an extraordinary resolution, which requires a three-fourths majority of the shareholders at a general meeting, with notice of the extraordinary resolution. It must then be confirmed by a majority at a general meeting, held not earlier than fourteen days or later than a month after the first meeting, and there must be due notice of the special resolution.

It is therefore a matter of no small difficulty to alter the articles of association. In this case they cannot be altered, because [113] the plaintiffs contol only 55 per cent of the share capital, while the defendants control 45 per cent.

Again, the company is what is known as a private company. This means, according to sect. 121 of the Companies Act, a company that by its articles – (a) restricts the right to transfer its shares; (b) limits the number of its members to fifty; (c) prohibits any invitation to the public to subscribe for debentures or shares.

On 16th April, 1908, this company passed resolutions forming itself into a statutory private company. This was carried into effect by articles 138-142. By article 138 the directors can refuse to sanction (inter alia) a transfer to any transferee not approved by them. They need give no reason for refusal, and their decision is final. Article 139 provides the formal procedure which must be gone through in effecting a transfer of shares. Shareholders must give notice in writing, to be left at the office of the company, of their desire to sell. The directors have then a month to look about for a desirable purchaser. If they find a purchaser within a month, the shareholder is obliged to sell to him. If they do not, the shareholder may after a month sell to a person found by himself, but even then the directors may refuse to register the transfer.

What is the intent and meaning of these provisions? There must be bona fides. There must be no indirect motives. The directors are to act strictly as trustees in the matter of the transfers: *Bennett's Case* (5 De G.M. & G.)

In all cases bona fides is the test of the valid exercise of powers by trustees. An opportunity for deliberation in the full light of the facts and circumstances is impliedly required. I must say that I think it is hardly within the spirit of the articles that shareholders holding 55 per cent. of the shares should be allowed to declare their desire to sell at 12.30, and that at 2.30 the chairman, who had previously refused to give any information, should disclose the names of the proposed transferees. We are not to forget the magnitude and importance of the proposed operation. It is a strong proposition to assert that a majority is to overbear and stifle a minority when the intention is to do such a serious thing as to give a controlling interest in one company to [114] another company that is engaged in the same line of business, and that may be to some extent a rival company. Article 70 prohibits a person engaged in similar business from being a director of this company, and excludes a director of a similar company.

When the test of bona fides comes to be applied, all these matters and the surrounding circumstances call for the most careful attention. I refer in this connexion to the weighty observations of Lord Lindley when Master of the Rolls in *Allen* v. *Gold Reefs Co. of West Africa* [1900] 1 Ch. 656 (ante p. 94). Even the statutory powers of altering articles of association by a special resolution must be exercised subject to those general principles of law and equity which are applicable to all powers enabling majorities to bind minorities. They 'must be exercised', says the learned Master of the Rolls, 'not only in the manner required by law, but also bona fide for the benefit of the company as a whole, and must not be exceeded. These conditions are always implied, and are seldom if ever expressed.' These observations refer to the exercise of powers by shareholders. They apply with augmented force when the powers are being exercised by directors.

There is one other matter of law affecting the case, and it is this: the powers given to directors are powers delegated to the directors by the company, and when once given the company cannot interfere in the subject-matter of the delegation unless by special resolution: *Automatic Self-cleansing Filter Co.* v. *Cuninghame* [1906] 2 Ch. 34 (ante p. 89).

I have stated the principles of law applicable to this case, and I now proceed to apply them. The first question that arises is whether Frank Workman was lawfully chairman of the meeting of directors on the 26th November. [Since he was not, (see ante p. 97)] everything that was done was ultra vires and wholly inoperative. . . .

[115] But it is contended that this is an irregularity that can be cured by acquiescence. The office of chairman becomes important in connexion

with the power to give a casting vote. The question of a casting vote never became material, so far as we know, until the meeting of the meeting of the 26h November, 1919. I am therefore of opinion that Mr Frank Workman was not legally chairman at that meeting, and that the whole of the resolutions which were carried by his casting vote are inoperative, and of no effect. This decision is of merly transient importance, inasmuch as by Article 82 the number of directors may by a resolution at a general meeting be increased, provided the total number shall not exceed ten. [116] Consequently a nominee of the defendants can be elected by the majority which the defendants possess.

I now proceed to examine the more important questions, whether the matter was one of internal management, with which the Court cannot interfere, and whether the defendant directors were acting bona fide, with a view to the interests of the company as a whole. It has been pointed out by the Solicitor-General that they were not altogether abandoning the company. They are retaining twenty-five shares each, which is the amount that would qualify them to be elected directors. But when we come to figures, the importance of their remaining is comparatively small. In value they are selling £1,562,037 and retaining £7,783. Whence it appears that those directors who remain are more vitally interested in the success of the company than those who are departing.

The Solicitor-General and Mr Whitaker contended that the Court has no jurisdiction to interfere in a question of internal management. That proposition cannot be disputed. The Court has no right to say how much is to be distributed in dividends or how much is to be added to the reserve account; what contracts for material are to be accepted, what remuneration is to be paid to their employees and such like. All these things must be dealt with by the directors, and no Court can interfere so long as they are acting within their powers.

But what was the nature of the contemplated operation as distinguished from its expediency? On the question of its expediency I am not called on to express any opinion whatever. I do not presume, with my limited knowledge of this particular kind of business, to express an opinion, on which these most eminent men of business hold divided views. Great combinations of business establishments, banks, and railways are now deemed expedient by many. On the other hand, it was no doubt present to the minds of the plaintiffs that the fine quality of their work might be watered down by the introduction of these English firms. The owners of the great shipping lines, who had found it a true economy to get the best work and the best material, might no longer resort to the company if it ceased to produce ships of the highest quality, as in the past. Which was right and which [117] was wrong I am not called on to decide. But I am obliged to decide whether it was a question of mere management or otherwise, and I am distinctly of the opinion that it was not. It was not a mere matter of the sale of shares. We must look at the contemplated results of the manifest intentions of the parties. It was a matter involving a complete transformation of the company – a fundamental alteration of policy from a policy of isolation to a policy of co-operation with a great syndicate in England, about which very little is known in this country. This operation could in no sense be held to be mere management. Furthermore, if it turns out that there was a breach of trust, that could never be a matter of internal management.

I must now consider the action of the defendant directors, their motives and intentions, and ascertain whether what they proposed and supported was, in the circumstances, inconsistent with a right performance of their fiduciary duty to the company. In the recent Scotch case of *Hindle and John Cotton Ltd.* (1919) 56 Sc.L.R. 625, Lord Finlay said: 'Where the question is one of abuse of powers, the state of mind of those who acted, and the motive in which they acted, are all important, and you may go into the question of what their intention was, collecting from the surrounding circumstances all the materials, which genuinely throw light upon that question of the state of mind of the directors, so as to show whether they were honestly acting in discharge of their powers in the interests of the company, or were acting from some by-motive, possibly of personal advantage, or for any other reason.'

I now refer to two uncontradicted statements in the affidavits. Par. 14 of R. W. Smith's affidavit: 'In my presence Frank Workman stated that he had promised the chairman of the Northumberland Shipbuilding Company, Ltd., that he would use his best endeavours to get the controlling interest in the defendant company into the hands of the chairman of the Northumberland Company, and that he would not attempt to get any better offer from anyone else.' We must take it that this represented the motives and intentions of Mr Frank Workman and those associated with him. By acting thus he had fettered himself by a promise to the [118] English syndicate, and had disqualified himself from acting bona fide in the interests of the company he was leaving. Again, take the affidavit of Sir George Clark, par. 10: 'I consider the offer of Robert Clark more beneficial to the shareholders who desire to sell than the offer of the Northumberland Shipbuilding Company or the Doxford Company, and I believe the defendant directors refused to consider it because they had entered into an agreement with the Northumberland Shipbuilding Company and the Doxford Company to force the sale of the control of the defendant company to them, even at the expense of the shareholders of the defendant company.' Sir George Clark swears that he believes the defendant directors are acting in the interest of the English syndicate, and not in the interest of the defendant company or its shareholders, and he states his belief that if the control is transferred to the syndicate the liquid assets of this company may be used for the purpose of buying debentures in the Northumberland Shipbuilding Company instead of for the benefit of the defendant company. Although this is not quite a statement as to facts, it is declared to be the belief of Sir George Clark. It was a challenge that required some answer, and no answer has been given. I desire it to be known that although I hold the defendants' action to have been wrongful and inconsistent with their duty as trustees, I do not in any way impute to them dishonourable conduct or anything in the nature of fraud. What they have done is analogous to cases we are all familiar with, where the donee of a power executes it in pursuance of an arrangement or bargain which he thinks erroneously he is entitled to make.

If I am right in my view of the law on the evidence, I am bound to make the two-fold order applied for, so as to prevent anything final being done to the prejudice of the plaintiffs before the trial of the action. When it does come to be tried it is quite possible that after discovery and interrogatories the case may assume a different complexion.

REMOVING DISSIDENTS

Re Bugle Press Ltd.
[1961] Ch. 270 (C.A.)

Bugle Press Ltd. had 10,000 issued £1 shares, two members holding 4,500 shares each and the third member holding the remaining 1,000 shares. After differences arose between the first two members and the third 'minority' shareholder, the first two established another company, which then launched a take-over bid for Bugle Press Ltd. The bid was accepted by the first two members; and with 90 per cent of the shares in its hands, the bidder than sought to 'take out' the third shareholder under the U.K. near-equivalent to §204 of the 1963 Act.

LORD EVERSHED M.R.: . . .[283] Mr Instone, in opening the appeal, put his case broadly as follows. First, he said: this case is within the four corners of the section upon the ordinary construction of its language; secondly, it follows that the onus must be upon the dissident shareholder to show that an order should be made otherwise than as the section envisages; and that argument, I interpolate, depends upon the language of the section which I have already read – 'the transferee company shall, unless on an application made by the dissenting shareholder. . . the court thinks fit to order otherwise, be entitled and bound to acquire,' etc. Thirdly, Mr Instone conceded that he cannot in this case rely upon the mere fact that 90 per cent of the shareholders in this company did accept or were prepared to accept this offer, but, says he, since there was an independent valuation of the interest in the company held by the minority shareholder, he fails to discharge the onus which the section puts upon him. . . . [285] He freely accepts that the mechanism of the section has here been invoked by means of the incorporation of this holding company, Jackson & Shaw (Holdings) Ltd., especially for the purpose, and in order to enable the two persons, Shaw and Jackson, to expropriate the shares of their minority colleague, Treby. He says that although that is undoubtedly true, nevertheless, in the result, the case does fall within the strict language of the section and falling within it the consequences must follow. If that argument is right it would enable by a device of this kind the 90 per cent majority of the shareholders always to get rid of a minority shareholder whom they did not happen to like. And that, as a matter of principle, would appear to be contrary to a fundamental principle of our law that prima facie, if a man has a legal right which is an absolute right, then he can do with it or not do with it what he will. . . .

[286] Nevertheless, when regard is had to the opening words and to the parenthesis, it seems to me plain that what the section is directed to is a case where there is a scheme or contract for the acquisition of a company, its amalgamation, re-organisation or the like, and where the offeror is independent of the shareholders in the transferor company or at least independent of that part or fraction of them from which the 90 per cent is to be derived. Even, therefore, though the present case does fall strictly within the terms of section 209, the fact that the offeror, the transferee company, is for all practical purposes entirely equivalent to the nine-tenths of the shareholders who have accepted the offer, makes it in my judgment a case in which, for the purposes of exercising the court's discretion the circumstances are special – a case, therefore, of a kind contemplated by Maugham J. to which his general rule would not be applicable. It is no doubt true to say that it is still for the minority shareholder to establish that the discretion should be exercised in the way he seeks. That, I think, agreeing with Mr Instone, follows from the language of the section which uses the formula which I have already more than once read 'unless on an application made by the dissenting shareholder the court thinks fit to order otherwise'. But if the minority shareholder does show, as he shows here, that the offeror and the 90 per cent of the transferor company's shareholders are the same, then as it seems to me he has, prima facie, shown that the court ought otherwise to order, since if it should not so [287] do the result would be, as Mr Instone concedes, that the section has been used not for the purpose of any scheme of contract properly so called or contemplated by the section but for the quite different purpose of enabling majority shareholders to expropriate or evict the minority; and that, as it seems to me, is something for the purposes of which, prima facie, the court ought not to allow the section to be invoked – unless at any rate it were shown that there was some good reason in the interests of the company for so doing, for example, that the minority shareholder was in some way acting in a manner destructive or highly damaging to the interests of the company from some motives entirely of his own.

McCormick v. Cameo Investments Ltd.
(McWilliam J., Oct. 27, 1978, H.Ct.)

The facts appear from the judgment.

McWILLIAM J.: This matter comes before me on a special summons issued by the applicants on 23rd January 1978, claiming that the respondent is neither entitled nor bound to acquire the shares of the applicants in Dublin and Central Properties Limited (hereinafter called the Transferor Company) upon the terms of a scheme or contract dated 18th November 1977, notwithstanding that it has been approved by nine-tenths of the shareholders of the Transferor Company.

The scheme or contract comes within the terms of section 204 of the Companies Act, 1963. [3] Subject to a question which has been raised about notice to the applicants, a matter to which I will return later, it is accepted that the requirements of this section have been satisfied by the respondent.

The Transferor Company was incorporated in 1901 as the Central Hotel Limited and was principally concerned with the operation of the Central Hotel in Exchequer Street, Dublin. What might be described as a complete reorganisation of the [4] Transferor Company took place in 1972 and 1973. A new issue of shares was made in November 1972, which gave a company called Charterhouse (Ireland) Limited through its subsidiaries a controlling interest in the Transferor Company. The hotel was closed at the end of 1973, the name of the Transferor Company was changed to Dublin & Central Properties Limited, and it became part of a property investment and development group. No attempt has been made to explain what was the purpose or what is the result of the involved inter-company transactions. Sufficient to say that the respondent, one of the subsidiaries of Charterhouse (Ireland) Limited, owned a substantial majority of the shares in the Transferor Company at the relevant date, and the Transferor Company had three wholly-owned subsidiaries one of which, Waterloo Holdings Limited, owned a valuable site for development in Baggot Street.

It appears from the accounts for 1973 that Charterhouse (Ireland) Limited made a loan of £473,849 to the Transferor Company. Presumably this was repaid as it does not appear in the subsequent accounts.

It also appears that, subsequently, a loan of £600,000 or thereabouts was made by the Transferor Company to [5] the respondent in a transaction which has variously been described as money with which property was to be purchased on behalf of the Transferor Company, money advanced to or deposited with the respondent and repayable with interest, and money to be invested by the respondent in property which was to be re-sold at cost to the Transferor Company when a suitable group of sites had been assembled, presumably to add to the site held by Waterloo Holdings

Limited. It is accepted that this money, then increased to £800,000 or thereabouts, was due by the respondent to the Transferor Company at the time of the offer under section 204. The circumstances of this transaction are relied upon strongly by the applicants in their opposition to the acquisition of their shares.

The object of a multiplicity of associated companies is to save tax, to conceal the operations of the effective owners, to conceal the actual ownership of property, to conceal the control of businesses, and, by means of the foregoing to increase the profits of the enterprise with particular regard to the interests of the people in effective control.

Such arrangements are (though some may think unfortunately) perfectly lawful under the provisions of the [6] Companies Act and it has to be borne in mind that a series of transactions designed primarily to benefit the people and the company in effective control may also be to the advantage of the people and companies associated in subsidiary capacities. I emphasise this aspect of the matter because the applicants' case is, essentially, that the scheme is not fair to them, and they claim that the circumstances of the loan of £800,000 have not been adequately explained and that this makes it impossible for them to form an accurate opinion about the scheme and confirms their view that they are incurring a substantial loss under it.

I consider it unsatisfactory that they and I do not understand the full implications of the scheme and that a full and simple statement elucidating the ramifications of the group or groups of companies involved and the purpose and effect of this scheme has not been made, but I am only concerned with the scheme as it stands and the provisions of the statute enabling it to be put through and, the statutory provisions being complied with, the onus is on the applicants [7] to establish that it is unfair to them. *Re Hoare & Co. Ltd.* (150 L.T. 374) *Grierson, Oldham & Adams Ltd.* [1966] 1 Ch. 17.

The applicants are the personal representatives of Frederick Brian McCormick and, as such, hold 4,000 shares of a nominal value of 25p. It appears that these shares represent a holding of 500 £1 shares purchased by the deceased for £500. He transferred these shares to Parkmore Estates Company in April 1964 for a sum of approximately £2,300. In 1967 these shares were divided into 2,000 shares of 25p and, in May 1967 there was a bonus issue of one for one giving a total of 4,000 held by Parkmore. In 1973 Parkmore transferred these shares back to the deceased for a sum alleged on behalf of the respondent to have been £500, estimated by reference to stamp duty, and alleged by the applicants to have been about £8,200. On this basis the applicants say that they will sustain a loss under the scheme whereas the respondent says they will make a profit. Whatever may have been the true value of this consideration I do not consider that it has any significance when considering the issues in this case, which merely concerns the present value of the shares whatever was originally paid.

[8] Be this as it may, the applicants say that, in the present state of the property and commercial world, this is a most unsatisfactory time for them to sell their shares and that they will become much more valuable in the future. This is denied by the accountants for the respondent and by a director of the Ulster Investment Bank Limited who was brought in in an independent advisory capacity before the scheme was submitted to the shareholders. His view was that the offer was a good one and that it is unlikely that the value of the shares will go above the price being offered although it is possible that it could do so.

The applicants further allege that there was oppression in that they were being expropriated by a company which has a majority shareholding. I was referred to the case of *Re Bugle Press* [1961] 1 Ch. 270 (ante p. 364) although it is not suggested that the position here is as clear as it was in that case. Not only is the position not so clear but it seems to me that there is very little resemblance between the two cases, the main difference being that here there were several active and fairly substantial shareholders [9] well-informed in business matters who have accepted the scheme, to whose views I should pay the greatest attention. See *Grierson, Oldham & Adams Ltd.*, and *Re Bugle Press Ltd.*

The applicants also allege that there was oppression in that the loan of £800,000 being payable on demand should have been called in by the Transferor Company and suggest that it was due to the controlling interest of the respondent that it was not called in and no interest was paid in respect of it during the past three years. As this policy was not queried by the applicants at general meetings or otherwise until the scheme was prop-ounded, I cannot accept that there is any evidence of oppression in this regard. It is not oppression for the directors to make an unsatisfactory decision in the conduct of the business of a company.

Finally, it is alleged that the scheme is, in effect, a breach of the provisions of section 60 of the Act in that the respondent owed the Transferor Company a great [10] deal more than is being paid for the shares and, therefore, it was the money of the Transferor Company which was being used to purchase its own shares. There is something to be said for this view of the scheme but I have the sworn testimony of Mr Crowley that he and another person were putting up the money by way of advance to the respondent for the purchase of the shares and that the respondent had not the money either to repay the loan or purchase the shares. I have no information as to the terms of this advance to the respondent but Mr Crowley stated that he and the other person were the main shareholders in the respondent, and they obviously thought it was to their advantage to make the advance. I am not satisfied that he is correct in saying that their major motivation was to see that the shareholders of the Transferor Company should receive the full price for their shares, but this does not alter the fact that the money for the purchase has been financed by another loan. Accordingly I hold that there has not been any breach of the provisions of section 60.

On the question of the notice required to be sent to the applicants under the provisions of section 204 (1), [11] the applicants say that it was sent to their mother's address, that they did not live there, and that they did not receive it until the end of December or the beginning of January. Wherever the applicants live now, the address endorsed on the share certificate as their address as executors is the address to which the notice was sent. There was no evidence as to the date on which it was delivered to this address but the evidence is that it was posted on 16th December and that it arrived at the address to which it was sent. Without evidence, I cannot assume that it did not arrive on 17th, 19th or 20th in the ordinary course of post even though it was the Christmas period. Accordingly, if it was so delivered, the summons was issued late and no application has been made to me to extend the time for issuing the summons and no argument has been addressed to me as to my power to do so. It appears from the affidavit of the first-named applicant that the notice was delivered a long time before the 16th January and his letter of that date is a little less than candid. Under these circumstances, it appears to me that the summons was issued out of time but I will not [12] make any ruling on this point as I have considered it more satisfactory to deal with the real issues in the case where the time involved is so very short.

In accordance with the views I have expressed, I will refuse to make the order sought.

In re National Bank Ltd.
[1966] 1 All E.R. 1006 (Ch.D.)

The National Bank, which had many branches in Ireland, also had branches in England, and the bank was registered as a company there and its head office was there. An elaborate scheme of arrangement was devised to enable the Bank of Ireland to take over National's Irish business and assets, and to enable a Scottish bank to take over its English business and assets. In brief, National's Irish affairs were to be transferred to a new Irish company, N.B.I., in return for shares in it; and those shares would then be sold to the Bank of Ireland in return for cash and renounceable loan stock, which would be distributed pro rata to National's shareholders once the scheme was approved by a special resolution. This was a scheme of arrangement under the U.K. equivalent of s. 201 of the 1963 Act. At a meeting convened to consider the scheme, 90 per cent of those attending (61 per cent of the voting shares) supported it.

PLOWMAN J.: . . . [1008] [I]f the scheme is sanctioned, the Irish business of National Bank will be vested in N.B.I., which will become a wholly

owned subsidiary of the Bank of Ireland, while the remaining business of
National Bank, that is to say, the other third of its business and its membership of the Committee of London Clearing Banks, will continue to
belong to National Bank, which will become a wholly owned subsidiary of
the Scottish Bank. Subject to this it will be a case of 'business as usual'.

The opposition to this petition comes in at sub-para. (d) and (e) of para.
4 of that circular, which I have just read and need not read again, and it
is based on two propositions. In the first place, it is submitted that the
court will not approve a scheme under s. 206 of the Companies Act, 1948
(cf. §201 of the 1963 Act) if the explanatory statement under s. 207 does
not fully and fairly disclose all material facts, and that circular which I
have just read and need not read again, and its based on is then said that
the circular to which I have been referring does not give this information.
The second proposition is this, that where an arrangement under s. 206
is in essence a scheme or contract for the purchase by an outsider of all
the issued shares of the company the court should not approve the arrangement unless both (i) the petitioner proves on full disclosure that the price
is fair and (ii) the arrangement is approved by the ninety per cent majority
referred to in s. 209 (it is 80 per cent in § 204 of the 1963 Act). It is said
that this arrangement is one of that s. 209 character and has not been
approved by the appropriate majority. I should perhaps add this, that no
part of the opposition's case here casts any reflection whatever on the bona
fides of anybody propounding the scheme.

As regards the first proposition the case put forward by National Bank
is this. It agrees that full disclosure of the value of the assets and the
amount of liabilities has not been made, but says that it is putting forward
this arrangement on the basis that a full disclosure of those matters shall
be deliberately withheld, and it submits that nevertheless the scheme is a
fair one which the court should sanction. This attitude arises from the fact
that National Bank is a bank and subject to the special statutory provisions
of Part 3 of Sch. 8 to the Companies Act, 1948. Those provisons exempt
banks from disclosing in their accounts certain information (which I will
call 'exempt information') which ordinary trading companies are required
by Part 1 of that schedule to disclose. . . .

[1011] I should perhaps also refer to an affidavit which was sworn by
Mr Carroll, the Governor of the Bank of Ireland, in which he says this:

> All the banks which were parties to the negotiations and which will
> be concerned in carrying the scheme into effect agreed and proceeded
> on the basis that none of the banks would be required to disclose any
> information which under the exemptions in Sch. 8 to the Companies
> Act, 1948, and the corresponding provision in Ireland, it would not
> be required to disclose in its accounts. As far as the Irish Bank is
> concerned this was a vital requirement. It was for the foregoing reason

and in order to protect the interests of all parties concerned that Messrs. Cooper Brothers & Co. were instructed to make an investigation of [National Bank] and they have stated that an aggregate consideration of 56s. 6d. in respect of each share of [National Bank] is fair and reasonable.

Mr Macdonald, the chairman of the Scottish Bank, swore an affidavit to the same effect as that of Mr Carroll. Mr Rait also gave evidence before me as to the reason why the disclosure of exempt information might prejudice the bank and its shareholders and he explained that if competitors have a greater knowledge of your business than you have of theirs you are at a disadvantage.

It was for reasons such as these that National Bank has put forward an arrangement which preserves inviolate exempt information but at the same time, within that framework attempts to produce a scheme which will appeal to an ordinary intelligent man as a fair commercial proposition.

[1012] Counsel for National Bank, in regard to the question of fairness, points out that independent accountants of eminence in their profession were instructed to make a detailed investigation and all relevant information, including the exempt information, was made available to them. They say in their report that the compensation offered was fair and reasonable. Secondly, two other firms of eminent accountants, namely, the joint auditors, are of the same opinion as Cooper Brothers & Co., and the board of National Bank unanimously recommended the acceptance of the proposals.

Reference was also made to the substantial profit which on current values the shareholders are able to see. In October last the Stock Exchange quotation for National Bank shares was a shilling or two under £2. In January of this year it had risen to 56s. 6d. A comparison was also made of the income position. On last year's dividend of sixteen per cent a holder of one hundred 10s. shares received £8 gross. If the arrangement is sanctioned he will get £100 of seven per cent loan stock producing £7 gross and £182 10s. in cash, which on a five per cent basis would produce £9 2s. 6d. gross, making a total of £16 2s. 6d. as compared with £8. All these matters are prayed in aid of the submission that within its self-imposed limits the scheme is a fair one.

The question, however, which I have to consider is whether the deliberate omission to disclose exempt information is fatal to the arrangement despite the weight of the evidence that the compensation is fair and despite the evidence that the disclosure of exempt information might result in damage to all the shareholders. In my judgment the answer to that question is No.

The principles on which the court acts in an application under s. 206 are well settled and are stated in *Buckley On The Companies Acts* (13th Edn.) p. 409 as follows:

> In exercising its power of sanction the court will see, first, that the provisions of the statute have been complied with [I interpolate there that no question arises with regard to that matter]; secondly, that the class was fairly represented by those who attended the meeting and that the statutory majority are acting bona fide and are not coercing the minority in order to promote interests adverse to those of the class whom they purport to represent [nothing arises on that] and thirdly, that the arrangement is such as an intelligent and honest man, a member of the class concerned and acting in respect of his interest, might reasonably approve.

I comment there that in fact very nearly four thousand shareholders did approve. Then the passage goes on:

> The court does not sit merely to see that the majority are acting bona fide and thereupon to register the decision of the meeting; but at the same time the court will be slow to differ from the meeting unless, either the class has not been properly consulted, or the meeting has not considered the matter with a view to the interests of the class which it is empowered to bind, or some blot is found in the scheme.

It is against the background of those principles that the opposition to this scheme has to be considered.

Section 206 and s. 207 say nothing about disclosure either of valuations or of profits or of assets or of liabilities. By s. 206 the court is given the widest possible discretion to approve any sort of arrangment between a company and its shareholders. It seems to me that to say that full disclosure must be made of all material facts begs the question of the nature of the scheme which is being propounded. The extent of the disclosure required must depend on the nature of the scheme. Here the scheme is one which is based on the withholding of exempt information. If the evidence satisfies me (as it does) that the scheme is fair I see no reason why I should not sanction it.

As regards counsel for the opposing shareholders' second objection, namely, that the scheme really ought to be treated as a s. 209 case needing a ninety per cent [1013] majority, I cannot accede to that proposition. In the first place, it seems to me to involve imposing a limitation or qualification either on the generality of the word 'arrangement' in s. 203 or else on the discretion of the court under that section. The legislature has not seen fit to impose any such limitation in terms, and I see no reason for implying any. Moreover, the two sections. . . involve quite different considerations and different approaches. Under s. 206 an arrangement can only be sanctioned if the question of its fairness has first of all been submitted to the court. Under s. 209, on the other hand, the matter may never come to the court at all. If it does come to the court then the onus is cast on the dissenting minority to demonstrate the unfairness of the scheme. There are, therefore, good reasons for requiring a smaller majority in favour of a scheme under s. 206 than the majority which is required under s. 209 if the minority is to be expropriated.

XIII. Transactions with Outsiders

The vast majority of companies are formed with a view to their doing business with persons other than their principal shareholders or directors, i.e. with 'outsiders'. A major problem, therefore, is when or in what circumstances contracts and engagements with outsiders which are purported to be entered into by or on behalf of a company are legally binding on it.Since companies by their very nature can act only through individuals, or agents, it must first be established that the person negotiating the transaction in question is authorised by the company to do so. Secondly, persons apparently authorised to act for the company in a particular way in fact may not have authority to do so. The transaction in question may even be *ultra vires*, or the company's regulations may place other restrictions on the agent's power to act. Subject to what is said below, since companies' memoranda and articles of association are public documents, outsiders dealing with companies are deemed to know the contents of such documents; and accordingly, they are deemed to have 'constructive notice' of companies' objects and any other restrictions that those documents impose on company agents' authority. In the past, companies would not be bound by contracts made on their behalf but contrary to such restrictions. Nor would companies be held to contracts made for them before they were incorporated. Nor could companies ratify either *ultra vires* or pre-incorporation contracts. Doing business with companies, therefore, presented special risks in that undertakings entered into with them could transpire not to be legally binding on them.

These very questions were the subject of the E.E.C. First Directive on Company Law. According to the central part of the Directive's preamble:

> Whereas the basic documents of the company should be disclosed in order that third parties may be able to ascertain their contents and other information concerning the company, especially particulars of the persons who are authorised to bind the company; Whereas the protection of third parties must be ensured by provisions which restrict to the greatest possible extent the grounds on which obligations entered into in the name of the compay are not valid; . . .

CAPACITY AND ULTRA VIRES ENGAGEMENTS

Ashbury Railway Carriage Co. v. Riche
(1875) L.R. 7 H.L. 653 (H.L.)
See ante p. 40.

Northern Bank Finance Corp. v. Quinn
(Keane J., Nov. 8, 1979, H.Ct.)
For background to this case, see ante p. 48.

KEANE J.: . . . [12] Counsel for the bank submitted that, even if the execution of the Guarantee were *ultra vires* the Memorandum, his clients were protected by s. 8 (1) of the Companies Act, 1963. [13] That sub-section provides as follows:

> Any act or thing done by a company which if the company had been empowered to do the same would have been lawfully and effectively done shall, notwithstanding that the company had no power to do such act or thing, be effective in favour of any person relying on such act or thing who is not shown to have been actually aware, at the time when he so relied thereon, that such act or thing was not within the powers of the company, but any director or officer of the company, who was responsible for the doing by the company of such act or thing shall be liable to the company for any loss or damage suffered by the company in consequence thereof.

Evidence was given on behalf of the Bank by Mr T. F. O'Connell who was in November, 1973, the Bank's Solicitor. He said that he received the title documents relative to the transaction from the security department of the Bank in November, 1973, with instructions to prepare the necessary mortgage documentation in connection with the loan. He was furnished with the Title Deeds to the properties concerned and with the Memorandum and Articles of the Company. He [14] investigated the title in the normal manner and drew up the necessary Resolution to be passed by the Directors of the Company, the Mortgage and the Guarantee. He also sent out the two sets of Requisitions on Title. He said that the first intimation that he had that there was any doubt as to the power of the Company to execute the Guarantee was contained in a letter from the Company's Solicitors to the Bank dated the 6th December, 1978.

Mr O'Connell said that he did not specifically recall reading the Memorandum and Articles. His normal procedure, before drawing up the Resolution of the Directors, was to check the objects clause. He could not, however, recall checking the objects clause in the present case. He said that it did not occur to him that the transaction was not within the powers of the Company. His normal practice was to mark the relevant objects in pencil, but he had not done so in this instance.

It is not surprising to find that Mr O'Connell had no positive recollection of reading the Memorandum and Articles, since, as he indicated, he has occasion to read so many [15] documents of this nature that he can hardly be expected to remember each of them, particularly when the transaction in question took place nearly six years ago.

I think that the probabilities are that Mr O'Connell did read the objects clause of the Memorandum; it would be surprising if he did not, since it was furnished to him so that he could satisfy himself as to the existence in law of the Company and its power to enter into the proposed transaction. It may well be that, as is not uncommon with busy practitioners when dealing with matters of this nature, his eye travelled reasonably rapidly over a number of the clauses. But I think that the probabilities are that he did read the Memorandum and came to the conclusion that the execution of the Guarantee and the Mortgage was within the powers of the Company. Had he come to any other conclusion, I have not the slightest doubt but that he would have advised his principals not to close the transaction until the necessary amendment had been effected to the Memorandum. It follows that Mr O'Connell was aware of the contents of the objects clause of the Memorandum, but must have mistakenly believed that they empowered the Company to [16] execute the Guarantee and Mortgage. It would not have been in accordance with his normal practice to dispense with reading the Memorandum and I have no reason to suppose that he departed from his normal practice on this occasion. It is, of course, inconceivable that he appreciated the lack of vires but simply did not do anything about it.

The question accordingly arises as to whether, in these circumstances, the bank were 'actually aware', within the meaning of s. 8 (1) of the lack of vires. Mr O'Neill submitted that the language of s. 8 (1) clearly demonstrated that the onus of establishing actual knowledge within the meaning of the section is on the person who asserts that such knowledge existed and that, accordingly, the onus was on the Company, to establish that the Bank were 'actually aware' of the lack of vires. This may very well be so, but I do not think it is material to the issue which has to be resolved in the present case. There is no conflict as to the facts in the present case; Mr O'Connell was the only witness on this issue and he was called by the Bank. The only question that arises is as to whether, having regard to that evidence and the inferences, which, in my view, necessarily follow from it, the [17] Bank can be said to have been 'actually aware' of the lack of vires.

Mr O'Neill submitted that actual, as distinguished from constructive, notice of the lack of vires was essential if a third party was to lose the protection of s. 8 (1). I accept that this is so: altogether apart from authority, the language used would suggest that what the legislature had in mind was actual and not constructive notice. Moreover, to interpret the section in any other way would be to frustrate its manifest object. While there is no authority of which Counsel were aware or which I have been able to discover on the section, the mischief which it was designed to avoid is clear. Prior to the enactment of the section, all persons dealing with a Company were deemed to have notice of the contents of the Company's public documents, including its Memorandum and Articles. If a transaction was *ultra vires*, the other party to it, speaking generally, had no rights at all. The manifest injustice and inconvenience which followed from this rule is amply illustrated by the decision in *Re John Beauforte Ltd.* [1953] Ch. 131, which was referred to in the argument. [18]

But if constructive notice can still be relied on in answer to a party claiming the protection of this section, the protection in question would be, to a significant extent, eroded. It is clear, moreover, that the doctrine of constructive notice should not normally be applied to purely commercial transactions, such as the advancing of money. (See the observations of Mr Justice Kenny delivering the Judgment of the Supreme Court in *Bank of Ireland Finance Ltd.* v. *Rockfield Ltd.* [1979] I.R. 21, ante p. 227).

But while I am satisfied that the doctrine of constructive notice does not apply to the sub-section under consideration, this does not dispose of the matter. The Bank, because of the knowledge of their Agent, Mr O'Connell, which must be imputed to them, were aware of the objects of the Company. There were no further *facts* of which they could be put on notice. But they failed to draw the appropriate inference from those facts, i.e. that the transaction was *ultra vires*. Mr O'Neill submits that, even accepting this to be so, this [19] is not the actual knowledge which the section contemplates.

A great number of transactions are entered into every day by companies, public and private, without any of the parties looking at the Memorandum in order to see whether the transaction in question is in fact authorised by the Memorandum. I think it probable that, on the occasions when the Memorandum is looked at before a transaction is entered into, it is normally because the company's solicitor or a solicitor for a third party wishes to satisfy himself that the proposed transaction is *intra vires* the Memorandum. I think it is clear that the section was designed to ensure that, in the first category of cases, persons who had entered into transactions in good faith with the company without ever reading the Memorandum and accordingly with no actual knowledge that the transaction was *ultra vires* were not to suffer. I can see no reason in logic or justice why the legislature should have intended to afford the same protection to persons who had actually read the Memorandum and simply failed to appreciate the lack of vires. The maxim *ignorantia juris haud neminem excusat* may not be of universal [20] application, but this is certainly one situation where it seems fair that it should apply.

This is best illustrated by an example. The Directors of a public company decide to invest the bulk of the company's resources in a disastrous property speculation as a result of which the company suffers enormous losses. The company in fact had no power to enter into any such transaction, but the Vendors' Solicitors, although furnished with the Memorandum and Articles, failed to appreciate this. If the submission advanced on behalf of the Bank in this case is well founded, it would mean that, in such circumstances, the innocent shareholders would be the victims rather than the Vendors. There seems no reason why the consequences of the Vendors' failure to appreciate the lack of vires should be visited on the heads of the blameless shareholders. I do not overlook the fact that the sub-section gives the company a remedy against any director or officer of the company who is responsible for the *ultra vires* act; but such a remedy may not necessarily enable the innocent shareholder to recoup all his losses.

It is interesting in this context to note that in the [21] United Kingdom the Jenkins Committee recommended that even actual knowledge of the contents of the Memorandum should not deprive a third party of his right to enforce a contract if he honestly and reasonably failed to appreciate that they precluded the company or its officers from entering into the contract. (See Cmnd. 1749, paras, 35-42). Writing in the early days of the operation of our Act, Mr Alexis Fitzgerald said of s. 8.

> The draughtsmen wisely reject the advice of the Jenkins Committee, which would have given contractual rights even to third parties with actual knowledge, where such a third party could prove he honestly and reasonably failed to appreciate the effect of the lack of power. Acceptance of this recommendation would have created uncertain and therefore bad law.

(See 'A Consideration of the Companies Act, 1948, the Companies Act (Northern Ireland) 1960, and Companies' Act, 1963: I', *The Irish Jurist* Volume One (New Series) Part One at p. 16)

In England, the ultra vires rule was modified by s. 9 (1) of the European Communities Act, 1972, and while the language of the section is different from that of s. 8 of [22] our 1963 Act, the requirement being that the third party should have acted in good faith, it is interesting to note that the editors of the 22nd Edition of *Palmer's Company Law* take the view that it would not protect the third party in circumstances such as the present. (See Volume One, p. 97).

I am satisfied that, where a party is shown to have been actually aware of the contents of the memorandum but failed to appreciate that the Company were not empowered thereby to enter into the transaction in issue, s. 8 (1) has no application. It follows that, in the present case, the bank cannot successfully rely on s. 8 (1).

Mr O'Neill next submitted that the execution of the guarantee was retrospectively validated by a special resolution of the Company passed on the 18th May 1974. It is conceded on behalf of the Company that this resolution effectively amended the memorandum so as to enable a guarantee to be executed. Mr O'Neill relied on s. 10(1) of the Act of 1963, which provides that:

> Subject to sub-section (2) a Company may, by special resolution, alter the provisions of its memorandum by [23] abandoning, restricting or amending any existing object or by adopting a new object and any alterations so made shall be as valid as if originally contained therein, and be subject to alteration in like manner.

He argued that the words 'shall be as valid as if originally contained therein' meant, in a case such as the present, that a transaction entered into prior to the passing of the resolution was, as it were, retrospectively validated.

I do not think that is correct. Were it so, the consequences would be strange indeed: as pointed out by Mr McCracken, if the Company in the present case originally had power to execute a guarantee and deprived itself of that power by the passing of a subsequent resolution, it could hardly be said that the execution of the guarantee prior thereto was thereby invalidated. I think that the meaning of the words in question is quite clear, if one considers the provisions of s. 7 which provides that

> the Memorandum must be printed, must bear the same stamp as if it were a deed, and must be signed by each subscriber in the presence of at least one witness who must attest the signature.

[24] The words relied on by Mr O'Neill were clearly designed, in my view, to relieve the Company from the necessity of having the Memorandum in its altered form signed again by the subscribers and attesting witnesses and then reprinted. This is also the view taken in one of the leading English text books on the subject: See Gower's *Principles of Modern Company Law* (3rd edition) at p. 90, n. 43.

Finally, Mr O'Neill submitted that the Company were estopped at this stage from contesting the validity of the guarantee. He concedes that the doctrine of estoppel could not enable the Company validly to perform an act which was *ultra vires*; but submits that as the Company had been empowered since the 18th May, 1974, to enter into the transaction, they cannot now be heard to say that it is *ultra vires*. In particular, he relies on a letter written by the Company to the Bank on 31st December, 1976, in which they said

> As you are aware, this Company has guaranteed the borrowings from the corporation of Mr Fursey Quinn.
>
> Please let us have details, in confidence, of the guaranteed borrowings in relation to the amount [25] outstanding including interest, the amount and timing of repayments made and interest paid to date.

Mr O'Neill points out that the Bank had power at any time to call in the amount of the loan; and that, following the receipt of this letter, they acted to their detriment by failing to call it in.

The ingredients of estoppel in pais are set out in volume 16 of Halsbury's *Laws of England.* 4th edition, para. 1505 as follows:-

> Where a person has by words or conduct made to another a clear and unequivocal representation of fact, either with knowledge of its false-hood or with the intention that it should be acted upon, or has so conducted himself that another would, as a reasonable man, under-stand that a certain representation of fact was intended to be acted on, and that (sic) the other has acted on the representation and thereby altered his position to his prejudice, an estoppel arises against the party who made the representation, and he is not allowed to aver that the fact is otherwise than he represented it to be.

[26] Can it reasonably be said that, in the present case, the Bank acted on the representation contained in the letter of 31st December – if rep-resentation it were – and thereby altered their position to their prejudice? There is no reason to suppose that at the date this letter was written the Bank entertained the slightest doubts as to the validity of the guarantee or mortgage. Had they entertained any such doubts, they would have immediately required the re-execution of the guarantee and the mortgage before allowing any further interest to accumulate. There is nothing to suggest that this letter had any effect on the attitude of the Bank towards calling in the loan. I do not think that it could be said that they in any way altered their position to their prejudice as a result of any representation that may have been contained in this letter. I think it is also clear that the mere fact that the Company sent to the Bank its Memorandum and Articles of Association at the time of its application for a loan could not in any sense be said to constitute a representation which was subsequently acted on to their detriment by the Bank. Their action in [27] so doing was not a representation that the Company had the power in question; it was no more than an invitation to the Bank to satisfy themselves that the transaction was *intra vires* and there is no reason to suppose that any request to alter the Memorandum would not have been immediately complied with. I am accordingly satisfied that this submission also fails.

In these circumstances, I am satisfied that the execution of the guarantee was *ultra vires* and that the Bank cannot successfully rely on any of the grounds advanced by Counsel. It is, I think, accepted that the mortgage is in turn dependent for its validity upon the guarantee; the Company could not validly execute a mortgage in order to secure an obligation which they had no power to accept in the first place. This is, in any event, made clear by sub-paragraph (f) to which reference has already been made. The claim of the Bank against the company will accordingly be dismissed.

In re M.J. Cummins Ltd.
[1939] I.R. 60 (H.Ct.)

The shareholders decided that the company's business should be sold to Mr Cummins for £3,000. He did not possess that money; but a scheme was made with the bank whereby the bank would advance money to the company, which would then put him into sufficient funds to acquire the company's entire share capital

JOHNSTON J.: . . . [64] The exercise by the company of its borrowing powers was, as I have indicated, clearly an act *ultra vires* the powers of the company, and it is contended on behalf of the liquidator that the bank, at the time when they advanced this sum were well aware that company was exceeding its powers and that no valid debt was thereby incurred which – so far, at any rate, as the innocent trade creditors of the company are concerned – can be relied upon by the bank.

Now, there are certain propositions of the law which have been advanced on behalf of the bank with which I entirely agree. For instance, it is the law that while a proposed lender in his dealings with a public company must be presumed to have notice of the provisions of its Memorandum and Articles of Association, he is not called upon in the case of a company which has a general power of borrowing, to make any inquiries as to the purpose of the loan in order to make sure that that purpose is within the powers of the company. That proposition is very conveniently illustrated in the case of *In re David Payne &* [65] *Co., Ltd.* [1904] 2 Ch. 608, where it was further decided that knowledge on the part of the lender that the money was intended to be misapplied will avoid the loan. In the same case it was held that knowledge, on the part of a director of the lenders, of the *ultra vires* purpose for which the loan is being got will not be imputed to the lending company if the person having such knowledge has a personal interest in the transaction. That principle, however, does not apply to the present case.

The main question in the case, therefore, is whether the bank had knowledge of the wrongful purpose for which this money was being raised; and, having analysed all the circumstances connected with the loan, I am satisfied that not only had the bank the fullest knowledge of that purpose, but the local Agent of the bank in Mullingar . . . was the person who arranged the ingenious plan by which the loan was carried through; so that, so far as the bank's participation in the affair is concerned, the case goes far beyond the question of mere knowledge. In saying so much I do not wish it to be thought that I am imputing to the bank blame of any kind. I think that the mistake took place through a failure to appreciate the limitations that must be read into Article 3 (o) of the Memorandum of Association and the realities as to the purpose of the loan. . . .

[69] [T]he matter that the liquidator has brought before me . . . involves

only a question as between the claims of a number of ordinary trading creditors and the claim of the bank founded upon an *ultra vires* transaction of the company of which they had notice; but, out of courtesy to the learned counsel for the bank, I think that I should say a word or two as to a number of extraneous matters.

First of all, it is almost unnecessary to say that a company cannot ratify an act of its own or an act of its directors which is outside and beyond the constitutional powers of the company. If such a thing were possible it would mean an end for ever of the salutary principle [70] of *ultra vires*. There are cases in which the *ultra vires* acts of directors have been held to be ratified by the conduct of the company; but those were cases in which the acts, if done by the company, would have been *intra vires*. In the case of the *Ashbury Railway Carriage and Iron Co.* v. *Riche* (L.R.7 H.L. 653 ante p. 40), Lord Cairns said: 'It would be perfectly fatal to the whole scheme of legislation. . . if you were to hold that, in the first place, directors might do that which even the whole company could not do, and that then, the shareholders finding out what had been done, could sanction subsequently what they could not antecedently have authorised,' and Lord Hatherly laid down a proposition which is very pertinent in the present case; 'I think that the Legislature had in view the object of protecting outside dealers and contractors with this limited company from the funds of the company being applied. . . for any other object whatsoever than those specified in the Memorandum of Association.' Similarly Lord Macnaghten in the case of *Trevor* v. *Whitworth* (12 A.C. 409), quoting Cotton L.J., said that no part of the capital of a company 'can be returned to a member so as to take away from the fund to which the creditors have a right to look as that out of which they are to be paid.' This matter has been very neatly summed up in the following proposition which I take from Mr Howard A. Street's excellent text-book on *Ultra Vires*. The learned author says: 'No act which is *ultra vires* of the corporation itself can be validated by ratification or acquiescence, or otherwise than by statute.'

The learned counsel for the bank then discussed at length the law as to subrogation and tracing orders, and endeavoured by some such means to place the bank's claim on an equality with the debts of the ordinary trading creditors. There is here a confusion of thought which must be set right. When an *ultra vires* act is committed by a borrowing company, on the one hand, and by a lending company, on the other, no debt, common law, equitable or otherwise, is thereby created in favour of the latter as against the former. The theory of the law is that the whole transaction is null and void and can give rise to no legal rights or claims whatever. In dealing with a limited company, which must act strictly within its constitution, a contracting party must watch his step; and in regard to this liability there is no difference between a family company and a great trading corporation. As was said by that master of clear-thinking and lucid exposition

– Lord Macnaghten – in *Trevor* [71] v. *Whitworth*, 'a family company. . . does not limit its trading to the family circle. If it takes the benefit of the Act, it is bound by the Act as much as any other company. It can have no special privilege or immunity.' In the *Ashbury Case*, Lord Cairns quotes with approval the following words of Blackburn J., in all their useful harshness, as to the effect of an *ultra vires* transaction: 'I do not entertain any doubt that if, on the true construction of a statute creating a corporation it appears to be the intention of the Legislature, expressed or implied, that the corporation shall not enter into a particular contract, every Court, whether of law or equity, is bound to treat a contract entered into contrary to the enactment as illegal, and therefore wholly-void.'

It frequently happened, however, that corporations, found themselves with surplus assets in their hands, after the ordinary creditors had been paid in full, and the anxious question then arose whether the shareholders of the company were to be allowed to make a profit for themselves by means of the money which had been wrongly or mistakenly advanced by their partner in the *ultra vires* transaction. That question was discussed at great length in the great case of *Sinclair* v. *Brougham* [1914] A.C. 398, (the celebrated Birkbeck Bank case) in which a building society had opened a bank and had taken huge sums, amounting to millions of pounds, from depositors. In the liquidation of the company, after the ordinary creditors had been paid in full, a large surplus remained in the hands of the liquidators, and the question arose whether that sum should be paid to certain classes of members of the building society – that is, whether the surplus in its entirety was assets of the society – or should be paid back in whole or in part to the depositors (the lenders). The problem before the House was how to work out 'the higher equity that no one has a right to keep either property or the the proceeds of property which does not belong to him,' without trenching upon the principle of *ultra vires* The anxious search of the Law Lords, set out in fifty pages of the Law Reports, for a formula which would on the one hand, be based upon sound principles of equity, and, on the other would not be a mere good-natured gesture, is the most remarkable illustration of which I am aware of the meticulous care with which that House approaches the task of reconciling what is called 'abstract justice' with the strict rule of law. In the result, it was pointed out [72] that that reconcilement could be effected either through the principle of subrogation (the principle, as Lord Dunedin explained, that if the lender could show that the borrowed moneys had been expended in paying the just debts of the borrower, the lender would be entitled *pro tanto* to the benefit of the relief that the borrower had thereby gained), or through the principle that the money that was lent was not a debt, but was trust money that the lender might follow by means of a tracing order.

But these considerations have no applicability to the present case. Neither principle could possibly be brought into operation in a contest between the genuine creditors of a company and a person who had lent money to the company under an arrangement that was 'illegal and therefore wholly void.' In the *Birkbeck Bank Case*, the ordinary creditors had been paid in full, and their right to that treatment was not controverted. Lord Dunedin (at p. 437) says that the trade creditors were, in his judgment, 'rightly paid, under the circumstances of the actual case, and had they not been, they would stand, after expenses of the liquidation, as first in the ranking. For, in a question with shareholders, we are told that they were debts of a character which the directors had a power to make. And in a question with the depositors [the lenders] they were incurred in a business, illegally carried on no doubt, as for the society, but yet one which the depositors had been willing that the directors should carry on.' That is exactly the question that arises in the present case, and it seems to me that this proposition of Lord Dunedin determines it. Lord Sumner seems to express the same view in a passage at p. 459, and the implications that are to be drawn from a passage in Lord Haldane's judgment at p. 414 are to the same effect.

The case of *Re National Permanent Benefit Building Society* (1869) L.R. 5 Ch. 309, seems to me to afford further authority – if such is needed – for the conclusion at which I have arrived. The case decides that if the bank had applied for the winding up of M. J. Cummins Ltd., claiming to be creditors by virtue of the loan that had been made, the Court would have been obliged to refuse the order. In that case a lender who had advanced an *ultra vires* loan was held to be unable to get a winding up order, and Romilly M.R. who had made such an order, was reversed. Giffard L.J. held that there was no debt, either legal or equitable owing to the petitioners and that therefore they could not ask for the [73] winding-up of the company. He said that if the lenders had any rights founded in equity, either against the property of this company, which was pledged to them, or against the persons to whom the money was lent, 'they can only be asserted by filing a bill and taking a very different proceeding from that which has been taken here.' In other words, he held that there could be no controversy between the *ultra vires* lenders and the creditors of the society, but that the former persons might establish rights as against the persons to whom the money was lent or against the property to which it could be traced.

The last case to which I need refer is that of the *Bank of Ireland* v. *Cogry Flax-spinning Co. Ltd.*, [1900] 1 I.R. 219, in which Porter M.R., in the course of the winding-up of a one-man company, found that certain debentures which had been issued to a supposedly secured creditor were 'issued without authority and without consideration' and that 'they do not bind the assets as against the creditors.'

In this judgment I have said nothing as to the collateral security which the bank insisted upon getting not only from Mr Cummins but from Mr

T. J. Dowdall as well – the guarantee for the whole debt from Cummins, the promissory note from the two of them and the guarantee for £500 from Dowdall; but it might be said that all this suggests at least a certain amount of misgiving in the mind of the bank as to the entire regularity of the transaction with M. J. Cummins Ltd. It is satisfactory to know, however, that the taking of this wise precaution on the part of the bank may have useful consequences in regard to the balance owing to them.

I shall therefore make the order which has been suggested by the liquidator.

AGENCY AND UNAUTHORISED TRANSACTIONS

Mahony v. East Holyford Mining Co.
(1875) L.R. 7 H.L. 869 (H.L.)

A group of fraudsters formed a company ostensibly to work a mine, and by a prospectus induced members of the public to invest in the company. But instead of spending those funds on developing the mine, the fraudsters withdrew it from the company's bank account for their own use. They misled the company's bank into believing that they were authorised to draw cheques on the company's behalf. When what transpired was discovered, the question arose who should bear the loss – either the investors or the bank.

LORD HATHERLEY: . . . [393] It is a point of very great importance that those who are concerned in joint stock companies and those who deal with them should be aware of what is essential to the due performance of their duties, both as customers or dealers with the company, and as persons forming the company, and dealing with the outside world respectively. On the one hand, it is settled by a series of decisions, of which *Ernest* v. *Nicholls* (1857) 6 H.L.C. 401, is one and *Royal British Bank* v. *Turquand* (1856) 6 E.& B. 327, a later one, that those who deal with joint stock companies are bound to take notice of that which I call the external position of the company. Every joint stock company has its memorandum and articles of association; every joint stock company, or nearly every one, I imagine (unless it adopts the form provided by the statute, and that comes to the same thing) has its partnership deed under which it acts. Those articles of association and that partnership deed are open to all who are minded to have any dealings whatsoever with the company, and those who so deal with them must be affected with notice of all that is contained in those two documents.

After that, the company entering upon its business and dealing [894] with persons external to it, is supposed on its part to have all those powers and authorities which, by its articles of association and by its deed, it appears to possess; and all that the directors do with reference to what I may call the indoor management of their own concern, is a thing known to them and known to them only; subject to this observation, that no person dealing with them has a right to suppose that anything has been or can be done that is not permitted by the articles of association or by the deeds.

This being the case, a banker dealing with a company must be taken to be acquainted with the manner which, under the articles of association, the moneys of the company may be drawn out of his bank for the purposes of the company. [I]n this case, the bankers were informed that cheques might be drawn upon the bank by three directors of the company. And the bankers must also be taken to have had knowledge, from the articles, of the duties of the directors, and the mode in which the directors were to be appointed. But, after that, when there are persons conducting the affairs of the company in a manner which appears to be perfectly consonant with the articles of association, then those so dealing with them, externally, are not to be affected by any irregularities which may take place in the internal management of the company. They are entitled to presume that that of which only they can have knowledge, namely, the external acts, are rightly done, when those external acts purport to be performed in the mode in which they ought to be performed. For instance, when a cheque is signed by three directors, they are entitled to assume that those directors are persons properly appointed for the purpose of performing that function, and have properly performed the [895] function for which they have been appointed. Of course, the case is open to any observation arising from gross negligence or fraud. I pass that by as not entering into the consideration of the question at the present time. Outside persons when they find that there is an act done by a company, will, of course, be bound in the exercise of ordinary care and precaution to know whether or not that company is actually carrying on and transacting business, or whether it is a company which has been stopped and wound up, and which has parted with its assets, and the like. All those ordinary inquiries which mercantile men would, in the course of their business make, I apprehend, would have to be made on the part of the persons dealing with the company. . . .

[897] Now if the question came to be which of two innocent parties (as it is said) was to suffer loss, I apprehend, my Lords, that in point of law what must be considered in cases of that kind is this: which of the two parties was bound to do, or to avoid, any act by which the loss has been sustained. I think there can be no doubt that in this case the shareholders of the company were the persons who were bound to see that nobody usurped or assumed the office of director unduly; that is to say, without that office having been properly conferred upon him. The shareholders of the company were persons some of whom had, though others perhaps had not, received the prospectus originally, when they did receive it they must have seen those persons named in the first or in the second prospectus

issued after the incorporation had taken place. At all [898] events the shareholders knew that if the company was to be carried on at all there must be some acting body, and as the subject matter of the prospectus to which they were invited to contribute was a mine, which was to be set at work, immediately, they must have known that if it was to be immediately set at work, there must be expenditure, and they must have known the expenditure would necessarily go on from time to time upon the ordinary business of the company, independently of that special work which they were undertaking amongst themselves to execute. Now whose business was it to see that that was all properly done? It was the business of the shareholders to see that it was done, and properly done, and if they allowed this duty to be assumed by persons who had no title to it, in their office at *12 Grafton Street,* the place where the office of the company was described in the prospectus as being – if they allowed persons who were not entitled to do it to carry on all the business of the company there – to act as directors and as secretary there; especially if they allowed them to perform the most important business of drawing cheques (for they must have known their own deed, which says that that can only be done by a draft of three directors, and they must have known that money must be had for the purposes of the company), if there is a fault on the one side or the other, it is on the side of those who allowed all these transactions to take place, when they were not conducted by persons legitimately appointed on the part of the company.

On the other hand, on the part of the bankers, I see no possible mode by which they might have pursued their inquiries in the manner contended for at the Bar without requiring all the minute-books of the company to be produced to them, and without conducting a detailed investigation into all the transactions of the company as to the appointment of directors and the like – a duty they were not called upon to perform, and a duty which, if it was objected to, they could not have insisted upon performing. I apprehend, my Lords, that the bankers having done all that was strictly their duty to do – having made themselves acquainted with the articles of the company, and having seen the offices of the company, with persons there affecting to perform all the duties of directors according to those articles, and having seen those who [899] had the power of appointing them continually present there, witnessing their performance – there can be no doubt that in this state of circumstances the bankers are not in any default whatsoever, and that the cheques must be taken, as between them and the company, to have been properly drawn, and the shareholders must be held liable to the loss.

Freeman & Lockyer v. Buckhurst Park Properties (Mangal) Ltd.
[1964] 2 Q.B. 480 (C.A.)

(From headnote) K. a property developer, and H. formed the defendant company to purchase and resell a large estate. K., personally, agreed to pay the running expenses and to be reimbursed out of the proceeds of the resale. K. and H. and a nominee of each were appointed directors of the company. The articles of association contained power to appoint a managing director but none was appointed. K. instructed the plaintiffs, a firm of architects, to apply for planning permission to develop the estate and do certain other work in that connection. The plaintiffs executed the work. The plaintiffs claimed their fees, the amount of which was not in dispute, from the defendant company. The county court judge held that, although K. was never appointed managing director, he had acted as such to the knowledge of the board of directors of the defendant company and he gave judgment for the plaintiffs. The defendant company appealed.

DIPLOCK L.J.: . . . [502] It is necessary at the outset to distinguish between an 'actual' authority of an agent on the one hand, and an 'apparent' or 'ostensible' authority on the other. Actual authority and apparent authority are quite independent of one another. Generally they co-exist and coincide, but either may exist without the other and their respective scopes may be different. As I shall endeavour to show, it is upon the apparent authority of the agent that the contractor normally relies in the ordinary course of business when entering into contracts.

An 'actual' authority is a legal relationship between principal and agent created by a consensual agreement to which they alone are parties. Its scope is to be ascertained by applying ordinary principles of construction of contracts, including any proper implications from the express words used, the usages of the trade, or the course of business between the parties. To this agreement the contractor is a stranger; he may be totally ignorant of the existence of any authority on the part of the agent. Nevertheless, if the agent does enter into a contract pursuant to the [503] 'actual' authority, it does create contractual rights and liabilities between the principal and the contractor. It may be that this rule relating to 'undisclosed principals,' which is peculiar to English law, can be rationalised as avoiding circuity of action, for the principal could in equity compel the agent to lend his name in an action to enforce the contract against the contractor, and would at common law be liable to indemnify the agent in respect of the performance of the obligations assumed by the agent under the contract.

An 'apparent' or 'ostensible' authority, on the other hand, is a legal relationship between the principal and the contractor created by a representation, made by the principal to the contractor, intended to be and in fact acted upon by the contractor, that the agent has authority to enter on behalf of the principal into a contract of a kind within the scope of the 'apparent' authority, so as to render the principal liable to perform any obligations imposed upon him by such contract. To the relationship so created the agent is a stranger. He need not be (although he generally is) aware of the existence of the representation but he must not purport to make the agreement as principal himself. The representation, when acted upon by the contractor by entering into a contract with the agent, operates as an estoppel, preventing the principal from asserting that he is not bound by the contract. It is irrelevant whether the agent had actual authority to enter into the contract.

In ordinary business dealings the contractor at the time of entering into the contract can in the nature of things hardly ever rely on the 'actual' authority of the agent. His information as to the authority must be derived either from the principal or from the agent or from both, for they alone know what the agent's actual authority is. All that the contractor can know is what they tell him, which may or may not be true. In the ultimate analysis he relies either upon the representation of the principal, that is, apparent authority, or upon the representation of the agent, that is, warranty of authority.

The representation which creates 'apparent' authority may take a variety of forms of which the commonest is representation by conduct, that is, by permitting the agent to act in some way in the conduct of the principal's business with other persons. By doing so the principal represents to anyone who becomes aware that the agent is so acting that the agent has authority to enter on behalf of the principal into contracts with other persons of the [504] kind which an agent so acting in the conduct of his principal's business has usually 'actual' authority to enter into.

In applying the law as I have endeavoured to summarise it to the case where the principal is not a natural person, but a fictitious person, namely, a corporation, two further factors arising from the legal characteristics of a corporation have to be borne in mind. The first is that the capacity of a corporation is limited by its constitution, that is, in the case of a company incorporated under the Companies Act, by its memorandum and articles of association; the second is that a corporation cannot do any act, and that includes making a representation, except through its agent.

Under the doctrine of ultra vires the limitation of the capacity of a corporation by its constitution to do any acts is absolute. This affects the rules as to the 'apparent' authority of an agent of a corporation in two ways. First, no representation can operate to estop the corporation from denying the authority of the agent to do on behalf of the corporation an act which the corporation is not permitted by its constitution to do itself. Secondly, since the conferring of actual authority upon an agent is itself an act of the corporation, the capacity to do which is regulated by its constitution, the corporation cannot be estopped from denying that it has conferred upon a particular agent authority to do acts which by its constitution, it is incapable of delegating to that particular agent.

To recognise that these are direct consequences of the doctrine of ultra vires is, I think, preferable to saying that a contractor who enters into a contract with a corporation has constructive notice of its constitution, for the expression 'constructive notice' tends to disguise that constructive notice is not a positive, but a negative doctrine, like that of estoppel of which it forms a part. It operates to prevent the contractor from saying that he did not know that the constitution of the corporation rendered a particular act or a particular delegation of authority ultra vires the corporation. It does not entitle him to say that he relied upon some unusual provision in the constitution of the corporation if he did not in fact so rely.

The second characteristic of a corporation, namely, that unlike a natural person it can only make a representation through an agent, has the consequence that in order to create an estoppel between the corporation and the contractor, the representation as to the authority of the agent which creates his 'apparent' authority must be made by some person or persons who have [505] 'actual' authority from the corporation to make the representation. Such 'actual' authority may be conferred by the constitution of the corporation itself, as, for example, in the case of a company, upon the board of directors, or it may be conferred by those who under its constitution have the powers of management upon some other person to whom the constitution permits them to delegate authority to make representations of this kind. It follows that where the agent upon whose 'apparent' authority the contractor relies has no 'actual' authority from the corporation to enter into a particular kind of contract with the contractor on behalf of the corporation, the contractor cannot rely upon the agent's own representation as to his actual authority. He can rely only upon a representation by a person or persons who have actual authority to manage or conduct that part of the business of the corporation to which the contract relates.

The commonest form of representation by a principal creating an 'apparent' authority of an agent is by conduct, namely, by permitting the agent to act in the management or conduct to the principal's business. Thus, if in the case of a company the board of directors who have 'actual' authority under the memorandum and articles of association to manage the company's business permit the agent to act in the management or conduct of the company's business, they thereby represent to all persons dealing with such agent that he has authority to enter on behalf of the corporation into contracts of a kind which an agent authorised to do acts of the kind which he is in fact permitted to do usually enters into in the ordinary course of such business. The making of such a representation is itself an act of management of the company's business. Prima facie it falls within the 'actual' authority of the board of directors, and unless the memorandum or articles of the company either make such a contract ultra vires the company or prohibit the delegation of such authority to the agent, the company is estopped from denying to anyone who has entered into a contract with the agent in reliance upon such 'apparent' authority that the agent had authority to contract on behalf of the company.

If the foregoing analysis of the relevant law is correct, it can be summarised by stating four conditions which must be fulfilled to entitle a contractor to enforce against a company a contract entered into on behalf of the company by an agent who had no actual authority to do so. It must be shown:

> [506] (1) that a representation that the agent had authority to enter on behalf of the company into a contract of the kind sought to be enforced was made to the contractor;
>
> (2) that such representation was made by a person or persons who had 'actual' authority to manage the business of the company either generally or in respect of those matters to which the contract relates;
>
> (3) that he (the contractor) was induced by such representation to enter into the contract, that is, that he in fact relied upon it; and
>
> (4) that under its memorandum or articles of association the company was not deprived of the capacity either to enter into a contract of the kind sought to be enforced or to delegate authority to enter into a contract of that kind to the agent.

The confusion which, I venture to think, has sometimes crept into cases is in my view due to a failure to distinguish between these four separate conditions, and in particular to keep steadfastly in mind (a) that the only 'actual' authority which is relevant is that of the persons making the representation relied upon, and (b) that the memorandum and articles of association of the company are always relevant (whether they are in fact known to the contractor or not) to the questions (i) whether condition (2) is fulfilled, and (ii) whether condition (4) is fulfilled, and (but only if they are in fact known to the contractor) may be relevant (iii) as part of the representation on which the contractor relied.

In each of the relevant cases the representation relied upon as creating the 'apparent' authority of the agent was by conduct in permitting the agent to act in the management and conduct of part of the business of the company. Except in *Mahony* v. *East Holyford Mining Co. Ltd.*, (1875) L.R. 7 H.L. 869, (ante p. 385) it was the conduct of the board of directors in so permitting the agent to act that was relied upon. As they had, in each case, by the articles of association of the company full 'actual' authority to manage its business, they had 'actual' authority to make representations in connection with the management of its business, including representations as to who were agents authorised to enter into contracts on the company's behalf.... [507] In *Mahony*'s case no board of directors or secretary had in fact been appointed, and it was the conduct of those who, under the constitution of the company, were entitled to appoint them which was relied upon as a representation that certain persons were directors and secretary. Since they had 'actual' authority to appoint these officers, they had 'actual' authority to make representations as to who the officers were. In both these cases the constitution of the company, whether it had been seen by the contractor or not, was relevant in order to determine whether the persons whose representations by conduct were relied upon as creating the 'apparent' authority of the agent had 'actual' authority to make the representations on behalf of the company. In *Mahony*'s case, if the persons in question were not persons who would normally be supposed to have such authority by someone who did not in fact know the constitution of the company, it may well be that the contractor would not succeed in proving condition (3), namely, that he relied upon the representations made by those persons, unless he proved that he did in fact know the constitution of the company. . . .

[509] In the present case the findings of fact by the county court judge are sufficient to satisfy the four conditions, and thus to establish that Kapoor had 'apparent' authority to enter into contracts on behalf of the company for their services in connection with the sale of the company's property, including the obtaining of development permission with respect to its use. The judge found that the board knew that Kapoor had throughout been acting as managing director in employing agents and taking other steps to find a purchaser. They permitted him to do so, and by such conduct represented that he had authority to enter into contracts of a kind which a managing director or an executive director responsible for finding a purchaser would in the normal course be authorised to enter into on behalf of the company. Condition (1) was thus fulfilled. The articles of association conferred full powers of management on the board. Condition (2) was thus fulfilled. The plaintiffs, finding Kapoor acting in relation to the company's property as he was authorised by the [510] board to act, were induced to believe that he was authorised by the company to enter into contracts on behalf of the company for their services in connection with the sale of the company's property, including the obtaining of development permission with respect to its use. Condition (3) was thus fulfilled. The articles of association, which contained powers for the board to delegate any of the functions of management to a managing director or to a single director, did not deprive the company of capacity to delegate authority to Kapoor, a director, to enter into contracts of that kind on behalf of the company. Condition (4) was thus fulfilled.

Cox v. Dublin City Distillery (No.2)
[1915] 1 I.R. 345

The company's regulations fixed the quorum of directors at two and provided that no director should vote on any matter in which he was personally interested. At a series of board meetings, the directors resolved to issue debentures to themselves as security for advances made by themselves to the company. At the same time, debentures were also issued to outsiders.

BARTON J.: . . . [353] I am of opinion that the three resolutions of the 12th and 16th May, 1903, and 20th January, 1904, were invalid. Article 94 of the Company's articles of association provides that no director shall vote in respect of any contract or matter in which he is individually interested, otherwise than as a member of the company. Article 109 fixes the quorum, [354] until otherwise determined, at two. At the meeting of the 12th May, 1903, three directors were present, Kennedy, Doherty, and Howes, who resolved to issue £4,000 debentures to a trustee, whom I treat as an outsider, in trust for Kennedy and Doherty by way of security for advances. The case is quite indistinguishable in principle from *In re Greymouth Point Elizabeth Railway & Coal Co.* [1904] 1 Ch. 32. By the resolution of the 16th May, five directors, Doherty, Kennedy, Churton, Trower, and Howes, resolved to issue £1,150 debentures to the same trustee in trust for themselves in various proportions by way of security for advances. This resolution cannot, in my opinion, be split up, and is equally bad. By the resolution of the 20th January, 1904, three directors, Kennedy, Doherty, and Howes, resolved to issue thirty-seven debentures to the same trustee in trust for those making advances for a new yeast-plant by way of security, and proceeded to sign, seal, and issue debentures to themselves and other directors. The resolution was a nullity, and the two other directors cannot be regarded as outsiders who took without notice of the board's minutes.

Next I come to the case of debentures issued to non-directors. Four debentures were issued to the same trustee on May 16th, 1903, in trust for Adam S. Findlater; one debenture was issued on May 12th, 1903, and four on 20th January, 1904, to the same trustee, for William Findlater. One of these gentlemen had been a director some years previously; the other was a trustee for the second debenture holders; but they were not directors in 1903 and 1904; and, *qua* the board of directors, I hold them to be outsiders, to whom notice of the board's minutes cannot be attributed. In such a case the onus lies, in my opinion, upon the party impeaching the debentures to show that a person who is prima facie an outside holder of a debenture, which is good on its face, had actual or constructive notice of the irregularity: *County of Gloucester Bank* v. *Rudry Merthyr Colliery Co.* [1895] 1 Ch. 629. Accordingly, I hold that, although these resolutions were invalid, the ten debentures issued to a trustee for the Messrs. Adam and William Findlater are valid and binding.

XIV Creditors and Debentures

While shareholder-protection is the dominant concern of company law, a major secondary theme is protecting those who give credit to companies. Because the debtor is the corporation itself and not its shareholders, and since the vast majority of companies possess limited liability, it is inevitable that there are special rules for companies' debts.

FLOATING CHARGES

In re Dublin Drapery Co.
(1884) L.R. Ir. 174

PORTER, M.R.: ... [189] The question remaining for me to decide is, whether the Company had power to charge future-acquired property. It was argued, on the authority [190] mainly of a doubt thrown out by the late Master of the Rolls (Sir George Jessel) in *Re Florence Land and Public Works Company, Ex parte Moor* (10 Ch.D. 535) that the debentures were invalid as to, and do not charge, anything which was not *in specie* the property of the Company at the time they were issued. The sum of £25,000, lodged in Court in pursuance of the order already mentioned, probably represents in money the sum realised by sale of the stock-in-trade of the Company, and the trade fixtures and other miscellaneous property. I have no information as to whether the debts were included. The stock-in-trade of a Company like the present is constantly fluctuating, and is from time to time disposed of and replaced in the course of business; and I cannot assume that any of the specific articles which were on the premises as stock-in-trade in 1883 was itself the property of the Company in 1876 and 1877; but no doubt substantially the stock on the premises in 1883 represented and corresponded with that which had been there in 1876 and 1877. That must, however, be the subject of inquiry if the general creditors desire it; and I shall, if it be pressed, direct a reference on this point, at the peril of costs. Should this course not be adopted, I shall assume the fact to be as I have mentioned.

It was contended by Mr White, on behalf of the general creditors, that the case of *Re Florence Land and Public Works Company, Ex parte Moor*, was not only well decided, but is supported by subsequent authorities. That was a remarkable case, and one of very considerable importance. The question was, whether a document called an 'obligation' was a charge on the property of the Company. Vice-Chancellor Hall had decided that it was not, on the authority of a decision of the Master of the Rolls (Sir George Jessel) in *Norton* v. *Florence Land and Public Works Company*, (7 Ch. D. 332), in which he had held that a similar bond of the same Company was not a charge on their property. The Company was ordered to be wound up, and the case of *Ex parte Moor* came before the Court of Appeal where Sir George Jessel sat, and in the course of the argument he made these observations (p.535): 'Can a Company, any [191] more than an individual, charge its future property? This is not a charge on the "undertaking", as in other debentures, but on the estate and effects. By the Judicature Act, 1875, s. 10, the administration of the estates of Companies in winding-up has been assimilated, as to the respective rights of secured and unsecured creditors, to the administration of estates in Bankruptcy. Would it not be contrary to the policy of the Bankruptcy laws that a mortgage security should affect after-acquired property?'

Two grounds are stated for the doubt thus thrown out: 1st, the incapacity of a Company to charge future property; 2nd, the effect of the Judicature Act, 1875, s. 10, which is identical with section 28, sub-sect. 1, of the Irish Judicature Act. There was no decision on the latter ground, as appears from the conclusion of the judgments of the Master of the Rolls and Lord Justice James; but, so far as any doubt was suggested on the construction of the Judicature Act, I take it to be set at rest by subsequent authorities. The 28th section of the Irish Act enacts that 'in the administration by the Court of the assets of any person who may die after the commencement of this Act, and whose estate may prove to be insufficient for the payment in full of his debts and liabilities, and in the winding-up of any Company under the Companies Acts, 1862 and 1867, whose assets may prove insufficient for the payment of its debts and liabilities, and the costs of winding-up, the same rules shall prevail and be observed as to the respective rights of secured and unsecured creditors, and as to debts and liabilities provable, and as to the valuation of annuities, and future and contingent liabilities respectively, as may be in force for the time being under the law of Bankruptcy, with respect to the estates of persons adjudged bankrupt in Ireland.' That section, read cursorily, no doubt might suggest that for all purposes the rules in Bankruptcy should be incorporated into the administration of assets in this Court. But I regard it as now perfectly settled that that construction is erroneous, and that the section has no such general application.

It was held in *Re Withernsea Brickworks*, (16 Ch.D. 337), after some con-[192]flict of decision, that section 87 of the Bankruptcy Act, 1869 (Eng.), which deprives execution creditors of the fruits of the execution, where the Sheriff has notice of bankruptcy within fourteen days after sale, is not made applicable to the winding-up of Companies by the Judicature Act, 1875, section 10; and in *Winehouse* v. *Winehouse* it was decided that the 10th section does not introduce into the administration of insolvent estates of deceased persons the provision of section 32 of the Bankruptcy Act, 1869, that all debts (with certain exceptions) are to be paid *pari passu*. It affects only the rights of the class of secured creditors as conflicting with those of the class of unsecured creditors. I regard it therefore as settled, that the doubt suggested by Sir George Jessel, as regards the operation of section 10 of the English and section 28, sub-section 1, of the Irish Judicature Act, rests upon no solid basis, and has no application to the question which I have now to decide. It is on the second ground suggested by Sir George Jessel that the strength of the argument rests: 'Can a Company, any more than an individual, charge its future property?'

In *Holroyd* v. *Marshall* (10 HL. Cas. 191), it was decided that, as in Equity it is not necessary that there should be a formal deed of conveyance, provided there be a valid contract for transfer, future property, contracted to be conveyed for valuable consideration, provided it is so identified as to be capable of being the subject of a decree for specific performance, passes at once when realised, and the vendor becomes a trustee for the vendee. That rule applies to personal property as well as to real estate. Such a contract, if made with respect to the sale or mortgage of future-acquired property, being capable of specific performance, tranfers the beneficial interest in the property as soon as it is acquired to the vendee or mortgagee, who may have an injunction to restain its removal. That decision rests on the principle of Equity that what is contracted for and ought to be done is treated as done. There is no doubt that at common law, as expressed by Pollock. C.B., in *Belding* v. *Read*, [193] 'a person cannot by deed, however solemn, assign that which is not in himself – in other words, there cannot be a prophetic conveyance'. But the doctrine of Courts of Equity, as shown by *Holroyd* v. *Marshall*, rests on a different principle; and if the contract be sufficiently specific, it will in Equity pass the property.

Ex parte Bolland (L.R.17 Eq. 115) was relied on, on behalf of the general creditors. There was a covenant in a marriage settlement to settle future-acquired property, and it was held to be invalid as against assignees in Bankruptcy. But it is to be observed that that decision is opposed to high authority in this country; and on that ground my predecessor, Sir Edward Sullivan, in *Galavan* v. *Dunne* (7 L.R. Ir. 144), refused to follow it, the decisions in Ireland not having been brought under the notice of the Court, and His Honor's opinion being against it. Therefore I cannot regard *Ex parte Bolland*, as an authority binding me in this Court.

In *Clements* v. *Matthews* (11 Q.B.D. 808), there was a bill of sale of growing and other crops which, at any time thereafter, should be on or about a particular farm, or any other premises of the grantor; and the Court of Appeal held, on the authority of *Holroyd* v. *Marshall*, that the bill of sale was valid, though only as to the future crops on the specified premises. Cotton, L.J., says 'an objection to the bill of sale has been taken on the part of the defendant with respect to the future crops, and it has been contended that it was not effectual as against Baggs; because, as appears from the judgment of the House of Lords in *Holroyd* v. *Marshall*, in order to be so effectual in Equity, the property which is not in existence at the time of the execution of the deed must be sufficiently specified, and that that was not done here, because the bill of sale describes such future crops as those on this farm and elsewhere; and this, it was said, was too vague and general. In my opinion it is not; and I agree with The Master of the Rolls that this is really an assignment of the future crops which Baggs may be entitled to.' Apply that principle to this case, and there is nothing in it in conflict with the claim of the debenture-holders. Crops are but stock-in-trade of a particular character. . . .

[195] Now, what do we find done by these debentures? The Company 'do hereby charge with such payments the undertaking, stock-in-trade, lands, premises, works, plant, property and effects (both present and future)' of the Company. If future property can be conveyed, these words do it. In *Ex parte Moor, Re Florence Company* (20 Ch.D. 545), the learned Judge laid stress upon the absence of the [196] word 'undertaking', which we have here. In *The Marine Mansions Company*, the debenture charged 'the property belonging to us for the time being, during the subsistence of the debenture, with all buildings and stock on, and connected with, our said property, and all the receipts and revenues to arise therefrom,' and declared that the entire debenture loan should be a first charge on 'our *undertaking* and property, and receipts and revenues aforesaid.' It was contended that they could not attach to chattels which might have been subsequently bought. But Lord Hatherley (then Vice-Chancellor Wood) referred to *Holroyd* v. *Marshall* and held that the debentures gave the holders a charge in priority to other creditors upon the land and other property of the Company.

In the *Panama and Royal Mail Company*, (3 H.& C. 955), a case in the Court of Appeal, it was held that the debenture-holders acquired a charge upon all the property of the Company, past and future, by the term 'undertaking', and had priority over the general creditors. Lord Justice Giffard said: 'What I have to decide in the present case is simply this: What are the rights of debenture-holders, the state of things being that the concern is being wound up, and that the whole of its property is being realised? I confess that I can have no doubt whatever as to what the effect of the debenture is. . . I have no hesitation in saying, that in this particular case, and having regard to the state of this particular Company, the word "undertaking" had reference to all the property of the Company, not only that which existed at the date of the debenture, but that which afterwards became the property of the Company. And I take the object and meaning of the debenture to be this: that the word "undertaking" necessarily infers that the Company will go on, and that the debenture-holder could not interfere until either the interest which was due was unpaid, or until the period had arrived for the payment of his principal, and that principal was unpaid. I think the meaning and object of the security was this, that the Company might go on during that interval; and furthermore, that during the interval the debenture-holder would [197] not be entitled to any account of mesne profits, or of any dealing with the property of the Company in the ordinary course of carrying on their business. . . But the moment the Company comes to be wound up, and the property has to be realised, that moment the rights of these parties beyond all question attach.'

To the same effect is the case of *The Anglo-American Leather Cloth Company Limited*, affirmed by the Court of Appeal (L.R. 4 Eq. 501; L.R. 5 Ch. 318), and in the case of the *Florence Company*, which was so much relied on for the general creditors, I find Lord Justice James saying, at p. 546, 'Then what is the meaning of binding the estate, property and effects of such a Company as this? In my opinion, the reasonable meaning, the only meaning which the persons who took it would have attached to it, was, that the words "estate, property and effects", were in fact exactly equivalent to the word "undertaking" which we find in the other cases; that is to say, it was to be, so far as the Company could make it, a special charge upon the assets of the Company, the assets which would be forthcoming at the time when the charge was to be made available; it was to be a special charge upon the assets in priority to the general creditors of the Company;' and Sir George Jessel (p. 542) says, 'My opinion is, that looking at the words of the bond, "estate, property and effects", and the terms of the articles, they do mean to charge, in the way I have mentioned, the estate, property and effects of the Company.' I consider that decision an authority favourable to the debenture-holders, on the meaning of the words 'undertaking, estate, property and effects', and other general words used in these debentures.

In my opinion, therefore, on every point the debenture-holders succeed, and I shall declare them entitled to be paid principal and interest, not only out of the £32,000 the produce of the real estate, but also out of the £25,000 representing general assets brought in to answer their demand, together with their costs.

Welch v. Bowmaker (Ireland) Ltd.
[1980] I.R. 251 (S.Ct.)

(From headnote) A company issued a debenture in favour of the first defendant. By clause 3 of the debenture the company charged its undertaking and assets, present and future, with the payment of moneys owed by the company to the first defendant, and also charged 'as a specific charge' the hereditaments 'specified in the schedule hereto'. The schedule described three of the company's four parcels of land. The debenture's fourth clause stated that it was issued subject to the conditions endorsed thereon which were to be deemed part of the debenture. The first condition endorsed on the debenture stated that the charge thereby effected was to be 'as regards the company's lands and premises for the time being' a specific charge and as regards the other assets of the company a floating security, and stated that the company was not at liberty to create any mortgage or charge on its property for the time being in priority to the debenture.

One month after the execution of the debenture the company deposited with the defendant bank the title deeds of the company's fourth parcel of land by way of equitable mortgage to secure the repayment of moneys owed by the company to the defendant bank. At the date of the equitable mortgage the defendant bank was aware of the existence of the debenture but was unaware of its terms.

The company became insolvent and its assets were insufficient to pay the claims of both defendants. In the course of the winding up of the company the first defendant claimed that, notwithstanding the terms of the debenture's third clause, the effect of the debenture's first condition was to create a specific charge on the company's fourth parcel of land and that, accordingly, the claim of the first defendant prevailed over the claim of the defendant bank as subsequent equitable mortgagee. The defendant bank claimed that the debenture created only a floating charge over the fourth parcel of land.

HENCHY J.: . . . [254] The complicating condition in the debenture is the first; it is in the following terms:

> This debenture is to rank as a second charge on the property within mentioned and such charge is to be as regards the company's lands and premises for the time being and all its uncalled capital a specific charge and as regards all other the property and assets of the company a floating security but so that the company is not to be at liberty to create any mortgage or charge on its property for the time being in priority to or pari passu with this debenture.

Read literally and on its own, this condition is in conflict with the charging provision which I have already quoted. The charging provision makes only the properties specified in the schedule subject to a specific charge: all else (including Ivy Lawn) is subject only to a floating charge. If the first condition is to be given prevailing force, it would make 'the company's lands and premises for the time being' (thus including Ivy Lawn) subject to a specific charge.

Relying on the first condition, counsel for Bowmaker contend that, with regard to the Ivy Lawn property, the bank's equitable mortgage must yield priority to the rights of Bowmaker as holders of a specific charge under the debenture. On the other hand counsel for the bank contend that it is the charging provision that is definitive of Bowmaker's rights; they claim that Bowmaker had only a floating charge over Ivy Lawn so that, when the bank became equitable mortgagees on deposit of the title deeds without (as is conceded) any actual notice of the prohibition in the debenture of the creation of a mortgage in priority to the debenture, the bank acquired rights over Ivy Lawn as mortgagees in priority to the rights of Bowmaker under the debenture.

In the High Court the judge, in an unreserved judgment, held with Bowmaker. He felt constrained to rule that the condition in the debenture gave Bowmaker a specific charge over Ivy Lawn. For my part, with the benefit of a fuller argument and after more mature consideration, I reach the opposite conclusion. I consider that the primary and dominant words and expressions delineating the extent of the powers and interests vested in Bowmaker by the debenture are to be found in the charging provision rather than in its attendant condition.

The relevant rule of interpretation is that encapsulated in the maxim [255] *generalia specialibus non derogant.* In plain English, when you find a particular situation dealt with in special terms, and later in the same document you find general words used which could be said to encompass and deal differently with that particular situation, the general words will not, in the absence of an indication of a definite intention to do so, be held to undermine or abrogate the effect of the special words which were used to deal with the particular situation. This is but a commonsense way of giving effect to the true or primary intention of the draftsman, for the general words will usually have been used in inadvertence of the fact that the particular situation has already been specially dealt with.

In this debenture the charging provision limits the creation of a specifc charge to the properties specially marked out with particularity in the schedule. If given its full literal meaning the subsequent condition, which provides that the charge created by the debenture is to be a specific charge 'as regards the company's lands and premises for the time being', would have such a generality of application as to make nonsense of the clear distinction that is drawn in the charging provision between the properties marked out for a specific charge and the company's other properties. In such a case, in order to effectuate the draftsman's true intention, it is the special rather than the general words that must prevail. Those special words show that the primary and transcendent intention was that the Ivy Lawn property, since it was not included in the schedule, was not to be subject to a specific charge. Therefore, I would hold that the debenture gave Bowmaker only a floating charge over it.

The words in the condition referring to 'the company's lands and premises for the time being' should be construed as if they read 'the company's lands and premises for the time being *as specified in the schedule herein',* in that way the charging provision and the condition are brought into harmony.

I am fortified in this conclusion as to the extent of the specific charge by the fact that, when particulars of the charge created by the debenture were lodged with the registrar of companies for registration, the 'short particulars of the property' charged were given (over the signature of Bowmaker's solicitor) as 'the company's undertaking and all its property and assets present and future including its uncalled capital for the time being, goodwill and as a specific charge the following premises. . .'. The words after 'the following premises' described the properties specified in the schedule to the debenture. It would seem that Bowmaker did not consider (or intend anyone [256] consulting the statutory register of charges to consider) that the debenture had created a specific charge over the Ivy Lawn property. Bowmaker represented to the registrar of companies, and to the public at large, that the charge over the Ivy Lawn property created by the debenture was only a floating charge. In my view, that was a correct representation of the effect of the debenture.

Counsel for Bowmaker has argued that, even if that be so, the bank should be fixed with constructive notice of the provision in the debenture precluding the company from creating a mortgage (such as the bank got) which would have priority over the debenture. Since such a prohibition is more or less common form in modern debentures, there would be much to be said for applying the doctrine of constructive notice to such a situation were it not that it is settled law that there is no duty on the bank in a situation such as this to seek out the precise terms of the debenture: *Re Standard Rotary Machine Co.* (1906) 95 L.T. 829, *Wilson* v. *Kelland* [1910] 2 Ch. 306, and *G. & T. Earle Ltd.* v. *Hemsworth R.D.C.* (1928) 140 L.T. 69. Actual or express notice of the prohibition must be shown before the subsequent mortgagee can be said to be deprived of priority.

Whatever attractions there may be in the proposition that priority should be deemed lost because a duty to inquire further was called for but ignored, and that such inquiry would have shown that the company was debarred from entering into a mortgage which would have priority over the debenture, the fact remains that it would be unfair to single out the bank for condemnatory treatment because of their failure to ascertain the full terms of the debenture when what they did was in accord with judicially approved practice and when such a precipitate change in the law would undermine the intended validity of many other such transactions. If the proposed extension of the doctrine of constructive notice is to be made, the necessary change in the law would need to be made prospectively and, therefore, more properly by statute.

I would allow the appeal and rule that the debenture did not give Bowmaker a specific charge over the Ivy Lawn property and that the bank's equitable mortgage over that property ranks in priority to Bowmaker's rights as the owners of a floating charge over that property under the debenture.

In re Keenan Bros. Ltd.
[1985] I.L.R.M. 641 (S.Ct.)

(From headnote) In May 1983, the company created a charge in favour
of Allied Irish Banks Ltd. and a debenture in favour of Allied Irish Investment Bank Ltd. The charge, which was stated to be a first fixed charge,
was in respect of all the book debts and other debts of the company, present
and future. The debenture charged by way of first fixed charge the present
and future book debts of the company and all rights and powers in respect
thereof. Clause 2 of the deed of charge provided that the company was
obliged to pay into a designated account with the bank 'all moneys which
it may receive in respect of the book debts and other debts hereby charged'
and that it could not without the bank's prior consent make any withdrawals
from the account. Clause 7 (1) of the debenture was in similar terms.
Clause 7 (3) of the debenture provided that the company '[s]hall not without
the consent in writing of the bank carry on its business other than in the
ordinary and normal course'. In August 1983, the company entered into
an agreement supplemental to the deed of charge. This provided for the
opening of a 'Book Debts Receivable Account', withdrawals from which
were to be in the joint names of the company and the bank. It also provided
that the bank might, at the company's request, make sums available for
the company's working account where required for carrying on its business;
and that the account would be closed on the happening of any event making
the money secured immediately repayable, when the bank could appoint
a manager over the book debts charged. The account envisaged by the
August 1983 agreement was opened in October 1983. A liquidator was
appointed to the company in November 1983, and he applied to the High
Court for directions as to whether the charge and debenture created fixed
or floating charges. Keane J. held ([1985] I.L.R.M. 254) that the intention
to be inferred from the instruments as a whole was that a floating charge
had been created. The banks appealed.

McCARTHY J.: [646] The banks appeal against the decision of the High
Court which held that the charges which had been created by the instruments of 3 May and 5 May 1983 were floating charges rather than fixed
charges over the present and future book debts of the company. The result
of that decision is that monies due to the Revenue have priority over the
claims of the banks on foot of the instruments of May 1983; the claim by
the banks is in respect of advances made between May 1983 and November
1983 when the company went into liquidation. It is unnecessary to detail
the sequence of events or to recite the provisions of the instruments all of
which are set out in detail in the elaborate judgment of Keane J. The
underlying basis was that the company, in May 1983, was in serious financial difficulties and the banks, if they could secure the advances, were
prepared to lend financial assistance. Because of the Companies Act 1963,

a floating charge would not secure the required priority, but a fixed charge would. In *Siebe Gorman & Co. Ltd.* v. *Barclays Bank Ltd.* [1979] 2 Lloyd's Rep 142, Slade J. had given a judicial blessing in [647] England to a claim by way of fixed charge on book debts where this was purported to be created by an instrument with marked similarities to those the subject of this appeal; during the course of the hearing, we were informed that they were, in fact, modelled on those in *Siebe Gorman*, although it was emphasised that monies received in respect of the book debts in the instant case were paid into a special account and not, as in *Siebe Gorman*, into the ordinary account of the mortgagor.

In *Re Armagh Shoes Ltd.* [1982] N.I. 59, Hutton J. in the High Court of Northern Ireland identified an apparent divergence of judicial view and legal precedent in a series of decisions; *Tailby* v. *Official Receiver* (1888) 13 App. Cas. 523; *Re Yorkshire Woolcombers Association Ltd.* [1903] 2 Ch. 284; *National Provincial Bank of England* v. *United Electric Theatres Ltd.* [1916] 1 Ch. 132; *Stave Falls Lumber Co. Ltd.* v. *Westminster Trust Co. Ltd.* [1940] 4 WWR 382; *Evans* v. *Rival Granite Quarries Ltd.* [1910] 2 KB 979; *Evans, Coleman & Evans Ltd.* v. *R.A. Nelson Construction Ltd.* (1958) 16 DLR 123 and the *Siebe Gorman* case.

It may well be that there are factual differences in the several cases but I think it desirable to identify some common ground so as to isolate the underlying principle and thereby resolve the two legal issues raised in this appeal, that is, (a) can a fixed charge be validly created in respect of future book debts? and (b) did the relevant instruments in this case do so?

Clearly, the parties wanted to secure the bank's advances in priority to all other claims, wanted to achieve this by a fixed charge whilst enabling the company to avail of advances from the bank covered, so to speak, by amounts received by the company in discharge of book debts and lodged to the special account; and wanted to achieve this result by using the *Siebe Gorman* scheme. It is not suggested that mere terminology itself – such as using the expression 'fixed charge' – achieves the purpose; one must look, not within the narrow confines of such term, not to the declared intention of the parties alone, but to the effect of the instructions whereby they purported to carry out that intention; did they achieve what they intended, or was the intention defeated by the ancillary requirements?

I turn, firstly, to the second issue, to determine the nature of the charge created by the instruments. In his judgment, Keane J. refers to the development of the floating charge in contrast to the fixed or specific charge, at pp. 257-258.

> I think that one has to bear in mind at the outset that this form of charge made its first appearance in England as a by-product of the joint stock companies which began to flourish after the enactment of the Joint Stock Companies Act 1844. In order to borrow money, such

companies offered as security not merely their fixed assets, but also, assets which were regulary turned over in the course of business such as the companies' stock in trade. It was obviously cumbersome and impractical to charge such assets specifically with the repayment of advances, since it would mean the constant execution and release of securities as the assets were disposed of and replaced. Hence the concept developed of a charge which did not attach to any specific assets of the company, remained dormant until the mortgagee intervened and in the interim did not prevent the mortgagor from using the assets in question in the ordinary course of his business.

It appears that what is now called a 'floating charge' on all property – [648] the 'undertaking' – of a company was first recognised in *Re Panama, New Zealand & Australian Royal Mail Co.* (1870) LR 5 Ch. App. 318, where it was held that the word 'undertaking' meant all the property present and future of the company, and that the charge thereon was effective and was to operate by way of floating security. In *Re Yorkshire Woolcombers Association Ltd.* [1903] 2 Ch. 284; sub nom. *Illingworth* v. *Houldsworth* [1904] AC 355, there are a number of judicial analyses, if not definitions, of the term 'floating charge', or of the distinction between a floating charge and a specific or fixed charge. Citations from these judgments are to be found in the *Armagh Shoes* case and in the judgment of Keane J. in the instant appeal. I am content to cite the relevant extract from the speech, of enviable brevity, of Lord Macnaghten, [1904] AC 355, at p. 358:

> I should have thought there was not much difficulty in defining what a floating charge is in contrast to what is called a specific charge. A specific charge, I think, is one that *without more* [emphasis added] fastens on ascertained and definite property or property capable of being ascertained and defined; a floating charge, on the other hand, is ambulatory and shifting in its nature, hovering over and so to speak floating with the property which it is intended to affect until some event occurs or some act is done which causes it to settle and fasten on the subject of the charge within its reach and grasp.

I do not overlook the fact that Lord Macnaghten expressly agreed with the judgment of Farwell J. in the court of first instance.

I emphasise the phrase 'without more' because it seems to me to be the badge that identifies the specific charge. The other side of the coin, when one looks at the characteristics of a floating charge is that, before what is called crystalisation of the floating charge, the company has power to create legal mortgages and equitable charges in priority to the floating charge: see *Re Florence Land and Public Works Co.* (1879) 10 Ch. D. 530; *Re Colonial Trusts Corp.* (1880) 15 Ch. D. 465, and *Wheatley* v. *Silkstone & Haigh Moor Coal Co.* (1885) 29 Ch. D. 715, where North J. said:

but it (the equitable charge by deposit of title deeds) is not intended to prevent and has not the effect of in any way preventing the carrying on of the business in all or any of the ways in which it is carried on in the ordinary course; and, inasmuch as I find that in the ordinary course of business and for the purpose of the business this mortgage was made, it is a good mortgage upon and a good charge upon the property comprised in it, and is not subject to the claim created by the debentures.

The breadth of the company's powers in this regard may be limited by the terms of the floating charge, but such a qualification is strictly construed and a legal mortgagee without notice would be entitled to his priority: see *Coveney* v. *Persse* [1910] 1 I.R. 194.

The learned trial judge laid particular emphasis on two clauses of the charging instruments. Clause 3(ii) of the charge dated 3 May 1983 in favour of Allied Irish Banks Ltd. provides:

The company shall pay into an account with the bank designated for that purpose all monies which it may receive in respect of the book debts and other debts hereby charged and shall not, without the prior consent of the bank in writing, make any withdrawals or direct any payment from the said account.

[649] Clause 7 (1) of the instrument of 5 May 1983 with Allied Irish Investment Bank Ltd. provides that the company:

shall not without the consent in writing of the bank carry on its business other than in the ordinary and normal course.

Clause 7 (1) contains a provision to the same effect as that quoted from the instrument of 3 May, in respect of which Keane J. commented [1985], at p. 260: 'it is patent that the parties intended the company to carry on its business so far as these assets were concerned. . . to collect the book debts, lodge them to its bank account and use them in the business in the ordinary way'. Mr Cooke S.C., for the banks, contends that this was a misconstruction of that clause, that its purpose was to give the bank a degree of control over exceptional transactions, but was far from directing the company to carry on its normal business, rather to trade subject to the express terms of the debenture with a provision for a cash flow set up by the bank in which the inflow of cash would go direct to the bank. In my view, this is the correct construction of that clause.

As to the earlier quoted clause (in respect of the bank account) Keane J. said, at p. 259;

Subject to the possible necessity to give notice in the case of the existing debts, the effect of the deeds was to vest the debts in the banks the moment they came into existence and to give the banks the right to collect them (on giving notice to the debtors); and the company, at the date of the execution of the deeds, ceased to have any interest in the debts whatever. If this, indeed, is what the parties intended, it is not easy to understand why it was thought necessary to provide that: (and he quotes Clause 3(ii) of the first instrument). On this view of the transactions, the company had no business collecting any debts once the securities had been executed. If the charge in each case was intended to be a specific or fixed charge, such a provision was wholly unnecessay and indeed virtually meaningless.

In my view, it is because it was described as a specific or fixed charge and was intended to be such that the requirement of a special bank account was necessary; if it were a floating charge, payment into such an account would be entirely inappropriate and, indeed, would conflict with the ambulatory nature of the floating charge to which Lord Macnaghten refers. In *Re Yorkshire Woolcombers Association Ltd.* [1903] 2 Ch. 284 at p. 295, Romer L.J. postulated three characteristics of a floating charge, the third being that 'if you find that by the charge it is contemplated that, until some future step is taken by or on behalf of those interested in the charge, the company may carry on its business in the ordinary way as far as concerns the particular class of assets I am dealing with'. Mr Cooke S.C. has argued that this latter characteristic is essential to a floating charge and that the banking provision in the instruments here negatives such a characteristic; I would uphold this view. I have sought to identify from the speech of Lord Macnaghten the badge of a specific or fixed charge; that of the floating charge seems to me to be the absence of immediate effect or possible ultimate effect – in short, it may never happen; if the advances made or the debts incurred are repaid or discharged, then the cloud is dispersed never to [650] return in that exact form. Towards the end of his judgment, Keane J. said, at p. 264:

> What the banks have sought to do in the present instance is to create a hybrid form of charge which incorporates all the advantages of a floating charge with none of the statutory limitations on its operation. The borrower continues to use the assets in the course of his business to his own benefit, and to the benefit of the lender who continues to earn interest on his loan in the knowledge that he can at any time realise his security if his prospects of ultimate repayment appear in peril. At the same time, he is protected from the consequences that would normnally ensue for a lender who offers money on the security of the floating charge within 12 months of a winding up or in circumstances where the preferential creditors are owed substantial sums.

The charge, whatever it nature, for its validity had to be registered under the Companies Act 1963 and its existence would have been known to anyone upon casual enquiry – its existence as what was described as a fixed charge. Whilst acknowledging that the charge is somewhat hybrid in form because of the concession in respect of the collection of debts and lodgment to a special account, I do not recognise in it the ordinary characteristics of a floating charge – that it may crystalise on the happening of some future event. If the borrower, the company, is driven to such financial straits that it is prepared to effect an immediate charge upon its book debts, the existence of which charge is, in effect, published to the commercial and financial world, I do not accept that an elaborate system set up to enable the company to benefit by the collection of such debts detracts from its qualifying as a specific or fixed charge.

The remaining question, as raised by the Revenue Commissioners, is whether or not it is possible in law to create a fixed charge on future book debts. There appears to be ample authority in England in support of this contention going back to the *Tailby* case (1888) 13 App. Cas. 523, and asserted in Canada in the *Evans, Coleman & Evans* case (1958) 16 DLR 123. I am content to adopt the observations of Davey J.A. at p. 127 of the latter report and hold that there is no legal bar to there being a fixed charge on future book debts. To echo Lord Watson in the *Tailby* case, at p. 536:

> I cannot understand upon what principle an assignment of all legacies which may be bequeathed by any person to the assignor is to stand good, and effect is to be denied to a general assignment of all future book debts. As Cotton L.J. said in *Re Clarke* (1887) 36 Ch. D. 348, at p. 353: 'Vagueness comes to nothing if the property is definite at the time when the court comes to enforce the contract'. A future book debt is quite as capable of being identified as a legacy, and in this case the identity of the debt, with the subjects assigned, is not a matter of dispute.

Each book debt is a separate entity; granted, that even though it was assigned to the banks, it may be altered in whole or in part by, for example, a contra-account. That may go to the amount payable but it does not affect the transaction; there is no logic in seeking to distinguish between an accepted validity of a floating charge on future book debts and an alleged invalidity in a fixed charge on such debts.

In my judgment, the instruments executed between the company and the [651] banks did effect what they were intended to effect and constituted fixed charges on all the book debts, present and future, of the company. I would allow the appeal accordingly.

REGISTRATION OF CHARGES

Welch v. Bowmaker (Ireland) Ltd.
[1980] I.R. 251 (S. Ct.)

See supra p. 398.

RECEIVERS

Airlines Airspares Ltd. v. Handley Page Ltd.
[1970] 1 Ch. 193 (Ch.D.)

(From headnote) The plaintiffs were the assignees of the benefit of an agreement dated December 23, 1966, and made between K. Ltd. and K. of the first part and the first defendants of the other part, under which the first defendants agreed, inter alia, to pay to K. Ltd. and K. a commission of £500 in respect of every aircraft of a type known as 'Jetstream' sold by the first defendants. On October 28, 1968, the first defendants issued a debenture to the bank; and on August 7, 1969, the bank, under the power contained in the debenture, appointed a receiver who was accorded the wide powers conferred on a mortgagee under the [Conveyancing Act, 1881]. The receiver, in order to carry out his duties in the most effective manner, caused the first defendants to create a subsidiary company, A. Ltd., to which the first defendants on August 15, 1969, assigned such parts of their undertaking as represented an economically viable business, namely, their business connected with the 'Jetstream' aircraft. The receiver then entered into negotiations for the sale of the shares of A. Ltd. to American interests, and notified K. and the plaintiffs that he could no longer comply with the agreement of December 23, 1966. The plaintiffs sought an injunction to restrain the sale of the shares, and a declaration that they were entitled to the agreed commission.

GRAHAM J.: . . . [196] Mr Lightman's argument is as follows: The first defendants are under an obligation, which is derived from an implied term of the contract and from general equitable principles, not to frustrate or put it out of their power to implement the agreement which the first defendants have entered into with the plaintiffs. In support of this proposition, he relies on [197] *Southern Foundries (1926) Ltd.* v. *Shirlaw* [1940] A.C. 701; see, in particular, pp. 716, 717. Secondly, if it is said against the plaintiffs that the undertaking has already been transferred and that it is now too late and nothing can be done about it, that argument is unsound. It is unsound because in such circumstances the subsidiary will be treated by the court as the alter ego of the parent and the plaintiffs can obtain relief in respect of their contract against the parent and its subsidiary or either of them. Aircraft is at present admittedly a wholly owned subsidiary of the first defendants, and, as long as it remains so, the court can and will enforce the agreement against it. In this conncection, he relies upon *Jones* v. *Lipman* [1962] 1 W.L.R. 832 (ante p. 63).

Thirdly, the defendants could only succeed if they could show that the receiver and manager appointed by a debenture holder is in a better position that the company, in that he can legitimately avoid a contractual obligation such as the present. Mr Lightman concedes that the receiver cannot be compelled to perform such a contract, but he contends that the receiver cannot legitimately frustrate the contract by a transfer to a subsidiary such as has been effected here. The onus is on the defendants to show that the receiver is in a better position than the company [the first defendants] and that the defendants can lawfully do what they have done. They have cited no authority which justifies such a contention. On the contrary, *In re Botibol, decd.* [1947] 1 All E.R. 26 is against it, and it may properly be said here that the receiver has, by his actions, rendered himself liable in tort by inducing the first defendants to commit a breach of contract. There is, it is said, a clear distinction between declining to perform a contract, which the receiver is entitled to do, and frustrating the contract by his own act, which he is not entitled to do.

Mr Lindsay, on the other hand, argues that the plaintiffs' contentions are misconceived. First, says Mr Lindsay, this case is entirely different from *Jones* v. *Lipman*. That was a case of specific performance of a contract to sell land where the first defendant had purported to frustrate the whole transaction by selling the land in question after the date of his contract with the plaintiffs to a company, the second defendant, which he had acquired purely for the purpose in question. The court held the whole transaction was a sham, that a decree of specific performance would be made against the first defendant, and that, as he controlled the second defendant, he was in a position to cause the contract to be completed. Here, says Mr Lindsay, there is no question of a sham transaction and the reciever is doing his best to realise the best price for those of the first defendants' assets which remain and are saleable, a course which is in the best interests of all the creditors, secured and unsecured.

Further, if, as in *Jones* v. *Lipman*, the contract is of such a nature that specific performance is a normal remedy, a plaintiff could expect to obtain it both against a parent and a subsidiary company, but if, as in the present case, breach of the contract normally only leads to damages – and it is accepted here that the receiver cannot be compelled to perform the contract – then the case of *Jones* v. *Lipman* cannot have relevance.

[198] Secondly, the defendants say that the plaintiffs are really trying, by their action, to get themselves placed in a preferential position over all other unsecured creditors, of which there are a large number. Yet, when the position is fairly examined, it will be seen that the plaintiffs are in no

different position from any other unsecured creditor, in that they have an ordinary trading contract with the first defendants which the receiver can either adopt or decline. There is no evidence that the option granted by clause 2 of the agreement has been adopted by the plaintiffs and all the plaintiffs stand to receive under that agreement is £500 per aircraft sold. It would not be equitable for the receiver to prefer the plaintiffs to other unsecured creditors, and it is in the best interests of all such creditors that he should be able to sell that part of the first defendants' business which will constitute a viable unit in the way which will secure the highest price. If, in so doing, he does decline to take over the plaintiffs' contract, he may, of course, render the first defendants liable in damages and may also, to some extent, at any rate, damage their reputation as a trustworthy company which can be expected to honour its contracts. This, however, the defendants say, he is entitled to do, so long as the realisation of the net assets of the company [the first defendants] to the best advantage is not impaired. There may be cases where declining to adopt a contract of the company would so seriously impair the goodwill of the company that such realisation would be adversely affected, but that is not the case here. There is no evidence that it would so impair such realisation, nor that it would seriously damage the prospects of the first defendants' trading successfully in the future if they ever do so, and in fact the only goodwill of any real value, namely, that connected with the design, manufacture and prospects of sale of the 'Jetstream', has been transferred to Aircraft. It is not suggested that the first defendants themselves are likely to do any active trading in the future.

Thirdly, it is said that to merit the grant of an injunction, the acts complained of must threaten an invasion of the plaintiffs' legal rights and the relief asked for must relate to those rights. Here, the relief asked for relates to the transfer of shares in Aircraft, and if that be so the plaintiffs must show that they have some legal rights in respect of the shares in question, and no such right has been shown. This argument seems to me to beg the real question the answer to which, in my judgment, determines the issue in this case. The question may be stated as follows: is a receiver and manager, appointed by debenture holders, in a stronger position, from the legal point of view, than the company itself, in respect of contracts between unsecured creditors and the company? Assuming that the company, on the authority of *Southern Foundries (1926) Ltd.* v. *Shirlaw*, cannot put it out of its own power to perform contracts it has entered into, can a receiver in effect do so on its behalf if, at the same time, he has made it clear that he is not going to adopt the contract anyway, and if, as is, in my judgment, the case here, the repudiation of the contract will not adversely affect the realisation of the assets or seriously affect the trading prospects of the company in question, if it is able to trade in the future?

[199] Counsel, when I asked them, were not able to produce any author-

ity which gave a direct answer to this question, but there is a helpful passage dealing generally with 'current contracts' in *Buckley on the Companies Acts,* 13th ed. (1957), p. 244. This passage, to my mind, makes it clear that, in the author's view, the answer to the question I have posed above must be 'yes'. It seems to me that it is common sense that it should be so, since otherwise almost any unsecured creditor would be able to improve his position and prevent the receiver from carrying out, or at any rate carrying out as sensibly and as equitably as possible, the purpose for which he was appointed. I therefore hold that the receiver, within the limitations which I have stated above, is in a better position than the company, qua current contracts, and that, in the present case, the receiver, in doing what he has done and is purporting to do, in connection with the transfer of Aircraft's shares, is not doing anything which the plaintiffs are entitled to prevent by this motion.

In re Ardmore Studios (Ireland) Ltd.
[1965] I.R. 1 (H.Ct.)

The net issue was whether a collective agreement that existed between the company and trade union was binding on the receiver and manager for the the company.

McLOUGHLIN J.: . . . [38] (referring to §316(2) of the 1963 Act) This sub-section is similar to sub.-s. 2 of s. 369 of the English Companies Act, 1948, as to the effect of which I have been referred to *Palmer's Company Precedents* (16th ed., 1952, Part 3), at p. 19: 'It is usual to provide that the receiver shall be the agent of the company so as to prevent him being held to be the agent of the debenture holders or being personally liable on contracts entered into by him. Sect. 369 (2), however, now provides that he is to be personally liable to the same extent as if he had been appointed by the Court, on any contract entered into by him in the performance of his functions, "except in so far as the contract otherwise provides."'

Now as of the date of his appointment, the 1st October, 1963, the receiver went into possession of the mortgaged property and took over the management of the business of the Company in exercise of the powers of the lender under the deed of mortgage delegated to him by the deed of appointment, and advertised the mortgaged property for sale.

In the course of the argument I have been referred to many cases as to the effect of the appointment of a receiver for debenture holders but I do not find it necessary to refer to all of them. I obtained most assistance in dealing with this branch of the case from those which I shall now refer to and I shall quote from the reports.

Re B. Johnson & Co. (Builders) [1955] 1 Ch. 634, is not directly in point on the issue whether or not the receiver is bound or not by the alleged seniority list agreement, but many of the views expressed by the distinguished judges who constituted the Court of Appeal in the case are certainly helpful. At page 644 Evershed M.R., after stating some of the powers given to the receiver under the debenture, which are similar to those in this case, continued: 'The situation of someone appointed by a mortgagee or a debenture holder to be a receiver and manager – as it is said, "out of Court" – is familiar. It has long been recognised and established that receivers and managers so appointed are, by the effect of the statute law, or the terms of the debenture, or both, treated, while in possession of the [39] company's assets and exercising the various powers conferred upon them, as agents of the company, in order that they may be able to deal effectively with third parties. But, in such a case as the present at any rate, it is quite plain that a person appointed as receiver and manager is concerned, not for the benefit of the company but for the benefit of the mortgagee bank, to realise the security; that is the whole purpose of his appointment; and the powers which are conferred upon him, and which I have to some extent recited, are. . . really ancillary to the main purpose of the appointment, which is the realisation by the mortgagee of the security (in this case, as commonly) by the sale of the assets.

'All that is perhaps elementary; but it bears upon what I shall have to say as regards the charges made against the receiver; for it appears to me inevitable to negative the proposition that a person appointed, as Mr. Aizlewood was appointed, owes some duty to the company to carry on the business of the company and to preserve its goodwill.'

Jenkins L.J., in the course of his judgment, says (for the sake of brevity I begin the quotation in the middle of a paragraph, at p. 661): '. . . whereas a receiver and manager for debenture holders is a person appointed by the debenture holders to whom the company has given powers of management pursuant to the contract of loan constituted by the debenture, and, as a condition of obtaining the loan, to enable him to preserve and realise the assets comprised in the security for the benefit of the debenture holders. The company gets the loan on terms that the lenders shall be entitled, for the purpose of making their security effective, to appoint a receiver with powers of sale and of management pending sale, and with full discretion as to the exercise and mode of exercising those powers. The primary duty of the receiver is to the debenture holders and not to the company.'

Finally, Parker L.J., at p. 664, says: 'What, however, in my judgment, is decisive of the case is that any work of management done by a receiver is not done as manager of the company. The powers of management are ancillary to his position as receiver, and, in exercising those powers, he is not acting as manager of the company but as manager of the whole or part of the property of the company.'

This case, of course, is not an authority binding on me, but the views expressed in it are very persuasive and deserving of respectful consideration.

Another up-to-date English case, *Robbie & Co.* v. *Witney Warehouse Co.* [1963] 3 All E.R. 613, is not directly in point, but, in effect, seems to support the contention that a receiver appointed by [40] debenture holders is not bound by a contract made by the company before his appointment.

During the course of the argument I was referred to many other English cases – no Irish cases were cited to me on this branch of the case – but I did not get much assistance from them, many of them being liquidation and winding up cases and cases where the receiver was appointed by the Court and subject to control as an officer of the Court.

The defendants' argument put most reliance on the clause in the debenture deed that the receiver is made the agent of the Company, but it should be pointed out that this does not make him the servant of the Company; the same clause – number 14 (c) of the debenture deed – also provides that the receiver shall in the exercise of the powers authorities and discretions conform to the directions from time to time given by the debenture holder. As agent for the Company, the Company is made fully responsible for his acts, but it is not a corollary to this that he is bound by all Company contracts and agreements entered into by the Company before the date of his appointment.

The mortgaged property of which the receiver entered into possession as defined by the deed includes also the property charged and assigned, i.e., all the undertaking and assets, machinery, book debts and goodwill; the argument of the defendants amounts to this: that he also took over, by operation of law, the obligations of the Company under the alleged agreement by the Company to employ the Union's electricians on the production of films in the studio. In as much as I find that it was the Union's insistence on this agreement that gave rise to the circumstances leading to the debenture holders putting in a receiver over all the Company's property and assets, this would seem to lead to an absurdity.

I have no hesitation in holding that there is no legal basis for their contention that the agreement as to the seniority list, even if it existed as an agreement on the date of the appointment of the receiver, became binding on him.

XV. Winding Up – Liquidations

Companies go out of existence through the formal process of being wound up or put into liquidation; these two terms mean the same thing. The leading work on the subject, B. H. McPherson's *The Law of Company Liquidation,* defines winding up or liquidation as 'a process whereby the assets of a company are collected and realised, the resulting proceeds are applied in discharging all its debts and liabilities, and any balance which remains after paying the costs and expenses of winding up is distributed among the members according to their rights and interests, or otherwise dealt with as the constitution of the company directs'. A liquidator is appointed (either by the members, the creditors or the court, as the case may be) in order to carry out the winding up. One major theme that runs through the various rules in this area of company law is protecting creditors' and investors' interests in the sense of conserving the company's property and asserting rights that the company may possess against persons who have wronged it. Many of the rules of bankruptcy law apply if the company being wound up is insolvent. Statutory Instrument No. 28 of 1966 contains the winding up rules for companies.

CATEGORIES OF WINDING UP

Davidson v. King
[1928] N.I. 1 (Ch.D.)

The company sold its undertaking and declared a tax free dividend which absorbed the entire proceeds of the sale.

WILSON J.: . . . [11] Outside a court of law I cannot imagine any one thinking that this 330 per cent. dividend is annual income or profit of this Lisnafillan Bleaching Company. If when the agreement of 28th April, 1925, was completed on 1st July, 1925, the Company had passed a voluntary resolution for winding up, the whole of this £33,000 now proposed to be divided amongst the shareholders would have been nett assets of the company returnable to the shareholders in proportion to the shares held by each of them. I say nothing about the 10 per cent. dividend in the Febuary 1926 accounts or about the 75 per cent. dividend in the 1st September 1926 accounts, all of which were adopted by the general meeting of the company on 7th October, 1926, as no question is asked about them in this summons. In my opinion the whole operations of this company from 1st July, 1925, were realization and liquidation and not trading or carrying on the business of the company authorised by their Memorandum of Association. Its objects were primarily to acquire the business premises, machinery, etc., in which William Gihon had been a partner and to carry on that or some similar business of bleaching, printing, or dyeing. The Company and the majority of its [12] directors contend that so long as they preserve the original £10,000, the capital of the company, they can cease to carry on the business they were incorporated to carry on and sell and realise it all, and by not passing, or by postponing the passing, of a resolution to wind up the company they can continue to exercise the powers given them for the purpose of carrying on the business of the company and put into force article 127 which says 'no dividend shall be payable except out of the profits of the company' and article 128 which says the declaration of the directors as to the amount of the nett profits of the company shall be conclusive which apply to profits of the company while its business is being carried on, and not to the entire assets of the company after the company and its directors have determined to realise all its assets and wind it up. The cases relied on by Mr Murphy relate to a profit made by a sale of part of a company's property in a year while the company still continues to carry on the business it has been incorporated to conduct. I can find no case where a limited company has been held entitled to realise its entire assets and after setting aside its nominal capital and paying its liabilities, to divide the surplus as income or profits under the guise of declaring a dividend. This in my judgment would be a fraud on the winding up provisions of the Companies Act.

In re Newbridge Sanitary Steam Laundry Ltd.
[1917] 1 I.R. 67

On the background to this case see *Cockburn v. Newbridge Sanitary Steam Laundry Co.* [1915] 1 I.R. 237, 249 (ante p. 282).

(From headnote) Llewellyn, the managing director of a laundry company, entered into contracts in his own name for work to be done by the company, the profits of which amounted to £3,268, of which he accounted to the company for £1,038 only. This he alleged was done with the consent of his co-directors. The capital of the company consisted of 2,000 £1 shares, the majority of which were controlled by the managing director, and a co-director who was a business partner of his. In an action brought by two shareholders against the company and Llewellyn, to compel an account of the profits so received, an order was made that he should so account; but no payment was made or account rendered by him, and no steps were taken by the company to compel him to account, and subsequent to the

action a resolution of confidence in his management was passed by a majority of shareholders at a general meeting.

The plaintiffs presented a petition to wind up the company on the ground that in the circumstances it was 'just and equitable' that the company should be wound up:

SIR IGNATIUS J. O'BRIEN L.C.: [78] This case comes before us on an appeal by the majority of the shareholders against an order of the Master of the Rolls for the compulsory winding-up of this small company. Counsel for the appellants have pressed upon us the argument that the Court has no jurisdiction to wind up the company, and further, that, if such jurisdiction exists, it ought not to be exercised in the circumstances of the present case. The appellants' main contention is that clause VI of sect. 129 of the Companies (Consolidation) Act, 1908, corresponding to sect. 129 of the Companies Act, 1862, confers no independent equitable or statutory jurisdiction to make an order for the winding up of a company, but that under this clause the Court is confined to the consideration of matters *ejusdem generis* as those dealt with in the preceding five clauses; and the judgment of Lord Cairns, then a Lord Justice of Appeal, in *Re Surburban Hotel Company* (L.R. 2 Ch.App. 737), has been relied upon as a strong authority in favour of the appellants' contention. I shall deal later on with this contention, but I must advert to the facts proved in the present case; and I may say in passing that, in my judgment, it would be a lamentable thing if the Court were, owing to any technical rule of construction, to find its hands so tied as to be unable to do what, as it appears to me, is only elementary justice to the petitioners. . . .

[86] Down to the present moment nothing has been done by the company to compel Llewellyn to account for the moneys, in respect of which this Court has decided that he is bound to account, and nothing will be done. It has been suggested that the company is actuated by high motives of economy in not pursuing remedies which might result in loss [87]. If so, I can only say that it would have been better if the company had acted in accordance with these motives at an earlier period, and had refrained from entering a defence to the action. Then it is said that it is for the Cockburns to make this order fruitful if they choose to do so; but the company will not do so. That is a singular way of discharging a serious obligation of a company towards a minority of its shareholders. If the company had not been in this very peculiar position, but had been deceived by Llewellyn but willing and anxious to discharge its duty, it would not have hesitated a moment before issuing a debtor's summons against him. The procedure by a debtor's summons would have enabled the true history of these transactions to have been ascertained, whether Llewellyn liked it or not; and the company could at the eleventh hour have been placed in a position such that the directors could say, 'We have done our best.'

I find as a fact that throughout this case the majority of the shareholders of the company have had no other intention than to shield Llewellyn, and I repeat that a winding-up order affords the only means of enabling justice to be done to the petitioners. It is said that the Court is paralyzed, and that there is no jurisdiction to make the order. I decline, however, to accede to the proposition that the words of sect. 129 of the Companies (Consolidation) Act, 1908, to which I have already referred, are not sufficiently wide to enable justice to be done. Now, in the earlier cases in which the corresponding section of the Act of 1862 was considered, there is no doubt that a somewhat restricted, not to say narrow, construction was placed on the words of the final sub-section, namely, that this 'just and equitable' clause ought to be construed on the *ejusdem generis* principle, and having regard to the matters dealt with in the preceding sub-sections. In the judgment of Lord Cairns in *Re Suburban Hotel Co.* to which I referred at the commencement of my judgment, I find the following passage:

'The next case referred to was the case of the *Anglo-Greek Steam Co.* (L.R. 2 Eq. 1). The precise point there decided by the Master of the Rolls was, that the misconduct of the directors and of the managers of the company, though it might render them liable to [88] a suit, was not a ground upon which the Court would consider it just and equitable to wind up the company. But his Lordship made these important observations. He said (L. R. 2 Eq. 5): "There are five different rules laid down in sect. 79, and the four previous rules are these." Then he enumerates the four previous rules which I have already mentioned. "Then the fifth is – Whenever the Court is of opinion that it is just and equitable that the company should be wound up." In that case Lord Cottenham laid down, and I have followed him, and all the other Courts, I think, have done the same, that these words are to be considered as referring to matters *ejusdem generis* with the four subject-matters previously stated in the four previous rules.'

There is no doubt, therefore, that Lord Cairns in that judgment did adopt what I have termed the restricted construction of this clause, which is first to be found in the judgment of Lord Cottenham. I do not think, however, that this view particularly appealed to Lord Cairns. Later in his judgment he says: 'At the same time I am of opinion that this principle would be satisfied if it were established that the company never had a proper foundation, and that it was a mere fraud, what is commonly called a bubble company. . . . In that case the Court would consider that it came within the fifth rule.' And he adds: 'It is not necessary now to decide it; but if it were shown to the Court that the whole substratum of the partnership, the whole of the business which the company was incorporated to carry on, has become impossible, I apprehend that the Court might, either under the Act of Parliament, or on general principles, order the company to be wound up.' Lord Cairns, I think, hesitated to dissent from Lord Cottenham's decision, but he was clearly of opinion that a company might be wound up under this 'just and equitable' clause, not only when it was a bubble company, or when the substratum of the company had disappeared, but also when the general principles on which Courts of equity act required it. That he would be right in so thinking is shown by the decision of Vaughan Williams J., and of the Court of Appeal, affirming that decision, in *Re Thomas Edward Brinsmead & Sons* [1897] 1 Ch. 406. There an order for the winding up of the company was made, [89] although it was not a bubble company, and although, as distinctly stated by Vaughan Williams L.J., part of the substratum of the company remained. I apply to the present case the words there used by A. L. Smith L.J., on the hearing of the appeal: 'Although the words "just and equitable" have had a narrow construction put upon them, they have never been construed so narrowly as to exclude such a case as this. If ever there was a case in which it was just and equitable that a company should be wound up by the Court, I cannot doubt that that case is this case' (p. 420). For my part I have always felt the greatest difficulty in placing this limited construction on the final clause of sect. 129, because I fail to see what effective force is to be given to it if it is confined to cases coming within the preceding clauses. In this view I am confirmed by modern authority. In Lord Justice Lindley's *Law of Companies* (6th ed., at p. 852) I find the following passage: 'At the same time, if it can be shown to the satisfaction of the Court that a company, although not insolvent, ought to be annihilated, the Court will order it to be wound up. Proof of inability to commence business after the lapse of a year, *or of continuing fraud*, will induce the Court to put an end even to a solvent company.' The statement of the law contained in the article in Lord Halsbury's Laws of England, vol. V, p. 397, dealing with 'companies', which is edited by that eminent authority Lord Justice Swinfen Eady, is explicit on this point. 'The words as to its being "just and equitable" to wind up are not to be read as being *ejusdem generis* with the preceding words of the enactment.' The authorities cited for that proposition are: *Re Amalgamated Syndicate*, [1897] 2 Ch. 600; *Re Brinsmead & Sons*; *Re Sailing Ship 'Kentmere' Co.* [1897] W.N. 38; and reference is also made to *Re Surburban Hotel Co.*, and *Re Langham Skating Rink Co.*, (5 Ch.D. 669). If that proposition, supervised as it has been by Lord Justice Swinfen Eady, is an accurate statement of the law, it disposes of the argument based upon Lord Cairns' judgment so strongly pressed upon us by the appellants' counsel. The matter is thus dealt with in the last edition of Lord Justice Buckley's work on the Companies Acts [90] (9th ed., 304-5-6): 'Sub-s. (vi), although thus worded in order to include all cases not before mentioned, should be interpreted in reference to matters *ejusdem generis* as those in the previous clauses; though the tendency of Court is now to give a somewhat wider meaning under special circumstances, e.g. if a winding up will be the means of getting rid of a complete deadlock, or putting an end to a vicious career, or if a winding up is desirable in order to enable a scheme of arrangement to be sanctioned. . . . The "just and equitable" clause gives the Court power to wind up a company in cases not coming under any of the first four heads, but there must be strong ground for exercising the power at the instance of a shareholder.'

An instance of the tendency of the Court to give a wider meaning to the words of the section is to be found in *Re Amalgamated Syndicate*, [1897] 2 Ch. 600, where Vaughan Williams L.J., after referring to the statement of the law on this question contained in the 7th edition of Buckley on the Companies Acts, said: 'without going into details, I repeat what I said during the argument, that the stringency of the *ejusdem generis* rule has been considerably relaxed of late.' I think that the view of the learned Lord Justice when he made use of these words, although he does not implicitly so state, was that not only was the stringency of the rule relaxed, but that it had no foundation in point of law.

The later cases which have been cited, *Re Chic, Ltd.* [1905] 2 Ch. 345; *Re Crigglestone Coal Co., Ltd.* [1906] 2 Ch. 327; and *Re Alfred Melson & Co., Ltd.* [1906] 1 Ch. 841, to my mind entirely support the view put forward by the repondents' counsel, but I shall not occupy public time by dealing with these in detail. I have arrived at the clear conclusion that the final clause of sect. 129 of the Companies Act, 1908, ought not to be construed in this restricted way, but that in all cases which cannot be brought under the preceding clauses, but where, having regard to the established principles of courts of equity, justice and equity require a company to be wound up, an order for its winding up ought to made. [91]

In re Murph's Restaurants Ltd. (No. 2)
(Gannon J., July 31, 1979, H.Ct.)

See ante p. 313.

In re Galway & Salthill Tramways Co.
[1918] 1 I.R. 62

O'CONNOR M.R.: [64] In this matter a petition has been presented for the winding up of the Galway and Salthill Tramways Co., and the petition on its face is that of the company. The petition is opposed by some of the shareholders, who make the legal objection that it was filed by the directors of their own motion, without the authority of the shareholders obtained at a general meeting of the company, and was ultra vires. It is admitted that there was no meeting of the company authorizing the petition for winding up, but it is contended that the directors had power under the general authority vested in them to present the petition, and that in the special circumstances of the case it was not only right that they should do so, but was the only course open to them. This is the point for decision. . . .

[65] But the question is, had the directors power to present the petition? I am satisified that the company is an unregistered company within the meaning of sect. 268 of the Companies Act, 1908, but that is not the point of the case. The point is, had the directors, without the authority of the company conferred by a general meeting of the shareholders, the right to present a petition for winding up? Counsel in support of the petition maintain that they have, and they say that the authority is conferred by section 90 of the Companies Clauses Act, 1845. That section enacts that the directors shall have the management and superintendence of the affairs of the company, and they may lawfully exercise all the powers of the company, except as to all such matters as are directed by that or the special Act to be transacted by a general meeting of the company. Counsel contend that all the powers of the company are thereby vested in the directors, except such as are specially excepted, and that the power of presenting a petition for winding up is not within the exceptions. But in my opinion that part of the section which gives the directors all the powers of the company subject to the exception must be read along with the opening words giving powers of management, and is merely in aid of the proper and effective exercise of such powers. If I am right in this, the powers of the directors are only powers of managing, and if the argument relied on is sound, a winding up of the company must come within the scope of its management. But the object of management is the working of the company's undertaking, while the object of a winding-up is its stoppage. On this ground alone I would hold that the directors had no power to present the petition in the present case, but there is another consideration which seems to me to be even more conclusive. A winding up was not at all within the purview of the Companies Clauses Act, 1845. A perusal of the Act shows that it [66] was only intended to prescribe generally for the carrying on of a company's business as distinguished from putting an end to it. I have not been referred to any authority on the point, and so far as my own researches have gone there is none.

It was forcibly pointed out by Mr Dickie that by sect. 91 there are certain powers which can only by exercised at a general meeting. These are the choice and removal of directors, the choice of auditors, the remuneration of directors, auditors, treasurer, and secretary, the determination as to the amount to be borrowed, &c. These are important powers specially reserved to the company in general meeting, and it would be a strange thing if the still more important power of putting an end to the company's business was left to the directors.

It may be that when the matter of winding-up is brought before a general meeting of the company the shareholders may feel obliged to recognize that it is no longer possible to carry on the undertaking, and that a winding-up is inevitable. That may be so; but the possibility, or even the probability, of such an event does not legalize the unauthorized act of the directors.

I am, for these reasons, of opinion that I ought not to make an order at present for the winding-up of the company, and that the proper course to adopt is to adjourn this hearing so as to enable the directors duly to summon a meeting of the shareholders, with the object of getting authority from them to proceed on the petition. I have been asked to dismiss the petition on the grounds that, as it was presented without authority and ultra vires, it cannot now legally be ratified. That is not my view. If the petition were ultra vires the company, of course it could not be ratified; but it was quite within the powers of the company to authorize the filing of a petition on its own behalf for a winding-up. That being so, it has now power to ratify the petition already filed without authority.

There are, no doubt, limits to the power of ratification. The person on whose behalf the unauthorized act was professed to have been done must have been in existence at the time. For instance, a contract purporting to be made on behalf of a proposed company not then in existence is void and incapable of ratification by the company as afterwards incorporated. But in the present case the [67] directors presumed to act on behalf of an existing company, and it is now open to the company to ratify their unauthorized proceeding. A case in point is *Irvine* v. *The Union Bank of Australia* (2 A. C. 366), in which directors exceeded their power of borrowing on behalf of their company, although the company had itself power to contract for the loans. The lenders, while admitting that the act was ultra vires, contended that it was ratified by the company. It was held by the Judicial Committee of the Privy Council that there was in fact no such ratification, but that it would have been competent for the company to ratify the loan and so bind the company.

It is not necessary for me, in the circumstances, to inquire what legal disabilities affect the directors by reason of the failure of the company to keep up the full number. If the company in general meeting authorize the petition, it will be their own act and not that of the directors. Indeed, the failure to maintain the directorate in its full strength may prove to be an additional reason for ordering the company to be wound up. I will reserve all questions of costs until the adjourned hearing, as I am satisfied that, though the directors have been mistaken in their rights, they acted bona fide and in the interests of the shareholders.

CREDITOR AND INVESTOR PROTECTION

In re Farm Machinery Distributors Ltd.
[1984] I.L.R.M 273 (H.Ct.)

(From headnote) In 1976 the respondent granted to Massey Ferguson (Eire) Ltd. a 35-year lease of factory premises at Naas Road, Dublin. Massey

Ferguson Holdings Ltd., a third party to the lease, guaranteed to the respondent the due payment of the rent and the performance of the usual leasehold covenants. In 1979 the T.M.G. Group acquired the issued share capital of Massey Ferguson (Eire) Ltd., (which was then re-named Farm Machinery Distributors Ltd.) and agreed to assume liability for the guarantee given to the respondent by Massey Ferguson Holdings Ltd. In January 1983 Farm Machinery Distributors Ltd. went into voluntary liquidation and the applicant in these proceedings was appointed liquidator. The applicant discovered that the lease of the Naas Road property represented a liability of some £1,250,000, the rent being above the going rate, a schedule of dilapidations having been served, and there being no prospect of assigning the lessee's interest other than at a 'reverse premium'. The applicant accordingly sought, pursuant to section 290 of the Companies Act, to disclaim the lease as onerous. The disclaimer was opposed by the respondent, and the court also entertained submissions from the two parties liable under the guarantee. It fell to the court to consider the position of the latter and to decide whether a disclaimer would put an end to the liability of the guarantors.

KEANE J.: . . . [277] It is clear, and accepted at the hearing, that whether an order should be made under s. 290 of the 1963 Act, and what terms, if any, should be imposed as a condition of granting leave, are matters for the discretion of the High Court judge. It is also clear, and was not seriously disputed at the hearing, that the premises in question are 'burdened with onerous covenants', that the leasehold interest is 'unprofitable' and that the leasehold interest is 'unsaleable or not readily saleable', to use the various expressions employed by s. 290 (1).

What is not immediately clear is the effect which any disclaimer might have on the rights and liabilities *inter se* of the lessors and the surety and the rights and liabilities *inter se* of the surety and the TMG Group Ltd. Moreover, while it is clear, and again was not seriously disputed by the parties, that the court, in considering whether to exercise its discretion, is bound to take into account the extent to which the interest of the creditors will be protected or otherwise by a disclaimer, it is not immediately clear to what extent, if any, the court may take into account the effect of any permitted disclaimer on the rights and liabilites *inter se* of the lessors, the surety and the TMG Group Ltd. In relation to both of these matters, it is necessary to bear in mind the concluding words of sub-s. (3) which make it clear that the disclaimer is not to affect the rights or liabilities of any other person 'except so far as is necessary for the purpose of releasing the company and the property of the company from liability.'

In relation to the first of these matters, two possibilities must be considered. In the first place, the effect of the disclaimer may be to put an end to the liability of the surety, and, as a consequence the liability of the TMG

Group [278] Ltd. This was the view taken by the Court of Appeal in England in *Stacey* v. *Hill* [1901] 1 KB 660, a decision to which it will be necessary to return; and it is based on the proposition that the liabilities of a surety are in law dependent upon those of the principal debtor and that, where the liabilities of the latter are determined, the former must inevitably be also determined. The alternative possibility is that the liability of the surety remains, notwithstanding the termination of the lessees' liability, because under the express language of s. 290 (3), the disclaimer is not to affect the rights or liabilities of any other person. In considering these alternative possibilities, it must be borne in mind that, if the liability of the surety continues notwithstanding the disclaimer, the surety will then be entitled to be indemnified by the lessees and, accordingly, to prove in the liquidation for the appropriate amount.

The question as to which of these two possible views of the effect of a disclaimer is correct only arises if the court is entitled to take into account on an application such as this the effect of the disclaimer on the rights and liabilities *inter se* of the lessors, the surety and the TMG Group Ltd. I accordingly propose to examine this question at the outset.

S. 290 of the Companies Act, 1963, is in virtually identical terms with s. 323 of the United Kingdom Companies Act, 1948. That section in turn replaced in virtually identical terms s. 267 of the Companies Act, 1929. That section represented the first appearance in the company legislation of either jurisdiction of the disclaimer provisions; but it reproduced with modifications the corresponding provisions of s. 54 of the U.K. Bankruptcy Act, 1914. There is a surprising dearth of authority on the relevant provisions of the Companies' Acts in both jurisdictions, but a wealth of authority on the corresponding provisions in the bankruptcy code. There is, however, one English decision which deals directly with the point now under consideration.

The case in question is *Re Katherine et Cie* [1932] 1 Ch. 70, where the circumstances were not dissimilar to those which have arisen in the present case. The liquidator of a company holding a lease applied for liberty to disclaim the lease. The lessors, who were relying on certain guarantors for the payment of the rent and performance of the covenants, opposed the application. It was held by Maugham J., (as he then was) that, as the lessors, who were entitled to appear, would suffer substantial injury if the disclaimer were allowed, the court, in the exercise of its discretion, would not allow it. Maugham J., in the course of his judgment, referred to the decision in *Stacey* v. *Hill* (which presumably he treated as binding on him) and observed that the lessors had said that the result of the disclaimer if allowed would be a loss of some thousands of pounds. Although he does not say so in express terms, I think it is a reasonable inference from the judgment that he considered that the inevitable effect of allowing the disclaimer would be to relieve the guarantors of liability because of the decision in *Stacey* v. *Hill,* thereby confining the lessors to proving in the liquidation for the amount of the injury sustained by them as a result of the disclaimer.

Maugham J., in the course of his judgment referred to the argument of counsel for the liquidator which was to the effect that the court could not [279] properly refuse to consent to a disclaimer because the interests of the liquidation were paramount and that, accordingly, the court had no right to consider whether the operation of a disclaimer would affect the interests of third parties. This contention was based on a decision of the Court of Appeal in *Ex parte East and West India Dock Co.: Re Clarke* (17 Ch.D. 759) where it was held that the corresponding power given to the court by s. 23 of the Bankruptcy Act, 1869, was to be exercised with a view to the administration in bankruptcy of the bankrupt's estate and for the benefit of all the persons interested in the administration; and that it followed that, if in a particular case it appeared that, looking at the object alone, the disclaimer ought to be allowed, the court would be introducing considerations foreign to the purpose of the legislature if, for collateral reasons connected with the position of other persons, it should refuse to allow it. Maugham J. considered that this view of the law was not easily reconcilable with an earlier decision of the Court of Appeal on the same section, viz. *Ex parte Buxton: Re Müller* ((1880) 15 Ch.D. 289). He also observed that a case of a disclaimer in a liquidation seemed to him very different from that of a disclaimer in a bankruptcy and that he saw no reason why, in exercising his discretion under s. 267 of the Companies Act, 1929, he ought not to take into account the injury to persons not directly interested. In the circumstances, he exercised his discretion by refusing to allow the disclaimer.

The editors of the 19th Edition of *Williams on Bankruptcy,* commenting on the supposed inconsistency between the two earlier cases, observe (at p. 390):

> This inconsistency was recognised, but not resolved in *Re Katherine et Cie.* . .

In *Ex parte Buxton: Re Müller (supra),* Müller had deposited a lease with Buxton to secure the repayment of moneys advanced by Buxton to Müller. Müller having become bankrupt, the Trustee in Bankruptcy applied to the Bankruptcy Registrar for leave to disclaim the lease. Notice of the application for leave to disclaim was served on the lessors and on Buxton. Buxton opposed the making of the order on the ground that the effect of it would be to destroy his title. He sought an assignment of the lease from the trustee, but the trustee was not willing to comply with this request unless he was indemnified by Buxton against liability on the covenants in the lease. Buxton insisted that he was not bound to indemnify the trustee. The registrar gave the trustee leave to disclaim and Buxton appealed.

On the hearing of the appeal, James LJ. made it clear that the trustee would not be allowed by his disclaimer to affect the rights of Buxton as an equitable mortgagee. The only question was as to the terms on which the trustee was to assign the lease. In delivering the judgment of the court, James LJ. said that, while Buxton as an equitable mortgagee was entitled to intercept the trustee's right to disclaim, he would have to take the property on terms that he indemnified the trustee against liability under the lease. It is a notable feature of the decision that the argument for Buxton proceeded on the basis that the Trustee in Bankruptcy was Trustee for the secured creditors as well as the [280] unsecured; and accordingly was bound not to exercise his power in such a way as to destroy the security of an equitable mortgagee.

The facts in *Ex parte East and West India Dock Co.: Re Clarke* (supra), were significantly different. This was the first engagement in a protracted legal battle which arose out of the leasing by the East and West India Dock Company of a public house called the Brunswick Tap to one Arthur Hill. Hill sold the premises to Clarke and the transaction was carried out by way of an assignment of the residue of the term, Clarke covenanting with Hill in the usual way to pay the rent and observe and perform the covenants. Clarke in turn mortgaged the premises to Truman Hambury and Co., the brewers, the mortgage being carried out by way of sub-demise. Clarke having become a bankrupt, Hill gave notice to the trustee in bankruptcy requiring him to decide whether he would disclaim the property comprised in the lease. The trustee then applied to the court for leave to disclaim the bankrupt's interest in the lease, on the ground that the property was not worth the rent. Notice of the application was served on Hill, the mortgagees and the Dock Company. The Dock Company opposed the application on the ground that the effect of the disclaimer would be to destroy the lease and to deprive them of their remedies against Hill upon the covenants; but they offered to undertake not to sue the trustee on the covenants and not to make any claim in respect of them on the bankrupt's estate. The mortgagees opposed the application upon the grounds that the disclaimer would destroy their underlease. The registrar having given leave to the trustee to disclaim, the Dock Company appealed.

On the hearing of the appeal, it was urged on behalf of the Dock Company that *Ex parte Buxton* showed that the court would have regard to what were described as 'the rights of third parties'.

Delivering the judgment of the court, Lord Selborne, LC. referred to the object of the disclaimer procedure and said:

> It appears to us that the object was to cut short by disclaimer all liability of the bankrupt's estate in the classes of cases which are there referred to, and which include beyond all question future liability under leases. The object was to cut it short by disclaimer, leaving any person who might be injured by the operation of the section to prove in the ban-

kruptcy for whatever he could establish to be the value of the injury done to him. On the face of this section it appears to us that the power given by it is to be exercised with a view to the administration in the bankruptcy of the bankrupt's estate, and for the benefit of all the persons interested in that administration. Therefore, if in a particular case it appears clear that, looking at the object alone, the disclaimer ought to be allowed, the court would be introducing considerations foreign to the purpose of the legislature if, for collateral reasons connected with the position of other persons, it should refuse to allow it, and thus leave on the bankrupt's estate a burden which under the section might be got rid of, and ought to be got rid of, if those collateral considerations did not prevail.

Then we must consider how that applies to the present case. No suggestion has been made that there is any reason for not allowing the disclaimer, which has been allowed by the order under appeal, *except the interest of the lessors as between themselves and (not the bankrupt's estate but) the person by whom the lease was assigned to the bankrupt*; and the proposition really comes to this, that the court ought never to allow a disclaimer under this section where the bankrupt is the assignee of the lease and the lessor is willing to offer such an undertaking as has now being offered to the court. (Emphasis supplied).

[281] The 'third party' rights which were under consideration in that case were accordingly, the rights *inter se* of the lessor and of the original lessee, i.e. a person who was not a creditor of the bankrupt's estate and was consequently not a person interested in that administration. By contrast, the equitable mortgagee in *Buxton's* case was clearly a creditor, albeit a secured one, and consequently a person interested in the administration of his estate. In my judgment, it follows that, with all respects to Maugham J, the two decisions are in truth reconcilable. Had the court in the *East India Dock* case declined to take into consideration the interests of the brewers as mortgagees, the cases would no doubt be irreconcilable. The registrar, however, had held that the disclaimer would not affect their interests, on the authority of a recent decision of the Court of Appeal, *(Smalley v. Hardinge)* 7 Q.B.D. 524; and the court in the *East India Dock Co.* case presumably took the same view, since the matter is not referred to in the judgment of Lord Selborne and counsel for the mortgagees was not called upon.

Maugham J., however, as I have noted, took the view that, in any event, the case of a disclaimer in a liquidation was very different from that of a disclaimer in a bankruptcy. This view seems to have been based, in part at least, on the fact that the property of the company remains vested in the company, notwithstanding the appointment of a liquidator; whereas in a bankruptcy the property of the bankrupt vests in the Trustee.

In Irish law, the position is different: there is no automatic vesting of the bankrupt's leasehold property in the official assignee. It is only upon his electing to take the property, that it so vests. The difference between the two jurisdictions is not, however, of importance in the present context, because a disclaimer procedure was provided in Ireland also by ss. 97 and 98 of the Bankruptcy (Ireland) (Amendment) Act, 1872. In both jurisdictions the object of the disclaimer procedure was the same: not merely to relieve the trustee or assignee of a personal liability, but also to free the estate of the bankrupt from burdensome covenants, unmarketable shares in companies and unprofitable contracts generally: in the words of Lush LJ. in *Ex parte Walton, Re Levy* (1881) 17 Ch.D. 757:

> Property which could be of no benefit to his estate, and which, if the Trustee could not get rid of it, would be a standing burden on the estate.

It is true that, in the case of a winding up of a company, there is no *cessio bonorum* such as occurs in a bankruptcy; but I cannot see why this should require one to impute any different intention to the legislature in enacting a similarly worded disclaimer provision in the companies code.

Maugham J. also took the view that the relevance of the *East and West India Dock Co.* case to the disclaimer section in the Companies Act, 1929, was limited by the fact that the Bankruptcy Act, 1869, upon which it was decided, was different from the more modern Bankruptcy Acts. It is certainly true that the wording of the relevant sections in the earlier and later Bankruptcy Acts is markedly different: whether it justifies the inference apparently drawn by Maugham J. that the *East and West India Dock Company* decision was no [282] longer applicable is a question which deserves closer scrutiny.

Section 23 of the United Kingdom Bankruptcy Act of 1869, upon which the *East and West India Dock Co.* case, and other authorities to which it will be necessary to refer, were decided was in the following terms:

> When any property of the bankrupt acquired by the trustee under this Act consists of any land or any tenure burdened with onerous covenants. . . the trustee. . . may, by writing under his hand, disclaim such property, and, upon the execution of such disclaimer, the property disclaimed shall, if the same is a contract, be deemed to be determined from the date of the order of adjudication, and if the same is a lease be deemed to have been surrendered on the same date. . . (I have omitted some words in the section which are not material).

In *Ex parte Walton, Re Levy*, to which I have already referred, the bankrupt lessees had made under leases of the property. When the trustee sought leave to disclaim, it was argued on behalf of the lessors that leave should be refused, because the effect of the disclaimer would be the same as an

actual surrender of the lease, which, under the relevant law, would bring
the under lessees into direct privity with the lessors, who would then be
unable to distrain for the higher rent reserved by the lease. The Court of
Appeal rejected the proposition that the effect of the disclaimer, over
which, of course, the lessor had no control, would be to work such an
injustice. It was held that the disclaimer operated as a surrender only so
far as was necessary to relieve the bankrupt and his estate and the trustee
from liability and did not affect the rights and liabilities of third parties.
James LJ. in a passage which was frequently quoted in subsequent cases,
said that:

> When the Statute says that a lease, which was never surrendered in
> fact (a true surrender requiring the consent of both parties, the one
> giving up and the other taking), is to be deemed to have been surren-
> dered, it must be understood as saying so with the following qualifi-
> cation, which is absolutely necessary to prevent the most grievous
> injustice, and the most revolting absurdity: 'shall, as between the lessor
> on the one hand and the bankrupt, his trustee and estate, on the other
> hand, be deemed to have been surrendered'.

It is of interest that, in coming to that conclusion, James LJ. bore in
mind the position of a guarantor for the rent, saying:

> Take the case of a lease with a surety for the payment of rent. Could
> it ever have been intended that the bankruptcy of the lessee was to
> release the surety?

That the views expressed by the Court of Appeal in that case – and, it
may be noted, views to the same effect were expressed by the Irish Court
of Appeal in *O'Farrell* v. *Stephenson* (1889) 4 LR (Ir.) 715 at p. 727 –
represented the correct construction of the section were put beyond doubt
by the further episodes in the *East and West India Dock Co.* saga. Following
upon the successful disclaimer by the trustee in bankruptcy of the lease of
the Brunswick Tap, the lessor brought an action against the original lessee
upon his covenant to pay rent for the rent accrued due since the appointment of the trustee. It was held by the Court of Appeal, affirming the
decision at first instance of Hall V.C., that, notwithstanding the disclaimer,
the lessee remained liable upon his [283] covenants. *Hill* v. *East and West
India Dock Co.* 22 Ch.D. 14 (1884) 9 App. Cases 448. On appeal, the
decision was upheld by the House of Lords, Lord Bramwell dissenting.
It was again argued on behalf of the original lessee that the effect of the
disclaimer was to put an end to the lease for all purposes and, that, accordingly, the original lessee was no longer liable upon his covenants. Earl
Cairns, LC, while admitting that the section seemed capable of that construction, approved the approach of James LJ. observing:

It is difficult to see upon what principle it can have been enacted by
Parliament – although Parliament has the power to enact it – that a
solvent man who has entered, with his eyes open, into a covenant with
the owners of property to pay rent to them and to be liable to them
for that rent and for other covenants, and who upon an assignment
has recognised that liability and has stipulated that it shall continue,
shall nevertheless be delivered from that liability, not by reason of
anything which has passed between him and the lessors, but from a
misfortune which has happened to the lessors, namely that the person
to whom the lease has been assigned has become a bankrupt.

He also remarked that the section in question had been repealed by a
Statute of the previous year which had substituted:

> An enactment of a very different and much more explicit kind upon
> this part of the bankruptcy law.

The Statute in question was the Bankruptcy Act, 1883; and, as Sir Robert
Megarry V.C., has recently pointed out in *Warnford Investments Ltd.* v.
Duckworth [1979] Ch. 127, the decisions of both Hall V.C. and the Court
of Appeal in the same case had been given in 1882, so that the draughtsman
of the Act of 1883 would have had the assistance of those authorities.
Section 55 of that Act contained a new provision for disclaimer in the
following terms:

> The disclaimer shall operate to determine, as from the date of dis-
> claimer, the rights, interests, and liabilities of the bankrupt and his
> property in or in respect of the property disclaimed, and shall also
> discharge the trustee from all personal liability in respect of the prop-
> erty disclaimed as from the date when the property vested in him, but
> shall not, except so far as is necessary for the purpose of releasing the
> bankrupt and his property and the trustee from liability, affect the
> rights or liabilities of any other person.

(This provision was re-enacted, virtually in so many words, in s. 54 (2) of
the Bankruptcy Act, 1914, which, as has been seen, ultimately provided
the model for s. 323 (2) of the United Kingdom Companies Act, 1948,
and the sub-section in our Companies Act of 1963 which I am considering).
It is difficult to quarrel with this summary of the relevant provision in the
1883 Act by Megarry V.C. in *Warnford Investments Ltd.* v. *Duckworth*:

> In this way the legislature sought to make explicit what the courts had
> held to be implicit for the purposes of avoiding injustice and absurdity.
> If that had been all, I should have said that it was clear beyond a
> peradventure that the legislature had resoundingly approved of the
> law which was shortly to find its final expression by the House of

Lords in *Hill* v. *East and West India Dock Co.* and had succeeded in making that law explicit. But that was not to be all. . . . [284]

He goes on to consider the effect of the decision which has been the subject of so much debate in the present case, i.e. *Stacey* v. *Hill.*

In *Stacey* v. *Hill,* the defendant had guaranteed the payment of rent which might from time to time be in arrear for twenty-one days under a lease. There had not been any under lease or assignment of the lease. The lessee having become bankrupt, the trustee in bankruptcy disclaimed the lease. The lessor sued the defendant for an amount which she claimed was rent in arrear in respect of the period subsequent to the disclaimer. It was held, by the Court of Appeal, affirming the judgment of Phillimore J. that the effect of s. 55 (2) of the Act of 1883 was that the lease was determined from the date of the disclaimer as between the lessor and the lessee and that, accordingly, the liability of the defendant for rent *in futuro* was also determined, and that therefore the action was not maintainable.

The judgment of Phillimore J. at first instance ((1900) 69 LJQB 796) appears to be laconic and unhelpful. In the Court of Appeal, the Master of the Rolls, Sir Archibald Smith, said that the question in the case was concluded by an earlier judgment of the Court of Appeal in *Re Finley, Ex parte Clothworkers Co.* (1888) 21 QBD 475. He quoted a passage from Lindley LJ. in that case to the following effect:

> Now the operation of those clauses in the simple case of a lease is not very difficult to ascertain. If there is nothing more than a lease, and the lessee becomes bankrupt, the disclaimer determines his interest in the lease under sub-s. 2. He gets rid of all his liabilities, and he loses all his rights by virtue of the disclaimer. There is no need of any provision for vesting the property in the landlord, but the natural and legal effect of sub-s. 2 is that the reversion will become accelerated.

The Master of the Rolls drew from this passage the conclusion that the lease was put an end to altogether as between the lessor and the bankrupt lessee and, accordingly, ceased to exist. He concluded that, in these circumstances, since no one was liable for the payment of rent, the surety could not be under any such liability. He had this to say about the concluding words of the sub-section:

> I think the defendant's counsel was right in the construction which he sought to put on the words at the end of the sub-section, except so far as is necessary for the purpose of releasing the bankrupt and his property and the Trustee from liability. If the surety is liable to pay rent *in futuro* on his guarantee, he would be entitled to indemnity against the bankrupt or his property. It is therefore necessary, in order to release the bankrupt and his property from liability under the lease

subsequently to the disclaimer, that the words at the end of the sub-section should be brought into play in such a case.

Collins LJ. and Romer LJ. gave short judgments to the same effect. It is noteworthy that in the *Ex parte Clothworkers Co.* case, Lindley LJ. expressly confined the comment to which the Master of the Rolls attached such weight in *Stacey* v. *Hill* to the 'simple case of a lease'. He goes on to deal with what he describes as the more complicated case of a lease and a sub-lease by way of mortgage and points out that, as between the original lessor and the sub lessee, 'their rights and liabilities are preserved by sub-s. 2'. It seems difficult to suppose that Lindley LJ, in the passage upon which so much reliance was [285] placed in *Stacey* v. *Hill*, had in mind anything more complicated than the position as between a lessor and lessee; and that the effect in law of the section upon the rights and liabilities of third parties, such as sub-lessees or sureties, can hardly have been intended by him to be epitomised by the passage in question.

It is an even more curious feature of the decision that, although referred to in the arguments of counsel and in the decision at first instance the decision of the House of Lords in *Hill* v. *East and West India Dock Co.* is not mentioned in any of the judgments. Yet the question inevitably posed itself: if the liability of the surety ceased as a result of the disclaimer, because the lease itself had ceased to exist, what became of the liability of the original lessee in a case where there had been an assignment? Had the effect of the decision in the *East and West India Dock Co.* been reversed by statute, thereby restoring the law to the state of 'the most grievous injustice and the most revolting absurdity' stigmatised by James LJ. in *Ex parte Walton, Re Levy?* If not, what was the distinction in logic and common sense between the position of a surety and the position of an original lessee?

The problem in that uncompromising form does not appear to have come before the courts in England until *Warnford Investments Ltd.* v. *Duckworth. (Stacey* v. *Hill* had in the meantime been followed by Swift J. in *Morris (D) & Sons* v. *Jeffreys* (1932) 148 LT 56). In *Warnford Investments Ltd.* v. *Duckworth*, the plaintiffs had granted the defendants a lease of business premises for a term of twenty years. The lease contained the usual covenant by the defendants for the payment of rent during the term. Later with the consent of the plaintiffs, the defendants assigned the lease to a company. The company went into liquidation and the liquidator dis-claimed the lease. The rent fell into arrears. On the plaintiff's action claiming arrears of rent from the defendants, it was held by Megarry V.C. that, when the liquidator disclaimed the lease which had been assigned to the company, the original lessee still remained liable to the lessor for the rent throughout the term and that the plaintiffs were accordingly entitled to the unpaid rent claimed from the defendants.

Having considered the earlier authorities to which I have already referred, Megarry V.C., stated his opinion that when a lease was disclaimed, there were very real distinctions between the case where it is vested in the original lessee and the case where it is vested in an assignee. A major distinction, he said, was that in the first case, disclaimer terminates the lease, which ceases to exist, whereas in the second case the lease continues to exist despite the disclaimer and may be made the subject of vesting order under the relevant provisions of the Bankruptcy Act 1914, or the Companies Act 1948. The learned Vice-Chancellor has this to say of the guarantor's position:

> Where it is the original lessee who is bankrupt, so that the lease comes to an end on disclaimer, a basic reason for holding that a guarantor of the rent is discharged from liability on his guarantee is that such liability ends with the termination of the obligation that is the subject of the guarantee. If there is no obligation to pay future rent, there can be no liability upon a guarantee of the payment of that future rent. Collins LJ. put it that way in *Stacey* v. *Hill.*

[286] The distinction between the case of a lease which is vested in an original lessee and one which is vested in an assignee does not, with respect, seem to me to be so clear-cut as it seemed to the learned Vice-Chancellor. I find it difficult to understand how, in the first case, it can be said that the disclaimer necessarily terminates the lease so that it ceases to exist for all purposes. The authorities make it abundantly clear that this does not happen where the lessee has made an under-lease: see *Re Finley, Ex parte Clothworkers' Co.* Indeed, in an authority referred to by Megarry V.C., (*Re Thompson and Cottrell's Contract* [1943] Ch. 97) Uthwatt J, said:

> It is quite clear that a disclaimer does not determine the lease and all interests carved out of it by way of sub-lease or otherwise and that it is limited to determining the rights, interests and liabilities of the Bankrupt in respect of the property. The rights of third parties remain on foot, except so far as it is necessary to release the bankrupt and his estate.

He was there considering the operation of the corresponding sections of the Bankruptcy Act 1914; but it is clear, as is acknowledged by Megarry V.C., that the same considerations apply to the similar provisions in the Companies Act 1948. In this context, I am bound to say that I do not altogether follow the reference by Megarry V.C., in his judgment in *Re Thompsom and Cottrell's Contract.* He says of it:

> Where the disclaimed lease was vested in an assigneee, the lease was discribed by Uthwatt J, in *Re Thompson and Cottrell's Contract* as being 'something like a dormant volcano. It may break out into active operation at any time', (Emphasis supplied).

I have read the facts of that case with some care and I cannot find any indication that the bankrupt was an assignee of the leasehold interest as distinct from the original lessee. I do not know on what basis it was concluded in *Warnford Investments Ltd.* v. *Duckworth* that there had been an assignment of the lessee's interest; and there is certainly nothing in the judgment of Uthwatt J. to suggest that he was considering the case of an assignee of the leasehold interest as distinct from the case of an original lessee. But I may have misunderstood the language used by the learned Vice-Chancellor; and, in any event, it seems to me that *Re Finley* is a clear authority for the proposition that, even in the case of an original lessor and original lessee, the lease will continue in effect where there is an under-lease, in the sense that failure to pay the rent reserved by it will justify distress and failure to perform the covenants contained in it will justify re-entry.

Megarry V.C. in his judgment then engages in a detailed analysis of the different effects which flow, in his view, in law from holding the original lessee liable on his covenants and holding the guarantor liable on his guarantee, in each case notwithstanding the existence of a disclaimer. While he canvasses various possibilities that may arise, it seems to me that in practical terms the consequences will very often be the same. In each case, the person sought to be made amenable to the payment of the rent and the performance of the covenants will have his right of indemnity as against the bankrupt's estate; and to that extent his release might be thought 'necessary for the purpose of [287] releasing the bankrupt and his property and the trustees from liability', to quote the words of the 1883 Act upon which so much reliance was placed in *Stacey* v. *Hill*. Megarry V.C. mentions the possibility of a break in a chain of assignments and indemnities which would preclude a lessee from having recourse to the estate of the bankrupt; but seems to concede that, even in those circumstances, a quasi contractual right of indemnity leading to a right of proof in the bankruptcy might remain. It seems to me, with all respect to Megarry V.C., that the distinction, if distinction there be, between the position of the surety and the original lessee must derive from the difference in the nature of their liability, the liability of the lessee being a primary liability and that of the surety a secondary or contingent liability. That indeed is a distinction understandably stressed by Megarry V.C. at many points in his judgment.

One can well understand the general conclusion reached by the learned Vice-Chancellor as to the intention of the legislature in enacting s. 55(2) of the Act of 1883. He summarises his views as follows (at p. 139):

Hill v. *East and West India Dock Co.* firmly established that prior to the Bankruptcy Act, 1883 the original lessee remained liable to the reversioner, notwithstanding an assignment and subsequent disclaimer. I think it was clear that the new wording in the Act of 1883 was not only intended to confirm the law laid down in *Hill's* case, but also actually did so. . . . In my judgment, the present wording is both more apt and more explicit for producing the result that in *Hill's* case was achieved on the old wording. If the draftsman had intended to reverse or alter the law laid down in that case he could scarcely have chosen more inept language for his purpose; and Mr Oliver was unable to advance any reasons why parliament should have wished to reverse or alter the law which the courts had wrested out of the old statutory language in order to avoid hardship and injustice.

It seems to me, however, that, if parliament intended to enshrine in statutory form the law as stated in *Hill* v. *East and West India Dock Co.* it is impossible to understand why that law was not also intended to apply to the position of a surety. It had been held prior to the decision of the House of Lords in the *East India Dock* case that, where an original lessee paid rent to the lessor and then claimed reimbursement from the surety, the surety remained liable to the original lessee, notwithstanding that the assignee's trustee in bankruptcy had disclaimed the lease: *Harding* v. *Preece* (1882) 9 Q.B.D. 281. The court so held for precisely those reasons which commended themselves to the House of Lords shortly afterwards in the *East and West India Dock Co.* v. *Hill*; although it is right to say that one of the two judges did so only because he considered himself bound so to hold by the decision of Hall V.C. in the *East India Dock* case. As I already observed, James LJ. in *Ex parte Walton, Re Levy*, which was expressly approved of in *Hill* v. *The East and West India Dock Co.* appears to have treated the case of a surety as no different from that of an original lessee who had assigned his interest.

No doubt, by constructing various hypotheses, one could establish situations in which continuing the surety's liability might be more or less injurious to the estate of the bankrupt than treating it as at an end. This indeed can be illustrated by reference to the facts of the present case. If the surety's liability [288] continues notwithstanding the disclaimer, the surety will be able to prove in the liquidation for any arrears of rent and damages for breach of covenant recovered from it by the lessors. This will depend in turn upon whether the lessors resume possession of the premises; because a resumption of possession will bring about a surrender of the lease by act and operation of law under s. 7 of Deasy's Act, which would in any event put an end to the liability of the surety. (See *Sexton* v. *Kelly*, 3 NIJR 60). That might have the effect of significantly reducing the liability of the surety and thereby the effect on the property of the company. On the other hand, if the liability of the surety is discharged by the disclaimer, the lessor's only remedy will be to prove in the liquidation, not merely for any arrears of rent which have accrued up to the date in which the disclaimer takes effect, but also under sub-s. 9 for the damages which they will sustain as a result of the disclaimer. It seems to me difficult to ascertain with any precision which consequence would be the more injurious to the estate of the company, particulary bearing in mind that, in the context of the huge deficiency which arises in the present case, the effect on the creditors will in any event be marginal. Moreover, on any view, the liability of the surety will only remain until the conclusion of the winding up and the dissolution of the company, at which stage the leasehold interest will become *bona vacantia* and vest in the Minister for Finance under s. 28 (2) and s. 29 (3) of the State Property Act 1954, subject to the right in turn of the Minister to disclaim it under s. 32 (2) of the same Act. If the Minister exercises that power of disclaimer the leasehold interest will thereupon vest in the person entitled to the reversion, i.e. the lessors. Again, it seems to me difficult to establish with any precision the extent to which the injury to the estate of the company will be more or less reduced by treating the surety's liability as continuing or as at an end, having regard to the various possibilities which may arise. Indeed, I mention these matters merely in support of my view that it is not particularly helpful to decide the issue by reference to niceties of that sort: indeed, I would echo the words of Megarry V.C. at another point in the judgment where he says:

> I do not think that the statute is directed to fine distinctions of fact which depend on the relative amounts for which proof could be made.

It also seems to me, however, that such an approach makes it inappropriate to draw distinctions between the position of a surety and the position of a lessee based on the possible differences in the relative amounts for which proof could be made by a surety held liable on the one hand and a lessee held liable on the other hand, depending in each case on a number of hypothetical possibilities that might or might not arise. By contrast, to treat the surety and the original lessee as on the same footing seems to me entirely consonant with the line of high judicial authority which preceded the 1883 Act and which repeatedly stresses the injustice and absurdity of treating lessor's rights as against both original lessees and sureties as at an end because of the effect of a disclaimer over which they have no control; and which, indeed, only arises because of the very circumstance against which the guarantee in the one case and the lessee's covenant in the other case was designed to protect them, i.e. the insolvency of [289] the original lessee or an assignee. As I have said, I entirely accept the conclusion that s. 55(2) of the 1882 Act was expressly designed and intended to shut the door on the possibility of any such injustice or absurdity in the future; but there seems no warrant in the sub-section for excluding sureties from its ambit which would not equally exclude original lessees who have assigned their interests. While *Stacey* v. *Hill* is authority to the contrary, I cannot regard it as a satisfactory decision and I am not prepared to follow it.

I should also point out, since some reliance was placed on it in the course of the argument, that no useful distinction is to be derived in my view, from the actual language used in the guarantee in this case which imposes the liability on the surety 'so long as the term hereby granted is vested in (the lessees)'. Clearly, as a result of the disclaimer, the liability of the lessees for the rent and covenants will come to an end and it may be that, in legal theory, the term may be regarded as no longer vested in them. But since the effect of the disclaimer is not to affect the rights and liabilities of third parties, it is immaterial whether the term is treated as still vested in the lessees: specifically, the surety and the TMG group remain liable on foot of the guarantee and letter of offer respectively.

The reason sometimes given for supporting the decision in *Stacey* v. *Hill* is, that any other view of the law would lead to a serious anomaly: the lessor, the lease having been disclaimed and thereby terminated as against an occupying lessee, could re-enter the land and make beneficial use of it, possibly by re-letting it, while at the same time continuing to recover the rent from the surety. Apart from the obvious comment that a similar anomaly arises where the original lessee remains liable, I have observed that, in this country at least, the effect of the lessor resuming possession would seem to bring about a surrender of the lease by act and operation of law under s. 7 of Deasy's Act, which would in any event put an end to the liability of the surety.

I also note that the correctness of the decisions in *Stacey* v. *Hill* and *Re Katherine et Cie* (supra) has been questioned in a number of leading English text books: See *Woodfall on Landlord and Tenant* (28th ed. vol. 1 par. 1-1805), *Gower's Modern Company Law* (4th ed. p. 737) and *Pennington's Company Law* (4th ed. 731/2).

I embarked on this lengthy excursus into the authorities with a view to establish whether one of the conclusion reached by Maugham J. in *Re Katherine et Cie* – that the change of wording in the disclaimer provisions introduced subsequently to the Bankruptcy Act 1869, warranted the court's taking into account the interests of third parties – was supported by authority. It has, however, produced the incidental benefit of enabling me to reach positive conclusions on the other perplexing problems which the case presents. I may summarise those conclusions as follows:

1. The exclusive concern of the court in an application for leave to disclaim must be the interests of all persons interested in the liquidation. I think it is clear that this was the over-riding intention of the legislature in both the bankruptcy and companies code and should be given effect to by the courts. The principle was established in law beyond doubt by *Ex parte Hill, Re East* [290] *and West India Dock Co.* and has not been significantly dislodged since then. To the extent that *Re Katherine et Cie* decides other-

wise, it should not in my view be followed.

2. In considering the extent, if any, to which the interests of those interested in the liquidation will be affected by the operation of a disclaimer it is necessary to consider whether the release of third parties such as (in the case of leasehold property) original lessees and sureties, is necessary 'for the purpose of releasing the company and the property of the company from liability'.

3. In the case of leasehold property which has been assigned by the original lessee to a company in liquidation, the release of the original lessee is not necessary for the purpose of releasing the company and the property of the company from liability. The position of a surety for the payment of the rent and performance of the covenants by a company holding property under a lease which goes into liquidation is no different; the release of the surety is not necessary for the purpose of releasing the company and the property of the company from liability.

4. The release of the surety, the case mentioned in the preceding paragraph, not being necessary for the purpose of releasing the company and the property of the company from liability, the liability of the surety is not affected by the disclaimer by the liquidator of the interest of the company in the property. This is consistent with the principles enunicated in *Harding* v. *Preece* (1882) 9 Q.B.D. 281 and *Hill* v. *East and West India Dock Co.* and avoids what James LJ. called 'the most grievous injustice and the most revolting absurdity' of permitting the lessor's rights against third parties to be adversely affected by the operation of a disclaimer which he has done nothing to bring about. *Stacey* v. *Hill* and *Re Katherine et Cie*, being founded on a different view of the law, should not be followed.

It remains to consider the application of these principles to the present case. There is not the smallest doubt, and the contrary was not seriously urged, that the giving of leave to the liquidator to disclaim could only be in the interests of those interested in the liquidation, although the financial benefit accruing to the unsecured creditors may be marginal in the extreme, having regard to the huge deficiency. The disclaimer, will, however, facilitate the liquidator in bringing the liquidation to a speedy close; and this can only be in the interests of all those interested in the liquidation. The rights and liabilities of the lessor, the surety and the TMG Group *inter se* having regard to the terms of the guarantee and the letter of offer dated 26 March 1979, will not be affected by the disclaimer.

There remains the question of the date at which the disclaimer should become operative. In *Peter Henry Grant* v. *Aston Ltd.* (1969) 103 ILTR 30, the only reported Irish case on s. 290, Kenny J. made an order that the liquidator should pay the rent under the lease from the date of the commencement of the liquidation until the date of the order of the court. The reported judgment is rather terse and, accordingly the decision does not afford me much assistance in determining what are the principles which are applicable in determining the date at which the disclaimer should be treated as operative. There is, however, [291] an English decision of *Re H.H. Realisations Ltd.* (1975) 31 P. & C.R. 249, in which Templeman J, considered in detail the principles which should be applied. He came to the conclusion that the only period during which it was equitable for the landlords to claim rent in full was the period during which the property was actually being retained by the liquidators for the benefit of the creditors in general. I am satisfied that I should apply the same principle in the present case; and it would follow that the lessors are entitled to the apportioned rent in full from the date of the appointment of the liquidator, 4 January 1983, to the date on which they were given notice of the liquidator's intention to disclaim, 4 February 1983. Accordingly, the order will provide that the disclaimer takes effect as and from 4 February 1983.

I will hear counsel as to the form of order that I should make in the circumstances.

(Having heard submissions from counsel, the judge concluded as follows):

It appears to me that, having regard to the conclusions I have reached, I should make a form of speaking order which should recite that the court is of the opinion that the release of the surety and the TMG Group from their respective liabilities under the lease and the acquisition agreement, the terms of which are set out in the letter dated 26 March 1979, is not necessary for the purpose of releasing the company and the property of the company from liability and that accordingly the rights and liabilities *inter se* of the lessors, the surety and the TMG Group will not be affected by the disclaimer of the lease by the applicant.

The question as to whether an order should be made under sub-s. 9 vesting the disclaimed property in one of the parties was canvassed during the original hearing. No application has been made to me for such an order at this stage; but, as the parties may wish to consider the position in the light of this judgment, the order will reserve liberty for each of the parties to apply.

The liquidator is entitled to his costs of the proceedings as part of the costs of the liquidation. There will be no order as to the costs of the other parties.

In re Creation Printing Co. Ltd.
[1981] I.R. 353 (S.Ct.)

(From headnote) On the 4th June, 1975, Creation Printing Co. Ltd., in consideration of the forbearance of the first defendant to demand the immediate repayment (by the parent company of Creation Printing) of moneys advanced to the parent company by the first defendant, issued a debenture in favour of the first defendant whereby a floating charge on the undertaking

and assets of Creation Printing was created to secure the repayment of those moneys by the parent company. On the 26th November, 1975, the first defendant appointed the plaintiff to be the receiver and manager of Creation Printing pursuant to the powers conferred by the debenture. On the 23rd December, 1975, it was resolved by the members of Creation Printing that it be wound up voluntarily. The plaintiff, as such receiver, sought an order of the High Court determining whether the debenture was valid, having regard to the provisions of s. 288 of the Act of 1963.

KENNY J.: [358] When a floating charge on the undertaking or property of a company is created and the company is ordered, or resolves, to be wound up within 12 months afterwards, the burden of establishing that the company was solvent at the date of the debenture rests on the debenture holder. The charge is invalid *unless* something is proved: Therefore, the proving of the conditions which exempt the charge from invalidity rests on the holder of the charge. . . .

'Solvent' and 'insolvency' are ambiguous words. It has now been established by the decided cases that, for the purposes of s. 288 of the Act of 1963, the test to be applied in determining this question is whether [359] immediately after the debenture was given, the company was able to pay its debts as they became due. The question is not whether its assets exceed in estimated value its liabilities, or whether a business man would have regarded it as solvent; *Ex parte Russell* (1882) 19 Ch.D. 588, *Re Patrick and Lyon Ltd.* [1933] Ch. 786. The question whether a company was solvent on a specified date is one of fact and it involves many difficult inferences. If there is, or is likely to be, a large deficiency of assets when the liquidation starts, the temptation to hold that the company was not solvent when the charge was given is strong. But the deficiency may have been caused by some change in economic or market conditions happening after the charge was given. So an examination of the financial history of the company, both before and after the charges were given, is necessary.

Although the solvency of a company is question of fact, some guidelines as to how this question is to be approached are given by the decided cases. *Ex parte Russell* related to s. 91 of the Bankruptcy Act, 1869, which provided that any settlement of property made by a trader (not being made in contemplation of marriage or in favour of a purchaser or incumbrancer) should, if the settlor became bankrupt at any subsequent time within 10 years after the date of such settlement, be void against the trustees in bankruptcy 'unless the parties claiming under such settlement can prove that the settlor was at the time of making the settlement able to pay all his debts without the aid of the property comprised in such settlement.' Mr Butterworth was a baker who had traded profitably and bought some houses as an investment. In 1878 he settled these in favour of his wife and children. He then purchased a grocery business in which he lost money. He filed a bankruptcy petition in 1881. He had continued to carry on his bakery business after the purchase of the grocery business. When the settlement was impeached he claimed that, in deciding whether he was solvent in 1878, the property, assets and stock-in-trade of the bakery business should be taken into account. Lindley L.J. dealt with this contention in these words at p. 601 of the report:

> I also think the settlement falls within the 91st section of the *Bankruptcy Act*. When we look at the words of that section, and have to consider whether a man is able to pay his debts, we must not merely look at the amount of his assets and liabilities, but we must consider the position which he is assuming. If, for example, this baker had been retiring from trade, of course we must have taken into account all his pots and shovels, the goodwill of his business, [360] and everything else; all those things would be the means of paying his debts. But, if he is going on with his baker's business, it appears to me idle that we should take such things into account as assets. He must be able to pay his debts in the way in which he proposes to pay them, that is by continuing his business.

Those words of Lindley L.J. were written in 1882 in relation to an individual. At that time floating charges by a company were rare. Their validity had been recognised only in 1870 in *Re Panama, New Zealand, and Australian Royal Mail Co.* (1870) 5 Ch.App. 318. His remarks show that when considering whether a company was solvent immediately after it had created a particular floating charge, in circumstances where its directors intended that the company would continue to carry on its business after that time, the fixed and moveable assets of the company are not to be taken into account. However, the capacity of the company immediately after the creation of the particular charge to borrow money on the security of another charge on its assets must be taken into account. This necessarily involves the court in an inquiry as to whether any creditor would advance money to the company on the security of another and later floating charge which would rank in priority after the particular debenture whose validity is in question. If a sum could be borrowed on the security of such a subsequent charge, it should be taken into the reckoning which has to be made when determining the company's solvency.

In re Station Motors Ltd.
(Carroll J., Nov. 22, 1984, H.Ct.)

The facts appear from the judgment.

CARROLL J.: There are three issues arising in this case:
1. Whether lodgments by the plaintiff ('the Company') to its account with the defendant ('the Bank') between the 15th September, 1980 (when the

directors decided to call a creditors' meeting with a view to creditors' voluntary winding up) and the 3rd October, 1980, (when the company actually went into liquidation) constituted a fraudulent preference within the meaning of s. 291 (1) of the Companies Act 1963.

2. Whether the Bank have a valid preferential claim under Section 284 (6) in respect of moneys paid by the company for wages during the four months prior to the 3rd October, 1980, out of its account with the Bank which was on an overdraft sanctioned by the Bank.

3. If so, whether the rule in *Claytons Case* applies.

[2] The facts are as follows: The company was incorporated on the 10th March, 1977. Mr William Murphy together with his wife effectively controlled the operation and existence of the company. The company's Bank account was guaranteed by Mr Murphy. On the 24th January, 1980, the Bank sanctioned an increase in overdraft to £30,000 to be guaranteed by Mr and Mrs Murphy. The company's overdraft increased, despite protest by the Bank, to £78,116.08 on the 16th June, 1980. On that date the Bank obtained a joint and several letter of guarantee from Mr and Mrs Murphy for the obligations of the company up to £75,000 with interest. Between the 16th June, 1980 and the 17th September, 1980, a total of £199,209.48 was credited and £187,649.65 was debited to the current account of the company.

On the 15th September, 1980, the directors of the company (including Mr and Mrs Murphy) passed a resolution that an extraordinary general meeting of the company be held on the 3rd October, 1980 at 10.30 a.m. to consider and if thought fit pass the following resolution:

> That it has been proved to the satisfaction of this meeting that the company cannot by reason of its liabilities continue its business and that it is advisable to wind up the same and that accordingly the company be and is hereby wound up voluntarily and that P. P. Carty F.C.A. [3] of Haughey Boland and Company, 60/62 Amiens Street, be nominated liquidator for the purpose of such winding up.

Mrs Murphy was instructed to convene a meeting of creditors for 11 a.m. on the 3rd October, and John Tobin was instructed to compile a full statement of the position of the company's affairs with a list of creditors and estimated amount of claims to be laid before the meetings on the 3rd October.

In his affidavit Mr Herlihy on behalf of the Bank said that on the 17th September, 1980, Mr Carty (then the proposed liquidator) and Mr and Mrs Murphy assisted the Bank in identifying wages cheques paid between the 16th June, 1980, and the 17th September, 1980, (totalling £32,519.11). He said the Bank was told of a proposed creditors' meeting for winding up and also that a wages account was opened on that day at the request of Mr and Mrs Murphy and Mr Carty. Mr Carty in a supplemental affidavit denied that he assisted in identifying wages cheques or that he requested with Mr and Mrs Murphy that a wages account be opened. On the 18th September, 1980, advertisements appeared in the newspapers concerning the creditors' meeting. On the 30th September, 1980, the wages account was debited with the said sum of £32,519.11 and the company's current account was credited in the [4] like sum. Between the 17th September, 1980, and the 3rd October, 1980, a further sum of £4,348.72 was debited to the wages account for wages.

Between the 15 September, 1980, and the 3rd October, 1980, lodgments were made to the company's account totalling £23,278.13. During the same period six cheques totalling £8,057.38 were honoured by the Bank. One of them was payable to Mr Murphy in the amount of £2,730 and was drawn on the 16th September. The other five totalling £5,327.38 were drawn prior to the 15th September. Mr Herlihy said that these cheques were paid following representations made by Mr Murphy. During the same period four cheques totalling £2,321.20 were presented but were not honoured.

With the exception of Mr Carty's disavowal in relation to identifying wages cheques and requesting a wages account to be opened, these facts are not in issue. Mr Murphy was represented at the hearing by Mr Nesbitt who said he did not wish to adduce evidence. The matter was heard on affidavit.

In relation to the first issue the relevant section is s. 286 (1) of the Companies Act 1963 which provides:

> Subject to sub-section (2) (which is not relevant here) any conveyance, mortgage, delivery of goods, payment, execution or other act relating to property made or done by or against a company within six [5] months before the commencement of its winding up which, had it been made or done by or against an individual within six months before the presentation of a bankruptcy petition on which he is adjudged a bankrupt, would be deemed in his bankruptcy a fraudulent preference, shall in the event of the company being wound up be deemed a fraudulent preference of its creditors and be invalid accordingly.

Also relevant is s. 53 of the Bankruptcy (Ireland) Amendment Act 1872 as amended by Section 399 of the Companies Act 1963 and set out in the 11th Schedule to that Act which provides:

> Every conveyance or transfer of property or charge thereon made, every payment made, every obligation incurred and every judicial proceeding taken or suffered by any person unable to pay his debts as they become due from his own moneys, in favour of any creditor or of any person in trust for any creditor, with a view to giving such creditor, or any surety or guarantor for the debt due to such creditor

a preference over the other creditors, shall, if the person making, taking, paying or suffering the same is adjudged bankrupt on a bankruptcy petition or a petition for arrangement, presented within six months after the date of making, taking, paying or suffering the same, be deemed fraudulent and void against the assignees or trustees [6] of such bankrupt; but this section shall not affect the rights of any person making title in good faith and for valuable consideration through or under a creditor of the bankrupt.

The payments which are queried are the lodgments made after the 15th September, 1980.

It is common case that the onus is on the liquidator to establish a dominant intention to prefer one creditor over another (see *Corran Construction Co. Ltd.* v. *Bank of Ireland Finance Ltd.*, 1976 No. 118. McWilliam J. delivered the 8th September, 1976). Since this is a company managed and run by Mr Murphy it is Mr Murphy's intention which falls to be considered. There is no direct evidence here by Mr Murphy as to what his intention was. Nevertheless the Court is not precluded from drawing an inference of an intent to prefer.

The case of *Re M. Kushler Ltd.* [1943] 2 All E. R. 22, deals with the following points:

1. The phrase 'with a view to giving such creditor a preference' means that the intention to prefer must be the dominant intention which actuates the payment (per Lord Greene M.R. at p. 24).

2. It is not enough to prove that there was actual preferment from which an intention to prefer can, with hindsight, be inferred. The liquidator [7] must prove an intention to prefer at the time the payment is made (per Goddard L.J. at p. 28).

3. Where there is no direct evidence of intention, there is no rule of law which precludes a Court from drawing an inference of an intention to prefer, in a case where some other possible explanation is open (per Lord Greene M.R. at p. 26).

Also in relation to the absence of direct evidence as to intention, Lord Greene M.R. says at p. 27

> . . . it does not seem to me that he (i.e. Lord Tomlin in *Peat* v .*Gresham Trust Ltd.* [1934] A.C. 252) could have meant that in every case where there is no direct evidence you are bound to say the onus is not discharged on the grounds that there may have been another explanation. Of course there may have been other explanations. One can scarcely imagine a case of circumstantial evidence where it would not be possible to say that there might be another explanation of the facts.

4. The method of ascertaining the state of mind of the payer is the ordinary method of evidence and inference, to be dealt with on the same principles

which are commonly employed in drawing inferences of fact [8] (per Lord Greene M.R. at p. 26). He goes on to say that because the inference to be drawn in a case of fraudulent preference is an inference of something which has about it at the very least the taint of dishonesty and in extreme cases very much more than a mere taint of dishonesty. That being so the Court on ordinary principles is not in the habit of drawing inferences which involve dishonesty or something approaching dishonesty unless there are solid grounds for drawing them.

As to the question of whether the taint of dishonesty is necessarily involved in a case of fraudulent preference, Maugham J. in *Re Patrick and Lyon Ltd.* [1933] 1 Ch.D. 786 at 790 expressed the view that a fraudulent preference within the meaning of the Companies Act 1929 or the Bankruptcy Act 1914 whether in the case of a company or of an individual possibly may not involve moral blame at all.

However, also in the *Kushler Case*, the same point was dealt with by Goddard L.J. at p. 28;

> The matter stands as it does in any matter relating to a state of mind where any criminal or civil court if the person upon whom the onus lies, proves no more than the state of facts which is equally consistent with guilt or innocence (using the expression [9] 'guilt' for convenience, because in bankruptcy, there is no question of crime or criminal intent). In such a case, the court is not entitled to draw the one unfavourable inference and find the payment was a guilty rather than an innocent preference and if any court is left in doubt as to the inference, then the trustee has not proved his case.

Having considered the established facts in this case, I am satisfied that the overwhelming inference to be drawn from those facts is that the lodgments made after the 15th September, 1980, were made with a composite intention to prefer (a) the Bank as the direct creditor and (b) the Murphys themselves as guarantors of the company's overdraft. The facts which support this view are:

1. This is a guarantee case. The attitude of Lord Greene M.R. in *Re M. Kushler Ltd.* to such cases is expressed as follows at p. 26:

> At the other end of the scale comes the type of case which is extremely familiar nowadays, where the person (such as a director) who makes the payment on behalf of the debtor is himself going to obtain by means of it a direct and immediate personal benefit. These cases of guarantees of overdrafts and securities deposited to cover overdrafts are very common indeed, and where, for example, [10] you have directors who have given guarantees, the circumstance of that strong element of private advantage may justify the court is attaching to the

other facts much greater weight than would have been attached to precisely similar facts in a case where that element did exist.

In this case a guarantee of £30,000 in January, 1980, was increased to £75,000 in June, 1980.

2. Because at the directors' meeting of the 15th September, 1980, it was resolved that an extraordinary general meeting and creditors' meeting be called for the purposes of a creditors voluntary winding up, one must draw an inference that on and from the 15th the directors knew that the company was insolvent and it was only a question of time until it went into liquidation and that the payment of any trade debtors on or after the 15th would have the effect of preferring them (see *Re F.P. and C.E. Matthews Ltd.* [1982] 1 All E.R. 338).

3. Only six cheques were paid out of the company's account on and after the 15th September and then only as a result of special representations made by Mr Murphy. Instead of inferring, as put forward in the Bank's affidavit, that the account was being operated normally in the ordinary course of business because of the payment of these six cheques, I find [11] exactly the opposite. It seems to me that the necessity to make a special case for these infers that the account was not being operated normally. Also there were four other cheques presented but not honoured during that period and this does not represent ordinary trading.

4. The fact that one of those cheques was drawn after the 16th September by Mr Murphy for himself does not weaken the inference of an intention to prefer the Bank. As I have said, the intention to prefer the Bank was coupled with an intention to prefer the guarantors. The payment of a cheque for £2,730 to Mr Murphy was a direct preferment of himself rather than an indirect one by reducing the amount payable on foot of the guarantee.

5. The payment of the five other cheques during this period, does not in my opinion negative an intention to prefer the Bank directly and the guarantors indirectly. For whatever reason, Mr Murphy decided those creditors should be paid even though as guarantor he would ultimately be responsible. In proportion to the lodgments totalling £23,278.13 the amounts involved in four of the cheques were very small.

6. Once the directors had decided on the 15th September to hold meetings for creditors voluntary winding up, there could not be normal trading as the [12] company at that stage must have been unable to pay its debts. The opening of the wages account on the 17th September was an indicator that the end was nigh.

I find the inference overwhelming that the lodgments after the 15th September were made to prefer the Bank directly and the guarantors indirectly and that this was the dominant purpose of the lodgments.

In relation to the second issue the relevant section is s. 295 (6) of the

Companies Act 1963 which provides:

> Where any payment has been made:
> (a) to any clerk, servant, workman or labourer in the employment of
> a company, on account of wages or salary: or
> (b) to any such clerk, servant, workman or labourer or, in the case of
> his death, to any other person in his right, on account of accrued
> holiday remuneration;
> out of money advanced by some person for that purpose, the person
> by whom the money was advanced shall, in a winding up, have a right
> of [13] priority in respect of the money so advanced and paid up to
> the amount by which the sum, in respect of which the clerk, servant,
> workman or labourer or other person in his right, would have been
> entitled to priority in the winding up has been diminished by reason
> of the payment having been made.

Mr O'Sullivan contends that the wages cheques paid out of the overdraft
were not paid out of money advanced by the Bank for that purpose; that
the Bank had not addressed its mind to the payment of wages and this
was proved by the fact that a separate wages account was not opened until
17th September 1980. Therefore there was no awareness by the lender
at the time of making the loan.

Mr Blayney on behalf of the Bank argued that ultimately it is a question
of fact were the moneys advanced by the Bank for the purpose of paying
wages; and that it must necessarily follow where cheques drawn in favour
of employees in discharge of wages and cashed week after week that the
money is advanced for that purpose.

One of the cases cited was *Re Rampgill Mill Ltd.* [1967] 1 All E.R. 56.
This was an action between a Bank and a liquidator and it was common
ground that within the limit of £500 per week, there was no restriction on
the purpose for which cheques could be drawn on the Bank.

[14] It was also common ground that the arrangement was made with
wages in mind. In that case, as in this, the Bank did not insist on a wages
account being opened and operated in such a way as to allow the Bank to
get maximum priority. In that case Plowman J. said at p. 60:

> In my judgment, Counsel for the liquidator seeks to apply too rigid a
> test. The object of s. 319 (4) (the equivalent of s. 285 of the Companies
> Act 1963) as I see it, was to establish a principle of subrogation in
> favour of banks (although its operation is not, of course, confined to
> banks), and the sub-section should, therefore, in my judgment, be
> given a benevolent construction rather than one which narrows the
> limits of its operation. . . . In the present case, the bank clearly had a
> purpose in advancing money to the company – namely, the purpose
> of enabling it to meet its commitments. I then ask myself, 'what com-

mitments', and my answer so far as the money provided under the Alston arrangement is concerned, is wages, which were the whole *raison d'être* of that arrangement.

He therefore held the money was advanced for the purpose of paying wages.

It is not possible to be quite as clear-cut in this case. The money was undoubtedly advanced in this case to meet the commitments of the company. It also seems clear to me that part of those commitments included wages and this must have been known to the Bank. Individual weekly wages cheques were drawn for each employee and were honoured by the Bank each week. I agree with Plowman J. that the section should be given a benevolent construction. The Bank in fact advanced money knowing part of it would be used for wages. Therefore in my opinion, insofar as that part is concerned they are entitled to the benefit of subrogation provided in s. 285 (6).

The last issue is whether the rule in *Claytons Case* (1816) 1 M.E.R. 572 applies. This is expressed as follows at page 608:

> In such a case (i.e. a banking account where all the sums paid in form one blended fund the parts of which have no longer any distinct existence), there is no room for any other appropriation than that which arises from the order in which the receipts and payments take place, and are carried into the account. Presumably it is the sum first paid in, that is first drawn out; it is the first item on the debit side of the account, that is discharged, or reduced, by the first item on the credit side.

[16] There were substantial lodgments made by the company during the period from the 3rd June to the 3rd October, 1980. According to the calculations made by the liquidator, the lodgments made up to the 3rd October were sufficient to clear the overdraft existing on the 3rd June and all cheques drawn up to the 20th August, 1980. If the rule in *Claytons Case* is applied, the lodgments must go to clear the earliest items in the account. Therefore subrogation could only be claimed in respect of wages cheques drawn after the 20th August.

The rule was applied in *Re Primrose Builders Ltd.* [1950] 2 All E.R. 334 where advances were made for the payment of wages. In each case the Bank insisted on being satisfied before honouring the cheques (some being made out to wages and some to cash) that lodgments substantially equal to or exceeding the amount would be paid in. Wynn Pary J. held not only that there was no sufficient evidence but that there was no evidence at all on which a Court could come to the conclusion that the rule was to any extent by agreement between the parties not to apply in any particular instance. So too in this case. There was no separate wages account until the 17th September. All lodgments went to reduce the general overdraft and the money advanced for wages formed part of the general overdraft. Insofar as the earlier wage cheques were cleared by subsequent lodgments, they cannot be the subject [17] of a claim by way of surbrogation.

However, the liquidator's calculations are not suitable to ascertain the amount because the lodgments made after the 15th September, which I have held to be a fraudulent preference, did not go to clear any of the earlier cheques. The line cannot be drawn at the 20th August. One must go back through debits totalling £23,278.13 (i.e. the equivalent of the amount of the preference payment) to find where the line is to be drawn for the rule in *Claytons Case*.

According to my calculations, lodgments up to the 15th September would only have cleared the overdraft and cheques drawn up to the 7th August. If my calculations are correct, if any of the cheques debited between the 11th August and the 20th August include wages or holiday cheques, subrogation may be claimed within the limits laid down by s. 285 (3).

The liquidator has already made calculations in respect of wages paid out of current account between the 20th August, 1980 and the 3rd October, 1980 which amount to £4,147.47. He does not appear to have included the sum of £4,348.72 which was paid out of the wages account after the 17th September, 1980. This sum is also eligible for subrogation, again within the limits laid down by s. 285 (3).

In re Hunting Lodges Ltd.
(Carroll J., June 1, 1984, H.Ct.)

The directors and secretary of a company that was insolvent and that owed large sums to the Revenue Commissioners arranged for the sale of the company's principal undertaking, a well known public house named *Durty Nellies*. But the full consideration was not paid to the company; part of the consideration was diverted to the directors' and the secretary's own bank accounts. The liquidator sought a declaration under s. 297 of the 1963 Act that those directors and the secretary should be made personally responsible without limitation of liability for all the company's debts.

CARROLL J.: . . . [17] The following issues are raised:
1. Can a single transaction be described as 'carrying on business' with the meaning of s. 297?
2. Was any business carried on with intent to defraud creditors of the company or creditors of any other person or for any fraudulent purpose?
[18] 3. Was each one of the persons sought to be made liable, 'knowingly' a party to the carrying on of such business with such fraudulent intent?

I am satisfied that carrying on business is not synonymous with trading. (See *Re Sarflax Ltd.* [1979] 1 All E.R. 529). In my opinion it is not necessary that all the company's business should be carried on with fraudulent intent nor is it necessary that there should be a course of dealing or series of transactions before the section can be called into operation.

The section refers to 'any business'. In the course of the conduct of its affairs, a company will have many different aspects of its business. One single transaction can properly be described as 'business of the company' and so also can constituent parts of a transaction. One single act committed with the fraudulent intent specified by the section can, in my opinion, suffice to ground a declaration under the section. The fact that the piece of business is a transaction which involves the sale of the entire assets of the company does not alter the position in any way (see *Re Gerald Cooper Chemicals Ltd.* [1971] 2 All E.R. 49).

[19] In this case, while the sale of the premises with a payment on the side can be viewed as one transaction, it also breaks into different elements. There are the negotiations culminating in the signing of the contract, the closing of the sale and the disposition of the purchase money. Each of these elements can be designated together or separately as 'business of the company'.

In particular I include the disposition of the purchase money as part of the business of the company. Unlikely though it was, Mr Porrit could have deposited the £160,000 to the credit of the company, which would have negatived an intent on his part to defraud creditors in respect of that money. Instead he concealed the money under false names in the building society accounts, thus completing the transaction which was part of the business of the company.

Having decided that any business of the company includes a single transaction or part thereof I intend to refer to the 'business' in this case as the sale or a constituent part thereof. This is the common denominator between Mr and Mrs Porrit and Mr O'Connor and Plage Services Limited.

I am satisfied that all four parties were 'parties' to the sale within the meaning of the section. The phrase in the corresponding section to the English Act (s. 32 of the Companies Act, 1948) has been defined in *Re Maidstone Buildings Ltd.* [1971] 1 W.L.R. 1085 at 1092, as indicating no more than 'participates in', 'takes part in' or 'concurs in'. Pennycuick, V.C., added that it seemed to him that involved some positive steps of some nature.

There is no problem in proving positive steps in this case as each of the parties participated in the sale. Mr Porrit participated from start to finish. He was involved in all the negotiations; he required the payment on the side; he produced at closing the resolution of the directors authorising the sale at £480,000; he countersigned the affixing of the seal to the conveyance; he took the additional £160,000 and he opened the accounts with the building society under false names.

Mrs Porrit participated in part of the sale. While she denied [21] any knowledge of the resolution of the directors, she attended the closing of the sale and countersigned the affixing of the seal to the conveyance without objection. She signed a false name to the signature cards in respect of the building society accounts. Therefore, she took an active part in the closing of the sale and the disposition of part of the purchase money.

Mr Humphrey O'Connor participated in the sale up to and including the closing. He negotiated directly with Mr Porrit and agreed to provide the money on the side. He co-operated by providing the three bank drafts in false names together with cash and the endorsed bank draft for the deposit and handed them over secretly to Mr Porrit without the knowledge of their solicitors or the company's auditor

Plage Services Ltd. is the actual vehicle which Mr O'Connor used to take the conveyance. It was therefore a party to the sale at closing.

The next issue is whether the sale or individual elements of it were tainted with an intent to defraud creditors (whether of the company or of any other person) or any fraudulent purpose and, if [22] so, did each of the parties knowingly participate.

In my opinion, in order for the section to apply, it is not necessary that there should be a common agreed fraudulent intent. If each of the participants acts for a fraudulent purpose then each may be liable. In this case I am satisfied that Mr Porrit intended to defraud the creditors of the company by abstracting money secretly from the company. Insofar as Mr O'Connor is concerned, he was a willing partner in completing the sale by paying part of the purchase money on the side in such a way that it could be concealed. It is irrelevant in my opinion whether he knew or did not know that the company was insolvent. He made the payment on the side in circumstances which could have had no purpose other than a fraudulent one. Either the creditors were going to be defrauded, if the company was insolvent, or the Revenue Commissioners were, if the company was solvent. The false names of the bank drafts were indicative of Mr O'Connor's guilty participation in Mr Porrit's scheme.

In addition both Mr Porrit and Mr O'Connor had the further fraudulent purpose of defrauding the Revenue of stamp duty on the [23] full consideration. While it appears to me that the avoidance of stamp duty was not their primary concern, it was nevertheless the necessary consequence of the secret payment. Since every person is deemed to intend the natural and probable consequences of his acts, so Mr Porrit and Mr O'Connor must be deemed to have intended the avoidance of stamp duty and thus added an additional fraudulent intent to their actions.

Plage Services Ltd. has the knowledge of Mr O'Connor as a director imputed to it. It therefore participated in the closing of the sale with the same guilty knowledge of Mr O'Connor.

As far as Mrs Porrit is concerned I am satisfied that she did not know of the payment of money on the side as part of the agreement with Mr

O'Connor but that does not absolve her from liability under the section. She knew about the sale itself and she countersigned the affixing of the company's seal to the conveyance to the purchaser without demur. When her husband brought home the signature cards from the I.P.B.S. she signed a false name. On her own evidence she assumed the money was part of the purchase money (which it was). It therefore [24] belonged to the company. She assisted in the concealment of that money by signing a false name. That could have had no purpose other than a fraudulent purpose. It is therefore immaterial as far as she is concerned that she did not know of the payment of money on the side. She was prepared to conceal and did assist in concealing the company's money arising from the sale of the property.

I am satisfied, therefore, that it is proper to make a declaration under s. 297 of the Companies Act 1963 that Charles Roger Porrit, Joan Porrit, Humphrey O'Connor and Plage Services Ltd. to be personally responsible for the debts of the Company.

The last remaining question is the extent to which each of them shall be liable. In this regard it is important to look to the entire circumstances.

In *Re Cyona Distributors Ltd.* [1967] Ch. 889 Lord Denning, M.R., says at p. 902:

> In my judgment that section (referring to the corresponding section in the English Act) is deliberately framed in wide terms so as to enable the court to bring fraudulent persons [25] to book. If a man has carried on the business of a company fraudulently the court can make an order against him for the payment of a fixed sum. . . . The sum may be compensatory. Or it may be punitive.

In *Re William C. Leitch Brothers Ltd.* [1932] 2 Ch. 71 at p. 79, Maugham, J. says:

> I am inclined to the view that section 275 is in the nature of a punitive provision and that where the court makes such a declaration in relation to all or any of the debts or other liabilities, it is in the discretion of the court to make an order without limiting the order to the amount of the debts of those creditors proved to have been defrauded by the acts of the director in question though no doubt the order would be in general so limited.

In the case of Charles Roger Porrit I am satisfied that at the time he entered into negotiations with Mr O'Connor the company was insolvent and that all his efforts were directed to getting as much money out of the company as he could before the Revenue moved against it. His personal drawings doubled; his personal overdraft at Allied Irish Banks was discharged out of the company's monies. He deliberately deceived the

Revenue officials about going to England in order to avoid a meeting, when in fact he did not go.

[26] In my opinion it is entirely proper that Mr Porrit should be personally responsible without any limitation of liability for all the debts of the company. The benefit of limited liability should, in my opinion, be totally withdrawn and he should be put in the same position as if he were a trader carrying on business personally.

In relation to Mrs Porrit, the case has been made on her behalf that she played no part in the running of the company.

The day has long since passed since married women were classified with infants and persons of unsound mind as suffering from a disability so far as responsibility for their acts was concerned, or since a married woman could escape criminal responsibility on the grounds that she acted under the influence of her husband. Mrs Porrit cannot evade liability by claiming that she was only concerned with minding her house and looking after her children. If that was the limit of the reponsibilities she wanted, she should not have become a director of the company, or having become one should have resigned.

Any person who becomes a director takes on responsibilities and [27] duties, particularly where there are only two. The balance sheet and profit and loss account and directors' report for each year should have been signed by her. A director who continues as a director but abdicates all reponsibility is not lightly to be excused. If she had reasonably endeavoured to keep abreast of company affairs and had been deceived (and there is no such evidence) it might be possible to excuse her.

Mrs Porrit was concerned with the concealment of £148,000 all of which has been recovered, therefore no loss arises. In deciding whether to make Mrs Porrit liable for debts where nothing was lost through her actions, it is necessary that there should be 'real moral blame' attaching to her. In my opinion this does arise because Mrs Porrit took all of the advantages and none of the responsibilities connected with the company. I consider that she should be personally liable without limitation of liability for all the debts of the company not exceeding the amount or value of any advancement from her husband since the 1st December 1976. I [28] have chosen that date as it is the start of the four year period when the accounts had to be reconstructed. I direct that Mrs Porrit make discovery on oath of any such advancement. She is already liable to the company on foot of the directors' loan account.

So far as Mr O'Connor and Plage Services Ltd. are concerned, I have decided that their liability should be limited to the sum of £12,000. This was the cash sum given to Mr Porrit which has disappeared and has not been accounted for. Mr O'Connor and Plage Services Ltd. are jointly and severally liable for this amount. I make this liability a charge on any debt or obligation due from the company to either of them. Mr O'Connor is already liable to the company in respect of the balance of monies due for the stock-in-trade.

In re S. M. Barker Ltd.
[1950] I.R. 123 (H.Ct.)

(From headnote) Shortly before the making of an order for its compulsory liquidation, a private limited company, voluntarily released a number of simple contract debts due to it and arising out of certain transactions between three persons in their personal capacity and the company. These three persons were, at the time, the sole directors of the company and the entire share capital of the company then stood in the names of the three persons and of another company the share capital of which was also owned exclusively by them. The entire share capital of the company was later transferred on a sale to another group of persons and subsequently the official liquidator, finding himself faced with a heavy deficiency of assets, moved the Court for an order under s. 215 of the Companies (Consolidation) Act, 1908, declaring that the former directors were liable to contribute to the assets a sum by way of restitution or as damages for misfeasance.

GAVAN DUFFY P.: . . . [134] To succeed in this motion the liquidator must prove damage to the Company at the hands of the respondent directors. So far, I think no such damage has been proved, unless the cancellation in the Latchmans' interest of an asset worth nearly £12,000, as I assume, so that the Company thereafter had nothing to show for that asset, is itself such an actual loss as to justify this claim under s. 215. At this point, it cannot be stressed too emphatically that on the evidence the three Latchmans were in truth the owners of the entire share capital, so that they were at liberty to do virtually whatever they chose, short of acting dishonestly or *ultra vires*. The transaction was the honest result of negotiations between the Latchmans and an external group of business men, eager for their own ends to gain control [135] of the Company and its assets without paying an excessive price for the shares which carried control. And I discern no moral obliquity in the deeds and omissions of the Latchmans as directors in this transaction: see *Dovey* v. *Cory* [1901] A.C. 477, in this connection.

Here was a small private company, owned and controlled by a family group, who acted unanimously, and in concert with the incoming members about to replace them, at the September and October meetings; and what they did they did in good faith and in natural reliance for the technical mechanics of their operations and of the deal upon an accountant-auditor belonging to a firm of high repute. However improvident the resolution releasing the Latchmans' indebtedness and however regrettable the failures to observe the requirements and the formalities of company law, quite beyond their ken, I think, the outstanding fact is the fact that the true owners of the property, acting with the full assent of their prospective assignees, all concurred at the two meetings and throughout in every step taken. Consequently, in my view, the Company cannot through its liquidator make the Latchman shareholders liable in their capacity of directors for the value of the released debts, unless the liquidator can show some act done *ultra vires* of the Company by the Latchmans as directors to have caused loss, or prove an improper pecuniary benefit acquired by the directors, for which they are accountable to the Company.

The undertaking was sold as a going concern by a transfer of the shares for a small deferred payment in cash and with no adequate provision for the payment of those creditors who had no personal guarantee; but I cannot on the evidence say that the very few among them still unpaid suffered at the hands of the Latchmans any damage cognisable in law. The liquidator is thrown back on the contention that the release, viewed as a gift or as a surrender of a large asset for a small return, was *ultra vires* of the Company, and he has to make that case and to assert the liability of the Latchmans on behalf of persons who gave credit to the Company after the Latchmans had severed all connection with it, both as directors and as members.

On the one hand, a large sum of money is here involved and that sum was conceded to men who constituted the Board on their undertaking to discharge a much smaller liability, due to the Company, and the directors are held up to me as the wrongful beneficiaries of their Company's singular bounty, which no clause in the memorandum of association seems to have anticipated; one naturally approaches a performance of that sort with suspicion and its propriety obviously looks very questionable indeed. On the other hand, a trading company may from time to time reduce or forgive a debt; and where is the line to be drawn? Max Latchman's debt to the Company at least was a large debt, but the Latchmans dealt with the whole affair straightforwardly and upon, as they must have supposed, competent advice, and the impugned resolutions, when acted upon, left the Company on the evidence a solvent going concern. Can such considerations as these be invoked to validate, as being *intra vires*, a costly indulgence, conceded at best for a small return, to an apparently solvent creditor at the expense of the corporation? And, if not, can the Latchmans, for their participation as directors, invoke s. 279 of the Act of 1908 and establish a claim that they ought fairly to be excused, having acted honestly and reasonably, if they did commit a breach of the trust?

In my view of this motion for summary redress under s. 215, based on the alleged misfeasance of directors and on nothing else, those interesting points, though much discussed, call for no decision here. I am unable to find any single thing wrongfully done by the Messrs. Latchman as directors and causing damage, to justify the application of sanctions under s. 215.

The Company's resolution releasing the debts describes them as indebtedness of the directors; that very convenient and very thoughtless description looks to me like a crass blunder; the ledger simply records the debts under the current accounts of Solomon and of Max and of Moss Latchman separately and the writing off, in pursuance of the resolution, of sums of £88, £12,354 and £2,098 respectively; the contra account discharge by the Latchmans is here disregarded, no doubt as being irrelevant to these particular ledger accounts; I do not pause on the inapplicability of the rule against set off under s. 215, if the two relevant resolutions can be taken as one. But the Latchmans owned the Company and, despite the wording of the main resolution, there was no point in treating their debts as directors' debts; surely, the reality is that they got their release because the Company was their *alter ego*, not because they made up the Board; if so, I cannot regard their acceptance of the benefit as misfeasance by them in their directorial capacity. So much for the Latchmans as recipients. Take them now as actors: the effective act releasing the debts was an act of the Company in general meeting, not an act of the Board: the facts that the meeting was not properly convened and [137] that the Universal Woollen Company was probably not invited are immaterial under the circumstances : see *Parker & Cooper, Ltd.* v. *Reading* [1926] 1 Ch. 975. And the next annual meeting, after the Latchmans had disappeared, expressly confirmed the minutes of the meeting in September. But to bring a case within s. 215, it is essential to show that pecuniary loss resulted to the company from acts constituting misfeasance by directors: *Re Irish Provident Assurance Co.* [1913] 1 I.R. 352.

The main resolution was altered by putting the date of release at the 12th October, instead of the 15th September. I accept Mr Max Latchman's evidence that (according to my own note) the alteration was made at a meeting on the 12th October; that must be the Board meeting; I accept his evidence that it was made by the accountant in the presence and with the assent of the members of the Cole group present; in fact, he says that it was done at their behest. That was probably done before the new Board was installed; it was done without any resolution of the Board, as the minutes are silent; and I do not infer from the evidence that it was done, nor that it was intended to be done, as an act of the Board; all that was really needed was the assent of all the members.

I observe that the sum total of the debts shown due by the three Latchmans at the altered date corresponds exactly with the figure given for their gross indebtedness by the accountant in his report to Mr Cole (being also the gross total now claimed by the liquidator); therefore the confirmation by the Cole Board meeting of the 22nd November, 1946, when the secretary was instructed to give effect to the release of the Latchmans in the accounts for the year, 1946, must have related to their indebtedness as at the 12th October, and not as at the 15th September, 1946; and the subsequent confirmation by the Company at its annual general meeting of the 10th April, 1947, must likewise have had the same indebtedness in view. One must come to the same conclusion, moreover, from the fact that the minutes of September had been deliberately altered to the knowledge of all concerned, so the confirmations necessarily related to the indebtedness as at the 12th October, 1946.

In the absence of the 'journal' from which the last ledger entries against the Latchmans are taken, one cannot be certain that any benefit whatever did accrue to the Latchmans or to any one of them from the change of date; one can only say that one or more of them may have gained. That is an unsatisfactory position. But that portion (if there [138] was a gain) of the forgiven liability the liquidator cannot recover on this motion, because I cannot impute the alteration to the Latchmans as a Board, nor as individual directors, and, if I did, I take the confirmation by the April general meeting to have ratified the altered minutes; this understanding of the general meeting's confirmation is borne out, if need be, since the Company had very few members, by the express direction of the Board in November to have the material resolution reflected in the accounts for the year, 1946.

To summarise the position, as I see it: the three Latchmans at the material times were the directors of the Company; naturally, because they were the owners of the entire share capital: and, because they were the owners, they were the complete masters of the Company's situation; it is as such that they were in a position to profit and did profit, and not as directors or trustees for the shareholders.

They had from time to time incurred simple contract debts to the Company individually for their own purposes; and the Company, instead of exacting payment of those debts, saw fit to annul, as if it were a single liability, that valuable indebtedness, or most of it, casually describing it in the ill-advised resolution as indebtedness of the directors. That annulment, whether valid in law or void or voidable, was the act of the Company in general meeting; and the comparatively small amendment of the amount forgiven, effected by the owners of the undertaking, was endorsed by another general meeting. There was, moreover, on the evidence, no concealment by the Latchmans, no trickery, and no fraud. In that state of the case, it would, in my judgment, be a distortion of the law to allow the liquidator to recover against the Latchmans in their capacity of directors under s. 215.

I cannot express the principle to be applied more tersely than in the words of Mr Justice Maugham, as he then was, in *Re Etic* [1928] 1 Ch. 861: 'The conclusion at which I have arrived is that s. 215 is. . . limited to cases where there has been something in the nature of a breach of duty by an officer of the company as such which has caused pecuniary loss to the company.'

I must refuse the liquidator's application, since any damage occasioned to the Company by the release of the Latchmans' debts was not the result of any breach of duty committed by them in their role of officers of the company, while the pecuniary gain to themselves from the same release was not acquired by them as directors, nor because [139] they were directors, nor in breach of their duty to the members of the Company, who, whether or not the profit be justifiable in law, were the real gainers in their personal capacity from the Company's largesse.

PROVING DEBTS

Civil Liability Act, 1961

Proof of claims for damages or contribution in bankruptcy.

61.—(1) Notwithstanding any other enactment or any rule of law, a claim for damages or contribution in respect of a wrong shall be provable in bankruptcy where the wrong out of which the liability to damages or the right to contribution arose was committed before the time of the bankruptcy.

(2) Where the damages or contribution have not been and cannot be otherwise liquidated or ascertained, the court may make such order as to it seems fit for the assessment of the damages or contribution, and the amount when so assessed shall be provable as if it were a debt due at the time of the bankruptcy.

(3) Where a claim for contribution or in respect of a judgment debt for contribution is provable in bankruptcy, no such proof shall be admitted except to the extent that the claimant has satisfied the debt or damages of the injured person, unless the injured person does not prove in respect of the wrong or debt.

Application of moneys payable under certain policies of insurance

62.—Where a person (hereinafter referred to as the insured) who has effected a policy of insurance in respect of liability for a wrong, if an individual, becomes a bankrupt or dies or, if a corporate body, is wound up or, if a partnership or other unincorporated association, is dissolved, moneys payable to the insured under the policy shall be applicable only to discharging in full all valid claims against the insured in respect of which those moneys are payable, and no part of those moneys shall be assets of the insured or applicable to the payment of the debts (other than those claims) of the insured in the bankruptcy or in the administration of the estate of the insured or in the winding-up or dissolution, and no such claim shall be provable in the bankruptcy, administration, winding-up or dissolution.

PRIORITIES

Finance Act, 1967

Schedule 19, Enactments Repealed:
(Inter alia) Finance Act, 1924, s. 38.

Finance Act, 1986

115.–(1) Where a person holds a fixed charge (being a fixed charge which is created on or after the passing of this Act) on the book debts of a company (within the meaning of the Companies Act, 1963) and the company fails to pay any relevant amount for which it is liable, then the said person shall, on being notified accordingly in writing by the Revenue Commissioners, become liable to pay such relevant amount on due demand, and on neglect or refusal of payment may be proceeded against in like manner as any other defaulter:

Provided that

(i) the amount or aggregate amount which the person shall be liable to pay in relation to a company in accordance with this section shall not exceed the amount or aggregate amount which that person has, while the fixed charge on book debts in relation to the said company is in existence, received, directly or indirectly, from that company in payment or in part payment of any debts due by the company to that person, and

(ii) this section shall not apply to any amounts received by the holder of the fixed charge from the company before the date on which he is notified in writing by the Revenue Commissioners that he is liable by reason of this section for payment of a relevant amount due by the company.

(2) In this section 'relevant amount' means any amount which the company is liable to remit –

(a) under Chapter IV of Part V of the Income Tax Act, 1967, and

(b) under the Value-Added Tax Act, 1972.

Alphabetical Table of Cases